THE
CLASSICAL
TRADITION

Helen, thy beauty is to me
  Like those Nicean barks of yore,
That gently, o'er a perfumed sea,
  The weary, wayworn wanderer bore
  To his own native shore.

On desperate seas long wont to roam,
  Thy hyacinth hair, thy classic face,
Thy Naiad airs have brought me home
  To the glory that was Greece
And the grandeur that was Rome.

THE
CLASSICAL
TRADITION

GREEK AND ROMAN INFLUENCES
ON WESTERN LITERATURE

BY

GILBERT HIGHET

OXFORD UNIVERSITY PRESS

New York   Oxford

Oxford University Press

Oxford   New York   Toronto
Delhi   Bombay   Calcutta   Madras   Karachi
Kuala Lumpur   Singapore   Hong Kong   Tokyo
Nairobi   Dar es Salaam   Cape Town
Melbourne   Auckland

and associated companies in
Beirut   Berlin   Ibadan   Mexico City   Nicosia

First published in 1949 by the Clarendon Press, Oxford
First issued as an Oxford University Press paperback, 1957
Reissued in paperback, 1985, by Oxford University Press, Inc.,
198 Madison Avenue, New York, New York 10016-4314

Oxford is the registered trademark of Oxford University Press.

Library of Congress Cataloging-in-Publication Data
Highet, Gilbert, 1906-1978.
The classical tradition.
Bibliography: p.
Includes index.
1. Literature, Comparative—Classical and modern.
2. Literature, Comparative—Modern and classical.
PN883.H5   1985   809   85-15477
ISBN 0-19-500206-7 (pbk.)

Printing (last digit): 9 8 7 6

Printed in the United States of America

PREFACE

THIS book is an outline of the chief ways in which Greek and Latin influence has moulded the literatures of western Europe and America.

The Greeks invented nearly all the literary patterns which we use: tragedy and comedy, epic and romance, and many more. In the course of their two thousand years of writing they worked out innumerable themes—some as light as 'Drink to me only with thine eyes', others as powerful as a brave man's journey through hell. These themes and patterns they passed on to the Romans, who developed them and added much of their own.

When the Roman empire fell civilization was nearly ruined. Literature and the arts became refugees, hiding in outlying areas or under the protection of the church. Few Europeans could read during the Dark Ages. Fewer still could write books. But those who could read and write did so with the help of the international Latin language, by blending Christian material with Greek and Roman thoughts.

New languages formed themselves, slowly, slowly. The first which has left a large and mature literature of its own is Anglo-Saxon, or Old English. After it came French; then Italian; and then the other European languages. When authors started to write in each of these new media, they told the stories and sang the songs which their own people knew. But they turned to Rome and Greece for guidance in strong or graceful expression, for interesting stories less well known, for trenchant ideas.

As these languages matured they constantly turned to the Greeks and Romans for further education and help. They enlarged their vocabulary by incorporating Greek and Roman words, as we are still doing: for instance, *television*. They copied and adapted the highly developed Greco-Roman devices of style. They learned famous stories, like the murder of Caesar or the doom of Oedipus. They found out the real powers of dramatic poetry, and realized what tragedy and comedy meant. Their authors modelled themselves on Greek and Roman writers. Nations found inspiration for great political movements (such as the French Revolution) in Greece and Rome.

This process of education by imitating Greco-Roman literature, emulating its achievements, and adapting its themes and patterns, has been going on ever since our modern languages were formed. It has a continuous, through very chequered, history from about A.D. 700 to 1949. No single book could give a complete description of the process. As far as I know, there is not even an outline of it in existence. This work is an endeavour to provide such an outline.

There are a number of books which treat separate phases of this process. They discuss classical influence on the writers of one particular country, or in one particular period; or they describe the changing fortunes of one classical author in modern times, showing how the Middle Ages neglected him, how he was rediscovered in the Renaissance and much admired, how he fell out of favour in the seventeenth and eighteenth centuries, and how he re-emerged, to inspire a new group of authors, in the nineteenth and twentieth centuries. These works are extremely useful, and I am much indebted to their authors.

It would be an enormous, a Sisyphean, task to compile a bibliography of the whole subject. At least a volume as large as this would be needed. However, I have mentioned in the notes a considerable number of books which I have found useful; and I have added a short bibliography of the most recent general surveys of various sections of the subject. From these it should be easy to branch off and follow any particular channel which seems interesting. A great deal of the territory is still quite unexplored.

All book-titles and all quotations are given in English, unless some special reason intervenes. All translations (unless otherwise noted) are mine; the original text and the references will be found in the notes. In a book dealing with several different languages, I felt it might be distracting to have German phrases jostling French and Italian jostling Spanish.

Many of my friends and colleagues have been kind enough to read and criticize various sections of this book, and many others have drawn my attention to points which I had overlooked. I should like, in return for their salutary criticisms and constructive suggestions, to express my warm gratitude to the following: Cyril Bailey; Jean-Albert Bédé; Margarete Bieber; Dino Bigongiari; Wilhelm Braun; Oscar Campbell; James Clifford; D. M. Davin;

Elliot V. K. Dobbie; Charles Everett; Otis Fellows; Donald Frame; Horace Friess; W. M. Frohock; Moses Hadas; Alfred Harbage; Henry Hatfield; Werner Jaeger; Ernst Kapp; J. A. Krout; Roger Loomis; Arnaldo Momigliano; Frank Morley; Marjorie Hope Nicolson; Justin O'Brien; Denys Page; R. H. Phelps; Austin Poole; Colin Roberts; Inez Scott Ryberg; Arthur Schiller; Kenneth Sisam; Herbert Smith; Norman Torrey; LaRue Van Hook; James Wardrop; T. J. Wertenbaker; and Ernest Hunter Wright.

I am also grateful to a number of my pupils who have been so good as to make suggestions—in particular Isabel Gaebelein and William Turner Levy. I have further to thank the members of the staff of Columbia University Library, especially the following, whose expert bibliographical knowledge has saved me many hours of searching: Constance Winchell, Jean Macalister, Charles Claar, Jane Davies, Alice Day, Karl Easton, Olive Johnson, Carl Reed, Lucy Reynolds, and Margaret Webb. And I must express my thanks to the Librarian and the staff of St. Andrews University Library, who gave me the traditional Scots hospitality.

One other debt, the greatest of all, is acknowledged in the dedication.

G. H.

COLUMBIA UNIVERSITY
NEW YORK

ACKNOWLEDGEMENTS

I SHOULD like to express my thanks to the authors, firms, and representatives who have been kind enough to grant me permission to print quotations from the following works, in which they hold the copyright:

George Allen and Unwin Ltd., London, from Lord Russell's *A History of Western Philosophy*; Appleton-Century-Crofts, Inc., New York, from *The Art of History*, by J. B. Black; Artemis-Verlag, Zürich, from Carl Spitteler's *Olympischer Frühling*; The Atlantic Monthly Press, Boston, from E. J. Simmons's *Leo Tolstoy*; C. H. Beck'sche Verlagsbuchhandlung, Munich, from Oswald Spengler's *Der Untergang des Abendlandes*; Cambridge University Press, from E. M. Butler's *The Tyranny of Greece over Germany*; A. S. F. Gow's *A. E. Housman: a Sketch*; A. E. Housman's *Introductory Lecture* of 1892 and his preface to his edition of Juvenal; J. E. Sandys's *A History of Classical Scholarship*; and A. A. Tilley's *The Literature of the French Renaissance*; Jonathan Cape, Ltd., London, from A. E. Housman's *A Shropshire Lad*; Chatto and Windus, London, from Lytton Strachey's *Books and Characters*; The Clarendon Press, Oxford, from W. J. Sedgefield's *King Alfred's Version of the Consolation of Boethius*; Columbia University Press, New York, from D. J. Grout's *A Short History of Opera*; S. A. Larrabee's *English Bards and Grecian Marbles*; E. E. Neff's *The Poetry of History*; and G. N. Shuster's *The English Ode from Milton to Keats*; J. M. Dent & Sons, London, from the Everyman's Library editions of Gibbon's *Decline and Fall of the Roman Empire* and R. K. Ingram's translation of the *Anglo-Saxon Chronicle*; Dieterich'sche Verlagsbuchhandlung, Wiesbaden, from W. Rehm's *Griechentum und Goethezeit* (*Das Erbe der Alten*, 2nd series, no. 26); E. P. Dutton & Co. Inc., New York, from the Everyman's Library editions of Gibbon's *Decline and Fall of the Roman Empire* and R. K. Ingram's translation of the *Anglo-Saxon Chronicle*; Éditions Bernard Grasset, Paris, from Jean Cocteau's *La Machine infernale* and Jean Giraudoux's *Électre* and *La Guerre de Troie n'aura pas lieu*; The Encylopædia Britannica, Chicago, from J. B. Bury's article 'Roman Empire, Later' and D. F. Tovey's article 'Gluck'; Faber & Faber, Ltd., London, from T. S. Eliot's poems and S. Gilbert's *James Joyce's 'Ulysses'*; Henry Frowde, London, from E. J. Dent's 'The Baroque Opera', in *The Musical Antiquary* for Jan. 1910;

Gallimard, Paris, from André Gide's *Œdipe* and Paul Valéry's *Poésies*; Harvard University Press, Cambridge, Mass., from D. Bush's *Mythology and the Romantic Tradition in English Poetry* (Harvard Studies in English 18); Harcourt, Brace & Co., Inc., New York, from Lytton Strachey's *Books and Characters*; William Heinemann Ltd., London, from E. Gosse's *Father and Son*; Henry Holt & Co. Inc., New York, from A. E. Housman's *A Shropshire Lad* and R. K. Root's *Classical Mythology in Shakespeare*; Alfred A. Knopf, Inc., New York, from S. Gilbert's *James Joyce's 'Ulysses'*; Librairie Ancienne et Éditions Honoré Champion, Paris, from E. Faral's *Les Arts poétiques du XIIe et XIIIe siècle* (Bibliothèque de l'École des Hautes Études, sciences historiques et philologiques, fasc. 238); Librairie Armand Colin, Paris, from the *Histoire de la langue et de la littérature française*, edited by L. Petit de Julleville; Librairie Hachette, Paris, from A. Meillet's *Esquisse d'une histoire de la langue latine* and H. Taine's *Histoire de la littérature anglaise*; Little, Brown & Co., Boston, from E. J. Simmons's *Leo Tolstoy*; Longmans, Green & Co., Ltd., London, from G. P. Gooch's *History and Historians in the Nineteenth Century*; K. S. P. McDowall, Esq., for the quotation from E. F. Benson's *As We Were*, published by Longmans, Green & Co.; Macmillan & Co. Ltd., London, from C. M. Bowra's *The Heritage of Symbolism*; J. W. Cunliffe's *The Influence of Seneca on Elizabethan Tragedy*; and M. Belloc Lowndes's *Where Love and Friendship Dwelt*; The Macmillan Company, New York, from C. M. Bowra's *The Heritage of Symbolism*; R. Garnett's and E. Gosse's *English Literature, an Illustrated Record*; A. S. F. Gow's *A. E. Housman: A Sketch*; and A. E. Housman's *Introductory Lecture* (1892); Methuen & Co. Ltd., London, from J. B. Black's *The Art of History*; John Murray, London, from Lady Gregory's *Gods and Fighting Men*; New Directions, Norfolk, Conn., from H. Levin's *James Joyce* and from the poems of Ezra Pound; Nouvelle Revue Française, Paris, from André Gide's *Réponse à une enquête de 'La Renaissance' sur le classicisme*; Nouvelles Éditions Latines, Paris, from André Gide's *Le Viol de Lucrèce*; Oxford University Press, London, from G. L. Bickersteth's lecture 'Leopardi and Wordsworth', and to the British Academy, before which the lecture was delivered; from C. M. Bowra's *A Classical Education*; H. Cushing's *Life of Sir William Osler*; T. S. Eliot's *The Classics and the Man of Letters*; T. E. Lawrence's translation of the *Odyssey*; H. Peyre's *Louis Ménard* (Yale Romanic Studies 5); W. L. Phelps's *Autobiography with Letters*; Grant Richards's *Housman 1897–1936*; A. J. Toynbee's *A Study of History*; and J. Worthington's *Wordsworth's Reading of Roman Prose* (Yale Studies in English 102); Pantheon Books Inc., New York, from André Gide's *Thésée*; Paul, Paris, from J. Giraudoux's *Elpénor*;

Picard, Paris, from G. Guillaumie's *J. L. Guez de Balzac et la prose française*;

Princeton University Press, from J. D. Spaeth's *Old English Poetry*;

Putnam & Co., Ltd., and G. P. Putnam's Sons, London and New York, from J. H. Robinson's and H. W. Rolfe's *Petrarch, the First Modern Scholar and Man of Letters*;

Random House, Inc., New York (The Modern Library), from Constance Garnett's translation of Tolstoy's *Anna Karenina*, and James Joyce's *Ulysses*;

Rheinverlag, Zürich, from W. Rüegg's *Cicero und der Humanismus*;

W. E. Rudge's Sons, New York, from J. S. Kennard's *The Italian Theatre*;

Charles Scribner's Sons, New York, from Nicholas Murray Butler's *Across the Busy Years*;

Simon and Schuster, Inc., New York, from Lord Russell's *History of Western Philosophy*;

The Society of Authors, London, as literary representative of the trustees of the estate of the late A. E. Housman, for quotations from *A Shropshire Lad*;

The State University of Iowa, from J. Van Horne's *Studies on Leopardi* (Iowa University Humanistic Studies, v. 1, no. 4);

Stock, Paris, from Jean Cocteau's *Orphée*;

B. G. Teubner Verlagsgesellschaft, Leipzig, from U. von Wilamowitz-Moellendorff's 'Geschichte der Philologie', in *Einleitung in die Altertumswissenschaft*, ed. Gercke and Norden, and from T. Zielinski's *Cicero im Wandel der Jahrhunderte*;

University of California Press, Berkeley, Cal., from G. Norwood's *Pindar* (Sather Classical Lectures, 1945);

University of Chicago Press, Chicago, from H. T. Parker's *The Cult of Antiquity and the French Revolutionaries*;

Vanderbilt University Press, Nashville, Tenn., from C. M. Lancaster's and P. T. Manchester's translation, *The Araucaniad*;

The Viking Press Inc., New York, from James Joyce's A *Portrait of the Artist as a Young Man*;

The Warburg Institute, London, from the *Vorträge der Bibliothek Warburg*, ed. F. Saxl;

Yale University Press, New Haven, Conn., from H. Peyre's *Louis Ménard* (Yale Romanic Studies 5) and J. Worthington's *Wordsworth's Reading of Roman Prose* (Yale Studies in English 102);

and to any other authors and publishers whose names may have been inadvertently omitted, and to whom I am indebted for similar courtesies.

CONTENTS

CONTENTS xvii

CONTENTS   xxi

CONTENTS xxv

CONTENTS xxxv

ABBREVIATIONS

The following conventions have been used for the sake of brevity:

bk.   = book
c.   = chapter; and also *circa*: about
cc.   = chapters
cf.   = *confer*: compare
ed.   = edition, or edited by
e.g.   = *exempli gratia*: for example
f.   = and following lines, or: and following pages
fin.   = *ad finem*: towards the end
fl.   = *floruit*: flourished, was active
ibid.   = *ibidem*: in the same place
i.e.   = *id est*: that is
init.   = *ad initium*: towards the beginning
l.   = line
ll.   = lines
med.   = *ad medium*: about the middle
n.   = note
n.F.   = *neue Folge*: new series
n.s.   = new series
op. cit. = *opus citatum*: the work quoted
p.   = page
para.   = paragraph
pp.   = pages
pt.   = part
suppl.   = supplementary volume
s.v.   = *sub voce*: under the heading
tit.   = *titulus*: title, or heading
tr.   = translated by
v.   = verse; and also *versus*: opposed to; and also volume
vv.   = verses; and also volumes

The abbreviations of the titles of books and periodicals are those shown in any standard list. Among the commonest are:

Aen.   = *Aeneid*
Aug.   = Augustine
Buc.   = *Bucolics*
Carm.   = *Carmina* (generally of Horace's odes)
Cat.   = Catullus
Ep.   = *Epistulae* (the Letters of Augustine, Horace, Seneca, and others)
FQ   = Spenser's *Faerie Queene*
Georg. = *Georgics*
HF   = Chaucer's *House of Fame*

Hom. = Homer
Hor. = Horace
Il. = *Iliad*
Juv. = Juvenal
LGW = Chaucer's *Legend of Good Women*
L.L.L. = *Love's Labour's Lost*
Met. = *Metamorphoses*
Od. = *Odyssey*
Ov. = Ovid
Proc. = Proceedings
PMLA = Proceedings, or Publications, of the Modern Language Association of America
Sat. = *Satires*, and also Petronius' *Satirica*
Serm. = *Sermones* (generally of Horace's satires)
Suet. = Suetonius
Verg. = Vergil.

A small superior number after a date shows the edition of the book produced on that date. So 1914³ means that the third edition of the book mentioned came out in 1914.

I

INTRODUCTION

OUR modern world is in many ways a continuation of the world of Greece and Rome. Not in all ways—particularly not in medicine, music, industry, and applied science. But in most of our intellectual and spiritual activities we are the grandsons of the Romans, and the great-grandsons of the Greeks. Other influences joined to make us what we are; but the Greco-Roman strain was one of the strongest and richest. Without it, our civilization would not merely be different. It would be much thinner, more fragmentary, less thoughtful, more materialistic—in fact, whatever wealth it might have accumulated, whatever wars it might have fought, whatever inventions it might have made, it would be less worthy to be called a civilization, because its spiritual achievements would be less great.

The Greeks and, learning from them, the Romans created a noble and complex civilization, which flourished for a thousand years and was overthrown only through a long series of invasions and civil wars, epidemics, economic disasters, and administrative, moral, and religious catastrophes. It did not entirely disappear. Nothing so great and so long established does. Something of it survived, transformed but undestroyed, throughout the agonizing centuries in which mankind slowly built up western civilization once more. But much of it was covered by wave after wave of barbarism; silted over; buried; and forgotten. Europe slipped backwards, backwards, almost into savagery.

When the civilization of the west began to rise again and remake itself, it did so largely through rediscovering the buried culture of Greece and Rome. Great systems of thought, profound and skilful works of art, do not perish unless their material vehicle is utterly destroyed. They do not become fossils, because a fossil is lifeless and cannot reproduce itself. But they, whenever they find a mind to receive them, live again in it and make it live more fully.

What happened after the Dark Ages was that the mind of Europe was reawakened and converted and stimulated by the rediscovery of classical civilization. Other factors helped in that reawakening, but no other worked more strongly and variously.

This process began about A.D. 1100 and, with occasional pauses and set-backs, moved on faster and faster until, between 1400 and 1600, western Europe seized on the arts and the ideals of classical Greece and Rome, eagerly assimilated them, and, partly by imitating them, partly by adapting them to other media, partly by creating new art and thought under the powerful stimulus they produced, founded modern civilization.

This book is intended to give the outlines of that story in one field only: in literature. It could be told from many other vitally interesting points of view. In politics, it could be shown how democracy was invented and its essential powers and mistakes explored by the Greeks, and how the ideals of democracy were adopted by the Roman republic, to be revived again in the democratic constitutions of the modern world; and how much of our thinking about the rights and duties of the citizen derives directly from Greco-Roman thought. In law it would be easy to show how the central pillars of American and British law, French law, Dutch law, Spanish and Italian and Latin-American law, and the law of the Catholic church, were hewn out by the Romans. (And it is unlikely that we should have constructed them, as they stood, without any help or stimulus from Rome. Our civilization is fertile in some kinds of invention, and particularly apt for the conquest of matter; but not in others. Judging by our inability to create new artistic forms and new philosophical systems, it is extremely improbable that, unaided, we could have built up anything comparable to the firm, lofty structure of Roman law.) In philosophy and religion, in language and abstract science, and in the fine arts—especially architecture and sculpture—it could equally well be shown that much of the best of what we write and make and think is adapted from the creations of Greece and Rome. There is nothing discreditable in this. On the contrary: it is discreditable to ignore and forget it. In civilization as in human life, the present is the child of the past. Only, in the life of the spirit, it is permitted to select our ancestors, and to choose the best.

However, this book will deal only with literature, and will refer to other fields of life only to illustrate important literary events. 'Literature' will be taken to mean books written in modern languages or their immediate ancestors. Although Latin was currently written and spoken in Europe until at least 1860,[1] although Latin is not only an ancient but also a modern European language, in which Milton and Landor, Newton and Copernicus, Descartes and Spinoza, wrote some or all of their best work, the history of Latin literature written by modern authors is so different from that of the other European literatures of our era that it must be treated separately. Still, the fact that Latin continued to live so long as an independent language, and for some purposes (such as Mass) still does, is itself one more proof that classical culture is an essential and active part of our civilization. And thoughts live longer than languages.

THE FALL OF THE GREEK AND ROMAN CIVILIZATION

It is not always understood nowadays how noble and how widespread Greco-Roman civilization was, how it kept Europe, the Middle East, and northern Africa peaceful, cultured, prosperous, and happy for centuries, and how much was lost when the savages and invaders broke in upon it. It was, in many respects, a better thing than our own civilization until a few generations ago, and it may well prove to have been a better thing all in all. But we are so accustomed to contemplating the spectacle of human progress that we assume modern culture to be better than anything that preceded it. We forget also how able and how willing men are to reverse the movement of progress: how many forces of barbarism remain, like volcanoes in a cultivated island, still powerfully alive, capable not only of injuring civilization but of putting a burning desert in its place.

When the Roman empire was at its height, law and order, education, and the arts were widely distributed and almost universally respected. In the first centuries of the Christian era there was almost too much literature; and so many inscriptions survive, from so many towns and villages in so many different provinces, that we can be sure that many, if not most, of the population could read and write.[2] The illiterates were probably (as they are in the United States) the poorest workers, the least-civilized immigrants, the slaves or descendants of slaves working on farms, and the inhabitants of remote districts of forest and mountain.

But two or three generations of war and pestilence and revolution destroy culture with appalling rapidity. Among the northern savages who fought each other over the body of the Roman empire, writing was not only uncommon. It was so rare that it was partly magic. The runes—which were really a northern European alphabet—could raise the dead, bewitch man or nature, and make warriors and even gods invincible. The word rune means 'a secret'. How barbarous were the people who believed that the purpose of writing was to keep a thing secret? Similarly, the word glamour, which we take to mean 'magic', really means 'grammar', the power of writing. During the Dark Ages—say about A.D. 600—civilization in the west had dropped back almost to the point whence it had risen in about 1000 B.C.: to something even rougher and simpler than the Homeric age. All through the *Iliad* and the *Odyssey* tokens and symbols are fairly common, but writing is mentioned only once, and then it is described in a vague and sinister way. Just as Hamlet's companions on his mission to England, in the original savage story, carried 'letters incised in wood', so Bellerophon was given 'baneful signs cut in a folding tablet' which called for his execution.[3] Like the runes, they were rare and uncanny.

The same story of a relapse into barbarism which is told in this retrogression in European ideas of writing can be read in many excavations of Roman remains in provinces which have been reclaimed, like Britain, or, like Asiatic Turkey and north Africa, still remain more barbarous than they were under the Romans. The excavator finds the outlines of a large and comfortable country house, in a beautiful site overlooking a valley or a river, with elaborate conveniences for living, and evidences of artistic taste such as mosaic floors and fragments of statuary. It is ruined. On its ruins it is sometimes possible to show that a later generation, still half-civilized, established a temporary home, patched up rather than rebuilt. Then there are new traces of burning and destruction; and then nothing more. The whole site is covered with the earth of the slow succeeding centuries, and trees are rooted high above the decorated floors.[4] What the Renaissance did was to dig down through the silt and find the lost beauties, and imitate or emulate them. We have continued their work and gone farther. But now, around us, have appeared the first ruins of what may be a new Dark Age.

THE DARK AGES

Civilization did not completely perish during the Dark Ages. How much of it survived? and through what channels or transformations?

First of all, the languages of the Greco-Roman world survived. But their fates were strangely different.

Greek was widespread all over the eastern Mediterranean. It was spoken not only by people of Greek blood but in Egypt, in Palestine, and elsewhere.[5] A simple colloquial Greek was the standard language for intercommunication between Near Eastern countries which had their own languages: that is why the New Testament is written in Greek.

In most of Italy, western Europe, and northern Africa Latin was spoken. Before it, nearly all the scores of native dialects and conquered languages like Carthaginian disappeared, leaving few traces in life and none in literature.[6] However, at its highest development, the Roman empire was not Latin-speaking but bilingual in Latin and Greek. Because of the flexibility of Greek, the Romans themselves used it as a social and intellectual language. Of course, they were (except for a few eccentrics) too strongly nationalist to abandon Latin altogether; but nearly all the upper-class Romans of the late republic and early empire used Greek not only for philosophical discussion and literary practice, but for social conversation and even for love-making. (French played a similar part in the court of Frederick the Great and in nineteenth-century Russia. Within living memory there have been noble families in Bavaria who never spoke German at home, but always French.) Thus it is that the last words of Julius Caesar, spoken at the actual moment of his murder, were Greek, and that the emperor Marcus Aurelius kept his private spiritual diary in Greek.[7]

But in the fourth century the two streams of language and culture which had flowed together to produce classical Greco-Roman civilization diverged once again. The essential fact here was *the division of the Roman empire*. Having proved impossible to administer and defend as a unit, the empire was in A.D. 364 divided into two: a western empire under Valentinian, with its capital at Milan, and an eastern empire under his brother Valens, with its capital at Constantinople. Thenceforward, although there were frequent contacts, the differences between east and west grew greater and greater. They increased sharply when in A.D. 476 the last emperor of the west (who bore the reminiscent names of Romulus, after the founder of Rome, and Augustulus, or 'little Augustus') was deposed and his power taken over by semi-barbarous kings; and thereafter they grew constantly more intense. After grave dissensions in the eighth and ninth centuries the Christian churches were finally divided in 1054, when the pope excommunicated the patriarch of Constantinople and the entire eastern Orthodox church as heretical. And at last the conflict became virtually a war. The Greek Christian city of Constantinople was sacked in 1204 by the French and Venetian Christian armies of the Fourth Crusade, representing the Roman and Catholic traditions of the west. The modern world still shows many powerful effects of this division between the empires. The pagans of western and west-central Europe were converted by the influence of the church of Rome, but those of Russia and the Balkans by Constantinople. The division runs down between Poland and Russia, and is shown in their writing. Although Polish and Russian are closely related languages, Poland (converted from Rome 965) uses the Roman alphabet, and Russia (converted from Byzantium 988) uses the Greek alphabet. But both the modern emperors called themselves Caesar—Kaiser in the west and Czar, or Tsar, in the east.[8]

Long before the sack of Constantinople, Greek had been forgotten in the west. It continued to be the official language of the eastern empire until the Turkish conquest in 1453, and a much-debased form of the language persisted, even under the Turks, in parts of Greece proper and of the islands. It has survived to the present day, and long bore the historical name of Romaic—i.e. 'Roman', the language of the Roman empire. But Greek culture was cut off from the western parts of Europe during the Dark Ages, except for the few trickles which penetrated through Arabian and Jewish channels; and it only returned to the west hundreds of years later, just in time to escape the mutilation which was to be inflicted on it in its home by the Turkish barbarians.[9]

The fate of the Latin language was different and more complex. Latin survived, not in one, but in three different ways.

First, it survived through seven modern languages and a number of dialects:

> Spanish, Portuguese, French, Italian, Rumanian, Catalan, Provençal; Corsican, Sardinian, Romansch, Ladin, &c.

These languages and dialects were not derived from the literary Latin which we know from Cicero's speeches and Vergil's poems, but from the simpler 'basic' Latin spoken by soldiers, traders, and farmers. Yet they are fundamentally Latin in structure and feeling, and it is through these Latin-speaking nations that most of classical culture was transmitted to western Europe and America.[10]

Also, Latin survived in the Catholic church. Here its life was more complicated. At first the Latin spoken and written in the church was kept deliberately simple and colloquial, to suit the simple speech of the Latin-speaking people who were its congregations. The Bible was translated into this simple Latin with the express purpose of being 'understanded of the people'. Again and again, many fathers of the church explain that they care nothing for fine classical language and style, nothing even for grammar. All they want is that *everyone* should be able to understand the gospels and their sermons. (For instance, the fighting pope, Gregory I (A.D. 590–604), was bitterly opposed to classical learning, and said that the colloquial and ungrammatical Latin he spoke and wrote was the only suitable language for Christian teaching. The monastic regulations drawn up for the order of St. Benedict (*c.* A.D. 530) are one of our best documents for the vocabulary and grammar of late colloquial Latin.[11])

But, as the barbarian invasions continued and the provinces of the empire split up into kingdoms and began their separate existences, that same colloquial Latin split up sectionally, and developed into the different languages and dialects mentioned above; and so they grew away, in different directions, from the simple Latin of the Bible and the church. At this point the church had one of the gravest decisions of its history to make: should it have the Bible and the breviary and the rituals translated again, into all the various languages of western Christendom, or should it keep them in the original Latin, which, although originally simple, was now becoming a dead language, a forgotten language that had to be studied? For the sake of unity it chose the second alternative: and so the Latin of the Vulgate, which had once been deliberately used in order to make the teaching of the church intelligible to everybody, became an obscure and learned tongue. The Irish monk, the French priest, who spoke Old Irish or a primitive French patois from childhood, and then had to learn church Latin for his vocation, therefore found it still more difficult and confusing to learn classical Latin—which was more elaborate, had a different set of words, and even used a different grammar.

Few churchmen did so; and, of course, there was always strong
opposition within the church to any study of classical civilization,
because it was the work of a world which was corrupt, pagan, dead,
and damned.

And yet the classical Latin language and literature did survive
in church libraries and schools. Manuscripts were kept, and were
copied by the monks as part of the monastic discipline. And
certain authors were taught to advanced students and commented
on by advanced teachers. But many, many other authors were lost,
in part or wholly, for ever. Pagan authors were much less likely to
survive than Christian authors. Informative authors were much
more likely to survive than emotional and individual authors.
Thus we have still the works of many unimportant geographers
and encyclopaedists, but hardly any lyrical and dramatic poetry—
although in the Greco-Roman world at its height there was far
more emphasis on pure poetry than on predigested information.
Moral critics were likely to survive, but immoralists not: so
Juvenal the satirist survived, and Horace survived chiefly as a
satirist, but Catullus reached us through only one manuscript,
preserved in his home town of Verona, and Petronius was, practically, lost for ever.[12]

Also, the scholars of the Dark Ages were more inclined to read
and copy authors nearer to them in time. Nowadays we are able,
as it were, to survey classical civilization in a single panorama, like
an aviator flying over a mountain range. But in the sixth or ninth
centuries the learned men were like Alpinists who see the nearer
peaks very big and impressive, while the more distant mountains,
although higher, fade into relative obscurity. Therefore they devoted a great proportion of their time and energy to authors who
are comparatively unimportant but who lived near their own day.

The second main channel for the survival of classical culture in
the Dark Ages was religion. Although the origins of Christianity
were Jewish, other elements not of Jewish origin were embodied
in it by the western and eastern churches. Its early supporters
introduced some folk-lore, for instance. The miraculous birth of
the baby who is to announce a new age of peace and happiness was
a dream of men all over the Mediterranean world in the last centuries of the pagan era. It appeared in a famous and beautiful
poem by young Vergil forty years before the birth of Jesus:[13] the
story as told in Matthew i–ii has little to do with the actual life

and teaching of Jesus, and is omitted from other gospels. Then, a little later, Greek philosophy was added. The teachings of Jesus himself are difficult to put into a single philosophical system; but God's purpose in sending him, the existence of the pagan deities, the position of Christianity in the state, and such topics were discussed, by the attackers and the defenders of Christianity, on a philosophical basis. St. Augustine himself, in his autobiography, actually says it was Cicero's introduction to philosophy, *Hortensius*, that turned his own mind towards religion, to Christianity.[14] Through his works, and the works of many other fathers of the church, classical philosophy was kept alive, converted to the service of Christianity, and transmitted to modern times.[15]

Even more important than the transmission of classical philosophy was the survival, through the church, of Roman law and Roman political sense. Even after the Roman empire dissolved and barbarian kingdoms succeeded it, the western church retained Roman law for its own use. This is clearly laid down in an early Germanic law of the sixth century, and although the principle developed, it did not change.[16] The canon law of the church grew out of the great civilizing achievement of Roman jurisprudence; and it carried on, even through the Dark Ages, not only the methods and principles of Roman law, but the fundamental conception that law is a lasting-embodiment of right, to be altered only with great care, and always higher than any individual or group. This is a conception more effective in western Europe and the Americas and the English-speaking world than anywhere else on the planet, and we owe it to Rome.

Roman political sense, chiefly as handed on to the church but also as revived in monarchs like Charlemagne, saved western Europe from degenerating into a Balkan disorder. Although Rome was not the city in which Christianity originated or first grew powerful, although a scholarly Roman at the end of the first century A.D. knew practically nothing about Christianity and met it only in the Near East,[17] we feel instinctively that it would be destroying an important value to transfer the seat of the Roman Catholic church from Rome to Jerusalem. And, although Catholicism is more firmly established in South America than in Europe, it would be still more improper to shift the centre of the church to Buenos Aires or Rio de Janeiro. It was St. Paul who first felt this: for, as Spengler points out,[18] he did not go to the oriental cities of

Edessa and Ctesiphon, but to Corinth and to Athens, and then to Rome. The Catholic church is the spiritual descendant of the Roman empire. The successorship was marked long ago by St. Augustine in his *City of God*; it was re-emphasized by Dante; and it is necessary. Even the geographical distribution of the power of the church (excluding America) bears a close resemblance to the geography of the Roman empire; and the great organization of the church, with its single earthly ruler, its senate of seventy 'princes of the church', its secure provinces under trusted administrators, and its expeditionary forces in rebellious or unconquered areas (*in partibus infidelium*), its diplomatic experience and skill, its immense wealth, and its untiring perseverance, is not only parallel in structure to the empire, but is the only continuously effective international system comparable to that created by Rome.[19]

And lastly, some knowledge of Greco-Roman history and myth survived through the Dark Ages, though often in a strangely mutilated and compressed form. Many, perhaps most, of the men of that time had no sense of historical perspective. As the early painters mix up in one single tableau scenes distant from one another in time, or draw in one plane, differentiated only by size, figures which really belong to several different levels of perspective, so the men of the Dark Ages confused the immediate with the remote past and the historical with the fabulous. A good non-literary example of this is the famous Franks Casket, an Anglo-Saxon box carved of whalebone about the eighth century A.D.[20] The pictures on it show six different heroic scenes from at least three very distant ages:

> Romulus, Remus, and two wolves (*c.* 800 B.C.?);
> the adoration of the Wise Men (A.D. 1);
> the capture of Jerusalem by the Romans (A.D. 70);
> the story of Weland and Beadohild (*c.* A.D. 400?);
> and an unknown myth, as well as an inscription about the
> whale itself.

Evidently the artist did not feel the long, receding corridor of fifteen hundred years, where these adventures, of different origins and natures, had their places, one behind another, this near and that remote. He saw one single unit, the Heroic Past; but some of that past was Greco-Roman. This unitary view of history grew more orderly and complex as the Dark Ages civilized themselves, and at last it found its highest manifestation in the great review of history which Dante called his *Comedy*.

THE MIDDLE AGES

The Dark Ages in western Europe were scarcely civilized at all. Here and there, there were great men, noble institutions, beautiful and learned works; but the mass of people were helpless both against nature and against their oppressors, the raiding savages, the roaming criminals, and the domineering nobles. The very physical aspect of Europe was repellent: a continent of ruins and jungles, dotted with rude forts, miserable villages, and tiny scattered towns which were joined by a few atrocious roads, and between which lay huge backwoods areas where the land and natives were nearly as savage as in central Africa. In contrast to that gloomy and almost static barbarism, the Middle Ages represent the gradual, steady, laborious progress of civilization; and the Renaissance a sudden explosive expansion, in which the frontiers of space and time and thought were broken down or pushed outwards with bewildering and intoxicating speed.

Much of the progress of the Middle Ages was educational progress; and one of its chief marks was that the knowledge of classical thought, language, and literature expanded and deepened.

Organizations were founded or reoriented in order to study the classics. The universities appeared, like street-lights going on one by one after a blackout: Salerno, the earliest, and Bologna, Paris, Oxford, Cambridge, Montpellier, Salamanca, Prague, Cracow, Vienna, Heidelberg, St. Andrews; and then schools, like Eton and Winchester. These universities, although their staff and most of their students were churchmen, were not clerical institutions. They were advanced schools rather than religious seminaries; and from their inception they had students who ranged more widely than divinity. They were devoted, not to language and literature as we understand the terms, but to philosophy: and philosophy meant the Greek philosophy of Aristotle, however deviously acquired and strangely transformed.

At the same time, the standard of scholarship rose within certain of the monastic orders. The Benedictines in particular built up a tradition of learning and aesthetic sensibility which still survives: many of our finest medieval manuscripts of the classics were written for or preserved in Benedictine libraries.

These scholarly activities were stimulated by correspondence, and still more by travel. The men of the Middle Ages were great travellers. Think of the Canterbury Pilgrims as types of the folk who longed to go on pilgrimages; and remember the travelling already done by the Knight (who had been in southern Spain, Russia, northern Africa, and Turkey) and by the Wife of bisyde Bath (who had been three times to Jerusalem, as well as visiting Cologne and Compostella). Relatively far more people travelled for education then than now. That strange cosmopolitan group, the 'wandering scholars', with their wits sharpened by travel and competition, played a considerable part in increasing the general knowledge of the classics.[21] They improved the standards of philosophical discussion; and by debate, competition, and criticism they helped to prepare the way for modern scholarship. Of course, they all spoke Latin and usually nothing but Latin. They argued, corresponded, delivered speeches, made jokes, and wrote satires in Latin. It was not a dead language but a living speech. It was the international language of the Middle Ages, not only for philosophical debate, but for science and diplomacy and polite conversation. (A. J. Toynbee, in *A Study of History*, 5. 495–6, is disastrously wrong in stating that this international language was directly descended from the 'Dog Latin' of the Roman slums. Low Latin actually grew into the modern Romance languages. The international Latin was a direct continuation of classical Latin, learnt through a continuous tradition of scholarly intercourse, with at most some Low Latin influence from early church writings.)

To-day many of us find it hard to understand why any intelligent man in the twelfth or thirteenth or fourteenth century should have spoken Latin and written books in Latin when he had a language of his own. We instinctively think of this as 'reactionary'. The explanation is that the choice did not then lie between Latin and a great modern language like Spanish or English, but between Latin and some little dialect which was far less rich, far less supple, far less noble in its overtones, and far less widely understood than Latin. If a medieval philosopher wanted to write a book about God, no single contemporary European tongue could provide him with enough words and sentence-patterns to do it, and very few with an audience which was more than merely parochial. And in addition, few of the dialects had ever been written down, so that their spelling and syntax provided still another difficulty for him to surmount in expressing his thoughts. We can understand this if we look at a modern parallel. Suppose an intelligent native of Curaçao in the Dutch West Indies wanted to write a novel about the life of his people. It would be appropriate if he wrote it in Papiamento, the local patois; but he would then find it very difficult to set down anything beyond simple dialogue and descriptions. And no one would read his book outside Curaçao until it was translated into Dutch, or English, or Spanish, or one of the *culture-languages*. It would be the same if he were an Indian writing Navaho, or a native of eastern Switzerland writing Romansch, or a New Orleans Creole writing Gombo,[22] or a Basque or a Neapolitan or a Finn writing in his mother tongue. The reason is that local languages and dialects are useful to their own groups, for daily life and for their own songs and stories, but only the great languages can be used for the higher purposes of communicating thought and spreading knowledge throughout the civilized world.[23]

Again, in the Middle Ages better books were read. During the Dark Ages readers had paid great attention to comparatively late and unimportant authors. The Middle Ages began to correct this attitude. Manuscripts of the greatest classical writers, so far as they were then known, began to increase in number. Libraries were enlarged and systematized in abbeys, monasteries, and universities. And—a sure sign of intellectual activity—translations from Latin into vernacular languages became much more frequent and much better.

Still Greek remained almost a closed field. Again and again one finds that the medieval copyist who writes Latin correctly and beautifully breaks down when he comes to Greek: he will copy a string of gibberish, or add a plaintive note saying 'because this was in Greek, it was unreadable'. The division of the empires was almost complete. In Latin there is an unbroken line of intellectual succession from ancient Rome to the present day: remote, but unbroken. We learn Latin from someone who learnt it from someone . . . whose educational ancestor was a Roman. But the knowledge of Greek in western Europe died out almost completely in the Dark Ages; the few islands of spoken Greek that remained in the west were outside the main streams of culture. It was almost as hard to get beyond classical Latin to classical Greek as it would be for us to reconstruct the language of the Incas. A knowledge of Hebrew and Arabic was probably commoner than a knowledge of Greek. Aristotle was read, not in the language he wrote, but in Latin translations—some made by Boethius soon after the fall of the empire, others written by Jews from Arabic translations, and others produced at the direction of St. Thomas Aquinas and forming part of the general re-education of Europe. Dante, whose scholarship was very considerable, appears to have known no more than a word or two of Greek. Nowadays, when both languages are equally dead, schoolboys who begin one of them always start with Latin: this is a survival of the curriculum of medieval schools and thus, at a distant remove, a result of the division of the empires.

However, the knowledge of Latin was constantly extending and improving. The effect of this was to improve the western European languages, most of which only took shape after the close of the Dark Ages. French, Italian, Spanish, all expanded their vocabularies by bringing in words from classical Latin—sometimes pedantic and silly additions, but more often valuable words to connote intellectual, artistic, and scientific ideas which had been badly or inadequately understood for lack of the language with which to discuss them. English expanded in a similar way. And, as any enlargement in language makes human thought more flexible and copious, literature immediately benefited, becoming subtler, more powerful, and far more varied. The study of Latin poetry, and the attempt to emulate its beauties in current European languages, assisted in the foundation of many modern national literatures and greatly extended the range of those which already existed.

THE RENAISSANCE

The life of the Middle Ages, though violent and exciting and prone to strange sudden outbursts of energy, was essentially one of slow gradual change from generation to generation. The medieval world was built as unhurriedly and elaborately as its own cathedrals. But the important thing about the Renaissance is its unbelievable rapidity. Recently we ourselves, within one or two generations, have seen an equally sudden change—the expansion in mechanical power, from the first electric motor and the first internal-combustion engine to far greater sources of energy, so great that the abolition of human labour is a possible achievement. In much wider variety, but in the same astounding accelerando, new possibilities burst upon the men of the Renaissance, decade after decade, year after year, month after month. Geographical discoveries enlarged the world—we can scarcely imagine how surprisingly unless we conceive of expeditions to-day piercing two thousand miles deep into the interior of the earth, or exploring the depths of the ocean to find new elements and new habitable areas, or visiting and settling in other planets. At the same time, the human body was discovered, both as an inspiration of beauty for the sculptor and painter and as a world of intellectual interest to be explored by the anatomist. Mechanical inventions and scientific discoveries made the world more manageable and man more powerful than ever before. Not only the printing-press and gun-powder, but the compass, the telescope, and the great mechanical principles that inspired Leonardo da Vinci, made it easier for man to master his environment; while the revolutionary cosmological theory of the Polish scientist Copernicus dissolved the entire physical universe of medieval mankind.

In literature, our chief concern, the tempo of change was quite as rapid. Much of the change was caused by new discoveries, characteristic of an age of exploration; but the scholars of that time called it rebirth.

Many manuscripts of forgotten Latin books and lost Latin authors were discovered, hidden in libraries where they had lain untouched and neglected since being copied hundreds of years before. The great book-finder Poggio Bracciolini (1380–1459) describes how he would talk his way into monasteries, ask to see the library, and find manuscripts covered with dust and debris, lying in leaky rat-ridden attics: with touching emotion he speaks of them looking up at him for help, as though they were living friends of his in hospital or in prison.[24] Discovering a manuscript of an author already known is scarcely very interesting, unless it is extremely rare or ancient; but the excitement of the Renaissance scholars came from discovering quite unknown works by authors whom they knew and admired, and sometimes from finding the books of writers whose works had been entirely lost and who had been known only from a few quotations in encyclopaedias. Their excitement was intensified by the precariousness of the operation. It was like looking for buried diamonds. A number of authors were found in only *one* manuscript, and no more copies of their books have ever been discovered.

This activity was paralleled by the rediscovery of classical works of art which had been buried in the ground for a thousand years and more: the famous statues, the cameos, coins, and medals which now fill museums all over the world. Thus, the *Laocoon* was dug up in a vineyard among the ruins of the Baths of Titus, and straightway bought by Pope Julius II for the Vatican Museum. When one particularly fine statue was excavated, it was carried in a special procession, with music and flowers and oratory, to be shown to the pope. This work was not scientific excavation but artistic investigation. It was art that was being searched for, and artists studied it when it emerged. As each new statue came to light, artists began to copy and emulate its special beauties, and sometimes to restore, with the dashing self-confidence of that era, its missing limbs. The Medici Pope Leo X appointed a general superintendent of antiquities for the city of Rome who produced a plan for excavating the innumerable hidden treasures that lay beneath the gardens, cottages, and ruins. His name was Raphael.

An even more important rediscovery was that of the classical Greek language. This was a slower event. It had two main aspects.

Western scholars learned Greek from Byzantine visitors to Italy. Petrarch was the first to make this attempt. He started in 1339, with the monk Barlaam, who was apparently a secret agent of the eastern empire. But he was too old, the lessons were broken off, and he had to be content with a Pisgah-sight. However, in 1360, his younger friend Boccaccio had one of Barlaam's pupils, Leontius Pilatus, made the first professor of Greek in western Europe— at Florence, which long remained the centre of this activity. With Leontius's help Boccaccio produced the first complete translation of Homer, into very wooden Latin prose. Subsequently other emissaries from Byzantium continued the work of teaching Greek in Italy.[25]

Now, the official and court language of Byzantium was recognizably connected with classical Greek through a continuous living chain of descent; but it was not classical Greek. Therefore, although the Byzantines could teach classical Greek to the Italians as a living, though archaic, language, they introduced Byzantine methods of writing and pronunciation which were false to classical standards and took a long time to eradicate. Gibbon illustrates the difficulty by an amusing note:[26] 'The modern Greeks pronounce the β as a V consonant, and confound three vowels and several diphthongs. Such was the vulgar pronunciation which the stern Gardiner maintained by penal statutes in the university of Cambridge (Gibbon was an Oxford man); but the monosyllable βη represented to an Attic ear the bleating of sheep, and a bellwether is better evidence than a bishop or a chancellor.'

As for writing, the first printers took for their models the best available standards of handwriting. Therefore, when they undertook to print Greek they asked Byzantine scribes to write out alphabets on which to model their founts. But Byzantine handwriting was very different from Greek as written in classical times. It was full of contractions, or ligatures, used to increase speed in cursive writing: ου, for instance, became ȣ, and καί became ϗ. In Roman type we still keep a few such contractions: fl, for instance, and &; but there they are not cumbrous, while the early Greek founts were full of them, so much as to be unreadable by non-specialists, difficult to set, and expensive. One Oxford Greek fount needed 354 matrices. They were gradually expelled during the sixteenth and seventeenth centuries; yet the slope of Byzantine Greek handwriting survives in the Greek type used by most university presses, and purists are still urging that the Greek founts be redesigned to cut out the last Byzantine influence and to present the language as the classical Greeks wrote it.[27]

The second aspect of the rediscovery of classical Greek was the appearance of manuscripts of Greek authors in the west. As the Turks drew nearer Constantinople, there was an exodus of scholarly emigrants, like the exodus from central Europe to America in 1933; and the Byzantine refugees brought Greek manuscripts with them. At the same time, Italian patrons of learning were eagerly searching for Greek manuscripts in both east and west. Gibbon quotes the statement that Lorenzo de' Medici of Florence sent his Greek agent, Janus Lascaris, to Greece to buy good books 'at any price whatever', and that Lascaris actually visited the remote monasteries of Mount Athos and found the works of the Athenian orators. Before Lorenzo the same activity had been carried on by his grandfather Cosimo and by Pope Nicholas V (who reigned from 1447 to 1455). It was Nicholas who created the present Vatican Library, employing hundreds of copyists and scholars, and 'in a reign of eight years, formed a library of five thousand volumes'.[28]

Thus the greater part of classical culture was discovered as though it were absolutely new, while men's knowledge of the other part, the Latin area, was immensely extended. The effect on modern languages and literatures was immediate and has not yet disappeared; it is a revelation of the amazing power and flexibility of the human mind that all the new ideas, emotions, and artistic devices could be so easily and sanely assimilated as they were. It was as though the range of colours visible to the eye had suddenly been enlarged, from the present small spectrum of seven to twelve, and as though artists had been supplied both with new media to work in and with new subjects to paint. We shall study the effects of this revolution in detail later, and meanwhile summarize them.

Of course classical scholarship took a tremendous forward leap. At last, men began really to understand and sympathize with the ancients. Difficulties of interpretation, confusions of personalities and traditions, stupid myths and silly misunderstandings which had existed since the onset of barbarism, perpetuated century after century by rationalization and misinterpretation, began rapidly to disappear. Vast areas of antiquity were explored, mapped, and became real. The Latin of western scholars improved until it was not far inferior to that of Cicero himself. Symonds particularly emphasizes the work of Coluccio Salutati, who became the chancellor of Florence in 1375 and for over twenty-five years wrote diplomatic correspondence and political pamphlets in Latin so pure and pointed that it was admired and imitated by the chanceries of all the other Italian powers, including the Vatican.[29]

The Romance languages were still further enriched by the incorporation of words taken directly from classical Latin and, to a smaller but still important extent, from classical Greek. English also assimilated Greek and Latin words, some directly from the classics and others from adaptations already made by French and Italian writers. Only lexicographers can trace the exact proportion between these two different types of loan-words in English. But they combined with the Anglo-Saxon and Norman-French bases of English to make it far wealthier than any Romanic tongue as a vehicle for literature. Again and again, Shakespeare makes his finest effects from a combination of genuine old English, simple

and strong, with the subtler Norman-French and the grander
Latin derivative: thus—

> This my hand will rather
> The multitudinous seas incarnadine,
> Making the green one red.[30]

But German and the other northern European languages—
Swedish, Flemish, &c.—were scarcely expanded at all by this new
knowledge of Latin and Greek. After all, English is akin to Latin
through one of its ancestors, Norman-French. German, having
no such close kinship, finds it more difficult to borrow and assimilate Latin words. Besides, the standard of culture in Germany
was then relatively low; and although classical scholars and
humanists existed, the interaction between them and the general
public in Germany was far more tenuous than, for instance, in
France and Italy.

During this period, the Poles wrote nearly all their prose and
poetry in Latin, the Russians in Old Slavonic. The native literatures went on in their own way, almost unaffected by the rediscovery of classical literature in the west. The Turkish conquest,
which cut the current of civilization that had been flowing into the
Slavic peoples from Byzantium, was a serious set-back to Russian
culture.

The rediscovery of the classics meant much more in western
Europe than an enrichment of the vocabularies of the Romance
tongues and of English. It improved and extended the styles used
by poets, orators, and prosaists. The Roman, and still more the
Greek, writers and orators were extremely subtle and experienced
artisans in language. There is hardly a single stylistic trick now
in use in modern writing which they did not invent. The vernacular writers of the Renaissance eagerly imitated all the newly
found devices of sentence-structure and paragraph-structure, of
versification, of imagery and rhetorical arrangement, copying and
adapting them in the modern languages as enthusiastically as the
Renaissance latinists did in Latin. It is this that really makes the
watershed between pre-Renaissance and post-Renaissance literature. We feel of many medieval writers that their style, by its
naïveté and awkwardness, cramps their thought: that it was
painfully difficult for them to get their ideas into words and their
words into groups. But from the Renaissance on there is no

such difficulty. In fact, the reverse: there are many good stylists who have little or nothing to say. The comparative fluency with which we write to-day is because we are part of the rich tradition of classical style that re-entered western European literature at the Renaissance.

Even more important than stylistic innovations was the discovery of literary forms. There has only been one people which could invent many important literary forms capable of adaptation into many other languages and of giving permanent aesthetic pleasure: the Greeks. Until the models which they perfected and the Romans elaborated were rediscovered, western Europe had to invent its own forms. It did so imperfectly and with great difficulty, apart from small folk-patterns like songs and fables. The revelation of the Greco-Roman forms of literature, coming together with the introduction of so many stylistic devices, the expansion in language, and the wealth of material provided by classical history and legend, stimulated the greatest production of masterpieces the modern world has ever seen:

tragedy in England, France, and Spain;
comedy in Italy, England, and France;
epic in Italy, England, and Portugal;
lyric and pastoral in Italy, France, England, Spain, and Germany;
satire in Italy, France, and England;
essays and philosophical treatises throughout western Europe;
oratory throughout western Europe: there is a continuous line of descent from the Renaissance stylists to such modern orators as Abraham Lincoln, who used, with great effect, dozens of naturalized Greco-Latin rhetorical devices.[31]

The Renaissance also opened up a vast storehouse of new material to western European writers in the form of classical history and mythology. Some of it was known in the Middle Ages, but not so fully realized. Now authors seized on this treasure and exploited it so enthusiastically that they often turned out elaborately polished trash. It is almost impossible nowadays not to be bored with their endless classical allusions—which if commonplace are hackneyed and if scholarly are obscure; with their classical comparisons—every orator a Cicero, every soldier a Hector; and with the mythological apparatus—Bacchus and the fauns, Diana and the nymphs, shepherds and harpies, Titans and cupids—which loads the literature of the sixteenth and seventeenth centuries, often to the exclusion of all matters of real interest. The best evidence that the myths invented by the Greek imagination are really immortal is the fact that they survived such treatment, and are still stimulating the imagination of poets and artists.

Finally, the rediscovery of classical culture in the Renaissance was more than the addition of books to the library. It involved an expansion in the powers and resources of all the arts—sculpture, architecture, painting, and music too—and a closer, more fruitful alliance between them. As in every great artistic era, all the arts stimulated one another. The sense of beauty was strengthened and subtilized. Pictures were painted, poems were written, gardens were designed and armour forged and books printed for the chief purpose of giving aesthetic pleasure; and the detestable medieval habit of extracting a moral lesson from every fact or work of art was gradually—although certainly not entirely—abandoned. The faculty of criticism, hitherto almost confined to philosophical and religious controversy, was now applied intensely to the arts—and not only to the arts, but by radiation from them to social life, to manners, costumes, physical habits, horses, gardens, ornaments, to every field of human life. The sense of beauty always exists in mankind. During the Dark Ages it was almost drowned in blood and storms; it reappeared in the Middle Ages, although hampered and misdirected. Its revivification as a critical and creative faculty in the Renaissance was one of the greatest achievements of the spirit of Greece and Rome.

2

THE DARK AGES: ENGLISH LITERATURE

OF all the great modern European languages, English has by far the largest and most important early literature. During the Dark Ages of history, between the fall of Rome and, say, the year 1000, there must have been some vernacular poetry in France, in Italy, in Russia, in Spain, and elsewhere—although it is unlikely that there was much more than songs and ballads in local dialects. But virtually none of it has survived: it may never have been written down. In German there is nothing but two or three fragments of war-poems; two poetic paraphrases of the Gospel story, with a section of a poem on Genesis and a short description of Doomsday; and several of Notker's philosophical and biblical translations. In the peripheral lands—Iceland, Ireland, Norway, Wales—there were growing up interesting collections of sagas and romances, mythical, gnomic, and occasionally elegiac poems; and in popular Greek some ballads and heroic tales have survived. Of course Latin books were being written in a continuous international tradition, while the Byzantine scholars continued, often with remarkable freshness, to compose in the forms of classical Greek literature. But scarcely anything else has survived in the language of the people out of so many centuries.

However, long before 1000, a rich, varied, original, and lively national literature was being created in England. It began soon after the western Roman empire fell; and it developed, in spite of frightful difficulties, during the dismal years known as the Dark Ages, when western European civilization was fighting its way up from barbarism once again.

ANGLO-SAXON POETRY

The most important poem in old English literature is an epic called *Beowulf*. It deals with two heroic exploits in the life of a warrior chief, but also covers his youth, his accession to the throne, his kingship, and his death. Beowulf is his name, and he is called prince of the Geatas. This tribe is believed to have lived in Götaland, which is still the name of southern Sweden; and the battle in which his uncle Hygelac was killed is known to have occurred about the year A.D. 520.[1] The chief tribes mentioned are the Angles, the Swedes, the Franks, the Danes, and the Geatas themselves. The material of the poem was therefore brought over from the Baltic area by some of the fierce war-bands who invaded Britain after the Romans left it.

Its chief interest is that it shows us an earlier stage of development in European civilization than any other comparable document, Greek and Roman books included. Compare it with Homer. The type of life described, a disorganized world of tribal states, raiding-parties, and gallant chiefs, is pretty much the same. Beowulf himself would have been welcomed in the camp of the Achaeans outside Troy, and would have won the swimming prize at Patroclus' funeral games. But there are important differences:

(a) In *Beowulf*, the conflict is between man and the sub-human. Beowulf's chief enemy Grendel is a giant cannibal living in a cave. (Apart from Grendel's terrific size, he is not necessarily a mere fable. As late as the seventeenth century there are reports from outlying parts of Europe of cannibal families inhabiting caves not unlike Grendel's. The most famous case is Sawney Bean, in southern Scotland.) The other opponent of Beowulf is a firedrake, a flame-spitting dragon guarding a treasure. So the story represents the long fight between brave tribal warriors on one side and, on the other, the fierce animals of the wilderness and the bestial cave-beings who live outside the world of men and hate it.[2] But in the *Iliad* the war is between raiding tribesmen from a Greece which, though primitive, is not empty of towns and commerce, and the rich civilized Asiatic city of Troy, with rich and civilized allies like Memnon. There is no prolonged conflict between men and animal monsters in Homer. (Bellerophon was forced to fight against a lion-goat-snake monster, the Chimera, which breathed fire; but that incident takes only five lines to narrate.[3] The chief Homeric parallels to this aspect of *Beowulf* are to be found in the *Odyssey*, where they are located in wild regions far outside the Greek world: Grendel's nearest kinsmen are the Cyclopes of the Sicilian mountains, or the man-eating Laestrygones in the land of the midnight sun.) Compared with Homer, Beowulf's adventures take place, not in the morning light of civilization, but in the twilight gloom of that huge, lonely, anti-human world, the forest primeval, the world so beautifully and horribly evoked by Wagner in *The Ring of the Nibelungs*; or that of the weird Finnish *Kalevala*, which is ennobled in the music of Sibelius.

(*b*) The world of *Beowulf* is narrower and simpler than that of Homer. Men's memories are very short. Their geographical range is small: north central Europe, bounded by pathless forest and serpent-haunted sea, with no trace of Slavs or Romans beyond. Within this frontier their settlements are lonely, scattered, and ill organized. When new champions face each other in the *Iliad*, or when Odysseus makes a new landfall in the *Odyssey*, there is usually a polite but clear exchange of information which shoots rays of light into the surrounding darkness. We hear of great cities in the distance and great heroes in the past. The result is that the epics gradually build up a rich collection of historical and geographical knowledge, rather like the books of Judges and Samuel in the Bible. But *Beowulf* contains far less such information, because its characters and composers knew far less of the past and of the world around. Any three thousand lines of *Iliad* or *Odyssey* take us into a wider, more populous, more highly explored and interdependent world than all the 3,183 lines of *Beowulf*; and the customs, weapons, stratagems, arts, and personalities of Homer are vastly more complex than those of the Saxon epic.

(*c*) Artistically, *Beowulf* is a rude and comparatively unskilled poem. Epic poetry is, like tragedy, a highly developed literary growth. Its wild ancestors still exist in many countries. They are short poems describing single deeds of heroic energy or suffering: the ballads of the Scottish borders, the songs about Marko Kraljević and other Serbian chiefs, the fine Anglo-Saxon fragment, *Maldon*, about a battle against the invading Danes. Sometimes these are roughly linked together, to make a cycle or a chronicle telling of many great exploits performed in one war, or under one dynasty, or by one group of strong men.[4] But still these do not make an epic. All the adventures of Hercules, or King David, or King Arthur and his knights, will form an interesting story, but they will not have the artistic impact of a real epic. An epic is made by a single poet (or perhaps a closely linked succession, a family of poets) who relates one great heroic adventure in detail, connecting it with as much historical, geographical, and spiritual background as will make it something much more deeply significant than any isolated incident, however remarkable, and causing it to embody a profound moral truth.

Now, most of the heroic poetry in the world belongs to the first stage of this development. It tells the story of Sir Patrick Spens, or the battle of Otterburn, and then stops. There is an Anglo-Saxon poem like this, called *Finnsburh*, which we can also find built into *Beowulf* in a different shape, like the little chapel which later architects have worked into a large and complex church.[5] The Icelandic sagas correspond to the second stage, the long chronicle—although a few, like *Njála*, have the nobility of true epic. *Beowulf* is a dogged, though unskilled, attempt to reach the third stage, and to make a poem combining unity and variety, heroic action and spiritual meaning. Here is its skeleton:

100–1,062   Beowulf fights the giant Grendel;
1,233–1,921   Beowulf fights Grendel's mother;
2,211–3,183   Beowulf fights the fiery dragon, and dies.

So the poem is mostly occupied by relating two (or at most three) heroic adventures, which are essentially similar, not to say repetitious. Two happen in a distant country and the third at the end of Beowulf's long life; while his accession to the throne and his fifty years' reign are passed over in less than 150 lines.[6] The other episodes, evoking the past,[7] comparing Beowulf with earlier heroes,[8] and foretelling the gloomy future,[9] were designed to co-ordinate these adventures into a single multidimensional structure; but the builder could scarcely plan well enough. It would have been astonishing if the age which made only the most primitive churches and castles and codes of law could have produced poets with the power to conceive a large and subtle plan and to impose it on the rough recalcitrant material and half-barbarous audiences with which they had to deal. The style and language of the poem, in comparison with the greater epics of Greece and Rome, are limited in range, sometimes painfully harsh and difficult; yet, even if awkward, they are tremendously bold and powerful, like the hero of whom they tell.[10]

There is apparently no direct classical influence on *Beowulf* and the other Anglo-Saxon secular poems.[11] They belong to a different world from that of Greco-Roman civilization. Attempts have been made to prove that *Beowulf* imitates the *Aeneid*, but they consist mainly in showing that both poems describe distantly similar heroic incidents in heroic language; and on these lines we could prove that the Indian epic poets copied Homer. The differences in language, structure, and technique are so striking as to make any material resemblance merely coincidental, even if it were probable that a poet working in one difficult tradition at such a period would borrow from another even more difficult. When early craftsmen like the creator of *Beowulf* know any classical literature, they are forced by its superior power and elaboration to adapt it very carefully and obviously.

There is, however, a certain amount of Christian influence— although it is evidently peripheral, and later than the main conception of the poem. *Beowulf*, like the world in which it grew, shows Christian ideals superimposed upon a barbarous pagan substructure, and just beginning to transform it. We see the same thing in some of the Icelandic sagas and in the Gaelic legends. Lady Gregory tells how Oisin argued with St. Patrick from the old heroic standpoint, and said to him:

'Many a battle and many a victory was gained by the Fianna of Ireland; I never heard any great deed was done by the King of Saints (i.e. Jesus), or that he ever reddened his hand.'[12]

So *Beowulf* both begins and ends with a thoroughly pagan funeral. It is significant also that, when Heorot the haunted palace was first opened, a minstrel sang a song about the first five days of Creation (evidently based on Genesis, like Cædmon's hymn); but later, when the ogre began to attack the palace, the chiefs who debated about preventive measures vowed sacrifices to 'the slayer of souls' (= the devil = a pagan divinity). Such inconsistency can be a sign either of interpolation or of the confusion of cultures. What Christian influence does appear is strictly Old Testament tradition. The audience of *Beowulf*, the 'half-barbarous folk' to whom Aldhelm sang vernacular songs, was scarcely at an intellectual and spiritual level which would permit it to appreciate the gospels and the Pauline epistles. God is simply a monotheistic king, ruler, and judge, venerable because of His power. There is no mention of Jesus Christ, of the cross, of the church, of saints, or of angels.[13] One or two early Old Testament stories appear, as it were grafted upon paganism: the giant Grendel, together with 'ogres and elves and sea-monsters', is said to come of the race of the fratricide Cain; and there is a mention of the Flood.[14] But all this, although it comes through the Latin Bible, is classical influence at its very thinnest. Greece and Rome had no immediate influence on *Beo-*

wulf and its kindred poems, any more than on the Welsh *Mabinogion*, the stories of Fingal and his warriors, the great legends of Arthur, and other heroic tales which grew up along the frontiers of the dissolving civilization of Rome. Classical influence, if it reached them and their makers at all, reached them through the church. After the Greek world had been cut off and the Roman world barbarized, the church civilized the barbarians. *Beowulf* allows us to see how it began: gradually and wisely, by converting them. After many dark centuries, Europe regained civilization, urged forward largely by feeling, once again, the stimulus of the spirit of Greece and Rome; but it was the church which, by transmitting a higher vision through that influence, began the reconquest of the victorious barbarians upon the ruins of the defeated empire.

In *A Study of History* Mr. A. J. Toynbee discusses the very odd fact that none of the northern epics describes the greatest war-like achievement of their peoples, the overthrow of the Roman empire.[15] His explanation is that the barbarians found the Romans too complex to write about, and the chiefs who conquered them (such as Clovis and Theodoric) too dull. This answer is incomplete. Not all the victors were dull. Many were memorable figures like Attila (= Etzel and Atli in epic and saga). But the Roman empire was indeed too vast and complicated. Its conquest therefore took too long for the tribesmen and tribal poets to see it as one heroic effort. The *Iliad* is not about the siege of Troy—although, because of Homer's genius, it implies the ten years' fighting and the final capture: still less is it about the whole invasion of the Mediterranean area by the men from the north. For primitive man the stimulus to action and to poetry is single: an insult, a woman, a monster, or a treasure. Further, although they looted cities in the Roman empire, although they displaced officials and occupied territories, many of the barbarians did not think they were subjugating an alien enemy so much as taking over their due share in privileges from which they had been kept. They did not abolish the empire. They moved in and took it over. To adapt a phrase of Mommsen's, the conquest meant the romanization of the barbarians even more than the barbarization of the Romans.[16] And lastly (as Mr. Toynbee hints) the very process of conquering the empire tended to abolish their urge towards epic literature, for it was a successful operation, and a success that made them richer and more staid. Heroic poetry seldom describes successes, unless against fearful odds. It prefers to tell of the defeat which makes the brave man even braver and rounds off his life.[17] Not through conquering Rome would the barbarians' will become harder and their hearts keener.[18] But centuries later they re-created the heroic style. When they themselves, led by a new Caesar (a Christian of barbarian descent), were threatened by new pagans no less formidable, then, over high mountain and dark valley, rang out the dying trumpet of Roland.

Christian English poetry is specifically stated by the greatest English historian of the Dark Ages to have sprung from the Anglo-Saxon poetic tradition. The story is in Bede's *Ecclesiastical History of the English Nation*. Bede explains that at parties it was often arranged that each guest in turn should play the harp and sing a song (the songs must all have been on non-religious subjects). A Northumbrian cowherd called Cædmon 'had lived to an advanced age without learning any poetry', so he used to leave the party before his turn came. But one night, after doing this and going away by himself to sleep in the byre, guarding the cattle, he was inspired in a dream to sing about 'the beginning of created things', in praise of God the Creator. When he woke he had firmly in his memory all that he had sung in his sleep, and to these words he later added others in the same noble religious style. After news of this was taken to Whitby Abbey, Cædmon was examined by the abbess Hilda and declared to be divinely inspired. The monks repeated to him the text of a sacred story or lesson to turn into verse, and he did it overnight. He could neither read nor write; but 'all he could learn by listening he pondered in his heart'. Taken into the abbey, he was taught the contents of the Old and New Testaments. Gradually, 'ruminating like a clean animal', he turned the stories and teachings of the Bible into Anglo-Saxon poetry.[19] And so—some time after A.D. 657, when Whitby Abbey was founded—the two great traditions, Anglo-Saxon and Latin, flowed together. When Cædmon ruminated the sublime chapters of the Bible and turned them into sweet songs, he was doing what secular poets like Deor and Widsith did with legends of old chieftains and battles long ago. But the material he was using was translated for him by scholars using the Latin Bible.[20] The synthesis is symbolized by the fact that Cædmon gave up his secular life and entered the monastery.

Of Cædmon's poetry nothing now remains except a fragment which is the right beginning for the long magnificent series of Christian poems in English—a short and beautiful hymn to God the Creator. But there are other Old English poems written later, on Cædmon's system and probably inspired by his example. They are poetic paraphrases and expansions of biblical narratives, apparently by authors who could read the originals in Latin. The essential fact about them is that they combine Bible tradition with Anglo-Saxon style and feeling. They are written in the same short rough metre and the same poetic language as *Beowulf*, full of fist-griping, teeth-grinding phrases. And they have all the martial energy and strength of will characteristic of Old English secular poetry. Abraham appears in *Genesis* as a bold Hebrew 'earl' rescuing Lot from the northmen. The grim resolution of Satan's rallying speech in *Genesis B* (which may conceivably have been known to Milton[21]) is that of a thousand northern chiefs who, although defeated, had courage never to submit or yield. The material of these poems is not Christian tradition but Jewish history and legend. Just as the few biblical reminiscences in *Beowulf* come from the very beginning of the Old Testament, so two of these works are on Genesis and one on Exodus. There is another on the book of Daniel—a story which, although it was written fairly late, is one of the most primitive and strongly nationalist Hebrew books. No doubt the simplicity and violence of the story appealed to the primitive people of England, who were themselves resisting cruel and powerful pagans. A similar paraphrase of biblical history is *Judith*, a fragment about 350 lines long, praising the national Jewish heroine who killed the general of the Assyrian invaders. It was of course attributed to Cædmon, as so many short Greek heroic poems were attributed to Homer or Hesiod; but it is now placed in the tenth century, during the long resistance to the invasion and occupation of England by the savage Danes. Along with two similar German works, these are the first translations from the Latin Bible into a modern vernacular: and they announce the great series of English renderings of the Bible which culminates in the King James Version.

Cynewulf, the next known Anglo-Saxon poet, represents the usual second stage in the development of primitive poetry. In lays, chronicles, and epics, as in other traditional stories (e.g. fairy-tales), the composer's own personality is suppressed. No one knows who put together the *Iliad*, the *Odyssey, Beowulf,* or *Judges*. But while the epic style still lives, there often appears a poet conscious of his own mission and proud of his skill, who inserts his own name in poems written within or near the epic tradition, and alters the conventional style to suit his personality. The earliest known Greek poet after the Homeric epics is Hesiod, whose *Works and Days*, although full of traditional lore and language, also embodies his name, some of his autobiography, and much of his personal outlook on life. In one of the hymns written in epic style long after the *Iliad*, the poet says he is a blind man living in rocky Chios: this was the origin of the tradition that Homer was blind.[22] Phocylides, who wrote poetic proverbs, 'signed' each of them by putting his name into the first line. And similarly in Old English poetry, after the traditionalist Cædmon, comes the much better-defined personality of Cynewulf.

We know that he existed, and know a little of his life, and know four of the poems he wrote. These are:

(*a*) *Christ*, a poetic paraphrase of a sermon on the Ascension by Gregory the Great;[23]

(*b*) *Juliana*, an account of the martyrdom of St. Juliana, evidently versified from a Latin martyrology;[24]

(*c*) *The Fates of the Apostles*, a short versified mnemonic summary of the missions and deaths of the twelve apostles;

(*d*) *Helena*, a long and detailed account of the journey of St. Helena, mother of the emperor Constantine, to Jerusalem, where she searched for the buried cross of Jesus, found it (by threatening to execute a large number of Jews), and instituted its cult.

All these poems contain the name of Cynewulf inserted in runes. This odd cipher is based on the fact that the letters of the runic alphabet had not only their own value as letters but also meanings as words. So they could be worked into a poem as words, but written as letters spelling out a name. (For instance, if a poet's name were Robb, he could insert his signature by using the words *are, oh, be,* and *bee* in prominent places close together in his poem, but writing them *R, O, B,* and *B*.[25]) *Helena* also contains auto-biographical information: Cynewulf says he was a poet, rich and favoured, but suffered sin and sorrow until he was converted to the Christian faith—or, more probably, to a more intense and sincere Christianity, centring on the adoration of the Cross. Cynewulf's work, like Cædmon's, is a synthesis of Anglo-Saxon poetic style with the Christian thought which came through Rome. His subjects, however, are not taken from the Old and New Testaments which were read aloud and translated for Cædmon, but from late Latin works of Christian doctrine and history. He thus marks a more advanced stage in the Christianization of Britain and in its penetration by classical learning. And his style is more orderly and smooth, with a new command of vocabulary and the structure of thought which is classical in origin.[26] For all that, his emotional tone is unmistakably Anglo-Saxon, tough and combative, full of naïve energy and love of the bolder aspects of nature: his zestful description of Queen Helena's voyage to Jerusalem contrasts sharply with the hatred of seafaring shown in most Greek and Latin poetry, and is an early expression of the long English sailor tradition. Even the fact that his signatures are in runes— which must have been obsolescent to a scholar like Cynewulf— is typical of English individualism and conservatism.

Although we cannot examine separate works in detail, two unique poems, often attributed to Cynewulf on grounds of style but not signed, deserve attention. *The Dream of the Rood* is a poem describing a vision of the Cross and of the Crucifixion. It is more individual than any other work of its time: although it is as intense as the fighting heroic poems, its intensity is that of a stranger, more difficult spiritual world. Some of it is in the tradition of early English art. For instance, the Cross speaks a long description of itself—which is like the inscriptions on Anglo-Saxon weapons and ornaments: the King Alfred jewel says *Ælfred mec heht gewyrcean*, 'Alfred had me worked'. No doubt that is why some of the poem was carved on the Ruthwell Cross in southern Scotland, so that the Cross could seem to tell its own story. Again, the author begins 'Listen!' as does *Beowulf*, and Christ is described as a 'young hero'.[27] But the poem contains some elements which are unlike anything in earlier English literature, and which are harbingers of the Middle Ages: the sensuous beauty of the descriptions—the rood drips with blood and glows with jewels, as though in the rose-window of a Gothic cathedral; the setting of the whole as a dream —that characteristic mark of medieval otherworldliness; the cult of the Cross—which was established in the eighth century, and was a novelty for the western church; and the adoration of Christ, neither as a powerful king nor as a moral teacher, but as a supreme and beloved person. As far as can be traced, the poem is neither a translation nor an adaptation, but an entirely original utterance, the mystical cry of one enraptured soul.

But the strangest synthesis of classical and English traditions in this period is the poem called *Phoenix*. Its author tells the story of the miraculous bird, the phoenix which lives far away near the gates of paradise; when it grows old, it builds its own funeral pyre, is burned, dies, and is resurrected. Then the poet goes on to draw the allegorical moral, of the type so dear to medieval zoologists: the fire symbolizes the fire of Doomsday, and the rebirth of the bird images the resurrection of Christ and Christian souls into eternal life. His description of the phoenix is an expanded translation of a late Latin poem on the myth, by the Christian writer Lactantius.[28] The allegory comes largely from a sermon by Ambrose on the resurrection of Christ, with additions from the Old Testament, Bede, and others.[29]

It is fascinating to see how the author of *Phoenix* has changed Lactantius's rather dull poem. The most important alteration is in emotional tone. Lactantius is, despite his remarkable theme, commonplace: full of clichés from earlier poets,[30] sinking into a peevish pessimism at the end, and seldom rising above conventional description, even in his account of the paradisiacal home of the phoenix. It is a gorgeous subject, even finer than the swan so beloved of the Elizabethans and the symbolists. It could have inspired lyrics like those of Tennyson on the eagle, Baudelaire on the albatross, Mallarmé on the swan. It could have been a mystical symbol full of breathless aspiration, like Hopkins's falcon. It could have been a piece of ornate and splendid Miltonic description. But all that Lactantius does with it is to stitch clichés together, and his chief emotion is the dreary early Christian hatred of life. The Anglo-Saxon poet, on the other hand, loves life and loves the subject. He describes the strange bird with an affectionate admiration. He gives far more detail about nature, both in picturing the rich home of the phoenix and in contrasting it with the hideous climate of Britain; and his imagination is far more alive. For instance, Lactantius says that the home of the bird is away in the east, where the gate of the sky 'opens' (*patet*)—a flat word used of any gate which was not permanently closed, and really worth not much more than 'is'. The English poet takes this, not as a conventional word, but as a stimulating image, and makes a beautiful new idea out of it. The gate of heaven not only stands open, but lets out the echoes of the anthems of the blest—to be heard by 'people' who really ought not to be there, since the home of the phoenix is unpeopled, but the conception is too good to lose:

> Peerless the island, peerless her maker,
> Glorious the Lord who laid her foundations.
> Her happy people hear glad singing
> Oft through Heaven's open door.[31]

Similarly, at the end, the Anglo-Saxon poet suppresses Lactantius's misanthropic reflections that the phoenix is happy because it has no mate and children and because it attains life through death:

> O fortunate in fate, of birds most blessed,
> whom God permits to give its own self birth!
> And, be its sex female, or male, or neither,
> blessed the being which knows nought of love!
> Death is its love, and death its only pleasure,
> and, that it may be born, it yearns to die.[32]

He changes the former observation into praise of the wonder-working power of God, and the latter into intimations of immortality.

Then the English poet liberates and expands. His Latin original is in tight couplets, often balanced couplet against couplet in narrow antithesis. He pays no attention to that. Following the Old English habit, he does not try to confine the sense within a couplet, but lets it run on, and even breaks off a speech or a description in mid-line. This is a fundamental difference between English poetry and poetry of the Romance tradition, and continues for many centuries.[33] In quantity, the English poet produces much more verse than his original, not because he is afraid of mistranslating or of being misunderstood, but because he wishes to heighten the emotional power of his descriptions. Lactantius's poem is 170 lines long, but the Anglo-Saxon poem has 677 lines, of which 380 more or less correspond to Lactantius's verses. Thus, 'there is a happy land' in line 1 of Lactantius inspires eleven lines of Anglo-Saxon poetry, plus the fine image of singing heard through the gate of heaven.

The Englishman modernizes to suit his audience. Lactantius writes:

> When Phaethon's flames had kindled all the zenith,
>   that place remained inviolate by fire,
> and when the deluge plunged the world in billows,
>   it overcame Deucalion's mighty flood.[34]

His translator, however, suppresses these remote Greek myths, substitutes the more real and terrifying Hebrew flood, and changes Phaethon's fires into lightning and the final fire of doomsday—the theme with which he is going to end his poem:

> No leaf shall waste,
> no branch be blackened with blast of lightning,
> till doomsday come. When the deluge swept
> with might of waters the world of men,
> and the flood o'erwhelmed the whole of earth,
> this isle withstood the storm of billows
> serene and steadfast 'mid raging seas,
> spotless and pure by the power of God.
> Thus blest it abides till the bale-fire come.[35]

And to the list of woes which Lactantius (following Vergil) says are absent from the home of the phoenix, the English poet adds two more, which often threatened Anglo-Saxon Britain:

> foe's assault, or sudden end.[36]

To conclude, he adds a long sermon in verse, ending with a curious blend of alliterative Anglo-Saxon verse and Latin hymnal phrases, half a line each. God, he says, has given us the chance to earn heaven by our good deeds, and to

> see our Saviour *sine fine*,
> prolong his praises *laude perenni*
> in bliss with the angels—*Alleluia!*[37]

Whoever this poet may have been, he was a good scholar (better than many 'clerks' in the Middle Ages centuries later), a powerful and positive poet who could outsoar his original, and a devout Christian. Obviously the cultural level of England was high to produce such a poet and his audience.

The greatest importance of the *Phoenix* is that it is the first translation of any poem in classical literature into any modern language. Its author knows his Latin, and is not at all afraid of his task. He feels that his own language with its poetic traditions, and his own energies and imagination, are fully equal to those of his Latin model. This is a concrete proof of the advanced civilization of Britain in the interim between the Saxon and the Danish invasions. In literature, the tide comes forward in five waves:

1. First, pagan poetry—*Beowulf* and the smaller heroic poems and fragments. In them, there is no traceable Greco-Roman influence; but a faint irradiation of Christianity from the Latin world.

2. Then Cædmon, writing in the second half of the seventh century, composed poems in the traditional Anglo-Saxon style on subjects from the Latin Bible. Following him, other poets read the Bible in Latin and produced free adaptations of several of its less Christian books.

3. About 800, Cynewulf adapted material from Latin Christian prose writers as subjects for Anglo-Saxon poems.

4. An imaginatively free translation, blending, and expansion of Latin poetry and Latin Christian prose works was made in *Phoenix*.

5. Finally, with *The Dream of the Rood*, an English poet created apparently new and original poetry on themes introduced to Britain through Latin Christianity.

It was to be many centuries before any other European nation would venture to make such translations and write such poems, at once so learned and so creative. The phoenix, miraculously reborn in the image of Christ, symbolizes the miraculous rebirth, in surroundings once barbarous, of Greco-Roman culture transformed through Christianity.

ANGLO-SAXON PROSE

The story of English prose literature during the Dark Ages is also the story of the much-interrupted upward struggle of civilization in the British islands. Poetry nearly always looks backwards, in form or matter or both, to an earlier age. Prose is more contemporary, reflecting the needs and problems and powers of its time. Therefore English prose literature in this period was primarily educational. Its intention was to civilize the British, to keep them civilized, and to encourage them in the struggle against the constantly recurring attacks of barbarism. To do this it used two chief instruments. One was the Bible and Christian doctrine.

The other was classical culture. There was nothing frivolous, no
fiction or fancy, about English prose in this era. It was resolutely
religious, or historical, or philosophical.

The effort to keep civilization alive in Britain was not a single
unidirectional process. It was interrupted and diverted by grave
conflicts. The first of these was the conflict between the British
church and the church of Rome.[38] The British church lost, but
the conflict was long and bitter. Most of the early British churchmen, St. Patrick probably and St. Columba certainly, were not
Roman Catholics. They did not consider themselves to be directly
under the authority of the bishop of Rome, and they interpreted
the Christian doctrine differently from their contemporary coreli-
gionists in Italy. Most of them have by now been appropriated
by the church as saints or expelled as heretics; but it was not
always so simple as that. One of the most interesting among the
pariahs was the Celtic priest Pelagius (c. 360–420), who originated
the doctrine later denounced as the Pelagian heresy. In opposition
to St. Augustine's view that man was totally depraved from birth
and absolutely incapable of saving himself from sin and damnation
without God's grace, Pelagius taught that God expects us to do
only what we can. Man can be good, or God would not punish him
for being bad. Obligation implies ability. It is possible, although
difficult, to live without sinning. Pelagius toured the Christian
world—Rome, Africa, Palestine—preaching this doctrine; but
he lost. Some see in him, Gael as he was, the earliest Protestant.

The Roman church set out to recapture the western outposts of
the empire, and to conquer its British rivals, in A.D. 596. Then the
great Pope Gregory I sent St. Augustine (not the bishop of Hippo
mentioned above) with a mission to establish himself in south-
eastern England. Because of the invasion of the pagan Saxons, the
mission was much needed. The struggle between the churches,
however, was long, and Augustine was not wholly victorious. He
failed to persuade the British churchmen to adopt the Roman
calendar with the Roman calculation of Easter, and there was also
some difficulty about the manner of tonsure.[39] But after winning
the great debate called the synod of Whitby (664), the Romans had
the upper hand. They at once improved their advantage by sending
out two cultural missionaries, Theodore and Hadrian. Theodore,
an Asiatic Greek from Tarsus, who knew Greek as well as Latin
(a rare thing then), was named archbishop of Canterbury.[40] The

two opened a school where Latin, Greek, sacred literature, astronomy, metrics, and arithmetic were taught. We can, however, trace the conflict of the two churches, and occasionally a synthesis, all through the first period of British prose literature.

It was the era of Cædmon and Cynewulf in poetry. In prose only Latin works have survived, but their cultural level is fairly high. The first known historical account of Britain in the Dark Ages was written by a Celtic monk, one Gildas (c. 500–70): he considers himself a direct survivor of the Roman civilization in Britain, calling Latin 'our language' and despising the fierce native chiefs as heartily as the early Americans despised the Red Indians. The earliest Saxon scholar, Aldhelm (abbot of Malmesbury in 675), was educated first by a Gael (Mældubh) and then by Hadrian the Roman.[41] His poetry is good, and much of it is lightened and charmed by Vergilian influence. The prose of his letters and articles on religion, morality, and education suffers from imitating the church fathers: evidently he read mostly late and tortuous Latin, and quotes Cicero only three times.

A much greater man followed him: the Venerable Bede (= Bates: c. 672–735), the first English author in whom we can trace the strong common sense and amiable directness which characterize the English at their best. He was a northerner, got his early schooling from Irish and north British churchmen,[42] and dedicated his greatest work to Ceolwulf, king of Northumbria. All his works are in Latin, many are compilations, and most are now obsolete or uninteresting; but none of them is silly, or obscure, or extravagant in the way that medieval works so often are.[43] Most are commentaries on scripture (the Old Testament still predominant) and on biblical subjects such as the temple at Jerusalem. The synthesis of classical and modern is greatest in his *Ecclesiastical History of the English Nation* from Caesar's invasion in 55 B.C. to A.D. 731. That he himself regarded this as the pinnacle of his life-work he showed by adding his autobiography and a list of his publications at the end.[44] It is an essential book, because:

it is one of the first of the great documents describing the reconquest of barbarism by civilization, after the fall of the Roman empire;

it is real history, giving more weight to central truth than to impressive details or propagandist lessons;

it is well constructed: by far the largest work of its kind in all early English literature, it contrasts very favourably with the patchy and discontinuous *Anglo-Saxon Chronicle*;

it was produced by genuine research: as well as incorporating the work of earlier annalists, Bede used invaluable un-published documents and verbal tradition, collecting evidence from sources as far distant as Rome. It is to him that we owe immortal stories like Cædmon's inspiration, Gregory's 'Angles with the face of angels', and the old thane who compared man's earthly life to the flight of a swallow through a lighted hall.

Bede was both an Englishman and a latinist. For him, Latin was still a living language, which took time and trouble to write, but which was clear and memorable and universally intelligible. European culture was profoundly influenced by his historical vision: for example, he was chiefly responsible for introducing the Christian era in dating events B.C. or A.D. He was the first English-man who transcended his age and who, as Dante saw,[45] belonged to all humanity.

(If *Beowulf* corresponds to Homer, and Cædmon to the authors of the early Homeric hymns, and Cynewulf to Hesiod, then to whom does Bede correspond, if not to the pious, patriotic, legend-collecting historian Herodotus?)

Another proof of the high standard of British learning in the Dark Ages is provided by two scholars who were so great that they were invited to help with the re-education of Europe. These were:

Alcuin of York (born 735), who went to teach in the school of classical learning founded by Charlemagne as part of his resistance to barbarism, and who left over 300 essays (in the form of letters) on literature and education, written while he was head of the school and later of the abbey at Tours;

John, who called himself emphatically Scotus Erigena or Eriugena, meaning 'the Gael from Ireland'. He was the greatest philosopher of the Dark Ages.[46] And he was another product of the Celtic church, which continued in existence all through this difficult time, leaving monuments of its work in the missions it founded and supported on the Continent as well as in many fine Latin manuscripts written in Irish hands. John, whose knowledge of Greek was unique in his age, succeeded Alcuin by heading the court school founded by Charlemagne's successor Charles the Bald. More of a philosopher than a churchman, he worked out a mighty pantheistic scheme of the universe, which shows that he had a genius for metaphysics, narrowed and strengthened, like the genius of the Gothic cathedral-builders, by the surrounding barbarism of his era.

But now, after the earlier invasions had ceased, and the tough Anglo-Saxons had been partly civilized and Christianized, new waves of pagan invaders were attacking Christendom. Only five years after Alcuin left England for France, in A.D. 787, the *Anglo-Saxon Chronicle* says:

'In these days the first three ships of the Northmen arrived, from the pirates' country.'

The sheriff, it goes on, dutifully went down to arrest the pirates, and was killed; and 'these were the first Danish ships that visited the land of the English'. From then on, the attacks got worse and worse. Repeated entries in the *Chronicle* carry no more than communiqués of disaster:

This year there was great slaughter in London, Canterbury, and Rochester.[47]

The Celtic monasteries and churches in Ireland and Scotland and elsewhere were attacked soon after 787, and destroyed piecemeal, so that their inhabitants were scattered all through western and central Europe as displaced persons.[48] The worship of Thor was set up in the holy city of Armagh.[49] In England the Danes settled as a permanent armed force of occupation: the *Chronicle* simply calls them 'the army'. It was King Alfred (848–901) who led the resistance and ensured that, in spite of frightening defeats, British culture was kept alive, and the Christian religion did not perish from the stricken island.

Alfred negotiated peace with the Danes in 878. This was really a Munich settlement made to hold off the invaders for a breathing-space, but it gave him time to revive British civilization within the territory that remained under his influence. Almost all the work of the Celtic church and of the Roman missions and teachers had now been undone. Alfred himself wrote[50] that there was *nobody* in southern England, *very few* in the midlands (south of the Humber),

and *not many* in the north, 'who could understand the Mass in
English or translate a Latin letter'—i.e. who knew what the Latin
ritual and prayers really meant, or who could read at sight the
ordinary current Latin which was the international language of
educated people. Britain was almost cut off from religion and
civilization. And that was only one aspect of her cultural losses
during the invasions. Schools, churches, the ordinary man's
consciousness of British history and world history and geography—
all had to be revived. It was a great and difficult work, which only
a great man could have carried out.

Alfred used a number of methods to revive civilization and
culture in Britain; but for our interests the most important is
translation. He chose four important Latin books, and with some
assistance turned them into Anglo-Saxon, for the instruction and
improvement of his people. They dealt with the four most
essential subjects.

1. *The practice of the Christian religion* was explained in Alfred's
Hierdeboc (= *Shepherd's Book*), a translation of the great Pope
Gregory's manual for parish priests, the *Regula pastoralis.*[51]
Gregory was the pope who expressly disowned any attempt to
write classical Latin and any interest in classical culture; but he
was a great fighter and teacher (it was he who sent Augustine's
mission to Canterbury) and his energy and ability and practical
wisdom were needed at this time. Alfred's preface—which has
been called the first important piece of prose in English[52]—
emphasizes the essential role played in education by translations,
and Alfred's determination to rebuild the mind of England by
translating such books.

2. *The Christian history and the continuous national existence of
the English people,* as well as the stage of culture it had attained
before the Danish invasions, were stressed in a translation, done
either by or for Alfred, of the *Ecclesiastical History of the English
Nation* by the Venerable Bede.

3. *World history and geography* were explained and interpreted
from a Christian point of view by a translation of the fifth-century
Spanish writer Orosius's *History against the Pagans.* Dedicated to
St. Augustine of Hippo, this book, like Augustine's own *City of
God,* gave a long proof that the introduction of Christianity was
not, as the pagan philosophers asserted, responsible for the fearful
sufferings of mankind which began when the declining empire was

attacked by plagues and savages. The historical sections of the book contain Greek and Roman mythology as well as history and some geography, in a convenient if sometimes distorted form. Alfred wisely omitted Orosius's geographical data about distant parts of the world which were then beyond the horizon of the English, and inserted some valuable chapters on the geography of north-western Europe, including verbatim narratives of two great exploratory voyages carried out by the sailors Ohthere, in the White Sea, and Wulfstan, in the Baltic.

4. *Moral philosophy in its relation to theology* was summed up in *The Consolation of Philosophy*, by Boethius. Since the influence of this book on European thought was far greater than that of the other three, it deserves a detailed examination.

The philosopher of late Rome, Anicius Manlius Severinus Boethius, born about A.D. 480, and brought up by the distinguished pagan statesman Symmachus (whose daughter he married), was for a thousand years one of the most influential writers in Europe. Rich and noble, he was highly educated, and was devoted to Greek —from which, just as the knowledge of the language was perishing in the western world, he translated a number of the important books that became the foundations of medieval science and philosophy.[53] As a patriotic Roman, who no doubt disliked the Ostrogothic rulers of Italy (although for some time he tried to collaborate with them), he was arrested by the Ostrogothic king Theodoric on the charge of inviting the eastern Roman emperor Justinian to drive out the barbarians. After some months in prison, he was executed in 524. The account of his death says that a cord was slowly tightened round his brain, and that, while enduring this torment, he was clubbed to death. It was while under sentence of death that he wrote his most famous work, *The Consolation of Philosophy*.[54]

This is a treatise in five sections, called 'books'. In form it is a cross between the Platonic dialogue, invented by Plato to reproduce the teaching methods of his master Socrates, and the Menippean satire, a mixture of prose and verse used for philosophical criticism by the Cynic Menippus.[55] Alternate chapters are in prose and verse; or perhaps we should say that each prose chapter is followed by a verse intermezzo. The prose is late Latin, struggling not without success to be classical; the verse is a collection of

many different metres, predominantly short-line patterns appropriate for lyric poetry, and many copied from the reflective choruses
of Seneca's tragedies: there is surprisingly little of the long rolling
didactic verse one would expect.[56] The style of the whole varies
from rapid, though dignified, conversation to stately rhetoric. The
general scheme is that of a conversation between Boethius, in his
cell, and his 'nurse and doctor' Philosophy.

After listening to his complaints, Philosophy tells him that he is
ill. His soul is ill, with ignorance and forgetfulness. He has
forgotten the real character of the power and wealth he has lost—
they are purely external and transitory things. He has forgotten
the truth about the world—that it is governed by God's providence.
He has forgotten the corollary of that fact—that not only happiness
but pain too is sent us for our own good, as punishment, or
exercise, or discipline.[57] So Philosophy questions him, as a doctor
questions a patient, carefully and firmly drawing out the errors
from his sick soul, and applying the remedy of truth.

Although Boethius's book ends nobly, it appears to be unfinished. It has no final dialogue to correspond to the initial
conversation between doctor and patient; it has no diagnosis, no
summing-up, no drawing-together of the results of the consulta-
tion, no prescription for the patient to take, and (although we
might expect it from Boethius's admiration for Plato) no poetic
and mythical conclusion. Why it is unfinished, we can guess.

Unfinished or not, it is a great book. Many who have glanced
into it, expecting to find a late-Latin cliché-monger or compilator,
have been surprised and moved by the depth of its feeling. There
are several reasons for its power.

It is individual. Although *The Consolation of Philosophy* is a
synthesis of the arguments of many other philosophers and the
images of many other poets, it is much more than a collection of
echoes. The noble character and able mind of Boethius himself are
manifest all through it; and they make it a unity. Then the
recurring poetic interludes, always sung by Boethius himself or
by his lady Philosophy, unify the book and keep it from resembling
a metaphysical treatise: no Ph.D. thesis is punctuated with songs.
And the book is closely connected with Boethius's own life and
death, which gives a real uniqueness to what might otherwise have
been an abstract dissertation. It has, therefore, as distinctive a
character as Plato's great dialogues, *Gorgias*, *Phaedo*, *The Republic*.

It is full of emotion, which transforms the book. Its setting is burningly dramatic: a condemned cell, in which a Roman nobleman, once rich, famous, and learned, once high in a great career, sits waiting for death at the hands of a half-civilized occupying army. The philosophical arguments, however dry and difficult, are made vitally moving by the urgency with which Boethius and his physician pursue them—much more so than in most earlier classical philosophy. (Even in Plato's *Phaedo* the proof of immortality, although it does serve as a consolation for the beloved master's imminent death, is presented as an impersonal analysis of the facts; and it is only in a few of Cicero's philosophical treatises, written when he himself was suffering bitter sorrow, that the same depth of emotion as in Boethius becomes apparent.) This sense of urgency is again heightened by the poetry: lyrical aspiration transcending the limits of a prison, beautifully expressed in songs of despair and consolation, which, to early Christians, must have sounded like the hymns of the persecuted church. The problem Boethius faces is one which every man and woman must face, and his difficulties are ours. Just as we all have bodily illnesses in which, although only for a moment, we feel the shadow of death touching us, so we all have periods of doubt and despair, profound spiritual illnesses when the whole life of the soul appears to ebb and falter. To see Boethius suffering from this illness, and to watch him being cured, must stir our sympathy. And there can be no doubt that the emotions of Boethius and his teacher are sincere. Boethius has literally nothing left to live for but to find the truth that will make him whole. Philosophy herself is not an abstraction. She is a stately lady, wise, loving, and kind— a type which appealed deeply to the men of the Middle Ages. She prefigures the medieval conception of the Virgin Mary, as well as such angelic guides as Dante's Beatrice. She was one of the first of a long series of gracious womanly spirits, such as Lady Holy Church in *Piers Plowman*, who move through medieval thought and soften the brutality of the times.

Boethius's book is very rich in content, for it is a synthesis of much of the best in several great realms of thought:

(*a*) Greco-Roman philosophy, Platonism above all. Boethius much admired Plato's *Gorgias*, *Phaedo*, and *Timaeus*. It is clear that the figure of Socrates, calmly preparing for death in his prison-cell and consoled by his own philosophy, was in Boethius's mind; he refers several times to the doctrine of reminiscence; and his entire book describes, step by step, a process of conversion like that which Plato held to be the necessary entrance to the philosophical life. Boethius also used the *Physics* and other works of Aristotle; and Cicero's philosophical writings, particularly the *Tusculan Discussions* (which deal with man's great unhappinesses) and *The Dream of Scipio* (which is a revelation of immortality). And, although he does not mention them, he depended very heavily on the treatises and commentaries of the Neoplatonists.[58] One of the greatest things in the book is Boethius's constant comparison of the physical universe, regarded as a rational system, to the moral law. The stars, he says, follow the same kind of law as the life and soul of man. We can see him, a condemned prisoner, looking up from his cell towards the serene heavens, and, like Kant, who declared that the two greatest things in the universe were 'the starry sky above, the moral law within',[59] assuring himself that wickedness, however powerful, was bound to sink and disappear before 'the army of unalterable law'.[60] (This thought also flowed into the medieval belief in astrology, since if man and the stars both obey laws ordained by God, it is easy to assume that they are part of a single interdependent system.)

(*b*) In classical literature, Boethius's emphasis is more on Roman than on Greek works: Seneca is his principal model in verse, he modelled his prose style on Cicero, while Vergil and Horace supplied many of the general maxims which he used, in those bad days, to prop his mind.

(*c*) Christian ideals are not expressed, but something close to them inspires the whole book. Although Jesus Christ is not mentioned, although Boethius never quotes the Bible explicitly and only once appears to allude to it, although it is not religion but philosophy that consoles him, still, the book is an expression of the belief in monotheism, begins by postulating immortality, emphasizes the importance of the moral life, mentions other Christian beliefs such as purgatory,[61] and embodies such Christian ideals as moral courage under persecution.

The fourth great merit of the book is its educational power. It is one of the supreme educational books of the world. Like Plato's dialogues, it educates the reader by carrying him through the process of education which it describes. It is moving to watch Socrates' interlocutors being forced or persuaded to see the light which they had denied; and so it is moving, but even more moving, to watch Philosophy curing Boethius (or Everyman) of the blindness into which his sufferings coming after his happiness had thrown him. It is touching to remember that his very name comes from the Greek word βοηθεῖν, which means (among other things) to *assist* a patient and *relieve* his illness. Just as Socrates often compared himself to a physician, so Philosophy here likens her work, not to that of a teacher with a pupil, but to that of a doctor with a patient: a mental patient undergoing psycho-analysis, we should now say. It is a mark of the difference between the Greeks and ourselves that for them all was health, and even the doctor told them chiefly how to keep fit (as a trainer advises a young athlete), while Boethius, like a modern man, feels himself to be suffering from a mortal disease of the soul.[62]

All these causes combined to make the influence of Boethius widespread and long-lasting through the Dark and Middle Ages.[63] And there was a personal reason for his popularity. He had faced the same problem which recurred for a thousand years, and he faced it nobly. He was a good man killed by vicious tyrants. He was a civilized man imprisoned and executed by the barbarians, but immortalized by his ideals. Many a Christian priest or knight hemmed in by savages took consolation from the pattern set up by Boethius. King Alfred himself, surrounded by Danes, on an island within an island, identified himself with the Roman hero: in his preface to the translation he says:

'King Alfred . . . set forth this book sometimes literally and sometimes so as to preserve the sense of it, as clearly and intelligently as he could, in the various and multiple worldly cares that often troubled him in mind and body. During his reign, the troubles that came on the kingdom to which he succeeded were almost innumerable.'

When translating Boethius, Alfred adapted the book to suit the audience for which he meant it. He omitted much which was too difficult for them, and perhaps for himself—including nearly all the difficult argument of book 5. Sometimes he substituted simpler paraphrases of the general drift of meaning, and sometimes little moral homilies of his own. Much as a modern translator might insert footnotes, Alfred adds explanatory phrases and extracts from the annotated editions which he used for his translation. He makes the whole thing much more of a Christian work. He mentions Christ by name, which Boethius does not; he brings in angels, the devil, Old Testament history, and Christian doctrine; and the name of God occurs much oftener than in the original. There is one touching personal addition. In his complaint Boethius tells Philosophy that, although he is not greedy for money or publicity, he had wanted to find some scope for his talents rather than to grow old uselessly.[64] To this Alfred adds his own thoughts:

'Now no man can get full play for his natural gifts, nor conduct and administer government, unless he has fit tools, and raw material to work on. By material I mean that which is necessary to the exercise of natural powers: thus, a king's raw material and instruments of rule are a well-populated country, and men of religion, men of war, and men of work.... Also he must have means of support for the three classes: land to live on, gifts (= money?), weapons, meat, ale, clothes, and anything else the three classes need. Without these means he cannot keep his tools in order, and without the tools he cannot perform any of the tasks entrusted to him.[65]

Still, many of his explanations are astonishingly naïve, and show the great decline in British scholarship, under the pressure of war, since the days of Bede.[66]

On his own grateful admission, Alfred was helped in his translations by four priests, notably a Celt from Wales named Asser, whom he calls 'my bishop', and who, like Aldhelm, became bishop of Sherborne.[67] It should also be remembered that Alfred had vital connexions with Rome and with the Holy Roman empire. His father married Judith, daughter of the emperor Charles the Bald; Alfred himself had visited Rome in his youth, and kept in communication with it.[68]

The last great pre-Norman educator in England was Ælfric (c. 955–1020), a southern scholar, bred at Winchester. He summed up the activity which preceded him by being almost bilingual in Latin and English. Many of his sermons are filled with Old English alliteration, and some are even dominated by a rhythmical beat comparable to that of the antique heroic poems. But he also wrote a Latin grammar, with prefaces in English and Latin and a Latin–English vocabulary. This was one of the very first modern Latin schoolbooks. He also made, or edited, a paraphrase of the first seven books of the Bible in English, with the dull and difficult parts left out. In his time, and partly through his work, English became a literary language—the earliest in Europe.

During the tenth century a number of English versions of the gospels were produced : the Lindisfarne Gospels in northern Northumbrian, the Rushworth Gospels in northern Mercian and southern Northumbrian, and the West Saxon Gospels. The manuscript of the Lindisfarne Gospels is one of the finest works of art preserved from the Dark Ages. Like Alfred's England, like British civilization, it was gravely endangered by the Danes: it was being removed from its home for safety when it was washed overboard in a storm; but, like the culture to which it belonged, it was recovered almost undamaged when the tide ebbed.[69]

During the Middle Ages and the Renaissance it became fashionable for British writers to translate and copy continental writers. But before the Danish and the Norman conquests, the standard of vernacular literature was so high, and the distribution of classical scholarship so wide, that culturally Britain was the most advanced state in Europe. That position she lost through the repeated attacks of the northern savages, and then through the conquest by their Norman kinsmen.[70] During all that long struggle to resist and to assimilate, there was growing up in Britain   at a level lower than that of Greco-Roman mythology, but soon to compete with the tale of Troy and the tale of Thebes—the splendid British legend of Arthur and his knights, the gallant band who resisted the heathen and the forces of darkness. The Danish conquest was a disaster. The Norman conquest was another disaster, alleviated only by the fact that it destroyed the Danish dominion and built a broader bridge to the Latin area of the Continent. The effect of the two was, first, to retard Britain—which had been so far in advance of the rest of Europe—and then, later, to link her more closely to the civilization of the Continent, in which she had once shared and which she had helped to revitalize.

3

THE MIDDLE AGES: FRENCH LITERATURE

THE focus of literature in the Middle Ages was France—both northern France and, until its destruction in the crusade against the Albigensian heresy, the gay southern land of Provence. From France, poetry radiated outwards, warmly to Italy and Britain, less strongly to Spain, Germany, and the Low Countries. Although languages and dialects differed greatly, and although there were political divisions through and between the European countries, on the spiritual plane western Europe was more of a unity than it is to-day. The world of scholarship, with its international language of Latin, was a unity. The world of the church was a unity—although it was troubled by heresies (Albigensians and Hussites), doctrinal disputes (St. Bernard *v.* Abélard), and schisms (the worst being the great schism between the rival popes). The world of courts and chivalry was a unity, however distracted by political and personal feuds. And, on the level above folk-poetry, the world of literature was also a unity. Before Italian, French was the literary language of northern Italy: at the end of the thirteenth century Brunetto Latini wrote his encyclopaedia, the *Treasure*, in French 'because the language sounds sweeter'; Marco Polo's travel memoirs were set down in French too. There was such an invasion of Italy by Provençal minstrels, and their poems were so warmly welcomed, that the magistrates of Bologna had to pass a law forbidding them to stand and sing in the streets.[1] The best symbol of the unity of the Middle Ages is the *Comedy* of Dante, in which scholars and poets and great men of all ages and countries known to him are brought together in a single, mainly medieval afterworld.

But it was in France, the nearest of the western provinces of the Roman empire, that the radiation of medieval thought and literature centred and grew strongest: it dominated and largely shaped that unity: so to France we turn first.

ROMANCES OF CHIVALROUS ADVENTURE

French literature (apart from a few small and unimportant religious works such as an eleventh-century life of the Syrian saint

Alexis) opens with *The Song of Roland*. Like *Beowulf*, which opens English literature, this poem is rather more primitive than Homer; and it is almost as unaware as *Beowulf* of the existence of classical civilization and Greco-Roman history. It is a 4,000-line epic, arranged in strophes bound together by assonance, and inspired by the Saracenic wars of Charlemagne. It relates the heroic death of Charlemagne's Lord Warden of Brittany, Hruodland, in A.D. 778. (Roland is his modern name, and he was actually killed not by the Saracens but by the Basques.) The few classical reminiscences that occur in it are feeble, and distant, and distorted. For instance, we are told that the pagan Saracens worship a trinity of idols. One is Mahomet; one is Tervagant, whose name survives in the word for a woman with a devilish temper; and the third is Apollo, in the strangest company that the Far-Darter ever kept.[2] Then once the poet, telling how a Saracen enchanter was killed by a Frankish archbishop, adds that the sorcerer had already been in hell, 'where Jupiter led him by magic'.[3] At a great distance, this might be a reminiscence of the visit of Aeneas to the underworld. Lastly, in the Baligant episode (which is not thought to be by the original poet of *Roland*), the emir of Babylon is said to be so old that he 'quite outlived Vergil and Homer'.[4] There is no other trace of classical influence, nor should we expect to find it in a poem whose author barely knew the Roman deities.

Roland is the earliest of an enormous series of heroic poems dealing with adventure and war all over the western world. These can be called romances.[5] The word *romance* simply means a poem or story written in one of the vernacular Romance languages instead of Latin—and so, by implication, less serious and learned; but in time it acquired the sense that indicates the essential quality of these works, their love of the marvellous. They were extremely long poems—not long and rich like Homer, but diffuse and rambling to suit the leisurely tempo of the Middle Ages. Homer's hexameters gallop forward with the irresistible rush of a chariot in a charge; the short-line couplets of the romances and other such medieval poems jog along, league after league, as patiently as the little horses that carried the knights on their interminable quests.

The earliest such poems dealt with the heroic exploits of Charlemagne and his court, or sometimes more distant contemporaries, during the Dark Ages. These were followed by romances on the exploits of Greek, Roman, and Trojan heroes, historical or mythical; and by tales of the adventures of the British King Arthur and his knights. Only the second of these groups concerns us here.

Before we begin to discuss it, it must be said that the appearance of a large and growing number of poems and prose works on subjects drawn from classical antiquity is only one aspect of the expansion of culture which was noticeable in the eleventh and admirable in the twelfth century.[6] This was the period when the universities began to assume something like their modern form, when a new spirit of questioning and criticism invaded and improved philosophy, and when a quantity of important Greek and Roman books were translated and taught for the first time since the onset of the Dark Ages. This was the century of the great logician and metaphysician Abélard, of John of Salisbury, and of many other progressive thinkers. It was also an age of increasing poetic production, and, very obviously, an age of broadening, though still shallow, knowledge of Greek and Roman things. Songs, satires, and romances poured out in overwhelming profusion. The songs and satires stop, but the romances seem to run on for ever. They are as endless as medieval wars.

The greatest of the romances on classical subjects is *The Romance of Troy*, *Le Roman de Troie*. It was written by Benoît de Sainte-Maure, a poet of north-eastern France, about A.D. 1160; and it runs to some 30,000 lines. The story begins with the Argonauts sailing eastwards to find the Golden Fleece and dropping off a detachment to capture and loot Troy. Troy is rebuilt by Priam. Priam's sister Esiona (= Hesione) is kidnapped by the Greeks. The Trojans send a punitive expedition to Greece which carries off Helen. The Trojan war then begins.

Obviously this alters the usual story so as to make the Trojans innocent and the Greeks brutal aggressors. This shift of perspective is maintained throughout the poem. The Trojans win nearly all the time; and Troy is only defeated when the Trojan prince Antenor, as a fifth-columnist, plots with the Greeks to admit a storming-party.

After the fall of Troy the romance describes the return of the Greek troops, and ends with the murder of Ulysses by his own son Telegonus: Circe's child.

Benoît says he takes the whole story from an eyewitness, who knew much more about it than Homer—since Homer lived more than a hundred years after the war—and who did not commit the foolishness of making gods and goddesses fight in human battles. The book written by this eyewitness (or a version of it) still exists. It is a very curious little thing.

It is called *The History of the Destruction of Troy* (*De excidio Troiae historia*), by 'Dares Phrygius', or Dares the Phrygian. (The Phrygians were neighbours and allies of the Trojans.) As we have it, it is a short work in bad, flat Latin prose of extreme simplicity, verging on stupidity, obviously written very late in the decline of Latin literature.[7] It is prefaced by an introduction in somewhat better Latin, saying that it was found by Cornelius Nepos (a contemporary of Julius Caesar) in Athens, written in Dares's own hand, and that it was then translated into Latin. Both the preface and the book are forgeries.

The book is really a late Latin translation and abbreviation of a Greek original, now lost but probably also in prose, which pretended to be a day-by-day description of the Trojan war written by one of the combatants. This is indicated by the sentence in the last chapter summing up the casualties with a transparently bogus pretence of accuracy:

'There fell on the Greek side, as the daily reports written by Dares indicate, 886,000 men.'[8]

We can reconstruct the original in its main outlines. It was a piece of pure fiction, probably written in the period known as the Second Sophistic (second and third centuries A.D.): we have other stories of adventure from that period, although none deals with Troy.[9] Historical romances of the same type have been produced in modern times: for instance, Tolstoy's *War and Peace*, which undertakes to prove that Napoleon did not really control the invasion of Russia, and Graves's *King Jesus*, which describes the career of Jesus as a pretender to the kingship of the Jews, from the point of view of an interested but unsympathetic contemporary. The peculiarities of this book were its special purposes:

> to justify the Trojans against the Greeks;
> to denigrate the Romans, by defaming their ancestor Aeneas: the author, instead of saying that Aeneas saved the remnants of Troy (as he does in Vergil), actually makes him join Antenor in opening the gates to the invaders; and the

founding of Rome is not mentioned—Aeneas is merely
dismissed in anger by Agamemnon, and sails away;[10]
to bring in love, which is not prominent in the *Iliad* and
Odyssey. Thus, the invulnerable hero Achilles is killed at
a secret rendezvous with Polyxena, the daughter of Priam.
Their story provides the main love-interest. It is peculiar
that, in the version of Dares which we have, there is nothing
corresponding to what later became the most famous love-
story of the Trojan war: Troilus and Cressida. But there
is a detailed description of the beautiful Briseis, Achilles'
captive, who appears under the name of Briseida;[11] and
Troilus' exploits are much emphasized (partly in order to
throw Aeneas into the shade): so it is possible that Benoît
used a fuller version of the story, which connected Troilus
and Briseis in a love-adventure parallel but opposite to that
of Achilles and Polyxena.[12]

The Greek author, like a good forger, made his falsification as
convincing as possible. He seems to have given far more detail
than we find in the *Iliad*: battle after battle, truce after truce,
covering the whole ten years instead of the brief episode of the
Wrath of Achilles. He omits all mention of the gods and their
constant interference in the course of the war: this looks more
reasonable and realistic. He gives precise eyewitness descriptions
of the appearance of the main characters, which Homer never does
directly. As for the fictitious author's name, there is a Trojan
warrior Dares mentioned by Homer in *Iliad*, 5. 9, but the book as
we have it does not call him the author—obviously because that
would be an appeal to the veracity of Homer, which the forger wants
to explode. And the story about the book's being hidden, and
discovered many centuries after the Trojan war, is the usual trick
to explain how, if authentic, it could have survived without being
mentioned by a single classical Greek writer from Homer through
Herodotus to Euripides and Plato. Basically, it is the same trick
as Poe's *MS. found in a Bottle*, and we shall meet it again later.[13]

As well as Dares, Benoît used another book of the same type.
It is the *Diary of the Trojan War* by 'Dictys of Crete', who pretends
to have been the official historian of the war on the Greek side.
The Latin translation of this is simple, but much better written
than Dares; and pieces of the Greek original have now turned up
among the Tebtunis papyri.[14] If one is prior to the other, then

Dictys is probably prior to Dares, for it is more intelligent and less extreme. Just as Dares's book was justified by a story about its being hidden and then discovered in Athens, so this is justified by the statement that it was found in a tomb in Crete, written in 'Phoenician characters'. The story about the death of Achilles in a love-intrigue with Polyxena occurs here too, and so does the betrayal of Troy by the fifth-columnists Antenor and Helenus. Aeneas does not appear as a traitor, but his founding of Rome, or of Alba, is not mentioned.[15] Neither Briseis nor Chryseis, the two beautiful captives who blended to make Cressida in the Middle Ages, is mentioned by name. The book ends with the return of the heroes and the adventures of Odysseus' illegitimate son Telegonus.

Now, why did Benoît use these two late and bogus books, which through him acquired such an enormous influence? Chiefly because they were easy to read. He had had a little classical education and had doubtless been taught some Latin at a monastery school: enough at least to follow the story-line of his authors; but it was not much more than a smattering.[16] Vergil, whom he might have used, is much more difficult than Dares and Dictys; and he does not tell the whole story of the war. Homer was lost, and the only existing Latin translation of the *Iliad* was little known and incomplete.[17] As well as being easy, the method of Dares and Dictys would be attractive to a medieval poet: for they both contain an enormous number of incidents (which is in the vein of all the romances), they emphasize romantic love, and they leave out the battles of the gods, which would have perplexed or repelled the twelfth-century Christian audiences. Benoît did not use them very intelligently. For instance, he made both Palamedes and Ajax die twice, in two different ways: because he was translating the two different versions given by Dares on the one hand and Dictys on the other.[18] But his book became extremely popular and extremely important.

The Romance of Troy virtually reintroduced classical history and legend into European culture—or rather spread it outside the scholarly world. Its essential act was to connect Greco-Roman myth with contemporary times. The tactics, sentiments, and manners of Benoît's characters are, of course, all twelfth century, but that means that the story and its heroes and heroines were quite real for Benoît and his readers. It is a seminal book, which announced and encouraged a whole new school of poetry and imagination.

Among other things, it stimulated one strange fashion: that of tracing genealogical connexions between modern families or nations and the peoples of antiquity. This had been a habit even in ancient Rome. Vergil and others spent much thought and care on proving that the Trojans, although defeated, were really the virtuous side, and that the survivor, Aeneas, had been the founder of the Roman stock and ancestor of Augustus. This kept the Romans from feeling themselves to be a parvenu tribe who had conquered the intelligent Greeks by sheer brute force, and it helped to legitimize the new imperial dynasty. We are told that Cassiodorus actually provided a Trojan family-tree for the executioner of Boethius, Theodoric the Ostrogoth.[19] In the Dark Ages men lost their historical perspective and the habit died away, but now it was revived. The Middle Ages and even the Renaissance were pro-Trojan. There was a contemporary parallel to Benoît's work in Geoffrey of Monmouth's *History of the Kings of Britain* (1135), which, in addition to containing the first detailed story of King Arthur, traced the ancestry of the British kings back to Troy.[20] Centuries later the idea still persisted. At the beginning of the Renaissance, Anthony à Wood says that a party in Cambridge University who opposed the introduction of Greek studies called themselves Trojans and nicknamed their leader Hector.[21] Sir Philip Sidney still believed the story when he wrote the *Apologie for Poetrie*, for he said it was 'more doctrinable' to read about 'the feigned Aeneas in Vergil than the right Aeneas in Dares Phrygius'[22] —i.e. Vergil was beautiful, but Dares was true. In France, Ronsard tried to use the myth as a theme for his epic, *The Franciad*. Seldom has there been such a successful forgery. Evidently it became ordinary slang, at least in English, for Jonson calls an amiable judge 'the honestest old brave Trojan in London', and Dekker says the patriotic cobblers are 'all gentlemen of the gentle craft, true Trojans'.[23] The idea still survives in the laudatory phrase 'to fight like a Trojan' rather than like a victorious Greek. In heroic legend, a glorious defeat is remembered longer than a victory.

The Romance of Troy was widely translated, and even more widely imitated.[24] It is appropriate for such a book that its imitations should have been even more influential than the original—particularly one which does not mention Benoît by name. This is the *History of the Destruction of Troy*, written in Latin late in the thirteenth century by Guido de Columnis.[25] Guido never mentions Benoît and often cites 'Dares' and 'Dictys', yet it is clear that Benoît was his chief source. This book had an overwhelming success all over Europe—partly because it was written in the international language—and was much oftener translated than *The Romance of Troy* itself, being turned into Italian, French, German, Danish, Icelandic, Czech, Scots, and English.[26] The tale of Troy as told by Benoît came to Britain by two different routes, equally interesting.

1. In about 1340 Boccaccio wrote a poem called *Filostrato*, expanding the incident in *The Romance of Troy* where Briseida, daughter of Calchas (a Trojan priest who deserted to the Greeks and left her behind in Troy), coquets with one hero for each camp, Troilus the Trojan and Diomede the Greek.[27] Possibly by confusion with Homer's beautiful captive, Boccaccio called the girl Griseida, and he emphasized the role of Pandarus as a go-between.[28] This is the poem which Chaucer adapted in *Troilus and Criseyde*.

2. Guido's Latin plagiarism was put into French by Raoul Lefèvre in 1464, as *Le Recueil des hystoires troyennes*. (He did not name Guido, any more than Guido named Benoît!) William Caxton turned this into English in 1474, and his version—together with Chaucer's poem and Chapman's Homer—is probably the source of Shakespeare's *Troilus and Cressida*. Shakespeare's bitter play is therefore a dramatization of part of a translation into English of the French translation of a Latin imitation of an old French expansion of a Latin epitome of a Greek romance.

The Romance of Troy was only one of many romances on classical themes; but the quality and historical function of them all was the same, and so, unfortunately, were most of their sources. To the men of the Middle Ages, most of the world and most of history was unknown: therefore they were ready and glad to believe marvellous tales about both. *The Romance of Aeneas*, which in essence is a rewriting of Vergil's *Aeneid* to serve as a sequel to *The Romance of Troy*, decorates and disguises its original with mythical details taken from commentaries on the *Aeneid*; marvels from books on the Seven Wonders of the World; erotic touches from Ovid; and incidents (possibly original) of romantic passion.[29] Thus Lavinia, who in the *Aeneid* is a quiet dutiful passive little girl, falls hotly in love with Aeneas the moment she sees him, and has her first love-letter shot to his feet by an archer.

The Romance of Thebes, another 10,000-line poem more or less contemporary with *Troy* and *Aeneas*, tells the story of Oedipus and the curse which he laid on his children, to work itself out in the fratricidal war of Polynices and the rest of the Seven against Thebes. There was a source for this at hand, in the *Thebaid* of Statius (written about A.D. 80), but the proportions and emphasis of the romantic poem are different. The author says he is using 'a Latin book called Statius', because laymen cannot read Latin: some of his work is careful transcription, apparently from an epitome of Statius, and the rest is romantic invention.[30]

There were many poems on that gallant figure Alexander of Macedon. *The Romance of Alexander* by Lambert le Tort and Alexandre de Bernay is a poem of over 20,000 lines, in the twelve-syllable metre to which it gave the name Alexandrine. This is medieval romance at its most absurd, although the actual outline is a recognizable account of the parentage, education, and campaigns of Alexander the Great. Its source is quite as curious as that of *The Romance of Troy*. The philosopher Aristotle was Alexander's tutor. Aristotle had a nephew called Callisthenes, who accompanied the king on his campaigns and left an unfinished history of them. It is lost. But Alexander soon after his death became a favourite subject for free fantasy—particularly his strange adventures in the East—and a number of forgeries or forged amplifications of Callisthenes' history were written.[31] These became frequent in the late Greek romantic period which produced Dares and Dictys. We have a vulgar Latin book of this kind by Julius Valerius, written in the late third century A.D., containing a 'letter from Alexander to Aristotle' about the marvels of India, full of travellers' tales which were, when revived in the Middle Ages, to be perpetuated form any centuries. The Arch-priest Leo, from Naples, that home of gossip and folk-tale, produced another version in the tenth century; and, to show the kind of milieu which produced this stuff, there are Syrian and Armenian versions.

Thus it is not only the best of the Greco-Roman world that comes down to us in modern adaptations, but the most trivial. Yet still it stirs the imagination. The Middle Eastern tales spun into late Greek and late Latin romances lived on to inspire that mendacious traveller 'Sir John Mandeville', whose very name is fiction, to make Rabelais compete with them in the voyage of Pantagruel, and finally to help Othello in bewitching Desdemona with tales of

> the Anthropophagi, and men whose heads
> Do grow beneath their shoulders.[32]

The *Lay of Aristotle*, which shows the philosopher saddled and bridled by a pretty Indian girl, and cavorting about the garden as an object-lesson for Alexander, is pure invention on the typical fabliau theme of the power and trickiness of women; and were it not that the Greek philosopher was the model, rather than King David or King Solomon, it would scarcely be worth mentioning.[33] But it was widely popular in the Middle Ages. In a number of French Gothic churches you can still see, among the carved grotesques, the philosopher (bearded, gowned, and wearing his doctoral bonnet) down on his hands and knees, with the Indian houri riding him side-saddle and whip in hand. This, at the time when the universities were developing the study of Aristotelian philosophy to the highest point it had reached for many centuries, is a fine example of the gulf between the scholars and the public in the Middle Ages.

OVID AND ROMANTIC LOVE

The conception of romantic love which has dominated the literature, art, music, and to some extent the morality of modern Europe and America for many centuries is a medieval creation; but there were important classical elements in its development. It took shape in the early twelfth century, as a fusion of the following social and spiritual forces (and in smaller degrees of many others):

the code of chivalrous courtesy, which compelled extreme deference to the weak;

Christian asceticism and scorn of the body;

the cult of the Virgin Mary, which exalted the purity and transcendent virtue of woman;

feudalism: the lover was his mistress's vassal, and she owned him like a serf;[34]

medieval military tactics: the process of winning a woman's

love was often compared to the alternative operations of storming a fortified place, or capturing it after a long blockade: the whole plot of *The Romance of the Rose* is a combination of the two;

the poetry of Ovid, who wrote a cynical intellectual discussion of love-making as a science, but whose other works contain many immortal stories of passionate devotion conquering death;

at a later period, in the dawning Renaissance, this conception was deeply influenced by Platonic philosophy; but at this time that influence was felt only faintly, through Neo-Platonic mysticism and even through Arab love-poetry.[35]

The ideal of romantic love had a long and rich artistic history, with a remarkable revival in the nineteenth century. It will be enough to mention a few of its greatest products:

Dante's *New Life*, and the guidance of Beatrice throughout his *Comedy*;

Spenser's *Faerie Queene*, and several aspects of Queen Elizabeth's personality;

Shakespeare's *Romeo and Juliet*, his Sonnets, and how much else?

Chopin's music, and Wagner's *Tristan and Isolde*, and most nineteenth-century Italian opera;

Heine's love-poems and the Schubert and Wolf settings for them;

Victor Hugo's *The Toilers of the Sea* and many modern novels;

the Sonnet of Arvers and countless modern lyrics;

Rostand's *Cyrano de Bergerac* and *The Distant Princess*;

and an infinite number of parodies and burlesques, notably *Don Quixote* and *Tom Jones*.

It is interesting that the conception should have died first in France, where it was born. In modern French literature, and for that matter in modern French society, there is scarcely any trace of it. There are many inversions of it, for instance the disgusting novels of Montherlant and Sartre's *Nausea*, and one great book symbolizes its corruption and decline. This is *Madame Bovary*, whose heroine ruins her life seeking for love and romance, while her husband treats her in a normal, sensible, French way, like most husbands throughout the modern world.

Although the ideal of romantic love was forming independently of the classics in the twelfth century, it was a great classical poet who gave it authority by his antiquity, illustrated it by his stories, and elaborated it by his advice. This was Ovid, who had been already known to scholars, but now entered the world of general literature.[36] Ovid was born in 43 B.C., and won quick fame with his love-poems, particularly *The Art of Love*. He was working on his masterpiece, an epic-romantic-didactic poem on miraculous transformations from the creation to the apotheosis of Julius Caesar, when, aged fifty-one, he was involved in the disgrace of Augustus' granddaughter Julia, to which his *Art of Love* apparently contributed. He was exiled to Tomi (now Constanţa in Rumania), where he died. He is one of the five or six greatest Roman poets, and, like Vergil and Horace, represents a fertile synthesis of Greek and Roman culture. His disgrace did nothing to injure his reputation after his death! Dante ranks him with Homer, Horace, Vergil, and Lucan.[37]

It is amusing to imagine that, just as the Latin language in different environments gave birth to the different modern Romance languages, so the different Latin writers produced different literary traditions in western Europe. The spirit of Vergil, with its solemnity, its devotion to duty, its otherworldliness, and its profound sense of the divine, is reincarnated in the Roman Catholic church and its greatest literary monument, the *Comedy* of Dante. Cicero produced the rhetoric and philosophical prose of England. Lucan the Spaniard had his imitators in Spanish epic.[38] But Ovid was the most French of Latin writers; and so he was the strongest classical influence on nascent French literature. Not only French: Ovid also typifies and helped to inspire the light, supple, amorous element in Italian literature—the spirit of Boccaccio and Ariosto. But the literature of France received his influence earliest and has retained it longest.

The medieval French romances dealt with three topics above all others: fighting, love, and marvels. As the years passed, as the medieval world became a little more sophisticated, fighting became less and less important, and love and marvels more and more. Now, Ovid was the master poet of love, and the greatest poet who had ever told of marvels—miraculous transformations and weird adventures, mostly motivated by sex. He was therefore a principal cause, and his popularity a symptom, of the increase

in the power of love and the marvellous in the twelfth century.
One example will illustrate this. An early and beautiful story of
romantic love is that of Héloïse and Abélard, a pair of star-crossed
lovers. Peter Abélard (1079–1142), master of Notre Dame, was
one of the greatest twelfth-century philosophers, but he was also
a popular and successful poet of love. Even after (with true Dark
Age savagery, surviving into these difficult centuries) he had been
castrated and silenced, he corresponded with his love Héloïse;
and, writing to her, he quotes the *Loves* of Ovid:

we yearn for the forbidden, desire the denied[39]—

while she, writing to him, quotes six lines from Ovid's *Art of Love*,
a moving passage on the multiplied power of love reinforced by
wine.[40] Even after their love was ruined, they still recalled the
subtle and sensuous Latin poet who expressed it, and perhaps
kindled it.

Early in the twelfth century we hear of a group of less desperate
and more consolable nuns holding a Council of Love to decide
whether it is better to love an aesthete or a soldier, a clerk or a
knight. The debate began by the reading of 'the instructions of
Ovid, that admirable teacher', just as a church service is begun by
the reading of the Gospel; and the reader was Eva de Danubrio,
'an able performer in the art of love, as other women say'.[41]

This argues a good deal of close interest in the amorous Ovid.
Not much later the stories he tells begin to enter European literature. Perhaps the first is *Pyramus and Thisbe*, a French poem of
some 900 lines. It is mostly in the dreary octosyllabic couplets of
the romances, but fantasy breaks in from time to time, and there
are some stanzas, and some dissyllabic lines. The story is a free
rendering of the tale of two unhappy lovers forbidden by their
parents to marry. Believing Thisbe to have died by a mischance,
Pyramus kills himself: she finds his body and follows him.[42]
Coming from Babylon through Rome to medieval France, this
story became very popular and had a long history. It is often
quoted from Ovid by Provençal troubadours and by French and
Italian poets from the end of the twelfth century onwards.
Chaucer makes it second in his *Legend of Good Women*; Gower
puts it into his *Confessio Amantis*; it is retold in *L'Amorosa Fiammetta* by Boccaccio, and it reappears in Tasso; there are some
remarkable correspondences between it and the plot of *Aucassin*

and Nicolete; it is essentially the same story as that of *Romeo and
Juliet*—the couple divided by the hatred of their parents, meeting
secretly, and dying separately under a mistaken belief in each
other's death; and one of its latest appearances is in *A Midsummer-
Night's Dream*, as

THE MOST LAMENTABLE COMEDY AND MOST CRUEL DEATH

OF

PYRAMUS AND THISBY.

Another of Ovid's stories, one of the most poignant, tells how
Philomela was ravished and mutilated by her sister's husband
Tereus. He cut her tongue out and kept her prisoner, but she
wove her story into a tapestry and sent it to her sister Procne.
With Philomela, Procne killed her son Itys and made Tereus eat
him, and then at the extreme of suffering changed into a bird:
she into a brown-blood-stained swallow, and Philomela into the
nightingale, which laments wordlessly in the darkness and yet
somehow tells her story.[43] This is one of the oldest legends in our
world. It appeared as early as Homer, and went all through Greco-
Roman literature, to be reborn in medieval French literature,
paraphrased from Ovid's version, under the softer title *Philomena*;[44]
it then passed into the Renaissance, where it was used and bruta-
lized in ? Shakespeare's *Titus Andronicus*. There Lavinia, like
Philomela, is ravished and has her tongue cut out, but her hands
are cut off too, so that she may not write. Nevertheless, she points
out the story in Ovid to show what happened to her:

> What would she find? Lavinia, shall I read?
> This is the tragic tale of Philomel,
> And treats of Tereus' treason and his rape;
> And rape, I fear, was root of thine annoy.
> See, brother, see! Note how she quotes the leaves![45]

Philomel was a convention for many years after that; was ignored
by Keats in his ode *To a Nightingale*; but revived in the thought
of later, more deeply troubled poets—in Arnold's *Philomela* and
in Eliot's *Waste Land*.

> So rudely forc'd.
> Tereu. . . .

In *Flamenca*, a Provençal poem dated to A.D. 1234, there is a list
of the well-known stories which minstrels would be expected to
sing.[46] Some of them are tales of Christian chivalry, but by far the

greater number are tales from Greco-Roman myth, and most of these come from Ovid. There is a large selection from his *Heroides*, the letters of famous ladies to their lovers, and there are others from the *Metamorphoses*. This was the period when many of the favourite stories like Pygmalion and Narcissus entered European literature.

Ovid's *Art of Love* was translated by the first great French poet, Chrétien de Troyes (fl. 1160). His translation is lost, but there are four others extant. One of them is an interesting modernization by Maître Elie. Ovid advises the young man in search of pretty girls to frequent public places in Rome—the porticoes, the temples, and above all the theatres. Maître Elie brings it up to date by inserting a list of good hunting-grounds in contemporary Paris.

Some time later, probably between 1316 and 1328, Ovid's *Metamorphoses* were not only translated but supplied with an intellectual and moral commentary, to the extent of over 70,000 lines of octosyllabic couplets. The author, who is unknown but seems to have been a Burgundian, first translates the fables as Ovid gives them, and then adds an instructive explanation.[47] For instance, Narcissus pined away for love of his own reflection and was transformed into a flower. This, explains the translator, is a symbol of vanity. What flower did Narcissus become? That flower spoken of by the Psalmist, which cometh up and flourisheth in the morning and dies by the evening: the flower of human pride.[48] Perhaps only the Middle Ages could have blended elements so diverse as the brittle, cynical, beautiful legends of Ovid and this pious Christian moralizing.

THE ROMANCE OF THE ROSE

To understand the Middle Ages through literature it is necessary to read three books: Dante's *Comedy*, *The Canterbury Tales*, and *The Romance of the Rose*. *Le Roman de la Rose*, incomparably the most important of the medieval love-romances, is a poem in some 22,700 octosyllabic verses, rhymed in couplets, of which the first 4,266 are by Guillaume de Lorris and were written about 1225–30, and the rest by Jean Chopinel or Clopinel, called Jean de Meun, who wrote them about 1270. It is the tale of a difficult, prolonged, but ultimately successful love-affair, told from the man's point of view. The hero is the lover, the heroine the Rose. The characters are mainly abstractions, hypostatized moral and emotional qualities, such as the Rose's guardians, Slander, Jealousy, Fear, Shame, and offended Pride. There are also anonymous human personages, notably Friend, who gives the lover some Ovidian advice, and an Old Woman, who advises the Rose's projection, Fair Welcome. Cupid, too, plays a part, and finally Venus herself appears, to win the definitive victory over Chastity. The entire poem takes place in a dream, and contains a great number of symbols, some of them emphatically sexual: thus, the action takes place in a garden, and the climax is the capture of a tower, followed by the lover's contact with the imprisoned Rose. The most permanently valuable elements in the poem are the romantic fervour and idyllic youthfulness of the first part, and the digressions in the second part, by the mature, satiric, and well-educated Jean de Meun: even in their confusion, they give a vivid and brilliant picture of the thought of the Middle Ages.

Classical influence in the romance is much more noticeable in the second part than in the first: still, it runs through the whole poem. We shall analyse it first as formal and then as material.

The general scheme of the poem is an adventure within a dream. Lorris actually begins with a reference to one of the most famous visions of antiquity, the *Dream of Scipio* which Cicero wrote to end his book *On the Commonwealth*. Most of the book is lost now, but the *Dream* was extant throughout the Middle Ages, having been preserved with the commentary written for it by the fifth-century author Macrobius. It was really Plato who introduced the habit of conveying deep philosophical ideas in dreams or visions, and Cicero merely copied him: of course, Lorris knows nothing of that, nor, indeed, is he clear about Cicero and Scipio: he says Macrobius

> wrote the vision
> that came to king Scipion.[49]

But the dream appears in many medieval authors who were not influenced by classical culture, and in contexts which are not borrowings from the classics: for instance, *The Dream of the Rood* and *Piers Plowman*. We may conclude that, in spite of Lorris's garbled reference to a classical author, the dream in *The Romance of the Rose* is not a classical device. It should rather be connected with the frank and powerful sexual symbolism of the poem. The rose is not, of course, exclusively a sexual symbol: in Dante (*Parad.* 30–1) the blessed appear as a great rose of light, and we recall the rose-windows which are among the most beautiful features of Gothic cathedral-architecture. But it is primarily sexual, and here it certainly is. A symbol of this kind is a disguised expression of a subliminal emotion; and dreams are the channels through which many subliminal emotions express themselves and find relief. We should therefore take the dream-form, together with the sexual symbolism of rose, garden, tower, &c., as expressions of the intense subconscious life which was produced by the new conception of romantic love. The two inharmonious partners, physical desire and spiritual adoration, are united in romantic love, in an extremely difficult and tense relationship.[50] That tension, and its expression by symbolism, are not classical but modern.

Within the dream, the plot of the romance is a quest, ending in a siege and a battle. Obviously this is the plot of many of the heroic romances, whether they deal with Arthur and his knights or the Greeks and the Trojans. The quest of the lover for the Rose is not far different from the quest of Arthur's knights for the Grail and many other such adventures. But when we examine the actual battle more closely, we find classical influence in it. For the entire conflict takes place, not between human beings, but between two parties of personifications (with the assistance of a few deities). This idea has a long history and a classical origin. The tale of allegorization in the Middle Ages would be endless. But the actual conception of representing a spiritual conflict as a physical battle probably entered modern literature from the *Psychomachia* or *Soul-battle* of the Christian Latin poet Prudentius (348–c.405), which describes the vices and virtues battling for the soul, and which was itself an elaboration and spiritualization of the older and simpler battles described by Homer and Vergil. Lorris did not take the idea from Prudentius, whom neither he nor Jean de Meun seems to have known, but that was its origin nevertheless.

But there is more talk than fight in the poem. The talk is in the form of dialogue—sometimes becoming monologue—and the talkers are usually abstractions. The most important talker is Reason, who comes to console the lover when, after having reached and kissed the Rose, he is temporarily separated from her. Reason is obviously an imitation of Boethius's Lady Philosophy, and the idea is obviously that of the *Consolation of Philosophy*.[51] Reason actually recites a series of extracts from Boethius;[52] and the entire tone of her sermon is that Fortune is not to be admired but (as

Philosophy explained to her patient Boethius) to be despised.[53]
She observes that 'he who translates Boethius on Comfort well will
do laymen a great deal of good',[54] and in fact, Jean de Meun did
translate it later. It should, however, be noted that many of Jean's
ideas came not directly from Boethius, but through his medieval
Latin imitator Alain de Lille, or Alanus de Insulis (1128–1202),
author of a Boethian dialogue with Nature on sodomy (*De planctu
Naturae*) and a great poem on the nature and powers of man,
Anticlaudianus.

The romance begins with an explicit reference to Ovid:

> This, the romance of the Rose,
> does the whole *art of love* enclose.[55]

And Ovid is quoted and referred to throughout: a little vaguely
by Lorris, frequently and in detail by Jean de Meun. There are
in both parts of the poem long passages on the art of love. The
Old Woman makes a speech nearly 2,000 lines long about the
methods a woman can use to improve her appearance, increase
her attractions, tease her lovers, and extract money from them.[56]
About 600 lines of it come directly from the third book of Ovid's
Art of Love. There is one amusing personal allusion. Ovid says
it is essential to bring girls presents:

> Although you brought the Muses with you, Homer,
> but took no gifts, you'd soon be shown the door.[57]

Jean alters this to bring in Ovid himself:

> To love a poor man she won't care,
> since a poor man is nothing worth:
> and were he Ovid or Homer's self,
> she wouldn't care two pins for him.[58]

Now, Ovid's *Art of Love* is a frivolous version of the didactic
treatise as written by so many classical philosophers and scientists;
and it is the didactic element in *The Romance of the Rose* that
echoes him. There is, however, an important difference, which is
not often pointed out. Ovid wrote a handbook whose wit consisted in treating love as a *science* (that is the real meaning of *ars*
amatoria): he gave the most efficient methods of starting and
continuing love-affairs, and he even wrote a book of *Cures for Love*
showing how to recover from an unsatisfactory liaison. There is
scarcely anything spiritual about the entire poem: physical, yes,

and social, and aesthetic in a high degree, but nothing spiritual. The girls are the reverse of ideals or symbols: they are Roman gold-diggers or Greek kept women. But *The Romance of the Rose* does not give the science of love. It begins by giving the good manners of love, the higher approach to the experience, and goes on to give the philosophy of love. Jean de Meun is not much interested in the good manners of love, but he philosophizes endlessly. His part of the poem is an intellectual exercise of the same type as the metaphysical debates of the twelfth-century and thirteenth-century universities. It is, of course, far less chivalrous and more satiric than the first part of the romance, and is inspired as much by Juvenal as by Ovid. He philosophizes in a harsh tone of cynicism and protest which sorts very ill with the ideal quest for the ideal Rose. We have suggested that the symbolism of the poem was produced by the sexual tension which came into the world with the modern consciousness. The conflict between the idealism of Lorris and the realism of Jean de Meun is another expression of that disharmony. However, despite the misogyny and cynicism of Jean's section of the romance, it has not the materialistic, non-moral outlook of Ovid's *Art of Love*, it deals far more in abstracts, and it insists incomparably more on moral ideals, even by satirizing those who fall short of them.

The Romance of the Rose contains the entire metaphysics of medieval love, as the *Divine Comedy* contains the metaphysics of medieval Christianity. Lenient observes that the subject became a dominant and permanent one in French literature.[59] The French have always been much more interested in the intellectual aspect of love than any other European nation. The disquisitions on the Passions, declaimed by the heroes of Corneille and Racine, the maps of Tenderness in baroque fiction, the treatise of Stendhal *De l'amour*, the surgical dissections of love in Proust and many modern authors, all these stem from the spirit that produced *The Romance of the Rose*. For that spirit, the odd blend of emotion and reasoning which issues in an intellectual discussion of the supreme human passion, the principal authority respected not only by the authors of *The Romance of the Rose*, but by their predecessors and contemporaries, was Ovid. The methods they used in discussing love came partly from Roman satire, and partly from contemporary philosophy, which itself was a direct heir of the philosophy of Greece. And for the psychological penetration that enabled them to enter deep into the heart of a tormented lover, and to vivisect it in soliloquies and anguished solitary debates, all medieval poets were indebted to the brilliant psycho-analytical poetry of both Ovid and Vergil.

We have examined various aspects of the form of the poem. But as a whole it is almost formless, in the sense that its parts bear no reasonable or harmonious proportion to one another. Its bitterest enemy, Jean Gerson, chancellor of Notre Dame, described it as 'a work of chaos and Babylonian confusion';[60] and not even its most convinced admirer could praise its arrangement and structural plan. In principle, this formlessness is the reverse of classical. We shall see later how, as the moderns became better acquainted with the great books of Greece and Rome, they learned to give better form to their own by learning the simple rules of proportion, relief, balance, and climax. *The Romance of the Rose* is in this respect a medieval product, comparable to the enormous tapestries, the endless chronicles, the omniscient encyclopaedias, bestiaries, and lapidaries, the vast Gothic cathedrals which grew slowly up, altering their plan as they grew, and sometimes, like *The Romance of the Rose*, ending with two different kinds of spire on the same building.[61] Nevertheless, there was a faint classical justification for formlessness in a quasi-philosophical work. The tradition of satire was that of a rambling, apparently extempore diatribe in which the author spoke as his fancy and humour moved him. It was in that tradition, crossed with the form of the philosophical dialogue (also fairly loose), that Boethius wrote his *Consolation of Philosophy*. But not even these two loose, roomy, disquisitive patterns can be held responsible for the shapeless garrulity of *The Romance of the Rose*.

Materially, the classical influence is very much stronger in the second part of the poem than in the first. It is seen chiefly in illustrative stories, in arguments, and in descriptions.

There are many illustrative stories. Jean makes the Old Woman say, with an unusual touch of self-criticism:

> Examples? Thousands I could give,
> but I should have to talk too long.[62]

The habit of using examples from history and myth to illustrate a moral lesson is very old in classical tradition. It can be found as early as Homer, where the great heroes of the still-earlier past are used as models and quoted in speeches, so that their successors can imitate their virtues, avoid their errors.[63] It spread through nearly all classical literature to an almost incredible degree. For instance, Propertius, who writes love-poetry, feels that his own passion is inadequate as a subject for a poem, unless it is objectified and exemplified by mythological parallels. The satires of Juvenal swarm with examples—some taken from contemporary or nearly contemporary life, but many others merely historical clichés: Xerxes = doomed pride; Alexander = boundless ambition. Both the authors of *The Romance of the Rose* use classical stories in this illustrative way. Guillaume de Lorris rewrites the tale of Narcissus from Ovid, although he simplifies it: he makes the nymph Echo merely 'Echo, a great lady' and omits the metamorphosis of Narcissus into a flower.[64] Jean de Meun takes the tale of Pygmalion from the same poem, the tale of Dido and Aeneas from Vergil, the story of Verginia from Livy, and many other illustrations from Boethius.[65]

Arguments derived from the classics are mostly in the second part of the poem. For instance, Jean de Meun's anti-feminist attitude is strengthened by arguments derived from Juvenal's sixth, the famous misogynist satire.[66] As for descriptions, a good example is Ovid's picture of the Golden Age, which is adapted in lines 9106 f.[67]

It goes without saying that the actual work of translation was done in a more scholarly way than in *The Romance of Troy* and works of that kind. Jean de Meun was more learned than Lorris. Although Lorris mentions Macrobius, Ovid, Tibullus, Catullus, and Cornelius Gallus, he really appears to have known only Ovid well.[68] Jean de Meun's chief sources were:

> Cicero's philosophical dialogues *On Old Age* and *On Friendship*;
> Vergil's *Bucolics*, *Georgics*, and *Aeneid*;
> Horace's satires and epistles, though not his odes;
> Ovid, who contributed about 2,000 lines to *The Romance of the Rose*;
> Juvenal, chiefly satire 6, but also satires 1 and 7;
> Boethius;

but there are minor mentions of other classical authors, enough to show that he was a remarkably well-read man.[69]

The Romance of the Rose had an immediate and long-lasting success. One remarkable proof of the popularity of Lorris's unfinished poem is the fact that Jean de Meun thought it worth while to take it over and make it the vehicle for his own ideas. And its wide appeal is proved by the existence of hundreds of manuscript copies, as well as by the fact that it was translated into English (by Chaucer) and German. Two hundred years after its appearance it was turned into French prose by Molinet (1483). Forty years later Clément Marot re-edited it, in a beautiful printed edition, with moral comments which remind us of *Ovid Moralized*. He said, for instance, that the Rose signified (1) wisdom, (2) the state of grace, (3) the Virgin Mary (who is defamed by Male-Bouche = heresy), and (4) the supreme good. Nevertheless, the poem was not universally approved. The poetess Christine de Pisan in 1399 reproached it for its unchivalrous attitude to womanhood; and the greatest of all its opponents was Jean Gerson, who wrote a *Vision* in 1402 describing it as an ugly and immoral book.[70] In the dispute which ensued, its morality was hotly debated on both sides. The poem which stirred up so much excitement more than a century after its publication was a very vital work of art.

4

DANTE AND PAGAN ANTIQUITY

DANTE ALIGHIERI was the greatest writer of the Middle Ages, and *The Divine Comedy* incomparably their greatest book. Now it is not possible to understand either Dante or his poem without recognizing that the aim of his life was to create, in fact, to *be* the closest possible connexion between the Greco-Roman world and his own. He did not think the two worlds equal in value: the Christian revelation had raised all Christendom above the antique pagans. But he held that the modern world could not realize itself without the world of classical antiquity, which was a necessary prior stage in the ascent of man. His work is a synthesis of ancient Rome and modern Italy (or rather modern Europe), so alive and natural that it is scarcely possible to disentangle the various elements without breaking the organic whole they make. Again, it was Dante who created the modern Italian language and inaugurated Italian literature. But he was also a competent writer in Latin: he was one of the few medieval authors who made considerable contributions to world-literature both in an ancient and in a modern tongue. That itself typifies the synthesis, and shows what is sometimes forgotten, that Greek and Latin are not dead languages so long as their literatures are living carriers of energy, and thought, and stimulus, to scholars and poets.

The Divine Comedy is great because it is rich. It is rich with much of the highest beauty and thought of the Middle Ages; and in that thought and beauty the Greco-Roman tradition played not only an important, but an essential, part. As usual in the Middle Ages, the tradition was, even by Dante, imperfectly understood, and in certain respects distorted; but he was a great enough man to apprehend its greatness.

The title of the poem is *The Comedy*.[1] Dante himself explains, in his important letter to Can Grande della Scala, why he chose this title. It is evident that he has little conception of its essential meaning—nor, indeed, of the meaning of drama as a *form*, a distinctive literary pattern. He says that comedy is a kind of poetic narrative which begins harshly and ends happily, and which is written in humble unpretentious language. He explains this further by distinguishing comedy from tragedy—which begins quietly and ends in horror, and is written in a lofty style. Apparently this is a garbled reminiscence of Aristotle's definitions of the two main types of drama.[2] When we recall that Dante makes Vergil himself describe the *Aeneid* as 'my tragedy',[3] we see that Dante considers 'comedy' to connote what we should now call an epic, a poem of heroic length, provided it has a happy ending. By calling his own work 'comedy' in contrast to Vergil's 'tragedy', he clearly means to set up his poem as a complement, not perhaps a rival but certainly a partner, to Vergil's *Aeneid*. (It should be added that such misapprehensions of the meaning of technical terms were widespread in the Middle Ages and were part of the general ignorance of literary patterns. Lucan was known as a historian; even *The Madness of Roland* was called a tragedy.[4]) So, like the *Odyssey* and *Paradise Regained*, Dante's poem is an epic with a happy ending.

Dante says the language is humble. Of course the original classical definition of comedy as low in style included the fact that such plays were full of slang and obscenity and broad verbal humour generally. Dante does not mean that. He means that his *Comedy* is in a straightforward unpretentious style compared with the grandeur and complexity of 'tragedy'. This explanation is supported by a passage in his essay on vernacular Italian style. There he declares that grand language should be kept for poetry written in the tragic manner, while comic writing should sometimes be intermediate in tone, and sometimes low. And, as we shall see, his poem is far less elaborate in style, and its vocabulary far plainer, than the work of Vergil and other classical heroic poets.

Yet it cannot really be called low and humble. It is sometimes very involved. It is often exalted and ecstatic. And although it has a supremely happy ending, it does not, like the comedies of Terence, deal with ordinary everyday life. In his earlier essay Dante went on to say that the grand style was reserved for lyric poetry on great subjects, such as salvation, love, and virtue. But these are the chief subjects of the *Comedy* itself, and it is difficult to believe that Dante really thought the style of his *Paradise* meaner than that of his own earlier lyric poems and those of his contemporaries. It is arguable, therefore, that by the time he wrote the letter explaining the *Comedy* he had dropped his earlier theories and subdivisions, and now meant that the language was 'low', not because it was a

plain style of vernacular Italian, but simply because it was vernacular Italian as contrasted with literary Latin. This would not be
mock modesty or classicist snobbery, but an acknowledgement of
the fact that, like all modern languages of the time, Italian was far
less flexible and sonorous, far more degraded by conversational
usages, and far less noble in its overtones, than the language of
Latin literature.[5]

The subject of the poem is a visit to the next world, the world
after death. This theme was common to poets and visionaries
in the Greco-Roman, and even more in the medieval Christian,
world.[6] The general structure Dante followed—a division into
hell, purgatory, and heaven—was Christian; and so was much,
though not all, of the theology and morality which Dante learnt
during his descent and ascent. Nevertheless, he does not mention
any medieval seer as his authority, or any medieval work as his
model. The essential point is that his guide into the next world,
through hell, and through purgatory is the Roman poet Vergil.
Before Vergil leaves him, the two are met by another Latin poet,
Statius—a pupil of Vergil, but described as a converted Christian[7]
—who takes Dante to paradise, where he is met, conducted, and
taught by his own first love Beatrice, in whom the ideals of
romantic love and Christian virtue are united. It is quite clear that
Dante means us to infer that, just as his poem is a complement to
the *Aeneid*, so the imagination and art which made it possible for
him to see and to describe the world of eternity were due (after
God and Beatrice) to Latin poetry, and in particular to Vergil.
Had it not been so, had there been a Christian model for the work,
Dante would have introduced a Christian mystic as his guide.

Dante's selection of Vergil as his guide was prompted by many
traditions (some trivial, some important) and by many profoundly
revealing spiritual factors.

First, Vergil was above all others the pagan who bridged the
gap between paganism and Christianity. He did this in a famous
poem (*Bucolics*, 4) written about forty years before Christ's birth,
foretelling the birth of a miraculous baby, which would mark the
opening of a new age of the world, a golden age corresponding to
the idyllic first beginnings, when there would be no more bloodshed, toil, or suffering. The child when grown was to become a
god and rule the world in perfect peace.

This fact has two aspects. The first is external. Mainly through this remarkable poem Vergil acquired the reputation of having been a Christian before Christ and of having, through divine inspiration, foretold the birth of Jesus.[8] St. Augustine held this belief[9] and many others after him. (Many modern scholars believe that Vergil actually knew something of the Messianic writings of the Hebrews.) The belief was strengthened by other interconnected facts:

> that the whole of the *Aeneid* (unlike any other classical epic) relates the fulfilment of a great and favourable prophecy, and that the prophecy led to the establishment of Rome;
> that at the climax of the *Aeneid* a famous prophetess, the Sibyl, appears to advise Aeneas;
> that the Sibyl is mentioned in Vergil's earlier poem (*Buc.* 4. 4) in connexion with the coming of the divine baby and the kingdom of God;
> that numerous Greek, Jewish, and Near Eastern prophecies and apocalypses were in existence during the two centuries before and after the birth of Christ, many of which, to give them authority, were known as Sibylline books;
> that in medieval Italian folk-lore Vergil was known as a great magician (although Dante himself does not pay any attention to that kind of story).

The internal aspect of Vergil's Christian mission is more important and has been less often considered. It is that his poem was not merely an accident. It was the expression of a real spiritual fact: of the profound longing for peace, the unvoiced yearning for a world governed by the goodness of God rather than the conflicting desires of men, which ran all through the Mediterranean world after a century of terrible wars.[10] The future emperor Octavian himself, with whose family the divine baby was doubtless connected, was hailed in many towns of the Middle East as God, Saviour, and Prince of Peace: the designations were apparently quite sincere or prompted by quite sincere motives.[11] It was this longing that prepared the way for the expansion of Christianity, and it is a tribute to Vergil's greatness that even as a young man he should have grasped it and immortalized it in an unforgettable poem.

Vergil's own character is the clue to this visionary power, and to his immortality as Dante's guide. Anyone who reads his poetry with intelligence and sympathy, as Dante did, recognizes that in essentials—in nearly all the essentials except the revelation of Jesus Christ—he was a Christian soul. So much so that throughout the *Aeneid* we feel the task of writing an epic about war and conquest to be repugnant to him.[12] He hated bloodshed. He had, and embodied in his hero, a deep devotion to selfless moral ideals: his *pius Aeneas* is far more of an idealist than the angry Achilles, the clever Odysseus, or even the patriotic Hector. Although passionate by nature, he had a singular refinement in sexual matters—which was recognized in the medieval misspelling of his name, Virgilius the virginal.[13] All we learn of his character from his friends and from his ancient biographers shows him as humble, and gentle, and loving-kind. But most of all, what marks out Vergil from other poets is his melancholy sense of the transitoriness and unreality of this life and his concentration, even in an epic of ardent passion and violent action, upon eternity.[14]

A third great factor influencing Dante's choice was that Vergil was a herald of the Roman empire. For Dante, the two most important facts in this world were the Christian church and the Holy Roman empire. The church and its revelation Vergil had only announced with a dim prophetic foreboding. But the empire he had sung better than any other. Essentially, the *Aeneid* is a proclamation of the Roman empire as established by the will of heaven, and destined to last for ever. This, Dante thought, was the same empire which governed central Europe in his day, and which he glorified in one of his two great Latin books, *De monarchia*—a proof that the existence of the empire was the direct will of God.[15] The same belief appears most strikingly in his climactic description of the lowest circle of hell, which is kept for those who have been traitors to their masters. In it, Dante and Vergil see the supreme traitor Satan, eternally immobilized in ice, and chewing in his three mouths the three worst earthly traitors. One is Judas Iscariot, and the other two are those who murdered the founder of the Roman empire, Brutus and Cassius.[16]

But apart from the Roman empire as a political entity, Dante loved Vergil because Vergil loved Italy. There is a superb description of Italy in Vergil's farming poem, which is the finest sustained tribute ever paid to a country by one of its citizens.[17] Far gloomier, but no less sincerely patriotic, is the apostrophe to strife-torn Italy in Dante's *Purgatory*,[18] which is introduced by the affectionate embrace of the modern Mantuan Sordello and the ancient Mantuan Vergil. Again and again Dante speaks proudly of Vergil as a fellow-citizen: *il nostro maggior poeta*, 'our greatest poet'.

And it should not be forgotten that, although neither Dante nor Vergil was a Roman born, they both assumed and preached that the ideals of Rome should cover and vivify all Italy. That is one of the main themes of Vergil's *Georgics*; it reappears constantly in the *Aeneid*; and it is often restated by Dante, who calls Italy simply 'Latin land'[19] and speaks of Italians whose souls he meets as 'Latins'.[20] For Dante the Roman world of the past was part of the Holy Roman empire to which he belonged, as limbo and hell were part of the eternal world that culminated in heaven.

Another factor, quite as important as the others, was that for Dante Vergil was the greatest poet in the world; and that he himself modelled his poetry upon Vergil. Although he referred to other classical poets, although he well knew the classics available to him then, he knew Vergil far best. It has often been said that, of Dante's two guides through the next world, Vergil represents Reason and Beatrice Faith. But it has been asked why, if Reason was to be one of Dante's guides, Dante did not choose 'the master of those who know', Aristotle.[21] He sees Aristotle in the next world, and pays him a high tribute, but does not speak with him. Instead, it is Vergil who takes Dante through hell and purgatory, helped by Vergil's warmest Latin admirer and imitator, Statius (whom Dante believed to have been converted to Christianity through Vergil's Messianic prophecy), and parting from him only when heaven and Beatrice are near. And if we read the *Comedy* we do not find that the influence of Vergil is predominantly that of Reason—although he is conceived as having encyclopaedic, or divine, eternal knowledge. What Dante first praises him for is his *style*:

> You alone are he from whom I took
> that beautiful style which has brought me honour.[22]

We must examine what Dante meant by this: for at first sight it is not more easily understandable than saying that Vergil, the poet of mystic imagination and haunting beauty and great distances, represents Reason.

To begin with, Dante did not imitate the verbal style of Vergil. This is obvious. It can be tested by comparing the passages where he uses Vergilian material and their originals in Vergil. For instance, in *Inferno*, 13, the two poets enter a wood where the trees bleed when broken, because they contain the souls of suicides. This is imitated from the *Aeneid*. But there, when Aeneas breaks the branch, Vergil describes the effect picturesquely and elaborately:

> Chill horror
> shook my limbs and cold fear froze my blood.[23]

But when Dante breaks the branch, and 'words and blood come out together', the effect is described with absolute, irreducible plainness:

> I let the twig
> fall, and stood like the man who is afraid.[24]

Again and again, where Vergil is elaborate, Dante is simple. His simplicity is none the less great poetry, but it is not the brilliantly ornate, highly compressed language of Vergil, loaded with various sounds and significances. It is a clear, direct style, and he was partly thinking of that quality when he called his poem a comedy.

But there is another passage where he speaks of his style. In purgatory, he meets a poet of the old school, who quotes one of Dante's own lyrics, praising it as 'the sweet new style'.[25] Now Dante's manner in his lyrics was a development of Provençal love-poetry, deepened and enriched by truer inspiration.[26] It was not Vergilian. It was not classical in origin at all.

And finally, what is the metre in which the whole *Comedy* is written? It is an elaborate system of triply rhymed hendeca-syllables: ABABCBCDC .... This, as one of the earliest com-mentators on Dante recognized, is an elaboration of a Provençal pattern called the *serventese*.[27] The metrical scheme, like the whole architecture of Dante's poem, is of course dictated primarily not by Provençal influence but by his wish to do honour to the Trinity: it is only the first example of the number-symbolism which penetrates the entire work. But the rhyme-scheme which he chose for this purpose, and the triple pattern of the poem in general, were Provençal, and not classical Latin.

The language is vernacular Italian, not classical Latin. The style is simple and direct, not rich and complex. The metre and rhymes are modern Italian developed out of Provençal folk-poetry. What is there left? What else can Dante mean by saying that he took his beautiful style from Vergil alone?

In a later passage of the *Inferno* a brother-poet, Guido Caval-cante, who wrote love-lyrics like Dante's, is described by him as 'perhaps despising Vergil'.[28] Dante means that most of the modern vernacular lyric poets thought nothing was to be learned from studying the classics: which, for their purposes, was true enough. But he himself tells Vergil that he has read the *Aeneid* 'with long study and much love'.[29] Therefore the essential qualities which differentiate the *Comedy* from Dante's early sweet lyrics, and which differentiate the *Comedy* from the work of all contemporary European poets, are the 'beautiful style' which Dante took from Vergil—as he says, *alone*. These qualities are grandeur of imagination and sustained nobility of thought. They are essentially classical and essentially Vergilian qualities; and Dante was the only modern poet who attempted to clothe them in modern language. Thus, by the testimony of Dante himself, one of the greatest of Dante's greatnesses, which raised him high above the jongleurs and amorists of his own day, was directly created by classical literature.[30]

This is borne out by a scrutiny of the actual imitations of Greco-Roman literature and of the ideas inspired by it which appear in the *Comedy*. There is an admirable analysis of Dante's debts to his classical teachers in Moore's *Studies in Dante*. To two of them Dante owes far more than to all the others. One is Aristotle, the thinker. The other is Vergil, the poet.[31]

The sixth factor which determined Dante to make Vergil his guide is the obvious one that Vergil had written a famous descrip-tion of a journey through the world beyond this world, in the sixth book of the *Aeneid*—and not only an account of its marvels, but a profound philosophical and moral exposition of the ultimate meanings of life and death. Vergil himself imitates and adapts so many of his forerunners that we tend to forget how original the final synthesis really is. His chief model is Homer (*Odyssey*, 11), but in Homer and in other poetic descriptions of the underworld there is no such intellectual content as Vergil has put into his poem, bringing together mystical ideas from Orphism, Platonism, and many other doctrines now unknown. True, Vergil's physical description of the other world is vague. Dante wished his to be realistic and exact and detailed: therefore he based his moral geography on Aristotle's arrangement of vices, with elaborations from St. Thomas Aquinas and alterations of his own.[32] But almost

all the supernatural inhabitants of his hell are taken from Vergil
rather than from medieval Christian belief: the ferryman Charon,
the judge Minos, the fiendish dog Cerberus, the Harpies, the
Centaurs, and many others.[33] It is fascinating to see how skilfully
he converts these classical myths into medieval figures: for example,
Minos is no longer the serene judge, the friend of Zeus, but a
snarling devil who gives sentence by twisting his tail round his
body again and again to show how many circles each sinner must
descend into hell.[34]
Lastly, I have sometimes thought that Dante chose Vergil as
his guide because, like Aeneas, he was himself a great exile.

The two essential classical influences on Dante's *Comedy* are the
ethical and physical system of Aristotle, and Vergil's imagination,
patriotism, and character. But the poem is penetrated with many
kinds of classical influences so deeply that there can be no talk of
mere imitation. The Greco-Roman world is as alive for Dante as
his own, is parallel to it, and is inextricably interwoven with it.
He describes very many great figures of classical myth and history
as inhabitants of hell. He places the noblest in limbo, a heaven
without God, because they lived before the Christian revelation.
In purgatory the seven cardinal sins, although expiated by modern
men and women, are emblematized by sculptures of classical personages mixed with figures from Jewish and Christian history: for
instance, Nimrod and Niobe, Saul and Arachne, as symbols of
pride;[35] and the guardian of purgatory is neither an ancient
Hebrew, nor a modern Christian, nor an angel, but the Roman
Cato.[36] Dante constantly alternates figures and ideas from the
ancient world with others from modern times, and balances
quotations from the Bible with quotations from the classics. The
two most striking of these interwoven pairs are, first, Dante's reply
to Vergil's summons: he says he dare not enter the underworld, for

I am not Aeneas, and not Paul—

St. Paul, whom a medieval legend made the hero of a descent into
hell.[37] And, second, the great moment when Beatrice at last
appears. The crowd of angels cries *Benedictus qui venis*, 'Blessed
art thou who comest (in the name of the Lord)'—the greeting of
the multitudes to Jesus at his entry into Jerusalem; and then
Manibus date lilia plenis, 'Give me, from full hands, lilies'—the

tribute of Anchises to the spirit of Marcellus in the *Aeneid*.[38] Again, throughout the poem Dante draws his comparisons from two chief fields: from his own observation of nature and from classical poetry and myth. But sometimes, as in his description of Paolo and Francesca approaching

like doves called by desire,[39]

he draws them from nature as observed by classical poets (in this case from Vergil[40]), and thus combines the beauty of reminiscence with the beauty of vision.[41]

Moore has analysed and listed the classical echoes in Dante, not only in the *Comedy* but in all his books, so admirably that it is merely necessary to summarize his work. The principal authors quoted and copied by Dante are these:

First, Aristotle, whom he knew through the Latin translation used by St. Thomas Aquinas. There are over 300 references, covering all the then available books of Aristotle, except the *Poetics*.

Next, Vergil, with some 200 references which show a profound study of the *Aeneid*. The *Bucolics* and *Georgics* Dante knew less well.

There are about 100 references to Ovid, whose *Metamorphoses* were Dante's main source for Greco-Roman mythology. He may also have known Ovid's other books—for instance, there are allusions to two of the *Heroides* in *Paradiso*, 9. 100–2—but not well.

Lucan appears in 50 references or so: Dante could scarcely admire his hatred of Caesarism, but was impressed by his powerful imagination.[42]

Cicero is quoted about 50 times also—not his speeches, but his moral essays. Dante himself[43] said the chief philosophical influences on him were Cicero's *Laelius, On Friendship*, and

Boethius, whom he cites 30 or 40 times.

Lastly, he knew something of Statius. He makes him a Christian poet, apparently because he inferred Statius had been secretly converted, and also because of Statius' vast admiration for Vergil. From his *Thebaid* Dante took several fine images, one being the forked flame which contains the souls of Diomede and Ulysses.[44]

These are the main authors in Dante's library—together, of course, with the Vulgate, St. Thomas, and the church fathers. He pays compliments to other poets. For example, Juvenal, when he arrived in limbo, told Vergil how much Statius admired the *Aeneid* —a thought inspired by Juvenal's own words.[45] But it is odd that the satires of Juvenal and Horace were so little known to Dante; and unfortunate that Tacitus, whose history he would have admired, was then virtually lost. On the other hand, it is notable that he deliberately ignores the late classical writers and the early Christian poets like Prudentius. It is sometimes said that he pre-figured the Renaissance. So far as that is true, it is justified by the intensity of his admiration for the Greco-Roman world, and by his knowledge of the *true* classics. He understands that Cicero is greater than Boethius, that Vergil is greater than Prudentius, and that Aristotle is the greatest of ancient thinkers. The sages and poets whom he meets in limbo are in fact most of those whom subsequent ages have agreed to regard as the supreme minds of that long and splendid civilization. It is a proof of Dante's vision that, even through the half-darkness of the Middle Ages, he saw the brilliance of the classical world, and knew at that distance who were the lesser lights in it, and who the greater.

5

TOWARDS THE RENAISSANCE

PETRARCH, BOCCACCIO, CHAUCER

THE Dark Ages were the victory of barbarism over classical civilization. The Middle Ages were the epoch during which, having been converted, the barbarians slowly civilized themselves with the help of the church and of the surviving fragments of classical culture. The Renaissance meant the enlargement of that growing civilization and its enrichment by many material and spiritual benefits, some acquired for the first time, others rediscovered after a long and almost death-like sleep. One of the treasures that most enriched us then was classical art and literature —only a small fraction of the original wealth possessed by the Greeks and Romans, but still inestimable riches: much of Greco-Roman art, many of the greatest Greek and Roman books, now emerged from the darkness of nearly a thousand years. The darkness had fallen last in Italy, and it was appropriate that it should there be lifted first. The darkness had begun with the separation of the western and eastern empires and the severance of Roman from Greek culture; it was fitting that it should lift again in the west, when a new and equally terrible Dark Age was invading the east—a Dark Age which in some ways has never yet lifted—and that in the west the real dawn should be heralded by the return of Greek culture to the lands which had once known it so well. It was to Italy that Greek returned first, and it was in Italy that the first of the rediscoveries were made, the first and most stimulating of all. The men who did most to recapture Greek and retrieve the rest of Latin were two Italians. They were, however, not purely Italians; but Italians who had a second home in France. Thus the two most highly civilized countries in Europe both shared, through their sons, in the rebirth of classical civilization. The two were Francesco Petrarca, customarily called Petrarch in English (1304–74),[1] and Giovanni Boccaccio (1313–75).

Petrarch belonged to the generation after Dante. His father was perpetually exiled from Florence by the same decree, at the same time, and for the same political offence as Dante himself.[2] The relation between Petrarch and Dante is highly significant. Although both are Italian poets of the same epoch, they differ in so many ways that the gap between them may be taken to symbolize the gulf between two stages of culture.

Himself a distinguished writer, Petrarch did not care for Dante's poetry: partly, perhaps, from jealousy of its unapproachable loftiness, partly because he claimed to despise books written in vernacular Italian (even his own), and partly because he found the Dantean austerity chilling and unsympathetic. In all his letters, he never mentions Dante by name. When he refers to him in a letter he calls him 'a fellow-citizen of ours who in point of style is very popular, and who has certainly chosen a noble theme';[3] and elsewhere he alludes to Dante's blunt speech and forbidding manner.[4] The greatest proof of his antipathy for Dante is that—although Petrarch himself was the first keen bibliophile—he did not possess a copy of the *Comedy* until Boccaccio wrote one for him and sent it to him in 1359.[5] (And yet before this he had written an ambitious series of poems on a theme partly suggested by Dante, and on a scope designed to rival the *Comedy* itself.) He saw Dante once, when he was eight. The relation between the two rather resembles that between Vergil and his junior Ovid, who says 'Vergil I only saw'[6] and who spent his life outdoing the elder master, in a style of greater grace and less depth.

Dante was exiled in middle life and never recovered. He always yearned to return to the little city-state of Florence. Petrarch was born in exile, and easily became what Dante hoped to be: a citizen of the world—travelling freely and with much enjoyment through Italy, France, and the Rhineland, having homes in various parts of France and Italy, staying as guest with numerous nobles and church dignitaries, but preferring no particular spot. Dante also was far-travelled—to Paris, and, some think, to Oxford; but it was the gloomy wandering of a displaced person, and, where Petrarch looked outwards with pleasure at the changing world, Dante always looked inward. Similarly, in the number and variety of his friends Petrarch far surpassed Dante. His correspondence, which was eventually collected into three sets of over 400 letters in all, is the first of the many international letter-bags assembled by scholars like Erasmus, and thus prefigures the world of free exchange of ideas and literatures in which we were brought up.

Dante had a bookshelf, a large one. But Petrarch had the first living and growing personal library, in the modern sense. The ideal which grew up in the Renaissance and has not yet died away, that of the many-sided humane thinker with a well-stocked head and a better-stocked library, the ideal personified in Montaigne, Ronsard, Johnson, Gray, Goethe, Voltaire, Milton, Tennyson, and many more—that ideal was, in modern times, first and most stimulatingly embodied in Petrarch. The books which Dante knew, he knew deeply; but they were not many. Petrarch knew neither the Bible nor Aristotle so well, but he knew classical literature much better than Dante, and he knew more of it. For he discovered much of it, and stimulated others to discover more. He did not discover it in the sense in which Columbus discovered America, or Schliemann Troy. The books were there, in libraries, and still readable. But they were in the same position as out-of-print works nowadays, of which only one or two copies exist, in basements or forgotten dumps. Hardly anyone knew they were there; no one read them; and they were not part of the stream of culture.[7] What Petrarch did was to *find* them by personal search, to *publish* them by copying them and encouraging others to make copies, and to *popularize* them by discussing them with his friends. For instance, when he was twenty-nine he visited Liège, heard there were 'many old books', sought them out, and found two hitherto unknown speeches by Cicero. He copied one himself and made his travelling companion copy the other, although they could hardly find any decent ink in the whole city.[8] Again, in 1345 he visited the cathedral library of Verona, and there found a manuscript containing a vast number of Cicero's personal letters. This correspondence was quite unknown at the time, and proved to be so interesting that it encouraged (among other things) the discovery of the remaining half of the corpus, which Coluccio Salutati turned up in 1392.[9] When Petrarch found the manuscript it was falling to pieces. He copied it out in his own hand. With the help of these letters he plunged into an exhaustive study of the many-sided character of Cicero, admirable as an artist, stimulating as a thinker, lovable as a man: the character which through Petrarch became one of the forces that formed the Renaissance ideal of humanism.[10] And he imitated them in his own voluminous and amusing Latin correspondence with scholars and writers throughout the western world. (One of his most charming ideas was to address letters to the great dead whom he admired: Homer,

Cicero, and others. After he found Cicero's correspondence in Verona, he wrote Cicero to tell him.[11])

Petrarch's library has been exhaustively described, for it was not merely a collection but a real cultural achievement.[12] His books make a striking contrast with Dante's. Both knew Cicero; but Dante only as a philosophical essayist and rhetorical writer, while Petrarch knew him as an orator through his speeches, and, through his letters, as a personal friend. Both knew Vergil well: Petrarch actually imitated him more closely and less successfully than Dante, in a Latin epic on Scipio, called *Africa*.[13] Dante and other men of the Middle Ages knew Horace 'the satyr' or satirist; but Petrarch, himself a lyric poet, quoted the odes of Horace freely.[14] Dante knew little about Latin drama, and thought comedy and tragedy were forms of narrative. Petrarch was familiar with the tragedies of Seneca and the comedies of both Terence and Plautus (at least with four of the eight Plautine plays then known): he had some idea of the meaning of drama, and in his youth attempted a genuine comedy. Dante was aware who Juvenal was, but paid him less attention than he deserved. Petrarch knew Juvenal's satires, and also those of his predecessor Persius. Dante knew probably no more than the first four books of Livy. Petrarch knew twenty-nine, and never gave up searching for the hundred or so that are lost: he wrote Livy to tell him of his eagerness to find them.[15] Dante had virtually no Greek. Petrarch tried to learn Greek in middle age, but failed, because his tutor Barlaam left Avignon.[16] Yet, from his study of Latin authors, he had realized something of the importance of their Hellenic teachers and predecessors. The hierarchy of Greek thinkers and poets was far more clear and precise for him than it was for Dante: and the few Greek writers mentioned in the *Comedy* compare poorly with those who appear in Petrarch's *Triumphs*.[17] Much to his grief, Petrarch never managed to read a book in Greek; but he did search for Greek manuscripts (he acquired a Homer and some sixteen dialogues of Plato) and finally, through Boccaccio, got hold of a Latin rendering of both the Homeric epics. Like a true book-lover, he was found dead in his library, stooping over a book; and the last large-scale work he began was to annotate the Latin version of the *Odyssey*.[18] Finally, Dante thought Aristotle the master of Reason; while Petrarch thought him a bad stylist and a thinker who was wrong in matters of great importance.[19] It is in Petrarch that we find the first modern admiration of Aristotle's master Plato, whose works he possessed and yearned to read.

Dante was a devout Christian. He placed classical learning almost on the same level as sacred learning, but, because it lacked divine revelation, lower. Petrarch also was a Christian, but less ardently absorbed in visions of life after death, less passionately interested in problems of morality and theology. Nevertheless it would be wrong to see him as foreshadowing, except in the gentlest hints, the positive paganism of many Renaissance humanists. Thus, while he loved Cicero more than all other men of the past, next to him he admired St. Augustine, whom he quotes many hundreds of times, and whom he introduced as his teacher and confessor in his *Secret*. We can, however, date his real interest in Christian literature to the latter part of his life, when he was about fifty;[20] and we cannot imagine Dante ever comparing his own attitude to religion (as Petrarch did) to the love of a son who takes his mother for granted until he hears her attacked.[21]

Like Dante, Petrarch wrote both in Latin and in Italian. His books in both languages are important. But he himself considered his work in Latin to be more valuable. He was wrong.

His main effort was spent on his Latin epic, *Africa*, its hero being Scipio Africanus and its model Vergil's *Aeneid*. But he made the mistake which Dante did not, the mistake of so many Renaissance authors, not excluding Milton. He believed that the more closely he followed the formal outlines of the classical poet he admired, and the more exactly each incident or image or speech corresponded with similar elements in his Latin model, the better his poem must be. This is an easy mistake to make, but it is disastrous. For it means that the creative mind cannot work freely, with reference only to the harmony of subject and form which it is building up. Everything must be referred, on this theory, to an external standard; and the author tests his own ideas by asking, not if they are original, beautiful, or appropriate, but if they are exact copies. He is producing, not original works of art, but plaster casts.

And yet many great modern writers—all those dealt with in this book—have copied subjects from the classics or adapted classical ideas, translated classical phrases or borrowed classical patterns. Why did they succeed, if Petrarch failed in what looks like a more careful attempt to do the same thing? (It was not that he wrote *Africa* in Latin, for Latin was a living language for him and his audience.) It was that the chief aim of those who succeeded was to produce something *original*. Whatever they took from the classics they used simply as material—like the material they acquired from other sources, from their observation of life, their own fancies, stories from gossip or contemporary journalism, phrases or ideas struck out by their contemporaries but only half-developed. Or, if they took over a classical form, they felt quite free to alter, and usually to expand, it in any way that suited their material. Those who failed allowed themselves to be benumbed by the weight of the material, paralysed by the rigidity of the form. Those who succeeded—like Dante, like Shakespeare—dominated either classical form or classical material or both, moulded and blended and changed them through their own creative imagination, and made a synthesis which, like a chemical compound of known elements, was nevertheless qualitatively different and genuinely new. Creative writing, though difficult, is always satisfying. Imitative writing, because of this conflict between imagination and external restrictions, is always a repugnant task for an original mind. Petrarch never published his *Africa*, worked on it very slowly, and apparently did not complete it: just as Ronsard later began a plaster cast of the *Aeneid* in French and gave it up after four books, with obvious relief.[22] Imitation is for hacks, not for good authors.

Petrarch's twelve Latin *Eclogues* are modelled on Vergil's *Bucolics*, but they are more of an original work than his epic. Although far less delicate and sensitive than Vergil's poems, they also are packed with many layers of meaning: the characters are not only nymphs and shepherds, but Petrarch's own friends, and contemporary dignitaries, and allegorical personages. Repugnant as this is to modern taste, it helps to account for the great influence these poems had in the Renaissance.

For us, his most interesting Latin work is the group of dialogues he called his *Secret*, in which he talks to St. Augustine about his own character. Three worlds meet in this book. Its conception and its dialogue-form come from Plato, through Cicero—and through Boethius, whose Lady Philosophy here reappears, on the same healing mission, as Lady Truth.[23] The choice of St. Augustine as interlocutor, and the concentration on thoughts of death and hell, and the hatred Petrarch expresses for the life of this world, show him as a medieval man: so too, on the other side of the conflict, does his romantic admiration for Laura, for which St. Augustine rebukes him. His acute self-examination, his psychical sensitivity, his self-distrust and worry are modern in so far as they are not a permanent part of human life.

His other works in Latin, philosophical, poetical, and historical, are less attractive. The most permanently valuable of all he wrote in the language he loved best continues to be his correspondence, where there were few fixed patterns to follow and he himself supplied all the material out of his rich and flexible mind.

In Italian his finest work is undoubtedly his love-lyrics to Laura, the *Canzoniere*, which inspired so many poets of the Renaissance, in France, in Italy, in England, in Spain and elsewhere, and much later were hotly reflected in the music of Liszt.[24] Although several classical currents flow through their thought, they are in the main purely modern, for they deal with romantic love, and their patterns are developed from folk-song.

In a set of *Triumphs* he endeavoured to rival Dante by revivifying a long series of the immortal dead, and by glorifying his beloved Laura after her death as Dante had exalted Beatrice. The poems describe a succession of triumphal processions modelled on those of the Roman conquerors: Love, Chastity, Death, Fame, Time, Eternity, they follow and surpass one another in a long crescendo of conquest which ends with Petrarch's aspiration towards heaven and Laura. The original idea, the Roman triumph, was classical. Petrarch had no doubt seen it transfigured in Dante's Triumph of the Church;[25] and he wrote in Dante's metre. However, this Italian poem fails as his *Africa* in Latin fails, and for a similar reason. The *Triumphs* are too obviously moulded on Dante, and have left Petrarch's invention little room to expand and live. Also, the idea, like so many of the ideas of devoted classicists, is static and therefore tedious. In Dante we are constantly moving. We are taken down, down through the earth's interior; we climb along the body of Satan, grappling to his hair; we pant upwards on the mountain of purgatory, and at last ascend into the true heaven, changing continually with the changing sights we see. In the *Triumphs* we stand still, and the procession passes, so far away and so dignified that we can hardly see more than the labels carried by each statuesque figure, and almost cry, with Macbeth:

> Why do you show me this? . . . Start, eyes!
> What, will the line stretch out to the crack of doom?

Like Dante, Petrarch was a synthesis of Greece and Rome with modern Europe. But, although a weaker, he was a more progressive spirit. He was more modern, by being more classical. He enriched the life of his time and of his successors by filling it with newly awakened powers from antiquity. This fact was recognized in his laureateship (1341). He was the first modern aspirant to the crown of laurel conferred on distinguished poets. The laurel coronation was a Greek idea which the Romans had taken over and formalized. Late in the Middle Ages it was revived (Dante in exile refused the honour), and Petrarch made it, for a time, real and important. After a formal examination by King Robert of Naples, he was adjudged worthy of the symbol of immortal fame, and was crowned with laurel in the heart of Rome.

His wreath meant more than poetic distinction. As a renewal of a Roman ceremony, the coronation symbolized the revival of the lofty aspirations and immortal glories of ancient Rome, and the creation of a new empire of intellectual and aesthetic culture. This was the empire which spread over half the world in the high Renaissance, which through many vicissitudes, shrinking here and advancing there, maintained its power for centuries, and which is still alive and strong. On the political side, the same ideals were held by Petrarch's friend, the Roman revolutionary Cola di Rienzo. A few years later he too was crowned with laurel, and named Tribune and Augustus. He dared (according to the pope's accusations) to abandon Christianity and restore the ancient rites of paganism. He attacked the medieval privileges of the Roman barons and proclaimed a restored Roman republic. His aim, like Petrarch's, was to renew the strength of Rome and of the civilization which had centred upon it, or, as his admirers saw it, to awake the sleeping princess, to restore her youth, and to become her bridegroom. In many of these aspirations he had been preceded by the astonishing emperor Frederick II.[26] The political plans of both these classically-inspired revolutionaries met an opposition too durable to overthrow. But the spiritual regeneration which they helped to initiate was a deeper need than any constitutional or national reform. It was not the revival of one nation, but the re-education of Europe. And, just as Dante's poetry means far more to the world than his statesmanship, so the laurels of Petrarch, poet and teacher, are still fresh, while the emperor's crown and the tribune's wreath have crumbled into dust.[27]

BOCCACCIO

Giovanni Boccaccio was born in 1313, perhaps in Paris, as the illegitimate son of a French girl and an Italian banker. As Dante had a sad, hopeless, romantic love for Beatrice, as Petrarch hopelessly loved Laura and lost her in the 1348 epidemic, so Boccaccio had a passionate and unhappy love-affair with Maria d'Aquino, the illegitimate daughter of King Robert of Naples: he is said to have made it the basis of the first modern European psychological novel, *Fiammetta*.

He was Petrarch's friend and pupil; and like him, he was active both in Latin and in Italian. The two sides of his life were not conflicting, but complementary—he was classicist and modern together. Although he greatly admired Dante, the contrast between his life and Dante's is even more marked than that between Dante and Petrarch. For instance, at the age of thirty-five, when Dante was lost in the dark wood and emerged through a vision of eternity, Boccaccio experienced the terrible disaster known as the Black Death; but his reaction to it was to produce the still popular, and still naughty, and perpetually profane *Decameron*.

This is a group of stories in Italian prose, mainly about adventure, love, and trickery, told during ten days of holiday (*decameron* is meant to be Greek for *a ten-day period*) by a group of seven ladies and three gentlemen who have fled from the plague-ridden city to a delightful carefree country-house. Although realistic, the *Decameron* is therefore escapist. There is no classical prototype for its pattern, the sets of characteristic stories told by a group of friends or accidental acquaintances (in Plato's *Symposium* they do not tell stories, but make rival speeches, and in Petronius they chat at random); and it probably stems from the million and one anecdotes and the infinite leisure and the long caravans and the multitudinous caravanserais of the Near East. Of the stories themselves, some have drifted westward from the bazaars and capitals of the Orient, some have scummed up from the same medieval underworld as the fabliaux, and others have crystallized from real incidents of contemporary western European life. The prose style, however, is not all ordinary and realistic, but is often elevated, leisurely, harmonious, and complex, with rhythms evidently based on those of the finest Italian prosateur, Cicero.

The characters of the *Decameron* frequently imply contempt for the Christian clergy. At the very beginning there is a story about a Jew who was trying to decide whether he should become a Christian or not. In order to make up his mind, he visited Rome. When he came back, he was baptized at once. Why? Because, he said, he had seen so much vice and corruption in Rome, the centre of Christianity, that if the Christian religion could possibly survive and progress as it did, God was obviously supporting the Christian religion. The extreme cynicism of this story is corroborated by a number of others about the sexual corruption of monks and nuns.

In Boccaccio's other works it is even less easy than in Petrarch's to separate the classical elements from the non-classical. The fusion is almost complete.

His most considerable poem is the first Italian epic—or rather the first after Dante: the *Theseid* or *Tale of Theseus* (*Teseida*). It is in the precise classical form, twelve books—no, to be more exact, it is in precisely the same number of lines as the *Aeneid*, and a piece of literary gossip says he actually started it sitting in the shadow of Vergil's tomb.[28] It is on a classical subject, the wars of Theseus; but since they were not sung at length by any extant classical poet, he was free to adapt most of his story from the French romancers and to invent the rest.[29] The metre itself, an eight-line stanza (ABABABCC), is Provençal in origin. Appropriately, this poem appealed to Chaucer's medieval Knight, who drew upon it for the tale he told the other Canterbury pilgrims. In the same metre, Boccaccio wrote another romantic-heroic poem, the *Filostrato*, which retells the Troilus and Cressida story. This poignant tale springs from the Trojan war, but, as we have seen, cannot be traced back beyond the medieval romance of Benoît de Sainte-Maure.[30] (This story too Chaucer took over from Boccaccio.)

Boccaccio was the begetter of the modern novel, by being the first author who ever wrote a long story in a modern prose vernacular about contemporary characters. This is *Fiammetta*. Because it is in ordinary Italian, and about romantic love, it is a medieval and non-classical production on the surface. Yet, if it is examined more carefully, it will be seen to be a blend of modern and classical artistic devices, and to have a deeply important strain of classical thought.

For instance, the entire conceptual background is Greco-Roman. On the very first page we read of Lachesis, the Fate, and of the teeth that Cadmus sowed. In book 3, the heroine wonders if her lover has been drowned ('like Leander') or marooned ('like Achimenedes' = the Achaemenides of Vergil and Ovid[31]); and at the end, desolate and deserted, she consoles herself with the examples[32] of 'Inachus his daughter' (Io), Byblis, Canace, Myrrha, Pyramus and Thisbe, Dido, and dozens of other classical lovers, mostly out of Ovid—among whom Sir Tristram and Lady Isotta appear rather lonely.

Then, most of the stylistic devices of the book have been absorbed from classical poetry: carefully and formally built sentences, long speeches which are almost dramatic monologues, rhetorical devices such as oaths, conjurations, elaborate comparisons, &c.

God, Christian morality, and the Christian world are not mentioned. Although the milieu is contemporary, the religion is pagan: we hear not of church but of 'the holy temples',[33] and people say 'the gods know' and 'let the immortal gods bear witness'.[34] When Fiammetta is dubious about yielding to her lover, the thought of God, or Christ, or Mary never passes through her mind. Instead, Venus appears to her, naked under a thin dress, makes a long seductive speech to her, and persuades her.[35] Both the morality and the strategy of this are inspired by Ovid. In *Fiammetta,* as in many earlier romantic French love-stories, Ovid became a modern.

As a scholar in his time, Boccaccio was second only to Petrarch, and complemented his work. Petrarch had failed to learn Greek; but, with the help of the Calabrian Leontius Pilatus, Boccaccio mastered it. He was the first western European of modern times to do so; and he encouraged his tutor to produce the first modern translation of Homer. (It was a flat literal version in Latin, but it was usable.) Petrarch had discovered many lost classical books. Boccaccio continued the search, and found treasures no less valuable—among them, the lost historian Tacitus. It was Boccaccio who told his pupils a story which, whether true or not, shows his deep feeling for buried antiquity, and epitomizes the difference between the Middle Ages and the Renaissance:

'Being eager to see the library [of Monte Cassino] . . . he . . . besought one of the monks to do him the favour of opening it. Pointing to a lofty staircase, the monk answered stiffly "Go up; it is already open." Boccaccio stepped up the staircase with delight, only to find the treasure-house of learning destitute of door or any kind of fastening, while the grass was growing on the window-sills and the dust reposing on the books and bookshelves. Turning over the manuscripts, he found many rare and ancient works with whole sheets torn out, or with the margins ruthlessly clipped. As he left the room, he burst into tears, and, on asking a monk . . . to explain the neglect, was told that some of the inmates of the monastery . . . had torn out whole handfuls of pages and made them into psalters, which they sold to boys, and had cut off strips of parchment which they turned into amulets to sell to women.'[36]

Like Petrarch, Boccaccio had been pushing forwards, toward the Renaissance. But after his conversion in 1361, he became once more a medieval man. He was still a classicist: he wrote nothing now except Latin, and his books were on scholarly subjects. But he looked backwards instead of forwards. In 1373 he became the first professor of the poetry of Dante. And somehow he became more and more like Petrarch. It is pathetic but charming to see the two old scholars settling down, towards the end of their lives, into compiling, translating, and re-reading. Petrarch's last book was a Latin translation of Boccaccio's famous *Patient Griselda*.

Yet Boccaccio had been a modern man. He was never a pedant who first accepted the classical patterns and then tried to squeeze his own imaginative material into them at the risk of distorting it. He was passionately alive, and wrote books whose amorous energy and lascivious languor can still be felt. Although he loved Latin and Greek, although he was far more of a productive scholar than many twentieth-century classicists, his real importance in a study of classical influence upon modern European literature is quite different, and much greater.

He was the first great modern author who rejected Christianity for paganism. True, he was converted late in life. But in the works for which he is best known, he had thrown aside Christian doctrine and Christian morality and turned towards Greco-Roman paganism as to a better world. The characters of the *Decameron* recognize the existence of the church, but despise it. Fiammetta turns her back on it, and gives herself up to the power of the Olympians.

This is not the first, but a very notable example of a vast and potent modern reaction towards paganism, away from Christian morality and theology. There were many earlier instances of it in the love-poets of twelfth-century France. The reaction is not merely rejection, but a positive assertion that Greek and Roman ideas of God and morality are better, freer, more real, because more closely corresponding to the facts of life in this world; more positive, less thin, less austere and misanthropic and other-worldly; happier; more human.

This movement is not the same as that which produced the Reformation, and in some ways is totally different. Yet its strength encouraged the Reformation, and in some channels the two ran parallel. We shall meet it again in the full Renaissance, where paganism competed with the ideals of Christianity and was often victorious. It recurred in the seventeenth and eighteenth centuries, disguised and distorted in the Battle of the Books. In the Age of Revolution, it was stronger than ever: Shelley hated the very idea of Christianity as fervidly as he adored the better aspects of Greek paganism. In the nineteenth century, the great writers of Europe can be divided into Christians like Tolstoy, pagans like Nietzsche, and unwilling, pro-pagan Christians like Arnold. And although, while the Catholics built neo-Byzantine churches and the Presbyterians neo-Gothic churches, the nineteenth-century pagans put up no buildings and no altars for their cult, yet they added a vast new sanctuary, or asylum, to the modern pagan shrines, one of the earliest of which was built by Boccaccio, on the still unobliterated ruins of the old.

CHAUCER

Throughout the Dark Ages, the Middle Ages, and the early Renaissance, we can trace, in the rise and fall of national literatures, the successions of war and peace which made the development of Europe so difficult and so uneven. Besides wars and crusades, there were other convulsions quite as grievous: for instance, the Black Death, which in 1348 killed so many of the friends of both Petrarch and Boccaccio, including their beloved women, Laura and Fiammetta. The Danish conquest, first, and then the Norman conquest had virtually taken Britain out of the current of European literature—as far as vernacular writing was concerned, although in Latin she was still able to play a part—while French, and Provençal, and Italian literature were building up. Now, in the fourteenth century, after a brilliant beginning, French literature almost died away, because France was caught in the Hundred Years war: with the exception of the patriotic historian Froissart, it became mediocre. Italian literature had begun its mighty ascent, and continued it with Petrarch and Boccaccio. Provençal culture was almost totally destroyed in the crusade preached against the

Albigensian heretics by the Roman Catholic church. But after long uncertainty and strife, modern England was at last coming into being. Although England too had its plagues and troubles in the fourteenth century, it developed a quiet serene depth of character which it has never yet lost, and which was best exemplified, for his time, in Geoffrey Chaucer.

Geoffrey Chaucer was a well-connected courtier and civil servant, the first of a long line of English civil servants who have done much for literature. Born about 1340, he served in France, visited Italy three times on diplomatic missions, and was M.P. for Kent. He does not seem to have been a university man, and indeed there was something amateurish about his learning; but it was good for his poetry.

Chaucer was the first great English poet who knew Europe. Part of his power lay in the fact that, taking up European vernacular influences, he used them to improve the English language and English literature. The modern tongues he knew were French and Italian. However, the French influence on him was less important than the Italian, which so deeply affected many of his successors— Milton, Byron, Browning.

The following poems of Chaucer were due to his knowledge of French and Italian; but most of them, through French and Italian, were derived from Greco-Roman literature:

part of a translation of *The Romance of the Rose*;[37]

a long chivalrous romance about the Trojan war, *Troilus and Criseyde*, modelled on Boccaccio's *Filostrato* (which was itself modelled on an Italian plagiarist's rewriting of a French poet's adaptation of a late Greek romance), but much longer than Boccaccio's poem.[38] This is one of the few works which guarantee Chaucer a place in the front rank of English poets;

a vision of history, literature, fame, and unhappy love, called *The House of Fame*: unfinished, it was inspired by Dante's *Comedy*, probably also by Boccaccio's *Vision of Love*, and certainly by Latin poetry ancient and medieval;

the Knight's Tale, greatest of the Canterbury stories: from Boccaccio's *Theseid*, which Chaucer naturalized by omitting much of the mythology and epic machinery and expanded by adding much material of his own, to make the story more expressive of real life.[39]

It is odd that Chaucer does not appear to have known the great contemporary Italian success, Boccaccio's *Decameron*, although his *Canterbury Tales* follow a similar plan. Even when he uses a story from it, the *Patient Griselda* of the Clerk's Tale, he uses Petrarch's Latin translation of it, and says so:

> I wol yow telle a tale which that I
> Lerned at Padowe of a worthy clerk,
> As preved by his wordes and his werk.
> He is now deed and nayled in his cheste,
> I prey to god so yeve his soule reste!
> Fraunceys Petrark, the laureat poete,
> Highte this clerk, whos rethoryke sweete
> Enlumined al Itaille of poetrye. . . .[40]

But besides these direct borrowings Chaucer received many broader intellectual and emotional suggestions from France and Italy. The medieval love-romance was one of the strongest formative influences in his poetry. Through Italy the smiling scepticism and humanist tolerance of the dawning Renaissance reached him. But he also knew Dante well, and admired his grandeur. He actually makes the Wife of Bath quote him by name:

> Wel can the wyse poete of Florence,
> That highte Dant, speken in this sentence;
> Lo in swich maner rym is Dantes tale:
> 'Ful selde up ryseth by his branches smale
> Prowesse of man; for god, of his goodnesse,
> Wol that of him we clayme our gentillesse.'[41]

Contemporary scholars have pointed out many passages in which Chaucer imitates Dante, and some of particular interest, in which he blends effects taken from Dante with effects taken from a Latin poet.[42] The whole plan of *The House of Fame* is a mingling of homage to Vergil with homage to Dante.

Chaucer was not a very deep or intelligent student of the classics. What he takes from them is always simplified to the point of bareness. His learning, too, is limited in scope: it is more confined than Dante's small bookshelf, and its books are not so well thumbed as those the great exile carried with him. On the other hand, there are a few books in it which Dante did not know, and a few glimpses of others which had been unknown throughout the Middle Ages.

Chaucer makes many shocking mistakes, far worse than any of

the small aberrations that appear in Dante. And, what is more disconcerting, he appears now and then to pretend to knowledge which he does not possess. Like all medieval writers, he makes a great show of quoting his ancient authorities: but sometimes Chaucer's authorities do not exist and are inventions based on his own misunderstandings. For instance, the Man of Law mentions the Muses, and then says

> Metamorphoseos wot what I mene.[43]

This looks like an ignorant allusion to Ovid's *Metamorphoses*, treated as if the poem were a man, with its name distorted. Perhaps that is a joke against pedants, lawyers in particular. In that case, how can Chaucer seriously quote one of Ovid's mistresses?—

> First folow I Stace, and after him Corinne—[44]

or has he remembered, very faintly, that Ovid wrote about Corinna in the *Loves*? Again and again in *Troilus and Criseyde* he says he is retelling the story told by 'myn auctor Lollius', who wrote an old book about Troy in Latin; and in *The House of Fame* he introduces Lollius as a real historian. There is no such historian, ancient or modern, known to the world under that name. A very clever explanation is that it is a latinization of Boccaccio (= 'big-mouth'), *loll* meaning 'thick-tongued'. But since Chaucer never mentions Boccaccio, although he often copies him, and since he does not show so much verbal dexterity in translation as this explanation would assume, something much simpler should be suggested.

The Roman poet Horace wrote to a young friend who was studying rhetoric, to advise him to read Homer for the moral and philosophical content of the epics. He began:

> The writer of the Trojan war, Maximus Lollius,
> while you practised speaking in Rome, I reread at Praeneste.[45]

The boy's name was Lollius Maximus—Maximus being a complimentary nickname attached to his family, which meant 'greatest', and which Horace playfully emphasized by inverting its usual order, so that it looked like Mighty Lollius. In Latin it is perfectly obvious, despite the order, that the writer of the Trojan war was Homer, whom Horace had been studying in the little country town of Praeneste. But anyone who knew little of Latin syntax and less of Greek literature, and who did not realize that Horace's epistles are letters to his friends with their addressees named in the first line or so, would easily believe that someone named Lollius was the greatest writer of the Trojan war.

Whether it was Chaucer who *first* made this mistake or not we cannot now tell.[46] Certainly he accepted it and believed it when he put Lollius on an iron pillar in the House of Fame beside Dares and Homer.[47] Perhaps by the time he wrote *Troilus and Criseyde* he may have known better; for then he obviously knew that he was not translating Lollius, but working from Boccaccio and other sources nearer and more real. His use of the name was half a joke and half a fiction: the same kind of fiction that led Guido de Columnis to pretend he was taking everything from Dares when he was really copying Benoît, and Boccaccio to claim that his *Theseid* was from a long-forgotten Latin author, instead of being modelled on Guido, Benoît, and Statius. Ultimately it is the stock device of the romance-writer—the map of Treasure Island, Captain Kidd's cryptogram found on Sullivan's Island 'near Charleston, South Carolina',[48] the mysterious old author unknown to others, the manuscript found in a bottle.

Chaucer made many other mistakes and wrong guesses of this kind. Like Dante but unlike Petrarch, he believed that 'tragedy' meant a kind of narrative. The monk on the Canterbury pilgrimage says:

> . . . first Tragedies wol I telle
> Of whiche I have an hundred in my celle.
> Tragedie is to seyn a certeyn storie,
> As olde bokes maken us memorie,
> Of him that stood in greet prosperitee
> And is y-fallen out of heigh degree
> Into miserie, and endeth wrecchedly.

He then adds a gratuitous piece of wrong information:

> And they ben versifyed comunly
> Of six feet, which men clepe *exametron.*

That is, they are not tragedies but epic poems.[49]

Chaucer had not read all the authors whom he quotes, and it would be quite mistaken to list their names as 'classical influences' on his work. He knew a few Latin writers fairly well, translating and adapting their books with some understanding and with genuine love. He had a surface acquaintance with a number of others. But any knowledge he had of their work was either at second hand (because their writings were used by someone else whom he knew), or through excerpts or short summaries in one of the numerous medieval books of encyclopaedic learning. For him the world of Greece and Rome was not peopled with many massive figures, clearly distinct even in the distance, as it was for Dante. It held four or five great 'clerks' who were his masters; behind them a multitude of ghosts faintly seen and heard through the mists of the past; and, flitting around them, a number of purely imaginary chimeras like Corinne and 'myn auctor Lollius'.[50]

The authors whom Chaucer really knew have been reviewed by various scholars. For the most part, the conclusions reached in separate studies agree.[51]

He knew Ovid best, without any comparison. Dryden actually saw a resemblance between the two poets:

'both of them were well bred, well natur'd, amorous, and libertine, at least in their writings, it may be also in their lives. . . . Both of them were knowing in astronomy. . . . Both writ with wonderful facility and clearness. . . . Both of them built on the inventions of other men. . . . Both of them understood the manners, under which name I comprehend the passions, and, in a larger sense, the descriptions of persons, and their very habits.'[52]

And although Ovid was far more sophisticated (it was not only that Chaucer affected *naïveté* more skilfully) there was indeed a certain sympathy between them, even to the gloom which enwrapped them both at the close of their lives. Chaucer began to use Ovid's *Metamorphoses* as soon as he started writing poetry. His first poem, *The Book of the Duchess*, opens and closes with the story of Ceyx and Alcyone from *Met.* 11. 410–748: although, like the authors of *The Romance of the Rose* and other medieval writers using Ovid, Chaucer cuts out the metamorphosis of the lovers into birds and makes it only a love-death. His next work, *The House of Fame*, was partly suggested by Ovid's description of the house of Fame in *Met.* 12. 39 f. Even in *The Canterbury Tales* there is an amusing passage where the Man of Law boasts that Chaucer has told more stories of lovers than Ovid himself, and then gives a list revealing that Ovid was his chief source.[53]

Then Chaucer was one of the first modern poets who made much use of Ovid's imaginary love-letters, which are usually called the *Heroides*. He mentioned them as the Epistles, in *The Legend of Good Women*, 1465, and summarized most of them in an interesting passage of *The House of Fame*.[54] There are many hints, too, in the letters Ovid wrote for Paris and Helen, which Chaucer used in his development of the pretty coquette Criseyde.[55] He also knew the *Fasti*, Ovid's historical expansion of the Roman calendar: which Dante did not. His tale of Lucretia in *The Legend of Good Women* is taken from Ovid's account, and opens with a translation of Ovid's own words:[56] from time to time he used Ovid to correct or amplify Boccaccio. Although he mentions Ovid's *Art of Love* and *Cures for Love*,[57] there is no way of showing whether he had read either of them.

Next best Chaucer knew Vergil, but apparently only the *Aeneid*.[58] He summarizes the story in *The House of Fame* and partly in *The Legend of Dido*. It was an ambitious work, *The House of Fame*. In some ways it was his assertion of his own high mission as a poet. Just as Dante describes how in limbo he was greeted as an equal by the great classical writers, so Chaucer here set out to parallel Vergil. In the dream whose story he told, he saw the temple of Venus with the incidents of the *Aeneid* graved on its walls. Just so had Aeneas, at the crucial point of his wanderings, his first landing in Italy, found the tale of Minos and Daedalus and Icarus—an earlier flight from alien domination into exile with an earlier landing in Italy—pictured on the doors of Apollo's prophetic temple at Cumae. Fame herself was modelled on the description of Rumour in *Aeneid*, 4; and in *The Legend of Dido* the famous love-story is retold. But there Chaucer, as an amorous poet, made Aeneas fickle instead of a martyr to duty: he implies that Aeneas' visions were invented; he calls him 'traitour' and makes poor Dido say that she may be with child—a shallower and more modern interpretation of Vergil's story.[59]

Less important for his language, but much more important for his thought, was Boethius. Chaucer translated *The Consolation of Philosophy* from the Latin original, with the help of a French version and an explanatory edition. Although his translation is not good, it contains many valuable new English words taken straight over from Latin or through French from Latin. And Boethius's book provided the most important part of Chaucer's philosophical thought.[60] (Its influence was strengthened by the fact that so many of its ideas appear in *The Romance of the Rose*.)

In particular, there are two passages concerning fate, or the relation between man's free will-power and God's providence, which come straight from Boethius.[61] There are other such borrowings of less importance. The finest example of Boethian influence on Chaucer, however, is not a copy but a real re-thinking of the Roman's thought. This is the noble and very personal poem *Truth*, or *The Ballad of Good Counsel*:

> Flee fro the prees, and dwelle with sothfastnesse.

Several of the finest lines in this poem are rebirths of immortal classical thought:

> Her nis non hoom, her nis but wildernesse:
> Forth, pilgrim, forth! Forth, beste, out of thy stal!
> Know thy contree, look up, thank God of al. . . .

is a renaissance of the thought of Plato on the difficulty of living a good life in this bad world[62]—the thought elaborated in his condemned cell over eight centuries later by Boethius, and now, over eight hundred years farther on, revived in Chaucer.[63]

Next, but far behind the others, comes Statius, the poet of the Theban war, whom Chaucer knew well and used directly. Pandarus finds his niece reading the 'romaunce of Thebes' right up to the end of the twelfth book, where the bishop Amphiorax falls through the ground to hell.[64] Towards the end of *Troilus and Criseyde* there is another summary of the *Thebaid*, longer, with the Latin added for good measure.[65] Although Statius was a Silver Age poet with a strong sense of his own inferiority to such as Vergil, he had a vivid imagination, and his poems suggested a number of striking incidents and decorative epithets to Chaucer.

Apparently from a medieval school anthology, Chaucer knew the late Latin poet Claudian's *Rape of Proserpine* and two of his minor works.[66]

Cicero he mentions. He did know the famous *Dream of Scipio*, on which (with suggestions from Dante) he based *The Parliament of Fowls*;[67] but he seems never to have read any more of Cicero's voluminous works.

That far-travelled and much experienced lady, the Wife of Bath, cites a distinguished array of philosophical authorities, as

> Senek and othere clerkes.[68]

Since there is little trace that Seneca's fundamental philosophical theories meant anything to Chaucer, he probably knew only isolated passages through intermediaries. The largest number of his quotations from Seneca is in *The Tale of Melibeus*, but they are all taken from *The Book of Consolation and Counsel* by Albertano of Brescia (1246). Still, there are some quotations from Seneca's moral epistles which do seem to argue that Chaucer had read them first-hand.[69]

Apparently these are all the classical authors whom Chaucer had read at any length. Others he had glanced at, or glimpsed in excerpts and commentaries. The most remarkable of these is Valerius Flaccus, author of an epic on the Argonauts.[70] Chaucer is the first modern writer to mention it. He speaks of it by name in *The Legend of Good Women*, l. 1457; and he knew what was in it— at least in its first book, for he refers to the list of the *Argo*'s crew as 'a tale long y-now'. And in the same legend Chaucer's description of the landing of the Argonauts in Lemnos contains one or two details which seem to come from Valerius Flaccus and no one else. The difficulty, however, is to conjecture where he had seen the *Argonautica*, for the manuscript of the poem was not discovered until 1416, sixteen years after his death.[71] Shannon makes a bold attempt to prove that, because some of the *Argonautica* manuscripts are written in insular script, one may have been known in England in Chaucer's lifetime; but it is hard to think of Chaucer as being a more successful research scholar than Petrarch.

Juvenal the satirist he names twice: both times with reference to the tragic satire 10 ('The vanity of human wishes').[72] One of these references he took from an explanatory note to Boethius; the other probably from a similar intermediary.

Other authors—Livy, Lucan, Valerius Maximus, &c.—he mentions without knowing except in the vaguest way. He also read a good deal of the current Latin poets, historians, and encyclopaedists. His favourites were Boccaccio's *Genealogy of the Gods* (he even makes the same mistakes as Boccaccio) and Vincent of Beauvais's *Mirror of History*, an outline of world history down to 1244, with 'flowers' or memorable quotations from the great writers of the past.[73] These books were summaries of the knowledge of the medieval scholars and preparations for the Renaissance. Chaucer, by knowing not only them but his own original classics, helped in that preparation.

In Chaucer's life there were three great interests. These were, in order of importance, contemporary English life; French and Italian romantic love-poetry; and classical scholarship—chiefly poetry and myth, and next to them philosophy. Late in his life, a poor fourth, appeared Christianity. No one would say that his scholarship helped his bright, clear vision of contemporary life, nor that it greatly enhanced his appreciation of romantic poetry, although it gave him more tales of passion to tell. But it improved his power to express what he observed. It enriched his historical and legendary knowledge. It suggested imaginative parallels. It stimulated his imagination to outsoar his own age and country— *The House of Fame*, although not wholly successful, is the first English work to approach Dante. It heightened his own conception of his art. It gave him a good deal more wisdom than the confused and shallow folk-beliefs which were otherwise the only thing available to a courtier who was not a strongly religious man; and it permitted him to put wiser thoughts in the minds and mouths of his characters.

The stylistic excellence of classical poetry had a great educational effect on Chaucer. Literature is a craft, although it can only be practised to its highest effect by craftsmen who also feel it to be a spiritual and intellectual release for their energies. Therefore it can best be learnt through the study of other craftsmen, through emulation of their achievements, and through conscious or unconscious adaptation of their methods to one's own material and age. All the ancient poets whom Chaucer knew were highly trained. They had behind them generations of experience in the crafts of developing long, complex, and difficult thoughts; of arranging speeches; of making vivid descriptions more vivid by similes; of varying sentences and building up paragraphs; and of handling large masses of material so as to mould them into poems of majestic length. Even the letters of the Heroides to their lovers were rhetorically worked out, and the monologues in the *Meta-morphoses* were glittering displays of declamatory fireworks. Chaucer's ability to write long passages of description, elaborate comparisons, and big speeches was derived from his training in the classics. It is the same debt, on the formal level, as that owed by Dante to Vergil. But Chaucer was a smaller, softer man than Dante: although he was inspired by his models to attempt large works, he seldom finished them. How much his classical studies helped his poetry, nevertheless, can be seen by comparison with a contemporary English poet who had the same clear vision and a deeper seriousness, but who had never been exposed to the guiding and encouraging and clarifying influence of Greco-Latin poetry: the author of *Piers Plowman*. It was with Chaucer that classical learning became a natural part of the greatest English literature. As soon as the *Prologue to the Canterbury Tales* opens, Zephyrus with his sweet breath meets us, as naturally and as pleasantly as his air visits the English holt and heath.

6

THE RENAISSANCE

TRANSLATION

CLASSICAL influence flows into the literature of modern nations through three main channels. These are:

> translation;
> imitation;
> emulation.

The most obvious channel is translation, although the effects of the power entering by it are much more various than one might suppose. Imitation is of two types. Either the modern author decides that he can write poems in Latin which are as good as those of Vergil and his other models; or else, much more rarely, he attempts to write books in his own language on the exact pattern of the Latin or Greek works he admires. The third stage is emulation, which impels modern writers to use something, but not everything, of classical form and material, and to add much of their own style and subject-matter—in the endeavour to produce something not only as good as the classical masterpieces but different and new. In this way the real masterpieces are produced: the tragedies of Shakespeare and Racine; the satires of Pope; Dante's *Comedy*; *Paradise Lost*.

Translation, that neglected art, is a far more important element in literature than most of us believe. It does not usually create great works; but it often helps great works to be created. In the Renaissance, the age of masterpieces, it was particularly important.

The first literary translation from one language into another was made about 250 B.C., when the half-Greek half-Roman poet Livius Andronicus turned Homer's *Odyssey* into Latin for use as a text-book of Greek poetry and legend. (Traditionally, it was about the same time that a committee of seventy-two rabbis was translating certain books of the Hebrew scriptures into Greek for the use of the Jews scattered beyond Palestine, who were forgetting Hebrew and Aramaic; but that version was not made for artistic purposes,

and was not such a great milestone in the history of education.)[1]
The translation made by Livius Andronicus was a serious and
partly successful attempt to re-create a work of art in the framework
of a different language and culture.[2] It was the first of many
hundreds of thousands.

To the precedent set by Livius we owe much of our modern
system of education. The Greeks studied no literature but their
own: it was so various, original, and graceful that perhaps they
needed nothing more. But the native Roman literature and Roman
culture were rude and simple: so, from the third century B.C.,
Rome went to school with the Greeks. Ever since then the
intellectual standards of each European nation have closely corresponded to the importance assumed in its education by the
learning and translation of some foreign cultural language. Roman
literature and Roman thought rose to their noblest when all
educated Romans spoke and wrote Greek as well as Latin.[3] The
poetry of Vergil, the drama of Plautus and Seneca, the oratory and
philosophy of Cicero, were not Roman, but, as we have often called
them, a perfect synthesis which was Greco-Roman. When the
western Roman empire ceased to know Greek, its culture declined
and withered away. But after that, throughout the Dark Ages,
culture was kept alive by the few persons who knew another
language as well as their own: by the monks, priests, and scholars
who understood not only Anglo-Saxon or Irish Gaelic or primitive
French, but Latin too. With the spread of bilingualism through
the Middle Ages and into the Renaissance, European culture
deepened and broadened. The Renaissance was largely created by
many interacting groups of men who spoke not only their own
tongue but Latin too, and sometimes Greek. If Copernicus,
Rabelais, Shakespeare, if Queen Elizabeth and Lorenzo de'
Medici had not known Latin, if they had not all, with so many
others, enjoyed their use of it and been stimulated by it, we might
dismiss Renaissance latinity as a pedantic affectation. But the
evidence is too strong and unidirectional. The synthesis of Greco-
Roman with modern European culture in the Renaissance produced
an age of thought and achievement comparable in magnificence to
the earlier synthesis between the spirit of Greece and the energy
of Rome.

Since then the culture of each civilized European nation has
been largely based on the teaching of some other language in its

schools and the constant flow of translations, imitations, and emulations into its literature. The other language need not be Latin or Greek. The Russians profited from learning German. The Germans profited from learning French. The essential thing is that the additional language should be the vehicle of a rich culture, so that it will expand home-keeping minds and prevent the unconscious assumption that parochialism is a virtue. The main justification for learning Latin and Greek is that the culture they open to those who know them is nobler and richer than any other in our world.

The intellectual importance of translation is so obvious that it is often overlooked. No language, no nation is sufficient unto itself. Its mind must be enlarged by the thoughts of other nations, or else it will warp and shrivel. In English, as in other languages, many of the greatest ideas we use have been brought in through translation. The central book of the English-speaking peoples is a translation—although it comes as a shock to many to realize that the Bible was written in Hebrew and Greek, and translated by a committee of scholars. There are many great books which none but specialists need read in the original, but which through translation have added essential ideas to our minds: Euclid's *Elements*, Descartes's *Discourse on Method*, Marx's *Capital*, Tolstoy's *War and Peace*.

The artistic and linguistic importance of translation is almost as great as its importance in the field of ideas. To begin with, the practice of translation usually enriches the translator's language with new words. This is because most translations are made from a language with a copious vocabulary into a poorer language which must be expanded by the translator's courage and inventiveness. The modern vernacular languages—English, French, Spanish, &c.—grew out of spoken dialects which had little or no written literatures, were geographically limited, and were used largely for practical and seldom for intellectual purposes. They were therefore simple, unimaginative, and poor in comparison with Latin and Greek. Soon after people began to write in them they set out to enrich them and make them more expressive. The safest and most obvious way to do so was to borrow from the literary language at their side and bring in Latin words. This enlargement of the western European languages by importations from Latin and Greek was one of the most important activities which prepared for the Renaissance; and it was largely carried on by translators.

The parent of the French language was a variant of colloquial Latin. But new transfusions, from literary Latin, appeared in French as early as the twelfth century, and increased in the thirteenth. By the fourteenth century there was a deliberate policy of borrowing Latin words to increase the scope of French. Contemporary writers sometimes give us their reasons for pursuing this policy. Clearly it was forced upon them as a solution to the problem of translating from a rich language into a poor one. Thus a Lorrainian translator of the *Books of Kings* writes:

'Since the Romance language, and particularly that of Lorraine, is imperfect, . . . there is nobody, however good a clerk he may be and a good speaker of Romance, who can translate Latin into Romance . . . without taking a number of Latin words, such as *iniquitas = iniquiteit, redemptio = redemption, misericordia = misericorde.* . . . Latin has a number of words that we cannot express properly in Romance, our tongue is so poor: for instance, one says in Latin *erue, eripe, libera me,* for which three words in Latin we have only one word in Romance: 'deliver me." '[4]

The policy was part of the cultural achievement of Charles V, in whom we recognize a precursor of the Renaissance. He cultivated scholars, got them good benefices, and encouraged them to translate the classics for his library. The most important of his protégés was Nicole Oresme (*c.* 1330–81), whom he made bishop of Lisieux.[5] A careful and skilful translator from Latin into French, he too complains of the poverty of his own language, and gives an interesting example suggested by his translations of Aristotle:

'Among innumerable instances we may use this common proposition: *homo est animal. Homo* means "man and woman", which has no equivalent in French, and *animal* means anything which has a soul capable of perception, and there is no word in French which precisely signifies that.'[6]

To remedy this condition Oresme and others set about latinizing, and even hellenizing, French. The result might have been disastrous had it not been for two factors: the close natural relationship between French and Latin, and the good taste of the

French people, both then and afterwards. Very early in his career
Pantagruel met a student with less reliable taste, who explained that
he too was making efforts to enrich the language:

'My worshipful lord, my genie is not apt . . . to excoriate the cuticle of
our vernacular Gallic, but viceversally I gnave, opere, and by vele and
rames enite to locupletate it with the Latinicome redundance.'[7]

Then Pantagruel took him by the throat, and his end was terrible.
Many such Latin loans were allowed to lapse, as awkward or
unnecessary, soon after they were made; but very many more
became part of the language and did really locupletate it.

We can distinguish several different channels by which Latin
(and Greek) entered French in the later Middle Ages. These are
typical. Other languages of western Europe made similar borrowings through some, or all, of the same channels.

Words were taken over from Latin and Greek and naturalized.
These fell into two main classes: abstract nouns, with the adjectives
related to them; and words connected with the higher techniques
and arts of civilization. In the former class come words which now
seem quite natural and indispensable, such as those in -tion:
circulation, décision, décoration, hésitation, position; those in -ité:
calamité, spécialité; those in -ant, -ance, -ent, -ence, such as absent,
arrogant, évidence; with many others less easy to group, such as
excès, commode, agile, illégal, and abstract verbs like anticiper,
assister, excéder, exclure, répliquer, séparer. In the latter class are
words now equally well accepted: acte, artiste, démocratie, facteur,
médecin. (One odd fact about the history of language is that some
of these words disappeared after their introduction and were
reintroduced into French at the beginning of the sixteenth century;
or, like compact, in the eighteenth; and a few, like raréfaction, in
the nineteenth.)

Verbal elements were extracted from naturalized Latin words
and adapted to broader uses throughout French: notably the
prefix in- (as in words like incivil, inouï), and the terminations -ité
and -ment for abstract nouns.

Quite a number of French words already existing, which had
originally been derived from Latin but had grown away from their
parentage, were corrected so as to conform more exactly with their
derivation. For instance oscur was changed back to obscur; soutil
became subtil, because it came from subtilis; esmer became

estimer. Sometimes both forms survived side by side: *conter* and *compter.*

Greek words were also introduced, although in a much smaller proportion. Usually they seem to be words which were already latinized through translations of the church fathers or of the Greek philosophers: for instance, *agonie, climat, fantaisie, poème, police, théorie, zone.* Oresme himself was responsible for bringing in a large number of important words dealing with politics and aesthetics: *aristocratie, métaphore, sophiste.*

Finally, *low Latin words* infiltrated French—not from the classical authors but from the current Latin of the law courts and the church: *décapiter, graduel, individu.*

The English language had not begun its life entirely devoid of Greek and Roman influence. Far back in the Dark Ages it drew in Latin and Greek words to cover activities which were not native to its people—religious, social, political—and even the names of foreign foods and drinks. *Church* and *kirk* come from the Greek; so do *bishop, monk, priest,* and (unless it be Latin) *wine.* Many Latin words entered indirectly at the Conquest, through Norman-French. Then, as the Middle Ages flowed towards the Renaissance, English began to grow in the same way, and for the same reasons, as French: very largely under the influence of French. Chaucer was the chief figure in this process.

He had some Latin, and knew French almost as well as English. We cannot tell now whether the Latin words naturalized in English during this period came directly from Latin or at one remove through French. But the majority seem, from their shape, to have been imported via France: for instance, the abstract nouns in *-ance* and *-ence,* like *ignorance* and *absence,* where the hard Latin terminations *-antia, -entia* have been softened down by French. Some words came by both routes. Jespersen quotes the Greco-Latin *machine,* which, as its pronunciation shows, came through French; while its relative *machination* entered directly from Latin. (Another relative, *mechanical,* came from the same Greek root directly into English via low Latin.) A similar pair is *example* and *exemplary.*

The Latin and Greek words brought into English by Chaucer, and by his contemporaries and followers, were (like similar importations into French) chiefly abstract nouns and adjectives or cultural and technical words. They included such abstract or semi-abstract words as *absolute, convenient, manifest, mortal, position, sensible*—all of which are said to be found for the first time in Chaucer's translation of Boethius,[8] a book that has been called 'the foundation of English philosophical prose'.[9] And Chaucer introduced such scholarly words as *astrologer, distil, erratic, longitude, native, occidental, orator*. Hundreds more words that we use every day were brought in at this time: words as simple as *solid*, as useful as *poetry*, as necessary as *existence*. It is difficult to overestimate the importance of the growth English experienced in the late Middle Ages: it started to become one of the great culture-languages of the world.

Similarly, Latin verbal elements like *-tion* and *in-* were imported and their use extended. And, as in French, the spelling of Romance words in English was corrected. For instance, *dette* was altered to *debt*; but the *b* of the original Latin *debitum* could not be inserted into the pronunciation, and we still pronounce *debt* in the Middle English manner derived from Norman-French. The same *b* was put into *doute* in English, to become *doubt* like the Latin *dubitatio*: but the pronunciation remained *dout* in English and *doot* in Scots. The French still call the fourth month *avril*; it was *Avril* or *Averil* in the early years after the Conquest, but by Chaucer's time became *Aprille*, 'with his shoures sote'.

Spenser called Chaucer a 'well of English undefiled'. This is nearly as false as Milton's description of Shakespeare: 'warbling native wood-notes wild'. There were many medieval English writers who thought and spoke pure English, as it then was. Some of them wrote well. None of them did much for the language or for its literature. The importance of Chaucer was that he became not only a well of pure English but a channel through which the rich current of Latin and a sister stream of Greek flowed into England.

Spanish early in the fifteenth century began to undergo a similar expansion, partly through direct imitation of Latin, partly under the influence of Italian culture. The importations into Spanish fall into the same classes as those mentioned above for French and English. There were abstract words from Latin: *ambición, comendación, comodidad, servitud, temeridad*. There were Greek words: *idiota, paradoja, pedante*. Existing Spanish words were corrected to make them more like classical Latin: *amos* became *ambos*, *veluntad* became *voluntad, criador* became *creador.* And sometimes, as in French and English, both forms survived:

blasfemar and *lastimar*	*colocar* and *colgar*
cálido and *caldo*	*íntegro* and *entero.*

(*Creador, criador,* and *criatura* all survive together.) The Spaniards, who love extremes, went farther than either English or French in adopting not only Greek and Latin words but Greek and Latin syntactical patterns which could not really be naturalized, and in authors like Góngora distorted both language and thought.

French, English, and Spanish were the languages which grew most markedly in strength and suppleness by naturalizing Latin and Greek words in the late Middle Ages and early Renaissance. German, Polish, Magyar, and other languages of northern and eastern Europe, however, lived on virtually untouched by the movement which was so strong in the west. Of course they had poets, and prose-writers, who wrote in the vernacular languages; and they had numerous authors working mainly or exclusively in Latin, the international language of culture. The essential point in which they differed from the western nations was this. They had few, if any, writers of talent who bridged the gap between their native cultures and the culture of Greece and Rome; and they had very few translators. Their authors were either wholly German (or Polish or Magyar) or else wholly Latin. But in the west many men like Chaucer and Gower in England, and Iñigo Lopez de Mendoza and Juan de Mena in Spain, wrote their own language, and at the same time enriched it by transfusions of Greek and Latin words and verbal patterns and stylistic devices; they translated from Latin into their own speech; they acted as a living channel through which the two cultures could actively intermingle, the older refreshing and strengthening the younger.

This movement, whose outlines have been briefly sketched, became ever stronger as western Europe moved into the full Renaissance. Learning became more widely distributed, geographically and socially. More difficult, more adult books were more carefully studied. The sense of language became more delicate. The flow of Latin and Greek words into the western European languages continued and increased. That continuing flow of rich energy, after it had been stabilized and refined by the later application of chosen Greco-Roman stylistic standards, made the rough strong simple dialects of the Dark Ages into the languages of western Europe and modern America.

Translation has another function, equally valuable and less obvious. It enriches the style of the translator's language. This is because any distinguished book when translated usually carries with it many stylistic patterns which the translator's language does not possess. It may, for instance, be written in a form which does not exist in the new language. When it is translated, the form will be naturalized. If it is in poetry, its metre may not exist in the new language, in which case it must be copied, or a satisfactory metre must be devised to render its effects. Almost certainly it will contain images which are new, and which can be imported with all the charm of novelty. And often it will embody fresh, interesting, and highly developed verbal devices produced by years or generations of experiment and evolution, which can be copied or adapted in the recipient language. From the translation, if it be a good one, these patterns are then imitated by original writers, and soon become a perfectly native resource.

Thus, Hebrew images have entered English in great numbers through the translation of the Old Testament.

Blank verse was devised by Italian poets of the Renaissance in order to render the effect of continuous flow, and the large scope, of the Latin hexameter and iambic trimeter.

Simply by copying their originals, translators into most of the modern languages have introduced Greco-Latin turns of style such as climax, antithesis, apostrophe, &c., which are now a regular part of modern style, but which scarcely existed in any European tongue until they became known through translations. One pattern which has become a great favourite is the tricolon. This was worked out by the later Greek rhetoricians, and used freely in Latin prose and poetry—above all others, by Cicero. It is an arrangement of words or phrases in a group of three. The three are related, usually expressing different aspects of the same thought. They are balanced in weight and importance. And they usually work up to a slight climax on the third. Abraham Lincoln's Gettysburg Address contains several such arrangements:

'we cannot dedicate—we cannot consecrate—we cannot hallow—this ground';
'government of the people, by the people, for the people'.

Lincoln could not read Cicero's speeches; but this device, which was not native to the English language, he had learnt by studying the prose of baroque writers such as Gibbon, who were steeped in the cadences of Ciceronian Latin and skilfully reproduced them in English. Now, of course, the tricolon is constantly used in English oratory. It is particularly useful because it both seems natural and is memorable. Another great president, no less an orator than Lincoln, created a deathless phrase on the same model when he spoke of 'one-third of a nation, ill-housed, ill-clad, ill-nourished'. And yet, natural as it now seems, this pattern was a Greco-Roman invention just as much as the internal-combustion engine was a modern western European invention; and in the same way it is now being used by millions who do not know its origin.

And even beyond this, it is important that there should be good translations of good books, because, by their vigour and intensity, they stimulate even artists who intend to write on other subjects or in different patterns. That was one of the highest functions of translation during the Renaissance. If great thoughts can be communicated—through whatever difficulties and distances—they will produce great thoughts. That justifies all translations, even the bad ones. That was the principle of the Renaissance translators.

The Renaissance was the great age of translation. Almost as rapidly as unknown classical authors were discovered, they and their better-known brothers were revealed to the public of western Europe by vernacular translations. The two chief factors in this phenomenon were the increasing knowledge of, and interest in, classical antiquity; and the invention of printing, which extended the distribution of culture by making self-education easier.

The countries of western Europe differ in the number and value of the translations they made. The order is, roughly, France first; then Britain and Germany; then Italy and Spain; and the rest nowhere. Many talented Italians chose, instead of translating Latin books into their own tongue, to write original works in Latin or Italian, or to translate from Greek into Latin. The French translations were numerous and splendid. The British translators were vigorous. But they were not really scholarly: they translated Greek books from Latin versions sometimes, and sometimes Latin books from French versions; and there was a dashing carelessness about them, the reverse of pedantry, which reminds us of Shakespeare, the author who 'never blotted out line' and would not see his own plays through the press. For example, Chapman *boasted* of having finished the second twelve books of the *Iliad* in less than four months. In Germany, the forces of classical culture made a far shallower penetration during the Renaissance. There was much writing in Latin; there were various adaptations of Roman comedies; there were a number of attempts at making classical learning accessible through translations; but there was, in literature, no real productive union between the German national mind and the art and thought of Greece and Rome. More Latin books than German books were printed every year until 1691.[10] Few of the translations had any literary value, and none stimulated the production of independent works of art. The small group of men like Reuchlin who knew Greek were quite isolated, although they and others in southern and western Germany were inspired by contact with Italy. The north and east were still sunk in medieval darkness.[11]

We can now survey the first translations into modern languages of the chief works of Greek and Latin literature, made during the Renaissance. (Translations into Latin, though they also were important channels for the transmission of classical influence, do not fall within the scope of this book. Nor do most of the fragmentary or unpublished translations, which had less effect on the general development of literature.)

EPIC

Some of HOMER'S *Iliad* was translated into Spanish from a Latin version, by the Marquis of Santillana's son, about 1445.[12] These early translations, however, were like the paraphrases of medieval times: such too was the French version of the *Iliad* (from Valla's Latin translation, with additions from 'Dares' and 'Dictys') made by Jean Samxon in 1530. Simon Schaidenreisser, also working on Latin versions, put the *Odyssey* into German prose in 1537. The first serious attempts at a modern verse rendering were made in France by Hugues Salel, with his 1545 version of *Iliad*, 1–10, and Jacques Peletier du Mans, who translated *Odyssey*, 1–2, in 1547. Salel's translation was completed by Amadis Jamyn in 1577. In England, Arthur Hall (who had no Greek) translated

Salel's version in 1581; but his work was soon outdone by the complete rendering made from the Greek by George Chapman, who produced the *Iliad* in English verse in 1611, the *Odyssey* in 1614, and the *Hymns* in 1616. (He had published a preliminary translation of *Iliad*, 1–2 and 7–11, in 1598.) This version, which Keats rightly calls 'loud and bold', was the first complete poetic translation of Homer in any modern tongue. We hear of Italian translations of the *Odyssey* into stanzas by Lodovico Dolce (1573), and into blank verse, together with the first seven books of the *Iliad*, by Girolamo Bacelli (1581–2); but they created little impression. In Germany a verse rendering of the *Iliad* by Johann Spreng of Augsburg appeared in 1610.

There was a prose translation of VERGIL's *Aeneid* in Gaelic before 1400—the *Imtheachta Æniasa*, in the Book of Ballymote.[13] During the fifteenth century prose paraphrases began to appear—in French by Guillaume Leroy, in Spanish by Enrique de Villena. Then about 1500 the first regular verse translation was produced, a naïve but faithful rendering in rhymed decasyllabic couplets by the talented French translator Octovien de Saint-Gelais.[14] A few years later, in 1515, T. Murner issued a German version of 'the thirteen books of the *Aeneid*', while in Scotland the energetic bishop Gawain Douglas had completed a strong, homely, and vivid translation in rough heroic couplets (1513). Political troubles kept this work from having any effect at the time, and it remained unpublished until 1553. The Earl of Surrey, beheaded in 1547, left versions of books 2 and 4 published posthumously, in which many passages of Douglas were copied almost word for word.[15] (It was in this poem by Surrey that blank verse was used for the first time in English, probably in imitation of the recently adopted blank verse used by Italian poets and translators.) Meanwhile there had been some renderings of parts of the epic in France: notably Du Bellay's version of books 4 (1552) and 6 (1561); and at last, after thirteen years of work, Desmasures produced a successful translation of the whole poem in 1560. An Alexandrine translation of all Vergil's works was published in 1582 by two Norman squires, the brothers Antoine and Robert Le Chevalier d'Agneaux. A translation of the *Aeneid* in English started by Phaer (books 1–7, 1558) was completed by Twyne in 1573, but it was poor stuff. Tasso's friend Cristobal de Mesa turned the *Aeneid* into Spanish, and the industrious Johann Spreng (d. 1601) made the first German verse rendering. Annibale Caro's Italian version, printed in 1581, was long famous. And equally famous was Richard Stanyhurst's English hexameter translation of *Aeneid*, 1–4 (1582), which has a strong claim to be the worst translation ever published—although competition in this field is very heavy. It will be enough to quote Dido's indignant exclamation on being deserted by Aeneas:

> Shall a stranger give me the slampam?

LUCAN was turned into French in the fourteenth century for Charles V. A Spanish prose version of 'the poet of Cordoba'—as the Spaniards proudly called him—was published at Lisbon in 1541 by Martin Laso de Oropesa; but it really belonged to the medieval tradition of treating him as a historian.[16] In English Marlowe produced a line-by-line translation of book 1 (dated 1600, but entered at Stationers' Hall in 1593). A complete English version was made by Sir A. Gorges in 1614, followed by a more successful one from T. May, who was secretary and historian of the Long Parliament, in 1626. The vogue of baroque poetry in Spain was encouraged against his will by Juan de Jauregui y Aguilar, who wrote a translation of Lucan which so vividly reproduced Lucan's conceits and distortions that it gave authority to the affectations of Góngora and his school.[17]

Versions of OVID's *Metamorphoses* have been mentioned in our chapter on the medieval romances.[18] Petrarch's friend Bersuire or Berçoir (who died in 1362) wrote a French paraphrase which long held the field, being even turned into English by Caxton in 1480—until Clément Marot translated books 1 and 2 in 1532, and Habert the entire poem in 1557. Hieronymus Boner issued a German translation in 1534; Halberstadt's old German paraphrase of 1210 reappeared in a modernized form in 1545, to be superseded by Spreng's verse rendering in 1564. In English Arthur Golding made a version rough but fluent (1567), which Shakespeare knew and used, adding to it the graces of his own imagination.[19]

HISTORY

HERODOTUS was put into Latin by Valla in 1452–7. Rabelais himself is said to have translated book 1 while he was a monk, but his work is lost and he never refers to it. Boiardo (1434–94) produced an Italian translation, and Pierre Saliat a French one in 1556. Books 1 and 2 were published in English by 'B. R.' in 1584.

There is a German version by H. Boner (1535) based on the Latin rendering.

THUCYDIDES also was given a famous Latin interpretation by Valla (1452), which became the basis for translations into the modern languages: into French by Claude de Seyssel, bishop of Marseilles, about 1512; into German by Boner in 1533; into Italian by Francisco de Soldo Strozzi in 1545; and into English from Seyssel's version by Thomas Nichols in 1550. A Spanish translation by Diego Gracián came out in 1564.

XENOPHON's *Anabasis* was put into French by de Seyssel in 1504; German by Boner in 1540; Italian by R. Domenichi in 1548; Spanish by Gracián in 1552; English by J. Bingham in 1623.

After PLUTARCH's *Parallel Lives* had been made accessible in Latin by Guarino and others in the early fifteenth century, they too entered modern languages. Twenty-six lives were turned into Italian by B. Jaconello in 1482; eight into German by H. Boner in 1534 and the rest in 1541; Alfonso de Palencia had already translated them into Spanish in 1491. In French, four were translated in 1530 by Lazare de Baïf, eight by George de Selve, bishop of Lavaur (who died in 1542), and others by Arnault Chandon, who followed de Selve, but was to be outdone by a greater man. In 1559 the great French translator Jacques Amyot, who rose from a professorship at Bourges to be bishop of Auxerre, issued his magnificent complete version of all the *Lives*. Montaigne said it was one of the two chief influences on his thinking, and it held its place in French literature for hundreds of years.[20] Thomas North turned it into English in 1579, and it then became an equally strong influence on William Shakespeare.[21]

CAESAR's *Memoirs* were turned into French for Charles V in the fourteenth century. His work *On the Gallic War* was published in German by M. Ringmann Philesius in 1507. Partial English versions having been made in 1530 by W. Rastell and 1564 by John Brend, Golding produced a complete version in 1565.

SALLUST (along with Suetonius) had also been translated for Charles V of France. In the next century he was done into Spanish—the Spaniards paid much attention to Roman history—by Francisco Vidal de Noya (1493). D. von Pleningen and J. Vielfeld issued German versions in 1513 and 1530. Meigret made a new French translation in the middle of the sixteenth century. *Jugurtha* was made English in 1520–3 by Alexander Barclay, the talented adaptor of *The Ship of Fools*; Thomas Heywood translated both the monographs in 1608.

LIVY, so far as he was known, was translated quite early. Boccaccio is reported to have made a version of the books then extant; and Petrarch's friend Bersuire produced a French rendering which was not superseded until 1582. In Spanish a very influential translation was made by Pedro Lopez de Ayala, Chancellor of Castile (1332–1407). B. Schöfferlin and J. Wittig translated all the books then known into German in 1505; their translation was reissued, with a rendering of the newly discovered books, by N. Carbach in 1523. The first complete English version was by the vigorous and learned Philemon Holland in 1600.

TACITUS, that difficult author, was put into German by Micyllus in 1535. In French the *Annals* were rendered by Étienne de la Planche (1–5, 1548) and Claude Fauchet (11–16, 1582). In English Sir Henry Savile translated *Agricola* and the *Histories* (1591), and R. Grenewey *Germany* and the *Annals* (1598).

In fact, history was probably the single most important field of translation during the Renaissance—which emphasizes one type of classical influence we are sometimes inclined to take for granted: the perspective of past events, the political experience, and the wealth of story laid open to us by the still unequalled historians of antiquity.

PHILOSOPHY

PLATO was less often translated than he deserved. However, there were many Latin versions, the greatest being a complete set made by Ficino in 1482 for the Medici. The first English translation appeared in 1592 (Spenser's *Axiochus*, a dubious work). Renderings of separate dialogues were made in French: the *Lysis* by Bonaventure des Périers about 1541, the *Crito* in 1547 by P. du Val, the *Ion* by Richard le Blanc in 1546, *The Defence of Socrates* by F. Hotman in 1549. Then the distinguished humanist Loys Le Roy began to issue a very valuable set of translations of more important dialogues: *Timaeus* (1551), *Phaedo* (1553,) *The Symposium* (1559), and *The Republic* (published in 1600). We are told that in 1546 Étienne Dolet was burned for publishing a version of *Hipparchus* and *Axiochus* which attributed to Plato a disbelief in the immortality of the soul.[22] This must be one of the most drastic punishments for mistranslation ever recorded.

ARISTOTLE's *Politics* had early been translated by Nicolas Oresme, whose version was printed in 1486 and superseded by that of Loys Le Roy in 1568. The first Italian translation was published by A. Bruccioli in 1547; 'J. D.' turned the book into English from Le Roy's French version in 1598.

Aristotle's *Ethics* were also translated into French under Charles V, and then again in the sixteenth century by Le Roy. Carlos de Viana made a Spanish version late in the fifteenth century. J. Wylkinson's English translation (1547) is from a third-hand medieval Italian version based on Brunetto Latini's work.

PLUTARCH's *Moral Essays* were always favourites, for their combination of charm, scholarship, and worldly wisdom. They were often translated separately: Sir Thomas Elyot's version of *On Education* (*c.* 1530) is an example. Wyat used Budé's Latin version to produce a translation of the essay *On Peace of Mind* in 1528; Wyer the printer turned out an English rendering of Erasmus's Latin translation of the essay *On Preserving Health* about 1530; and Blundeville translated four between 1558 and 1561. Complete versions were issued in German by M. Herr and H. von Eppendorf in 1535, and by W. Xylander (completed by Jonas Löchinger) in 1580; in French by Amyot in 1572—another of his essential translations; and in English by Holland in 1603.

CICERO's little dialogues *On Friendship* (*Laelius*) and *On Old Age* (*Cato Maior*) were widely popular. Laurent Premierfait, who died in 1418, turned them into French. The former was translated into English before 1460 by John Tiptoft, earl of Worcester, whose version was printed by Caxton in 1481 along with a translation of *On Old Age* made from Premierfait's French version (probably by Botoner). They were both included in a collection of translations called *The German Cicero*, by Johann, Freiherr zu Schwarzenberg (1534), which also contained the *Tusculan Discussions*; Jean Colin turned them into French again in 1537–9; John Harington (father of the poet) translated *On Friendship* from the French version in 1550; R. Whittington *On Old Age* about 1535; and Thomas Newton did both in 1577. Cicero's big treatise *On Duties* had been anonymously translated into German as early as 1488, and again in 1531 by Schwarzenberg. Whittington made a poor English version of it in 1540, and Nicolas Grimald a good one in 1553. The *Tusculan Discussions* were put into French by

Étienne Dolet (1-3, 1542) and into English by John Dolman in 1561. Schaidenreisser turned the *Paradoxes* into German in 1538, Whittington into English in 1540, and Thomas Newton again in 1569, together with one of Cicero's finest works, the fragmentary *Dream of Scipio*.

SENECA's *Letters* and moral treatises on moral subjects were usually read in Latin—their popularity being increased by Erasmus's fine edition in 1515. However, we hear of a fourteenth-century French version and of a German compendium by Michael Herr (1536). Dietrich von Pleningen translated the *Consolation to Marcia* into German in 1519. The treatise *On Benefits* was Englished in 1577 by Arthur Golding, the translator of Ovid, and all Seneca's prose works by Lodge in 1614.

DRAMA

Translations of drama were surprisingly patchy and infrequent. A grave disservice to literature was done by the Renaissance translators who neglected the Greek playwrights. Aeschylus and Aristophanes were scarcely ever turned into modern languages, Sophocles and Euripides poorly and incompletely. The Roman comedians and the tragedies of Seneca were very much better treated. The reasons for the neglect of Greek drama were, first, the extreme difficulty of its thought and language; second, the superior attraction of the flashier Seneca; third, the existence of handy Latin translations, such as those by Erasmus and Buchanan; and fourth, the fact that anyone who could read Greek and write poetry usually preferred to spend his efforts not on translating but on emulating the classical poets.

SOPHOCLES' *Electra* was turned into Spanish as *Revenge for Agamemnon* by Fernan Perez de Oliva (*c.* 1525), and into pretty heavy French in 1537 by Lazare de Baïf, whose son Jean-Antoine published his own version of *Antigone* in 1573.[23] Alamanni's rather free Italian rendering of *Antigone* was issued in 1533, and in 1581 Thomas Watson produced a translation into Latin.

The most notable translations of EURIPIDES were the Italian ones made between 1545 and 1551 by Lodovico Dolce: *Hecuba*, *Medea*, *Iphigenia at Aulis*, and *The Phoenician Women*. *Hecuba* was put into Spanish by Fernan Perez de Oliva in 1528 and in 1544 into French by Bochetel and Amyot.[24] In 1549 Thomas Sébillet produced a French version of *Iphigenia at Aulis* exactly twice as long as the original. No other Greek play appeared in French for 120 years. In German the Strasbourg humanists issued a fair number of translations of Greek drama from 1604 onwards; and there was one sixteenth-century translation, Michael Babst's *Iphigenia at Aulis*. Very few English versions of Greek plays were made during the Renaissance. Peele is said to have translated one of the Euripidean plays on Iphigenia while he was at college, but it is lost. The only published translation was a rendering of *The Phoenician Women* put out in 1566 by Francis Kinwelmersh and George Gascoigne, who took it from Dolce's Italian and called it *Jocasta*.

ARISTOPHANES' easiest and most popular play, *Plutus*, was turned into French about 1550 by Ronsard (to be acted by his friends at the Collège de Coqueret) and into Spanish in 1577 by Pedro Simon Abril.[25]

PLAUTUS was a favourite. The court poets of Ferrara were translating his comedies as early as 1486, and scores of Italian versions appeared later. An early translation of his *Amphitryon* into Spanish prose was produced in 1515 by Francisco Lopez de Villalobos. *The Brothers Menaechmus* was Englished by 'W. W.' in 1595, possibly to the benefit of Shakespeare's *Comedy of Errors*;[26] and it had long before been turned into German, along with *The Bacchides*, by the German scholar Albrecht von Eyb. (He died in 1475, but the translations were not published until 1511.) A German version of *The Pot Comedy* was made by Joachim Greff in 1535, of *Stichus* by C. Freyssleben in 1539, of *The Brothers Menaechmus* by Jonas Bitner in 1570, and there were numerous others. Many playwrights, beginning with the Italians, produced modrneizations and adaptations of Plautine comedies.[27]

TERENCE, although less popular as a dramatist, was easier, politer, and more edifying: so he was translated early and often. A French prose rendering by Guillaume Rippe and one in verse[28] by Gilles Cybille were published together about 1500. *The Eunuch* was turned into German as early as 1486 by Hans Nythart. In 1499 a complete German Terence in prose appeared at Strasbourg, possibly made by the Alsatian humanists Brant and Locher. It was followed by another prose translation by Valentin Boltz in 1539, by Johannes Bischoff's rhymed version in 1566, and by many versions of single plays. Complete translations appeared in French, by C. Estienne, J. Bourlier, and 'Anon', in 1566; in Spanish, by Pedro Simon Abril, in 1577; and in English, by the Puritan divine Richard Bernard, in 1598.

The earliest dramatic translation of SENECA was a version of *Medea*, *Thyestes*, and *The Trojan Women* (with fragments of others) made in Catalan by Antonio Vilaragut. It can be placed not far from 1400; and we hear of a complete translation of Seneca's tragedies into Spanish in the fifteenth century. The most influential vernacular dramatic translation of the period was certainly the English version of the *Ten Tragedies*, produced by six different translators between 1559 and 1581.[29] As well as a regular translation made by Dolce in Italy about 1550, there were many versions specially written for stage presentation. There appear to have been none in German. In France Charles Toutain produced the first Senecan translation with his *Agamemnon* (1557). This was followed by another *Agamemnon* (Le Duchat, 1561), an important series made by Roland Brisset (*The Madness of Hercules*, *Thyestes*, *Agamemnon*, and the bogus *Octavia*) in 1590, and finally by a complete set of the tragedies translated by Benoît Bauduyn (1629).[30]

ORATORY

Oratory also was ill represented in translations during the Renaissance. Much public speaking was still being done in Latin —for instance, we hear of Queen Elizabeth delivering a fiery extempore speech in fluent Latin to the envoys of Spain. It was a little later, during the baroque period, that modern oratory really developed—using classical originals and translations as its models.

DEMOSTHENES' *Olynthiacs* were put into French in 1551 by Loys Le Roy, and into English in 1570 by T. Wilson, who designed them to be read as propaganda against the aggressions of Philip of Spain.[31] Boner produced a German version of the *Philippics* in 1543, while Loys Le Roy published his French *Philippics* and *Olynthiacs* together in 1575.

ISOCRATES was not really an orator, but a political philosopher. However, his ideas were set out in the form of speeches or letters, polished to a rhetorical brilliance. Three of these works were particularly popular in the Renaissance. *To Nicocles* is an address by Isocrates himself to one of his princely pupils, and discusses the duties of the monarch. It was translated into German by

J. Altenstaig in 1517 and into English by Sir Thomas Elyot in 1531.[32] *To Demonicus*, an essay on practical morality, was put into German in 1519 by W. Pirckheimer, and into English in 1557 by Bury, and, following him, by Nuttall in 1585. *Nicocles*, an address by the young prince to his subjects on the principles of government, was turned into French by L. Meigret in 1544. Loys Le Roy produced a French translation of all three in 1551, and T. Forrest an English one, working on a Latin version, in 1580.

Ten of CICERO's speeches were rendered into French by Macault in 1548. R. Sherry did the speech for Marcellus into English in 1555 (C. Bruno had put it into German in 1542), and T. Drant the little speech for Archias in 1571. Centuries earlier, Brunetto Latini had turned the speeches for Marcellus, Ligarius, and King Deiotarus into Italian.

SMALLER WORKS

Smaller works, being easier to publish and appreciate, were frequently translated.

ARISTOTLE's *Poetics*, which is not only incomplete but forbiddingly difficult, was scarcely known until the sixteenth century. Thenceforward it was often edited, translated into Latin, and excerpted, but seldom put into modern languages. The earliest Italian version was issued in Florence by Bernardo Segni in 1549, and was followed by a translation with commentary by Lodovico Castelvetro (Vienna, 1570). In France the Pléiade appear to have known the book only through the Italian critics; there was no direct translation during the Renaissance. Ascham and Sidney quote it in England, and in 1605 Ben Jonson is said to have made a version of it—certainly he knew its doctrines well. But the general public throughout Europe, having scarcely any translations available, did not.

THEOCRITUS was put into Italian by the talented Annibale Caro (1507–66). Six of the idylls appeared anonymously in English in 1588.

LUCIAN, with his polite but cynical wit, was a favourite of the Renaissance. About 1495 Lapaccini rendered one of his *Dialogues of the Dead* into musical Italian verse. He was the most popular Greek author in Germany, where at least eleven translators worked on him during the period 1450–1550.[33] Thirty of his dialogues were turned into French by Tory in 1529. In England, Rastell

(d. 1536) produced a translation of *Menippus*, also called *The Necromancy*, while Elyot translated *The Cynic* before 1535 and 'A. O.' the *Toxaris* in 1565.

THE GREEK ROMANCERS were very popular too. Annibale Caro put *Daphnis and Chloe* into Italian, and Amyot in 1559 made a superb French translation which A. Day turned into rather clumsy English in 1587. Amyot also translated the *Aethiopica* in 1547. James Sandford turned some of this romance into English in 1567, and in 1568–9 Thomas Underdown produced a complete version, based on a Latin translation by the Pole Stanislas Warshewiczki.

CICERO's correspondence with his friends was put into French by the unfortunate Dolet (1542) and F. de Belleforest (1566).

VERGIL's *Bucolics* were freely paraphrased in Spanish, with the addition of much medieval philosophical and religious doctrine, by Juan del Enzina (1492–6), and translated into octaves, along with the *Georgics*, by Cristobal de Mesa about 1600. Bernardo Pulci had written an elegant Italian version in 1481. The earliest French translation of the *Bucolics* and *Georgics*, by Michel Guillaume de Tours (1516 and 1519), contained pious expositions like some of the medieval versions of Ovid.[34] Clément Marot translated *Bucolics* 1 in 1532, and Richard le Blanc completed the set in 1555; he had translated the *Georgics* in 1554. The *Bucolics* were put into German by Stephan Riccius in 1567 and into English in 1575 by Abraham Fleming, who added his version of the *Georgics* in 1589. The great Spanish poet Luis de León (*c*. 1527–91) made fine translations of the *Bucolics* and of the first two books of the *Georgics*; while Giovanni Rucellai's adaptation of *Georgics*, 4, *The Bees*, finished in 1524, began a long succession of didactic poems in Italian.

About twenty of HORACE's odes were turned into Spanish by Luis de León.[35] It has always been splendid practice for young poets to try their skill on translating these little lyrics, so tightly packed with thought, so iridescent with subtle shades of emotion, so delicate in their use of language. Many, many individual translations appeared in every western tongue: witness Milton's remarkable version of the Pyrrha ode, *Carm.* 1. 5.[36] Still, they are so complex and so reflective that Renaissance versions of the complete collection are relatively few. There were none in English or German. In French they appeared in a complete translation of Horace's works by Mondot in 1579, and in Italian Giorgino issued a version in 1595. Horace's longest *Letter* (*Ep.* 2. 3, usually called 'The Art of Poetry') was a very important formative factor in Renaissance literary theory and was often translated. Dolce produced an Italian version in 1535; it was paraphrased in an influential Italian critical work by Robortelli in 1548; it was put into French by Grandichan in 1541 and by Peletier du Mans in 1544; into Spanish in 1592 by Luis Zapata; and into English, along with the other *Letters* and the *Satires*, by T. Drant in 1567. The *Satires* appeared in Italian, by Dolce, in 1559; and in French, by Habert, in 1549. Dolce did the *Letters* in the same year and 'G. T. P.' translated them into French in 1584.

OVID's minor works came out in French in 1500–9. In English, translations of the *Heroides* were produced by Turberville in 1567, of the *Tristia* by the appropriately named Thomas Churchyard in 1572, and of the *Loves* by Christopher Marlowe himself in about 1597.

The obscure but memorable satirist PERSIUS is still a severe test of a translator's ingenuity and taste. Renaissance versions were very few. There were two in French: by Abel Foulon in 1544, and by Guillaume Durand in 1575. An Italian translation by Antonio Vallone was published at Naples in 1576. No others appeared in the sixteenth century; but it is worth mentioning a good effort by Barten Holyday, issued in England in 1616.

An abridged French version of PLINY's *Natural History* by Pierre de Changi came out in 1551, and an English version by 'I. A.' in 1566—which perhaps inspired Shakespeare with the travel-tales that Othello told to Desdemona in a pliant hour.[37]

Clément Marot (1496–1544) translated MARTIAL's epigrams into French, but they are so easy to read that translations were scarcely necessary in the Renaissance.

JUVENAL was translated into Italian by G. Summaripa in 1475. The tenth satire was put into Spanish by Geronimo de Villegas in 1515 and into English by 'W. B.' in 1617; in 1544 Michel d'Amboyse issued 8, 10, 11, and 13 in French.

APULEIUS's *Metamorphoses* were rendered into Italian by Boiardo, who died in 1494; into French by Guillaume Michel and German by Johann Sieder; and in 1566 into English by William Adlington, whose translation, though less brilliant than the original, is still readable and enjoyable.

During the Middle Ages, each of the European countries in the west had two literatures. They had books written and songs sung in their own dialects or languages; and they had Latin literature old and new. Thus there were separate national literatures, and there was an international literature—both constantly growing.

Sometimes the two interpenetrated. When they did, the synthesis could be a nobler creation than any purely national or purely Latin work of its age. Such was Dante's *Comedy*. As the Renaissance approached, they interpenetrated more often and more deeply. The contacts which had been rare and difficult became easy, delightful, fertile. New ideas poured into the national literatures; new patterns were learned and utilized and developed; the ardently competitive spirit of the men of the Renaissance was challenged, and their greedy intellectual appetite was fed, by newly revealed books in Latin and Greek, greater than any their fathers had written, but not (they felt) greater than they themselves could write.

The inspiration they drew from these books was sometimes direct, as when Montaigne digested Seneca's essays and made Seneca's thoughts into part of his own mind. Sometimes it acted remotely, by intensifying the nobility of their work and subtilizing their art. A Renaissance comedy on contemporary persons and themes is far more comically complicated than anything the Middle Ages ever conceived, because its author has enjoyed, at first or second hand, the intricacies of Plautus. But, more and more often during and since the Renaissance, writers who wish to live in both worlds and make the best of both, find that translations of classical books will serve them well. The current flows between the two worlds more and more richly. Amyot translates the Greek biographer and moralist Plutarch into French. Montaigne seizes on the translation and lives with it the rest of his life. North turns Amyot's translation into English. Shakespeare changes it into *Coriolanus, Antony and Cleopatra, Julius Caesar*. Great books, in Milton's words, are the life-blood of a master spirit. Through translations the energy of that life-blood can be given to other spirits, and can make some of them as great, or greater.

7

THE RENAISSANCE

DRAMA

IN the Middle Ages there were various types of rude popular
plays and religious pageants, and an occasional half-realized
drama in Latin on classical or biblical subjects, for the church, the
learned, and sometimes the nobles. But it is little likely that any
of these would ever have grown up to the full power of the modern
theatre without the new impulses provided by the Renaissance,
and in particular by the rediscovery of classical drama in the
fifteenth and sixteenth centuries. The modern stage was created
by the impact of Greco-Roman drama on Renaissance life.

It owes the following debts to the playwrights of Greece and
Rome.

(a) *The conception of drama as a fine art.* The plays of the
Middle Ages had been performed either by amateurs or by strolling
players of low culture and status: touchingly human as their
efforts were, they scarcely even deserve to be called a craft. The
improvement in the prestige and skill of actors and writers came
only when they tried to rise to the heights attained by classical
drama. Renaissance drama was an aristocratic art. It began in the
ducal palaces of Italy. It developed in the royal courts, the noblemen's houses, the great schools, and the colleges of western
Europe. During its development it was written predominantly for
audiences who had an exceptional education and a lively understanding of Greek and Latin culture. They had high critical
standards. Even their clowns had to be learned or to pretend
learning. The establishment of these high standards, and the
increasingly numerous contemporary discussions of the principles
of criticism, made it impossible, during the Renaissance, to continue producing the rude old farces and the naïve old religious
spectacles on the customary low level. It was necessary to equal
not only the skill but the dignity of the ancients, for whom the poet
was not a mountebank but a teacher, a legislator, almost a priest.

(b) *The realization of drama as a type of literature.* As we have
seen, neither Dante nor Chaucer nor their contemporaries understood the essential difference between drama and narrative.[1] This

vagueness about the real character of the great literary patterns was characteristic of the Middle Ages and helps to account for the formlessness of much medieval literature. (Even the old-fashioned inscription on Shakespeare's bust at Stratford compares him to Nestor, Socrates, and Vergil.) It was not until nearly 1500 that scholars had gone far enough ahead to make out the general structure of drama, and to put translations and imitations of classical plays on the stage in Italy and France; and only then, with experiment and experience, did the full potentialities of the drama start to make themselves plain. Then, by testing, and discarding, or imitating, or adapting the patterns used by the Greeks and Romans, the Renaissance playwrights and critics established the genera which have ever since been called by their Greek names: drama, comedy, tragedy. Some of them tried to go too far, and specialize and classicize too much. In Polonius's introduction of the players Shakespeare satirizes his contemporaries who were ready not only to play the four recognized types of drama (three of them classical) but to mix them to the customer's own taste:

'The best actors in the world, either for tragedy, comedy, history, pastoral, pastoral-comical, historical-pastoral, tragical-historical, tragical-comical-historical-pastoral, scene individable, or poem unlimited: Seneca cannot be too heavy nor Plautus too light.'[2]

But still, until the essential character of the type of literature we call drama was understood, with all its possible varieties, the real beauties of tragedy and comedy could not be achieved.[3]

This must not be taken to mean that drama reached perfection in the Renaissance when it copied Roman and Greek comedy and tragedy. No: it culminated when, in each of the western countries, it met and mingled with the spirit of the nation, and helped that spirit to express itself more eloquently. In Italy, after many ambitious but unsuccessful attempts, it reached its nature in opera, which was a well-thought-out attempt to reincarnate Greek tragedy. In France it failed in the sixteenth century and came to fruition later, in the tragedies of Corneille and Racine, in the comedies and near-tragedies of Molière. In England and Spain there was scarcely any classicizing drama which was successful. But the English and Spanish dramatists assimilated much of the classical drama, and added their own imagination to it, reshaped its characters, its humour, and its conventions to suit their peoples, and left the rest. The magnificent result was Marlowe, Lope de Vega, Webster, Calderón, Shakespeare.

(c) *The theatre-building and the principles of dramatic production.* The Middle Ages had no theatres. What plays they had were given on temporary platforms, or on 'floats', or in buildings meant for other purposes. There is only one late exception: the Fraternity of the Passion had the Hôtel de Bourgogne in Paris for their mystery plays.[4] But permanent theatres were built in the Renaissance, for the first time since the fall of Rome: partly to accommodate the audiences, which had grown immensely larger and more demanding since the drama had improved,[5] and partly to provide a Greco-Roman setting for so many plays done on Greco-Roman subjects or on Greco-Roman principles. At first no one knew how to build a theatre. There were various amateurish attempts, which grew a little more elaborate with experience. But in 1484 the first edition of the Roman architect Vitruvius was printed, and producers, playwrights, architects, and illustrators at once began to try to reconstruct the splendid buildings he described. During the high Renaissance the problem of theatrical design was not fully solved. When Shakespeare began his career the finest theatre in London was the Swan, which a Dutch visitor sketched 'because it looked so like a Roman amphitheatre'.[6] But from his sketch it is clearly a hybrid. It is a cross between a medieval inn-yard and a Renaissance conception of a Greco-Roman stage. Like *King Lear*, it is a synthesis of classical and medieval. But after further experiment and further realization of the meaning of classical design, the modern theatre was constructed. Mr. Allardyce Nicoll, in his admirable book *The Development of the Theatre*, picks the Olympic Theatre at Vicenza as the point at which, in 1580, the possibilities of modern stage construction were fully realized on classical models.[7] It was started by the famous classicist architect Palladio, and, although its stage was evidently far too ornate for modern (or for Greek) taste, it explored such essentials of theatrical design as permanence, dignity, symmetry, and long-receding perspective. These discoveries were elaborated during the baroque age. The work of the baroque architects and theatrical producers, with their renewed and strengthened emphasis on Greek and Roman art, is responsible for the fact that most of the great theatres in the world, from the Teatro Colon in Buenos Aires to the Scala in Milan, from the

Residenz in Munich to the Opera of Paris and New York and London, are re-created Greek and Roman theatres—even to the semicircular auditorium, the arch above the stage, the side-pillars, the decorative garlands of fruit and symmetrical wreaths of flowers, the sculptured masks of Comedy and Tragedy, the busts and medallion portraits of great writers and actors, the staircases, vaults, and columns, the noble draperies, the statues of poets, of Muses, of the god of poetry, Apollo himself.

(d) *The structure of modern drama* comes to us from Greece via Rome: in particular, the following elements are classical importations.

First, the proportions of our plays, which last from two to three hours, and seldom much more or less. We now accept this as natural; but it is not. The Middle Ages ran to short plays, interludes and the like; the Spaniards love brief *zarzuelas*; in the early days of moving pictures there were hundreds of ten-minute farces; and the Japanese have raised tabloid drama to a high art in their *Nō* plays. Extreme length also appeared in the Middle Ages, with cycles of miracle plays which took a whole day to perform. This goes even further in the serial dramas of the East (e.g. the *kabuki* plays of Japan) which continue for weeks at a time, and in the serials of the early movies, which, like comic strips, are designed to provide interminable excitement. We get our sense of proportion, in drama as in so much else, from the Greeks.

We also get the symmetrical division into three, four, or (usually in the Renaissance) five acts, each embodying a major part of the action. This too was an invention of the Greeks, who punctuated the plot with choral songs and dances, although the performance was continuous—like a modern film rather than a modern play.

The chorus was another Greek invention. All modern choruses are its direct descendants: from the narrative Chorus of *Our Town* to the explanatory Chorus of *Henry V*, who opens the play with a noble appeal to the imagination of the audience:

> O! for a Muse of fire, that would ascend
> The brightest heaven of invention;
> A kingdom for a stage, princes to act,
> And monarchs to behold the swelling scene;

from the pretty girls of musical comedy to the troubled Russian people of *Boris Godunov*.

The idea of having an intricate plot was Greek and Roman in origin and in transmission to us: a dramatic story built on strongly marked and complex characters, on conflicts between individual people and collisions of spiritual forces, and on the mounting suspense produced by the increasing intellectual complexity and emotional tension of such a plot.

Modern dramatic verse, which has produced so many of the sublimest moments of our theatre, was created to rival the eloquence of Greek and Roman drama. The verse of the medieval plays was more like lyric, or farce, or doggerel; and the early emulations of classical drama were written in completely unsuitable metres.[8] Probably it was the actual imitation of the chief metre of Greek and Roman tragedy—a 12-syllable iambic line—that produced modern blank verse, Italian and English.[9]

(*e*) No less important than all these was the fact that Greek and Roman drama, when rediscovered, provided *high standards* to admire, to compete with, and if possible to outdo. The response to this formidable challenge was Renaissance and baroque drama.

The classical playwrights whose works survived (in pitifully small numbers) to influence modern drama were these:

(*a*) *Athenian tragedians* of the fifth century B.C.:
Aeschylus (525–456), seven of whose plays remain;
Sophocles (495–406), seven of whose plays remain;
Euripides (?481–406), nineteen of whose plays remain.

(*b*) An *Athenian comedian* of the same age:
Aristophanes (?444–?385), who has left eleven plays.

(*c*) *Roman comedians*, working on material, characters, and styles largely created by the Athenian Menander and his colleagues of the fourth and third centuries B.C. (the works of these men are almost wholly lost):
Plautus (?254–184), of whom we have twenty-one plays;
Terence (?195–159), who left six.

(*d*) A *Roman tragedian*:
Seneca (?4 B.C.–A.D. 65), writing on Greek myths and models in an extreme style of his own, and possibly not for stage-performance:[10] we have nine of his plays and a contemporary imitation on a contemporary subject, Nero's destruction of his wife Octavia.

As Shakespeare saw, and made Polonius say, the chief classical stimuli acting upon Renaissance drama were not the Greeks but the Romans Seneca and Plautus.[11] Almost equally influential (in forming critical standards) were Aristotle's *Poetics* and Horace's 'Art of Poetry'.[12] After these came Terence, and then Euripides and Sophocles. The much greater difficulty of the language of Greek tragedy, in which the style of Euripides is the simplest, probably accounts for its otherwise inexplicable neglect, and for the general lack of interest in the greatest and most difficult of all, Aeschylus.[13] The neglect of Aristophanes may be explained by the oddity of his form, the extreme topicality and indecency of his humour, and the complexity of his language. Rabelais had a copy of his works; but, although he closely resembled Aristophanes in wit and language, there are very few traces that he actually quoted or imitated him.[14] But Plautus is far more straightforward; and when twelve of his lost plays were discovered and brought to Rome in 1429,[15] the discovery encouraged Italian playwrights to imitate him.

It was Seneca in particular who stimulated and instructed the Renaissance dramatists of Italy and England. From him they took certain characters, attitudes, and devices which, although partly obsolete on the stage to-day, were new and valuable then. For example, the ambitious ruthless tyrant, best exemplified in Shakespeare's Richard III. He is an eternal figure. He was created in drama by the Greeks; but he was intensified into diabolism by Seneca, eagerly taken up by the Italians because their own cities produced so many of his type, and copied both from Rome and from Italy by the horrified but interested English poets.[16] The ghost of a monarch calling on his kin to avenge his murder, and thereby bringing on new crimes and horrors, appears in Greek drama as early as the *Oresteia* of Aeschylus; Seneca used such phantoms frequently and violently; Italy, with its passion for vendetta, took the revengeful ghost from Seneca, and the English from them both. The ghost seems silly nowadays: even in Queen Elizabeth's reign Lodge said its miserable calls for revenge sounded 'like an oyster-wife';[17] but we cannot despise the lendings which Shakespeare changed into the perturbed spirits of Banquo, Caesar, and King Hamlet.

It was partly to recent history in Italy and England, but even more to Seneca, that the Renaissance playwrights owed their

passion for the darker sides of life: for witchcraft and the supernatural (as in *Macbeth*), for madness impending or actual (*Hamlet*,
The Spanish Tragedy, *The Duchess of Malfi*, *King Lear*), for the
display of torture, mutilation, and corpses (*King Lear*, *Titus
Andronicus*, *Orbecche*, *The Duchess of Malfi*), and for murder
committed and multiplied before the eyes of the audience. Finally,
it was Seneca, strengthening the energy of their own souls, who
stimulated the Elizabethan dramatists to the tremendous outbursts
of pride and passion, half heroic and half insane, in which they

> raise cavalieros higher than the clouds,
> And with the cannon break the frame of heaven,
> Batter the shining palace of the sun,
> And shiver all the starry firmament.[18]

The wellhead of modern drama is Italy. The Italians first felt
the stimulus of classical drama, and under it they produced the
earliest modern comedies, tragedies, operas, pastoral plays, and
dramatic criticisms. It turn, they stimulated the French, the
English, and, less directly, the Spaniards. The best way to see how
their stimulating influence spread outwards is to survey the 'firsts'
in each field—translations, imitations, and original modern plays
emulating the classics.

Translations of Latin and Greek plays were being acted in Italy
from the second half of the fifteenth century onwards. The first
comedy to be acted in translation was *The Brothers Menaechmus*
of Plautus, done by Niccolo da Correggio for the Duke of Ferrara
in 1486. (The noble house of Ferrara did more than any other
family, and more than most European nations, for the development of the modern theatre.) Tragedy took longer to develop. We
hear of performances of Senecan tragedies in Italian about 1509,
and of an Italian version of Sophocles' *Antigone* by Luigi Alamanni
which was acted in 1533.

In France poets and scholars began, in the latter half of the
fifteenth century, to translate classical plays both from the original
and out of Italian adaptations; but they were not acted. Instead,
we hear of men like the brilliant Scottish scholar George Buchanan
producing Latin versions of Greek dramas. The turning-point
came in 1548. In that year Henri II and Catherine de' Medici
were sumptuously entertained at Lyons by Ippolito d'Este,

cardinal of Ferrara, who showed them a comedy in modern Italian prose adapted from a Latin play, performed by skilful actors and beautiful actresses. (It was an adaptation of *The Brothers Menaechmus* called *Calandria—calandro* means 'booby'—and written in 1513 by Bernardo Dovizi, who became Cardinal Bibbiena.) Five months later Joachim Du Bellay brought out *The Defence and Ennoblement of the French Language*, calling among other things for the production of comedies and tragedies on the classical model to emulate the ancients, instead of medieval farces and morality plays; and soon the modern French drama was launched.[19] (In 1567 another member of the Pléiade, Jean-Antoine de Baïf, produced a modernization of Plautus' *The Boastful Soldier*, called *The Hero*, which is still readable.)

In Britain, although there were productions of Latin plays in the original at schools and colleges, we rarely hear of the production of such plays in translation. In Spain there was an adaptation of Sophocles' *Electra* made by Fernan Perez de Oliva in 1528, and called *Revenge for Agamemnon*, and a version of Plautus' *The Brothers Menaechmus* (called *Los Menemnos* or *Los Menecmos*) by Juan de Timoneda in 1559, which was entirely modernized and set in contemporary Seville: but it is improbable that they were ever produced. In Portugal, Camoens wrote a good translation and adaptation of Plautus' *Amphitryon*, apparently for performance at a festival in the university of Coimbra between 1540 and 1550. Some time later, in the early years of the seventeenth century, a group of humanists working at Strasbourg began to produce a number of classical plays (including several Greek tragedies) in the original and in German translations.

Imitations of classical drama in Latin were really a step closer to genuine Renaissance drama, since they were original plays on original subjects. The most remarkable was the earliest. This was *Eccerinis* (*c.* 1315), a tragic poem on the life of the fiendish Ezzelino da Romano, who became tyrant of Padua in 1237. It was specially written for the city of Padua as propaganda against future attempts to seize power there. The author—who was richly rewarded—was Albertino Mussato (1261–1329), a pupil of Lovato de' Lovati, the first modern scholar who understood the metres of Seneca's tragedies. *Eccerinis* is like a classical drama in having five acts, a chorus, dialogue, and dramatic metres; but it is very short, and was not conceived as a drama for performance on the stage. Mussato himself, with a confusion which we have seen in his contemporary Dante, compared it to the *Aeneid* and the *Thebaid*, and intended it to be read rather than acted. Still, it was for its time a work of bold and admirable originality.[20]

Later, particularly with the great improvement in classical education at schools and colleges, Latin plays were written and acted all over Europe. In Germany they were the commonest form of high drama. George Buchanan wrote some of great distinction, in which his pupil, Montaigne (aged 12), acted. Latin tragedies on biblical subjects were particularly popular. In Poland, too, Jesuit teachers wrote a considerable number for their pupils to act.[21]

As for the fact that such plays were written in Latin, it must be remembered that in many European countries there was no choice between Latin and a fully developed national language, but rather between Latin and one or other local dialect. As J. S. Kennard points out,

'humanism embraced the several districts of Italy in a common culture, effacing the distinctions of dialect, and bringing the separate elements of the nation to a consciousness of intellectual unity. . . . Divided as Venetians, as Florentines, as Neapolitans, as Lombards, and as Romans, the members of the Italian community recognized their identity in the spiritual city they had reconquered from the past. The whole nation possessed the Latin poets as a common heritage; and on the ground of Plautus, Florentines and Neapolitans could understand each other.'[22]

If for 'the whole nation' we read 'all educated men and women', that is true and important: although, in the instinctive nationalism of to-day, we assume that any national language is more alive and more powerful than an international language, like Latin, which covers many centuries and many realms of thought.

Emulation of classical drama in modern languages was the essential starting-point of the modern theatre. The chief stages in its earliest development were marked by the following plays.

The earliest dramatic production on a classical theme in a modern language was *Orpheus*. This is a slender but moving piece, half pastoral drama, half opera, on the tragic love and tragic death of the musician Orpheus. It was written for the court of Mantua in 1471, by the brilliant young Angelo Ambrogini of

Montepulciano, called Politian.[23] Although there is some action on the stage, and much dramatic tension, the metres are almost wholly lyrical. Similar works followed it: such as Correggio's *Cephalus*, a dramatization of the story from Ovid, in *ottava rima* and lyrical metres, produced at Ferrara in 1487; and dramatizations of tales from the *Decameron* in the same light graceful forms.

The earliest original comedy in the modern manner was Lodovico Ariosto's *The Casket Comedy* (*Cassaria*), written in 1498 and played (at Ferrara, of course) in 1508. It was adapted from several classical comedies: *The Casket Comedy*, *The Ghost Comedy*, and *The Little Carthaginian* of Plautus, and *The Self-punisher* of Terence; but it also embodied some satire on contemporary personalities. Others soon followed—indeed Mantovano's *Formicone* was actually produced before *The Casket Comedy*. Ariosto's *The Masqueraders* (*Gli Suppositi*), written in 1502–3 and acted in 1509, was based on Plautus' *The Prisoners* and Terence's *The Eunuch*. In 1566 George Gascoigne translated it into English to be played at Gray's Inn and Trinity College, Oxford, under the imaginative title of *Supposes*. In this shape it provided material for Shakespeare's *The Taming of the Shrew*. However, Italian comedy went sour with the plays of Machiavelli and Aretino, who took the structure, plot-line, and characters of classical comedy, modernized them, and added dirt derived partly from the medieval fabliaux and partly from their own experience and imagination.[24]

Not quite the earliest, but the first influential tragedy in a modern language was *Sophonisba*, by Giovan Giorgio Trissino (1515). This is a dramatization of the story of the African queen told by Livy (28–30), and imitates Greek models, in particular the *Antigone* of Sophocles and the *Alcestis* of Euripides. Its particular originality lies in the facts that it is not on remote myth but on factual history; that it is in blank verse; and that it is an early effort to exploit the emotions mentioned by Aristotle as essential for a tragedy—pity and terror. The author was strongly conscious of the epoch-making character of his work: we shall shortly meet him again as the writer of the first modern epic in classical style. Unfortunately, although an original writer, he was not a great one.[25]

Although published in 1515, *Sophonisba* was not acted until many years later. The first original modern tragedy which made a wide impression and founded a school was *Orbecche* (1541), by Giovanni Battista Giraldi, called Cinthio—a historical tragedy on the feuds within the Persian royal family, and the earliest to put on the stage the sexual crimes and bloody murders which the Renaissance audiences so much adored. Audiences wept; women fainted; it was a tremendous success.[26]

In French the first tragedy was Jodelle's *Captive Cleopatra*, produced in 1552, and written on the model of Seneca's tragedies although boasting Greek drama as its predecessor and claiming

to sing in French the tragedy of Greece.[27]

Its metres were ten-syllable iambic couplets, alexandrine couplets, and lyrical choruses. It was stately but dull.

Produced on the same day, the first French comedy, Jodelle's *Eugene*, was really a descendant of medieval farce, in its octo-syllabic metre, its farcical fabliau-like subject, and its manner—except for its full-length, five-act scale, its setting (in the street outside the homes of the main characters), and a few reminiscences of Plautus and Terence. Subsequent French comedies were equally unclassical. The true nature of French comedy was only to be realized much later, in a different age of classicism, by Jean-Baptiste Molière.

The first English tragedy was Sackville and Norton's *Gorboduc* (or *Ferrex and Porrex*), played at the Temple in 1562. It is in blank verse. It does not observe the 'laws' of unity—which had scarcely yet been invented or disseminated—but it is on a theme allied to that of the fratricidal civil war between the sons of Oedipus; and it contains Greek devices acquired through Seneca, such as the Furies and the messenger describing off-stage calamities. The story is localized in an earlier region of classical influence —the mythology of Trojan Britain.[28]

Long before this, a few years earlier than 1500, English audiences had seen the interlude called *Fulgens and Lucres* (or *Lucrece*), a love-story evidently inspired by Renaissance fantasy on Roman republican history, in which a good plebeian and a voluptuous patrician compete for the hand of a virtuous maiden. This had a funny sub-plot; and in fact the English comic spirit, which had been obstreperously active in the medieval plays, now gradually clothed itself in plots of Greco-Roman intricacy and in grotesque characters derived from Greek and Roman story or drama. An early attempt of this type was *Thersites* (c. 1537), a coarse farce adapted from a Latin original written by the French Renaissance scholar Ravisius Textor, and based on the comic vulgarian in Homer's *Iliad*—whom Shakespeare was later to make the clown of *Troilus.and Cressida.*[29] Such also was *Jack Juggler* (*c.* 1560), a 'wytte and very playsent Enterlued' rudely adapted from Plautus' *Amphitryon.*

The first full-scale English comedy was *Ralph Roister-Doister*, written about 1553 by Nicolas Udall for a cast of schoolboys who evidently knew their Plautus. Its main character is a braggart like Thersites, modelled on Plautus' boastful soldier (*Miles gloriosus*), who was himself drawn from the swaggering foreign legionnaires of the successors of Alexander the Great. Attached to him there is a typical Plautine parasite called Merrygreek. The complexity of the plot and its layout in acts are classical in origin, and a number of the best jokes come from Plautus; but the rest is genuine energetic native humour.[30]

Spanish drama grew, like the national drama of other countries, out of the grave religious pageants of the Middle Ages and the crude little conversational pieces of the fairs and festivals, sometimes countrified and sometimes farcical. The Shakespeare of Spain, Lope de Vega, composed some of these latter trifles in his youth. Then, about 1590, almost exactly in the same year as Shakespeare, he began his real work. He himself well described his relation to classical drama. In his *New Art of Making Comedies* he said that before starting to write he locked up all the rules, banished Plautus and Terence, and then constructed his plays by popular standards. The result was that he and his chief successor Calderón produced the greatest wealth of drama with which any modern country, during the Renaissance, was enriched. It has, however, made less impression on other nations than the Renaissance drama of England.[31] From the classical stage it appears to have taken the complex intrigues and the clash of character, and the knowledge that (even locked up) there were classical masterpieces to outdo. What Lope did not take over was the fine taste and richness of poetic thought which enable a play to be created, not only for the day that dawns as the last lines are written, but for the world beyond and for other times.

Other types of drama were taking shape in the Renaissance, or were contributing their own force and brilliance to the growing modern theatre.

Masques, for instance, were being produced with increasing splendour at almost all the Renaissance courts; and, as Professor Allardyce Nicoll points out, greatly influenced the development of theatrical scenery and dramaturgy.[32] The most famous for English readers is Milton's *Comus*, produced at Ludlow Castle in 1634. It is much more than a mere masque. It is also a pastoral play: the Attendant Spirit disguises himself as a shepherd called Thyrsis,

> Whose artful strains have oft delayed
> The huddling brook to hear his madrigal,
> And sweetened every musk-rose of the dale,[33]

and at the end the river Severn is personified as a Greek nymph with a Latin name. But Milton's thought, even in his twenties, was so rich that he infused into his little drama many other elements. The dramatic scene where Comus is put to flight is modelled on the conquest of Circe (Comus' mother) by Odysseus in *Odyssey*, 10.274 f.; and there are long discussions of ethical questions, modelled on Plato, from whom Milton actually translates an important passage.[34]

Pastoral drama was a peculiar creation of the Renaissance, a new synthesis of existing classical elements.[35] The characters were idealized shepherds and shepherdesses (the types created by Theocritus and etherialized by Vergil) with the nature-spirits Pan, Diana, satyrs, fauns, and nymphs. The introduction of hopeless love into Arcadia was really an invention of Vergil's[36] but was made more complex in the Renaissance. In several of Vergil's *Bucolics* two characters speak, and dispute, and compete, so much so that the poems were actually staged in the theatre of Augustan Rome.[37] The rediscovery of classical drama suggested to modern playwrights that they might create complete plays on the romantic love-themes appropriate for pastoral characters, with the charming costumes, music, and scenery of Arcadia. The earliest play in a vernacular language on a secular subject, Politian's *Orpheus*, was set in pastoral surroundings, and its subordinate characters included shepherds and a satyr. This idea was doubtless suggested partly by the fact that Orpheus was associated with wild nature, and partly by the legend which said Eurydice died from a snake-bite received while she was running away from the passionate shepherd Aristaeus.[38] Pastoral plays continued to develop as an independent genre; but they also contributed something to dramas like Shakespeare's *As You Like It*, while they became, because of their lyrical music and imaginative settings, a remote ancestor of modern opera.

The earliest large-scale pastoral drama was Beccari's *The Sacrifice*, produced (at Ferrara) in 1555.[39] This set the pattern which many pastoral dramas were to follow—the assortment of ill-matched lovers. *A* loves *B*, *B* loves *C*, *C* loves *D*, and *D* is vowed to chastity; *E* loves *F* and his love is returned, but they are forbidden by a cruel kinsman to marry. (Beccari solved the latter problem by changing the kinsman into a boar.)

The two supreme masterpieces of the pastoral drama are Torquato Tasso's *Amyntas* (*Aminta*, in Italian), produced at Ferrara in 1573, and the much longer *Faithful Shepherd*, by Battista Guarini, produced in 1590. These are extremely complex dramas of love and adventure. Aminta is not (as he has since become) a girl but a nephew of Pan, bearing the Macedonian name Amyntas which Theocritus had introduced into his idylls. He loves Diana's niece Sylvia, who hates men and loves only hunting. Even when a satyr strips her naked and binds her with her own hair to a tree, with the most reprehensible intentions, and when Amyntas frees her at the last moment, she is not grateful; she goes on hunting; she melts only after Amyntas commits suicide by throwing himself over a cliff—but fortunately he is saved by a bush which breaks his fall. Guarini's play, which was intended to outdo *Amyntas*, is much more complicated. All action takes place off stage, and is reported and then commented upon in song or declamation. The poetry of *Amyntas* is exquisitely, poignantly beautiful, and has well been compared to music and to Renaissance painting.[40] *The Faithful Shepherd* was imitated all over Europe, and was more often translated into foreign languages than any other work of Italian literature.

According to one theory, there is another direct descendant of the Greek and Roman theatre. This is the popular farce, which survived (particularly in Italy) through the tradition carried on by strolling players, through puppet shows, and through such institutions as the fools kept by monarchs and noblemen. In particular, it is suggested that certain stock characters have come straight down from the Roman comedians: for instance, the fool who combines shrewdness with folly, and looks deformed or ridiculous: he wears a cock's comb or is bald-headed. Certainly there is much in common between the Italian *commedia dell' arte* and the spirit of the comedies of Plautus, enough to make us believe that the same funny people, and funny gestures, and funny situations, may well have continued to please sixty generations of Italian audiences. The most famous of such survivals known to modern spectators is Mr. Punch, the Pulcinella of the Italian comedies.[41]

Opera also was coming gradually into life. It was created by classical scholars who loved the drama, and who knew that in Greek tragedies music was an essential part of the production. They tried therefore, by interweaving musical accompaniment with dramatic declamation and lyrical comment, to heighten the emotion of the entire piece. One of their chief problems was to decide whether the Greeks set the dramatic speeches and arguments to music as well as the choruses. This is, of course, a perennial problem in opera: the baroque composers solved it by using recitative, soaring up to an occasional aria, and Wagner by what he called 'song-speech'. (It should be remembered that Wagner thought he was emulating Greek tragedy, and, while composing *The Ring of the Nibelungs*, wrote music all morning and read the Athenian dramatists all afternoon.)

The first experimental opera was produced at Florence in 1594. This was *Daphne*, by Ottavio Rinuccini, with music by Peri and Caccini: a dramatization of the story in Ovid, which tells how Apollo killed the dreadful dragon Python, and then, shot by Cupid's jealous arrow, fell in love with the obdurate Daphne, who at last became the laurel-tree.[42] (I do not know whether the authors were aware that one of the most famous pieces of music in ancient Greece was a programme piece depicting the conflict between Apollo and the Python.)[43] The essential novelty of this production and of *Eurydice*, which succeeded it in 1600, was 'the fusion of two apparently incompatible elements, the spoken comedy of the theatre and the lyrical melody of chamber-music'. Plays with incidental music were not new, but the great departure made by the authors of *Daphne* and *Eurydice* was to construct 'a magic circle of unbroken musical sound from the beginning of the story to its end'.[44] That magic, which raises so many of us into a higher world with the first notes of the overture to *Don Giovanni* or the prelude to *Das Rheingold*, was first made by men who were endeavouring to re-create the original beauty and power of Greek drama.

A few years after this, the first great operatic composer, Monteverdi, entered history with a setting of the immortal legend of the immortal musician, *Orpheus*. He was the first to realize the possibilities of opera on the grand scale, for earlier operatic productions had been designed for a small room and an intimate audience of friends. Modern opera and modern verse-drama are the two children of Greek tragedy, and they constantly aspire towards one another.

Modern standards of dramatic criticism were being built up through the Renaissance, partly by experiments in new forms, and partly by study and discussion of Greco-Roman literary theory—represented chiefly by Aristotle's *Poetics*, Horace's 'Art of Poetry', and, much less influentially, by 'Longinus's' essay *On the Sublime*. Much of Renaissance drama was created by the lofty standards of Renaissance critics, who, in spite of their frequent pedantry, would not tolerate slovenly work.

Joel Spingarn, in his valuable *History of Literary Criticism in the Renaissance*, has traced the development of the theory of the Three Unities into a code of literary law. The only rule that Aristotle lays down is the sensible one that in poetry the story must deal with *one action*.[45] As for time, he says that—as a matter of fact—tragedy endeavours to keep within a single circuit of the sun, one twenty-four-hour period, or something near it; although the early tragedies did not.[46] According to Spingarn, the first critic to make this a definite rule was Cinthio (p. 136 above), who was professor of philosophy and rhetoric at Ferrara. He laid down this rule in his *Lectures on Comedy and Tragedy* (c. 1545); and then Robortelli, in his 1548 edition of Aristotle's *Poetics*, explained that Aristotle really meant twelve hours (because people are asleep at night); and Segni, in his translation of the *Poetics* (1549), countered by saying that, since many highly dramatic events take place at night, the period meant was twenty-four hours. Pedantic as all this sounds, it was an attempt, not to impose classical rules on a brilliant and original modern drama, but to improve a faltering and often feeble modern drama by pointing out that it would achieve its best effects by concentration, rather than by hanging out a sign marked THIRTY YEARS LATER before each act.

The unity of place was added by Castelvetro in his 1570 edition of the *Poetics*. He too gave a sensible reason for it, although he did not say that Aristotle had laid it down. He said Aristotle insisted on verisimilitude. The action of the play must seem probable. It will not seem probable if the scene is constantly being changed to 'another part of the field' or 'Bohemia. A desert part of the Country near the Sea'. Trissino also, in his *Poetice* (1563), contrasts the practice of the Unities with the sloppiness of 'ignorant poets'. Therefore the doctrine of the Three Unities was useful for the time at which it was created. It was an attempt to strengthen and discipline the haphazard and amateurish methods of contemporary dramatists—not simply in order to copy the ancients, but in order to make drama more intense, more realistic, and more truly dramatic.

Modern drama works in four different media: the stage and the opera, the cinema and television. The second two are extensions of the two first, differentiated mainly by the physical and mechanical conditions of production and transmission. The essential first pair were created in the Renaissance, not by the mechanical reproduction of classical material, but by the creative adaptation of classical forms, with all their potentialities unrealized by medieval dramatists, and the challenge of classical masterpieces, previously misunderstood or unknown.

8

THE RENAISSANCE

EPIC

ONLY one poem which could be called epic in grandeur was written in a vernacular language during the Middle Ages: Dante's *Comedy*, which in form is unlike any previous epic, and indeed any previous poem in the world. We have traced the debt which Dante owed, and most nobly acknowledged, to Vergil. The debt of the Renaissance epics to classical poetry is more obvious, and goes no less deep.

Epics in Latin, such as Petrarch's *Africa*, are not to be considered here. The vernacular epics of the Renaissance which interest us fall into four classes, according to their subject-matter and the type of classical influence working in them.

The first class is easily disposed of: *direct imitation of classical epic*. This is represented only by *The Franciad* (*La Franciade*) by Pierre de Ronsard (1524–85), four books of an unfinished poem published in 1572. This was designed to be a plaster cast of the *Aeneid*. It was to tell how, just as Aeneas escaped from Troy to found Rome, so a hero of even higher descent, Astyanax, son of Hector (now called Francus or Francion), survived the fall of Troy, reached Gaul, founded the city of Paris (named after his brother), and established the beginnings of modern France. It is in decasyllabic couplets, much too short for the French language and the ambitious subject. A romantic love-affair between Francus and a Cretan princess was introduced. The poem was a total failure: Ronsard could not even finish it.[1]

Next come *epics on contemporary heroic adventures*, mainly or wholly written in the classical manner. The greatest of these is *The Sons of Lusus* (i.e. the Portuguese, *Os Lusiadas*), published in 1572 by Luis de Camoens (1524–80). This tells the story of Vasco da Gama's exploration of east Africa and the East Indies: Camoens himself had been one of the earliest explorers of the Far East. His poem is luxuriously classical in style, incident, and background.[2]

Much simpler is *The Poem of Araucania* (*La Araucana*), by Alonso de Ercilla y Zuñiga, one of the Conquistadores of South America (1533–94). He began to publish it in 1569 and produced the complete edition in 1590. It tells in thirty-seven cantos, partly poetry, partly doggerel, how the resistance of the Chilean Indians was broken by the Spanish invaders.[3] This is the first important book written in America. (The author, who was well connected at the Spanish court, rather like Chaucer but on a higher level, was court-martialled and sent home from Chile, after just escaping execution: he took his revenge by leaving his commanding officer almost entirely out of the poem.) It had a tremendous success and was much imitated. When the curate and the barber were going over Don Quixote's library and throwing out the trash, they kept *La Araucana*, saying it was one of the best three heroic poems in Spanish.[4] There are, of course, others of its type: for instance, *La Dragontea* by Lope de Vega, telling of the last voyage and death of that devilish dragon, Sir Francis Drake . . .

The third class contains *romantic epics of medieval chivalry*, with considerable classical influence. These are a blend of three chief ingredients: complex chronicles of knightly adventure long ago, romantic love-stories in the manner which began in the Middle Ages and continued through the Renaissance, and Greco-Roman enrichments of all kinds, from the trivial to the essential. The best known is *The Madness of Roland* (*Orlando Furioso*) published in 1516 by Lodovico Ariosto (1474–1533)—a huge and delightful phantasmagoria telling of the adventures in love and war of Roland and other champions, in a period roughly identifiable as that which saw the invasion of France by the Saracens and their defeat by Charles Martel.[5] It was a continuation and improvement of an unfinished *Roland in Love* (*Orlando Innamorato*) by Matteo Maria Boiardo, Count Scandiano (1434–94). The plot and its treatment are wildly unhistorical. Orlando (in whom few could recognize Hruodland, the grim warden of the Breton marches) goes mad through his hopeless love for Angelica, daughter of the Grand Khan of Cathay. He recovers only when the sorcerer Astolfo visits the moon, riding on a winged horse and guided by St. John the author of the Apocalypse, and brings back a bottle containing his common sense. The lost wits of many people are stored in the moon. Astolfo had not thought lunacy had undone so many. He examined them bottle after bottle for Roland's,

> and then the wizard recognized it, since
> it bore the label: ROLAND'S SANITY.[6]

To rival Ariosto in art and to surpass him in seriousness, Edmund Spenser (?1552–99) started *The Faerie Queene*. Six books and a fragment remain. He intended twelve books, each telling the story of one chivalrous adventure connected with Arthur's Round Table, and exemplifying one moral virtue. In form and in type of subject his poem follows Ariosto, but its moral tone and many of its subsidiary features were modelled on Homer and Vergil.[7] Boccaccio's *Theseid*, whose manner is medieval although its subject is Greek, is an earlier, less developed example of this type.

Two poems of this group are in a sub-class by themselves. The greater is *The Liberation of Jerusalem* by Torquato Tasso (1544–95), a magnificent poem which was finished in 1575, published without the author's sanction in 1581, and reissued, after he had revised and spoilt it, in 1593.[8] It relates the story of the first Crusade (1095) in highly romantic terms, concentrating on the devil's attempts to hinder the Crusaders from capturing Jerusalem, his chief assistant being a charming witch, Armida. This is an almost unrecognizably different story from that soberly told by Gibbon[9] and his authorities. Externally this poem resembles Ariosto's, but it is different in one essential point. Constantly, and quite seriously, it introduces Christian doctrine and the Christian supernatural.

In this it had a predecessor, once famous. This was *The Liberation of Italy from the Goths* (*La Italia liberata da Gotti*), by Giovan Giorgio Trissino (1478–1550), a poem in twenty-seven books of blank verse describing, much in the style of medieval romance but with Christian and classical trimmings, how the eastern Roman emperor Justinian attacked the Goths who dominated Italy in the sixth century, and defeated them.[10] It is often said that this epic is a failure because it adheres rigidly to the rules of Aristotle. It is indeed a failure. But that is not because it observes any particular set of rules. The principles suggested by Aristotle for epic are not numerous or rigid enough, even if misapplied, to cramp any writer. The poem fails, like Trissino's tragedy *Sophonisba*, simply because its author is a bad poet: his verses are flat, his plot boringly arranged, and his imagination feeble.[11] Still, it was once famous as the first modern epic in the classical manner, and its very title symbolized the chief current of the Renaissance.

These two poems make a bridge to the fourth and last class of Renaissance epic: *Christian religious epics*, on subjects from Jewish and Christian history and myth, but arranged almost wholly in the classical manner.[12] These are *Paradise Lost* and *Paradise Regained*, published in 1667 and 1671 by John Milton (1608–74), telling, in twelve and four books of blank verse respectively, the majestic stories of the fall of man and of the temptation of Jesus in the wilderness.

Classical influence in these poems, in every one of them, is all-pervading. It is not predominant in them all; but it is one of the main presuppositions without which they cannot be understood. In several of them medieval ideals are quite as strong, or stronger. Elsewhere in the Renaissance we can trace the survival of medieval habits of thought: for example, in the splendid suits of armour designed for nobles and kings (often with Greco-Roman designs on them) long after the practical usefulness of armour was over, and in some of the anachronistic festivals at which they were worn. Milton himself at first thought of writing on Arthurian themes. But, relatively weak or relatively strong, classical thought and imagination penetrates all the Renaissance epics. Even the simplest, *La Araucana*, cannot be properly appreciated by anyone who knows nothing of Greco-Roman literature; while, in order to understand all of Milton, one must be a classical scholar.

It is interesting to trace how this influence varies from one poem to another in importance, strength, and penetration.

The subjects of only two poems are classical. These are *The Franciad*, which is a failure, and *The Theseid*, which is medieval in manner. Apparently it is impossible for a modern poet to write a good classical epic in the classical manner. The failure of Petrarch's *Africa* confirms this.

In structure, some of the poems have the typical medieval pattern, wandering, intricate, voluminous. But *Paradise Lost* is in twelve books—the same number as the *Aeneid*—each semi-independent and all carefully balanced. *The Sons of Lusus*, again, is in ten books; and *The Faerie Queene* was planned in twelve.[13] These poems are classical in structure; and even *The Madness of Roland*, although rambling, has more symmetry and order than a real medieval gallimaufry like *The Romance of the Rose*.

An essential part of epic is the supernatural, which gives the heroic deeds their spiritual background. We find that in the epics on contemporary subjects Greco-Roman mythology provides practically all the supernatural element. Thus, one of the grandest conceptions in *The Sons of Lusus* is the spirit of the stormy Cape of Good Hope, who appears as a gigantic genie of cloud and storm to Vasco da Gama as he sails towards India. His name is Adamastor, Unconquerable. He explains that he was once a Titan, and that he was changed into a mountain (apparently Table Mountain) for trying to seduce Thetis, the sea.[14] Again, in *The Poem of Araucania*, the Indian sorcerer Fiton, who conjures up a vision of the battle of Lepanto for the narrator's benefit, invokes such classical demons as Cerberus, Orcus, and Pluto; he lives in a cave copied from the witch's cave in Lucan 6, and has a collection of snakes copied from the ophiology in Lucan 9: cerastes, hemorrois, &c.[15]

On the other hand, in the romantic epics, most of the supernatural element is provided by medieval fantasies: magic, sorcerers, enchanted objects such as helmets and swords, fabulous animals such as flying hippogriffs.[16] But classical mythology is blended with it to provide important ancillary material. (This blend of medieval and Greco-Roman is a deliberate device all through these poems.) For instance, hell as described in *The Faerie Queene* is almost wholly the Greek and Roman underworld. In 1.5 Sansjoy, the wounded paynim, is taken down by the same route and past the same figures as those described in the *Aeneid* (Tityus, Tantalus, &c.) and is cured by the god Aesculapius.[17] And in *The Liberation of Jerusalem*, 4, there is a similarly classical hell, with harpies, hydra, Python, Scylla, Gorgons, and all—although the enchanters, witches, and fiends of the poem are quite medieval. Then most of the subordinate deities in these poems are creations of Greek and Roman fancy. In *The Faerie Queene*, 1.6, Una is freed from the ravisher Sansloy by a passing group of fauns and satyrs. (Satyrs appear often in Spenser's epic, and sometimes engage in remarkably satyric activities.) When a bad spirit is called in, it is usually a classical spirit. Both in *The Madness of Roland* and in *The Liberation of Jerusalem* strife has to be kindled in one of the opposing armies. In the former it is done by Discordia, the spirit of Strife who caused the Trojan war; in the latter by the fury Alecto, who did the same job in Vergil's *Aeneid*, 7. Some taste of the gay confusion of Ariosto can be got from the fact that Discordia was dispatched by the archangel Michael, and *en route* met

Jealousy, accompanied by a tiny dwarf sent by the beautiful Doralice to the king of Sarza; and something of Tasso's grandeur can be gathered from the fact that Alecto's appearance is made more terrifying than in Vergil—she comes as a headless trunk, holding in her hand a head from which her voice proceeds.[18] Again, Circe, with her magic palace and her habit of changing unwary guests to animals, reappears as Armida in Tasso, and as Acrasia (personifying Incontinence, and named by Aristotle) in Spenser. But again Tasso adds something: he borrows Ovid's technique of metamorphosis, and makes her change the knights into something which they physically resemble: fish, with the scales corresponding to their glistening plate-armour.[19]

In the Christian epics practically all the supernatural element is provided by God, Jesus, the angels, and the devils. But their actions, and even their appearance, are largely described in terms invented by the classical epic poets. For instance, when Milton's archangel Michael comes to expel Adam and Eve from Paradise, he is in full uniform, wearing 'a military vest of purple', dyed by the Greek goddess of the rainbow:

Iris had dipt the woof.[20]

And when Raphael flies down to warn Adam of the tempter's visit, he is, like the biblical seraphs, wearing six wings; but two of them are on his feet, like those of Hermes/Mercury, to whom he is then compared:

Like Maia's son he stood.[21]

In the early books of the Old Testament and now and again in the gospels, angels are sometimes sent to intervene in human affairs. On this pattern, Christian epic writers constantly make angels carry messages from God to man, and assist or hinder the chief characters. But their interventions are so elaborate and systematic that they more closely resemble the minor deities of classical epic. Thus, at the beginning of *The Liberation of Jerusalem* God sends Gabriel to ask Godfrey de Bouillon why he is not taking action against the paynims; and at the beginning of *The Liberation of Italy* God dispatches the angel Onerio (disguised as the pope) to stir up Justinian against the Goths. Again, in one of the duels in *The Liberation of Jerusalem* God sends a guardian angel to interpose an invisible diamond shield between Raymond and the sword of Argantes, much as the deities in the *Iliad* and the *Aeneid* safeguard their favourites;[22] and in *Jerusalem*, 7.99 f., a devilish phantom persuades one of the pagans to break the truce in the same way as Athene persuades Pandaros to break the truce in *Iliad*, 4.68 f. Occasionally the devils are equated with the Olympian deities. The architect of Pandemonium in *Paradise Lost* is Vulcan; and in *Paradise Regained* Belial is identified with the various deities of Greek myth who seduced women in disguise.[23] The debate of the devils in *The Liberation of Jerusalem*, 4, and *Paradise Lost*, 2, is like the debates of the gods in so many classical epics, and is vastly unlike the behaviour of devils as conceived by the Middle Ages (for instance in Dante, *Inferno*, 21).[24] In *Paradise Lost* there is a terrible battle between the angels and the devils. It is copied from the battle of the gods in *Iliad*, 20–1; the overthrow of Satan is modelled on the overthrow of Ares; and the climax in which the angels tear up mountains and throw them on the devils, with jaculation dire, is adapted from the war of the Titans against the Olympians in Hesiod's *Theogony*.[25]

Milton's God himself does things which were done, not by Jehovah, but by Zeus and Jupiter. Thus, when Satan first entered Eden he was arrested by Gabriel and his angelic squadron, and there would have been a battle,

> had not soon
> The Eternal, to prevent such horrid fray,
> Hung forth in Heaven his golden scales, yet seen
> Betwixt Astraea and the Scorpion sign,
> Wherein all things created first he weighed . . .
> In these he put two weights,
> The sequel each of parting and of fight:
> The latter quick up flew, and kicked the beam.

Jehovah never did this; but Zeus did it for Achilles and Hector in the *Iliad*, and Jupiter for Aeneas and Turnus in the *Aeneid*, and Milton has added the reference to the use of the scales in the work of creation.[26] Even in that great work as described by Milton, when God decided to create man and this earth, he did not do so simply, as in the Bible:

And God said, Let us make man in our image, after our likeness. . . . So God created man in his own image, in the image of God created he him; male and female created he them.[27]

No: like Zeus and Jupiter, he took an oath:

> so was his will
> Pronounced among the Gods, and by an oath
> That shook heaven's whole circumference, confirmed.[28]

That Milton, thinking of the angels, should use the word 'Gods' here and elsewhere shows how completely he conceived his divinities in the image of the Olympian pantheon.

Throughout all these poems the culture of Greece and Rome provides a noble background. There are many aspects of this.

Modern history (however fabulous) is conceived as a continuation of Greco-Roman history, the Dark Ages being curtailed or forgotten. (*Paradise Lost* and *Paradise Regained* are exceptions here, for Milton has a profound sense of the perspective of ancient and biblical history.) For instance, at the end of *The Madness of Roland* the nuptial tent of Ruggiero is described. It was woven by Cassandra as a gift for Hector, and, since she was a prophetess, it showed all the descendants of Priam, ending with Ruggiero himself. Similarly, its history was a continuous chain: it was captured by Menelaus at the fall of Troy, taken to Egypt and given to Proteus in exchange for Helen, inherited by Cleopatra, and taken from her by the Romans, from whom it now descended to Ruggiero—and the description ends with a quotation of Caesar's famous epigram 'I came, I saw, I conquered'.[29] Again, in *The Sons of Lusus* the Portuguese explorers are described by Jupiter as outdoing Ulysses, Antenor, and Aeneas by their discovery of new worlds.[30] Paridell in *The Faerie Queene* gives a summary of the story of the *Aeneid* leading up to the story of Aeneas' descendant Brute, who founded Troynovant in Britain.[31]

The deeds of modern heroes are constantly compared to those of Greek and Roman epic and legend. Thus, in *Paradise Lost* Satan was

> in bulk as huge
> As whom the fables name of monstrous size,
> Titanian, or Earth-born, that warred on Jove,
> Briareos or Typhon, whom the den
> By ancient Tarsus held. . . .[32]

The valiant Indians in *The Poem of Araucania* are said to be braver than the self-devoting Decii and many other Greek and Roman heroes; and the sack of Concepción is called worse than the sack of Troy.[33] In *The Madness of Roland*, Grifon at the siege of Paris inflicts wounds which might have come from the hand of Hector, and (in a noble line which Ariosto borrowed from Petrarch) looks like

> Horatius alone against all Tuscany.[34]

Nature is usually described in classical terms—sometimes very inappropriately. The great ordeal in *The Poem of Araucania* where the Indian chief Caupolicán holds up a huge log for twenty-four hours is timed by the appearances of Tithonus' lady (Aurora) and the sun-god Apollo.[35] In *The Sons of Lusus* the Portuguese conquest of the sea is symbolized in an ebullient Rubens revel when all Vasco da Gama's sailors marry Nereids, in happy islands which are probably the Azores.[36] When there is a storm, in *The Faerie Queene*,

> angry Jove an hideous storm of rain
> Did pour into his leman's lap.[37]

Striking scenes are compared with beauties known from classical poetry. Even the garden of Eden, in *Paradise Lost*, is so presented: the garden where, since Milton could not keep out the lovely Greek nature-spirits,

> universal Pan,
> Knit with the Graces and the Hours in dance,
> Led on the eternal Spring. Not that fair field
> Of Enna, where Proserpin gathering flowers,
> Herself a fairer flower, by gloomy Dis
> Was gathered—which cost Ceres all that pain
> To seek her through the world—nor that sweet grove
> Of Daphne, by Orontes and the inspired
> Castalian spring, might with this Paradise
> Of Eden strive. . . .[38]

Pandemonium, built by the devils, is specially said to be like a Greek temple;[39] and in *The Liberation of Jerusalem* Armida's palace has golden doors decorated with pictures which show the triumph of Love, embodied in Hercules and Iole, Antony and Cleopatra.[40]

In all these epics, many, many episodes from Greco-Roman heroic poetry are imitated and adapted. Here is one striking example. Early in *The Faerie Queene* the Red-Cross Knight plucks a branch from a tree,

> out of whose rift there came
> Small drops of gory blood, that trickled down the same.

The tree speaks to him, and says it is a human being, bewitched; and we recognize a haunting fancy of Vergil's, which Dante took up and, in the grove of suicides, made far more terrible.[41]

Some of these adaptations are of the greatest artistic and spiritual importance. Such, for instance, are evocations of the heroic dead, and prophecies of the great unborn. In *The Liberation of Jerusalem* Rinaldo is given a suit of armour showing the exploits of his ancestors fighting the Goths; and later, the archangel Michael appears to Godfrey at a grave crisis, and shows him the spirits of the dead crusaders and the angels of heaven all fighting on his side. The first of these ideas is adapted from the divinely made armour of Aeneas in the *Aeneid*, and the second from the battles of the gods in the *Iliad*: Tasso has made the latter more sublime than its original.[42] In *The Poem of Araucania* a magician conjures up a vision of the battle of Lepanto, so that Ercilla may see it although he is on duty in Chile, at the other side of the world; in *The Sons of Lusus* a prophetic nymph describes the future history of the East Indies: both scenes are reworked from the underworld visit which gives Aeneas his long glimpse into the Roman future.[43] There are similar visions in *The Madness of Roland* and *The Faerie Queene*. The ghost of Merlin prophesies to the beautiful Bradamante that, with Ruggiero, she will have a long and glorious line of descendants, culminating in the family of Este, Ariosto's patrons; and Spenser makes Merlin foretell the coming centuries of British history to Britomart. The grandest of all such prophecies is in *Paradise Lost*, where one angel reveals the whole temporal past of the universe to Adam, and another the whole future, as far as the Day of Judgement.[44]

Again, both heroic adventures and grand crowd-scenes are often imitated from Vergil and Homer and others. In *The Madness of Roland* King Norandin rescues his wife from a cattle-keeping ogre by putting on a goatskin and crawling on all fours among the animals—the stratagem devised by Odysseus in the cave of the Cyclops.[45] In the same poem the rescue of Angelica from the sea-monster is inspired by the tale of Perseus and Andromeda in Ovid's *Metamorphoses*: indeed, Ingres's picture of the episode

emphasizes the similarity.[46] *The Madness of Roland* ends with a
crucial duel between Ruggiero and the paynim champion Rodomonte—as the *Aeneid* ends with the duel between Aeneas and
Turnus.[47] Even the final sentences of the two poems are almost
the same; but the modern author introduces a characteristic
difference of tone. When Turnus received the death-blow,

> his limbs slackened and grew cold,
> and with a groan his life fled grieving to the dark.[48]

So the poem ends, not as it might in triumph and peace, but in the
hopeless sorrow for young life cut short—just as the pageant of
mighty Romans yet unborn, in *Aeneid*, 6, ended with the sad
phantom of young Marcellus, who was to have such promise and
to die before his time. But *The Madness of Roland* ends when
Ruggiero, much less reluctantly, gives Rodomonte the death-blow,
not once, but twice and thrice, and then

> loosened from the body colder than ice,
> cursing and damning fled the angry soul
> that was in life so proud and so disdainful.[49]

The pagan knight does not grieve, but blasphemes. The victory
is complete—not marred by the inevitable waste of life which, for
Vergil, makes triumph into tragedy, but enhanced by the strength
and bravura of the defeated champion. Sympathy for him? No,
there is none, any more than in the original poem of Roland:

> Pagans are wrong, and Christian men are right![50]

So, instead of ending on a tremulous minor chord, Ariosto's poem
finishes on a bold major flourish of trumpets, like the sweep of
black plumes, haughty and orgulous.

So many of the crowd-scenes in these epics are inspired by
Greek and Roman epic poetry and history that it is impossible to
treat them in a general survey. Like the Greeks of *Iliad*, 23, and
the Trojans of *Aeneid*, 5, the victorious Indians in *La Araucana*,
10, hold elaborate games, with prizes formally awarded. The great
formal debates of gods, heroes, or devils (note 24) and the catalogues
of warriors derive from Homer and Vergil. The ambassador in
Tasso who says he has both peace and war in the folds of his
cloak, and asks which he shall shake out, is modelled on a real
Roman: none less than Quintus Fabius Maximus, on the momen-
tous embassy to Carthage before the second Punic war.[51]

Homeric similes, in all their elaboration, occur in every one of these poems. Sometimes the actual comparison is borrowed from Homer or Vergil—as when Ariosto compares Rodomonte, glittering and dangerous in his armour, to a snake gleaming in its new skin.[52] Sometimes the poets have used their own experience or imagination—as when Ercilla compares an Indian army surrounding a few Christians to an alligator swallowing up fish,[53] or when Milton likens Satan flying through hell (Satan, who later appears as vast as an island mountain) to an entire fleet, which far off at sea

> Hangs in the clouds, by equinoctial winds
> Close sailing from Bengala, or the isles
> Of Ternate and Tidore, whence merchants bring
> Their spicy drugs; they on the trading flood
> Through the wide Ethiopian to the Cape
> Ply stemming nightly toward the Pole.[54]

Several of the most vivid characters of Renaissance epic are imitated from, or partly inspired by, the figures of Greco-Roman epic. For example, the warrior girl, beautiful, virginal, agile, strong, and valiant, who fights on the wrong side, performs prodigies of bravery, is defeated (and usually killed), but inspires passionate love and regret in one of the opposing heroes. Clorinda in *The Liberation of Jerusalem*, Bradamante in *The Madness of Roland* are such heroines, and their younger sister is Spenser's Britomart. Although women soldiers like Joan of Arc and Caterina Sforza existed in real life, the model for these formidable girls was the Amazon queen Hippolyta, whom Theseus conquered, and whose virgin girdle he captured; and that other bare-breasted Amazon, Penthesilea, slain by Achilles; and Vergil's own imitation, Camilla.[55] Other fantasies were blended to make the modern Valkyries, but most of them were classical in origin. Tasso's Clorinda, for instance, was the white daughter of a negro queen —a compensatory fantasy from the late Greek romance of Heliodorus; she was suckled by a tigress—as Romulus and Remus were suckled by a she-wolf; and she was carried over a raging river first by her foster-father and then by miraculous winds and waters—as Camilla, tied to a spear, was thrown across by her father in the *Aeneid*.[56]

Several of these poems also invoke one or more of the Greek Muses. (Such invocations appear as early as Dante himself.)[57] In important passages the poets remember that the Muses were

pagan deities, and justify the invocation by Christianizing them,
like that of Tasso

> who dost not with soon-fallen bays
> adorn thy forehead on Mount Helicon,
> but high in heaven among the blessed choirs
> hast of immortal stars a golden crown.[58]

The assumption on which the Christian epics are based is that,
other things being equal, they will be superior to the epics of
Greece and Rome because their subject, through the revelation of
Jesus Christ, has been exalted to a far higher level: it is an

> argument
> Not less but more heroic than the wrath
> Of stern Achilles on his foe pursued
> Thrice fugitive about Troy wall; or rage
> Of Turnus for Lavinia disespoused;[59]

and the spirit which inspires the poets is therefore not an earthly
but a heavenly Muse.

And, by the more intense of these poets, many memorable
utterances from Greek and Roman poetry are translated or
imitated. Today many readers find this hard to understand. They
believe that the poet who echoes a phrase from Vergil or Ovid is
lacking in originality; that he cannot think of things for his characters to say, and must go to the ancients and 'borrow' their words.
This may be true of minor poets and hack writers, but it is very far
from true of great creative writers like Milton and Dante. The
truth is that quotation of beautiful words deepens the meaning,
and adds a new beauty, the beauty of reminiscence. For instance,
in *Paradise Lost* the first words spoken by Satan are his address
to Beelzebub, as they lie vanquished in hell:

> If thou beest he—but Oh how fallen! how changed
> From him!—who, in the happy realms of light,
> Clothed with transcendent brightness, didst outshine
> Myriads, though bright. . . .[60]

This is a deliberate quotation of the words in which Aeneas
described the ghost of Hector:

> Ah, how he looked! how changed from his old self,
> the Hector who brought back Achilles' armour![61]

It is a poignant phrase in the *Aeneid*. Milton's translation of it has the same piercing sadness, and has the additional charm of reminiscence: for the reader who knows Vergil feels another chord vibrating in his heart as he recognizes the words.

But the meaning also is enriched. When Milton uses the words in which Vergil described Hector's ghost, he is telling us that Satan and Beelzebub, though fallen, are still powerful heroic figures; but that Beelzebub, once 'clothed with transcendent brightness', now bears frightful wounds received in the rebellion against God—just as Hector's phantom appeared with its hair matted with dust and blood, and its face indescribably mutilated by being dragged around Troy behind the victor's chariot. And so, without any more direct description, merely by the brief allusion to the hero doomed to perpetual exile and visited on the night of danger by the ghost of his dead friend, he makes us feel the atmosphere of anguish, and foreboding, and defeat.

Similarly, when T. S. Eliot wishes to describe a rich and beautiful woman, he writes:

> The Chair she sat in, like a burnished throne,
> Glowed on the marble . . .,

which is a reminiscence of Shakespeare's superb description of Cleopatra:

> The barge she sat in, like a burnished throne,
> Burned on the water. . . .[62]

Thus, in half a sentence, he not only delights his readers by causing them to remember a phrase and a picture of great beauty, but evokes all the loveliness and luxuriousness of the woman he is describing.

It is a difficult art, the art of evocative quotation. The theory held by the romantics that all good writing was entirely 'original' threw it into disrepute. It has been further discredited by the misapplication of scholarship and the decline in classical knowledge (on which see c. 21): for readers do not like to think that, in order to appreciate poetry, they themselves ought to have read as much as the poet himself. Also, they feel, with justice, that hunting down 'allusions' and 'imitations' destroys the life of poetry, changing it from a living thing into an artificial tissue of copied colours and stolen patches. Still, it remains true that the reader who knows and can recognize these evocations without trouble gains a richer pleasure and a fuller understanding of the subject than the reader who cannot. Compared with the classically educated reader of Milton—or for that matter of Shelley or Eliot —the reader who has never interested himself in the classics is like a child reading Dickens 'for the story', without understanding the larger significances that are clear to every adult.

Further, it is an art that is often misused. In Tasso, Godfrey tells the Egyptian envoy that the Crusaders are not afraid to be killed in battle for the Holy Sepulchre:

> Yes, we may die, but not die unavenged

—which is an allusion to the last words of Dido in the *Aeneid*.[63] Pathetic, no doubt; but quite inappropriate that, in a speech where the Christian heroes offer their lives to the Cross, there should be a reminiscence of the pagan princess killing herself for love. Tasso is not a pedant, but far too many inferior poets have also used classical imitation and allusion as props to support an inadequate structure of imagination, or as a display of learning designed to ornament the commonplace.

Yet, when properly employed, the art is magically powerful. It may be compared with the art of imagery. When a poet describes a soldier standing alone against heavy odds, and preparing to counter-attack, he will not lessen the clarity of his picture, but add something to it, if he compares the solitary fighter to a fierce and noble animal, a lion or wild boar, surrounded by hunters and hounds, yet not helpless or frightened but filled with rage and strength and the exultation of combat, pausing only to find the best point of attack before, with burning eyes, taut muscles, and resistless energy, it charges. In just the same way, five words of apt allusion will, for the alert reader, evoke a scene more vividly, bring out all the force of an event, ennoble both the poet and his creations.

When emulating classical poetry, it is impossible not to envy the strength and flexibility of the Greek and Latin languages. Therefore all these poets, in varying degrees, broadened their style by introducing new words and types of phrase modelled on Latin, and to some extent on Greek. Portuguese critics (according to Mr. Aubrey Bell[64]) hold that real poetic diction in their language begins with Camoens, because he raised the language to a fuller power by introducing many latinisms. This is true of the others, in varying degrees: of Milton, in a special sense.

What Milton did in *Paradise Lost* and *Paradise Regained* was to create a new style to fit the subject 'unattempted yet in prose or rhyme'. It was intended to be grand; to be evocative; and to be sonorous—three different aspects of sublimity, differing only in the means by which sublimity is achieved. The closest parallel to him in this is Vergil, who, feeling that the Latin language was painfully poor and stiff compared with Greek, elaborated its syntax, enlarged its vocabulary, and refined its rhythms until it produced in his hands an effect scarcely less rich than that of Greek poetry. Just as Milton quotes many Latin and Greek poets (although remarkably little from the Bible), so Vergil quoted Ennius and Lucretius and even his contemporaries and immediate predecessors in Latin poetry, and translated or adapted innumerable beauties from the Greek. As Milton introduced Latin syntax into English, so Vergil introduced grecisms into Latin; and just as many English critics accuse Milton of barbarizing the language, so Vergil was accused of distorting the Latin tongue by unnecessary 'affectations'. It is worth recalling that Milton was a musician: any writer who really understands and practises music will tend to work over his style and elaborate it in detail inconceivable to an unmusical person. It is strange, though, and perhaps in the last analysis it is a proof of the failure of his method, that so few of his phrases (in comparison with those of Shakespeare or even of Pope) have become part of the English language.

One of his strangest devices is to use existing English words, not in their current sense, but in the sense which their Latin root possesses. Strange, certainly, and to an etymologist interesting; but to others rather pedantry than poetry. For instance: the bridge between hell and the earth was built

> by wondrous art
> Pontifical . . .

—not bishop-like, nor pope-like, nor pompous, but 'bridge-building', literally.[65] At the beginning, Satan asks why the fallen angels should be allowed to

> Lie thus astonished on the oblivious pool—

—which does not mean 'lie surprised on the forgetful lake', but lie

attoniti, 'thunder-struck', on the pool which causes forgetfulness.[66]
Or when a speaker, in the evil days before the Flood, preached of
religion, truth, and peace,

> him old and young
> Exploded . . .

—i.e. 'hissed off', not 'blew into pieces'.[67] Sometimes these distortions of English are literal transferences from the Greek or
Latin, as when the army of rebellious angels bristled with

> shields
> Various, with boastful argument portrayed . . .

—not dispute, or even challenge, but 'subject', as in Vergil's
Aeneid.[68]

Not only the original Latin root-meanings of English words are
substituted for their acquired meanings, but latinisms in syntax
delay and distort the thought. The Romans disliked using abstract nouns, which in Latin were vague and heavy; they would
rather say 'from the city founded' than 'from the foundation of the
city'. So Milton calls his poem *Paradise Lost*, although it is not
about Paradise after it had been lost, but about the loss of Paradise.
For this he had models in *Orlando Furioso* (which we have translated *The Madness of Roland*) and *Gerusalemme Liberata* (= *The
Liberation of Jerusalem*). And so he says:

> the Archangel paused
> Betwixt the world destroyed and world restored[69]

—between telling of the destruction and describing the restoration
of the world. This is intelligible enough, but what does it mean to
anyone except a practising teacher of Latin (with the *licet* plus
subjunctive idiom in his head) when Belial asks

> Who knows,
> Let this be good, whether our angry foe
> Can give it?[70]

This habit of Milton's differs in an important point from his
other displays of learning. They are made in order to bring in as
many as possible of the riches of the spirit, to express the grandeur
of his subject by showing that it illuminates many different levels
of art and history. But to use a word in *only* its Latin sense cuts
out part of its meaning, and the most important part. The effect

is not richness but obscurity. In language Milton sometimes stepped over the narrow and almost imperceptible boundary which divides wealth from ostentation, eloquence from pedantry, art from technique. This is exactly the mistake that Dante did not make, the danger he avoided and signalized by calling his poem a humble *Comedy*. It is the mistake of the poet who is obscure, not because of the intensity of his thought and the variety of meanings he is evoking, but because he wishes to be dignified through obscurity. In this, Milton was not a Renaissance artist but a baroque artist. Much contrapuntal music, ending with Bach's *Art of the Fugue*, suffers from the same defect. The weakness of the fugue, and of linguistic cleverness such as Milton's, is that it appeals to only a few levels in the human mind. The epic, like the symphony, addresses all the spirit of man.

In spite of all their debt to the classics, the great epic poets of the Renaissance were not copyists. Their poems are all unlike one another, and unlike the epics of Greece and Rome. To write a work of heroic grandeur needs such strength of mind that one cannot succeed in it without being vigorously original and completely individual.

But, as well as strength, epic poetry needs richness. If it is to have its maximum effect, it must have sumptuously varied imagination or deep philosophical content, or both. It must stretch far back into the past and look forward into the future. It must work upon many emotions, use many arts, contain the achievements of many ages and nations, in order to reflect the energies and complexities of human life. All these poets recognized this. They felt the authority of Greco-Roman myth, they knew the excellence of Greco-Roman poetry, they realized that the world of Greece and Rome, so far from being dead, was much of the living past of which our world is a continuation, and therefore they enriched their own work by emphasizing that continuity. Where they failed it was because they went back into the past and forgot the present—like Ronsard, or like Milton studding his poetry with verbal fossils. Where they succeeded it was by using the multiple radiance of the classical past to deepen the bright single light of the present, and thus, with the power given only to great imaginative writers, illuminating the whole majestic spectacle of man's destiny.

9

THE RENAISSANCE

PASTORAL AND ROMANCE

PASTORAL and romance are two styles of literature which, although allied and sometimes combined, have different origins, different histories, different methods, and different purposes. For instance, the ideal of the pastoral is uneventful country life, 'easy live and quiet die', while the ideal of romantic fiction is wild and unpredictable adventure, becoming more and more unlifelike in its very length and complexity. Nevertheless, the two have their similarities. At bottom there are deep psychological links between them. And they combined to produce many books which had a great success, once towards the end of Greco-Roman civilization and again during the Renaissance. They are still being combined to-day.

Pastoral poetry and drama (seldom plain prose) evoke the happy life of shepherds, cowboys, and goatherds on farms in the country. Ploughmen and field-workers are not introduced, because their life is too laborious and sordid. Nymphs, satyrs, and other flora and fauna also appear, to express the intense and beautiful aliveness of wild nature. Pastoral life is characterized by: simple love-making, folk-music (especially singing and piping), purity of morals, simplicity of manners, healthy diet, plain clothing, and an unspoilt way of living, in strong contrast to the anxiety and corruption of existence in great cities and royal courts. The coarseness of country life is neither emphasized nor concealed, but is offset by its essential purity.

The type of literature was invented by the poets of one of the earliest great metropolitan cities of the world, Alexandria; and, it is believed, specifically by Theocritus, an admirable poet of whom little is known, except that he was born about 305 B.C. and lived at the courts of Alexandria and Syracuse.[1] His bucolic 'idylls'[2] were mostly placed in Sicily: their characters spoke the local Doric dialect of Greek, with its broad *a*'s and *o*'s. As well as the charm of their subject, Theocritus' poems are marked by the exquisite music of their sounds and rhythms—a music which, like the sound of a brook or the glow of sunlight through leaves, transfigures even ordinary thought and commonplace figures with an unforgettable, inimitable loveliness.

The great new departure adopted by most subsequent pastoral writers was made by Vergil in his *Bucolics*, published in 39 B.C.[3] A number of them were direct copies of Theocritus, with exact translations of his Greek verse into Latin. What was original—as always in Vergil—was the additions he made to his model. Some of his poems were placed (like Theocritus') in the Sicilian country-side; one or two in his own home-country of northern Italy; but two (7 and 10) were placed in Arcadia. Vergil was the discoverer of Arcadia, the idealized land of country life, where youth is eternal, love is sweetest of all things even though cruel, music comes to the lips of every herdsman, and the kind spirits of the country-side bless even the unhappiest lover with their sympathy. In reality, Arcadia was a harsh hill-country in the centre of the Peloponnese: it was known to the rest of Greece chiefly for the very ancient and often very barbarous customs that survived in it long after they had died elsewhere. We hear hints of human sacrifice, and of werewolves.[4] But Vergil chose it because (unlike Sicily) it was distant and unknown and 'unspoilt'; and because Pan—with his love of flocks, and nymphs, and music (the un-tutored music of pan-pipes, not the complex lyre-music of Apollo and his choir, the Nine)—was specifically the god of Arcadia.[5] It was in this unreal land of escape that Vergil placed his friend Gallus, a poet and an unhappy lover, to receive consolation from the wild scenery of woodland and caves, from music, and from the divinities of art and nature.

Romance is the modern name for a long story of love and adventure in prose. The first known to us were written in Greek, under the Roman empire.[6] Such stories were probably told for centuries before any were written down; but they seem to have entered literature in the early centuries of the Christian era, when literary stylists took them up as vehicles for the display of elaborate rhetoric, dazzling epigram, and brilliant invention. (Apparently it is to the same period that the original forgeries of the Trojan history by 'Dares the Phrygian' and 'Dictys the Cretan' belong, although they were more distinguished for cleverness than for grace.)[7] A number of these stories survive. There must have been hundreds. They are immensely long and, unless the reader decides to believe them, immensely tedious; but if given belief they are delightful. Their main elements are:

the long separation of two young lovers;

their unflinching fidelity through temptation and trial, and the miraculous preservation of the girl's chastity;

a tremendously intricate plot, containing many subordinate stories within other stories;

exciting incidents governed not by choice but by chance— kidnappings, shipwrecks, sudden attacks by savages and wild beasts, unexpected inheritance of great wealth and rank;

travel to distant and exotic lands;

mistaken and concealed identity: many characters disguise themselves, and even disguise their true sex, girls often masquerading as boys; and the true birth and parentage of hero and heroine are nearly always unknown until the very end;

a highly elegant style, with much speechifying, and many elaborate descriptions of natural beauties and works of art.

The Greek romances which were best known in the Renaissance are:

(a) *Aethiopica*, by a Syrian author called Heliodorus: the adventures of two lovers—the daughter of the queen of Ethiopia, and a Thessalian descended from the hero Achilles—in Egypt, Greece, and the eastern Mediterranean generally. This was translated into French by Amyot in 1547, and into English by Underdown in 1569.

(b) *Clitophon and Leucippe*, by Achilles Tatius: the adventures of another nobly descended pair in Tyre, Sidon, Byzantium, and Egypt. This was translated into Latin in 1554; into Italian in 1550; into French in 1568; and into English by Burton's brother (in a version which was suppressed) in 1597.

(c) *Daphnis and Chloe*, by Longus: the adventures of two foundlings among the shepherds and peasants of the island of Lesbos. It was translated into French by Amyot in 1559, and from Amyot's French into poor English by Day in 1587.

The first two are adventure-stories pure and simple, with the love-affair a continuous thread running through them. *Daphnis and*

Chloe is an important departure from the pattern, for it is a successful combination of stirring romantic adventure with pastoral atmosphere and charm.

Now although the pastoral, with shepherds and nymphs singing exquisitely and loving innocently in a sweet country-side, seems to us tedious and unreal, and although the romances with their absurd melodrama and stilted speeches and exaggerated emotions are practically unreadable, they are not intrinsically worthless. Both serve a real purpose. They are obsolete because the purpose is now served by something else. They are not high literature, as tragedy or epic is high literature, employing all the mind and all the soul. They are escape-literature, they are wish-fulfilment. And, as such, they fulfilled (both in their day and in the Renaissance) the useful function of idealizing aspects of life which might have been gross, and adding poetic fantasy to what is often dull or harsh prose. They are meant for the young, or for those who wish they were still young. All the leading characters in them are about eighteen years old, and think almost exclusively about their emotions. No one plans his life, or works towards a distant end, or follows out a long-term career. The hero and heroine are buffeted about by events without deserving it—as young people always feel that they themselves are buffeted—and yet no irremediable damage happens to them, they are united while they are still fair and young and ardent and chaste. In these, as in modern romantic stories, the Cinderella myth is one of the chief fantasies: a typical wish-fulfilment pattern, in which one does not have to work for success or wealth, but is miraculously endowed with it by a fairy godmother and the sudden passion of a prince. (A pathetic note in the *Aethiopica*, which tells us something about the author and the audience he expected, is that the heroine, although the daughter of coloured parents, is miraculously born white.) Even the style reflects youth: for the commonest devices are antithesis and oxymoron. Everything in youth is black or white, and these devices represent violent contrast and paradoxical combination of opposites. The idealistic tone of the romances often had a real effect. Many a young man exposed to vice in the roaring metropolitan cities of the late Roman empire, or the corrupt courts of the Renaissance and baroque era, was drawn for a time to think more highly of love, by imagining himself to be the faithful shepherd and his beloved the pure clean Chloe. The manners of all the chief characters, even the shepherds, are intensely courtly: no one speaks gross rustic patois, everyone has fine feelings, and speaks gracefully, and behaves nobly—because youth has sensitive emotions.

The same yearning is satisfied to-day by fantasies about other milieux and by different social customs. Instead of reading about nymphs and shepherds in Arcadia, we read about idyllic peasants or idealized countrymen outside our own megapolitan cities: sometimes we even create them and support them. The Swiss; the Indians of the south-western United States; the Bavarians (with their wonderful Passion Play); Steinbeck's drunken but angelic paesanos; seely Sussex; salty Vermont; the pawky Highlanders; the cowboys of Wyoming; and the fishers of the Aran Islands—all these, and many more, and the modern works of art made out of them by Giono, Ramuz, Silone, Bartok, Rebecca West, Selma Lagerlöf, Grant Wood, Villa-Lobos, Chavez, Grieg, many more, and the innumerable converted farm-houses and rebuilt cottages and primitive pictures and rustic furniture which we covet—all are the products of a real need, which is becoming more poignantly felt as city life becomes more complex, difficult, and unnatural. Pastoral dreaming has produced some very great things. We need only think of Beethoven's Sixth Symphony. We need only remember that Jesus, although he was a townsman and an artisan, called himself a shepherd.[8]

Greek and Roman pastoral and romance had so many important incarnations, together and apart, during the Renaissance that we can point out only the chief works they produced. Even before the Renaissance the pastoral spirit appeared. The medieval French play of *Robin and Marion* (by Adam de la Halle, *fl.* 1250) is a shepherd-story; so is the pretty fourteenth-century poem, *Le Dit de Franc Gontier*, by Philippe de Vitri (who was, however, a friend of the classical scholar Petrarch). *Robin and Marion* has been plausibly derived from the *pastourelles*, little dialogues in which a minstrel courts a shepherdess: there were many of these gay little things, invented by the Provençal poets, and not directly built on classical models.[9] But it was with the rediscovery and imitation of the Latin pastoral poets, and the publication of the Greek romances, that the two styles were really reborn in modern literature.

Boccaccio's *Admetus* (*Ameto*, *c.* 1341) is the very first vernacular reappearance of either ideal. It is a blend of pastoral poetry with allegory of an uncomfortably lofty type. A rude countryman is converted from physical love to spiritual adoration by hearing the several songs and stories of seven lovely nymphs, who prove to be the seven cardinal virtues. Crude as this contrast is, it contains the essential idealism of the pastoral. And *Admetus* set one pattern which was followed, in varying proportions, by all the other Renaissance works of its kind—the blend of prose narrative with verse interludes which raise the simple story into the realm of imaginative emotion.

Richer, more elaborately written, and more successful in its international effect, was the *Arcadia* of Jacopo Sannazaro. The author was the son of Spanish immigrants into Italy (his name is a doublet of Salazar): born in Naples, he spent his youth in the beautiful valley of San Giuliano near Florence, and devoted much of his life to his monarch Frederick of Aragon, whose exile in France he shared. His *Arcadia* circulated in manuscript before 1481 and was published in 1504. It is in twelve chapters of prose separated by twelve 'eclogues' in lyrical metres. It tells how an unhappy lover goes away to Arcadia (like Gallus in Vergil's *Bucolics*) to escape from his misery, is temporarily diverted by the idyllic country-life of the people and by other tales of love, and, at last, is conveyed back to Naples by a subterranean journey, to find his beloved lady dead. *Arcadia* is a very complex and rich pastoral, enlarged by reminiscences of the heroic poem, the romance, and even the philosophical dialogue. Its model in modern literature is Boccaccio's *Admetus*; but the allegorizing of Boccaccio has been dropped, and instead many vivid details of rural life and landscape have been inserted from Homer, Theocritus, Vergil, Ovid, Tibullus, Nemesianus, and other classical authors, as well as from personal observation. In Sannazaro's pretty Italian prose they all sound natural enough, and the literary reminiscences blend with the other harmonics of his dream. (For instance, when the shepherds hold games, two of them wrestle. Neither can throw the other. At last one challenges his opponent 'Lift me, or let me lift you'—for a decisive fall. Quite a natural and vivid detail; but Sannazaro has copied it directly from the match between Odysseus and Ajax in Homer.)[10] *Arcadia* had an enormous success: it was translated into French in 1544 and into Spanish in 1549, and often imitated. Its rich wealth of description and allusion made it 'the most complete manual of pastoral life that could possibly be imagined'.[11]

Even more successful was *Diana*, by Jorge de Montemayor or Montemôr (1520–61), a Portuguese who, after visiting Italy and seeing the popularity of *Arcadia*, went to Spain in the suite of a royal bride and wrote his own book there: his premature death left it unfinished, but it was none the less popular. (Notice that, just like the original Greek and Roman pastoral idylls, the Renaissance pastorals and pastoral romances were nearly all written by courtiers.) Montemayor was not such a learned man as Sannazaro, but he took most of the pastoral setting and a number of incidents in his book from *Arcadia*. What he emphasized above everything else was love. Although shepherdesses are mentioned in *Arcadia*, they do not appear. *Diana* is full of shepherdesses, real or disguised, nymphs, and other enchanting creatures. Its chief novelty is that it is a continuous story, with a central thread of love-interest and a number of subordinate love-stories, making a vastly more elaborate fiction than any of its predecessors. It is really, like *Daphnis and Chloe*, a romance with a pastoral setting; but it contains more adventures and much less psychological analysis than Longus's sensitive story. Its complex intrigues, its lofty tone and the amorous sensibility of its characters, made it famous throughout western Europe. Shakespeare used one of its stories in *The Two Gentlemen of Verona*, and probably thought of it when he disguised Viola in *Twelfth Night*. Cervantes attempted to rival it in his *Galatea*: in *Don Quixote* he first saved it (a little mutilated) from the burning of the books, and then made the knight turn from the profession of arms to imitate it:

'I will buy a flock of sheep, and everything that is fit for the pastoral life; and so, calling myself the shepherd Quixotis, and thee the shepherd Pansino, we will range the woods, the hills, and the meadows, singing and versifying. . . . Love will inspire us with a theme and wit, and Apollo with harmonious lays. So shall we become famous, not only while we live, but make our loves as eternal as our songs.'[12]

And so the sixteenth-century Spanish idealist, having once adapted his name to sound like a medieval knight, now proposes to change it again to sound like a Greek shepherd: and not a mere shepherd, but a poet like Gallus and Vergil, under the patronage of the Greco-Roman god Apollo.

We have already seen that in Boccaccio's love-story *Fiammetta* there is a marked avoidance of Christian sentiment, and a deliberate substitution of pagan morality and pagan religion.[13] The same applies to all these pastoral books: the Christian religion, its creed and its church, are never mentioned. Even when the characters are quite contemporary and the story (as it becomes now and then) autobiographical, only Greco-Roman deities appear: and they are not stage properties, but powerful spirits, who are sincerely worshipped and can protect their votaries. Their hierarchy, however, is unlike that of Olympus. Venus, the goddess of love, Pan, the god of wild nature and animal husbandry, and Diana, goddess of hunting, of the moon, and of virginity, are far more prominent than any others. This was not merely a fad, or a wish for dramatic propriety. It was a genuine rejection of the austere and otherworldly Christian ideals, and an assertion of the power of this world and human passions, as personified in those Greek figures who were called immortal because the spirits they hypostatized lived on for ever in the heart of man.

Other types of long adventurous stories were being written in various countries of western Europe during the Renaissance. Some of them owed nothing whatever to classical influence: for instance, the picaresque tale (*Lazarillo de Tormes*) and the romance of medieval chivalry (*Amadis de Gaula*, i.e. *Amadis of Wales*—a belated Spanish revival of the Arthurian legends). These too were currents which flowed into modern fiction; but the influence of Greek romance and pastoral was quite as powerful. In Renaissance England it is represented, among others,[14] by Sir Philip Sidney's unfinished book dedicated to his sister, *The Countess of Pembroke's Arcadia*. This is a long, complex, and gracefully written story of love and chivalrous adventure set in the Greek land of Arcadia. It is sometimes said that Sidney took nothing but the name from Sannazaro's *Arcadia*; but he also borrowed, and slightly altered, a number of vivid and charming details such as the statue of Venus suckling the baby Aeneas.[15] However, he owed more to Montemayor's *Diana*. He imitated the form of some of Sannazaro's poems,[16] but he translated some of Montemayor's; and on *Diana* he designed the complicated network of plots and sub-plots and the disguises of some of his main characters. In addition, he enriched these imitations by his own classical reading, being especially indebted to Longus's *Daphnis and Chloe*.

His Arcadia is a far less restful place than Vergil's or Sannazaro's. There is a great deal of terrifying danger and bloody fighting. Hands are struck off, heads roll on the ground, the clash of armour harmonizes grimly with the groans of the dying. The jousts and battles come from his own chivalrous imagination, stimulated by tales like *Amadis* and *The Madness of Roland*. But other adventures, such as kidnappings and pirate-raids, are imitated directly from the Greek romances, which abound in them. Thus, in *The Countess of Pembroke's Arcadia* the two Greek currents of Arcadian pastoral and romantic adventure have blended in a new proportion, along with other elements of fantasy, to make a story which is one of the sources of modern fiction.[17]

In France the most successful pastoral romance was *Astraea* (*Astrée*, the name of the spirit of Justice, who left earth at the end of the Golden Age to become the Virgin in the zodiac), by Honoré d'Urfé. Published in 1607, it was tremendously popular for many years. Like those of *Diana*, its characters are not real shepherds and shepherdesses, but ladies and gentlemen, who have adopted shepherds' clothes for the reason (psychologically true, even if improbable in the plot) that they wish to live more quietly and pleasantly (*vivre plus doucement*). The scene and period are fifth-century Gaul at the time of the barbarian invasions; and the characters have a vast number of complicated chivalrous adventures in the noblest medieval manner. But long afterwards another French author recombined romance and pastoral, with less emphasis on aristocratic sentiments and more upon the inherent goodness of man and nature. One of the leading novels of the eighteenth century, Bernardin de Saint-Pierre's *Paul and Virginia* (1788), told the story of a young couple who, in settings of idealistic beauty, had a series of romantic adventures culminating in the triumph of pure love. This book once more proved that men distant in time can be, as Spengler said, contemporaries: for it was modelled on Longus's *Daphnis and Chloe*, and obviously both Saint-Pierre and his friend Rousseau were profoundly sympathetic to the ideals Longus had expressed.

The pastoral ideal had many other expressions, apart from its blend with romance. In fact, it was very much more influential in Renaissance and baroque European literature than it ever was in Rome and Greece. It is scarcely necessary to describe in detail the numerous collections of bucolic poems that were written, both in Latin and in the various national tongues, in emulation of the ancients. The most famous in Renaissance Latin were those by the Italian humanist, Baptista Mantuanus. Shakespeare makes his pedantic schoolmaster quote them in *Love's Labour's Lost* and praise the author by name.[18] In Spanish Garcilaso de la Vega (1503–36) wrote several long, sweet, melancholy 'eclogues' adapted both from Vergil's *Bucolics* and from Sannazaro's *Arcadia*. In France the first pastorals of the Renaissance were written by Clément Marot (1496–1544), who sang of peasants with French names in a French setting, but under the protection of the god Pan. His successor and conqueror Ronsard began with a free translation of Theocritus, 11 (*Cyclops in Love*), and proceeded to six melodious 'eclogues' partly drawn from Vergil, Vergil's imitator Calpurnius, and Sannazaro (who had been turned into French by Ronsard's friend Jean Martin in 1544). Some of them at least are dramatic enough to be performed as little masques at festivals. True to the traditions of French aristocracy, he dressed his shepherds in court clothes, and (like d'Urfé later) assured his audience:

> These are not shepherds out of country stock
> who for a pittance drive afield their flock,
> but shepherds of high line and noble race.[19]

In English the most distinguished pastoral poem of the Renaissance was Spenser's *Shepherd's Calendar* (1579). Although it was given out as a re-creation in English of the themes and manner of Greco-Roman pastoral, modern research has shown that Spenser depended much less on Theocritus and Vergil than on Renaissance pastoral writers in France and Italy. Several of his poems on the months are simply free adaptations of 'eclogues' by Marot and Mantuanus, while most of the classical reminiscences come through Politian, Tasso, and the leading poets of the Pléiade, Baïf, Du Bellay, and Ronsard.[20] For much of his language and metre Spenser went back to Chaucer. The names of his shepherds— Cuddie, Hobbinol, Piers, Colin—are native English, but are far more homely and less melodious than the Doric names of Theocritus' singing herdsmen; and less melodious, alas, is his verse.

Still, some of the sweetest and most sincere songs in all English

literature were written in the pastoral convention. It is scarcely
a convention. It is really more natural for a young lover to imagine
himself as a wanderer through the country-side,

> Seeing the shepherds feed their flocks
> By shallow rivers to whose falls
> Melodious birds sing madrigals,

than as a merchant in the city or a diplomat in the court; and he
is less happy in dreaming of his sweetheart as a housewife keeping
the furniture and the children clean than as a girl who, wearing

> A cap of flowers and a kirtle
> Embroidered all with leaves of myrtle,
> A gown made of the finest wool
> Which from our pretty lambs we pull,

is the quintessence of all the beauties of eternal spring and kind
Nature.[21] The English poets of the Renaissance poured out
hundreds of pastoral songs, which united their genuine love of the
classics to their equally genuine love of youth and beauty and the
country-side.

Pastoral poems and stories are not, as is sometimes assumed,
completely empty and artificial. Very often they contain charac-
terizations of the author and his friends under a thin disguise,
and stories of their lives and loves. Theocritus began this; his
seventh idyll contains himself, under the name of Simichidas, and
(probably) his friend Leonidas of Tarentum, bearing the name
which has since become famous in pastoral—Lycidas. Vergil is
his own Tityrus, while his friends Gallus and Varius and his
enemies Bavius and Maevius appear in his *Bucolics* without even
the disguise of a rustic name.[22] Vergil also introduced allusions to
important incidents in his own life, such as his recovery of his
father's estates through the favour of Octavian.[23] Sannazaro's own
unhappy love is thought to have inspired the close of his *Arcadia*,
which also takes his hero to his own favourite city, Naples.
Similarly, Montemayor's *Diana* stops with a journey to Coimbra,
and to the castle of Montemôr o Vello, the author's birthplace.
D'Urfé includes many stories of contemporary court intrigue in
Astraea. Tasso puts both his friends and himself, and perhaps
his hopeless love for Leonora d'Este, into *Amyntas*. Two generations after Spenser, a young English poet of even nobler promise

symbolized the two sides of his own nature in two lonely rhapsodies, which, starting from Greek myth and pastoral idyll, wandered far into the realms of music and philosophy. They were Milton's *L'Allegro* and *Il Penseroso*.[24]

Sometimes, again, the personal element in pastoral issues in satire against persons and causes of which the author disapproves. Vergil's reference to his rivals Bavius and Maevius is brief but bitter. It follows a similar attack in Theocritus. However, in the Renaissance pastoral, aesthetic criticism is less common than ecclesiastical criticism. We have already pointed out that Jesus called himself a shepherd. For the same reason, Christian clergymen are called pastors (= shepherds), and the bishop carries a shepherd's crook. It is therefore quite easy to criticize abuses of the church in a pastoral poem. Petrarch did so in his Latin eclogues, one of which introduces St. Peter himself under the attractive name of Pamphilus. Mantuanus continued the idea, and Spenser brought it into the *Shepherd's Calendar*. St. Peter appears again in Milton's *Lycidas*, to utter a formidable denunciation of bad pastors:

> Blind mouths! that scarce themselves know how to hold
> A sheep-hook, or have learnt aught else the least
> That to the faithful herdman's art belongs![25]

A few lines before, Milton complains that such unworthy ones

> Creep, and intrude, and climb into the fold—

an image which, long afterwards, he remembered, and turned into an epic simile, and applied to the enemy of mankind:

> So clomb this first grand Thief into God's fold:
> So since into his Church lewd hirelings climb.[26]

Autobiography takes a nobler turn in the pastoral elegy, in which poets mourn the premature death of their friends, and, to emphasize the youth and freshness of the dead, depict them in a wild woodland setting, lamented by shepherds, huntsmen, and nature-spirits. The origin of this pattern is Theocritus' lament for Daphnis who died for love (*Id.* 1) and the anonymous Greek elegy on the later pastoral poet Bion. During the Renaissance the pattern spread all over western Europe. In English the earliest pastoral elegies are Spenser's *Daphnaida* (1591) and *Astrophel*

(1595), the latter being a tribute to Sir Philip Sidney. The three greatest English pastoral elegies are Milton's *Lycidas*, written in 1637 for his friend King, Shelley's *Adonais* (1821) for poor Keats, and Arnold's *Thyrsis* (1866), inspired by the death of Clough.[27] And one of the most famous poems in the English language, although not a lament for any single person, is a blend of pastoral idealism and elegiac melancholy: Gray's *Elegy in a Country Churchyard*.

The pastoral convention also produced drama. It was natural that the singing contests of shepherds, the dialogues based on 'flyting' or mutual abuse, and the occasional love-conversations should suggest dramatic treatment. We have seen that Vergil's *Bucolics* were recited in the theatre.[28] One of the first modern dramas, Politian's *Orpheus*, placed the tragic tale of Orpheus and Eurydice within a Vergilian pastoral frame;[29] we hear of many 'dramatic eclogues' recited by two or more speakers in Italian festivals during the early sixteenth century;[30] and in 1554, at Ferrara, the first regular full-scale pastoral drama was produced, Beccari's *The Sacrifice*.[31] This fashion too spread from Italy to other countries. In France the first such work was *The Shades* by Nicolas Filleul, a five-act drama produced in 1566, about a loving shepherd and a cruel shepherdess, paralleled by a loving satyr and a cruel naiad, with a chorus of amorous phantoms.[32] Two of the most popular plays ever written belong to this genre: Tasso's *Amyntas*, first acted in 1573, and Guarini's *The Faithful Shepherd*, issued in 1590 with even greater success.[33] Despite the artifice of the interlocking love-stories which compose their plots, their youthfulness gives them charm, and the verse of Tasso and Guarini is often so enchantingly melodious that it almost sings. In several of Shakespeare's comedies there are pastoral elements; and a number of regular pastoral dramas appeared in England during the first half of the seventeenth century.[34] The poetry in Fletcher's imitation of Guarini, *The Faithful Shepherdess* (c. 1610), is full of delicate and charming brush-work; and Jonson's *The Sad Shepherd* (published incomplete in 1640) ought to have been finished, for it contains a fine native set of English pastoral figures.

Huntsmen as well as herdsmen always played a part in pastoral poetry. They too live close to nature, they prefer animals to people, they pray for Pan's favour. In Vergil's tenth bucolic poem the lovelorn Gallus hopes to cure the sickness of love by hunting the wild boar among the craggy Arcadian highlands. The hero of Boccaccio's *Admetus* is not a cowherd but a hunter; and several of the pastoral books of the Renaissance introduced huntresses and huntsmen as prominent characters. In Italy cattle did not regularly pasture on low-lying fields, but up on the hill-sides and among the woods, so that it was easy to think of the forest as the common home of hunters and herds. Also, herding was a commoner's occupation, hunting a nobleman's. Tasso and other authors of Italian pastoral plays therefore often called their pieces *favole boschereccie*, 'tales of the woods', so that they would cover both activities. So when Jonson decided to make the characters of his pastoral not Greco-Roman herds but native English woodsmen, he could easily go one step further and choose the gallant outlaw hunters, Robin Wood (alias Hood) and his merry men. The same change appears in Shakespeare's *As You Like It*, where the exiled duke and his companions take to the maquis and become huntsmen;[35] while honest shepherds like Corin and Audrey, although part of the same sylvan society, are inferior to them.

Milton's masque of *Comus* (1634), which has been mentioned in another connexion,[36] proves together with his other poems in this vein that he was one of the world's greatest pastoral poets. Allied to pastoral drama and pastoral masque is pastoral opera, which began comparatively early—as early as Rinuccini's *Daphne* (1594).[37] The first sacred opera was in the pastoral manner: *Eumelio*, produced in 1606 by the church composer Agostino Agazzari.[38] The advantage of pastoral opera was that folk-melodies and folk-rhythms could be introduced into it. It could therefore re-emphasize natural emotion and simple expression when conventional operatic style became too grand and florid. Among the most famous and charming are Handel's *Acis and Galatea* and Bach's *Peasant Cantata* and *Phoebus and Pan*. The framework of Gluck's beautiful *Orpheus and Eurydice* (first produced 1762), which was designed to be a return to natural expression in opera, is pastoral, and it ends with an Arcadian merrymaking. Gluck's friend, the child of Nature, Rousseau, produced *The Village Soothsayer* and began *Daphnis and Chloe* with the same artistic purpose. During the nineteenth and twentieth century the pastoral opera followed Rousseau's lead, and left imaginary Arcadias for the real (though still a little distant) countryside, where it created Smetana's *The Bartered Bride*, Mascagni's *Rustic Chivalry*, Vaughan

Williams's *Hugh the Drover*, and most recently Rodgers and Hammerstein's *Oklahoma!* And yet Arcadia itself has never died. Among the most remarkable of modern ballet suites is Ravel's music for the immortal loves of *Daphnis and Chloe*.

The ideals of Arcadia were perfectly real and active for several hundred years—particularly during the baroque age, when the social life of the upper classes tended to be intolerably formal and hypocritical, and when the art created for them was too often pompous and exaggerated. Dresden-china shepherdesses and Marie-Antoinette's toy farm in the Petit Trianon look childishly artificial to us now; but they were closer to reality than the enormous operas about Xerxes and the enormous mural paintings representing His Serene Highness as Augustus or Hercules. Arcadia meant an escape to purer air, out of the gloomy solemnity of courts and churches. Its most remarkable avatar was in Italy. Queen Christina of Sweden, after abdicating and becoming a convert to Roman Catholicism, settled in Rome and gathered round her a number of friends with ideals similar to hers. In 1690, a year after her death, they founded a society to keep her memory and her ideals alive. It was called Arcadia; its arms were a pan-pipe garlanded with laurel and pine; its home was a 'Parrhasian grove' on the Janiculum, one of the seven hills of Rome; and its leading members took the names of Greek shepherds. Dozens of Arcadian societies were formed on its model both in Italy and elsewhere, and produced vast quantities of lyric poetry. Hauvette sums up the result in the acid phrase, 'a long bleating resounded from the Alps to Sicily';[39] but a society which endeavoured to encourage art and insisted on natural feeling in poetry cannot be dismissed as wholly ridiculous.[40]

The pastoral tradition continued through the era of revolution (when it produced the graceful *Bucolics* of André Chénier) into the nineteenth century, where Matthew Arnold and many others gave it new life. That it is still alive in modern poetry and art is shown by Mallarmé's *Afternoon of a Faun*,[41] by Debussy's *Prelude* expressing the poem in exquisite music, and by Nijinsky's memorable ballet on the same theme. A recent group of paintings by the energetic experimentalist Picasso includes a *Joy of Life* (1947), in which a centaur and a faun play Greek clarinets to a dancing, cymbal-clashing nymph, while two young kidlings skip beside her with ridiculous but charming gaiety. Sometimes, as in

Goethe's delightful love-song set to Wolf's even more delightful music,[42] nothing survives of the tradition of Sicily and Arcady except the flute, the shepherd names (Damon, Chloe, Phyllis, or Ophelia), and the love of nature. But even then the essential genius of Greece and of poetry still burns clear: the power to idealize the simple, the happy, the natural, the real.

10

RABELAIS AND MONTAIGNE

L IKE many other great French writers, Rabelais is far from being the cool, well-balanced, classical figure which is the accepted ideal of French literature. On the contrary, he is difficult to understand and difficult to admire. Those who enjoy his vigour are repelled by his pedantry; those who like his idealism hate his coarseness; those who prize his humour seldom prize all of it, or else ignore his seriousness: everyone feels that, although much is there, something is lacking—yet what it is that Rabelais lacks is not easy to say.

The difficulty which his readers feel is based on a lack of harmony between conflicting factors in Rabelais's book; and it is evident that, since more than most writers he is a one-book man, the disharmony reflects a profound conflict in his own character and life.

We have observed the same type of conflict in other Renaissance writers, and it exists in many important figures who do not come within the scope of this book: for instance, Leonardo da Vinci and Queen Elizabeth. The chief difference between the later Renaissance (with the baroque age which succeeded it) and the early Renaissance is that in the later Renaissance form and matter, character and style, are more completely interpenetrated, while in the earlier period there are many conflicts and wastages. Doubt and insecurity, experiment and divagation, are notable by their absence in such baroque figures as Molière, Rubens, Dryden, Corneille, Purcell, and Titian. There were, of course, even in the opening of the Renaissance, many well-balanced characters such as Lorenzo de' Medici; but on the whole the age brought in changes too violent for most men to experience without doubt and difficulty and frequent error.

This conflict has no very obscure psychological cause. Like some modern neuroses, it was due to the divergence of stimuli acting on sensitive people. The word Renaissance means 'rebirth'; but in fact only Greco-Roman culture and its concomitant spiritual activities were reborn, while all the rest of the Renaissance period was marked not so much by rebirth as by sudden change and abolition and substitution of ideas and systems already long established and very powerful. The Renaissance was a spiritual revolution: a civil war in which both sides were strong and determined. Often that civil war was waged within one man's soul. We see it in Shakespeare's work, whether it takes the form of the passionate debate of some of the Sonnets or of Hamlet's excited despair. It is imaged in the suicidal incompleteness of Leonardo's art. It appears in the madness of poor Tasso. On some souls whose strength was less than their sensitivity the conflict produced a numbing effect, and issued in that inexplicable melancholy, which is less often a persistent *taedium vitae* than a manic depression alternating aimless violence with motionless gloom. In others it evoked desperate courage, wild daring, a gallantry whose chief purpose was not the achievement of an external end but self-assertion and self-display, as in Sir Philip Sidney, Sir Richard Grenville, and Cyrano de Bergerac. But the strongest men of the early Renaissance were able, partly by psychical insight, partly by sheer strength of will, but chiefly because of the immense optimism produced by the Renaissance, to dominate the conflict, and to compel its conflicting elements to meet in great works of art to which, despite disharmony and incongruity, all the spiritual enemies contribute one common quality, energy.

Before we examine Rabelais's life and his book we must summarize the main conflicts which, like volcanoes in one of the great ages of geological formation, were boiling and erupting throughout the early Renaissance. They were these:

1. The conflict between the Catholic and the Protestant forms of Christianity. (Here it is odd to observe that the division was deepened by some of the liberal elements within the Catholic church, who sided rather with the classical pagans than with the primitive Christians: for the priest who closed his breviary and opened his Cicero, in order to improve his style, was thereby diminishing the prestige of Mother Church.) There is reason to believe that this conflict affected the life and work of William Shakespeare, whose greatest characters, even when they live in Christian milieux, are very far from being devout Christians.[1] It is even more visible in the life of the converted Catholic Donne, whose *Pseudo-Martyr* and *Ignatius his Conclave*, aimed at converting or convincing the members of his own former church, are practically contemporary with his *Biathanatos*, aimed at proving that suicide is not inevitably sinful.

2. Akin to this was the conflict within the Roman church between the liberals and the conservatives: the liberals were unwilling to leave the Catholic communion entirely, but refused to subscribe to all its doctrines, and often made some significant gesture of revolt or renunciation at critical times. This is one of the main conflicts within the life of Rabelais: it appears also in the career of Erasmus, who refused the sacraments on his death-bed although he was an ordained priest.

3. There was also the conflict between the upper class and the self-assertive middle class. In England, for instance, the university wits were mostly not rich men's sons but ambitious boys from the *bourgeois* class, striving to enter or conquer the aristocratic clique. Not many Renaissance figures believed it possible to overthrow the entire social structure, or even to force the oligarchy to behave more liberally. But many of the greatest works of the period are disguised symbols of hatred for the oligarchs and the wish to dominate them. Marlowe's tragedies seethe with the lust for power. Shakespeare's greatest plays all deal with rebels: *Hamlet* with the legitimate heir, expelled by a less intellectual, more energetic ruler; *Othello* with the greatest servant of a state of which his colour forbade him to be more than a servant; *Macbeth* with a usurper—not a deliberate, Italianate, Machiavellian usurper, but a sorely tempted man of feeling; *King Lear* with a rightful monarch dethroned and impotent.

4. As the age of scientific exploration, the early Renaissance was split by the conflict between science and its two enemies: superstition on the one hand, and the authority of traditional philosophy and theology on the other. Galileo is the classical example, but there are many others. It should, however, be noted that much of the new scientific spirit was based on, and authorized by, the new knowledge of the Greco-Roman classics. Just as Renaissance architecture and Renaissance scenography received their great stimulus from the study of Vitruvius, so one of the two great impulses that founded modern medicine and zoology was the study—by philologists even more than by scientists—of the works of Greek and Roman scientific writers.[2] Rabelais himself lectured on the text of Hippocrates and Galen to a large audience at Montpellier; and in 1532 he published an edition of Hippocrates' *Aphorisms* and Galen's *Art of Medicine*. To say this is not to underestimate the essential part played in Renaissance medicine

by experiment and discovery; Rabelais knew, and boasted of knowing, a great deal of anatomy; but he started towards his anatomical knowledge from the rediscovery of the classics. The comic over-emphasis with which medical descriptions are elaborated and medical authorities cited and multiplied in *Gargantua* and *Pantagruel* shows that for Rabelais medicine with its new discoveries was not an ordinary activity to be accepted and used like commercial law, but an exciting proof of the power of the newly awakened human mind.[3]

5. Containing the social and scientific conflicts, but transcending them, was the conflict between authority and individuality. This was far from new—witness those great medieval personalities Reynard the Fox and Tyl Ulenspiegel—but now it increased in violence. Some of the greatest documents for it are Machiavelli's *The Prince*, in which the individual politico is shown how to succeed by ignoring all moral, social, and religious restraints on his own action; Montaigne's *Essays*, in which the humanist, writing his own autobiography, declares the superior importance of his own personality (however inconsistent it may be) to any conventional or philosophical system; and Rabelais's *Gargantua* and *Pantagruel*, where the only authority under God is that of the huge philosopher-kings, who rule by an unquestionable and unapproachable greatness of body and mind, while every other authority, from holy church to court and university, except only the authority of science and learning, is questioned, outwitted, lampooned, befooled.

Most of these conflicts can be traced in the life and work of François Rabelais even more clearly than in those of other Renaissance authors. Born towards the close of the fifteenth century, he entered a Franciscan monastery early in life; but he found the ignorance and simplicity enjoined by St. Francis irksome, and began to study the classics for himself, with such energy that the authorities tried to stop him. His books were seized, and he and his friends were put under restraint. In 1524, by special licence from Pope Clement VII, he became a Benedictine, transferring his allegiance to the order which had long stood for culture and learning. But this too was not free enough. Next he attached himself to a prince of the church who liked learned men. Then for a time we lose track of him. He appears to have become a wanderer, giving up the Benedictine's garb for that of a secular priest. At last, finding his true career, he emerged as a physician and teacher of Greek and modern medical doctrines. Even in that position he had conflicts, with the Lyons hospital (for taking absence without leave), with the Sorbonne (for publishing irreverent remarks about its doctors), and with the monks (for making fun of them and their orders). He died in 1553, still fighting and still laughing.

His book describes the adventures and encounters of two giant kings, father and son, living in an idealized France more or less contemporary, and vitalized by all the currents of humour, energy, travel, pleasure, satire, intellectual enterprise, art, and learning which flowed through the Renaissance. Both the kings, Gargantua and Pantagruel, are borrowed from medieval heroic poetry and fairy-tales. Gargantua comes out of a cheap little book sold at fairs, *The Great and Inestimable Chronicles of the Great and Enormous Giant Gargantua*, published in Lyons in 1532, and spiritually an ancestor of to-day's Superman. Pantagruel is his son, better educated and more modern. The name, according to Plattard, comes from a mystery-play where a special devil called Panthagruel was allotted to drunkards, to keep them for ever thirsty.[4] The exploits of the two giants, and their court and their attendants, are inspired by the comic Italian epics of medieval prowess such as Luigi Pulci's *Morgante* (1483), which are also creations of the naive popular fairy imagination that produced Gargantua before Rabelais transformed him.[5] There are other Renaissance tales based on medieval themes, such as *The Madness of Roland*. They all have something cheerfully immature about them; but Rabelais's book is quite literally the most childish of all Renaissance works. It is a long *wish-fulfilment*: not in all realms of life (not in sex, for example), but in most—eating, drinking, physical energy, travel, fighting, practical joking, talking, learning, thinking, and imagining. In this it reflects the enormous expansion of self-confidence, the love of man's natural functions, which characterized the Renaissance: it should be compared with the insatiable appetites of such anti-ascetics as Benvenuto Cellini. And yet to write a long book full of perfectly impossible wish-fulfilments is a sign of curious spiritual disharmony; and to put a contemporary Utopia full of bold philosophical thought into the framework of a childish fairy-story shows that Rabelais stood with one foot in the Renaissance and the other in the Middle Ages.

A similar incongruity appears in the content of the book, for its two most prominent features are (a) a considerable amount of classical learning and up-to-date scientific and philosophical thought, and (b) an equally large amount of dirty jokes. Most of the dirt is unclassical in origin. It comes out of the spiritual underworld which was part of the Middle Ages, which is documented in the fabliaux, which appears again and again in Chaucer's *Canterbury Tales*, and which is essentially anti-cultural, opposed to the spirit of the Renaissance. These contrasts could be further developed; but our particular interest is the nature of Rabelais's classical learning and its effect on his work.

Although the main characters and the general scheme of his book are medieval in origin, the subordinate characters are often classical in name, and many of the principal themes are classical in character. For example, Gargantua's tutor is Ponocrates, which means Power through Hard Work; the page who reads aloud to him is called Anagnostes (= Reader); his nimble squire is Gymnast (= Athlete); his eloquent and good-natured courtier is Eudemon (= Happy); his steward is Philotimus (= Lover of Honour); and the angry king who makes war on him is Picrochole (= Bitter Bile).[6] The ideal abbey which he founds is called Thelema, a Greek word meaning 'will', because its motto is DO WHAT YOU WILL.[7] Similarly, Pantagruel (who makes everyone thirsty) conquers the Dipsodes (= Thirsty People, a word Rabelais found in Hippocrates); his own nation is the Amaurots (= Obscure), who are obscure because they live in Utopia (= Nowhere). His tutor is Epistemon (= Knowledgeable), and his favourite courtier Panurge, whose name means Clever Rascal.[8]

One of the most important classical themes in Rabelais is the humanistic education which is given by Ponocrates to the young Gargantua after he has had a simple, natural, beastly, and unprofitable education: see *Gargantua*, 21–4. The description of his curriculum—which was perhaps inspired by that of the great educator Vittorino da Feltre[9]—is an essential document for anyone who wishes to study the re-emergence of classical ideals in the Renaissance. Not only does Gargantua become a philosopher-king, the hope of Plato, but he is educated in a manner befitting a descendant of Plato, and ultimately endows a community which partly resembles that of the Guards in *The Republic*. Even the style of the letter on education which he sends to his son

(*Pantagruel*, 2. 8) is deliberately classical, with rich Ciceronian periods, careful antitheses, rhetorical questions, and triple climaxes.[10] It is true that, in the actual routine followed by Gargantua, there are odd survivals from the Middle Ages: for instance, he never writes his lessons (apart from practising calligraphy) but learns everything orally and memorizes a great deal. But the gargantuan appetite for education, for learning *all* languages, for reading *all* the great books and assimilating *all* the useful sciences, is characteristic of the Renaissance. It is also characteristic of Rabelais himself, and was a reaction against the early limitation of his studies. In fact, since the whole war between the aggressive king Picrochole and Gargantua and his father Grandgousier is described as taking place on the estates of Rabelais's own family, since the names of Gargantua's fortresses are those of Rabelais's family properties, and since his headquarters, La Devinière, is the farm where Rabelais himself was born, it is clear that the good giant Gargantua is Rabelais himself.[11]

In a careful and intelligent book Jean Plattard has analysed the classical authors whom Rabelais knew and from whom he borrowed. Like many medieval writers and some in the Renaissance, he owed a great deal to anthologies and to Reader's Digests—even for his knowledge of authors so closely akin to his own vein of humour as Aristophanes. His greatest debt in this region was to the *Adages* of Erasmus, a collection of 3,000 useful quotations from the classics, with explanations.[12] His chief original sources were prose writers rather than poets; Romans more than Greeks (like many men of the Renaissance he found Latin far easier than Greek, and annotated his Greek texts with Latin translations of difficult words); and writers of fact rather than imagination—with one exception, the Greek philosophical satirist Lucian. He quotes eighteen or twenty good classical authors in such a way as to show that he knew them; but it is clear that he was not familiar with Greek and Roman epic, drama, lyric, or (more surprisingly) satire. His favourite authors were scientists, philosophers, and antiquarians. Among the scientists are Aristotle, Galen, Hippocrates, and the elder Pliny. The philosophers he admired most, whom Gargantua puts first in his reading-list, were Plutarch and Plato.[13] The antiquarians mentioned by Gargantua are Pausanias and Athenaeus, and Rabelais also read Macrobius. His favourite writer was Lucian, the laughing Greek sceptic of the Roman empire, whose work also influenced Erasmus's *Praise of Folly* and More's *Utopia*. It was to Lucian that he owed such inventions as the imaginary conquests of Picrochole,[14] the description of hell where the great are made small,[15] and the interrogation of Trouillogan by Panurge.[16] Lucian was his spiritual comrade, sharing with him the laughter which delights without condemning.

Serious conflicts, such as those which existed in the life of Rabelais, can be resolved only by strong will or by great art. No one would say that Rabelais was a great artist. His work is often too rough and often too silly. But there can be no doubt that he was a great man; and the two solutions which he applied to his own difficulties and suggested for those of the world were, first, education, and second, enjoyment—gusto—the simple, energetic, life-giving gaiety of the joke and the bottle. . . .

'. . . and therefore . . . even as I give myself to an hundred pannier-fulls of faire devils, body and soul, tripes and guts, in case that I lie so much as one single word in this whole history: after the like manner, St Anthonies fire burne you; Mahoom's disease whirle you; the squinance with a stitch in your side and the wolfe in your stomack trusse you, the bloody flux seize upon you, the curst sharp inflammations of wilde fire, as slender and thin as cowes haire, strengthened with quicksilver, enter into your fundament, and like those of Sodom and Gomorrha, may you fall into sulphur, fire, and bottomlesse pits, in case you do not firmly beleeve all that I shall relate unto you in this present chronicle.'[17]

MONTAIGNE

It is a strange contrast, almost like turning from lunacy to sanity, to turn from Rabelais to Michel de Montaigne (1533–92), whom Sainte-Beuve well called 'the wisest of all Frenchmen'. Rabelais knew much, lived hard, travelled widely, absorbed huge gulps of thought and experience; but the result was confusion, which would have meant strain and indigestion had it not been for his humour, his health, his tireless energy. As it is, we find it difficult and unsettling to read him—a disharmony which shows that he was not through and through sympathetic to the ideals of classical culture. Montaigne, on the other hand, is not a straightforward imitator of the classical writers; but he knew them better than Rabelais, he had thought more about them, his spirit was largely formed by them, his culture was principally based upon them, and it was his constant intercourse with them which raised him high above the place and time in which he lived. One of the two prime facts about Montaigne is that he was an exceptionally well-read man—he knew much more about the classical authors than many professional scholars in the sixteenth, or for that matter the twentieth, century. The other is that he had a sufficient experience of life and a large enough soul to master, to use, and to transform his knowledge into something active and vital not only for himself but for other modern men.

The first of these facts is the result of an unusual, but admirable, education. He came of the family Yquem or Eyquem (whose estates produce one of the finest wines, Château Yquem), which had only recently enriched and ennobled itself. But, because his father was sympathetic to the ideals of the Renaissance, by which he had been stimulated in Italy, he did not simply teach young Montaigne hawking and courtly behaviour or expose him to the bad old education under which young Gargantua became healthy and beastly, but instead gave him one of the most thorough classical trainings ever known. Montaigne describes it himself in one of his essays.[18] Before he could speak he was put in charge of a German tutor who knew much Latin and no French whatever; and it was a rule that nothing but Latin should be spoken to the little boy and in his presence, even by the servants. As a result, the first book he enjoyed reading was Ovid's *Metamorphoses*:

'for, being but seven or eight years old, I would steal and sequester myself from all other delights, only to read them: forasmuch as the tongue in which they were written was to me natural; and it was the easiest book I knew, and by reason of its subject the most suitable for my young age. For of King Arthur, of Lancelot of the Lake, of Amadis, of Huon of Bordeaux, and such idle, time-consuming, and wit-besotting trash wherein youth doth commonly amuse itself, I was not so much as acquainted with their names.'[19]

The little boy could scarcely be taught Greek in the same way, since he was learning Latin on the direct principle; his father started him on it, as a game, which would probably have been an excellent idea had it been continued; however, he was sent off to school at the Collège de Guienne, the best in France. He says that there he lost much of the ground gained by his extraordinary education. The truth probably is that he had to turn back in order to learn how to speak French and play with other children. By the age of twelve he was acting leading parts in school productions of Latin tragedies by Buchanan and Muret.[20]

In his teens his life became more normal. He entered on the usual course of life of a prosperous gentleman: studied law, took part in local government, went to court. But at thirty-eight, in 1571, he retired from what he himself called 'the slavery of the court and public duties'[21] to a tower—not indeed an ivory one, but a book-lined one, where he studied and thought and wrote for most of the rest of his life. Montaigne did not like to do anything determinedly or consistently, so that we are not surprised to see that he came out of retirement now and then. He became a not very energetic mayor of Bordeaux, he travelled in Italy, Austria, and Switzerland, and he entertained the Protestant king of Navarre at his home. But from thirty-eight onwards most of his life was absorbed in lonely study and self-examination. One of the main motives for his retirement was his wish to avoid taking sides in the religious civil wars which were then devastating France: his father had been a Roman Catholic, while his mother was a lady of Spanish-Jewish descent, and three of his brothers and sisters were either bred as Protestants or converted later.

In 1580 he published two books of *Essays*, with great and immediate success. They ran into five editions during his lifetime. As successive editions were called for, he added much material. The last (1588) contained a whole new book, as well as hundreds of additions to the other two. After his death his 'adopted' daughter brought out a still larger edition, containing supplements from Montaigne's own manuscript notes. The importance of this is that the alterations and additions have been used by Villey and other scholars to show the development of Montaigne's thought during the most important years of his life, and his deepening knowledge of the Greek and Roman classics.[22]

Montaigne himself, in one of his most interesting essays, gives an account of his favourite reading.[23] Two general points emerge. The first is that he read for pleasure. He would not be bored. He would not read tedious authors. He would not read difficult authors at all, unless they contained good material. The standard he constantly uses is one of pleasure. However, his pleasure was not merely that of pastime, but that which accompanies a high type of aesthetic and intellectual activity, far above the vulgar escape-reading and narcotic-reading. Two authors he read for profit and pleasure combined, 'whereby I learn to range my opinions and address my conditions': these were Plutarch, in French (i.e. in Amyot's translation), and Seneca. The remark shows us the second point. Montaigne had much Latin, but little Greek. He could read Latin so easily that he was able to choose his Latin reading for pleasure; but not Greek.[24] That still puts him head and shoulders above the moderns, but it explains a certain slackness we often feel in his thinking, a certain lack of clarity in his appreciation of the ideals of antiquity.

The poets whom he himself names as his favourites are Vergil (particularly the *Georgics*), Lucretius, Catullus, Horace, Lucan, and the gentlemanly Terence. In prose, next to Plutarch and Seneca, he likes Cicero's philosophical essays, but complains that they are verbose—although not so bad as Plato's dialogues. He also likes Cicero's letters to his friends; and he concludes by saying that historians are his right hand, and Plutarch and Caesar chief among them.

Villey has gone over Montaigne's reading with a magnifying-glass, and listed a formidable array of authors whom he knew well. There are not less than fifty. The striking absence of Greek classics is at once observable. Montaigne knew no Greek trage-dians at first hand, quoted Lucian (so familiar to Rabelais) only once, knew nothing of Aristophanes, met Thucydides only at second hand, and had not even read Homer properly. Still, he knew and with qualifications admired Plato and Plutarch; and although he began by abusing Aristotle, he apparently read the *Nicomachean Ethics* with care towards the end of his life and made considerable use of it.[25] Here is Villey's list:

Aesop
Ammian
Appian
Aristotle (the *Politics* and *Ethics* only)
Arrian
St. Augustine (the *City of God* only)
Aulus Gellius
Ausonius, because he came from Bordeaux
Caesar, whom he mentions 92 times
Catullus
Cicero, whom at first he disliked and later came to admire, and
    quoted 312 times
Claudian

Diodorus Siculus

Diogenes Laertius, with his memorable anecdotes about philosophers

Heliodorus

Herodotus (in Saliat's translation, which he never mentions and always uses)

the *Historia Augusta*

Homer, at second hand

Horace, who with Lucretius is his favourite poet—both were Epicureans: 148 quotations

Isocrates, in translation

Josephus

Justin

Juvenal, quoted 50 times

Livy, whom he used freely

Lucan

Lucian, once or twice

Lucretius, 149 quotations

Manilius the philosophical poet of the stars

Martial, with 41 quotations

Oppian

Ovid, 72 quotations

Persius, quoted 23 times

Petronius, apparently only at second hand: most of the *Satirica* was still undiscovered

Plato, in whom his interest increased after 1588: he makes over 110 quotations from at least 18 of the dialogues, including 29 from that difficult book *The Laws*

Plautus scarcely at all: Montaigne thought him very vulgar

Pliny the elder, a few moral aphorisms

Pliny the younger

Plutarch, mentioned by name 68 times and quoted 398 times

Propertius

Quintilian

Sallust, less than we should expect

his favourite Seneca, from whom he lifted entire passages, often without acknowledgement[26]

Sextus Empiricus, the only Sceptic philosopher whose work survives

Sidonius Apollinaris, of Lyons

Suetonius, quoted over 40 times

Tacitus, particularly the *Annals*

Terence

Tibullus
Valerius Maximus and other minor historians and anecdotards
   like Nepos and Stobaeus
Vergil, quoted 116 times
Xenophon.

Now, what use did Montaigne make of this enormous mass of learning? The very catalogue of the authors whom he knew is apt to repel modern readers. We forget that we read countless ephemeral books, magazines, and newspapers, far less worth reading: stuff which bears the same relation to literature as chewing-gum does to food. But as soon as we read the *Essays*, we feel more at ease. We see that he did not remember and quote these classical books merely in order to dazzle his contemporaries with his learning. Burton's *Anatomy of Melancholy* is a work in which, despite the interest of its subject-matter, the deployment of authorities from abstruse regions of literature is an end in itself, and one we cannot now admire. But Montaigne took his reading naturally, and was a little embarrassed by knowing so much less than men like Budé. His relation to his books was not a mechanical but an organic one. He did not imitate the ancients as Ronsard imitated Vergil. He did not want to be a classic in modern dress any more than he wanted to be a polymath. He wanted to be Michel de Montaigne, and he loved the classics because they could help him best in that purpose. So he assimilated them, and used them, and lived them.

As material for literature, he used them in three ways.

(*a*) He employed them as sources of general philosophical doctrine. He selected sayings from them which seemed to him particularly true and valuable, and then proceeded to discuss and illustrate these apophthegms from his own knowledge of books and life.

(*b*) He used them as treasuries of illustration. After he had laid down some general truth which he wished to examine (whether taken from one of the ancients, or worked out by himself, or quoted from a modern), he then sought illustrations to prove it, qualify it, or elaborate it. Some of the illustrations came from his own contemporary reading, many from recent history, very many from the classics. For instance, in *Essays*, 1. 55, *Of Smells and Odours*, he discusses body-odour. The essay begins with the report that Alexander the Great had sweet-smelling perspiration, goes on to condemnations of perfume taken from Plautus and Martial, a remark about Montaigne's own sensitivity to smells, confirmed by a repulsive quotation from the equally sensitive Horace, jumps to a note from Herodotus about the perfumed depilatories used by Russian women, a personal reminiscence about the way perfume clings to Montaigne's moustache, a reference to Socrates' freedom from infection during the plague, and stops abruptly with a story about the contemporary king of Tunis.

(c) He found stores of compact well-reasoned argument in the classics: for there were no modern philosophers available who had put so much hard thinking into such small space. Montaigne is often indebted to the classics for his arguments even when he does not acknowledge the debt: without mentioning the source, he will translate entire paragraphs out of Seneca and lift whole sections from Amyot's Plutarch; and sometimes he will make what Villey calls a 'parquetry'[27] out of sentences drawn from different parts of an author like Seneca whom he knows well.

Turn now to the two most important problems about Montaigne's work, his two chief claims to literary greatness. He was the inventor of the modern essay. Where did he get the idea? And he was one of the first modern autobiographical writers, attempting what Rousseau long afterwards called 'a daring and unheard-of task', psychological self-description. What was the origin and motive of that innovation?

The origin of the essay, as far as content goes, is made fairly clear by the subjects of the first two volumes which Montaigne published. The themes are predominantly abstract questions of ethics, and sometimes single moral precepts: *Cruelty, Glory, Anger, Fear, Idleness*; *That we should not judge of our happiness until after our death*; *To philosophize is to learn how to die*; *All things have their season*. The moral treatises of Seneca and Plutarch, although on the average longer than Montaigne's first essays, are on similar subjects with similar titles: *Anger, Kindness, On the Education of Children, How to distinguish Flatterers from Friends*. In addition, many of Seneca's ethical treatises are in the form of letters to his friends: a shape which Montaigne apparently borrowed for his essay on education.[28]

Nevertheless, Montaigne did not call his works treatises, or discussions, or even letters. He called them 'essays'. The word may mean 'assays', weighings and testings; or, more probably, 'attempts'. More probably the latter, because they follow no systematic scheme, such as they would have if they were really weighing facts and opinions. And in the first two volumes the 'essays' often consist merely of a string of quotations and illustrations of a single generalization, which is itself not discussed. Villey therefore suggested that Montaigne began by copying the collections of memorable apophthegms which were so popular in the time when his style was forming—particularly the *Adages* of Erasmus, which went into 120 editions between 1500 and 1570. If this is true, the debt of the essay to the classics is a double one, both to the systematic philosophical discussions of men like Seneca and to the isolated fragments of philosophical wisdom collected by the Renaissance humanists.

(As the essay developed, other influences entered it and enlarged its form and purpose. One of these was classical: the psychological character-sketch, invented by Theophrastus, and embodied in the characters of comedy by his pupil Menander. This, after the appearance of Casaubon's great edition of Theophrastus in 1592, was practised as an independent form by Hall and Earle and La Bruyère; and, through the essays of Addison and others, helped in the growth of the modern novel.)[29]

But one important element differentiates Montaigne's *Essays* both from the classical treatises on ethical questions and from the collections of apophthegms: that is the subjective factor, which makes them vehicles for Montaigne's own autobiography. At one time or another he tells us nearly everything about himself: his height, his health, his education, funny things he has seen, a ghost-story he has just heard, the fact that he seldom dreams, &c. This gives the *Essays* an intensely real, vivid, individual style: we hear him talking, more to himself than to us. He begins where he likes, ends where he likes, and is content to come to no conclusion, or several, or half a one. Yet for this subjectivity he himself quotes a classical model. He says it is like the Roman satirist Lucilius, who, as Horace tells us, spread out his whole life and character in his satires, as if in a realistic picture;[30] and he might well have cited Horace too, whose moral *Letters* are, like Montaigne's *Essays*, a blend of philosophical meditation and personal musing.

Nevertheless, the intensely personal wish-fulfilment dream-story of Rabelais, the autobiography of the artist with the Gargantuan appetites (Benvenuto Cellini), the rise of autobiographical writing elsewhere (as in the unhappy Greene), and the great success of Montaigne's *Essays* show that the new spirit of autobiography was largely a creation of the Renaissance. It was called into being by the wish for freedom. Rabelais made himself into a giant in power, appetites, benevolence, and learning. Cellini would be bound by no law, obliged to no potentate, and equalled by no artist. Montaigne believed nothing without testing it, and then believed it only until it confined him. His favourite poets were Epicureans, and his motto, *What do I know?*, was an assertion of philosophical doubt based on the wish to remain absolutely free from all systems. The Renaissance gave humanity many things: some good, some doubtful, some evil. For good or evil, its greatest gift was the sense of moral and intellectual freedom. This sense was given almost infinite scope by the new aesthetic, historical, geographical, and cosmological discoveries of the fifteenth and sixteenth centuries: hence, for example, the relativism of essays like Montaigne's *On the Cannibals*. The same sense was stimulated by the rapid extension of the knowledge of human psychology which resulted both from contemporary social revolutions and from the revelation of Greco-Roman drama, erotic poetry, satire, and philosophy. And it was propelled by the reaction against medieval authority—the authority of the church, of feudal society, of the close social structure of small states and tightly organized trades, of philosophical dogma,[31] of inherited privilege. Because it asserted the fundamental dignity of man, the spiritual achievement of the Renaissance is called Humanism; and Montaigne was one of the greatest, and most human, of the humanists.

II

SHAKESPEARE'S CLASSICS

THERE is no doubt whatever that Shakespeare was deeply and valuably influenced by Greek and Latin culture. The problem is to define how that influence reached him, and how it affected his poetry.

Forty large works, including the two long narrative poems and the sonnet-sequence, are attributed to Shakespeare. Of these:

six deal with Roman history—one with the early monarchy, three with the republic, two with the empire;[1]

six have a Greek background;[2]

twelve concern British history, chiefly the period of the dynastic struggles in the late Middle Ages and early Renaissance;

fourteen are played in Renaissance Europe. In these, even when the story is antique, the settings and the manner are quite contemporary. For instance, in *Hamlet*, the prince whose companions (in the original tale told by Saxo Grammaticus) carried 'runes carved in wood'[3] now forges a diplomatic dispatch and its seal,[4] and in his own court discusses the stage of Elizabethan London.[5] Half of these plays are localized in Renaissance Italy,[6] while two are set more or less in France (*As You Like It* and *All's Well*). The other five are in vaguely defined places which are Italianate (*Measure for Measure*, *Twelfth Night*, and *The Tempest*), Frenchified (*Love's Labour's Lost*), or northern European (*Hamlet*);

one play, *The Merry Wives of Windsor*, is laid in an England almost wholly contemporary in feeling; but its hero is Falstaff, who started life in the fourteenth century. Only the Sonnets can be said to deal directly with Shakespeare's own time and country.

Of course Shakespeare took little care to exclude geographical and historical incongruities, or to create a complete illusion of local and temporal colour. All his plays have touches, and many have complete scenes and characters, which could only be contemporary English. But from this broad classification of his themes it is evident that three great interests stimulated his imagination. The first was the Renaissance culture of western Europe. The second was England, and particularly her monarchy and nobility. The third, equal in importance to the second, was the history and legends of Greece and Rome.

From his characters and their speech we derive a similar impression. To begin with, most of Shakespeare's writing is English of the English. No poet has ever expressed England, its character, its folk-speech and song, its virtues and its follies and some of its vices, and even its physical appearance, so sensitively and memorably. Rosalind is the daughter of a banished duke (therefore not an English girl, but French or Italian); yet she goes into exile in the forest of Arden, which is near Stratford-on-Avon,[7] and her nature and her way of talking are English to the heart's core. Then, intertwined with the Englishness of Shakespeare's characters, there is a silken strand of Italian charm and subtlety. A number of his best plays are stories of the intricate villainy which flourished in Renaissance Italy: Iago is only one such villain; think of Sebastian and Antonio in *The Tempest* and the beastly Iachimo in *Cymbeline*. And much of the wit and fine manners (particularly in the early dramas) is of the type cultivated by Englishmen Italianate —for instance, Osric's ridiculous courtesies in *Hamlet*. Pandarus actually calls Cressida by an Italian pet-name, *capocchia*.[8] But lastly, there is an all-pervading use of Greek and Latin imagery and decorative reference, which is sometimes superficial but more often incomparably effective. Think of the aubade in *Cymbeline*:[9]

> Hark, hark, the lark at heaven's gate sings,
>   And Phoebus 'gins arise,
> His steeds to water at those springs
>   On chaliced flowers that lies.

Or of Perdita's garland:[10]

> . . . violets dim,
> But sweeter than the lids of Juno's eyes
> Or Cytherea's breath.

Or of Hamlet's godlike father:[11]

> See, what a grace was seated on this brow;
> Hyperion's curls, the front of Jove himself,
> An eye like Mars, to threaten and command,
> A station like the herald Mercury
> New lighted on a heaven-kissing hill.

Or of the idyllic love-duet:[12]

> In such a night
> Stood Dido with a willow in her hand
> Upon the wild sea-banks, and waft her love
> To come again to Carthage.

The poet who wrote like that knew and loved the classics.

The power of the classical world on Shakespeare can also be proved negatively. We have seen how many of the writers of the Renaissance belonged spiritually to both worlds: that of the Middle Ages, with knights and ladies and enchanters and magical animals and strange quests and impossible beliefs, and that of Greco-Roman myth and art. Such, for example, were Ariosto, and Rabelais, and Spenser. But Shakespeare, like Milton, rejected and practically ignored the world of the Middle Ages. Even his historical dramas are contemporary in tone, far more than they are medieval: who could dream that Sir John Falstaff was supposed to be a contemporary of the Canterbury Pilgrims?

It is significant to observe Shakespeare's few allusions to medieval thought: they are pretty or quaint, but they show that he did not feel the Middle Ages vital and stimulating. Mistress Quickly, when describing the death of Falstaff, declares that he must be in heaven. The biblical phrase is 'in Abraham's bosom', but the hostess says:

> He's in Arthur's bosom, if ever man went to Arthur's bosom,

for unconsciously she finds it easier to think of Sir John being received by the old symbol of immortal British chivalry than by a Hebrew patriarch.[13] Again, one of the men whom Shakespeare most despises, Mr. Justice Shallow, explains the technique of drill by recalling 'a little quiver fellow' whom he knew when he himself played 'Sir Dagonet in Arthur's show'.[14] And sometimes there are echoes of the Middle Ages in proverbs and in songs: Edgar as a madman sings snatches of old ballads, among them a beautiful anachronism which was to inspire another English poet to revive the medieval tradition:

> Child Rowland to the dark tower came.[15]

The only important element in Shakespeare's work which can really be called medieval is the supernatural: Oberon and his fairies, the witches and their spells. Even in that there are Hellenic touches, and the rest has been shrunk and softened by distance, the fairies have grown smaller and kinder, the gargoyles and fiends have vanished for ever.

Now we must analyse Shakespeare's classical knowledge in more detail. The first fact we observe is that he knows much more and feels much more sensitively about Rome than about Greece, with the single exception of the Greek myths which reached the modern world through Rome. The Roman plays—plus some anachronisms and some solidly English touches—are like Rome. The Greek plays are not like Greece. Although Shakespeare took several of his best plots from the Roman biographies of Plutarch, he almost entirely ignored the Greek statesmen whom Plutarch described as *parallel* to his Roman heroes, and used only Alcibiades and Timon. In *Timon of Athens* itself there are only two or three Greek names; all the rest are Latin—some of them, such as Varro and Isidore, ridiculously inappropriate; and the Athenian state is represented by senators, which shows that Shakespeare wrongly imagined it to be a republic like Rome. It is true that in *Troilus and Cressida* his warriors were not the anachronistic chevaliers who appear in the medieval romances of Troy; and that he has borrowed some things from the *Iliad*—the duel of Hector and Ajax, the speech of Ulysses in 1. 3. 78 f., the stupidity of Ajax, and certainly the character of Thersites, who does not appear in the romances.[16] (No doubt he had been reading Chapman's translation of *Iliad*, 1-2 and 7–11, which came out in 1598.) But even so, the whole play is not merely anti-heroic: it is a distant, ignorant, and unconvincing caricature of Greece.

The Roman plays are far more real and elaborate in detail than the Greek. Sometimes they are wrong in secondary matters like costume and furniture. But the touches of reality in the Greek dramas are fewer, and the anachronisms are far worse: Hector quotes Aristotle,[17] Pandarus talks of Friday and Sunday,[18] and the brothers Antipholus are the long-lost sons of an abbess.[19] In the Roman plays there are few large misrepresentations and much deep insight into character. The strong, law-abiding, patriotic plebeians of the early republic appear in *Coriolanus*, because of Shakespeare's contempt for the mob, as an excitable degenerate rabble like the idle creatures of *Julius Caesar*. Antony is made a much better man than he was; but there Shakespeare has exercised the dramatist's right to re-create character, and has made him a hero with a fault, like Leicester, like Essex, like Bacon, like so many great men of the Renaissance. For the rest, he has rendered better than anyone else, better even than the sources which he used, the essence of the Roman republic and its aristocracy. On the other hand, the Athenian noble Alcibiades, who appears in *Timon*, was a complex personality who would have much interested Shakespeare if he had known anything about him; but he never understood the Greeks enough to portray him properly.

Just as Shakespeare has more command over Roman than Greek themes, so the spirit of his tragic plays is much less Greek than Roman. Of course the Greeks founded and developed drama; without them, neither we nor the Romans could have written tragedies; and most of the essentials of Latin as of modern tragedy are borrowed from them. Nevertheless, the English Renaissance playwrights did not as a rule know Greek tragedy, and they did know Seneca, whose tragedies appeared severally in translation from 1559 onwards, and complete in 1581. Less than ten years later the sharp and satirical Nashe was sneering at the writers who from Seneca 'read by candlelight' copied 'whole *Hamlets*, I should say handfuls, of tragical speeches'.[20] Ghosts, and revenge, and the horrors of treachery, bloody cruelty, and kinsmen's murder, and a spirit of frenzied violence unlike the Hellenic loftiness—these Shakespeare found in Seneca, and he converted them into the sombre fury of his tragedies.

Shakespeare's free use of Greek and Latin imagery has already been mentioned. He is fluent and happy in his classical allusions. No writer who dislikes the classics, who receives no real stimulus from them, who brings in Greek and Roman decorations merely to parade his learning or to satisfy convention, can create so many apt and beautiful classical symbols as Shakespeare. Except the simplest fools and yokels, all his characters—from Hamlet to Pistol, from Rosalind to Portia—can command Greek and Latin reminiscences to enhance the grace and emotion of their speech. It is of course clear that Shakespeare was not a bookman. Miss Spurgeon's analysis of his similes and metaphors[21] shows that the fields from which he preferred to draw likenesses were, in order: *daily life* (social types, sport, trades, &c.), *nature* (in particular, growing things and weather), *domestic life* and *bodily actions* (which are surely both very closely connected with 'daily life'), *animals*, and then, after all these, *learning*. And even within the range of his learning Shakespeare's classical knowledge occupies a comparatively small space. He knew more about mythology than about ancient history—he knew the classical myths far better than the Bible. But he had far fewer classical symbols present to his mind than Marlowe. Learning meant little to him unless he could translate it into living human terms. It is mostly his pedants who quote the classics by book and author, and such quotations are either weak or ridiculous, and almost always inappropriate, as when Touchstone tells his poor virgin:

'I am here with thee and thy goats, as the most capricious poet, honest Ovid, was among the Goths.'[22]

But the classical images which, for Shakespeare, emerge from books to become as real as animals, and colours, and stars—these images are used so strikingly as to show that classical culture was for him a spectacle not less vivid, though smaller, than the life around him. The loveliest, most loving girl in his plays, waiting for her wedding-night, gazes at the bright sky, sees the sun rushing on towards evening, and urges it to hurry, hurry, even at the risk of destroying the world. She does not say so: the direct wish would be too extravagant; but it is conveyed by the superb image:

> Gallop apace, you fiery-footed steeds,
> Towards Phoebus' lodging; such a waggoner
> As Phaethon would whip you to the west,
> And bring in cloudy night immediately.[23]

It would scarcely be possible to distinguish between Greek and Roman imagery in the plays; at most one might point to the predominance of Rome among his historical images. But in language it is clear that, as Ben Jonson said, Shakespeare had 'small Latin and less Greek'.[24] He uses only three or four Greek words.[25] He does bring in Latin words and phrases, but not so freely as many of his contemporaries, and with less sureness than he uses French and Italian. Latin is quoted most freely in the early plays. *Love's Labour's Lost* has a comic schoolmaster who talks Latin,[26] but, like the rest of Shakespeare's latinists, he is not a really learned pedant, on the same level as the Limousin student in Rabelais.[27] He can only string a few schoolbook Latin words together—

and this in a play where Berowne's speech on love introduces
some exquisite classical allusions, used with fine imaginative
freedom:

> Subtle as Sphinx: as sweet and musical
> As bright Apollo's lute, strung with his hair.[28]

Few are the sentences in Shakespeare that seem to have been suggested by a direct memory of a Latin phrase, while in Milton,
Tasso, Jonson, Ronsard, and other Renaissance poets they are
myriad. But he often uses English words of Latin derivation in
such a way as to show that he understands their origin and root-
meaning. Occasionally he makes an eccentric attempt to 'despu-
mate the Latial verbocination', such as the word *juvenal* for
youngster; and when he experiments with the importation of Latin
into English he is as likely to fail (*exsufflicate* in *Othello*, 3.3.182)
as to succeed (*impartial* in *Richard II*, 1.1.115). All this matters
little. Shakespeare wrote the English language.

To quote phrases from Roman poetry, either in Latin or in
translation, and to imitate striking passages, was not pedantry in
the Renaissance poets. As we have seen,[29] it was one of their
methods of adding beauty and authority to their work. The taste
and learning of the individual poet determined how frequently he
would use quotations, how far he would disguise or emphasize
them, how carefully he would follow the original text or how freely
he would adapt memorable words, images, and ideas. No great
modern writer has ever surpassed Milton in his ability to embellish
his work with jewels cut by other craftsmen. Of the Renaissance
dramatists Ben Jonson, easily the best scholar, was much the
busiest borrower and the most sedulous translator: some of his
most important speeches are almost literal renderings of passages
from the Roman historians who gave him his plots. Compared
with Milton and Jonson, Shakespeare quotes the classics seldom;
but by other standards (for instance, in comparison with Racine)
he quotes freely and often.

Ben Jonson's judgement of Shakespeare's classical knowledge
has often been misquoted, and often teased into a comparative
rather than an absolute judgement: that Shakespeare merely knew
less Latin and much less Greek than Jonson—which would still
allow him to be a fair scholar. But the way in which Shakespeare

quotes the classics is, like his use of Latin words, proof that Jonson was literally correct. Shakespeare did not know much of the Latin language, he knew virtually no Greek, and he was vague and unscholarly in using what he did know. But he used it nearly all with the flair of a great imaginative artist. What Jonson could have added, and what we must not forget, is that Shakespeare loved Latin and Greek literature. What he had been taught at school he remembered, he improved his knowledge afterwards by reading translations, and he used both what he remembered and what he got from translations as verbal embellishment, decorative imagery, and plot material throughout his career.

Beginning in 1767 with Richard Farmer's *Learning of Shakespeare*, there have been many, many discussions of Shakespeare's use of his classical sources—too many to treat here. It is a specialist field of considerable interest, still incompletely covered, since not many scholars who know enough about Shakespeare and his time have had the classical training which would enable them to make all the right connexions. Its chief value for the general reader is that it keeps him from conceiving Shakespeare as an Ariel warbling his native woodnotes wild. Shakespeare was indeed part Ariel; but he was more Prospero, with volumes that he prized above a dukedom.[10]

The most convenient way to assess Shakespeare's classical equipment and the use to which he put it is to distinguish the authors he knew well from those he knew imperfectly or at second hand. The difficulty of making this investigation accurate is the same difficulty that meets every student of the transmission of artistic and spiritual influence. It is seldom easy to decide whether a similarity between the thought or expression of two writers means that one has copied the other. It is particularly hard when one of those writers is as great as Shakespeare, whose soul was so copious, whose eloquence was so fluent. We can be sure, for instance, that he had not read Aeschylus. Yet what can we say when we find some of Aeschylus' thoughts appearing in Shakespeare's plays? The only explanation is that great poets in times and countries distant from each other often have similar thoughts and express them similarly. On the other hand, we are reluctant to believe that, given the opportunity, a great writer would borrow anything valuable from a lesser man. Yet some resemblances are too striking to be denied; and it is folly to imagine that Shakespeare could take his plot from one book and his names from another and yet balk at borrowing a fine image from a third.

This is perhaps a suitable place to suggest a simple set of rules by which parallel passages in two writers can be taken to establish the dependence of one on the other. First, it must be shown that one writer read, or probably read, the other's work. Then a close similarity of thought or imagery must be demonstrated. Thirdly, there should be a clear structural parallelism: in the sequence of the reasoning, in the structure of the sentences, in the position of the words within the lines of poetry, or in some or all of these together.

Sometimes it is impossible to prove that the later writer read the works of the earlier, but possible to conjecture that he heard them discussed. In periods of great intellectual activity a man with a lively imagination and a retentive memory often picks up great ideas not from the books which contain them (and which may be closed to him) but from the conversation of his friends and from adaptations of them in the work of his contemporaries. We know that Ben Jonson was a good scholar. We know that Shakespeare had long and lively discussions with him. Often Jonson must have tried to break the rapier of Shakespeare's imagination with the bludgeon of a learned quotation or an abstruse philosophical doctrine, only to find Shakespeare, in a later tournament or even in a play produced next season, using the weapon that had once been Jonson's, now lightened, remodelled, and apparently moulded to Shakespeare's own hand. The channels by which remote but valuable ideas reach imaginative writers are as complex and difficult to retrace as those by which they learn their psychology and subtilize their sense of words; but in estimating a various-minded man like Shakespeare we must make the widest possible allowance for his power of assimilating classical ideas from the classical atmosphere that surrounded him.

There is a good example of this in one of Shakespeare's most imaginative scenes. Plato made known to the modern world the noble idea that the physical universe is a group of eight concentric spheres, each of which, as it turns, sings one note; and that the notes of the eight blend into a divine harmony, which we can hear only after death when we have escaped from this prison of flesh. Somewhere Shakespeare had heard this. He had not read it in Plato: because he altered it—freely, and, for a student of

Plato, wrongly, but, for all his readers, superbly. In a scene where two lovers have already recalled much beauty from classical legend and poetry, he made Lorenzo tell his mistress, not that the Ptolemaic spheres sang eight harmonious notes, but (with a reminiscence of the time when 'the morning stars sang together') that every single star in the sky sang while it moved, with the angels as the audience of the divine concert:

> There's not the smallest orb which thou behold'st
> But in his motion like an angel sings,
> Still quiring to the young-eyed cherubins;
> Such harmony is in immortal souls;
> But, whilst this muddy vesture of decay
> Doth grossly close us in, we cannot hear it.[31]

Shakespeare was therefore, directly and indirectly, a classically educated poet who loved the classics. They were his chief book-education. They were one of the greatest challenges to his creative power. His classical training was wholly successful, because it taught him their beauties at school, encouraged him to continue his reading of the classics in mature life, and helped to make him a complete poet, and a whole man.

He knew three classical authors well, a fourth partially, and a number of others fragmentarily. Ovid, Seneca, and Plutarch enriched his mind and his imagination. Plautus gave him material for one play and trained him for others. From Vergil and other authors he took stories, isolated thoughts, and similes, sometimes of great beauty. Because of his early training he was able to respond to the manifold stimuli which the reading of translations gave to his creative genius.

Shakespeare's favourite classical author was Ovid. Like other English schoolboys of the time, he very probably learnt some Ovid at school.[32] He read him later, both in the original Latin and in Golding's translation of the *Metamorphoses*. He often imitated him, from his first work to his last. His friends knew this. In a survey of contemporary literature published in 1598 Francis Meres said Shakespeare was a reincarnation of Ovid:

'As the soul of Euphorbus was thought to live in Pythagoras, so the sweet witty soul of Ovid lives in mellifluous and honey-tongued Shakespeare; witness his Venus and Adonis, his Lucrece, his sugared sonnets among his private friends.'[33]

The first book he published, and, according to him, the first he wrote,[34] was a sumptuous blending and elaboration of two Greek myths which he found in Ovid's *Metamorphoses*;[35] and he prefaced it with a couplet from Ovid's *Loves*.[36] The quotation throws a valuable light on his artistic ideals. It reads

> Vilia miretur vulgus; mihi flavus Apollo
> pocula Castalia plena ministret aqua;

which means

> Let cheap things please the mob; may bright Apollo
> serve me full draughts from the Castalian spring.

His other long poem, *The Rape of Lucrece*, is based partly on Livy, partly on Ovid's *Fasti*, with several close correspondences of language and thought.[37]

Several quotations of Ovid's own words are scattered through the plays. In *The Taming of the Shrew* Lucentio poses as a Latin tutor in order to make love to Bianca. He conveys his message to her through the device used by schoolboys in classroom repetition and convicts in hymn-singing:

Bianca: Where left we last?

Lucentio: Here, madam:
  Hac ibat Simois; hic est Sigeia tellus;
  Hic steterat Priami regia celsa senis.

Bianca: Construe them.

Lucentio: Hac ibat, as I told you before, Simois, I am Lucentio, hic est, son unto Vincentio of Pisa, Sigeia tellus, disguised thus to get your love; Hic steterat, and that Lucentio that comes a-wooing, Priami, is my man Tranio, regia, bearing my port, celsa senis, that we might beguile the old pantaloon.[38]

(Of course the translation is not meant to make sense, but there is an allusion to the original meaning in 'the old pantaloon'.)

Direct quotations also occur in two of the doubtful plays.[39] And there is one very famous echo which Shakespeare has made his own. The name of the fairy queen in *A Midsummer-Night's Dream* is not taken from Celtic legend like her husband's. It is a Greco-Latin word, Titania, which means 'Titan's daughter' or 'Titan's sister'. The name is well liked by Ovid, who uses it five times, and, in the two best-known passages, of Diana and Circe.[40] From these two queens of air and darkness and from their melodious title, Shakespeare has created a new and not less enchanting spirit.

Golding's translation of Ovid's *Metamorphoses* was a coarse free version in lumbering 'fourteeners', very unlike the suave graceful original. But Shakespeare could read the original, he had incomparable taste, and, as T. S. Eliot has remarked,[41] he 'had that ability, which is not native to everyone, to extract the utmost possible from translations'. Therefore several fine passages, which we now regard as heirs of his own invention, were borrowed—no, not borrowed, but transmuted from Ovid through the Golding translation.

> Like as the waves make towards the pebbled shore,
> So do our minutes hasten to their end;
> Each changing place with that which goes before,
> In sequent toil all forwards to contend.

This famous quatrain in Sonnet 60 is a transmutation of Ovid, as Englished by Golding:

> As every wave drives others forth, and that which comes behind
> Both thrusteth and is thrust himself: even so the times by kind
> Do fly and follow both at once, and evermore renew.[42]

But that is only one aspect of a complex philosophical idea, the idea that nature is constantly changing, so that nothing is permanent and yet nothing is destroyed. This is expounded in the sermon of Pythagoras towards the end of the *Metamorphoses*, and is the theme of several of Shakespeare's finest sonnets.[43]

There is, however, not much philosophy in either Ovid or Shakespeare—indeed, one of Shakespeare's characters explicitly distinguishes Ovid and philosophy, implying that the former is far more delightful.[44] But most of the *Metamorphoses* is concerned with sex and the supernatural, both of which interested Shakespeare. His most sensual poem, *Venus and Adonis*, was inspired, as we have seen, by episodes in the *Metamorphoses*. Again, when Juliet says:

> Thou may'st prove false; at lovers' perjuries,
> They say, Jove laughs,

she is quoting Ovid's *Art of Love*,[45] the book which Lucentio also says is his special subject.[46] In his other great love-drama Shakespeare based the character of Cleopatra on Dido as drawn by Ovid,

and actually made her quote an angry line from Dido's reproaches.[47]
As for magic, Prospero's incantation in *The Tempest*:

> Ye elves of hills, brooks, standing lakes, and groves;
> And ye, that on the sands with printless foot
> Do chase the ebbing Neptune and do fly him
> When he comes back; you demi-puppets, that
> By moonshine do the green sour ringlets make
> Whereof the ewe not bites; and you, whose pastime
> Is to make midnight mushrooms; that rejoice
> To hear the solemn curfew; by whose aid—
> Weak masters though ye be—I have bedimmed
> The noontide sun, called forth the mutinous winds,
> And 'twixt the green sea and the azured vault
> Set roaring war: to the dread-rattling thunder
> Have I given fire, and rifted Jove's stout oak
> With his own bolt; the strong-based promontory
> Have I made shake; and by the spurs plucked up
> The pine and cedar; graves at my command
> Have waked their sleepers, oped, and let them forth
> By my so potent art[48]. . . .

this splendid speech, apart from some light, inappropriate, and
quite British fairy-lore, is based on Medea's invocation in Ovid,
Met. 7. 197 f., as translated by Golding, thus:

Ye Ayres and Windes; ye Elves of Hilles, of Brookes, of Woods alone,
Of standing Lakes, and of the Night approche ye everychone.
Through helpe of whom (the crooked bankes much wondring at the
   thing)
I have compelled streames to run cleane backward to their spring.
By charmes I make the calme Seas rough, and make ye rough Seas plaine
And cover all the Skie with Cloudes, and chase them thence againe.
By charmes I rayse and lay the windes, and burst the Vipers jaw,
And from the bowels of the Earth both stones and trees doe drawe.
Whole Woods and Forestes I remove: I make the Mountains shake,
And even the Earth it selfe to grone and fearfully to quake.
I call up dead men from their graves; and thee O Lightsome Moone
I darken oft, though beaten brasse abate thy perill soone.
Our Sorcerie dimmes the Morning faire, and darkes ye Sun at Noone.

Some of the ingredients of the witches' cauldron in *Macbeth*[49] came
from Medea's pharmacopoeia in Ovid,[50] which also provided the
vaporous drop profound that hangs upon the corner of the moon.[51]

In another field, it was Golding's rather Jorrocksy translation of Actaeon's kennel-book[52] that inspired the heroic hunting-conversation in *A Midsummer-Night's Dream*.[53] A number of passages contain explicit references to Ovid's own personality[54] and to his books.[55] But Shakespeare's greatest debt to Ovid is visible all through his plays. It was the world of fable which the *Metamorphoses* opened to him, and which he used as freely as he used the world of visible humanity around him, now making a tale of star-crossed lovers into a clownish farce,[56] and now exalting the myth of Pygmalion to symbolize a higher love.[57]

Shakespeare knew one other Latin author fairly well. This was that enigmatic and decadent figure Seneca, the Stoic millionaire, Nero's tutor, minister, and victim, the Spanish philosopher who taught serene fulfilment of duty and wrote nine dramas of revenge, cruelty, and madness. For the English playwrights of the Renaissance Seneca was the master of tragedy; and even although, at first glance, Stoicism would not appear to be a creed sympathetic to that stirring age, the pithy energetic thinking of his letters and treatises impressed many contemporary writers. He is never quoted in the original by Shakespeare, except in the doubtful *Titus Andronicus*.[58] But he deeply influenced Shakespeare's conception of tragedy, and added certain elements of importance to his dramatic technique, while several memorable Shakespearian speeches are inspired by his work.[59]

Shakespeare's great tragedies are dominated by a hopeless fatalism which is far more pessimistic than the purifying agonies of Greek tragedy, and almost utterly godless. None of them shows any belief in 'the righteous government of the world', except in so far as successful evildoers are later punished for their own cruel schemes. Sometimes his tragic heroes speak of life as ruled by fate inhuman, unpredictable, and meaningless;[60] and sometimes, more bitterly, cry out against vicious mankind which is unfit to live,[61] and cruel gods who 'kill us for their sport'.[62] That much of this hopeless gloom came from Shakespeare's own heart, no one can doubt; but he found it expressed decisively and eloquently in the Stoical pessimism of Seneca.[63]

To the realization that life is directed by forces indifferent or hostile to man's hopes, there are several possible responses. One, which Seneca's philosophy teaches, is taciturn indifference:

emotionless, or even proud, obedience to an irresistible fate. This philosophical disdain of external events occasionally appeared in the Renaissance, where it was strengthened by chivalrous (particularly Spanish) traditions. Shakespeare's heroes usually die in eloquence, but some of his villains withdraw into Stoical silence, and the Stoicism which challenges and even welcomes death appears in the death-scenes of later Elizabethan dramatists.[64] Another response is a furious protest, the yell of suffering given words, the raving self-assertion which grows close to madness. The two responses both appear in Seneca's own works. The Elizabethans, and Shakespeare in particular, preferred the second. We hear it in the ranting of Laertes and Hamlet in Ophelia's grave,[65] in Hotspur's boasts,[66] in Timon's curses.[67] Not so much single speeches as the general tone of tremendous emotional pressure in his tragedies, of a boiling energy which repression only increases and which threatens to erupt at every moment—that, however strengthened by the pains and ardours of his own life and increased by the excitements of the Renaissance, is Shakespeare's inheritance from Seneca.

In technique, the general Elizabethan use of stock Senecan characters—ghosts, witches, and others—has already been mentioned.[68] It has also been suggested that Shakespeare's gloomy, introspective, self-dramatizing heroes are partly inspired by those of Seneca, so unlike the heroes of Greek tragedy.[69] There was moreover an interesting device of dramatic verse invented by the Greeks, which reached Shakespeare and his contemporaries through Seneca's plays. It was a series of repartees in single lines, or occasionally half-lines, in which two opponents strove to out-argue one another, often echoing each other's words and often putting their arguments in the form of competing philosophical maxims. Called stichomythia, it sounds in Euripides and Seneca like a philosophers' debate; in the Elizabethans it is more like the rapid thrust and counter-thrust of fencing. It is most noticeable in Shakespeare's early play, *Richard III*, where the hero and the plot are also shaped on Senecan models.[70]

A number of scenes in Shakespeare's histories and tragedies are closely parallel in thought or imagery to passages in Seneca; and in some of them there are structural similarities also. There are examples in early plays—*Richard III* and *King John*—and in *Titus Andronicus* and *Henry VI*;[71] but there are also several striking instances in that great tragedy of witchcraft, oracles, ghosts, murder, and madness, *Macbeth*. After his stepmother has polluted him by an attempted seduction, Seneca's Hippolytus cries out:

> What Tanais will wash me? what Maeotis,
> urging strange floods into the Pontic sea?
> No, not the mighty father with all his Ocean
> will wash away such sin.[72]

In a second tragedy Seneca elaborates the same idea, adding the dreadful half-line:

> deep the deed will cling.[73]

This is certainly the model for the great scenes in which Macbeth and Lady Macbeth, married in their sin like two parts of a guilty soul, vainly hope to clean the hands stained with their crime:

> Will all great Neptune's ocean wash this blood
> Clean from my hand? No, this my hand will rather
> The multitudinous seas incarnadine. . . .

and later, in the woman's words:

> All the perfumes of Arabia will not sweeten this little hand.[74]

Again, after recovering from his murderous frenzy, Seneca's Hercules says:

> Why this my soul should linger in the world
> there's now no reason. Lost are all my goods—
> mind, weapons, glory, wife, children, strength,
> even my madness.[75]

Even so Macbeth, at the end of his crimes, mutters:

> I have lived long enough: my way of life
> Is fallen into the sear, the yellow leaf;
> And that which should accompany old age,
> As honour, love, obedience, troops of friends,
> I must not look to have.[76]

In the same passage[77] Hercules cries:

> A mind polluted
> No one can cure.

And in the same scene[78] Macbeth asks:

> Canst thou not minister to a mind diseased?

Other Senecan parallels in *Macbeth* are no less powerful.[79]

The third of Shakespeare's favourite classical authors was Plutarch, the Greek moralist and biographer who wrote *Parallel Lives* of Greek and Roman statesmen. Plutarch entered western culture in 1559 through the fine translation made by Jacques Amyot. (Montaigne was one of its most enthusiastic readers, and it continued to be part of French thought for centuries: we shall see it as one of the forces inspiring the French Revolution.)[80] Sir Thomas North turned Amyot's version into English in 1579, and through him Plutarch became the author who made the greatest single new impression on Shakespeare. *Julius Caesar*, *Coriolanus*, *Antony and Cleopatra*, and *Timon of Athens* all come from the *Lives*. Plutarch was not a great historian. North was not an accurate translator. Shakespeare was sometimes careless in adapting material from him,[81] sometimes almost echoic in versifying his prose. Yet the results were superb.

Once again we see how incalculably various, how unpredictably fertile, is the stimulus of classical culture. The tradesman's son who attended an unimportant provincial school, who was far from scholarly and went to no university, who toured and acted and collaborated and adapted and wrote plays from all sorts of material, who read Latin keenly but sketchily and Greek not at all, who was more moved by life than by any books, still was so moved in middle life by a second-hand English translation of a second-rate Greek historian that he wrought it into dramas far more tense and vigorous, far more delicate in psychical perception, far fuller in emotion than the biographical essays that introduced him to Roman history.[82] Long afterwards a young English student who wanted to be a poet was lent the translation of Homer made by one of Shakespeare's contemporaries. After reading and thinking all night, he wrote a poem saying it had been for him like a new planet for an astronomer, or, for an explorer, a new ocean. And so for Shakespeare the reading of Plutarch was an unimagined revelation. It showed him serious history instead of playful myth. And it showed him more. Listen.

> Since Cassius first did whet me against Caesar,
> I have not slept.
> Between the acting of a dreadful thing
> And the first motion, all the interim is
> Like a phantasma, or a hideous dream.[83]

That is a new voice. It is the voice of Brutus. But beyond it we can hear the sombre brooding voices of Macbeth; of Hamlet. *Julius Caesar*, the first of Shakespeare's plays from Plutarch and one of his greatest dramas, marked a climax in his experience. It was his entrance into the realm of high tragedy.[84]

Analysis of Shakespeare's sources will not dull, but intensify, our admiration for his art. To read a chapter of North's plain prose, full of interesting but straightforward facts, and then to see the facts, in Shakespeare's hand, begin to glow with inward life and the words to move and chime in immortal music, is to realize once again that poets are not (as Plato said) copyists, but seers, or creators.[85] Take North's version of Plutarch's life of Caesar, chapters 62.4 to 63.3. The passage deals with the jealousies, hatreds, and omens threatening Caesar's life. Every single sentence in it is used by Shakespeare in *Julius Caesar*, but the details, instead of being crowded together, are scattered over the first three acts. What Plutarch made flat narrative, Shakespeare makes energetic description or crescendo action. As a dramatist, he initiates at least one important change. Plutarch speaks of Caesar as suspecting and even fearing Cassius. Shakespeare could not make an heroic figure out of an apprehensive dictator: he felt that if Caesar had really feared Cassius he would have protected himself or eliminated the danger; doubtless he remembered the many anecdotes of Caesar's remarkable courage. Therefore he altered these incidents, to show Caesar not indeed as quite fearless, but as affecting the imperturbability of marble. Plutarch writes:

'Caesar also had Cassius in great jealousy and suspected him much: whereupon he said . . . to his friends, "What will Cassius do, think ye? I like not his pale looks." Another time, when Caesar's friends complained unto him of Antonius and Dolabella, . . . he answered them again, "As for those fat men and smooth-combed heads," quoth he, "I never reckon of them; but these pale-visaged and carrion lean people, I fear them most." '

In Shakespeare's mind, this changed into:

Caesar: Let me have men about me that are fat;
    Sleek-headed men and such as sleep o' nights.
    Yond Cassius has a lean and hungry look;
    He thinks too much; such men are dangerous.

Antony: Fear him not, Caesar, he's not dangerous;
    He is a noble Roman, and well given.

Caesar: Would he were fatter! but I fear him not:
Yet if my name were liable to fear,
I do not know the man I should avoid
So soon as that spare Cassius.[86]

Again, Plutarch mentions the omen of the sacrificial victim which had no heart; but all he can add is the obvious comment 'and that was a strange thing in nature, how a beast could live without a heart'. Shakespeare cannot show the sacrifice on the stage. But he has the omen reported, and invents a lofty reply for Caesar:[87]

Caesar: What say the augurers?
Servant: They would not have you to stir forth today.
Plucking the entrails of an offering forth,
They could not find a heart within the beast.
Caesar: The gods do this in shame of cowardice:
Caesar should be a beast without a heart
If he should stay at home today for fear.

So indeed Caesar must, or should, have spoken.

One example is enough to show how Shakespeare turns Plutarch's prose descriptions into poetry—keeping the touches of beauty which were part of the original scene described, colouring it with fancies and images, and adding his own eloquence. In chapter 26 of his life of Marcus Antonius, Plutarch describes the first appearance of Cleopatra:

'Therefore, when she was sent unto by divers letters, both from Antonius himself, and also from his friends, she made so light of it and mocked Antonius so much, that she disdained to set forward otherwise, but to take her barge in the river of Cydnus, the poop whereof was of gold, the sails of purple, and the oars of silver, which kept stroke in rowing after the sound of the music of flutes, howboys, citherns, viols, and such other instruments as they played upon in the barge. And now for the person of herself: she was laid under a pavilion of cloth of gold of tissue, apparelled and attired like the goddess Venus commonly drawn in picture; and hard by her, on either hand of her, pretty fair boys apparelled as painters do set forth god Cupid, with little fans in their hands, with the which they fanned wind upon her. Her Ladies and gentlewomen also, the fairest of them, were apparelled like the nymphs Nereides (which are the mermaids of the waters) and like the Graces, some steering the helm, others tending the tackle and ropes of the barge, out of the which there came a wonderful passing sweet savour of perfumes, that perfumed the wharf's side, pestered with innumerable multitudes of people. Some of them followed the barge all alongst the river's side; others also ran out of the city to see her coming in. So that in th' end, there ran such multitudes of people one after another to see her, that Antonius was left post alone in the market place in his Imperial seat to give audience.'

In Shakespeare[88] this becomes:

Enobarbus: When she first met Mark Antony she pursed up his heart, upon the river of Cydnus.

Agrippa: There she appeared indeed, or my reporter devised well for her.

Enobarbus: I will tell you.
    The barge she sat in, like a burnished throne,
    Burned on the water; the poop was beaten gold,
    Purple the sails, and so perfumed, that
    The winds were love-sick with them, the oars were silver
    Which to the tune of flutes kept stroke, and made
    The water which they beat to follow faster,
    As amorous of their strokes. For her own person,
    It beggared all description; she did lie
    In her pavilion—cloth-of-gold of tissue—
    O'er-picturing that Venus where we see
    The fancy outwork nature; on each side her
    Stood pretty dimpled boys, like smiling Cupids,
    With divers-coloured fans, whose wind did seem
    To glow the delicate cheeks which they did cool,
    And what they undid did.

Agrippa: O! rare for Antony!

Enobarbus: Her gentlewomen, like the Nereides,
    So many mermaids, tended her i' the eyes,
    And made their bends adornings; at the helm
    A seeming mermaid steers; the silken tackle
    Swell with the touches of those flower-soft hands,
    That yarely frame the office. From the barge
    A strange invisible perfume hits the sense
    Of the adjacent wharfs. The city cast
    Her people out upon her, and Antony,
    Enthroned i' the market-place, did sit alone,
    Whistling to the air; which, but for vacancy,
    Had gone to gaze on Cleopatra too,
    And made a gap in nature.

Agrippa: Rare Egyptian!

Nearly every phrase in North contains something flat, or repetitious, or clumsy: 'and such other instruments as they played upon in the barge'; 'apparelled and attired'; 'commonly drawn in picture'; 'with the which they fanned wind upon her'; 'a wonderful passing sweet savour of perfumes that perfumed'. And consider the structure of the first sentence. It is still possible for the reader to understand that the scene was exquisitely beautiful; but the words dull it. Shakespeare omits or emends the infelicities, invents his own graces, and adds verbal harmonies, which, like the perfumes of Cleopatra's sails, draw the world after them.

Ovid, Seneca, Plutarch: these were Shakespeare's chief classical sources. A fourth author helped him early in his career, but did not stay long with him. This was the Roman comedian Plautus.

In *The Brothers Menaechmus* Plautus told (from the Greek) a merry tale of identical twins separated in childhood, grown to manhood ignorant of each other, and suddenly brought together in the city where one has a wife and a home while the other, his exact duplicate, is a stranger. The resulting confusions and the ultimate recognition made a good comedy. This was the basic plot Shakespeare used in *The Comedy of Errors*; but, by adding a great deal to it, he improved it. He altered the names of the characters, and changed the locale from a little-known port to a famous city. He made the twin brothers have identical twin servants—multiplying the confusion by eight, at least. He made the stranger brother fall in love with his twin's sister-in-law. He made the early separation more real by making it more pathetic: the father who has lost both sons appears in the first scene, under sentence of death as an enemy alien, and only in the last scene, where he meets his sons and his wife supposed dead, is he reprieved.

Some of these enlargements Shakespeare himself invented. Some he took from sources outside the drama: the shipwreck, apparently, from the romance *Apollonius of Tyre*. But the grand complication, the creation of twin servants, he took from another of Plautus' comedies, *Amphitryon*. And a careful reading of *The Comedy of Errors* with Plautus' two plays will show that Shakespeare did not merely lift the idea from *Amphitryon* and insert it *en bloc* into the other play, but blended the two plays in an organic fusion to make a new and richer drama.

Amphitryon was not translated into English until long after Shakespeare was dead. The only known translation of *The Brothers Menaechmus* was printed in 1595, some years after the accepted date for Shakespeare's *Comedy of Errors*. The conclusion is virtually certain. Shakespeare read Plautus' comedies in the original Latin.[89] He used them just as he used the stories he took from all his other sources—as a basis of interwoven action which he made into poetry by adding deeply human characterization and the poetry of his own inimitable words. As a result *The Comedy of Errors* is more of a drama than most of Plautus' comedies: more carefully wrought, more finely characterized, more various, less funny but more moving, and, despite its naughtiness, nobler in moral tone.[90]

Still, the limitations of his classical knowledge came out clearly in his adaptation of Plautus. They are those we have noticed already. For a great imaginative poet, they were not defects but advantages. We must, however, recognize their existence. Shakespeare knew Latin enough to get the story of the plays when he read them, but not enough to appreciate the language as well as the dramatic art of the poet. Plautus is a very witty writer, full of puns and deft verbal twists and comic volubility. Anyone who can read his language fluently is bound to be infected by the rattling gaiety of his words. Shakespeare (who could not even get the name of Epidamnus right) failed, in *The Comedy of Errors*, to take over Plautus' verbal skill, although he mastered his plotting and surpassed his characterization. But we cannot be anything but grateful for this. A more intimate knowledge of the style of other comedians might well have hindered the development of Shakespeare's own incomparable eloquence. If he had stopped at *Lucrece* and *The Comedy of Errors*, we could regret that his classical learning was so much inferior to Marlowe's, to Spenser's, to Milton's. But even then, he was Ovid reincarnated; and now he became Plautus romanticized. He was still growing and learning. Plautus gave him another part of his education: the ability to build a long story out of coincidences and complications which, although credible, were always fresh and unexpected. What Plautus might have given him in verbal dexterity he later achieved for himself; and thereby made his language indistinguishably a part of his own characters, the very voice of his own thought.

Other authors he knew, but only in outline, or by quotations learnt in school and remembered afterwards, or by extracts published in the Reader's Digest type of collections which were so common in the Renaissance. Some of them gave him a beautiful line or a powerful description, but none deeply affected his thought. In an exhaustive work called *William Shakspere's Small Latine and Lesse Greeke*, Mr. T. W. Baldwin has analysed the educational system of England in Shakespeare's boyhood, inferring from that, and from echoes in the dramas, what were the books he probably read in school. To begin with, Shakespeare used the standard Latin grammar written by the two great Renaissance educators, John Colet and William Lily, for he quotes and parodies it several times.[91] It contained many illustrative quotations from classical authors. Even if Shakespeare did not read their works, he remembered the excerpts, and used them as they were given in the grammar.[92] This accounts for some otherwise inexplicable coincidences: they are due to Shakespeare's memory for good poetry. For instance, one of his first Latin texts was a collection of pastoral poems by the Italian humanist Baptista Spagnuoli, known as Baptista Mantuanus. The schoolmaster Holofernes in *Love's Labour 's Lost* actually quotes a line from it and praises the poet.[93] Again, in *Hamlet*,[94] Laertes utters a beautiful epitaph over Ophelia:

> Lay her i' the earth,
> And from her fair and unpolluted flesh
> May violets spring!

It is impossible to escape the conclusion that this is a reminiscence of a sentence of the same shape, thought, and rhythm in the satirist Persius:[95]

> Now from his tomb and beatific ashes
> Won't violets grow?

Only it is equally impossible to believe that Shakespeare ever read that most difficult author. But Mr. Baldwin has pointed out that the passage from Persius is quoted in full in the explanatory notes on Mantuanus' elegies, where Shakespeare no doubt read and remembered it.[96]

Shakespeare also read some Vergil at school, but apparently only the early books, as elementary Latin pupils still do. The descriptions of the fall of Troy in *Lucrece*, 1366 f., and *Hamlet*, 2.2.481 f., are partly modelled on, partly exaggerated from Aeneas' account in *Aeneid*, 2; and the line with which Aeneas begins that famous history—

> You bid me, queen, renew a grief unspeakable

—is echoed at the opening of *The Comedy of Errors*:

> A heavier task could not have been imposed
> Than I to speak my griefs unspeakable.[97]

That standard text-book, Caesar's *Gallic War*—or at least the part dealing with Britain (a suitable selection for English beginners)—was also known to Shakespeare. In *2 Henry VI*[98] old Lord Say, attempting to persuade Jack Cade and his Kultur-Bolshcviks that they should not lynch him, quotes it:

> Kent, in the Commentaries Caesar writ,
> Is termed the civil'st place of all this isle.

Of Livy, Shakespeare knew at least the first book, with the story of Tarquin and Lucrece.[99]

From other classical authors, he seems to have known only a few memorable passages. For instance, when Brutus is facing his doom, he cries

> O Julius Caesar, thou art mighty yet!
> Thy spirit walks abroad, and turns our swords
> In our own proper entrails.[100]

Apparently this is an echo of the opening lines of Lucan's poem on the civil war:[101]

> a mighty nation,
> its conquering hand against its vitals turned.

Like everyone in the Renaissance, Shakespeare brings in scientific and other information from Pliny's *Natural History*, but without naming its author. And when Polonius accosts Hamlet,[102] and asks him what he is reading, the bitter reply:

'Slanders, sir: for the satirical rogue says here that old men have grey beards, that their faces are wrinkled, their eyes purging thick amber and plum-tree gum, and that they have a plentiful lack of wit, together with most weak hams'—

points to only one satirical rogue known to us: the Roman Juvenal, whose tenth satire contains a terrible description of the ugliness and weakness of old age.[103] Slight as these and other such reminiscences are, they show Shakespeare's liking for the classics, his sensitive ear, his retentive memory, and the transforming magic of his eloquence. Others, like Jonson, stud their pages with quotation-marks, and talk in italics. When Shakespeare's characters speak, only the pedants quote: the rest speak from the fullness of their own heart, and of his.

Shakespeare was an Englishman of the Renaissance. It was a wonderful time—scarcely less wonderful than the world's great ages of Greece and Rome which returned again in it. One of the vital events which then gave vigour to men's minds and depth to their souls was the rebirth of classical culture. It was not the only such event. There were revolutions, explorations, and discoveries in many other regions distant, although not utterly alien, from it. But it was one of the most important: for it was a revolution of the mind. Like all sensitive and educated men, Shakespeare shared in its excitements. It was one of his great spiritual experiences. True, England was more important to him; and so was the social life of contemporary Europe, with its subtleties, its humours, and its villainies; and most important of all was humanity. But he was not the unschooled poet of nature. For him great books were an essential part of life.

He had a fair introduction to the Latin language, not enough to make him a scholar, not enough to allow him to read it fluently, but enough to lead him (like Chaucer and Keats) to love Greek and Roman myth, poetry, and history. He lived among men who knew and admired classical literature, and he learnt from them. His first books were adaptations of Greco-Roman originals, affectionately elaborated and sumptuously adorned by his superb imagination. Until late in his career he continued to read and use translations of Greek and Latin books; twelve of his forty works (and those among the greatest) dealt with themes from classical antiquity; and classical imagery was an organic part of his poetry from first to last. Greek and Roman literature provided not only the rhetorical and dramatic patterns which he and the other Renaissance poets used, not only rich material to feed his imagination, but the challenge of noble humanity and of consummate art. To that challenge many great souls in the Renaissance responded, none more greatly than the man who had small Latin and less Greek.

12

THE RENAISSANCE AND AFTERWARDS

LYRIC POETRY

SONGS are the simplest, commonest, and most natural kind of poetry. The people of every nation, every little clan or county, make up their own songs, and sing them to their own tunes, and often dance with them. Songs need not all be gay. They and their music can be sorrowful, or stately and severe. They need not always make their hearers dance. But they must be meant for music; and within the music must be felt the pulse of dancing, whether the body dances like King David the Psalmist,[1] or the heart alone.

Lyric poems are songs. They have developed out of the dance-rhythms and folk-melodies and verbal song-patterns worked out by each people for itself. In the names of nearly every kind of lyric we can hear singing or dancing. Ballad (like ballet) comes from *ballare*, which means 'dance': so does the word 'ball', used for a dancing-party. A sonnet is a sonetto, a little sound or song. Ode and hymn are simply Greek words for 'song'. Chorus means 'round dance'. Psalm and lyric are both 'harp-music'.[2]

Lyric poetry becomes more intense and complex when it grows away from music and the dance. If a song is not meant to be danced, and yet has a strong rhythm, its emotion is usually heightened. Everyone feels this with ballads. When a particular song-pattern becomes popular, and then, while being elaborated for the sake of the words, subordinates or abandons its music, it usually makes up for that loss by having a rich verbal melody, with intricately interwoven patterns of sound (such as rhyme), haunting music of vowels and consonants, and phrases beautiful enough to sing by themselves.

Every country can create its own songs, and some can develop them into poetry. (For instance, ballads were produced all over western Europe in the later Middle Ages, from Spain to Scotland, from Germany to Iceland; not all, but some, grew into great poems.) Certain nations, more gifted in self-expression than others, made more numerous and beautiful patterns of song, which were borrowed and copied by their neighbours. The Provencal minstrels set not only France but Italy singing, and then the other western countries. More than anyone else, the southern French gave us rhyme. Although there are rhyming poems in church Latin (from which the first rhymes in vernacular languages may have come), there is no regular rhyme in classical Greek and Latin poetry and none in Old English. In spite of this it has given a perfectly new beauty to most of the finest European poetry, from Dante to yesterday. Rhyme, with many of the patterns based upon it, couplet, ballad, multiple-rhymed stanza, sonnet, grew up in the later Middle Ages, spreading from country to country in a springtime exuberance, song by song.

Song and dance are so instinctive that we should not expect modern lyric poetry, starting from them, to be deeply influenced by the lyrics of Rome and Greece. After all, Greek and Roman music has disappeared; we cannot see their lovely dancing; it is difficult even to trace the rhythms in their lyric poems, and impossible to feel them to be as natural as our own dance songs, like

> It was a lover and his lass,
>   With a hey, and a ho, and a hey nonino

or

> O, my luve's like a red, red rose,
>   That's newly sprung in June.

All we have left of them now is the words: few even of the words. Nearly all Greek and Roman lyric poetry was destroyed or allowed to disappear during the Dark Ages. Sappho is lost, except for a few scattered jewels. Nearly all Alcaeus is gone, and most of Pindar, and all but a few words of many more Greek poets whose names we know from encyclopaedias and quotations. In Latin we have four priceless books of Horace, some lyrics by Catullus, the work of a few third-raters like Sidonius Apollinaris, and rare anonymous gems like *The Vigil of Venus*. These poems are few altogether, and they are nearly all difficult to understand. In the Middle Ages Greek lyric poetry was unknown to the west. Horace's odes were read by scholars, but seldom by poets and never by the public. By the time the surviving Latin lyric poets were read more widely and the remains of Greek lyric poetry began to be published, every modern western country had its own lyrics well advanced and still developing. Greco-Roman influence in this field was therefore late, and only partially effective.

Simple, private, emotional lyrics, voicing the pain of longing or the joy of possession, the delight of spring or the violence of hate, must be pure songs. They can borrow very little from the classics. But when lyric poetry grows less private and more reflective, then it can and often does enrich itself by subtilizations of thought, elaborations of pattern, new devices of style and imagery, adapted from Greco-Roman lyric and fused into a new alloy. It was partly under Latin and even more under Greek influence that the modern European countries built up their formal lyric poetry; and to its most prominent type they gave a Greek name, the ode.

The chief classical models for the modern formal lyric were Pindar and Horace; and then, far behind them, Anacreon (with his imitators), the poets of the Greek Anthology, and Catullus.

Pindar was born about 522 B.C., was trained at Athens in music and poetry, wrote hymns, songs of triumph, and festal lyrics all his life with the greatest success, and died about 442.[3] Coming from the territory of Thebes, which lay a little apart from the full current of Greek life and thought, he seems to belong to an age earlier than the busy, revolutionary, thought-searching fifth century. He is more, not less, intense. But his intensity is emotional and aesthetic; in his poems we see few of the struggles and triumphs of the intellect. His spiritual energy, however, is compellingly strong, his power to see visions and to make them intensely and permanently alive in a few speedy words is unsurpassed in any poetry, and the inexhaustible wealth of his vocabulary and sentence-structure makes readers (unless they prefer prose to poetry) as excited as though his subjects equalled his eloquence in greatness.

His surviving poems (apart from some fragments discovered very recently) are four books of choral songs intended to celebrate the victories of athletes at the national sports festivals held every year at the great shrines of Greece. They pay little or no attention to the actual contests, and not much more to the personality of the winner, unless he is a great ruler; but they glorify his family—both for its past achievements (in which the victory is a unit) and for the grand legends with which it is linked. Above all they exalt *nobility* of every kind, social, physical, aesthetic, spiritual. These poems were not recited, but sung by a large choir, with Pindar's own music and a beautiful intricate dance to intensify the effect of the superb words.

The two chief difficulties in understanding Pindar are not the results of our own ignorance, or of our distance from him. They have always existed. They troubled his readers in classical times. Horace, himself a skilful and sensitive poet, felt them too.

The first difficulty is the actual structure of his poems—their metre and their pattern. They are of every kind of length, from a trifle twenty-four lines long to a titan of just under 300. Being dance-songs, they must be built up of repeated and varied rhythmical units. But what are the units? How are they repeated and how are they varied?

The odes are all divided into sections—groups of verses which we might call stanzas.

In a few poems the stanzas are all exactly the same. Evidently the dance here was a single complex evolution, repeated again and again.

Most of the odes are in a form like A–Z–P: where A and Z are two stanzas almost exactly equal, and P is a briefer, quieter stanza, differently arranged but on a similar rhythmical basis. The same A–Z–P pattern is then repeated throughout the poem. Here the dancers apparently performed one figure (A), then retraced it (Z), and then performed a closing movement (P) to complete that section of the poem. Or else, after dancing A and Z, they may have stood still singing the closing group of verses (P). These units are called, in Greek, strophe (A), antistrophe (Z), and epode (P). Poems built on a single stanza-pattern are called monostrophic; the A–Z–P poems triadic.

So far, good. But can these stanzas be broken down further—into verses or lines—as a ballet can be dissected, not only into movements, but into separate elements and subordinate figures? At this point scholars usually stopped, until the nineteenth century. They saw the single or triple stanza-division (which they knew from Greek tragedy, where the choruses sang and danced in similar patterns), but they could not be sure of the component units of each stanza. In the first editions of Pindar the stanzas were chopped up into series of short lines, more or less by guess-work, and their readers assumed that he wrote 'irregularly', varying the length and pattern of his lines by caprice, and balancing only stanza against stanza.

Scholars now know, however, that Pindar divided his stanzas by breathing-spaces into verses, rhythmical units of varying length and pattern—not so much like the regular lines of a modern poem as like the varying musical phrases that make up a 'romantic' symphonic poem. The verses in each stanza correspond to each other almost exactly. In the *A–Z–P* pattern, the units composing the *A* and *Z* stanzas correspond all through the poem; and the units of the *P* stanzas correspond all through the poem.[4]

The result is more complex than most of our poetry, and much more like our music. For instance, a sonnet is made up of fourteen iambic lines, all of the same length within a syllable and all on exactly the same rhythmical basis. The variety is produced by the rhyme-scheme, which makes the lines interweave on a pattern like this:

$$
\begin{array}{ll}
\text{— — — — — — — — — — — — —} & a \\
\text{— — — — — — — — — — — — —} & b \\
\text{— — — — — — — — — — — — —} & a \\
\text{— — — — — — — — — — — — —} & b \\[6pt]
\text{— — — — — — — — — — — — —} & c \\
\text{— — — — — — — — — — — — —} & d \\
\text{— — — — — — — — — — — — —} & c \\
\text{— — — — — — — — — — — — —} & d \\[6pt]
\text{— — — — — — — — — — — — —} & e \\
\text{— — — — — — — — — — — — —} & f \\
\text{— — — — — — — — — — — — —} & g \\
\text{— — — — — — — — — — — — —} & e \\
\text{— — — — — — — — — — — — —} & f \\
\text{— — — — — — — — — — — — —} & g
\end{array}
$$

The stanzas of Pindar's odes, on the other hand, have no rhymes, and they hardly ever have more than two lines the same in shape, so that one stanza may look like this

$$
\begin{array}{ll}
\text{— — — — — —} & a \\
\text{— — — — — —} & a \\[4pt]
\text{— — — —} & b \\
\text{— — —} & c \\
\text{— — — —} & b \\[4pt]
\text{— — — — — — — — — —} & d \\
\text{— — — — — — —} & d'\text{ (shortened)} \\[4pt]
\text{— — — — — —} & e \\
\text{— — — — —} & f \\
\text{— — — — — —} & e \\
\text{— — — — —} & f
\end{array}
$$

And then the same pattern will be echoed in the next stanza; and there will be a rhythmical kinship running through *a, b, c, d, e,* and *f,* so that a few basic dance-movements can be felt pulsing through them all despite their differences. If you read aloud one of Pindar's odes with a strong but fluent rhythmical beat, you will sense behind it the intricately interweaving rhythm and music of choir and ballet. The odes could even be set to music and sung and danced, now that these patterns have been worked out by devoted scholars; but until the nineteenth century nothing of them was known, except the broad stanza-grouping *A–Z–P* (with an occasional *A–A–A–A*), built up out of metrical units irregular and apparently haphazard in length and rhythm.

The second difficulty in Pindar has not yet been solved. This is that no one can follow his train of thought. Horace, the calm, restrained, elegant, enlightened Epicurean, said Pindar's poetry was like a torrent rushing down rain-swollen from the mountains, overrunning its banks, boiling and roaring.[5] We feel its tremendous power, we are excited and exalted and overwhelmed by its speed and energy, it is useless to argue and analyse, we are swept away as soon as we begin to read. True; but does it make sense?[6]

In eras when reason was stronger than emotion or imagination, people thought Pindar wrote like an inspired lunatic. He was a madman like Blake, who saw fine visions and rammed them together without sequence or even coherence, or filled in the intervals with meaningless spouting. Malherbe called his poems balderdash, *galimatias.*[7] Boileau saw them as 'beautiful disorder'.[8] Horace felt them to be imaginative energy uncontrolled, and he had read more of Pindar than any modern man. Contemporary scholars have constructed various schemes to make Pindar's thought seem continuous. An admirable recent book by Dr. Gilbert Norwood of Toronto suggests that each poem is dominated by a single visual image—a harp, a wheel, a ship at sea—symbolizing the victor and his family and circumstances.[9] Others have tried to link stanza to stanza by finding repetitions of key-words and key-phrases at key-points. I believe myself that it is not possible for us to find either a continuous train of thought or a central imaginative symbol or a series of allusive links in every one of Pindar's odes. The unity of each poem was created by the single, unique moment of the festival for which it was written. The nation-wide contest, the long training and aspiration, the myth of city or family that inspired the victory, the glories of the earlier winners in the same city or family, the crises of contemporary Greek history, the shrine itself and its god—all these excitements fused into one burning glow which darted out a shower of brilliant images, leapt in a white-hot spark across gaps unbridgeable by thought, passed through a commonplace leaving it luminous and transparent, melted a group of heterogeneous ideas into a shortlived unity, and, as suddenly as a flame, died. It is difficult to recapture the full significance even of Greek tragedy or early comedy, without the acting, the scenic effects, the chorus, the dancing, the great theatre, and the intense concentration of the Athenian audience. In reading Pindar's triumphal odes it is almost impossible to understand them unless, simultaneously, we revive in our own minds the high and unifying excitement created by the poetry and the music and the dancing and the rejoicing city and the glorious victor and the proud family and the ennobling legend. We have nothing left but the words and a ghost of the dance. The thoughts and images of Pindar's poems do not always succeed each other in logical sequence. They are chosen for their beauty and their intensity and their boldness. They are often grouped by a process like free association, and linked simply by contrast, by the poet's wish *not* to be logical, but to be nobly inconsequent, divinely astonishing, as unique as the triumphal moment.

The greatest Roman lyricist, Horace (65–8 B.C.), said it was too dangerous to try to rival Pindar.[10] He wrote at a time when the Greco-Roman world, still trembling with the fury and exhaustion of generations of war and civil war, needed no excitement, no audacity, no excess, but calm, moderation, thought, repose. His odes were not composed for a single unique moment, but for Rome and its long future. They are all in precisely arranged four-line stanzas, or (less often) couplets. Unlike Pindar's lyrics, they fall into a comparatively small range of variations on traditional line- and stanza-forms. The patterns which Horace prefers are based on models created by the Greek lyric poets Alcaeus and Sappho, who worked in the seventh and sixth centuries, several generations earlier than Pindar. From them, too, he adopted a number of themes—although we cannot certainly tell how many, since nearly all they wrote has vanished. He could not copy Sappho's deep intensity of emotion, nor the songs of fierce hatred and riotous revelry which Alcaeus sometimes sang; but he reproduced and deepened Alcaeus' political sensibility, the keen love of nature felt by both Alcaeus and Sappho, something of their bold independent individualism, and much of their delicate grace, which produces effects as surprising in their subtlety as Pindar's in their power.

After describing the dangers of emulating the dashing energy of Pindar, Horace compares Pindar to a swan. For the Italians this did not mean the mute placid beautiful creature which floats somnolent on the lake, but the strong-winged loud-voiced bird which in flight soars high above everything but the eagle.[11] Why not the eagle itself, the bird of Jove? Probably because, although a conqueror, the eagle is not a singer; it symbolizes power to be feared more than beauty to be admired. Still, one of his followers preferred to think of Pindar as the Theban eagle.[12] Eagle or swan, he flies too high (says Horace) for us to attempt to follow him on man-made wings, without falling, like Icarus, into the sea.

I, Horace goes on, am like a bee, hard-working, flying near the ground on short flights, gathering sweetness from myriads of different flowers. Certainly the swan is stronger, more distinguished, more beautiful; but the bee makes honey, the substance which is unique in the world, fragrant of innumerable blossoms, and not only a food but a symbol of immortality. Rarely has one poet contrasted his work and character so emphatically with that of a great predecessor.[13] The contrast is important, because it images the division between the two most vital ideals of formal lyric poetry in modern literature. Among the lyricists who follow classical inspiration, consciously or unconsciously, some are descendants of Pindar, some of Horace. The Pindarics admire passion, daring, and extravagance. Horace's followers prefer reflection, moderation, economy. Pindaric odes follow no pre-established routine, but soar and dive and veer as the wind catches their wing. Horatian lyrics work on quiet, short, well-balanced systems. Pindar represents the ideals of aristocracy, careless courage and the generous heart. Horace is a *bourgeois*, prizing thrift, care, caution, the virtue of self-control. Even the music we can hear through the odes of the two poets and their successors is different. Pindar loves the choir, the festival, and the many-footed dance.

Horace is a solo singer, sitting in a pleasant room or quiet garden with his lyre.

Characteristically, Horace often undervalued his own poems. Brief, orderly, tranquil, meditative, they are less intense and rhapsodical but deeper and more memorable than those of Pindar. Cool but moving, sensitive but controlled, elusive but profound, they contain more phrases of unforgettable eloquence and wisdom than any other group of lyrics in European literature.

Inspiration and reflection; passion and planning; excitement and tranquillity; heaven-aspiring flight and a calm cruise near the ground. These are not only differences between two individuals or two schools of lyric poetry. They are the distinguishing marks of two aesthetic attitudes which have characterized (and sometimes over-emphasized) two different ways of making poetry, music, painting, oratory, prose fiction, sculpture, and architecture. Detach Pindar and Horace from their background, and read them as poets in their own right. Pindar, the bold victor who sang with the same conquering energy that possessed his own heroes, who made his own medium, who dominated the past and future by the comet-like intensity of his moment, is he not 'romantic'? Horace, the man who ran away in the civil war, the ex-slave's son who worked his way up to become the friend of an emperor, the poet who built his monument syllable by syllable as carefully as bees build their honeycomb, the apostle of thought, care, self-control, is he not 'classical'?

The distinction has often been misapplied. All Greco-Roman literature and all its imitations and adaptations in modern languages have been called 'classical'. Modern literature which shuns regular forms, which is conceived as a revolt against tradition, which gives full and free expression to the personality of the writer, which values imagination more than reason and passionate emotion more than self-restraint, has been called 'romantic' and very often 'anti-classical'. The distinction between the two attitudes to art is useful enough, although it tends to make us forget that there are many others. But it is a dangerous mistake to call one 'classical' and the other 'anti-classical', and to assume that *all* Greco-Roman literature with its modern descendants is 'classical' in this sense. It is painful to hear such a poet as Shelley described as 'romantic', when 'romantic' is taken to mean 'turning away from Greek and Latin literary tradition': for very few great English poets have loved Greco-Roman literature more deeply or understood it better.[14] And it ruins our appreciation of Greco-Roman literature, of which a large and important part is tensely emotional and boldly imaginative. The word *classical* simply means 'first-class', 'good enough to be used as a standard'; and by derivation it came in the Renaissance to be a general description for all Greek and Latin literature. It is still employed in that sense at those universities which have a Chair of Classics or profess Études Classiques; and in this book it has been used to mean that, and nothing more.[15]

Pindar and Horace, then, are both classical poets—in the sense that they belong to the same literary tradition, the tradition which sprang from Greece and grew through Rome. But in many of their aims and methods they are quite different; and much of the greatest modern lyric poetry can be best understood as following the practice of one or the other. There are bold exuberant free-patterned odes, which derive from Pindar. There are brief, delicately moulded lyrics, seriously meditative or ironically gay, which derive from Horace. And in the work of some poets we meet both styles. Milton produced both Pindaric odes and Horatian sonnets. Ronsard began by soaring up with Pindar, and then, with Horace, relaxed. This is possible because the two attitudes are not polar antitheses. After all, both Pindar and Horace were lyric poets; Pindar, for all his excitement, kept a firm control of his language and thought; Horace, though usually restrained, sometimes breaks into plangent grief or daring imagery. Therefore the two schools, Pindaric and Horatian, are not opponents, but complements and sometimes allies.

Other Greek poets, and one other Roman, were admired by modern lyricists, but much less than Pindar and Horace. The most famous of these Greeks was Anacreon, who sang of love, wine, and gaiety in the sixth century B.C. Nearly all his poems have been lost; but a certain number of lyrics on the same range of subjects, written by later imitators, survived and for some time passed under his name. To them we owe many pleasant little images of the lighter aspects of life, frail pleasure or fleeting melancholy: youth as a flower which should be plucked before it withers, love not an overmastering daemon but a naughty Cupid. In form, the Anacreontics (as the imitators are called) were simple and easy and singable. (*The Star-Spangled Banner* was written to the tune of a modern Anacreontic song called *Anacreon in Heaven*). They are slight things, but charming. For instance

> In the middle of the night-time,
> when the Bear was turning slowly
> round the hand of the bright Keeper,

came a knocking, came a tapping; and when the poet opened his door, there entered, not a raven, but a little boy with a bow. The poet warmed and sheltered him; in return, after he had dried his bowstring, he fitted a sharp arrow to it, and . . .[16]

There was also the Greek Anthology, an enormous collection of epigrams and short lyrics on every conceivable subject, from almost every period of Greek literature. It contains a vast quantity of trash, some skilful journeyman work, and a surprising number of real gems: small, but diamonds. Some of our poets have been indebted to it in developing the modern epigram,[17] and many of its themes were taken up, partly through the Renaissance Latin poets and in part directly, into the sonnets and lesser lyrics of France, Italy, England, and other countries.[18]

Catullus, who belonged to the generation before Horace and lived a life as short and passionate as his own poems, left a handful of love-lyrics which have never been surpassed for intensity of feeling and directness of expression. Every lover should know the greatest:

> I hate and love. You ask how that can be?
> I know not, but I feel the agony.[19]

Some, like the poems on Lesbia's pet sparrow,[20] are buoyant and colloquial. Others are epigrams and lyrics forged out of white-hot pain and passion, yet with perfect craftsmanship. Most of them are too great to copy, but modern poets have adapted some of the themes, and sometimes disciplined themselves by emulating Catullus' rapidity and his truth.

Long before the Renaissance began, lyric poetry already existed in Europe. Provençal, French, Italian, English, German, Spanish poets had made song-patterns of much beauty and intricacy. Perhaps in the very beginning the songs of the vernacular languages had grown out of the Latin hymns of the church; but they soon left behind any link with the parent language. Therefore, when Pindar and Horace and the other classical lyric poets were rediscovered, the discovery did not create modern lyric poetry. It was not like the theatre, where the emergence of Greek and Latin comedy and tragedy was a complete revelation of hitherto undreamed-of forms and creative possibilities. Poets who already commanded the rhyme royal, the sonnet in its various shapes, ottava rima, and many more complex stanza-forms scarcely needed to borrow many patterns from the classics.

What they did borrow was, first of all, thematic material. Not the broad subjects—love and youth and the fear of death and the joy of life—but a number of clear and memorable attitudes to the subjects of lyric poetry, images or turns of thought that made them more vivid; and, of course, the whole range of imagery supplied by Greco-Roman myth. More important, they enriched their language on the model of Pindar's and Horace's odes, taking it farther away from plain prose and from conventional folk-song phraseology. And in their eagerness to rival the classics, they made their own lyrics more dignified, less colloquial and song-like (with a tra-la-la and a hey nonino), more ceremonial and hymn-like. This was the most important change that classical influence brought into modern lyric: a graver, nobler spirit. To mark these debts and their general kinship with the classics, the Renaissance lyric poets frequently copied or adapted the verse forms of Pindar, Horace, and the others; and, for more ambitious and serious lyrics, they chose the name *ode*.

It is a Greek word, meaning *song*, brought into modern speech through its Latin form *oda*. Neither Pindar nor Horace used it as a name for their poems, but it is so firmly linked with them now, and so clearly indicates their qualities of loftiness and formality, that it can scarcely be abandoned. Many modern lyrics are songs, written for the moment. An ode is a song in the classical manner, written for eternity.

PINDAR

Horace was known throughout the Middle Ages, although seldom imitated in the vernacular languages.[21] Pindar was unknown; and his poetry was stranger, more brilliant and violent. Therefore, when he was rediscovered, he made a deeper impact on the Renaissance poets. The modern formal lyric became, and remained, more Pindaric than Horatian. The first edition of Pindar's odes was printed at Venice by the great publisher Aldus

in 1513. Educated men already knew Horace's admiring reference
to Pindar's unapproachable loftiness.[22] This was a challenge, and
the Renaissance poets were not men to refuse it.
The earliest vernacular imitations of Pindar were in Italian.
Probably the hymns of Luigi Alamanni (published at Lyons in
1532–3) have priority.[23] But the loudest and boldest answer to the
challenge of Pindar's style and reputation came from France a
few years later, and made the name of Pierre de Ronsard,

> the first who in all France
> had ever Pindarized.[24]

Ronsard was born in the Loire country in 1524. Like Chaucer
and Ercilla,[25] he was a royal page, and in his early manhood
travelled abroad in the king's service. One of his young companions infected him with enthusiasm for Vergil and Horace, and
while still in his teens he began to write love-poems on themes
drawn from the classics.[26] But a serious illness, which made him
partly deaf, debarred him from continuing a diplomatic and courtly
career. Aged twenty-one, he determined to turn to poetry and
classical learning—for the two were then, in the expanding
Renaissance, almost indissolubly allied. He had already had the
good fortune to find an excellent teacher, Jean Dorat, and followed
him to the Collège de Coqueret, a small unit of the university of
Paris. Dorat (c. 1502–88) was one of the many superb teachers,
with a strong but winning personality, learning both wide and
deep, a mind constantly in pursuit of new beauties, and a sensitive
literary taste, who helped to create the Renaissance and its literature.[27] He was the formative influence, while Ronsard and his
young friends were the energy and the material, of the group of
poets who rebelled against the traditional standards of French
poetry and proclaimed revolution in ideals and techniques. They
called themselves the Pléiade, after the group of seven stars which
join their light into a single glow.[28]
The revolution preached by the Pléiade was neither so violent
as they believed nor so successful as they hoped. It was, nevertheless, important enough. In a sentence, it amounted to a closer
synthesis between French poetry and Greco-Latin literature, the
two meeting on an *equal* basis. Its three chief landmarks were:

> the publication of *The Defence and Ennoblement of the French
> Language* by Ronsard's friend Joachim Du Bellay in 1549;[29]

the appearance of Ronsard's *The First Four Books of the Odes* in 1550;

the staging of Jodelle's *Captive Cleopatra* and *Eugene* in 1552.[30]

As young men do, the Pléiade issued extravagant claims to originality, heaped contempt on their predecessors, and made daring experiments from which they later recoiled. But in the main they were right, and successful.

Du Bellay's thesis was this. It is unpatriotic for a Frenchman to write in Latin. It is an admission of inferiority for a Frenchman to write in French without trying to equal the grandest achievements of Greek and Latin literature. Therefore French poetry should 'loot the Roman city and the Delphic temple', raising the literature of France to a higher power by importing into it themes, myths, stylistic devices, all the beauty of Greece and Rome.[31] Abandon the old medieval mystery-plays and morality-plays. But also abandon the idea of writing plays in Latin. Write tragedies and comedies as fine as those of the classical dramatists, but in French. Abandon the old-style French lyrics, leave them to provincial festivals and folk-gatherings: they are 'vulgar'.[32] But also abandon the idea of writing lyrics in Latin or Greek.[33] Write 'odes still unknown to the French muse' containing all that makes Pindar great, but in French.

Du Bellay was right. Nationalism narrows culture; extreme classicism desiccates it. To enrich a national literature by bringing into it the strength of the continent-wide and centuries-ripe culture to which it belongs is the best way to make it eternally great. This can be proved both positively and negatively in the Renaissance. It was this synthesis of national and classical elements that produced, in England, Shakespeare's tragedies and the epics of Spenser and Milton. It was the same synthesis in France that, after a period of experiment, produced the lyrics of Ronsard, the satires of Boileau, the dramas not only of Racine and Corneille but of Molière. It was the failure to complete such a synthesis that kept the Germans and certain other nations from producing any great works of literature during the sixteenth century, and made them spend their efforts either on imitating other nations, writing folk-songs and folk-tales, or composing faded elegances in faded Latin.

Ronsard and his friends claimed that he was the first Frenchman to write odes, and even to use the word *ode*. The brilliant investigations of M. Laumonier and others have made it quite clear that, as his opponents pointed out at the time, he invented neither the word nor the thing. The word *ode* had been used in both French and current Latin years before Ronsard started writing; and the actual invention of the French ode is due to Clément Marot quite as much as to Ronsard.[34] It is not even clear whether, as he declared, Ronsard was the first of his group to write odes in the manner of Pindar.[35]

What is absolutely certain is that Ronsard was the founder of elevated lyric poetry on classical models, not only for France, but for all modern Europe. He achieved this by the bold step of publishing a huge single collection of ninety-four odes all at once, *The First Four Books of the Odes*. This act he conceived as rivalry with Pindar (who left four books of triumphal odes containing forty-four poems)[36] and Horace (who left four books of odes, 103 poems in all, but on the average much shorter than Ronsard's), and as the annunciation of a new trend in French poetry. Although he drew subjects and models for these poems not only from Pindar but from Horace, and Anacreon, and many other sources both within and without classical lyric, the most striking and ambitious of his odes were written in rivalry with Pindar,[37] and with them we can begin a survey of Pindaric odes in modern literature.

Horace said that following Pindar's flight was like soaring on artificial wings, and was apt to end in a spectacular failure.[38] Did Ronsard succeed?

Pindar's odes deal with victories at the Olympic and other national games. Ronsard tried to find subjects even nobler. The first one in book 1, for instance, praises King Henri II for concluding a successful peace with England, and the sixth glorifies François de Bourbon on the victory of Cérisoles. But most of them were written for a friend or a patron with no particular occasion to celebrate, and are merely encomia. Therefore the sense of exultation and immediate triumph which swept through Pindar's victory odes is often absent from Ronsard's, and is replaced by an elaborate but sometimes frigid courtesy.

In power of imagination and richness of style, Ronsard falls far below Pindar. His sentences are straightforward, often coming very close to rhyming prose. Often enough their meaning is obscure, because he felt that, to be a poet like Pindar, he must cultivate the dark profundity of an oracle. He usually achieved this, however, not by writing sentences in which every word is charged with deep significance, their order too is meaningful, and whole phrases contain many different layers of thought, through which the reader must slowly penetrate; but by using lofty periphrases and alluding to strange myths, all of which become quite clear as soon as one recognizes the reference. The sentences themselves are far simpler and less various than those of Pindar.[39] His vocabulary is bright, ingenious, and attractive, although perhaps too much addicted to diminutives; but, apart from proper names, it seldom has anything comparable with the blazing new-forged compounds and the white-hot poetical words of Pindar. The myths he introduces are far from being flat and conventional. Some are deliberately abstruse. Some are as rich as a Renaissance tapestry. *Odes*, i. 10 contains a fine, and largely original, description of the birth of the Muses, their presentation to their father 'Jupin', their song of the battle between the Gods and the Titans, and the power with which Jupiter rewarded them. Such myths are not pedantic. But they are not heroic. They have not Pindar's burning intensity. They contain no pictures like Pindar's lightning-flash vision of the maiden Cyrene straining motionless in combat with a lion;[40] and we feel that Ronsard could not see such things, because his eyes were not opened.

Ronsard's Pindaric odes are divided into strophes, antistrophes, and epodes. In itself this is uselessly artificial, since they were not meant to be sung by a choir and danced. The stanzas are made up of blocks of short lines, mostly varying between six and nine syllables from poem to poem. Each stanza is practically uniform; there is none of Pindar's ebb and flow. The rhymes are usually arranged in couplets interspersed among quatrains. What is most important is this: nearly every stanza is hermetically sealed off, to form one group of sentences without carry-over; and within each stanza the sense nearly always stops at the line-ending, and seldom elsewhere. This is far more limited and hampered than the style of Pindar, whose thought flows on from line to line, stanza to stanza, triad to triad, without necessarily pausing at any point not dictated by the sense, until the end of the poem. Evidently Ronsard still has the little two-forward-and-two-back rhythms of the folk-dance running in his head. That epitomizes the differences between his odes and those of Pindar. Ronsard's are a simpler, more naïve, thinner, less melodious imitation of a rich, polyphonic, warmly orchestrated lyrical work.

In 1551 Ronsard gave up the attempt to rival Pindar. In fact he had neither the character nor the environment which would enable him to become a second Pindar; he was too soft, and his public too shallow. In the odes he often refers to his attempt to copy Homer and Vergil in a plaster cast of the *Aeneid*, called *The Franciad*;[41] but his soul was not deep enough and strong enough to enable him to complete such a task, and he abandoned it after four books. In the same way, he gradually dropped the manner and matter of Pindar, and returned to the poet whom he had once boasted of surpassing.[42] He abandoned the *A–Z–P* arrangement in strophe, antistrophe, and epode, and took to writing in couplets and little four-line and six-line stanzas. His tone became quieter, melancholy instead of heroic, frivolous instead of triumphant. He boasted less often of playing a Theban string, and turned towards the softer, more congenial music of Horace, Anacreon,[43] and the Greek Anthology.

Still, his attempt, and the supporting work of the Pléiade, were not useless. He set French lyric poetry free from the elaborate stanza-forms in which a very few rhymes, difficultly interwoven, confined the poet's thought.[44] He shook off much of the heritage of folk-song, which had originally been natural and had become conventional and jejune. He and his brother-stars in the Pléiade added many valuable words and stylistic devices to the French language, from their study of Greek and Latin poetry. He showed that French lyric could be noble, and thoughtful, and equal in majesty to the greatest events it might choose to celebrate.

The Italian Ronsard—or, as he hoped, the Italian Pindar—was Gabriello Chiabrera (1552–1638), whose epitaph, written by Pope Urban VIII, boasted that he was the 'first to fit Theban rhythms to Tuscan strings, following the Swan of Dirce (Pindar) on bold wings which did not fail', and that, like his great fellow-townsman Columbus, he 'found new worlds of poetry'.[45] In his youth Chiabrera was made enthusiastic for the study and emulation of classical literature by association with Paulus Manutius, son of the publisher Aldus, and by hearing the lectures of Marc-Antoine

Muret, the brilliant friend and commentator of Ronsard. His Pindaric poems are partly independent creations, but partly modelled on those of Ronsard and the poetry of the Pléiade.[46] They are only a small proportion of his large output, which includes several epics, dramas, pastorals, and 'musical dramas' (opera libretti written in an attempt to re-create the true effect of the combination of music and words in Greek tragedy). His *Heroic Poems* (*Canzoni eroiche*) contain about a hundred odes, of which twelve are divided like Pindar's into strophes, antistrophes, and epodes. They are all composed in stanzas of six, eight, ten, and sometimes more than ten lines. The lines are uneven in length, sometimes having three beats, or four, or five. The rhymes are unevenly distributed: a typical pattern being *abab cddc efef*.[47] So both rhythm and rhyme are irregularly balanced; but the pattern struck out in the first stanza is carefully preserved in all the others. The general effect is therefore quite like that of Pindar's odes, except that the turning triadic movement of the dance is lost. The few triadic poems run in shorter, simple stanzas.

Chiabrera had genuine victories to celebrate. He wrote a number of these poems after naval battles in which the galleys of Florence played a successful part against the Turks, enslaving Turkish prisoners and liberating Christian slaves. However, neither in them nor in his numerous poems glorifying various Italian dignitaries of state and church did he achieve anything like Pindar's volcanic blaze: only a mild and pleasing warmth. The besetting sin of baroque poetry is already traceable in his poems—the habit of introducing a classical allusion not to support and add beauty to the poet's own invention, but as a substitute for imagination. The odes are crowded with Greco-Roman deities and myths, Apollo and the Muses, the tears of Aurora for Memnon, the beams of bright Phoebus, and the roars of the Titans; yet Chiabrera puts them in, not because they excite him, but because they are expected. The melody of his odes is very charming, for he is skilful at interweaving rhyme and rhythm, but they do not sound so much like Pindar's triumphal odes as like gracefully elaborated Italian canzoni. Like Ronsard, whom he admired and strove to emulate, Chiabrera was really a songster.

The word *ode* was introduced into English in Shakespeare's time. For Shakespeare it meant a love-poem. He used it to describe one in *Love's Labour's Lost*,[48] and in *As You Like It* Rosalind complains that her lover (true to one of the conventions of pastoral) is carving ROSALIND on the tree-trunks, hanging odes upon hawthorns and elegies upon brambles.[49] Spenser's exquisite *Epithalamion* is not a Pindaric ode, despite its metrical complexity: apparently it is a blend of the Italian canzone with Catullus' wedding-poems. The earliest extant English poem actually called an ode is an address to the Muses printed in the introduction of Thomas Watson's ἑκατομπαθία, or *Passionate Century of Love*, and signed by one C. Downhalus (1582): it is a pleasant little piece in six-line stanzas, but very far from the Pindaric pattern.

The first actual imitations of Pindar in English came two years later. They were in *Pandora*, published in 1584 by John Southern. The book contains three odes and three 'odellets'. The first ode, addressed to the earl of Oxford, promises to capture 'the spoyle of Thebes' and cries:

> Vaunt us that never man before,
> Now in England, knewe Pindars string.[50]

However, Southern does not really know Pindar's string; he is roughly and ignorantly copying Ronsard.[51] His odes are merely poems in a regular four-beat rhythm, arranged in couplets and quatrains and divided into stanzas called strophes, antistrophes, and epodes—but not even keeping the *A–Z–P* Pindaric pattern which Ronsard understood and followed. Southern's sole importance is historical. Even at that it is not very great, for his 'imitation of Pindar' was only an ignorant copy of the work of another imitator.

The first truly Pindaric poem in English is one of the greatest. This is Milton's prelude and hymn *On the Morning of Christ's Nativity*, which he began on Christmas morning, 1629. Not long before, he had bought a copy of Pindar: it is now in Harvard University Library, and shows by its annotations how carefully he read it.[52] After a short prelude—in which he calls on the Heavenly Muse to give the poem as a Christmas present to Jesus— Milton breaks into a rich, powerful, and beautiful descriptive hymn in a regular succession of eight-line stanzas. The lines are of irregular length, rhyming *aabccbdd* and rising to a final alexandrine. The hymn is therefore not written in triads like most of Pindar's odes. What enables us to call it Pindaric is the dancing metre with its controlled asymmetry, the vivid imagery, and, most of all, the splendid strength and vividness of the myths, both the dying deities of Greece and Rome:

> In consecrated earth,
> And on the holy hearth,
> The Lars and Lemures moan with midnight plaint

and the glorious new spirits of Christianity, visiting the earth to celebrate the incarnation of God:

> The helmèd cherubim
> And sworded seraphim
> Are seen in glittering ranks with wings displayed.

At last, a modern pupil of Pindar, meditating on the greatest theme in Christian thought, and using all the eloquence and imagination with which both classical antiquity and biblical learning had endowed him, had achieved an even stronger and loftier flight than the eagle of Thebes.

Ben Jonson also attempted the Pindaric vein, with interesting and original results. In the same year as Milton wrote his Pindaric hymn on Christmas, Jonson completed his *Ode on the Death of Sir H. Morison*.[53] This is actually built in the triadic form *A–Z–P*; and, although the rhymes are arranged in couplets in the 'turn' and 'counter-turn', and not much more elaborately in the 'stand', the lines are so widely varied in length and so skilfully married to the meaning that the effect is broader, more Pindaric, than the rather operatic stanzas of Chiabrera, and more thoughtful than the lilting odes of Ronsard. And yet, the thoughtfulness, the slow pace, the frequent epigrams (more spacious than Pindar's brief aphorisms), are really derived from Jonson's favourite poet Horace. One famous stanza will show the free form and the meditative tone:

> It is not growing like a tree
> In bulk, doth make man better be;
> Or standing long an oak, three hundred year,
> To fall a log at last, dry, bald, and sere:
> A lily of a day
> Is fairer far in May,
> Although it fall and die that night;
> It was the plant and flower of light.
> In small proportions we just beauties see;
> And in short measures, life may perfect be.

This, then, is the first of many great modern odes in which the styles of the two great classical lyricists, Pindar and Horace, interpenetrate to form a new beauty.

The modern ode was created very slowly, after many failures. In these two poems of Milton and Jonson it was newly born. We can now attempt to define it. In modern literature an ode is a poem combining personal emotion with deep meditation on a subject of wide scope or broad public interest. It is short enough to express one emotion in a single movement, but long enough to develop a number of different aspects of that emotion. It is either addressed to one person (human or superhuman) or evoked by one occasion of particular significance. Its moving force is emotion more than intellect; but the emotional excitement is tempered, and its expression arranged, by intellectual reflection. The emotion of the ode is stirred and sustained by one or more of the nobler and less transient events of human life, particularly those in which temporary and physical facts are transfigured by the spiritual and eternal. The interplay of the emotions and reflections which make its material is reflected in the controlled irregularity of its verse-form.

'Who now reads Cowley?' asked Pope, adding

'Forgot his epic, nay Pindaric art.'[54]

Abraham Cowley (1618–67) was a precocious and talented poet who claimed to be the inventor of the English Pindaric ode, and for a long time imposed this claim upon the public. His rhapsodic odes (published in 1656) were indeed directly suggested by his study of Pindar; and he said in his preface that he tried to write, not exactly as Pindar wrote, but as he would have written if he had been writing in English (and, by implication, in the seventeenth century). He was rightly determined not to make a plaster cast, but to re-create and rival. Therefore he abandoned Pindar's triadic form and replaced it by irregular verse, without even the stanzaic regularity of Milton's and Jonson's odes. If it had not been rhymed and had not possessed a certain basic pulse, we should now call it free verse. This, however, was not Cowley's invention. Madrigals in free asymmetrical patterns, bound together only by vague rhyme-schemes, were common before his day; Milton himself, Vaughan, and Crashaw had already published more serious poems in equally free forms.[55] If Cowley made any innovation, it was in using a free form, not to follow the ebb and flow of song, but to represent the gush and lapse and swell of emotional excitement. The real effect of his work was to make the concept of a Pindaric ode, in which the poet's emotion masters him and is imaged in the irregular metre, familiar to English poets and their readers. His poems themselves are negligible.

Ode means 'song'. Poets knew this, in the Renaissance and the baroque age: they endeavoured to enhance the beauty of their odes by having them set to a musical accompaniment, or by making them reproduce, in words, the movement and harmony of music. Those who wrote Horatian lyrics, if they thought of music, usually designed their work for one singer, or at most a small group.[56] But with its broad sweep and surging emotion, the Pindaric ode was fully able to reproduce or to evoke the music of a choir and an orchestra.

In a very early ode of this kind Milton emphasizes the juncture of poetry and music:

> Blest pair of sirens, pledges of heaven's joy,
> Sphere-born harmonious sisters, Voice and Verse,
> Wed your divine sounds, and mixed power employ.

And he goes on to describe the eternal music of heaven, where the bright seraphim and cherubim are the orchestra, and the blessed souls sing everlastingly to their music. He does not, however, attempt to echo musical sounds in his own beautiful lines.[57]

The first English opera (*The Siege of Rhodes*) was performed in 1656, and, after the Restoration, English musical taste turned eagerly towards the new Italian music—highly emotional yet extremely dignified, gorgeously decorative and often quite unreal.[58] In 1683 the London Musical Society inaugurated annual performances of musical odes in honour of the patron of music, St. Cecilia. Purcell himself set the first. In 1687 John Dryden produced a technical masterpiece, his *Song for St. Cecilia's Day*, to be set by the Italian composer Draghi. Beginning with a reminiscence of Ovid, proceeding to a combination of biblical and pagan musicology, then evoking the sound of trumpets, drums, flutes, violins, and the organ, it ends with a Grand Chorus on the Last Judgement.

This was little more than a skilful trick; but ten years later Dryden changed skill into art, and wrote, for the same occasion, *Alexander's Feast*. It was a great success. Dryden thought it the best poem he had ever writ; and long afterwards it was splendidly reset by Handel.

This was only one, although the greatest, of the many musical Pindaric odes written in the baroque period. They are Pindaric in the studied irregularity which reflects their connexion with music (and of course in much else beside—in their use of myths, their loftiness of language, &c.); but where Pindar designed his poems for the dance, these odes are written for orchestra and stationary singers. (I have sometimes thought that the Horatian odes with their musical settings find their best parallel in the fugue, the Pindaric odes like *Alexander's Feast* in the grand toccatas and chaconnes which Bach wrote to test the fullest powers of his own art, and the odes of the revolutionary period in the symphony.) A recent writer has distinguished four classes of these works— sacred odes, cantata odes, 'occasional' or laureate odes, and odes for St. Cecilia's Day—and has worked out from contemporary criticisms and parodies (such as Swift's *Cantata*) the qualities which were considered necessary to make a good musical ode.[59] Clearly it was a difficult art, but—like opera and oratorio—an art in which success was much hoped for and highly rewarded. Contemporary poets have made few attempts to marry their poems to music in this way, and the most moving recent works have been made by blending new music with literature already accepted: Copland's *Lincoln Portrait* and Vaughan Williams's *Serenade for Music*.

The greatest lyricist of the eighteenth century did not write a Pindaric ode for music. Instead, he wrote a Pindaric ode which contained music, the music not only of the orchestra but of nature:

> The rocks and nodding groves rebellow to the roar—

the light dance of spirits and the floating grace of Venus herself. Gray's *Progress of Poesy* begins and ends with an allusion to Pindar, and, with true Pindaric dignity, sets Gray himself in the direct line of mighty poets with Shakespeare, Milton, and Dryden. Perhaps, as a Bard, he could foresee his successors, Keats and Wordsworth and Shelley.

Most of the Pindaric odes written in the baroque period were not musical but ceremonial. With the aid of Pindar, poets celebrated the births, marriages, and deaths of the nobility and gentry; the accessions, coronations, birthdays, jubilees, and victories of monarchs; the founding of a society, the announcement of an invention, the construction of a public building, any public event that expressed the pomp and circumstance of the age. The result was exactly as Horace had predicted—a series of spectacular, bombastic failures. More bad poems have been written in the intention of rivalling Pindar than in any other sphere of classical imitation. True poets are genuinely inspired by their subjects: energy and eloquence are breathed into them, they are excited, mastered, dominated, they *must* write. Their problem is to control their emotions, and to direct them to the point of maximum expressiveness. But mediocre poets are not overwhelmed by their subjects, not even excited by them. They try, therefore, to borrow the themes and expressions of true poetic excitement from some other poet who was deeply moved and memorably eloquent. With the best available wax, and selected high-grade feathers, they construct artificial wings, launch themselves off into the azure air in pursuit of Pindar, the Theban eagle, and fall into the deep, deep bog of bathos with a resounding flop.

It was particularly difficult to be truly Pindaric in the seventeenth and eighteenth centuries. Pindar lived in an age abounding in great poets, where prose, and the type of thought best expressed in prose, were not yet fully developed. The baroque period was an era of orderly thought, measured prose, and cool, symmetrical verse. Even the lyrics of such an age usually chime with all the regularity and less than the harmony of church bells. The distinction between ordinary common sense and emotional excitement, whatever its cause, was then marked by a broad, almost impassable frontier. Therefore the poets who announced that they felt themselves transported by Pindaric excitement convinced neither themselves nor their audience nor posterity.

> 'What wise and sacred drunkenness
> This day overmasters me?'

—cries Boileau; but he knows perfectly well that he is stone sober, and determined to write a Pindaric ode.[60]

Even if the baroque poets had been capable of feeling and

expressing genuine enthusiasm, the subjects of their Pindaric odes were seldom such as to generate it. That is the fatal defect of 'occasional' poetry. Pindar loved the great games, the handsome youths striving against one another, the horses and the chariots and the shouting crowds. Countless baroque poets were personally quite indifferent to the marriage of His Serene Highness or the erection of a new Belvedere in his lordship's grounds, but made odes on such subjects as a matter of duty. Boileau, who detested war, wrote an ode on the capture of Namur.[61] The results of the spurious excitement produced by poets labouring their wits on tasks like these are painful to the lover of literature, unless he has a hypertrophied sense of humour. If he has, he may even collect some of the finer examples, such as Edward (*Night Thoughts*) Young's panegyric on international trade:

> Is 'merchant' an inglorious name?
> No; fit for Pindar such a theme;
> Too great for me; I pant beneath the weight.
> If loud as Ocean were my voice,
> If words and thoughts to court my choice
> Outnumbered sands, I could not reach its height.
>
> Kings, merchants are in league and love,
> Earth's odours pay soft airs above,
> That o'er the teeming field prolific range.
> Planets are merchants; take, return,
> Lustre and heat; by traffic burn;
> The whole creation is one vast Exchange.[62]

When Shadwell was made Poet Laureate in 1688, and began the practice of producing annual birthday odes for the king, he initiated a long, heavy tradition of laureate poetry in which inspiration was replaced by perspiration.

Truly great Pindaric odes unite strong and rapid eloquence with genuine and deep emotion. It is a rare combination. The baroque era, for all its talk about the poetic sublime and the need of rivalling Pindar, seldom achieved it. Even although the themes of death and virtue and young womanhood were, and are, profoundly significant, Dryden failed to make anything really moving out of them in his ode *To the Pious Memory of the Accomplished Young lady, Mrs. Anne Killigrew*. It has been called 'the finest biographical ode in the language';[63] but it contains so much verbal cleverness that Dryden clearly either did not feel deeply about the girl's death, or was unwilling to give his emotions free expression. It was nearly a century later that Thomas Gray, with his sensitive spirit and his love of wonder, found subjects to excite both himself and the readers of his Pindaric odes, and, not only in the passion of the words and rhythms, but in the gloomy forebodings and defiant challenges of the Bard, announced the age of revolution.

HORACE

It is more difficult and less attractive to follow Horace than Pindar. Poets are eager to believe that they can soar above the Andes, but seldom willing to undertake to polish a twenty-four-line poem for seven years. There are, accordingly, fewer Horatian lyrics than Pindaric odes in modern literature; but their quality is higher.

Horace's lyrics were known in the Middle Ages, intermittently. They were not, however, greatly loved.[64] Petrarch, who discovered so many other beauties, was the first modern enthusiast for their discreet and lasting charm. But he had his own style of lyric poetry, and although he incorporated thoughts and graceful phrases from Horace in his poems, he did not form them on the Horatian models. Even his enthusiasm failed to bring Horace back into full favour. It was late in the fifteenth century that the Florentine scholar Landino, and his greater pupil Politian, founded Horace's modern reputation.[65]

The Italians were the first to appreciate Horace. The Spaniards were the first to cultivate the Horatian manner intensively in their lyric poetry. Having learnt from the Italian humanists to appreciate Horace (with the bucolic poets and others), they began to emulate his odes very early in the sixteenth century. They used modern metres, in short stanzas which could easily be adapted to Horatian material; and the result was a new and natural beauty.

That doomed elegant Garcilaso de la Vega (1503–36) wrote the earliest Horatian lyrics in Spanish,[66] using the stanza called 'the lyre': three seven-syllable and two eleven-syllable lines, borrowed from Bernardo Tasso, it became the favourite medium for the reproduction of Horace's neat four-line stanzas.

Fernando de Herrera (1534–97) received Greek mythological material and lyrical impulses through Horace—for it is clear that he knew no Greek.[67] His poem to Don Juan of Austria is really a triumphal ode, inspired by two of the few poems in which Horace allowed himself to become airborne on a long ambitious flight.[68] Horace implied that Octavian, by conquering Mark Antony, had become one of the gods whose wisdom overthrows Titanic brute force. Herrera also tells the story of the battle between the gods and the giants; he implies that Don Juan, by conquering the rebels, has merited heaven; and, like Horace, he compares the god of song to himself, the poet of the event.

Greatest of the Spanish lyricists was Luis de León (*c.* 1527–91), who said that his poems 'fell from his hands' while he was young.[69] This means that, among them, his emulations of Horace and other poets were not tasks (like so many classicizing works) but spontaneous expressions of real enthusiasm. He did fine translations of Vergil's *Bucolics* and the first two books of the *Georgics*—he actually called *The Song of Solomon* a pastoral eclogue with two lovers answering each other, as in Vergil. From Horace he translated over twenty odes, sometimes (like many Renaissance translators) incorrectly, but always beautifully and naturally; and in middle life, while imprisoned by the Holy Inquisition, he got hold of a Pindar and translated the first Olympian ode. But several of his own original poems are modelled on Horace and Vergil: notably the famous *Prophecy of the Tagus*, which is inspired by the Tiber's prophecy in the *Aeneid* and the warning of Nereus in the *Odes*.[70] To him, as to Garcilaso and others, the idyllic description of country life beginning

> Happy the man who far from business cares
> Like Adam in the Garden,

given by Horace in the *Epodes*, meant more than the sour satiric twist at the end; and they both embodied in poems of their own its pastoral charm—which for the warlike Spaniards was then as great a relief as for the exhausted Romans 1,600 years before.[71]

In Italy the first Horatian odes were published in 1531 by Tasso's father Bernardo. Since they were more purely classical in form than the sonnets and canzoni which were the accepted Italian lyrical patterns, Tasso was leading the same kind of revolution that Ronsard was to make in France a few years later.[72] He was followed by many others, notably Gabriello Chiabrera, whom we have already met as a Pindaric.[73]

Chiabrera in Italy, some of Ronsard's friends in France, Gabriel Harvey and others in England attempted to go farther than using Horace's themes and imitating the structure and tone of his odes. They tried to re-create his metres. There were two possible ways of doing this. The first was exceptionally difficult, virtually impossible. It was repugnant to the movement of history. It meant, not strengthening one tradition by another (as the best classical adaptations do), but substituting a dead one for a living one. It was an effort to abolish the stress accent of modern languages, in order to impose on them the system of scanning lines by quantity, counting syllables long or short, which was created in Greek and successfully taken over into Latin. The two systems are fundamentally different. Even in Latin they competed. There they were reconciled by the acceptance of a series of intricate rules, intelligible to few but the educated who knew and felt the rhythms of Greek. When the Roman spoke the first line of Horace's best-known ode, he said

$$\acute{} \qquad \acute{} \qquad \acute{}\ \acute{} \qquad \acute{}$$
integer uitae scelerisque purus;

but when he sang it or declaimed it as verse, he paused on long syllables, and made it

$$\bar{}\ \bar{}\ \bar{}\ \bar{} \qquad \bar{} \qquad \bar{}$$
integer uitae scelerisque purus—

a slower, more complex, difficult, and beautiful pattern.[74] The aim of the strictly classicist metricians in the Renaissance was to try to introduce patterns of the second type into modern languages. Music was actually written for verses of this kind; but music and verses are both forgotten now.[75]

Although it was impossible to try to make modern poetry scan by quantity, it was not out of the question to take the patterns of Horace's lyrics, and other classical metres, and adapt them to modern stress-accent. (This is the plan on which Longfellow wrote the familiar hexameters of *Evangeline* and Goethe those of *Hermann and Dorothea*.)[76] In Spain, for instance, Villegas took the Sapphic stanza, and, without too much violence, hammered its pattern of longs and shorts into the mould of stressed and unstressed syllables; Chiabrera managed it in Italian, and bequeathed the result to a greater lyricist in the nineteenth century, Giosuè Carducci;[77] and Ronsard did the same in French.

In France it was the Pléiade which naturalized Horace; and chiefly it was Ronsard. But before Ronsard published his odes, Peletier in 1544 turned the 'Art of Poetry' into French verse; and then, in 1547, brought out a collection of his own *Poetic Works* containing three translations and fourteen imitations of Horace's lyrics. Like the Horatian poems published in Spain, they were not in a form modelled on Horace's Alcaic or Sapphic stanzas, but in native patterns designed to produce a similar effect,[78] to lay less emphasis on rhyming tricks and minor elegances than the earlier poets, and to reproduce something of the sculptural restraint and economy of Horace's lyrics.

Although Ronsard boasted that he rivalled Pindar and surpassed Horace,[79] he could not do so, and he knew it. He did not even want to, for long. He had begun to imitate Horace when he was only seventeen;[80] and the chief classical model for the poems with which he started to form his collection of *Odes* was Horace, the material being drawn mainly from Horace and Vergil.[81] During the productive years 1545–50 he was, as he himself asserted, both the French Horace and the French Pindar.[82] However, the collection contained only fourteen Pindaric odes; and, after the publication of the first four books, it was with obvious relief that he came down from yonder mountain height and rejoined Horace among the flowers of the meadow. Even although he maintained his interest in Greek, from 1551 onwards he turned away from Pindar towards the elegiac poets and the Greek Anthology, particularly the Anacreontics.[83] His tone became lighter, less aggressive, more frivolously gay or mildly melancholy.

Why did he turn again towards Horace? He might have abandoned him as he abandoned Pindar.

He loved him sincerely. Their natures were genuinely sympathetic. Both were pagans. Not that Ronsard was anti-Christian, nor Horace atheistical, but neither felt that religion was deeply connected with morality, and neither believed that the powers of heaven were closely interested in his own personal affairs. (That is the main reason why Ronsard, in his preface to the *Odes*, dates his first poetic experiments to coincide, and contrast, with Marot's rhymed version of the Psalms.)[84] It is amusing to see how neatly Ronsard takes over Horace's favourite Epicurean consolation— 'don't worry, leave everything to the gods'—and transfers it to Christian surroundings, while still allowing himself and his friends the same freedom of action and enjoyment of life. It was in enjoyment of life that the two were most sympathetic. When Ronsard writes a love-poem or a drinking-song, he is not imitating Horace even if he quotes one of the odes. He is writing because he loves women and wine, and he is quoting Horace because he loves literature, Horace in particular. Laumonier has a fine page on the drinkers of the Vendôme country, where Ronsard was born, and where he felt at home.[85] The plump grey-haired Roman with the quizzical eyes would have felt at home there with him.

In England Horace's lyrics were taught in schools, and quoted in Latin, for some time before poets took to imitating them.[86] The first Horatian in England was Ben Jonson, who admired and often copied the satires and letters, translated the 'Art of Poetry' and based his own critical principles on it, and transmitted to his poetic 'sons' his admiration for the odes.[87] We have already seen (p. 238) that Jonson's own odes are Horatian as well as Pindaric. Herrick, in his own ode to Sir Clipseby Crew, shows that these imitations were not pedantry but based on real human sympathy:

> Then cause we Horace to be read,
> Which sung, or said,
> A goblet to the brim
> Of lyric wine, both swelled and crowned,
> Around
> We quaff to him.

Herrick's and Jonson's work is so penetrated with the poetry of Horace that it is inadequate to speak of imitation. Line after line, stanza after stanza, is good in itself for lovers of poetry, and better for those who recognize the voice of Horace, now speaking English.

Andrew Marvell's *Upon Cromwell's Return from Ireland* has often been called the finest Horatian ode in English. Certainly it shows how a good classical metre like the Alcaic can be simplified, changed to a stress-pattern, and yet keep its original beauties of thoughtfulness and dignity. But although there are fine stanzas in it, there is too much prose, like:

> And now the Irish are ashamed
> To see themselves in one year tamed,

and too many conceits.

His friend Milton has one translation of a delightful Horatian love-poem, into a similar, but slightly richer metrical form:

> What slender youth, bedewed with liquid odours,
> Courts thee on roses in some pleasant cave?[88]

Although it shows signs of the fault which sometimes mars Milton's epic poetry,[89] it helped to teach him the art of compression, of getting the maximum of meaning into the minimum of space. This lesson he carried into the English sonnet. By making the sonnet stronger and richer, he gave it new life. Nine of his sonnets begin with an address, as Horace's odes so often do; and one:

> Lawrence, of virtuous father virtuous son

actually with a close imitation of Horace's

> O lovelier daughter of a lovely mother.[90]

Horace's inspiration goes throughout the sonnets, from a tiny comic trick like this:

> Some in file
> Stand spelling false, while one might walk to Mile-
> End Green;[91]

to the deep moral, political, and educational purpose which inspires the greatest of them, and which Milton's example transmitted to Wordsworth and many a later English poet.[92]

Respected as a critic in the baroque period, Horace was less admired as a lyric poet than he deserved; but when the better poets felt a deep but tranquil emotion, which could not issue in 'Pindaric rage', they often turned to Horace's manner, sometimes to his very metres.[93] Pope's early *Ode on Solitude* and Collins's beautiful odes *To Evening* and *To Simplicity* show how natural the adaptation was. *The Oxford Book of English Verse* contains a less natural blend from the same period, in a Horatian metre: Watts's *Day of Judgment*. With the Greek lyric metre now known as Horace's Sapphic stanza, it mingles the most fearful medieval imaginings of Doomsday: open graves, shrieking victims, devils, stop here, my fancy! Inappropriate as the metre appears, it has a terrifying momentum from the very first stanza:

> When the fierce North-wind with his airy forces
> Rears up the Baltic to a foaming fury;
> And the red lightning with a storm of hail comes
> Rushing amain down. . . .

There could be no better example, in small space, of Christian thought and myth carried by a purely classical poetic form.

A generation or two later, with the poets of the revolutionary era, a new vigour and richness, a stronger self-assertion sang through the odes. The two strains can still be clearly traced. Horace has his followers, and Pindar; some of the greatest poems of the period made a new synthesis which both would have admired.

The heirs of Pindar in this epoch include Goethe, Shelley, Hugo, Wordsworth, and Hölderlin. (Once more we see how mistaken it is to call this period anti-classical. Victor Hugo, for example, began his career with a series of odes, in which, just like his predecessors, he calls on the Muses, sings to his heroic lyre, and describes classical scenes and landscapes. The essential differences are his *style* and his *purpose*.) The Pindaric ode became very free in form. Its rhythm was stronger, but more varied. It was still a dance, but the dancers, instead of repeating one triple figure, or one complex inwoven movement, moved through a series of patterns governed only by the will of the poet, or his fiery imagination.

Bad as Cowley's odes are, perhaps it was they which established this dithyrambic form in English. Shelley's *Ode to Naples* is in ten irregular stanzas, marked epode, strophe, and antistrophe, even numbered and Greek-lettered; but the names and numbers have no real sequence.[94] It is the difference between a 'classical' and a modern ballet; between a Haydn symphony and a modern symphonic poem. The Pindaric ode has in fact always aspired towards free improvisation: poets knew that he had written dithyrambs 'without law', and yearned to have his authority for a mode of expression which would, without being incoherent, be absolutely free.

The content of the Pindaric ode had always been highly emotional. It now became more energetic than it had been during the baroque period, and its emotion, though not less intense, more supple and varied—and therefore more Greek. Finally, with the general liberation of the spirit that came with the close of the eighteenth century, the range of subjects which the ode covered became much wider, and its aspirations, both individual and social, loftier.

Goethe admired Pindar more than any other non-dramatic Greek poet except Homer.[95] He was reading and translating Pindar in his early twenties. From 1772 onwards he began to write spirited lyrics in short irregular lines, sometimes with scattered rhymes and sometimes entirely rhymeless, characterized by a tone of bold defiant energy which he himself felt to be Pindaric.[96] Schiller too left a number of Pindaric poems, including a *Dithyramb* and the two famous odes, *The Gods of Greece* and *To Joy* (exalted in the last movement of Beethoven's Ninth Symphony); they are full of genuine love for Greek myth and Greek truth, but they are monotonous in rhythm, sometimes cheap in phrasing. The unhappy Hölderlin was the truest Grecian of his generation in Germany. He translated about half of Pindar's lyrics; and, although he did not fully understand the metres and sometimes strained the meanings, they stimulated him to produce a number of lofty and difficult hymns in free verse, which were scarcely appreciated until a century after he died.[97]

Through his *Odes and Ballads* Victor Hugo is more often Pindaric than he is Horatian;[98] and often we see him, with characteristic love of excess, attempting to surpass Pindar by outshouting, outsinging, and outdancing his predecessor and all the Olympian choirs. The strings of exclamations become monotonous; but they are redeemed by the fine imagery, and by the sweeping, constantly changing rhythms.

Shelley's *Ode to the West Wind*, although its form is a stanza derived from a simple Italian lyric pattern, succeeds so magnificently in making the autumn wind into a powerful and impetuous superhuman presence, and in personifying many aspects of nature from the fallen leaves to the sleeping Mediterranean, from tiny seed and buds to vast clouds, 'angels of rain and lightning', that it recaptures something more essentially Pindaric, more Greek, than any of its baroque or Renaissance predecessors.

The greatest modern Pindaric poem, however, is Wordsworth's *Ode—Intimations of Immortality from Recollections of Early Childhood*. It seems at first to be far, far from Pindar's world and Pindar's clear energy. Yet, just as the form is Pindar's, adapted to the stresses of the modern poetic mind, so, turned inwards and darkened with modernity, is the spirit. The ode opens with rejoicing, and closes with triumph renewed. It is the festival of spring:

> Land and sea
> Give themselves up to jollity,
> And with the heart of May
> Doth every Beast keep holiday.

But the poet, within the rejoicing, is alone, with a thought of grief. Again and again he declares that he is one with the gay birds and winds and children; and again and again he pauses, doubtfully and sadly, looking for a lost radiance, the visionary gleam that has gone with his youth. The ode is not a glorification of triumph, but a description of a painful conflict, gradually resolved. Through a series of irregular stanzas, some dancing and lyrical, some brooding and meditative, Wordsworth moves on to the final proclamation of victory, out of the suffering which (as Aeschylus wrote) teaches wisdom:

> Another race hath been, and other palms are won.

Few in the age of revolution could admire Horace's moral and political message. It was an era of youth; he seemed middle-aged. Yet he was a superb artist in words, he loved nature, he knew beauty, he had a spiritual depth and serenity that communicated themselves to some of those who cared little for his social creed. The Horatian tradition was altered much more deeply than that of Pindar, yet something of it survived.[99] The stanza of the meditative odes became, although still regular, more intricate. The thought, while still tranquil, was often made more private. Nature was observed in more vivid and elaborate detail. Sometimes the complexity and exultation of Pindar were taken into the poet's own heart, and blended with the thoughtful depths of Horace's lyrics.

The tradition of Horace was most fertile in the baroque age when it produced Collins's exquisite odes.[100] In this, Collins had a far greater successor. The odes of John Keats are not like Horace, because they are not like the work of anyone but John Keats himself. But they are in the direct line of descent from Horace, whose work helped to bring them into being; and they look back beyond him to reach something younger and richer. The greatest, the *Ode to a Nightingale*, opens with a direct, unmistakable echo of Horace's voice, over twenty centuries.[101] But in all the superb 1819 odes there is something quite new, a change made by the mind of Keats and by the sensibilities of his era upon the

inheritance which Horace passed to him from Greece. The odes of
Pindar had been intense realizations of the moment of public
triumph, with everything vividly alive, crowded and active, ablaze
with energy. The exultant city surrounded the family of the
champion, the procession moved on with dance and music, the
poet spoke for all Greece, and all Greece listened. In Horace,
although the lyric was often a lonely song, it was to be heard by
a friend, it was to influence others by charming them, it was
uttered for Rome. But for Keats, the public has disappeared.

The poet is alone; silent; nearer to grief than to rejoicing. He
contemplates a Greek vase; he sits 'in embalmed darkness', half
in dream, listening to a lonely bird; he recalls a vision of 'two fair
creatures, couchèd side by side', or evokes the mellow season of
Autumn, the cloud of Melancholy. And out of this quietness and
this reflection, he mounts into an imaginative excitement akin to
Pindar's. He sees the figures on the vase as alive, panting and
young; he hears their melodies, piped to the spirit. As the nightingale moves from tree to tree, he takes wings to fly to it. Autumn
appears to him in a shape no less human and real than any
Hellenic deity, and Melancholy as a mighty veiled figure in her
secret shrine. The excitement does not blur, but sharpens his
senses, giving him keener perception of a thousand details—the
dew in the musk-rose, the piping of gnats, the iridescent ripple
on the sandy shore. His very thoughts grow into branching
trees, and murmur in the air. Only the dance which Wordsworth felt around him in the festival of spring is absent from
these odes. Keats, like Horace, has become a solitary singer;
but he has no hearers, and his lyre is a bird's song or the night
wind.

In the English 'romantic' odes the original purpose of Pindar has
been quite reversed and mellowed by blending with the subtleties
of Horace. Yet many essentials of the Greek and Roman lyric
remain, transfigured. Piercing vividness of imaginative detail;
creation of great superhuman visions transcending ordinary life;
profound spiritual ecstasy, the adoration of beauty and the
exaltation of noble ideals—all these elements of poetry have been
transmitted, through the tradition of the ode, from Horace and
Pindar to modern poets. The song and the festal dance have
passed away. In these lyrics, the structure of the ode reflects the
subtler excitements of the lonely human soul.

Since the revolutionary era closed, dozens, hundreds of poets have composed odes: but none finer. A moving book could be written on the nineteenth-century odes alone, and a noble anthology of them needs to be made. Most of those produced in the last hundred years are Pindaric rather than Horatian—some consciously (Hart Crane said 'I feel myself quite fit to become a suitable Pindar for the dawn of the machine age')[102] and some, like Walt Whitman's, unconsciously. Although musical odes were composed less often, the ode kept its natural kinship with music and the dance; Swinburne's technical virtuosity and corybantic energy are closely parallel to the rhapsodies of Liszt.

From the mid-nineteenth century onwards there was a movement of growing strength to break the regular patterns of verse, to allow it to sound wholly spontaneous, like immediate improvisation. Much of this came from the desire for originality, the hatred of tradition, the urge to twist the neck of eloquence, down with everything fancy and artificial, away with thou and thee, abolish Parnassus and the Muses, damn anything that's lofty, I cannot bear it.[103] But much of it was strengthened by the sense that real poetry had always been free, that Greek art, at its best, meant freedom. (It was largely the Hellenic improvisations of Isadora Duncan which set the modern ballet free, during the same period and for the same reasons.) Thus, when Gerard Hopkins was impelled to write poems on the tragic shipwrecks of the *Eurydice* and the *Deutschland*, he knew he was writing in the manner of Pindar—although the words, the syntax, even the rhymes he used were boldly unprecedented.

Hopkins's verses flowed molten into a strange mould. Part of it he had made, part of it was English, part of it (for he was a trained classical scholar) was Greek and Roman. Since he died, all moulds have been broken. Some modern lyrical free verse is merely typographical cleverness. Some represents the dialogue of half-heard figures in an interior drama. But in so far as the rest is rhythmical, it is a descendant of the excited songs of the Bacchic revellers, which Pindar was one of the first to make into art, and which many of his admirers have since heard through the irresistible mountain-torrent energy of his poems of triumph.

13

TRANSITION

WE have seen how, after Greek and Roman civilization was almost overwhelmed by repeated floods of barbarism, it managed to survive, in strangely altered but still powerful forms; how its influence continued to exist throughout the Dark Ages; and how it was one of the great currents which flowed with increasing strength through the Middle Ages, until at last it became one of the most powerful urges in that tidal wave of energy, emotion, and thought which we know as the Renaissance. We have now to trace its power, sometimes diminishing, sometimes increasing, always changing, and never dying, throughout the literature of modern Europe and America. Within this period-from the end of the Renaissance to the present day—we can make a rough but useful division. The first part, which ran from about 1600 to about 1770, can be called the age of monarchies, or the Counter-Reformation, or, comprehensively, the baroque age. The second part is the truly modern age, from the American and French revolutions and the industrial revolution down to our own times.

This twofold division is not merely a convenience. It reflects a real change both in the nature of our civilization and in the power exerted upon it by classical culture. Since about 1850 the whole tone, much of the purpose, and many of the methods of literature have undergone a revolution of great importance: not an abrupt shallow transformation, but a strong and permanent change of direction. This change accompanied and was conditioned by the great novelties of the nineteenth century:

industrialism and the rise of applied science;

a tremendous increase in the actual population of Europe and America;

a move away from government by inherited privilege—monarchy, aristocracy, landed property, inherited capital—towards government by the people or through the people—democracy, socialism, communism, and fascism;

the abolition of serfdom and slavery (temporarily, in some countries);

the provision of a much wider education for the mass of the people in many lands.

In literature the change takes several important forms:

(*a*) A huge increase in the amount of literature produced.

(*b*) A shift in emphasis towards literary standards acceptable to large masses of people and types of art which would influence the greatest possible number of paying customers or recipients of propaganda. Poetry has been, and still is, losing ground to prose. Poetic drama is very rare and special, while prose drama (on the screen as well as the stage) flourishes. No one writes didactic poems, while there are thousands of books of 'serious non-fiction'. Epics have disappeared, novels are superabundant. Similarly, there is less and less emphasis on style; but immense stress is laid on 'power' and 'appeal', which in practice mean emotional intensity within certain limited fields. There are a large number of very popular new, or newly re-created, literary patterns, none of them strict, but all designed to please a large public of fairly low cultural standards: the detective film and detective story, the musical comedy, the strings of unrelated jokes which compose many radio shows, the reporter's diary of ephemeral on-the-spot observations. Since about 1900 no single literary type has raised its standards, but all have broadened them.

(*c*) As a reaction to this, extreme specialization and 'coterization' in the work of artists who are determined not to aim at mass effects. T. S. Eliot is the best-known example, and often the growth of specialization can be traced within the career of a single artist: for instance, Joyce, Rilke, Picasso, Schönberg. It goes all the way from the invention of a private language (Joyce, Tzara), through the use of unintelligible symbols, to the creation of works of art out of purely private material: personal experiences unexplained and unknown to others (Auden, Joyce, Dali), odd myths, haunting quotations, obscure symbols, references to abstruse books or religious practices or almost unobserved events (Eliot's *Waste Land*, on the Fisher King and the meaning of *Datta Dayadhvam Damyata*, Pound's *Cantos*, the French surrealists who admired the murderers of Le Mans), and the foundation of new quasi-religious cults (Stefan George).

(*d*) And finally, in literature at least, one unquestioned gain: a great increase in vigour, spiritual energy multiplying as it finds more voices, and an enlarged and deepened field of subject-matter for the author.

In literature, these are among the deepest effects of recent social changes. Only the third seems to have much to do with classical influence. However, the power of Greco-Roman culture is more pervasive and penetrative than one might at first imagine. We have mentioned the spread of education. This is one of the most important factors in the civilization of the last three or four hundred years. It was not by any means nation-wide in any country, until quite recently; yet education was diminishing nowhere, and spreading slowly but continuously, throughout western Europe and America, from the Renaissance onwards. And from the beginning of this period—say, 1600—until about 1900 (and in several important countries much later) the focus of higher education was the study of the classical languages and literatures. Until well within living memory it was the exception rather than the rule to find, in America, Belgium, France, Germany, Great Britain, Holland, Poland, and other civilized lands, a school which went any distance beyond the three R's without compulsory Latin and optional Greek—far less a college or a university.[1] Technical and vocational schools were invented only after the rise of mass-production in industry.[2] Until the First World War knowledge of the classics was increasing. More was discovered about them, and, until at least 1900, more people were learning about them.[3]

A final general remark. During the period from 1600 to the present, classical influence has affected life and literature most directly and intensely in France; it has produced the richest effects in literature among the English; and it has evoked the largest quantity of scholarship in Germany.

The generation which was alive in 1600 saw the end of the Renaissance. It sounds unreasonable to speak of the end of a rebirth: for surely the classical literatures and so much of modern civilization as depends on them were reborn in the fifteenth and sixteenth centuries; and they did not die. Still, this rebirth and regeneration were only one aspect of a much broader revolutionary change which included events as diverse as the Protestant reformation and the discovery of America. The most characteristic thing about this change was not its concrete effects so much as its emotional, its vital qualities: 'bliss was it in that dawn to be alive, but to be young was very heaven.'[4]

But it ended sombrely.

With the latter half of the sixteenth century a cold wind seems to blow in upon the world. Poets turn harsh; heroes die ingloriously; men begin to hate more than they love; aspiring societies and noble works are cut short by violence; freedom, often extravagant or licentious, is succeeded by repressive laws and organizations, sometimes stupid and often cruel; even the classical books which had once connoted stimulus and liberation come to mean regulation and law and the multiplication of rules. Perhaps this reaction was inevitable; possibly some of it was necessary and salutary; but it was painful. However, the reaction that followed the Renaissance did not everywhere mean a contraction of the human spirit, without any compensation. In some countries (such as Spain) it did. In other countries it meant that, after a pause, literature and the arts and human thought left a period of wild uncoordinated expansion and entered on a period of regulated progress. Whether the progress would have been greater if the regulation had been less is a question no historian can answer without guess-work.

Certainly the period of reaction saw a great number of those disasters of civil and international war which deserve the name of public crimes. It saw needless waste of lives, and property, and objects of art, and products of learning. This history of the late sixteenth century is full of broken lives: scholars who were murdered because some drunken soldier thought they had money concealed, who fled from their native country because they belonged to the wrong sect or party, who like Casaubon had to study Greek in a cave in the hills while their parents hid from the S.S. (I have sometimes thought that the discovery of manuscripts, which helped to start the Renaissance, did not come to any *necessary* end in the sixteenth century—most of Petronius turned up in Dalmatia in 1650—but that it was discouraged and then stopped, by war, looting, and political oppression.) The history of England in the Dark Ages (p. 39 f.) and many similar stories show that scholarship can scarcely be blotted out except by total barbarization; but it can be gravely weakened, the main arteries cut, the few uninfected areas tied off, the healthy interflow broken, decay creeping over every section, and growth discontinued for generations, for centuries.

Here are the peaks in the counter-wave which rolled back the tide of Renaissance.

1. First, and most important—since Italy had been the chief stimulus to other European nations—the sack of Rome in 1527 by the armies of two peoples which had not experienced the full effects of the Renaissance: the Germans and the Spaniards.[5] The effect of this was clinched by the Spanish occupation of Italy, according to the treaty of Cateau-Cambrésis (1559).

2. The wars of religion spoilt many a valuable life. One key-date is the massacre of St. Bartholomew (1572).[6]

3. Still more frightful was the Thirty Years war in Germany, which effectively crushed out any chance the German states had had of reaching the same level of civilization as their neighbours.

4. It should be remembered that the barbarians were still pressing on in the east. They put Hungary out of European civilization for centuries, with the battle of Mohacs in 1526. The Balkans were occupied and partially paganized, while Poland and Austria were perpetually under threat.

5. The Counter-Reformation had many good effects, but several bad ones. The Spanish Inquisition, established as a national organization by Ferdinand and Isabella in 1480, now became more powerful. The Inquisition was not only anti-Protestant and anti-Jewish, but deadened, or tried to deaden, many of the most active impulses of Catholicism; it twice imprisoned St. Ignatius Loyola, while St. Theresa was several times denounced, and her *Conceptos del amor de Dios* was prohibited. The Society of Jesus, an institution great for both good and evil, was founded in 1540. After the Council of Trent, in 1564, an index of books prohibited to Catholics was issued, and censorship in the modern manner began with its ordinances.[7]

6. In Britain, Switzerland, Germany, and other Protestant countries the puritan and Lutheran reaction was equally active. A ban was placed on the British theatre in 1642 which lasted virtually until 1660; and even after its removal its ill effects were felt for many generations—first in the Restoration comedies (whose lewdness was quite unparalleled in English literary history) and then in a cutback in British stage-design and stage-management which lasted until well into the nineteenth century, and may

have been responsible for the failure of British drama to produce worthy successors to Marlowe and Shakespeare.[8]

Some of these reactions were purely military or political. There was a very important spiritual reaction which found its opponents among poets, scholars, and thinkers. The conflict between the two sides, almost evenly matched, lasted for nearly a century, and is not yet solved. It was called the Battle of the Books.

14

THE BATTLE OF THE BOOKS

THERE was a very famous and very long-drawn-out dispute in the seventeenth and eighteenth centuries which agitated not only the world of literature but the worlds of science, religion, philosophy, the fine arts, and even classical scholarship. It was never decided; it involved a number of comparatively trivial personal enmities, temporary feuds between men and women and pedants who are now forgotten; the issues were not always clearly stated on either side; some of the protagonists missed their aim, like the Player King's Priam, 'striking too short at shadows'; and there was far too much emotion involved, so that the entire dispute became a subject for laughter, and is now remembered under the satiric titles of LA QUERELLE DES ANCIENS ET DES MODERNES and THE BATTLE OF THE BOOKS.[1]

Nevertheless, it was an important dispute. In the first place, it was remarkable that an argument about taste should have lasted many years and occupied much attention, for that meant that the standards of criticism, and therefore of literature, were pitched very high. In the second place, the personalities interested were among the greatest of the time: Pascal, Boileau, Bentley, Swift. In the third place, the issues debated were of deep significance, and continue to be significant at the present day. They recur (although often disguised or misunderstood) in nearly every contemporary discussion of education, of aesthetic criticism, and of the transmission of culture. The battle waged in France and England at the turn of the seventeenth century was only one conflict in a great war which has been going on for 2,000 years and is still raging. It is the war between tradition and modernism; between originality and authority.

The chronology of the affair is not of the chiefest importance. Nor are the books that marked its various stages. There were many violent skirmishes on minor issues; sometimes important victories seemed at the moment to be defeats, and the losers built a trophy and went away rejoicing. But as a test of the vitality of taste in various European nations during the baroque age it is worth observing that the battle started in Italy, or rather that the early frontier encounters occurred there; that the real fighting took place in France; that an interesting but secondary struggle went on in England; and that no other European or American country played any part except that of spectator. Yet though the part played by English writers was secondary, the works they produced were more permanently interesting than anything which came out of France: for they included Bentley's *Dissertation upon the Epistles of Phalaris* and Swift's *Battle of the Books*.

Later we shall survey the authors who appeared as champions on one side or the other, and describe the phases of the battle. First, it is essential to analyse the issues which were being debated and the arguments used on both sides.

The question was this. Ought modern writers to admire and imitate the great Greek and Latin writers of antiquity? or have the classical standards of taste now been excelled and superseded? Must we only follow along behind the ancients, trying to emulate them and hoping at most to equal them? or can we confidently expect to surpass them? The problem can be put much more broadly. In science, in the fine arts, in civilization generally, have we progressed beyond the Greeks and Romans? or have we gone ahead of them in some things, and fallen behind them in others? or are we inferior to them in every respect, half-taught barbarians using the arts of truly civilized men?

Since the Renaissance many admirers of classical literature, charmed by the skill, beauty, and power of the best Greek and Roman writing, had assumed that it could never be really surpassed, and that modern men should be content to respect it without hope of producing anything better. After the rediscovery of Greco-Roman architecture this assumption was broadened to include the other arts; and it took in law, political wisdom, science, all culture. It was now attacked by the moderns on many grounds. The most important of the arguments they used were four in number.

1. *The ancients were pagans; we are Christians. Therefore our poetry is inspired by nobler emotions and deals with nobler subjects. Therefore it is better poetry.*

This is a far less simple argument than it sounds. Stated in these terms, it appears excessively naïve; yet it is a thesis which shallow minds might well accept or deny without question, and deeper thinkers might ponder for years. Obviously the fact that a bad writer is a Christian does not make him a better writer, although it should make him a better man. Some books and buildings and pictures produced by devout Christians and full of devout feeling have been artistically indefensible. J. K. Huysmans, himself an ardent Catholic, believed that much Catholic art of the nineteenth century was directly inspired by the Devil, in order to turn sensitive souls away from the true religion. And yet, in great works of art, the presence of the spirit of Christ, with its intense psychical sensitivity, its rejection of so much human unworthiness and inadequacy, and its moral nobility, must add greatness; its absence leaves a spiritual lacuna which no artistic skill can compensate or conceal.

The three greatest modern heroic poems are all blends of pagan and Christian thought, dominated by Christian ideals—Dante's *Comedy*, Tasso's *The Liberation of Jerusalem*, and Milton's *Paradise Lost*. In them all, the Christian religion is the essential moving factor. But in none of them could Christianity have been so well expressed without the pagan vehicle. Dante found no Christian teacher able to conduct him through the terrors of hell and the disciplines of purgatory towards his spiritual love Beatrice in heaven. He was guided by the pagan poet Vergil, to whom his poem owes more than to any other mortal except the pagan philosopher Aristotle. Milton makes Jesus say, in *Paradise Regained*, that Greece derived its poetry and its music from the Hebrews;[2] but that is not true, nor did Milton himself believe it. At the opening of his own *Paradise Lost* and again later in the poem, he summoned the aid of a Heavenly Muse, who was really the spirit of Christianity, but embodied in a pagan shape.[3] There are no Muses in the psalms of David or the songs of the prophets; nor does Milton, except in minor details, ever copy Hebrew poetry, while Greek and Roman literature is a constant inspiration to him.

The Roman Catholic church and the Protestant churches have long been internally divided on the question: Do the pagan poets teach nothing but evil, so that they should be cast out? or do they teach some good, so that they can be accepted and fitted into the pattern of Christian education? St. Augustine thought their beauties were not all bad, and their wisdom not all deceit, so that they could be used to broaden the mind and enlarge the soul of Christians. In Aristotelian terms, his answer means that some of the pagans were potentially good, and could be formed into real good by being put to a Christian use. And that is how many medieval teachers took them. Others, like St. Jerome, thought all the pagans were bad; they were the voices of the world which Jesus came to destroy; their very charms were evil, and Vergil was a beautiful vase full of poisonous snakes. This belief recurs again and again throughout modern history: in Savonarola, in Father Rancé, founder of the Trappists, and in many a fundamentalist preacher to-day. (In essence, it goes back to Plato; and the counter-view goes back at least to Aristotle.) The churches, however, usually inclined towards the broader opinion, that many pagan writers were potentially valuable. The baroque period was marked by the work of many brilliant Jesuit teachers who used the classics as 'hooks to draw souls', as well as by the steady expansion of classical education in Protestant countries.

2. The second argument is the most popular nowadays. It is this. *Human knowledge is constantly advancing. We live in a later age than the Periclean Greeks and Augustan Romans: therefore we are wiser. Therefore anything we write, or make, is better than the things written and made by the ancient Greeks and Romans.*

The emotional pressure towards accepting this argument was strong in the Renaissance, when worlds which the ancients had never seen were being discovered every generation, every decade: worlds in the far west, in the antipodes, in the sky. But in the Renaissance the discovery of the great classical books was still too new to allow men to vaunt one achievement of thought and will above the other. All the discoveries were equally wonderful: the new world of unknown nations and strange animals found by Columbus, the new worlds revealed by science, and the new world of subtle writing and trenchant psychology and glorious myth created by antiquity. In the baroque age, on the other hand, the classics were growing familiar, especially the Latin classics, less daring than the Greeks. Their thoughts had so long been current that their majesty had become customary and their daring had been equalled. Meanwhile, the science of the ancients, Vitruvius the architect, Hippocrates the doctor, and the few others, had been examined, equalled, surpassed, and discarded; while the self-perpetuating fertility of modern experimental science was asserting itself more emphatically every year. Men forgot that Lucretius and his master Epicurus and Epicurus' master Democritus had known that matter was constructed of atoms; men forgot that the Greeks had inferred, by thought alone, that the planets revolved round the sun; men forgot that Hippocrates had laid the foundations of medicine. They saw that, by experiments which had never been conceived before, modern men had found out things which had never been proved or believed possible of proof. They concluded therefore that civilized humanity as a whole had become better, and that their moral conduct, their arts, and their political intelligence had improved also. This is now the commonest attitude to the question, and looks like being the most persistent. The diagram of human history which most European and American schoolchildren have in their heads is simple. It is a line, like the line on a graph, rising continuously at a 45° angle, from the cavemen, through ancient Egypt, past Greece and Rome, through a nebulous Middle Age, past the Renaissance, upwards, ever upwards, to the ultimate splendour of to-day. Much of this belief, however, is false. Sir Richard Livingstone sums it up thus: we think we are better than the Greeks, because, although we could not write the superb tragic trilogy, the *Oresteia*, we can broadcast it.

Yet part of this modern optimism is true and justified. The ancients never believed in the noblest and most ennobling ideal of modern science—that man can change and improve nature. The abolition of disease; the curtailment of labour; the suppression of physical pain; the conquest of distance, planetary and interplanetary; penetration of the heights and the depths, the deserts and the poles; interrogation of nature far beyond the limits of our own senses, and the construction of machinery to continue that questioning and then change the answers into acts—these magnificent achievements have given modern man a new freedom which raises him higher above the animals, and allows him, with justice, to boast of being wiser than his ancestors.

But the argument is false when applied to art, and particularly false when applied to literature. (In philosophy it is highly questionable, and in politics and social science it cannot be accepted without careful examination.) Great works of art are not produced by knowledge of the type which can be accumulated with the lapse of time, can grow richer with succeeding generations, and can then be assimilated by each new generation without difficulty. The material and the media of art are the human soul and its activities. The human soul may change, but it does not appear to grow any greater or more complex from generation to generation, nor does our knowledge of it increase very markedly from age to age. One proof of this is that the ordinary problems of living, which have been faced by every man and woman, are no less difficult to-day than they were 2,000 years ago: although, if the argument from scientific progress were universally true, we ought to have enough knowledge at our disposal to enable us to solve the great questions of education, and politics, and marriage, and moral conduct generally, without anything like the per-plexities of our forefathers. In one of his finest poems Housman comforts himself by the same sad reflection.[4] Watching the storm blowing over Wenlock Edge, he remembers that the Romans once had a city there.

> Then, 'twas before my time, the Roman
>   At yonder heaving hill would stare:
> The blood that warms an English yeoman,
>   The thoughts that hurt him, they were there.
>
> There, like the wind through woods in riot,
>   Through him the gale of life blew high;
> The tree of man was never quiet:
>   Then 'twas the Roman, now 'tis I.

And is it not truer to say that to-day our scientific progress has made the problems of life not easier, but more difficult? Now that we have learnt to change the world, the world has become less stable, so that it is more difficult to understand: new problems are constantly arising, for which no clear precedents exist. And our naïve confidence in applied science has to some extent dissuaded the common man from thinking out problems of conduct as earnestly as our forefathers did, in conversation, in public debate, in meditation, and in prayer.

To the assertion that man has progressed through the accumu-lation of scientific knowledge there is a counter-argument which is sometimes overlooked. This is that many arts and crafts have been forgotten during the past centuries, crafts of great value, so that our scientific advance has been partly offset by the loss of useful knowledge. Some such crafts were the property of skilled tradesmen, who never wrote their secrets down; others were part of the mass of folk-lore which has only recently perished; others again were the result of generations of skilled practice in work that is now done, more copiously but not always more satisfactorily, by machinery. For example, the pharmacopoeia could be greatly enlarged if some of the valuable herbal remedies known to country folk a few generations ago were available; but many have been lost. The art of oratory was studied by the ancients for many centuries. During that time they discovered thousands of facts about applied psychology, about propaganda, about the relation between thought, artifice, and emotion, about the use of spoken language—facts which became part of a general tradition of rhetorical training, and were lost in the Dark Ages. Men make speeches to-day, and still move their hearers; but they cannot calculate their results so surely, and the speeches themselves have a narrower influence than those of the great classical orators because the rules of the craft have been forgotten.[5]

Even if we know more than the ancients, does that prove that we are better? Does it not mean that they did the great work, and that we only use it, adding a little here and there? This objection was put very forcefully by the twelfth-century philosopher Bernard of Chartres, in the famous phrase, 'We are dwarfs standing on the shoulders of giants.'[6] However, it was taken up and turned round, wittily though falsely, by the partisans of the modern side in the Battle of the Books. They pointed out that we ought not to call Plato and Vergil 'ancients' and think of ourselves as their young successors. Compared with us, Plato and Vergil and their contemporaries are young. We are the ancients. The world is growing up all the time.[7]

Now, this is the commonest modern assumption, and it is one in which the deepest fallacy lies. The assumption is that the whole of human civilization can be compared to the life of a man or an animal—as a continuous process in which one single organism becomes steadily more mature.[8] It is the great merit of Spengler to have shown, in *The Decline and Fall of the West*, that this is false, because it is over-simplified. Toynbee, in his *Study of History*, has elaborated and strengthened the view which Spengler stated. This view is that civilization all over the world, or for that matter civilization in Europe, is not one continuous process but a number of different processes. Different *societies*, groups of races, grow up at different times, forming separate civilizations (he calls them 'cultures', but he means the set of activities we call civilizations). At any given moment there may be three or four different civilizations alive at once, all of different ages. There have been several in the past, which have died or been destroyed. One civilization can come into contact with another, can destroy it or imitate it or learn from it. But one civilization does not grow out of another and surpass it, any more than one full-size tree grows out of the top branches of another. Spengler proceeds to infer that the growth, maturity, and decay of all the different civilizations follow the same rhythmic pattern, and manifest themselves in comparable intellectual, social, and artistic phenomena. Thus he says that our present time is preparing for 'the era of warring Caesarisms'—a name he devised as early as the First World War, before the emergence of Mussolini, Hitler, and those others—and says it is *contemporary* with the Hyksos period in Egypt (*c.* 1680 B.C.), the Hellenistic period in Greco-Roman civilization (300–100 B.C.), and the age of the contending states in China (480–230 B.C.). (One of the smaller, but not less striking, aspects of this theory is that it helps to explain the sympathy which men of one civilization often feel for their 'contemporaries' in another, and the repulsion or lack of understanding with which they confront art or thought of a period too early or too late for them to grasp. For instance, Tacitus was a great historian; but we have not yet arrived at the period when we can fully appreciate his spiritual attitude and his strange style, because he belonged to an age later than ourselves; while the mystery religions of antiquity, the stories of the saints in primitive Christianity, and the religious beliefs of more recent 'primitives' such as the founders of Mormonism are too early for most of us to understand nowadays.)

If this theory is true, the moderns in the Battle of the Books were mistaken in saying that they were later than the Greeks and Romans, and therefore wiser. They were later in absolute time, but not in relative time. Spengler holds that, on the chart of the growth of civilizations, they were at an earlier stage. Louis XIV looks like Augustus Caesar; his poets read like the Augustan poets; and the Louvre corresponded to Augustus' reconstruction of central Rome. But both the monarch and the arts of seventeenth-century France look *less mature* than those of Augustan Rome.

And apart from theories, the cold facts of history are enough to disprove the argument. The development of civilization has *not* been continuous since the flourishing of Greco-Roman culture. It has been interrupted. It has been set back many centuries by wars, savages, and plagues. The European of the tenth century A.D. was not ten centuries in advance of the European of the first century B.C., but, in everything but religion, many centuries behind him.

3. Some of the participants in the battle used a third argument, which dovetails with the second. It was put succinctly by Perrault, in the sentence *Nature does not change*.[9] The lions of to-day are no less fierce than those of the days of Augustus Caesar; roses smell no less sweetly; men are no taller nor shorter. Therefore the works of men are as good to-day as they were in classical times.

This argument also is at least half-true. The great things of life, out of which art arises, change very little: love, sin, the quest for honour, the fear of death, the lust for power, the pleasures of the senses, the admiration of nature, and the awe of God. Yet that does not prove that, in all times and places, men are equally skilful at making works of art out of this material. Art is a function of society. The ability of men to create works of art out of these universal subjects depends largely on the character of the societies in which they live: their economic structure, their intellectual development, their political history, their contacts with other civilizations, their religion and their morality, the distribution of their population between various classes and occupations and types of dwelling-place, even the climate they enjoy. Everyone has a voice and can sing; people are always singing; but the art of song, and the craft of writing solo or choral music, take long to develop, and reach a high level only in special periods and places. Throughout history men have enjoyed looking at beautiful women (and beautiful women have enjoyed being looked at). But in Islam it is against the law of the Prophet to make a representation of any living thing, so there are no Arabian artists comparable to Giorgione or Rubens. In colonial America it was indecent to paint nudes, money was not plentiful enough to support schools of art, and life was often hard: so there are no colonial American pictures of women comparable to those by the contemporary French painters Boucher and Fragonard. At all times men *can* produce great works of art; but sometimes the impulse and often the necessary social conditions and skills are absent, and without them it is impossible. The argument therefore neither proves nor disproves the primacy of classical art and literature.

4. The fourth argument is the argument from taste. Many

modernists, as well as defending contemporary art, reversed the charge and attacked the classics, saying that they were badly written and fundamentally illogical. This is a consequence of, and a natural reaction to, an exaggerated admiration of the classics. It is painful to be told that Homer is absolutely above criticism, that Vergil's *Aeneid* is the perfect poem; and such assertions always provoke a revolt. As early as the fourth century Plato was breaking down the belief that Homer's teachings were always right and always noble.[10] Orthodox Greek thinkers declared Homer to be a repository of all known wisdom (a theory amusingly burlesqued by Swift in *A Tale of a Tub*); and among them up rose Zoilus, who tore the *Iliad* and the *Odyssey* to pieces for bad taste and improbability. A common expression of this reaction is parody. Parody was common in antiquity, particularly among the Sceptic and Cynic philosophers, who used, by parodying Homer's greatest lines, to attack his authority, and through him the inviolability of tradition and convention. Epic parody began again in the Renaissance as soon as men became really familiar with the *Aeneid*, and has continued until very recently. One of the earliest attacks on the authority of the classics, introducing the Battle of the Books, was Tassoni's *Miscellaneous Thoughts*. Now, Tassoni (1565–1635) was the author of a good and celebrated epic parody, *The Ravished Bucket* (*La secchia rapita*), a mock-heroic poem about a war between Modena and Bologna which broke out in the thirteenth century, and which was actually caused by the theft of a bucket belonging to a Bolognese. This was copied by Boileau in *The Lectern* and then through him by Pope in *The Rape of the Lock*. Just before the battle began in France, Scarron had a considerable success with two such parodies, *Typhon or the Battle of the Giants* (1644) and *Vergil travestied* (1648–53, on an Italian model), and he was followed by others. Two of the most amusing books produced during the dispute were similar epic parodies: François de Callières's *Poetic History of the War lately declared between the Ancients and the Moderns* (1688), and Jonathan Swift's *The Battle of the Books* (1697–8, published in 1704).

This attack on the classics has two chief aspects, which are sometimes confused. Briefly, it consists in saying that *the Greek and Roman writers are either silly, or vulgar, sometimes both.* For example, their dramatic conventions—such as the introduction of gods into human conflicts—are described as stupid. Lucan thought so as early as the first century A.D., and (to outdo Vergil) wrote an epic which makes no use of divine characters. It will be recalled that the forger who produced 'Dares Phrygius' said it was authentic because no gods appeared and intervened in the action (pp. 51–2). In this part of the argument the moderns seem to have the advantage. Still, it is difficult to write on sublime subjects without introducing the supernatural, and in a critical age the appearance of tangible and audible divinities can always be made to look ridiculous. The most ambitious works on this scale produced in modern times already look a good deal the worse for wear: Hardy's *The Dynasts* and Wagner's *The Ring of the Nibelungs*.

Again, the early history and legends of Greece and Rome, when read without historical and imaginative perspective, contain many absurd inconsistencies. In an age of myths, when an exceptionally brave man or beautiful woman becomes famous, stories from the lives of other people are soon attached to the name of the hero or heroine, whether they fit in with the rest of the facts or not. Little local deities are, through time, identified with well-known gods and goddesses, who thus acquire many different and often paradoxical characters. When all the legends are written down, some of them are obviously contradictory. It is easy for a strict rationalist to conclude therefore that they are all nonsense. Pierre Bayle was among those who took this view. He calculated that (on the assumption that *all* the legends about Helen of Troy were true) she must have been at least sixty, and probably 100, at the time of the Trojan war—scarcely worth fighting for.[11]

Similarly, the stylistic mannerisms of the classical poets can be criticized: Perrault and his friends used to have great fun parodying the long Homeric similes, with their irrelevant conclusions. And the sequence of ideas in classical poetry can sometimes be described as naïve or unreasonable. Perrault in his *Parallel between the Ancients and the Moderns*[12] tells an excellent story about an admirer of the classics who was praising Pindar with enormous enthusiasm, and recited the first few lines of the first Olympian ode, with great feeling, in Greek. His wife asked him what it was all about. He said it would lose all its nobility in translation, but she pressed him. So he translated:

'Water is indeed very good, and gold which shines like blazing fire in the night is far better than all the riches which make men proud.

But, my spirit, if you desire to sing of contests, do not look for any star brighter than the sun during the day in the empty heavens, nor let us sing any contest more illustrious than Olympia.'

She listened to this, and then said 'You are making fun of me. You have made up all this nonsense for a joke; but you can't fool me so easily.' And although her husband kept trying to explain that he was giving her a plain literal translation, she insisted that the ancients were not so stupid as to write stuff like that.

But are the ancients vulgar? The second aspect of the argument is one of much interest and importance. In brief it is this. The classical poets are vulgar, because they describe common things and use undignified words; their heroes and heroines give way to violent emotions, and even work with their hands. Modern poets, of the age of Louis XIV, do not write of such things: therefore modern poets are superior. Perrault scoffs at Homer for describing a princess going down to the river with her maids-of-honour to do her brothers' laundry;[13] Lord Chesterfield, a most gentlemanly personage, raised his eyebrows at 'the porter-like language of Homer's heroes';[14] readers of refined taste and aristocratic sensibilities were deeply and genuinely shocked at the very mention of such things as domestic animals and household utensils—or, to put it with Homeric bluntness, cows and cooking-pots.[15] One of the passages most generally objected to was the famous simile in Homer where the hero Ajax, slowly retreating under heavy Trojan attacks, is compared with a donkey which has strayed into a field and is stubbornly eating the grain, while boys beat it with sticks to make it move on.[16] The very *word* 'donkey', said the modernists, could not be admitted into heroic poetry; and it was ineffably vulgar to compare a prince to an ass. The poet of the *Odyssey* was even worse when he described Odysseus' palace as having a dunghill at its gate.[17] The general attitude of these critics resembled that of the old Victorian lady who went to see Sarah Bernhardt in *Antony and Cleopatra*, and, after watching her languish with love, storm with passion, and rave with despair, murmured 'How unlike the home life of our own dear Queen!'

The answer to this argument is twofold. In the first place (as Tasso observed), 'those who are accustomed to the refinements of the present day despise these customs as old-fashioned and obsolete'.[18] There is really nothing disgraceful for a princess in superintending the washing—particularly since Nausicaa is not described as doing any dirty work, but rather making a trip to the riverside with her maidens as a sort of gay picnic, more real and not less charming than Arcadia. The manners and customs of the Homeric epics are indeed primitive, but they are nobly primitive, and only a very limited mind can despise them as gross.

On the other hand, words and images drawn from ordinary life *are* sometimes used in classical literature; although not in all of it. (The historian Tacitus, for instance, deliberately avoids calling a spade a spade, and uses the periphrasis 'things by which earth is extracted'; he will not even use the common word 'taverns' for the pubs where Nero went on his night excursions, but calls them 'resorts' or 'restaurants'[19]). But what the baroque critics did not realize is that, even in Homer, the vulgar words to which they objected were carefully chosen and sparingly used. For instance, 'donkey' occurs only once in all the Homeric epics, in the image of Ajax retreating; and immediately before it the poet compares Ajax to a lion at bay—although he seldom uses double comparisons. What Homer meant, therefore, was that Ajax was as brave as a lion and as stubborn as an ass; that his bravery and his stubbornness were closely connected aspects of his personality. This is comic. Homer meant it to be so. But it is true to life. To omit such brave stubborn soldiers from a poem about war would be to falsify the poem. Ajax *is* a comic hero, the only one in the epic—although both Nestor and Paris have a humorous side. As for Odysseus, his adventures during his return go far beyond anything in the *Iliad*. Odysseus is extremely clever, and utterly determined. He *will* get home in spite of every kind of temptation and trial; he *will* regain possession of his own house, wife, and wealth, although they are all claimed by younger rivals. To do this, he has to suffer. He is shipwrecked naked on a strange island. He escapes from a cannibal giant by hanging on to the underside of a ram. In order to get near his own house, he has to disguise himself as a ragged beggar, and have bones thrown at his head; but he endures. Sometimes during these trials he is pathetic, and sometimes he is grotesque—as when, during a sleepless night of anxiety, he is compared to a black-pudding which is being turned over and over before a blazing fire. But his humiliation and grotesquerie are part of his trials, and his endurance of them is necessary, to make him more truly heroic.

At bottom, the question is whether humour and the heroic can go together. Can the sublime emotions admit comic relief without being weakened? If they cannot, Dante's *Comedy*, Shakespeare's *Macbeth* and *Hamlet*, Tolstoy's *War and Peace*, along with many other great works, must be purified or discarded. And it must be remembered that at the supreme crises in the Homeric epics, there are no images and no words except those of the utmost nobility.

Behind these attacks on the art of the classical poets lay a number of preconceptions, which deserve examination, since the participants in the battle were not always aware of them.

The first was the assumption that contemporary taste—the taste of the baroque age, or rather of France, or rather of the French aristocracy, or rather of a small group within the French aristocracy—was the supreme judge of all art. It was a monarch as absolute as Louis. It could judge even things beyond the province of art. The Maréchale de Luxembourg is said to have exclaimed, after a shuddering glance at the Bible, 'What manners! what frightful manners! what a pity that the Holy Spirit should have had so little taste!'[20] Yet, although believed impeccable, this taste had certain limitations. Its standards were partly made by women, and by women who did not read with much care: so that they were apt to pronounce a book or a play barbarous if it did not pay much attention to love, and they could damn even the most important work by calling it tedious.[21] Again, taste was overwhelmingly dominated by reason, and almost ignored the irrational beauties of poetry. Assuming that poetry was merely an elaborate method of saying what might be clearer in prose, it expected a prose translation to contain all the beauties of the poetic original. And, most important, it was fearfully snobbish. It could scarcely bear the mention of anyone beneath the rank of marquis. No person worth writing about (it held) ever does any work, or experiences anything but the grandest emotions. From this it is an easy step to a limitation of language that makes it impossible even to mention everyday things, because ordinary means common, and common means vulgar. There was an uproar once in a French theatre, long after this, when a translation of *Othello* actually used the word *mouchoir* for the object which is the key of the plot; while a baroque poet avoided the word *chien* by calling the animal

de la fidélité le respectable appui.[22]

This habit was largely responsible for the growing cult of poetic clichés which ruined French poetry in the eighteenth century: it carried the chill upward, and upward, until even *love* began to sound common, and it was better to say *fires* or *flame*. Some of this was originally attributable to Spanish influence, for in aristocratic detachment from the ordinary world no one (at least in western civilization) has ever excelled the Spanish nobles of the seventeenth century. Certainly, it produced a drastic limitation of the vocabulary and syntax of French drama, and helped to kill a promising literary form. Doubtless these conventions were, as Hugo and the other revolutionary writers who attacked them believed, part of the old social system; but they took longer to destroy than the monarchy itself. They outlasted the revolution and the Terror: it was a generation later that

with breasts bare, the nine Muses sang the Carmagnole.[23]

The second assumption behind the modern attack was nationalism. From the time of Alfred in England, from the time of Dante in Italy, we have seen that the national language of each country is used as a tonic to strengthen patriotism. Statesmen and thinkers who are eager to increase the solidarity of their own people vaunt their language as equal or superior to Greek and Latin. This was the inspiration of Dante's essay *On Vernacular Style*.[24] In French it had already appeared in Du Bellay's *Defence and Ennoblement of the French Language*.[25] After him it was restated by Malherbe (who, although a purist and a 'classicist', despised much of the best of classical literature), and then in 1683 by François Charpentier, who argued in his treatise *On the Excellence of the French Language* that to admire the Greeks and Romans would keep the French from cultivating their own tongue. At the time this seemed reasonable enough. It was impossible to foresee that it was part of the general movement towards nationalism which, in the nineteenth and twentieth centuries, was to have such disastrous results, not only in politics but in literature, and occasionally in art and music. It would be a darkening of the light if any European or American country were to fall victim to the delusion that it has its *own* literature and its *own* culture. Politicians can be nationalists—although the greatest are something more. But artists, like scientists, work in a tradition which covers many countries and histories, transcending them all. The finest creative artists are those who live most fully both within their own nation and time, and within the much larger cultural stream of civilization, to which even the most powerful state is only a small channel, a single tributary.

A third impulse behind the modernists' attack was their opposition to traditional authority.[26] They felt that the prestige of the ancients was a dead hand, which kept the rising age from developing its full power, kept men from thinking clearly and boldly, discouraged aspiration and invention. In this they were speaking for the Renaissance, and they represented the best of its spirit. When first discovered and when properly used, the great achievements of classical antiquity were challenges to generous rivalry, not commands to laborious imitation. In the age of revolution, early in the nineteenth century, they became so again. But in this period they too often acted as a chilling weight on the imagination. The scientists and philosophers in particular attacked them for this narcosis, and boasted of ignoring all tradition in the advance of their own work. Bacon had been the first aggressor here. Some of his successors, supporters of the Royal Society, 'went so far as to express the opinion that nothing could be accomplished unless all ancient arts were rejected . . . everything that wore the face of antiquity should be destroyed, root and branch'.[27] Descartes, who prided himself on thinking out philosophy on his own account, boasted that he had forgotten all his Greek; and although he actually wrote two of his works in Latin, he had them carefully translated later.

The moderns also wished to assert naturalism, as opposed to the conventional loftiness and highly stylized unreality of classicizing literature. One of the leaders on the modern side was Charles Perrault, who gave us some of the most famous fairy-tales in the western world: *Puss in Boots*, *Little Red Riding Hood*, *Bluebeard*, and *Cinderella*. In this also the modernists had more right than wrong on their side. The greatest works of baroque literature are those in which, even when the language is correct and the setting formal and symmetrical, the eternal realities of the human heart find their most direct and complete expression. This conflict has been immortalized in a famous scene from Molière's *Misanthrope*, where Alceste bitterly attacks a formal elegiac love-poem, and says he far prefers a pretty little folk-song because it is closer to nature.[28] (And yet, in the same play, an admirable speech on the blindness of lovers is translated by Molière—who had an excellent classical education—practically word for word from Lucretius.)[29] The weakest of the modernist preconceptions was the fifth. Most of the moderns knew little or no Greek. And they all assumed that translations were amply sufficient to allow them to estimate the best works of antiquity—translations which were often in prose, and often (as we now know) positively incorrect. Perrault himself wrote a four-volume comparison of the ancients and the moderns although he could not read Greek at all, and knew little Latin literature outside the works of Cicero, Horace, Ovid, and Vergil.[30] It is true that good translations of classical books are few, but that does not mean we can take bad ones as our authority, any more than we should judge a picture by a blurred monochrome photograph. It is also arguable that, consciously or unconsciously, the moderns were asserting a preference for the Latin over the Greek tradition. Homer was attacked dozens of times more often than Vergil; the chief defenders of the ancients (Racine, Dacier, Boileau) were good Greek scholars; and when the regeneration of classical studies came, in the late eighteenth century, it was through a deepened understanding of Greek. By that time (see Chapter 20) a new Battle of the Books was about to begin.

Phases of the Battle

As full of confusion, uproar, false boasts, missed blows, and unexpected defeats as any Homeric battle, the Dispute of the Ancients and Moderns in France is difficult to describe in any easily intelligible and memorable sequence. It was complicated by the facts that irrelevant personal feuds, such as that between Boileau and the Jesuits, and those which set the supporters of Corneille against Racine, often clouded the issues; that second-rate men sometimes brought out first-rate arguments to prove wrong conclusions; and that really important critics such as Boileau never did themselves and their cause full justice. However, if the chief arguments are kept clearly in view, the course of the actual battle will be easier to follow.

The first blows were struck in Italy at the beginning of the seventeenth century. Homer and his Greek admirers were attacked by the brilliant Alessandro Tassoni, author of the mock-epic, *The Ravished Bucket*. In his *Miscellaneous Thoughts* (1620), he applied argument 4 to the *Iliad* with ruthlessly sharp intelligence and lofty baroque taste.[31] Most of the objections raised by later critics—improbable incidents, weak structure, vulgar imagery, the absence of a single grand subject, the interventions of the gods and the inconsistencies of the heroes—all these and many more were heaped on Homer's white head. And Tassoni went on to the positive argument that in fact modern men are far superior to the ancients of Greece and Rome in nearly every sphere of life and art.

The conflict became hotter in France. Here its first phase centred in the French Academy, which was founded in 1635. The very name of this institution implied that seventeenth-century France was intellectually at least as far advanced as Greece: for the Academy was not a mirror-copy of Plato's research institution, but a rival—and even, it was hoped, an improvement. We now think of the French Academy as a rather dictatorial authority on questions of language and taste, a closed corporation with a talent for not electing the greatest authors. But we must beware of thinking that, when it was founded, it was either unified or conservative. On the contrary, the majority of its early members were what we should now call advanced progressives; Boileau, who admired tradition, was in the minority throughout his career as a member; and one of the side-issues that confused the Dispute of Ancients and Moderns was a struggle for the control of the Academy and the power to write its regulations.

The fourth speech delivered before the Academy, at its meeting on 26 February 1635, was an attack on classical literature by the dramatist Boisrobert. He also used argument 4: for his purpose was to prove that his own plays had failed merely because his audiences had a mistaken admiration for the Greco-Roman poets, and that the ancients, though no doubt inspired by genius, were inferior in taste and grace to his contemporaries and himself. The speech is stated to have been bitterly combative in tone, but provoked no immediate reaction (which confirms that the Academy was inclined towards the 'modern' side), and is now lost.

A more sustained and violent attack on the classics was delivered a generation later by one of Richelieu's most powerful civil servants, Jean Desmarets de Saint-Sorlin (1596–1676), whom Boileau called 'the prophet Desmarets'. This man was an exact contemporary of Milton; he was converted in middle life, to become a fiery and resolute Catholic; and his ambition, like Milton's, was to write a great poem of Christianity which would equal by its technique and surpass by its subject the epics of pagan antiquity. He made two chief attempts: *Clovis*, on the conversion of the pagan Frankish king to Christianity (1657, republished with a polemical preface 1673), and *Marie-Magdeleine* (1669), on the conversion of the Jewish harlot to Christianity and her attainment of sainthood. Although these poems are not great works of art, the theory on which they were written is admirable, and it was a mistake of Boileau to condemn it.[32] It is justified not only by *Paradise Lost*, but by the tragedies of Corneille and Racine, some of which are on biblical or Christian subjects (*Polyeucte, Esther, Athalie*), while others (*Phèdre* in the queen's repentance, *Iphigénie* in the martyr's resignation) are Christian in spirit. But Milton, Tasso, Racine, and other great Christian poets acknowledged that the works of the ancients were noble, and then tried to surpass them. The prophet Desmarets made the mistake of trying to prove that his own and his contemporaries' works must be good because the works of the ancients were bad. (This is argument 4 again.) It is an amusing proof of his self-deception that one of his critical treatises maintains the superiority of the moderns, in an argument set out as a Platonic dialogue between two characters with the Greek names of Eusèbe and Philédon.[33] Before his death he solemnly called on Charles Perrault to continue the struggle:

> Come, Perrault, and protect your fatherland,
> Join in my fight against this rebel band,
> This gang of weaklings and of mutineers
> Who praise the Romans, greet our work with jeers . . .[34]

and then, like Hamilcar after dictating to Hannibal his oath of eternal hatred for Rome, fell asleep in peace.

There was another demonstration in 1683, when the witty Bernard Le Bovier de Fontenelle (1657–1757) published his *Dialogues of the Dead*. The main idea of these imaginary conversations is an expansion of argument 3, for they place ancients and moderns on exactly the same level: Montaigne talks with Socrates, and Erasistratus the physician with Harvey the surgeon. But they also emphasize argument 2. Fontenelle believes that progress in the arts and sciences is not a possibility, but an inevitable 'law'; and at most he qualifies it by his own enlightened cynicism, as when both Harvey and Montaigne, after explaining modern scientific and material progress, concede that, although men have learnt more than their ancestors, they have not become any better. There are also several trenchant assertions of argument 4: in a conversation with the little fable-teller Aesop, Homer is ridiculed for the absurd conduct of his gods and heroes. Fontenelle delivered further flank-attacks on the ancients in his *Discourse on the Nature of the Eclogue*, where he defended his own atrociously artificial pastorals by declaring Theocritus vulgar and Vergil affected; in his *Digression on the Ancients and Moderns*; and in his *Remarks on the Greek Theatre*, which called Aeschylus 'a sort of lunatic', as he no doubt was to that serene and narrowly focused intelligence.

These were skirmishes. The main battle was launched on 27 January 1687 by Charles Perrault, who read before the Academy a poem on *The Age of Louis the Great*. This work was based mainly on arguments 3 and 4, attacked the bad taste of the Homeric epics, and listed a number of contemporary Frenchmen who, said Perrault, would in due time be just as famous as the great Greeks and Romans. His list includes such household words as Maynard, Gombauld, Godeau, Racan, Sarrazin, Voiture, Rotrou, and Tristan, together with Régnier and Malherbe, who are slightly better known, and Molière, who really is a world figure; it omits Racine and Boileau.

While the poem was being read Boileau was scowling and chafing and muttering, like Alceste listening to the sonnet. Before it was finished he went out, saying that it was a disgrace to the Academy. For a long time, however, he made no systematic reply. He wrote a few epigrams comparing Perrault and his sympathizers to the savages of North and South America and to lunatics;[35] and he proposed that the Academy should adopt as its symbol a group of monkeys admiring themselves in a clear well, with the motto *sibi pulchri*, 'beautiful in their own eyes'; but it looks as though he had been too angry to construct a real answer.

Encouraged by his own success and his opponents' silence, Perrault went on to cover the ground more completely, by publishing a series of dialogues between contemporary characters (one of them personifying himself), called *Parallel between the Ancients and the Moderns*. These came out at intervals between 1688 and 1697, and dealt with architecture, sculpture, painting; oratory; poetry; and science, philosophy, and music. They also included a very injudicious and inexact defence of his own knowledge of Greek and Latin. All four of the chief arguments were used in various places; but argument 4 was employed only in the discussion of literature, while Perrault was wise enough to keep argument 2 ('progress is continuous') for subjects like architecture and science.

Before any answer could be composed, a diplomat called de Callières produced an amusing parody, *A Poetic History of the War lately declared between the Ancients and the Moderns*, which drew off some of the heat from the contest, and which Swift later indignantly denied copying—although it bears the same relationship to his *Battle of the Books* as Boileau's *The Lectern* does to Pope's *Dunciad*. Like Swift's parody, it ended with the victory of the ancients, and the glorification of their greatest modern supporters: by which de Callières meant Boileau and Racine.[36]

Still, no systematic reply was attempted from the classical side. Boileau got involved in a feud with the Jesuits (although, as devoted to classical education, they should have been on his side) because he had supported Pascal: so that the odds were further shifted against him. Meanwhile, Bayle was incorporating Perrault's and his own modernist ideas in his *Philosophical Dictionary* —particularly the weakest of all the arguments, the argument from taste: he said, for instance, that Achilles raging for the loss of Briseis (and his honour) was like a child crying for a doll.[37] This argument was answered in 1692 by Huet, in a *Letter to Perrault*, and in 1694 by Boileau, in his rather ill-humoured *Critical Reflections on Longinus*. Although Boileau's criticism of Perrault's ignorant blunders were perfectly justified, their effect was diminished by the tone of sour pedantry in which they were written. We shall see a similar phenomenon in Britain in the next generation.

Soon afterwards the great Jansenist and anti-Jesuit Arnauld addressed a letter to Perrault, suggesting a reconciliation between the two groups of opponents, for the sake of reason and of Christian charity. Boileau followed this up by a handsome letter to Perrault, in which he abandoned many of his strongest positions. He agreed that the seventeenth century was the greatest age of mankind, and conceded that the men of his own day surpassed the Augustans in tragedy, philosophy, lyric poetry, science, and novel-writing, while the Augustans retained the primacy in epic, elegy, oratory, and his own field of satire. There was a formal reconciliation, and this phase of the battle closed, leaving the moderns with a very marked advantage.

The bridge between the first French phase of the battle and the English phase was Charles de Marguetel de Saint-Denis, Seigneur de St. Évremond, born in 1610, exiled in 1661 after Fouquet's fall, and prominent in London (where his daughter had a salon) for a quarter of a century: he died in 1703 and was buried in Westminster Abbey. Rigault begins his chapter on the subject with an acid description of the cultural relations between France and England: 'True to her general habits,' he says, 'England has taken a little more from us than she has given us.'[38] And, with perhaps a touch of imagination, he relates how St. Évremond sat in Will's coffee-house and instructed the barbarian English—Dryden, Wotton, Temple, and such—in the necessity of reading the classics in the original rather than in translation. The relations between English literary society and France during the baroque age were very close and rich, so that, although St. Évremond no doubt created a liaison, he was certainly not the only channel of ideas.

The first shot of the battle in England was fired by the cultured, intelligent, and above all discreet diplomat Sir William Temple, patron of Jonathan Swift. In 1690 he published a little book dedicated to his alma mater, Cambridge, called *An Essay upon the Ancient and Modern Learning*. This is a ridiculously exaggerated assertion of the primacy of the classics. It takes up arguments 2 and 3, and inverts them. Yes, it says, we have progressed; but most of the really important discoveries were made by the ancients; we have added little: let us respect our superiors. And, although the moderns assert that nature does not change, that merely proves it is more difficult for us nowadays to surpass the ancients, who have already said everything worth saying. 'There is nothing new in astronomy to vie with the ancients, unless it be the Copernican system; nor in physic, unless Harvey's circulation of the blood.' Like Perrault, he gives a list of the moderns whom he thinks worthy of lasting fame; and it is worse, if anything, than Perrault's. The Italian immortals, for instance, are Boccaccio, Machiavelli, and Fra Paolo Sarpi; and the English are Sidney, Bacon, and Selden. His list proclaims him a determined admirer of the second-rate. And then, in one very celebrated passage, he declared that the oldest books were also the best:

'The two most ancient that I know of in prose, among those we call profane authors, are Aesop's Fables and Phalaris's Epistles. . . . As the first has been agreed by all ages since for the greatest master in his kind, . . . so I think the Epistles of Phalaris to have more grace, more spirit, more force of wit and genius than any others I have ever seen.'

He adds that some have questioned the authenticity of these letters, but that taste and discernment are enough to show they are genuine.

Phalaris was a powerful Sicilian monarch who reigned despotically and, it is said, with savage cruelty in the sixth century B.C. More than 700 years after his death a forger composed a collection of letters and published them under Phalaris' name. This was another of these mystifications like the eyewitness accounts of the Trojan war by 'Dares' and 'Dictys'.[39] Perhaps it is unfair to call it a forgery. Perhaps it should be called an imaginative exercise, like many a modern historical romance told in the first person. But it produced the same results as if it had been a forgery: it deceived generations of readers, and obscured the truth of history. The chief merit of Temple's essay was that it caused the real facts to be made known at last.

Meanwhile, however, another Cambridge man replied to Temple. This was the brilliant William Wotton: he had been an infant prodigy, and knew more about the classics than Temple had ever dreamt of. His *Reflections upon Ancient and Modern Learning* (1694) is the best book directly concerned with the dispute. It distinguishes the sciences, which progress, from the arts and philosophy, which do not; and it answers argument 1 by proving that it is to the advantage of the Christian faith to use the best of pagan literature, to transform and transcend it. Wotton was a friend of the man who was the best scholar not only in Cambridge but in all England, and not only in England but in the whole world. This was Richard Bentley.

Now, because of the advertisement given to the 'Letters of Phalaris' by Temple's remarks, a new edition of their Greek text was called for. It was published in 1695, by a group of the dons and undergraduates of Christ Church, Oxford, headed by the dean, Aldrich; but signed, according to a convention by which each new book produced in the House was attributed to one of the group, by the Hon. Charles Boyle, second son of the earl of Orrery and a kinsman of the distinguished scientist. The preface contained a tart reference to Bentley, who, as librarian of St. James's

Library, had refused to allow a manuscript of the letters to be kept out more than a few days. Like his disciple Housman, Bentley never forgot or evaded an attack.

In 1697 he produced a *Dissertation* on Aesop and Phalaris, which was published in the second edition of Wotton's book. Boyle and his friends replied, wittily and amateurishly. In 1699 Bentley issued an enlarged and final version of his *Dissertation*, which, although it did not at once carry conviction (because of the very loftiness of its standards), 'marked an epoch in the history of scholarship'.[40] It was as scientific as any modern savant could desire. By clear and sensible analysis of the letters themselves, by subjecting them to historical, philological, and literary examination, he proved that they were written in the wrong dialect of Greek, that they referred to men and cities that flourished long after the death of the real Phalaris, and that they contained quotations from poets centuries younger than the Sicilian tyrant. He added the best of all culminatory arguments, that from spirit. The letters, he says, are not vigorous, vivid, Medicean, but artificial and jejune:

'You feel, by the emptiness and deadness of them, that you converse with some dreaming pedant with his elbow on his desk; not with an active, ambitious tyrant, with his hand on his sword, commanding a million of subjects.'

In the same treatise Bentley exposed three other forgeries of the same type, the 'Letters of Themistocles', 'Letters of Socrates', and 'Letters of Euripides'; and he gave the true descent of the so-called 'Fables of Aesop'.

Nevertheless, the *Dissertation* had one serious fault, which stemmed from Bentley's own character. He argued so haughtily and violently that his tone created opposition in many readers who were genuine lovers of the classics. For instance, Pope, who was no fool, might have wished to put the Christ Church group into his *Dunciad*, but instead he introduced Bentley as an example of Pedantry.[41] (Housman himself pinned him in the phrase 'tasteless and arbitrary pedant'.[42]) The nemesis, the Agamemnonian tragedy, followed inevitably. Bentley produced an edition of Milton's *Paradise Lost*, in which nearly all the poetry was altered to suit his own taste and the criteria of contemporary style. He asserted that the poem contained so many unintelligible phrases that—having been dictated by Milton in his blindness—it must have been deformed by a careless editor: just as a number of the Greek and Latin classics have been deformed. Thus,

> No light, but rather darkness visible[43]

was obviously ridiculous, since darkness reveals nothing. Milton must have meant 'darkness in which it is still possible to see'; what could the correct version be?—I have it:

> No light, but rather a transpicuous gloom.

And thus, by applying the standards of his own age and the limitations of his own imagination to Milton's poetry, Bentley fell into exactly the same faults and follies as the 'moderns' had committed in criticizing Homer.[44] This was not the last time that an arrogant professor was to spoil great poetry in the belief that, while the poet had been blind, he himself could see perfectly.

Swift, who was Temple's secretary, had been watching this conflict. He had a certain amount of sympathy for both sides, for he was a good classical scholar, but admired and cultivated originality; and he viewed both sides with his own ingrowing contempt, for he hated pedants and polymaths, he loathed upstarts and ignoramuses, and he despised the pettiness which causes mankind to divide Truth and squabble over her mangled body. In 1704 he published two of his earliest satires, *A Tale of a Tub* and *The Battle of the Books*. The first of these contained, among many side-blows at the innumerable species of human folly, several savage cuts at Bentley and Wotton. The second was a description of the battle, told in the manner of Homer. Although Swift declared with some violence that he had never heard of de Callières's *Poetic History of the War . . . between the Ancients and the Moderns*, there are some close parallels;[45] still, it is amusing enough and original enough, as epic parodies go.

It contains one episode more interesting than the various mock-heroic adventures: a fable (told partly in epic style[46]) of a dispute between a spider and a bee. The spider reproaches the bee, who has broken his web, with being a homeless vagabond with no possessions, living on loot; and he boasts that he himself is the architect of his own castle, having both designed it and spun the material out of his own body. (This was the reproach which the moderns aimed at the ancients, calling them copyists, the thieves of others' thoughts, while they themselves claimed to be entirely original in all they wrote.) The bee replies that it is possible to rely exclusively on one's own genius, but that any creative artist who does so will produce only ingenious cobwebs, with the addition of the poison of selfishness and vanity; while the bee, ranging with infinite labour throughout all nature, brings home honey and wax, to furnish humanity with sweetness and light.

By this fine phrase (which later became a favourite of Matthew Arnold) Swift stood out unequivocally as a partisan of the 'ancients', a believer in Greco-Roman culture as the essential preparation for creative art and thought. Although he did not mention Horace, he was surely thinking of the poem in which Horace compared himself to the hard-working bee, gathering sweetness from innumerable flowers.[47] He knew Horace's poetry well; and perhaps he liked it better because of his own crushing failure to write odes in the manner of Pindar.[48] And yet—and yet Swift himself, in his own best work, was far more of a modern than an ancient. Compared with those of Boileau and of Pope, his satires are boldly original, owing relatively little to his satiric predecessors; and sometimes, like his own spider, they are marked by 'an overweening Pride, which feeding and engendering on itself, turns all into Excrement and Venom'.

Just as Bentley, by the chances of conflict and the twists of character, was manoeuvred into the false position of seeming to defend the moderns, so we feel that Swift misplaced himself on the side of the ancients, whom he doubtless admired but could not follow. This maladjustment was largely due to Bentley's own singularly offensive character, and to the wit and charm displayed, although on a flimsy framework, by his opponents.[49] The essential distinction between ancients and moderns was really not summed up in the contrast of Politeness and Pedantry: it had been obscured by the dust of dispute and the clash of personalities.

Many years afterwards, in 1742, Mr. Pope took a belated part in the battle, bringing a caricature of Bentley into The Dunciad.[50] Bentley himself put this down to the directness (and justice) of his own criticism of Pope's translation of the Iliad: 'a very pretty poem, but you must not call it Homer'. At this juncture scarcely anything of the original Battle of the Books was left; but the point of Pope's attack, that scholarship without broad humanity is repellent, still holds good.

The third phase of the war takes us back to France, but since it was fought over nearly the same terrain we need not follow all the operations in detail. This time the ancients took the offensive. Madame Dacier (1654–1720), a lady as noble as she was learned, published in 1699 a translation of the *Iliad* into French prose, in which she endeavoured to do the fullest possible justice to the beauties obscured by other translations. She added a laudatory preface, in which she took up and destroyed argument 4. Some years later, in 1714, her work was undone and the argument re-asserted by Antoine Houdar de la Motte, in an abridged translation of the *Iliad*, which he altered, abbreviated, and bowdlerized so as to omit the boring speeches, vulgar words, disgusting passions, and useless or unpleasant supernatural effects which offended the taste of the baroque age.[51] Madame Dacier replied in a treatise *On the Causes of the Corruption of Taste* (1714), which was not only an attack on contemporary taste in literature but a denunciation of some of the standards of contemporary civilization. In reply, Houdar de la Motte prepared a set of *Reflections on Criticism* (1715). This argument, like that between Boileau and Perrault, was reconciled in 1716 by the kind offices of mediators; but not solved. It has scarcely been solved to this day.

So ended the great Battle. It has been resumed since, but not on exactly the same ground, or by the same opponents. Although it was less neatly conducted than the chessboard wars of Vauban and other baroque strategists, its results were similar: a limited gain on one side, a smaller gain and a retrenchment of forces on the other, a certain amount of loss for both, and a general readjustment of diplomatic weights and counterweights. The 'ancients' won their contention that the virtues of the great Greek and Roman writers were not all on the surface, required careful and well-informed appreciation, and could not be approved or denied by the taste of one generation and one country alone. Critical standards were constantly improving from the sixteenth century onwards, and the Battle of the Books did a great deal to refine and sharpen them. The defenders of the classics thus prepared the death of rococo and similar trivialities, and helped to create the deeper understanding of Greek poetry which came with the end of the eighteenth century. They defended, and expanded, the highest traditions of the Renaissance.

The main damage done by the battle was that it created, or widened, a gap between scholars and the general public. It confirmed certain pedants in their exclusiveness; and it encouraged the belief that the man in the street is capable, without any conscious training of his taste and knowledge, of deciding what is and what is not a good work of art.

The 'moderns', on the other side, carried the essential point—which their opponents had never sincerely disputed—that modern books *can* be just as good as anything written in Greece and Rome. They did not succeed in convincing anyone that modern literature, even if elevated by Christian doctrine, *must* be better than the classics. But the real benefit of the battle for both sides was that it discouraged slavish respect for tradition, and made it more difficult for future writers to produce 'Chinese copies' of classical masterpieces, in which exact imitation should be a virtue and original invention a sin. (Had some such broadening of the significance of tradition been possible in Rome, the literature of the later empire would be far more valuable.) The idea of progress may sometimes be a dangerous drug, but it is often a valuable stimulant; and it is better for us to be challenged to put forth our best, in order to surpass our predecessors, than to be told the race is hopeless.

A NOTE ON BAROQUE

T HE word 'baroque' comes from the Spanish *barroco*, 'a large irregular pearl'. A regular pearl is a perfect sphere; an irregular pearl is a sphere straining outwards at one point, bulging and almost breaking, but yet not bursting into fragments. Therefore 'baroque' means 'beauty compressed but almost breaking the bounds of control'.[1]

Renaissance art is the perfect pearl. The art of the seventeenth and eighteenth centuries, during the period between the Renaissance and the age of revolutions, is the baroque pearl. The essential meaning of the word is the interplay of strong emotion and stronger social, aesthetic, intellectual, moral, and religious restraints. What we, nowadays, usually see in baroque art and literature is its formality, its symmetry and frigidity. What the men and women of the baroque era saw in it was the tension between ardent passion and firm, cool control. This conflict appeared in their own lives and characters. It was epitomized in the Grand Monarch himself, turning from the voluptuous Montespan to the serene and spiritual Maintenon. It has been finely described by Macaulay in his character of William the Third:

'He was born with violent passions and quick sensibilities: but the strength of his emotions was not suspected by the world. From the multitude his joy and his grief, his affection and his resentment, were hidden by a phlegmatic serenity, which made him pass for the most coldblooded of mankind. Those who brought him good news could seldom detect any sign of pleasure. Those who saw him after a defeat looked in vain for any trace of vexation. He praised and reprimanded, rewarded and punished, with the stern tranquillity of a Mohawk chief; but those who knew him well and saw him near were aware that under all this ice a fierce fire was constantly burning. It was seldom that anger deprived him of power over himself. But when he was really enraged the first outbreak of his passion was terrible. It was indeed scarcely safe to approach him. On these rare occasions, however, as soon as he regained his self-command, he made such ample reparation to those whom he had wronged as tempted them to wish that he would go into a fury again. His affection was as impetuous as his wrath. Where he loved, he loved with the whole energy of his strong mind. When death

separated him from what he loved, the few who witnessed his agonies
trembled for his reason and his life.'[2]

That same tension characterizes the work of the baroque artists
and writers. It can be seen

in their satires and epigrams, venomous but polite;

in their tragedies, passionate but stilted and formalized;

in the statues of female saints and mystics, yearning, swoon-
ing, almost expiring, almost flying up to heaven, but richly
and conventionally draped and elegantly posed;

in the solemn, strictly symmetrical churches, cathedrals, and
palaces, where a grand and austere design is blended with
soft, charming decoration—flower-and-leaf motives, graceful statuary and portrait-heads—with sumptuous colours,
crimson, purple, and gold, with elaborately curving pillars
and swooping arches, with brilliant lighting and rich
fabrics;

in music, in the contrast between the free and emotional Bach
prelude or toccata, and the rigidly formal and intellectually
disciplined fugue which follows and dominates the dual
composition; and again, in the unbelievably intricate
cadenzas through which the voice of the opera-singer, like
a bird struggling to escape, fluttered upwards, soared, and
sank at last, returning to the keynote and the waiting
orchestra, to complete the formal aria.[3]

The greatest baroque artists, who most intensely characterize their
age, are these:

Adam in architecture	Góngora in poetry
The brothers Asam in interior decoration	El Greco in painting
	Handel in music
Bach in music	Lully in music
Bernini in architecture	Metastasio in operatic tragedy
Boileau in satire and criticism	Molière in comedy
Bossuet in oratory	Monteverdi in music
Churriguerra in architecture	Pope in satires and poetic epistles
Corneille in tragedy	
Dryden in tragedy and satire	Poussin in painting
Fielding in the mock-heroic novel	Purcell in opera
	Racine in tragedy
Gibbon in prose history	Rubens in painting

Alessandro and Domenico Scar-
  latti in music
Swift in satire
Tiepolo in painting

Titian in painting
Vanbrugh in architecture
Veronese in painting
Wren in architecture.

In the work of all these diverse artists, in so many countries, what part did Greek and Roman influence play?

First, it supplied themes, which ranged all the way from tragic stories to tiny decorative motifs on a vase, a wall, or a cabinet. Despite the resistance of the 'moderns', Rome was reborn in the gorgeous palaces, the immense cathedrals, the long straight roads and geometrically designed towns which grew up all over Europe during that era. (Some of the 'moderns', like the architect Perrault, actually helped in the rebirth.) Racine's greatest heroine was a prehistoric Greek princess. Purcell's finest opera is about Dido and Aeneas. Handel's best-known song comes from an opera about Xerxes. Pope and Boileau both strove to reincarnate Horace in themselves, and partially succeeded. Gibbon spent his life writing the history of the later Roman empire, in cadences which themselves were consciously Roman.

Secondly, it supplied forms—the forms of tragedy, comedy, satire, character-sketch, oration, philosophical dialogue, Pindaric and Horatian ode, and many more.

More important, it acted as a restraining force. As such, it was welcomed. The men and women of that period felt the dangers of passion, and sought every proper means of controlling it. Religion was one: the greatest. Social prestige was another: to display extreme emotion was ungentlemanly. No less powerful was the example of Greco-Roman morality (particularly Stoicism) and of Greco-Roman art, with its combination of dignity and purity. Greek and Roman art is very, very rarely grotesque and ignoble, as much medieval art is. (Compare the punishments of the damned in the classical underworld, with the more terrible but often mean and filthy tortures of the damned in Dante's hell.) Therefore its example can help modern men and women to ignore or minimize the baseness which lies in every human heart, and, even at the apparent sacrifice of individuality, to achieve nobleness. Those subtle psychologists the Jesuits knew that, properly taught, classical literature will purify the heart and raise the soul; and they became the greatest group of classical teachers the modern world has seen. A list of the pupils whose minds they developed through the classics would include an astonishing number and variety of geniuses: Tasso, Molière, Descartes, Voltaire. . . .

To use classical literature and fine art as a moral restraint was well judged. Its use as an aesthetic control was at first well judged, too, and then was exaggerated until it became, not a moulding principle, but a numbing and paralysing force. For instance, baroque tragedy subjected itself, in the name of Aristotle, to a number of rules which Aristotle had never conceived as rules, and, as part of the same restraining movement, to many others which would have amused or appalled him. This exaggeration is sometimes called *classicism*, which is a good enough name in English, provided it is not taken to mean 'the use of classical models' in general.[4] Later, the revolutionary era was to discover that Greco-Roman literature and thought can mean not only restraint, but liberation; and when it cast off the classicism of the baroque age it was not discarding Greece and Rome, but exploring them more deeply.

Lastly, classical literature, myth, art, and thought helped to produce the intellectual unity of Europe and the two Americas. Through the seventeenth and eighteenth centuries they provided a common realm of imagination and discussion in which minds separated by language, distance, and creed could meet as equals. It transcended nationality and bridged religious gulfs. Like the Roman Catholic church in the Dark Ages and the Middle Ages, it was a spiritual, and therefore a more lasting, rebirth of Greek and Roman culture in the form of an empire in the souls of western men.

16

BAROQUE TRAGEDY

IN poetry the most considerable production of the baroque age (excluding the latest of the Renaissance epics, *Paradise Lost*) is a body of tragedies in English, French, and Italian. The finest of these are the work of Pierre Corneille (producing from 1635 to 1674), Jean Racine (producing from 1664 to 1677, with two later works on biblical subjects), and John Dryden (producing from 1664 to 1694). There are also a number of interesting singletons such as Milton's *Samson Agonistes*, Addison's *Cato*, and Johnson's *Irene*; there is a large body of operatic dramas by Metastasio; and there were thousands of mediocrities now forgotten—such as Voltaire's tragedies, which would still be buried had they not been disinterred and momentarily galvanized into ludicrous life by Lytton Strachey in *Books and Characters*. All these tragedies are in a form very closely resembling that of Greco-Roman tragedy, and many, including the greatest, are on subjects taken from Greek mythology or Roman history. Some, such as Racine's *Phèdre*, are actually on themes already worked out by Greek and Roman dramatists, and use ideas originated by classical playwrights.[1] Baroque tragedy was what Spengler calls a pseudomorphosis: the re-creation in one culture of a form or activity created by another culture distant in time or space.

Baroque tragedy was more intensely classical than almost any other type of modern literature. Certainly it depended much more on Greco-Roman literature and mythology than the great bulk of English, French, and Spanish Renaissance drama. There were several reasons for this: all important, because they mark significant changes in the society and civilization of western Europe.

The authors were much more thoroughly educated than those who produced Renaissance tragedy, and even after the end of their schooling they continued to steep themselves in the classics.

Corneille was educated by the Jesuits, which means that he had a sound and sympathetic classical training. Although he was the least well read of the three chief tragedians, his knowledge of ancient literature was far wider than that of Shakespeare: it was he who founded French classical tragedy by seizing the essentials and discarding the unusable elements in Greco-Roman tragedy. Although we cannot measure a poet's gifts and achievements by the quality of his learning, still it is interesting to know that Racine was much more learned than Corneille. Racine could be called a skilled hellenist, whereas Corneille, like many of his contemporaries, had much Latin and small Greek. Even in character Corneille was a Roman, proud, simple, rather inarticulate, while Racine was a sensitive, thoughtful, and complex Greek.

Racine was educated very well and carefully by the Jansenists at Port-Royal. They got him late, at the age of seventeen, but they did a remarkable job of making him understand and love the classics. We hear of his roaming the woods of Port-Royal alone with his Euripides, and learning Heliodorus' *Aethiopica*² off by heart. The feat sounds very improbable; yet the book, which contains a story of a proud king meditating the sacrifice of his own daughter (as in *Iphigénie*) and another of a stepmother in love with her stepson (as in *Phèdre*), must have affected him deeply: one of his early plays was on a theme frankly borrowed from it. We have said that Corneille was the Roman, Racine the Greek. The difference reflects the difference in their education, for the Jesuits did little to encourage Greek studies while the Jansenists specialized in them. It is strange to see how the tragedians of the modern world, having started to understand classical tragedy through the latest of all the tragic poets, Seneca, gradually work their way back from the estuary to the source, from the Roman back to the Greeks. Corneille's early *Médée* is the only baroque tragedy in French which comes from Seneca, and except in the Latin tragedies written by Jesuit playwrights Senecan influence shrinks rapidly in this period. But even Racine did not penetrate farther upstream than Euripides.

Only one poet of the period knew and assimilated all three Greek tragedians. This was John Milton, who has left us one tragedy on a hero like himself, blind and surrounded by Philistines. *Samson Agonistes*, unlike the other dramas of the baroque era, is a pure re-creation of Greek tragedy. Like *Paradise Lost*, it blends classical technique and emotion with Hebrew and Christian thought. While its parallelism to Milton's own life and to the apparent defeat of the cause which he served is clear, it is far less contemporary in feeling than the plays by professional dramatists like Corneille and Dryden. It is also less dramatic; and it is far less effective than its Greek models.[3] The conflicts are less urgent and the subordinate characters more shadowy than in Aeschylus' *Prometheus Bound* (which was Milton's chief pattern), and there is a subtlety in Sophocles which Milton could scarcely achieve. Although the conception of the play is majestic, and the single character of Samson is grand, and several speeches and choruses contain immortal poetry, the work was written for the study and not for the theatre, so that it lacks the tension of Greek drama, and of all true drama.

John Dryden was educated at Westminster School and Trinity College, Cambridge. Both the style of his prefaces and prose writings, and the frequent quotations in them, made without affectation, show that he knew ancient literature familiarly and held it dear. His translations from Roman and Greek classics are of a purity rare at any time, and of a range which many professional scholars could not now equal.

Johnson, like Corneille, was a poor Grecian; but he was an excellent latinist. He read a great deal by himself in his father's bookshop, was well educated by the time he reached Pembroke College, Oxford, and as an undergraduate turned Pope's *The Messiah* into Latin verse. One of the earliest of his many literary plans was to edit the poems of the Renaissance humanist Politian and to produce a history of modern Latin poetry; and he made his name with an adaptation of Juvenal's third satire.

Addison went to Charterhouse, and then to Oxford, where he became a fellow of Magdalen and wrote admirable Latin verse. Among his early work in the field of classics are a translation of the fourth book of Vergil's *Georgics* and an archaeological *Essay on Medals* written during his tour of Italy.

As for the phenomenal Metastasio (1698–1782), he translated the *Iliad* into Italian verse at the age of twelve, and wrote an original tragedy in the manner of Seneca at fourteen.

This mass of learning comes out not only in the plays these men wrote but also in their prose works: Dryden's *Essay on Dramatic Poesy*, Corneille's *Trois discours sur le poème dramatique*, Racine's careful commentaries on Pindar and Homer, Addison's essays on Milton, and Milton's superb *Areopagitica*.

But the audiences, although better educated than those of the Renaissance, were not nearly so well educated as their poets. Few of the ladies, whose taste had so much to do with the success of a play, knew their classics. Few of the gentlemen were more than amateur scholars, like Charles Perrault, with a strictly limited range of reading. Baroque tragedy is not the first literary type, nor the last, in which classical influence has led to the adoption of artistic standards too high for a contemporary audience.

On the other hand, the audiences were far from unsympathetic. Society had now lost many of the vivid, vital qualities of the Renaissance; but it acquired, or retained and enhanced, those which were suited to encourage the new style of drama. In France, and to a less extent in England, Italy, and elsewhere, society was now becoming much more urbanized. For the first time since the fall of Rome, western European societies were organized around great capital cities, each with a regal court at its heart. Where such cities did not exist, it was necessary to create them—as the Prussian monarchs created Berlin, as Peter the Great both built St. Petersburg as a city and inaugurated it as the centre of government. The leisured classes in these cities provided a keen and permanent audience for the dramatists.

Grandeur was the ideal of western Europe. It was an era of magnificent display. We see this in architecture—not only great buildings like Versailles and Blenheim but elaborate formal gardens and vast parks, entire sectors of cities, even whole towns were laid out on a hitherto-unexampled scale which recalled Rome. We see it in interior decoration. The grandiose conception, the very size, of the Hall of Mirrors at Versailles would have staggered any Renaissance prince. Social and diplomatic ceremony also show it, and so does costume, where there were many non-functional adjuncts such as wigs, lace, and dress swords. It appeared in music: this was the age of the organ, when the counterpoint of Bach built an invisible Versailles to the glory of God, and it was the age of the enormous trained choirs. Stage design, too, showed it: production, *décor*, and costumes reached a new peak of elaboration and opulence. Nowadays we are apt to think that, behind all this magnificence, beneath the periwigs and the jewelled orders, people were empty shells. Some were; but the letters and memoirs and portraits of the time remain to show us that many still felt and suffered deeply—perhaps all the more intensely for the repressions that surrounded them. It was this combination of formal grandeur and passionate emotions which made tragedy and opera, with all their conventions, the truest expression of the baroque era.

(Always close, the kinship between tragedy and opera now became closer still. Dryden joined Purcell in writing *King Arthur*. The works of Metastasio were scarcely less fine when viewed as pure tragedies than when they were sung as operas. The Franco-Italian composer Lully collaborated closely with Molière, and himself felt that his work was allied to that of the dramatists: he said, 'If you want to sing my music properly, go and hear la Champmeslé'—a favourite actress of the Comédie who had received lessons in speech and acting from Racine himself.)

Baroque tragedy was, in its day, greatly admired. Its actors and actresses, together with the famous virtuosi singers, almost raised the stage to the dignity of a profession. Its achievements in stage-design and production are still unequalled. It produced some interesting critical discussions, a few marvellous plays, and many fine speeches. But can we say that it was a success? Can it be equalled with Greek tragedy, or with the tragedy of the Renaissance?

Clearly it cannot. Not as a whole. In France, the baroque tragedians did produce finer plays than any of the *French* Renaissance playwrights; but we must survey the tragedy, not of one country, but of the entire epoch. Not only did the genus fail to produce a sufficient number of good plays to offset the enormous bulk of bad plays born from it; not only do few of its products hold the stage to-day; but its own poets, from Metastasio to Dryden, abandoned the stage before finishing their careers, and sank into a silence which confessed a sense of failure.

Two reasons can be assigned for this failure. The first is social and cultural, the second aesthetic; but they connect

Socially and culturally, the error of the baroque tragedians was that they addressed too small an audience, and that they themselves limited the audience still further. The greatest drama has usually appealed to, and drawn its strength from, a broad section of the nation that gives it birth. That does not mean that it cannot be aristocratic in tone. Usually it is, but it appeals to the middle class and sometimes to the working class as well; and what gives it real fertility is a large literate public with good taste. But the audience of baroque tragedy was (except for Italian opera) confined to the upper classes, 'the court and the capital', and not all of those.[4] And its themes were on an even loftier social plane, moving among princes, kings, emperors, and their faithful attendants. It has been suggested that this was due to a misunderstanding or exaggeration of Aristotle's advice that only great men should be made the subjects of tragedies, but it is easier to believe that it was a reflex of the monarchical structure of society. Nor can it be said that, in spite of this, the problems of baroque tragedy are all universal problems. On the contrary, many of the plots concern the dynastic struggles of autocratic monarchs. Consider Racine's *Iphigénie*. Some fathers, it is true, do sacrifice the happiness of their daughters, and so far the problem is a universal one; but very few fathers have to decide whether to have their daughters liquidated as part of a political and military operation. Dryden's *Aureng-Zebe* is an intricate story of intrigue and power-politics in the Mogul court, and every major character has a band of trusty mutes or a private army.

The learning which the baroque playwrights displayed also alienated some of their audiences. Although their works are rarely pedantic, they do presuppose a knowledge of the classics more considerable than that possessed by some of the men and nearly all the women in the aristocratic audiences. Poetry written by scholars has this inevitable weakness, that even when it is good it creates a feeling of discomfort and even resentment among those who are not classically educated. The basic conflict which lies beneath this feeling is the conflict between art as education and art as amusement. Most of the audiences of baroque tragedy felt, when they saw a classical play, that it was elevated, but in danger of becoming pedantic. Quinault, with his lyrical dramas, and Thomas Corneille, whose romantic *Timocrate* was the greatest success of the era, were really more popular than the great Pierre Corneille and the subtle Jean Racine.

The second, or aesthetic, reason for the failure of baroque tragedy is a peculiar one. It is often misunderstood by modern critics. They are apt to think that the seventeenth-century and eighteenth-century tragedians were hampered and limited by their obedience to Greek and Roman rules of form. But the truth is that they imposed limitations on themselves which were far more complex, far more rigid, than anything to be found in classical drama.

These limitations were not so much a reproduction of the conventions of the Greco-Roman stage as a reaction against the extravagances of the Renaissance. The baroque era despised the Renaissance drama for bad taste: for its wildly confused plots, unbelievable incidents, vulgar buffoonery, ranting speeches, eccentric and incredible characters; for offensive morality—with its obscene jokes and its tortures, lusts, and treacheries; and for improbabilities which insulted not merely scholarship but ordinary common sense—as when Macbeth's porter (who lived in A.D. 1055) made up-to-the-minute jokes about Elizabethan London. But, more important than that, the baroque conventions were *social* restrictions. To make a good play is to create a work of art. To observe *les bienséances* is to conform to an aristocratic social code. The baroque playwright had to do both. He could not do the former without doing the latter. About his artistic success opinions might differ; but if his work was socially offensive he was surely damned. His task was therefore excessively, unnecessarily difficult: and, except for the greatest geniuses, and not seldom even for them, impossible.

One of the chief social limitations which interfered with the work of the baroque playwrights was the rule that 'low' words could not be used. Had this meant the avoidance of obscene or repulsive words, it would have been a limitation possible to accept. (It carried with it the condemnation of Hamlet's

I'll lug the guts into the neighbour room,[5]

of much of his denunciation of Gertrude,[6] and of many great speeches not only in drama but in other kinds of poetry such as Roman satire.) The Greek and Roman tragedians and epic poets on the whole avoided such words too, although Homer and Aeschylus, Seneca and Lucan, all permit themselves to employ one or two for special effects. But in the baroque age the vocabulary was limited much further than the great classics had ever imagined necessary, by the exclusion of working-class words. Dr. Johnson objected to Lady Macbeth's tremendous invocation:

Come, thick night,
And pall thee in the dunnest smoke of hell,
That my keen knife see not the wound it makes!

—on the ground that a knife was 'an instrument used by butchers and cooks in the meanest employments'.[7] Shakespeare well knew that it was used by butchers. Yet he did not think Lady Macbeth any less a queen for saying the word. Racine himself recognized that in this the language of his contemporaries was much more confined than that of the Greco-Roman poets, who did not find it shocking to hear the word 'cow' or 'dog'.[8]

The reader who compares baroque drama with the tragedies of the Greeks or the Elizabethans will notice another strange limitation: the avoidance of vivid imagery. Sometimes this may be put down to the avoidance of objectionable words—for instance, Aeschylus' comparison of the Greek fleet attacking Troy to an eagle striking a pregnant hare[9] would be impossible in the seventeenth and eighteenth centuries. Part of it was due to the wish not to fall into the extravagance of the Renaissance; and part to the desire for complete concentration on the character and emotions of the personages. Still, even those metaphors which do occur are uncomfortably often like clichés: brows are clouded, tendernesses are frozen, and every now and then a startling image proves to have little real imaginative force, but to be a clumsy mixture of two accepted metaphors. A crowned flame is a strange and evocative idea, which might come from Dante; but in Racine it only means 'love triumphant'.[10]

Then the metre of the baroque tragedies was far more strictly limited than anything in Greek, Latin, or Renaissance tragedy. It has its virtues: tautness and tension. But it never allows a character to make a great, long, rich, continuous speech, with emotion surging and welling and falling back and urging upwards again: because every line must hesitate for the caesura in the middle, and pause at the end of the line, and halt at the end of the couplet. On the whole, the English tragedians are freer than the French, but still less fluent than their predecessors. In French there is another constriction. Two lines with a masculine rhyme must be followed by a couplet with a feminine rhyme—so that every long speech is broken down, by the listener's ear, into neat four-line packets. It is astounding that the playwrights managed to produce such powerful effects as they did with such a metre. It is a splendid vehicle for expressing rapid changes of purpose and conflict of motives (provided they are clearly realized and described) within the mind of one character; and for giving the rapid thrust-and-parry of altercation; but it can never rise to the heights of imaginative rhetoric that are possible to freely moving blank verse, as in Clytemnestra's beacon-speech in *Agamemnon*,

Clarence's dream in *Richard III*, Prospero's dismissal of the spirits in *The Tempest*; and it can never portray the incoherent wanderings of a tormented soul on the edge of madness, as in Hamlet's soliloquies, or the ravings of Lear when he calls on the thunder to destroy mankind. In many passages it becomes straight prose, without even the complexity which is possible for prose:

Clytemnestre: Ma fille, il faut partir, sans que rien nous retienne,
Et sauver, en fuyant, votre gloire et la mienne.
Je ne m'étonne plus qu'interdit et distrait
Votre père ait paru nous revoir à regret:
Aux affronts d'un refus craignant de vous commettre
Il m'avait par Arcas envoyé cette lettre. . . .[11]

Greek tragedy and Renaissance tragedy are full of varied emotion. There are crowd scenes in both; the Greeks have choric songs and dances; the Elizabethans have comic relief. Seneca, more restricted than either, still kept a chorus and introduced ghosts and furies. Compared with them all, the baroque tragedians are monotonous, with an intense monotony which reflects the smallness of the court society for which they worked. The technique by which they compensated this limitation was the use of magnificent *décor*, costumes, and stage effects; but of all that little survives in their poetry.

The symmetry of baroque tragedy was a thing unknown to the Greeks. It is virtually impossible to guess who were the chief and who the subordinate characters of a lost play by Euripides, far less of an Aeschylean tragedy. But after one has read or seen a few baroque tragedies, the grouping of the characters, with their carefully balanced loves and hates, confidants and rivals, becomes familiar and even obvious.

Lastly, the rules. The Unities, above all. It cannot be too often repeated that these were not laws laid down by the Greeks. There were few if any laws restricting the Greek poets. There were only customs, and the customs were often broken. Aristotle says that a play must have unity of action, because any work of literature must; but he cares little for the unity of time, and still less for the unity of place, except in so far as they assist the drama. It was the Italian theorists of the Renaissance who first established these principles as *laws*:[12] that essentially second-rate character, the elder Scaliger, proved to be ultimately the most influential among them; yet his judgements (as that Vergil was superior to Homer) were not based on the opinion of classical antiquity but on his own prejudices. It is true that, as a contemporary scholar has pointed out,[13] discipline is necessary for the artist, and the limitations which a great genius accepts and surmounts purify and intensify his work. But the rules of the baroque pedants went much farther than this. Combined with the savage criticism which—sometimes for reasons purely social and personal—was levelled at many great tragedies on their appearance, the rules at first hampered and finally silenced the tragedians whom they ought to have assisted. As a code of laws, these rules did not exist in Greece and Rome. They were extracted, elaborated, and exaggerated from hints in Aristotle; and what gave them their legislative force was not classical precept or example but the fear of anarchy and the love of social and political order which were the ruling motives of the baroque age.

These, then, are the reasons for the comparative failure of baroque tragedy. It was not caused by 'excessive admiration for classical models' or 'the laws of Aristotle', but by social and political limitations. The baroque poets were far more *limited* than the Greek playwrights they admired; and their classicism was *unappreciated* by most of their public. Even at that, it was a wholesome influence on their work. We can see that by comparing Corneille and Racine, in whom it was strong, with the shallower Dryden, in whose dramas it was less strong; and by contrasting these three with the balderdash which was poured out by their less educated contemporaries to divert the admirers of Scudéry's romantic adventure-stories. Louis XIV once asked Boileau who was the greatest contemporary French poet. Boileau gave him a name. Louis replied 'Really? I should never have believed it!' But Boileau was right. The finest product of the baroque stage came from France. It was in a genre where classical precision of form is invaluable and where the excesses of classicizing pedantry are excluded by definition. That was the comedy of Molière.

17

SATIRE

THE word 'satire' has nothing to do with satyrs, but comes from the same root as 'saturate', and means 'a medley' full of different things. Originally it had none of the sense of invective which we now associate with it. It was simply a catch-all term like 'revue', or *mélange*, or 'farce'.[1] Imprecise as its name might be, satire was the only literary form invented by the Romans; and it was a Roman satirist who gave it its modern sense and purpose. In Latin there were two main groups of satirists.

(a) The more important were the satiric poets, usually specializing in invective against clearly identifiable or thinly disguised personalities. (The verse, in all the complete poems that have survived, is hexameter—the most flexible and interesting hexameter in Latin literature.) The inventor of this vein was Lucilius (*fl.* 150–102 B.C.), whose works unfortunately did not survive the Dark Ages. He was followed by Horace (65–8 B.C.), who began with rather sour social criticism and gradually mellowed into philosophical and aesthetic discursiveness; towards the middle of his life he gave up satires for his gentler epistles.[2] The next extant Roman satirist is Persius (A.D. 34–62), a rich young puritan who was a passionate admirer of Stoicism, and wrote remarkably realistic satires in a strange, vivid, crabbed, slangy style. The last and greatest is Juvenal (*c.* A.D. 55–130, publishing *c.* 100–130), who produced the most bitter and eloquent social satires ever written: his best-known and oftenest-imitated works are Satire 3, on the horrors of megapolitan life, Satire 6, a thoroughly relentless attack on women, and Satire 10, a sombre but noble meditation on the vanity of human hopes.

(b) The others were the Menippean satirists, writing in prose, with short interludes of verse which are often parodic. This style was invented by the Greek (or rather Syrian) Cynic philosopher Menippus of Gadara (*fl.* 290 B.C.), who apparently used it for making fun of his philosophical opponents. Cicero's friend Varro (116–27 B.C.) brought it into Latin, but his work is lost. One whole Menippean satire survives, the *Joke on the Death of Claudius* or *Pumpkinification* by Seneca (*c.* 4 B.C.–A.D. 65), a cruel but very funny parody of the deification of the drooling old emperor Claudius.[3] We also have a fragment of a huge Epicurean satire in the form of a picaresque romance, the *Satirica* of Nero's friend Petronius (d. A.D. 66);[4] but the main part of it was not discovered until 1650, so that it has had little effect on modern satire.

Apparently there was no essential difference of function between the two types of Roman satire: although as far as we can see the Menippean satire is looser, more slangy, less often serious and eloquent than satire in verse.

On this Roman form, it is possible to trace certain Greek influences which are still active in modern satirical works.

The desire to improve society and purge its abuses by attacking notorious fools and villains was taken by the Romans from Athenian Old Comedy, whose only surviving representative is the brilliant and fearless Aristophanes. This is a natural enough function of poetry. Since the Romans had no drama suitable to fulfil it, they used satire (which was originally semi-dramatic) for the purpose.

The Romans also borrowed many devices used by the Greek street-preachers, usually Cynics and Sceptics, to attract and hold attention. These men used to give ostensibly improvised sermons (called 'diatribes') on themes drawn from their own doctrines— usually on paradoxes which would attract a crowd; and they illustrated and decorated them with anecdotes, character-sketches, fables, dialogues against imaginary opponents, topical references, parodies of serious poetry, obscene jokes, and slang phrases.

However, the moral seriousness, the direct violence, and the cruelty of satire are rather more Roman than Greek, and come out most emphatically in the most Roman of the satirists.

From the second century A.D. there survives the work of one philosophical satirist writing in Greek prose. He was born in Syria about A.D. 125, and his name is Lucian. His tone is one of amused disillusionment. 'Lord!' he says, 'what fools these mortals be!'—but there is more gentleness in his voice and kindness in his heart than we feel in his Roman predecessors. His work is unlike nearly everything else that survives from Greco-Roman literature. It forms a bridge between the dialogues of creative philosophers like Plato, the fantasy of Aristophanes, and the negative criticism of the satirists. He was Rabelais's favourite Greek author. Swift may have recalled his fabulous travel-tales when he wrote about Gulliver;

and Cyrano de Bergerac certainly did when he went to the moon. With such distinguished descendants, Lucian has earned the right to be called by the title which would have amused him, 'immortal'.

A definition of Roman satire, largely applicable to modern satire in so far as that is still a form in itself, would be:

Satire is a continuous piece of verse, or of prose mingled with verse, of considerable size, with great variety of style and subject, but generally characterized by the free use of conversational language, the frequent intrusion of its author's personality, its predilection for wit, humour, and irony, great vividness and concreteness of description, shocking obscenity in theme and language, an improvisatory tone, topical subjects, and the general intention of improving society by exposing its vices and follies. Its essence is summed up in the word σπουδογέλοιον = *ridentem dicere uerum* = 'joking in earnest'.

Like the gift of song and dance, the urge to make fun of fools and scoundrels always exists in all kinds of barbarian, half-savage, and fully civilized societies. Although the men of the Middle Ages understood neither the pattern nor some of the important devices of the classical satirists, they wrote many satirical works. Sometimes they spoilt their material by putting it in inappropriate forms. For example, the second part of *The Romance of the Rose* is full of satirical thinking and satirical expressions, even of translations from Roman satires; but they are painfully out of place as digressions in a visionary love-story.[5] During the Middle Ages there was more satire written in Latin than in the vernacular languages— evidently because learned clerks were more likely to possess a sharp critical intellect, and because the Latin classics provided them with ready-made turns of thought and expression. The twelfth century produced some very remarkable poems of this type. One of the most powerful invectives against the moral corruption of society ever written is the poem *On the Contempt of the World* by Bernard of Morval, a monk of Cluny (*fl.* 1150). We know it only from a few brief passages which have been translated to be sung as hymns (*Jerusalem the Golden* is one), but in intensity of feeling and deftness of language it is a masterpiece which does not deserve its neglect.[6] But the authors of these works do not draw a clear distinction between satire and didacticism, they think they are preaching sermons, and wander off into long descriptions and digressions which weaken the force of their satire by dispersing it. Vernacular satire, during the Middle Ages, is almost always either temporary lampoon or else disguised in the people's own favourite forms: as a collection of anecdotes, like *Tyl Ulenspiegel*, or a group of animal-fables, like *Reynard the Fox*.

As we have seen, one of the main effects of the rediscovery of classical literature in the Renaissance was that men learnt much more about the precise character of the various literary types, and about the methods appropriate for each. They came to realize that it spoilt the desired effect if they mixed up satire and other types of writing unsympathetic to it—love-poetry, for instance, or high philosophical argument. And they saw more clearly than ever before—partly through study of the Roman satirists, partly through reading the epigrams of Martial (which are akin to satire and in particular to Juvenal's satires), and partly through their own increased experience of the subtleties of style—how the damage a satirist can do with a loud and long denunciation can be exceeded by a short, biting, and memorable epigrammatic sentence. Juvenal himself has never been surpassed in the craft of etching on the human heart with pure acid. It was he who created many phrases which are now household words, such as 'bread and circuses', *panem et circenses*.[7] There are hundreds of such utterances in his work: they have the permanence of a great inscription and the ring of sincere and perfect poetry. The tragic irony of his attitude to life, and the superb style that enables him to comment on an eternal problem in three or four words, have reached many modern poets who have worked in quite different media. It is traceable, for instance, in Donne: 'a bracelet of bright hair about the bone' could come straight out of Juvenal. It is certainly obvious in the lyrics of Housman (who made his scholarly reputation in part by a careful edition of Juvenal's text). For instance, in the sixty-second poem of *A Shropshire Lad* he recommends his readers to digest his bitter poems, in order to immunize themselves against the bitterness of life—like the Asiatic king Mithridates, who

> gathered all that springs to birth
> From the many-venomed earth;
> First a little, thence to more,
> He sampled all her killing store;

And easy, smiling, seasoned sound,
Sate the king when healths went round.
They put arsenic in his meat
And stared aghast to watch him eat;
They poured strychnine in his cup
And shook to see him drink it up:
They shook, they stared as white's their shirt:
Them it was their poison hurt.
—I tell the tale that I heard told.
Mithridates, he died old.

The tale is told in many places, but it was Juvenal, in the last words of his satire on women's treachery, who gave it to the luckless lad.[8] In another of his most powerful poems he wishes for death, crying that

All thoughts to rive the heart are here, and all are vain;
Horror and scorn and hate and fear and indignation—
Oh why did I awake? when shall I sleep again?[9]

That *indignation*, the last of the emotions mentioned and the most constantly powerful, is the driving force which Juvenal himself says made him a poet, and which Swift wrote on his own tomb as the worst of his torments.[10]

However, our special interest is the influence directly exerted on modern satirists by their Roman predecessors. The first thing to observe is that the effect of verse satire was primary, the effect of prose satire only secondary. There was not enough classical prose satire known to tempt many modern writers to emulate it; and in any case the form itself seems to have been too vague and loose to provide real technical standards to adapt. Therefore modern satires written in prose have usually adopted the form of some other branch of literature, and injected satiric matter and spirit into it: as Lucian did before them. For example, Swift's *Gulliver's Travels* is a parody of the traveller's tale; his *Battle of the Books* pretends to be a prose translation of a fragment of heroic epic Voltaire's *Candide* is a picaresque travel-romance, and so is *Der abenteurliche Simplicissimus*; Rabelais's work is a distorted romance of chivalry, ending in a parody of the Grail quest. The advantage of this is that it gives great freedom and variety to the authors of satire. The disadvantage is that it tends to diffuse the satiric spirit, so that it becomes confused with the peculiar attitudes and methods of other literary types; and so nowadays few authors write complete satires in prose, but tend to produce novels like *Bleak House* and *Bouvard et Pécuchet* which contain some satiric elements but are not completely transfused with satire.

One of the most vigorous of modern satiric writers working in prose was a preacher whose sermons represent an interesting synthesis of the spirit of classical satire, with its profound cynicism, and the spirit of Christianity, with its ultimate optimism, and of many of the methods used by the Roman satirists with modern devices, equally striking and genuine because derived from the inexhaustible treasury of popular language. This was Abraham a Sancta Clara (1644–1709), a peasant boy from a Bavarian village who was outstandingly clever at school, was trained as a Catholic preacher in the order of Barefooted Augustinians, and at a remarkably early age was appointed court preacher to the Imperial Court of Vienna. In such a post one might think such a man would be solemn, learned, and orotund, like Bossuet and other baroque preachers. On the contrary, Abraham is serious only at the most serious moments—and then he is overpoweringly impressive. But for the rest of the time he is a laughing philosopher, a brilliant wit, who (like the Greek philosophical preachers) uses every device to attract, interest, hold, and dominate his audience: puns, funny stories, dialect jokes, riddles, parodies of poetry and of medical prescriptions and even of Christian rituals, frequent quotations from his vast reading in both the classics and the literature of the church, ingenious rhythmical patterns, which a good speaker, as he was, could make absolutely gripping and enthralling. His audience must have been constantly amused and stimulated, and yet they were being edified all the time: perhaps that is the only way to teach Austrians. He is almost unknown to-day. There is, however, an imitation of his style by Schiller, in the Capuchin monk's sermon in *Wallensteins Lager*, taken over by Piave in his libretto for Verdi's *Forza del Destino*. Unjustly neglected, he is a memorable and brilliant writer, an important voice of the baroque era, and, in his use of the system of teaching through 'joking in earnest', solidly within the tradition of Greek and Roman satire.[11]

Verse satire

Most modern satirical prose owes little directly to any classical satirist except Lucian. Indirectly, the natural indignation of its writers gained additional force and variety of expression from the study of Greco-Roman satire in general. Most of the modern satirists whose work has lived were well-educated men; and most, having read the classical satirists, had been stimulated by their immense moral energy, and encouraged to emulate their ironic amusement, their vigorous brevity, their surgical economy of effort.

Most modern verse satire, on the other hand, was directly inspired by the form, or the matter, or both the form and the matter, of the Roman verse-satirists. Probably this is the reason for the comparative scarcity of verse satires in the high Renaissance, and for the absence of great satiric writers in countries which were partly outside the Renaissance, like Spain and Germany. Greco-Roman drama, elegy, ode, pastoral, and romance were studied and understood fairly early; the first appearance of these literary types in western European literature closely follows the publication of the first editions of each classical model. But satire is a difficult and eccentric form, which was mixed up with the satyric play, and not fully understood until Isaac Casaubon in 1605 published an elucidation of its history and meaning, attached to his edition of Persius.[12]

The Italians, who discovered most of classical antiquity, also discovered and emulated classical satire long before Casaubon wrote on it. It suits their nature: they have produced many brilliant satirists, working in every key from the high classical to the improvisatory and popular. The earliest verse satires we hear of are six poems of general moral reflection by Antonio Vinciguerra (1440–1502). Luigi Alamanni (1495–1556) included thirteen Juvenalian satires on the woes and vices of Italy in his *Opere Toscane*. Ariosto himself, between 1517 and 1531, wrote seven satiric discourses on social corruption—covering boorish patrons and wicked women, corrupt priests and immoral humanists—and blended the honey of Horace with Juvenal's acid. He was followed by Lodovico Paterno, the first modern satirist to use blank verse. However, the most successful Italian satirist of the Renaissance was certainly Francesco Berni (1498–1535), who was not an imitator of the classics, but used verse-forms worked out during the Middle Ages. He specialized in farcical effects obtained by the accurate description of incredibly sordid places, objects, adventures, and people; in parodies, even of such great poetry as Dante's *Comedy*; and in wildly bizarre subjects—for instance, a eulogy of

eels. His harsh realistic attitude, which made a valuable corrective
to the sometimes hypertrophied nobility of the Renaissance, was
really a survival from the Middle Age.

Another largely medieval satirist was the Alsatian scholar
Sebastian Brant (1458–1521). Born in Strasbourg, he was educated
in Basle and trained as a lawyer. A fluent Latin poet and a fervent
supporter of the Holy Roman Empire, he stood, like Rabelais, with
one foot in the Middle Ages and one in the Renaissance. His chief
work was *The Ship of Fools*, which was published in 1494, went into
six editions during his lifetime, and was translated into several
other European languages, including Latin.[13] It is a rambling,
staccato, planless collection of short character-sketches, describing
and denouncing the various types of fools in the world. Although
numerous translations of epigrams from Latin verse-satirists and
other poets show that Brant knew their subject-matter, he had not
mastered their form.[14] Even the idea of putting all the fools in one
boat appears only towards the end, and is not carried through. *The
Ship of Fools* reminds the reader of the huge catalogue-pictures by
Pieter Brueghel, in which dozens and dozens of little figures and
groups are engaged in playing different games or exemplifying
different proverbs, all over the canvas, with no principle of unity
except their one common genus and the four sides of the frame.
But, as one can spend long hours looking at these pictures, so one
can enjoy reading *The Ship of Fools* for its crisp and lifelike
photographs of the manners of a distant age.

An English translation and adaptation of this satire, under the
same name, was made in 1509 by a Scots priest, Alexander Barclay;
Skelton and others took ideas from it; and, also in 1509, Erasmus
wrote his fine Latin satire, *The Praise of Folly*, containing a long
procession of fools like those described by Brant, but binding them
together with a stronger central plan, including many more
important types, and treating the whole subject with far more
grace and wit. Because Erasmus wrote it in the international
language, Latin, it falls outside the scope of this book—an idea
which would have amused Erasmus greatly.

Verse satire in the Roman style reached England rather late,
because the models were little known. Sir Thomas Wyat (1503–42)
was moved by Alamanni's example to write three satires (published
after his death) on the thanklessness of ambition and court life and
the rewards of retirement. Reminiscences from Horace, Persius,

Juvenal, and Alamanni are blended, without any trace of ostentation or pedantry, in these rather immature, but easy and sincere, poems.[15] Not long afterwards, George Gascoigne published *The Steel Glass*, the first English blank-verse satire—a long tirade against many varieties of vice and folly, from which classical influence and the sense of form are equally absent.[16] Then suddenly, just before Casaubon published his definitive essay, a small group of young Englishmen began to write thoroughly contemporary satiric poems, stimulated by their discovery of Roman satire. Their chief model was an eccentric youngster like themselves—Persius—but, like him, they also took much from Horace; and one of them knew and followed Juvenal. The most famous now is John Donne, who wrote three grotesquely warped and wry-mouthed satires in 1593 and several others a few years later. Then there was Joseph Hall—according to his own claim, the first satirist in English— who published six books called *Virgidemiarum*, three issued in 1597 being 'toothless satires' modelled on Horace and Persius, and three in 1598 'biting satires' modelled on Juvenal, with many resounding echoes from his work. These are good poems, suffering only from a youthfully excessive bitterness which becomes a little shrill, but which long afterwards no less a man than Milton thought fit to reprimand.[17] John Marston's *Scourge of Villainy* (1598), an attack on Hall and others, was even more bitter. But in June 1599 the archbishop of Canterbury ordered that 'no satires or epigrams be printed hereafter'; and so closed the first period of modern British satire.[18]

In France of the Renaissance there were several spirited outbreaks of the satiric spirit. We have already met the greatest French satirical writer, Rabelais, and discussed his debt to the Greco-Roman writers.[19] The religious wars produced two invectives against the Roman Catholics, one amusing, one deadly solemn, both effective. The first was the *Menippean Satire*, written in 1594 by a group of supporters of Henri IV against the Catholic League. The name refers to the fact that it is a mixture of prose and verse, and indeed of languages: the papal legate speaks both Latin and Italian. Its many topical allusions make its interest mainly historical.[20] A much finer work is *Les Tragiques* of Agrippa d'Aubigné, published in 1616: a successful attempt by a very remarkable genius to raise the satiric spirit higher and blend it with the heroic

and divine spirit of epic: the poem is too lofty to allow us to call it
a true satire.

The first regular French verse-satirist was Mathurin Régnier
(1573–1613).[21] He himself, in phrases which remind us of Ronsard,
boasts of it:

> This highway has felt many poets' tread,
> but by French rhymers is unvisited;
> I enter it, following Horace close behind,
> to trace the various humours of mankind.[22]

He is a competent and interesting poet, much better at satire
than his contemporary Donne, knowing more of life, and owning
a sparkling sense of humour. Five different interests combine to
enrich his work, making it reflect both his character, his education,
and his era.[23]

Most important is his knowledge of human nature: he was a
courtier, a traveller, and a versatile lover. His portraits, of fops
bores, and hypocrites are predecessors of those in the comedies of
Molière.

His philosophy is a gentlemanly liberalism, rather like that of
Montaigne, though less mature, and traceable ultimately to Horace
and the Epicureans.

Latin literature, particularly satire, he knows well: he quotes
from it and assimilates its ideas freely and unpedantically and
naturally. Who could guess that, when he complains 'I am un-
employable at court, because

> I do not know the courses of the planets;
> I cannot guess another courtier's secrets . . .'

he is translating and adapting Juvenal?[24] Many of his most vivid
phrases, such as

> the darlings of their age, sons of the white hen,

are just as effortlessly borrowed; while the main ideas of his third,
seventh, eighth, twelfth, thirteenth, and fifteenth satires are taken
from Rome.[25] Although once he calls Horace too discreet, and says
he will follow the free Juvenal,[26] both his character, with its innate
drollery and friendliness, and his style are much more reminiscent
of Horace; and on the whole he quotes Horace more extensively.

He visited Italy six times, in the retinue of the cardinal de
Joyeuse, French representative at the Vatican. Evidently he did

not like it much better than Du Bellay, but it stimulated him more. He was very struck by Berni's comically photographic descriptions of repulsive people and things, and by the work of Berni's follower Caporali. His tenth satire is a Bernesque description of a frightful dinner, which begins by being like the bad meal in Horace, and then goes on to such details as this:

> Next, an enormous plate of soup arrives,
> where famished flies are swimming for their lives.[27]

This is followed by an equally amusing description of a terrible lodging for the night, where one of the people he meets is an old woman fearfully, unbelievably thin:

> so that through her bones
> we saw quite clearly right inside her head
> how her ideas prompted all she said.[28]

And with incredulous horror he details all the squalid things he found in his room, including

> three teeth from a corpse's mouth, wrapped in blank parchment.[29]

Lastly, Régnier was a true Frenchman, and thought a great deal about *l'Amour*. He wrote more about it than any other modern satirist; he struck out a new line by incorporating into the satiric tradition themes which he first found in Latin love-elegy. It is significant that Jean de Meun, the author of the second part of *The Romance of the Rose*, made a similar innovation by introducing themes from Latin satire into what was fundamentally a poem about ideal love; and in fact Régnier borrowed some of Jean de Meun's ideas, which thus, at second hand, returned to their original home in satiric poetry.[30]

Most of the good baroque satires in verse were written within the classical tradition, enriched by ideas from modern sources outside it. The cultural predominance of France is obvious; but no less obvious is the moral and intellectual vigour, the superior gusto, of Britain.

After Régnier there came many satirists in France. There was no gap between Régnier and his formidable successor Boileau. Men like Furetière and Boileau's own elder brother Gilles were writing satire with unremitting zest and, if anything, with excessive violence, through the first half of the seventeenth century. But the greatest of all was Nicolas Boileau, called Despréaux, whose satires, modelled closely on those of Horace and Juvenal (with the main emphasis on the former), were mostly published between 1657 and 1667. Some epistles in the manner of Horace and three larger satires appeared later; and his most considerable achievement was his Horatian *Art of Poetry* and his mock-heroic poem on an ecclesiastical dispute, *The Lectern* (both 1674); but he made his reputation by his earlier satires, and never surpassed them.

Dryden was middle-aged before, in quick succession, he produced the satires that place him high among the world's best. *Absalom and Achitophel* (part 1) appeared in November 1681; part 2 (mostly by Nahum Tate) a year later; *The Medal* was published in March 1682 and *MacFlecknoe* in October 1682. Thereafter he wrote no more straight satire; but, with some assistance, he did produce the best English version of Juvenal (1693),[31] headed by a well-written and instructive preface based mainly on Casaubon's essay. The relation between the baroque satirists and the Roman satirists was so close that the moderns not only imitated and adapted but often translated their models. However, Dryden's satiric poems were more quickly produced than the usual baroque satire, dealt with exceptional subjects, and were more original than those of Boileau and Pope.

(*a*) *Absalom and Achitophel* and *MacFlecknoe* are mock epics, with identifiable characters as their mock heroes. This is new. Mock-heroic episodes do occur in Roman satire, but they are only a few dozen lines long—with one exception, Juvenal's description of an imperial council held by Domitian on a ridiculously trivial subject, related in grandiose terms appropriate to Homeric or Vergilian heroes.[32] But there is no mock epic on this scale in classical literature known to Dryden which deals with political criminals like Absalom or dunces like MacFlecknoe. Dryden himself told Dean Lockier he was indebted to Tassoni's *Ravished Bucket* and Boileau's *Lectern*. It may not be extravagant to conjecture that he had been attracted to the powers of epic, serious or comic, by that which he had tried, some years before, to turn into an opera: Milton's *Paradise Lost*.

(*b*) Classical satire, particularly the poems of Juvenal, contains a number of character-sketches; but none so independent and full as those in Dryden's satires, which were followed by the more sharply incised, if less bold, portraits drawn by Pope. The ancestry of these character-sketches is complex. To begin with, they were created by Dryden himself, who knew and disliked his subjects. In literary tradition they go back to the humours of the late Middle Ages, and to the interest in psychology shown by the writers of the Renaissance (e.g. Montaigne). In satire, such character-portraits appear both in Donne and in Butler's *Hudibras*; in psychological essays, they are beautifully exemplified in the baroque age by Earle's *Microcosmographie* (1628) and La Bruyère's *Characters* (1688)—themselves based on the work of Aristotle's pupil Theophrastus. Perhaps these are the greatest contribution of English satire to the literature of the world. There is nothing in other languages, ancient or modern, like Dryden's Og and Pope's Sporus, the painted child of dirt, that stinks and stings.

Alexander Pope produced the prettiest of all mock-heroic satires, and one of the earliest of rococo poems, in *The Rape of the Lock* (1712)—forty years after Boileau's *Lectern*, which, with hints from Ozell's translation of *The Ravished Bucket*, had inspired it.[33] His *Dunciad*, a larger and coarser mock-epic, out of Dryden by Swift, appeared in 1728;[34] and the *Imitations of Horace* at various times from 1730 on.[35] Like Boileau, Pope also produced a number of milder didactic *Epistles*, as well as poetic *Essays* on the principles of literature and life.

Samuel Johnson's two fine imitations of Juvenal appeared towards the middle of the eighteenth century: *London*, adapted from Juvenal's megapolitan satire 3, in 1738, and *The Vanity of Human Wishes*, built on Juvenal 10, in 1749.[36] His publisher paid him ten guineas for the former, and, for the latter, fifteen.

As the era closed, an Italian produced one of its finest satires. It was a complete description of the daily routine of a young Italian dandy, done with cruelly accurate attention to every detail and a venomous pretence of awe and admiration for the useless gentry. This was *The Day*, by Giuseppe Parini (1729–99), a social revolutionary poem if ever there was one. Part 1, *Morning*, came out in 1763, part 2, *Midday*, in 1765, and the others after his death. Parini was well read in the classics, and published a number of competent classicizing odes, but his reputation depends on this remarkable satire. Its relation to the Roman satires has not yet been fully examined; but it appears to have been inspired by Juvenal's brief chronological account of a day in the client's life and by Persius' ironical address to a lazy young nobleman.[37] This inspiration does not lessen its striking force and essential originality, which put it on the same level as the work of those great realists Crabbe and Hogarth.

Boileau, Dryden, Pope, and other baroque satirists are universally known as 'classical' satiric poets, heirs of the Romans. It is held that both their weaknesses and their virtues derive largely from the fact that they imitated Roman models. This is a dangerous half-truth. The differences between their work and that of the Roman satirists are very considerable, and the relation between the two is substantially the same as that between the baroque tragedians and Greco-Roman tragedy. This is apparent in several aspects of their poetry.

First, take metre. All the Roman verse-satirists write in a bold, free-running hexameter, which has a range unequalled by that of any other metre except perhaps English blank verse at its fullest development. They can make it do almost everything from comical light conversation to sustained and lofty declamation. But the verse satirists of the baroque age (except Parini) write in the stopped couplet—a metre capable of great delicacy and wit, but quite unable to attain a wide range of emotion, or a copious variety of effects. Compared with their classical models, therefore, the baroque satirists are severely limited in their choice of medium.

The Romans did use couplets for certain poems which had a purpose not far removed from satire: notably for invective epigram. Juvenal's friend Martial developed the metre and the genus almost to perfection. But such poems have a much more constricted field than that of satire proper, which ought always to be able to sink to coarse farce, to burst out into virtuoso sound-effects, or to rise to proud and sombre pessimism. The stopped couplet has so much in common with the Latin elegiac couplet that its use was probably authorized in part by the example of Ovid, Propertius, and Martial, who were popular in the seventeenth and eighteenth centuries. But the poets themselves sometimes felt its limitations. Boileau complained that his most difficult task was *managing the transitions*.[38] He thought in couplets, and rode Pegasus on the snaffle.

Another awkwardness of the stopped couplet is that it inevitably makes its users over-indulge in certain arrangements of thought. Its logical pattern is a pair of balances. The statement made in line 1 is exactly balanced by the statement made in line 2: the two are linked and the second is driven home by the rhyme. Then within each line there is a caesura, which more or less divides the single line into halves: into precise halves in the French alexandrine. The result of this is that antithesis between line 1 and line 2, and antithesis between the ideas expressed in the halves of each single line, are used far more than any other stylistic and logical pattern—so much so that 'point' becomes almost synonymous with antithesis, and satire becomes the art of finding crushing or piercing antithetical contrasts. Here is Pope:

> Beeves, at his touch, at once to jelly turn,
> And the huge boar is shrunk into an urn:
> The board with specious miracles he loads,
> Turns hares to larks, and pigeons into toads.[39]

Here again is Boileau:

> Cet animal, tapi dans son obscurité,
> Jouit l'hiver des biens conquis durant l'été.
> Mais on ne la voit point d'une humeur inconstante,
> Paresseuse au printemps, en hiver diligente,
> Affronter en plein champ les fureurs de janvier,
> Ou demeurer oisive au retour du Bélier.
> Mais l'homme, sans arrêt, dans sa course insensée,
> Voltige incessamment de pensée en pensée:
> Son cœur, toujours flottant entre mille embarras,
> Ne sait ni ce qu'il veut ni ce qu'il ne veut pas.
> Ce qu'un jour il abhorre, en l'autre il le souhaite.[40]

And here is vigorous John Dryden:

> From hence began that Plot, the nation's curse,
> Bad in itself, but represented worse;
> Raised in extremes, and in extremes decried;
> With oaths affirmed, with dying vows denied;
> Not weighed or winnowed by the multitude;
> But swallowed in the mass, unchewed and crude.
> Some truth there was, but dashed and brewed with lies,
> To please the fools and puzzle all the wise.[41]

Where the two halves of a couplet are not antithetical, they are too often composed of a statement redoubled into a tautology. As long as verse is subject to such strict and monotonous control it cannot reproduce the full variety, energy, and flexibility of human thought and emotion.

Turn to the question of vocabulary. The Roman satirists did not shrink from 'low words'. On the contrary, they all used words which can be found nowhere else in Latin literature, only in actual echoes of the slangy talk of the common people, in private letters, in inscriptions scrawled on walls, in curses and jokes. Their vocabulary is very large indeed, very varied: it is full of the charm of the unexpected, it interests even when it shocks. Among the baroque satirists, Boileau refused to do this. He would not use a vulgar word. Indeed, he probably thought that by using ordinary words like 'rabbit' and 'hammer' he was being daringly vivid. In his *Art of Poetry*, after surveying the Latin satirists and his predecessor Régnier, he concluded that both Régnier and the Romans were too free with their language.

> Le latin dans les mots brave l'honnêteté,
> Mais le lecteur français veut être respecté;
> Du moindre sens impur la liberté l'outrage,
> Si la pudeur des mots n'en adoucit l'image.[42]

It is significant to compare this refinement with Boileau's attitude to comedy: he said that Molière would have been the greatest of comedians if he had not been so much 'a friend of the people', blending the polite Terence with the farcical Tabarin.[43] And it is worth observing that, by looking with distaste at the vulgar vocabulary of the Roman satirists and shunning it in his own practice, he is in fact making a tacit admission of argument 4 used by the moderns in the Battle of the Books: he is agreeing that the ancients are vulgar.[44] Similarly, although his picture of the horrors of Paris is modelled on Juvenal's description of the horrors of Rome, he tones the whole picture down: instead of giving a drunkard's insults verbatim, he merely mentions 'two lackeys abusing each other' and bandits shouting 'Your purse!'[45]

Dryden, however, and (partly under Swift's influence) Pope, both used a certain number of low words with great vigour and effectiveness. Dryden calls Og

> A monstrous mass of foul corrupted matter,
> As all the devils had spewed to make the batter.[46]

Mr. Pope is more refined, and actually makes his vulgarities melodious:

> Yet let me flap this bug with gilded wings,
> This painted child of dirt, that *stinks* and *stings*.[47]

However, all the 'classical' satirists of the baroque period avoided the oddities, the neologisms, the metrical and verbal tricks which the Roman satirists enjoyed, and which were cultivated in modern times by satirists like Butler and Byron. Sound-effects do occur in Dryden and Pope, and occasionally in Boileau, but they are rare, and there is nothing so effective as the line (one among many such) in which Persius reproduces the bubbling sound made by a soul sunk, like the melancholy in Dante's hell, deep in the mud:

demersus summa rursus non bullit in unda.[48]

It is not only that the baroque limitations on the vocabulary of poetry made the satirists too polite. Sometimes they made baroque satire dull, by compelling it to be abstract instead of concrete and real. This can be seen by comparing the many imitative passages with their Roman originals. In Boileau's largest and most realistic satire, the tenth, on women, he warns the husband to wait until his wife takes off her make-up:

Dans sa chambre, crois-moi, n'entre point tout le jour.
Si tu veux posséder ta Lucrèce à ton tour,
Attends, discret mari, que la belle en cornette
Le soir ait étalé son teint sur la toilette,
Et dans quatre mouchoirs, de sa beauté salis,
Envoie au blanchisseur ses roses et ses lis.[49]

Here the lowest words are *cornette*, *blanchisseur*, *salis*, and the infamous *mouchoir*. But listen to Juvenal on the same subject, in the passage which Boileau is adapting:

Meanwhile, a foul and funny show, her face
bulges with bread, or steams with fat Poppaean
creams, that smear the lips of her poor husband.
(She'll clean them off to visit her adulterer.)
Tell me, that thing, so overlaid and dosed
with drugs and medicines, covered with lumps of moist
newly baked dough—is that a face, or an ulcer?[50]

With this fearful vividness, contrast Boileau's abstractions and politenesses: the verbs *étaler*, *salir*, *envoyer* with *bulge*, *steam*, *smear*, *dose*; the nouns *teint*, *toilette*, *beauté*, *roses*, *lis* with *bread*, *dough*, *lumps*, *ulcer*! Again and again this reserve ruins modern satire, particularly that of the French. Juvenal says

This criminal gains the gallows, that a crown,

and Régnier translates it

> L'un est justicié, l'autre aura recompence.[51]

In this artificial limitation of the vocabulary of what must be a
brutally realistic type of poetry, Boileau and other baroque satirists
may have been 'classicists', but they were not following the example
of the Romans.

Consider, lastly, the subject-matter of the baroque satires.
Dryden wrote only a few, on rather limited and special subjects.
Régnier wrote more, but still his field was not broad. Boileau was
a professional satirist; yet his themes do not cover the whole of
life or even of Parisian society, nor do his attacks on fools and
knaves include very many of his contemporaries. The subjects he
might have chosen are fascinating to think of. What would we not
give for a mock-heroic description of the contest for Louis XIV's
love, between Montespan and Maintenon—like Ajax and Hector
fighting over the body of Patroclus! or an account of the dinner
given by Condé, where the chef Vatel killed himself because the
fish was late in arriving; or, instead of the abstract disquisition
against Jesuitry called *Equivocation*,[52] a factual account of a day
in the life of a high Jesuit official; or a court-satire, showing
Colbert and Louvois as good and evil spirits fighting for the soul
of France; or a satire on the building-mania of the king and his
nobles, ending with a description of Versailles as being grander
than heaven itself and making the Almighty envious:

> et bientôt le bon Dieu lui-même aura bâti
> sa Versailles au ciel, pour imiter Louis!

Contrast the limited range of Boileau with the absolute fearlessness
of Rabelais and d'Aubigné in an earlier generation; or with the
ruthlessness of his own contemporary Saint-Simon. Only Pope,
who had more courage, who lived in a freer country, and who was
a friend of Swift, lashed out as freely as the great Romans did; and
even Pope became infected by the disease of abstract moralizing
which overcame Boileau and paralysed his initially mordant wit.[53]

So then, with the exception of Pope, the chief baroque verse
satirists were narrow in style and limited in subject. They missed
opportunities; they avoided describing crimes and naming criminals; they shrank from strong themes: as Pope said of Addison,
they were 'willing to wound, and yet afraid to strike'.[54] They
used a painfully constricted metrical scheme, a narrow gamut of

poetic and emotional effects, and too often a tame and abstract vocabulary, to deal with a relatively small range of material. These limitations were not the direct result of their imitation of the classical satirists, since Roman satire is much bolder and richer. They were created by two rather complex and difficult situations.

The first of these was the realization on the part of poets in the Renaissance, and still more, much more, in the baroque era, that the standards set for them by the poets of Greece and Rome were extremely high; and that those high standards were achieved by amazingly subtle versification, fastidious choice of words, and quintessential compression of both thought and emotion. In the effort to attain similar standards, the baroque poets concentrated on regularity and tightness of form and purity of language, and often (as in the case of satire) introduced that regularity and purity into literary forms where they were deleterious to the poetry.

The second was the aristocratic and authoritarian structure of society in the baroque age. This made it difficult for the language of satire to be suitably forceful in England, and impossible in France. It also made it unwise for a satirist to attack the nobility and impossible for him to attack the monarch. Dryden was cudgelled by Rochester's thugs in 1679. Voltaire was put in the Bastille in 1717, was cudgelled by Rohan's thugs in 1725, and lived much of his life in the safety of exile. Pope was threatened several times, and perhaps only his being a cripple saved him. Boileau, who had suffered much in youth, from his harsh upbringing and from his painful operation at the age of fourteen, was a timid soul,

assez faible de corps, assez doux de visage.[55]

Dryden gave up satire after his brief triumphant excursion into the field, and spent the end of his life on translations. Boileau abandoned it too, and spent many years on writing a history of Louis XIV.

The formality of baroque art comes from its attempt to emulate the dignity and the tension of Greco-Roman art. The limitations of baroque art are products of the peculiar character of seventeenth-century society. Most portraits of baroque monarchs show them wearing the Greek laurel, Roman armour, and a wig. The Romans too portrayed their rulers as divinities or armoured warriors; but it took the baroque age to invent, and to respect, the curled, horned, and dyed periwig.

BAROQUE PROSE

THE seventeenth and eighteenth centuries have been called 'the age of prose'. Certainly the prose then written was superior in quality (although probably not in quantity) to the poetry produced by thousands of amateur and professional poets throughout western Europe. Recognizing this, Fénelon suggested that verse should be abolished. The reason for the superiority of baroque prose is plain, and may sound like an over-simplification; but no better has been suggested. It is that intellect predominated over emotion and imagination in the life of the time, and controlled them: prose is the language of the intellect. This is the age in which a best-selling love-romance began with a neat *map* of the Land of Tenderness;[1] in which Lord Chesterfield laughed only twice or thrice in his life and Fontenelle never; in which young Edward Gibbon, ordered to give up his sweetheart, 'sighed as a lover but obeyed as a son'.

We have discussed the relation of baroque tragedy and baroque verse-satire to the classical poems they were emulating, and have endeavoured to show that they were in fact much more limited than their models. The prose of the baroque era also imitated and emulated Greco-Roman prose, but with fewer limitations, more variety, and more marked success. To begin with, its authors were more familiar with the books they set out to rival; and so were their audiences. Then the models were much more often Latin than Greek. Greek prose has many beauties—flexibility, subtlety, precision, brevity, and the power to rise from ordinary conversation or logical analysis to poetic excitement without the appearance of artificiality and strain. But the structure of western European languages is very much more closely akin to that of Latin than to Greek: it was well, therefore, that Latin provided the principal models on which modern prose was formed.

PROSE STYLE[2]

There were two different schools of prose style in the baroque age. Both turned to classical models for inspiration and to classical theories for authority. Both were continued in the prose of the nineteenth and twentieth centuries; and both were actually re-creations of rival schools of prose-writing which had flourished in Athens, in the empire of Alexander, in Rome, and in the early Christian church. The history of European prose demonstrates perhaps more clearly than that of any other branch of literary art that contemporary literature can be neither understood nor practised unless it is seen as part of a continuous and permanently vital tradition.

One of these styles was of course founded on the work of the greatest master of prose who ever wrote: the Roman Cicero (106–43 B.C.). He himself had a number of styles—colloquialism in his private letters, half-formal dialogue in his philosophical and critical treatises, and a tremendous variety of modes of oratory in his speeches. But the style in which he is most powerful and most fully himself is a full, ornate, magnificent utterance in which emotion constantly swells up and is constantly ordered and disciplined by superb intellectual control.

Even while Cicero was reigning as the greatest orator in Rome, his style was attacked by his friends and critics. They pointed out that it was a development of the manner of the Athenian orator Isocrates, which in its careful symmetry is often painfully affected; and that the tricks of Isocrates had been taken over and elaborated and pumped full of even more artificial emotionalism by the Greek orators and rhetorical schools of Asia Minor. They called it 'Asiatic', and set up against it their standard of 'Attic' brevity, simplicity, sincerity.[3]

After Cicero's death the writers and orators of Rome, realizing that they could go no farther in elaborating his characteristic style of balanced orotundity, turned towards the ideals of Atticism. Sentences now became brief. Clauses were curt, often jolty in rhythm. Connectives were dropped, balance avoided; the thought-content became denser; where Cicero built up his paragraphs to a crescendo of crashing sound, the writers of the early empire ignored harmony, cultivating epigrammatic brilliance and preferring paradox to climax. This was not pure Atticism. There was little or nothing like it in the work of the Athenian orators and prosateurs. But in its short sentences, its simple vocabulary, its apparent informality, it was quite Attic: its less likeable exaggerations were force-grown in the hot competition of the rhetorical schools and the literary salons of the empire. Its greatest master was Seneca (*c.* 4 B.C.–A.D. 65); and something of it can be seen in the poetry of his nephew Lucan, who turned away from Vergil's mellifluous harmonies as Seneca had turned away from Cicero's organ-tones. A generation later the historian Tacitus (*c.* A.D. 55– *c.* 120) worked out an even stranger style, within the same school, based on the calculated surprises of asymmetry. And in the writings of the early church fathers the same contrasting schools appeared—one sonorous and complex, symmetrical and smooth and richly nourished, the other brief, vigorous, thought-loaded, often eccentric, sometimes obscure. Lactantius was the Christian Cicero, and the other school was headed by the brilliant Tertullian.

With the beginning of the Renaissance, the amazing strength and flexibility of Cicero's style was recognized once more. It was copied by writers of Latin prose on almost every subject. For centuries the diplomacy of the European chanceries was carried on not only in the language, but in the precise vocabulary, and word-order, and cadences of Cicero's speeches. There was a long and fierce dispute between scholars who held that Cicero was an un-challengeable 'authority' and that no modern writer could use Latin words or constructions not found in his works, and those, more liberal, who pointed out that Latin was still a living language which modern authors could expand and alter to their own needs. Since this was a dispute about the use of the Latin language, it does not come within the scope of our book. But it was closely con-nected with another dispute which does.

Many writers in the vernacular languages felt that the 'big bow-wow' style of speaking and writing was bogus. All style is artificial, no doubt; but they held that prose should at least give the appearance of being natural. They therefore turned away from Cicero and most of the devices he had developed, and, as models for modern prose, picked Seneca and Tacitus. Some of them went farther back, to Demosthenes and Plato. The aim of them all was to be personal, to avoid formalism. On the models of Seneca's moral essays and Tacitus' histories—and, to a much smaller extent, Demosthenes' plainer speeches and Plato's quieter dialogues—they created the prose of most modern essays and character-sketches, the prose in which some great modern sermons have been written.

Of this second style the chief masters were:

Francis Bacon (1561–1626)
Sir Thomas Browne (1605–82)
Robert Burton, author of *The Anatomy of Melancholy* (1577–1640)
Jean de La Bruyère (1645–96)
John Milton (1608–74)
Michel de Montaigne (1533–92)
Blaise Pascal (1623–62).

The prose of this school has again been subdivided into two types—the loose manner, in which short clauses are built up into larger sentences and paragraphs by light and informal connexions, with little symmetry; and the curt manner, where there are no connexions whatever, and thought after thought is dropped from the writer's mind as it is formed.[4] The reader supplies the links.

Here is a beautiful example of the loose manner, from Burton's *Anatomy of Melancholy*.[5] Burton is talking about the dangers and delights of building castles in the air, and how the habit grows on those who indulge in it:

'So delightsome these toys are at first, they could spend whole days and nights without sleep, even whole years alone in such contemplations, and fantastical meditations, which are like unto dreams, and they will hardly be drawn from them, or willingly interrupt, so pleasant their vain conceits are, that they hinder their ordinary tasks and necessary business, they cannot address themselves to them, or almost to any study or employment, these fantastical and bewitching thoughts so covertly, so feelingly, so urgently, so continually set upon, creep in, insinuate, possess, overcome, distract, and detain them, they cannot, I say, go about their more necessary business, stave off or extricate themselves, but are ever musing, melancholizing, and carried along, as he (they say) that is led round about a heath with a Puck in the night, they run earnestly on in this labyrinth of anxious and solicitous melancholy meditations, and cannot well or willingly refrain, or easily leave off, winding and unwinding themselves, as so many clocks, and still pleasing their humours, until at last the scene is turned upon a sudden, by some bad object, and they being now habituated to such vain meditations and solitary places, can endure no company, can ruminate of nothing but harsh and distasteful subjects.'

It is a style, not for speaking, but for reading and lonely brooding: it gives the impression of overhearing Burton's—or the melancholiac's—actual thoughts as they ramble on and grow out of one another and become ever more intricately involved in a world of their own. Its modern descendant is the profoundly meditative, luxuriantly evocative style of Marcel Proust.

The curt manner is more pithy, more drastic:

'In the great Ant-hill of the whole world, I am an Ant; I have my part in the Creation, I am a Creature; But there are ignoble Creatures. God comes nearer; In the great field of clay, of red earth, that man was made of, and mankind, I am a clod; I am a man, I have my part in the Humanity; But Man was worse than annihilated again.'[6]

However, most of the anti-Ciceronian authors passed fairly freely from one of these manners to the other, according to their subject-matter, and some were not averse to an occasional flight of Ciceronian rhetoric, provided they could return to firm ground after it.

This style, in its two developments, 'loose' and 'curt', was not only a method of arranging words. It was a way of thinking. It carried with it some potent moral and political implications. Since Ciceronian style was that of the church, of the universities, of the Jesuits, of the foreign offices, and of orthodoxy generally, this Senecan and Tacitean manner was associated with unorthodoxy and even libertinism. It was the voice of Seneca the Stoic, boldly independent and subject to God's will alone, the philosopher who was driven to death by a tyrant. It was the voice of Tacitus, the bitter historian who denounced tyranny by describing it, whose books were often made a cloak for the exposition of Machiavellian political theory.[7] Pascal's brilliant letters against the Jesuits were partially modelled on the Stoic discourses of Epictetus, in which thought appears, like an athlete, stripped and ready for the contest. Seventeen centuries earlier a pupil of the Stoics had upheld simplicity of style against Cicero, and the rights of the citizen against Caesar: he was Brutus, the champion of the republic.

This was the style used by most of the great seventeenth-century prose writers. With the eighteenth century its eccentricities were planed down, and its wilful asymmetries discouraged: it began to assume the tone of polite semi-formal conversation; in time, it merged into the unassuming, straightforward, graceful simplicity of light eighteenth-century prose.

Meanwhile another style had been building up, a perfect echo of Cicero in vernacular prose. Varying from one language to another, varying also between authors and between subjects, it still was so fundamentally Ciceronian that it is often easier to detect the Roman cadences in a page of it than to tell which of the baroque stylists wrote the page. The greatest names in this field are:

Joseph Addison (1672–1719)
Jean-Louis Guez de Balzac (1597–1654)
Jacques-Bénigne Bossuet (1627–1704)
Louis Bourdaloue (1632–1704)
Edmund Burke (1729–97)
François de Salignac de La Mothe-Fénelon (1651–1715)
Edward Gibbon (1737–94)
Samuel Johnson (1709–84)
Jonathan Swift (1667–1745).

They were all highly educated men. As Johnson said of Greek, 'Learning is like lace: every man gets as much of it as he can.' Some of them hated the institution to which they went—like Gibbon; or the people who taught them—like Voltaire; some, like Addison, loved the university; some did badly at it through bad discipline, like Burke and Swift; but all did a great deal of quiet solitary thinking and reading in large libraries (poor Johnson in his father's bookshop), usually enough to form their minds before they were twenty years of age.

The most obvious benefit derived from their classical reading is shared by both schools of baroque writers, Ciceronians and anti-Ciceronians alike. This is a rich variety of imaginative and intellectual material derived from Greco-Roman literature. All the works of all of them are full of it. They could not keep it out. They would not keep it out: any more than a well-educated man nowadays would choose to suppress his knowledge of art and music. It makes a bond between them all, whether they are separated by time, like Browne and Burke, or by country and religion, like Bossuet and Gibbon. They seem to belong to a single society of cultured men. Sometimes their membership in that society appears to exclude those of us who know no Greek and Latin. That may be one reason for the comparative neglect of these authors nowadays, when we would rather read a biography of Gibbon than his history. Yet it gave their writings much beauty,

a fund of noble and powerful allusions, memories, and comparisons
for which no satisfactory modern substitute has been found, a richness of imagination which offsets their cool rational style, and an
impersonality which, by taking them out of their immediate
present, helps to make them immortal.

Baroque prose was as full of classical allusions as the poetry of
the Renaissance. Sometimes these were direct historical parallels.
When the House of Commons was discussing British policy towards
Russia, in 1792, the town of Ochakov at the mouth of the Dnieper
was mentioned. It was regarded as the key to Constantinople, but
few of the debaters had ever heard of it. The whole strategic
situation was at once made clear when the speaker referred to
Demosthenes' fourth *Philippic*, citing the paragraph in which
Demosthenes told the Athenians that the northern towns whose
names they scarcely knew were the keys by which Philip would
enter Greece to conquer it.[8] The danger of Napoleon's insatiable
aggressions was much more easily realized by those who knew the
story of the Macedonian conqueror of the Greek states—for there
was no parallel in recent European history. The earliest work of
the German scholar Niebuhr was an anonymous translation of the
first *Philippic*, published in Hamburg in 1805, with a dedication
to the Tsar and an explicit comparison of Napoleon to Philip of
Macedon: a work which, like the Demosthenic speeches of the
younger Pitt, formed a bridge between the baroque age and the
oratory and political sentiments of modern times.[9] When Burke
impeached Warren Hastings for misgovernment in India he
modelled his attack on Cicero's successful prosecution of Verres,
the corrupt Roman governor of Sicily; and the whole court knew
it. When Voltaire wished to publish his own unorthodox deistic
views on religion, he wrote them in the form of letters from Memmius to Cicero, 'found by Admiral Sheremetof in the Vatican,
and translated from the Russian rendering by Voltaire';[10] and
when poor Calas was condemned to be tortured, broken on the
wheel, and burnt alive, Voltaire, at the head of the movement for
annulment and legal reform, denounced the tyranny of his own age
as compared with the Roman courts, where 'the witnesses were
heard in public, face to face with the accused, who could answer
and cross-examine them either personally or through his counsel.
That was a noble, generous system, worthy of the magnanimous
Romans. Among us, everything is done in secret.'[11] One last

example. In March 1775 Burke was speaking with great emotion on the most important event in modern history—the impending dissolution of the political bond between Britain and the British colonies in North America. He examined three possible methods of dealing with the complaints of the colonists. One suggestion was to blockade them. Burke warned the House that this would not remove the cause of complaint, and that their discontent would increase with their misery; and he ended with a formidable epigram from Juvenal's warning to a tyrannous Roman governor:

Beggared, they still have weapons.[12]

All thoughtful men in the House recognized the phrase and saw its implications.

Indirect allusions were even commoner than direct parallels. Under the pen of a great writer, in the mouth of a brilliant speaker, such references can, like quotations in epic,[13] give an additional and unexpected grace to the subject, can intensify the emotion of prose discourse into that of poetry. Sir Thomas Browne, discussing the medical and psychological fact that the sense of smell is dull during sleep, makes it not only memorable but beautiful by saying that the sleeper, 'though in the bed of Cleopatra, can hardly with any delight raise up the ghost of a rose'.[14] The younger Pitt was trained by his father, who caused him to translate aloud, and at sight, passages from the Greek and Latin classics. It was largely to this that he owed his immense command of language and his fertile imagery. During the peroration of his great speech on the abolition of the slave-trade, even his opponents listened to him as to a man inspired. The debate had lasted all through the night, and the rays of the rising sun were streaming into the House of Commons, when he closed a splendid passage on the coming dawn of a brighter day for the natives of Africa, with the fine quotation from Vergil:

On us breathes early dawn with panting horses:
for them red evening kindles her late lamps.[15]

It is scarcely necessary to point out how all these writers were stimulated by contact with the great minds of Rome and Greece. Even when they did not quote the classics directly, they grew greater by their consciousness of eternity. Before writing his finest sermons Bossuet used to read the best of classical poetry, in order to raise his thoughts to the highest attainable pitch of nobility; and, preparing himself to compose the funeral sermon on Queen Marie-Thérèse, he shut himself up alone, and for many hours read nothing but Homer.[16]

Besides this, the Ciceronian writers all used, in very various degrees, a number of stylistic devices derived from Latin and Greek prose, which through their work have now become naturalized in most modern languages. Their aim was to produce an impression of *controlled power*. They chose to do this by making their prose sonorous; rich; and, most important, symmetrical.

To achieve sonority they used long words derived directly from Latin, rather than short ones derived from Anglo-Saxon or smoothed down by passage through Old French. Bossuet, for instance, speaks of the Virgin as *chair angélisée* (a phrase taken straight out of Tertullian); he is the first to use the word *appréhensif*, and one of the first to write *régime, sapience, locution*.[17] Samuel Johnson's predilection for ponderous Latin nouns, adjectives, and verbs is well known: bipartition, equiponderant, vertiginous, expunge, concatenation, irascibility, and his favourite, procrastination.[18] Boswell observed that he actually thought in simple Saxon terms, and then translated into Latin, or rather into Johnsonese. '*The Rehearsal*', he said, 'has not wit enough to keep it sweet'; and then, after a pause, 'it has not vitality enough to preserve it from putrefaction.'[19] This was what Goldsmith laughed at when he said that if Johnson were to write a fable about little fishes he would make them talk like whales. It should be remembered, however, that few of the baroque prose-writers introduced many new words from Latin. On the contrary, they cut many out which had been tentatively brought in by the men of the Renaissance. What they really did was to apply their taste to those already introduced as experiments, and to select and naturalize those which we now use. Johnson's mistake was to use so many words of Latin derivation and heavy intellectual content closely together without relief to the ear or the mind.

This mistake was not made by the French prosateurs. Balzac, chief of the founders of French baroque style, set his face sternly against every kind of word that kept French from being clear and harmonious: provincial expressions, archaisms, neologisms, and latinisms—not *all* words of Latin derivation, but those which, to a sensitive ear, sounded strange, heavy, pedantic, incompletely

naturalized.[20] By such careful discernment he and others forged
the fine, sharp, glittering steel of French prose, one of the best
tools of thought ever created by man.
Yet prose is not only a tool. It can also be an instrument of
music. The most skilful, least monotonous, and subtlest of the
baroque musicians in words was Browne, who produced his finest
effects by blending simple Anglo-Saxonisms with organ-toned
words from Rome:

'We whose generations are ordained in this setting part of time, are
providentially taken off from such imaginations; and, being necessitated
to eye the remaining particle of futurity, are naturally constituted unto
thoughts of the next world, and cannot excusably decline the considera-
tion of that duration, which maketh pyramids pillars of snow, and all
that's past a moment. . . . Gravestones tell truth scarce forty years.
Generations pass while some trees stand, and old families last not three
oaks.'[21]

For the sake of richness the baroque prose-writers chiefly cultivated repetition—either the use of synonyms, which is repetition
of meaning, or the use of homophones, which is repetition of
sound. Of this style, synonyms in twos and threes are a sure mark
and unmistakable characteristic:

'supporting, assisting, and defending';[22]
'deliberate and creeping progress unto the grave';[23]
'la vertu du monde; vertu trompeuse et falsifiée; qui n'a que la mine
et l'apparence';[24]
'the bonds and ligaments of the commonwealth, the pillars and the
sustainers of every written statute';[25]
'de donner (aux maux) un grand cours, et de leur faire une ouverture
large et spacieuse';[26]
'read not to contradict and confute; nor to believe and take for
granted; nor to find talk and discourse; but to weigh and consider'.[27]

Homophones are more difficult to manage, but often very
powerful:

'we are weighed down, we are swallowed up, irreparably, irrevocably,
irrecoverably, irremediably';[28]
'prose admits of the two excellences you most admire, diction and
fiction';[29]

and a famous modern example:

'government of the people, by the people, for the people'.[30]

An effective variation of this device, practised by none more magnificently than by Cicero, and learnt from him by most modern orators, is anaphora—repetition of the same word or phrase in the same position in successive clauses, hammering the idea home. Thus:

> 'Ce n'est là que le fond de notre misère, mais prenez garde,
>   en voici le comble
>   en voici l'excès
>   en voici le prodige
>   en voici l'abus
>   en voici la malignité
>   en voici l'abomination
>   et, si ce terme ne suffit pas,
>   en voici, pour m'exprimer avec le prophète, l'abomination de la désolation.'[31]

The noblest achievement of the baroque writers of prose is symmetry. Symmetry does not necessarily mean $1 = 1$ balance, although it can mean that. A baroque cathedral, with a single great dome in the centre of its structure, is symmetrical. In prose as elsewhere, symmetry means a balanced proportion of parts corresponding to their importance in the general structure. Cicero was such a master of this art that he could extend it all through a long speech, balancing clauses in a sentence, sentences in a paragraph, paragraphs in a section, and sections one against another throughout the entire oration. This is not an external trick. The essence of it is logic; and it was during the baroque age, from the study of Cicero's oratory, that the leading speakers became fully familiar with the necessity for dividing each subject into large, easily distinguished, easily correlated aspects, and then subdividing those aspects into smaller topics to be handled separately. Bad speeches by uneducated men usually fail in this. Adolf Hitler, for example, had very little idea of it, and never wrote a good speech except when he happened to hit on a good idea for a framework before beginning; but emotional as they were, most of his speeches (public and private) were rambling and ill digested. Jesuit orators, on the other hand, are particularly skilful in the art of division, or logical analysis, which is emphasized in their training. A good instance is the second retreat sermon in Joyce's *A Portrait of the Artist as a Young Man*,[32] but any Jesuit sermon will show it. In his sermon *On the Kingdom of God* Bourdaloue says the kingdom of God is

1 like a treasure, hidden away;
2 like a victory, to be fought for;
3 like a reward, kept in store;

and then subdivides each of these divisions—for instance, in 2, the victory must be won, first over the flesh, then over the Devil, then over the world.[33]

On a smaller scale, the commonest methods of achieving symmetry in sentences and paragraphs are antithesis and climax. Both are familiar to us; we use them constantly; but it was the writers of the Renaissance and the baroque age who learnt them from the Greco-Roman prose authors, and developed them for us.

Antithesis can range all the way from the opposition of single words to the opposition of clauses, sentences, and paragraphs.[34]

'No man is an island, entire of itself; every man is a piece of the continent, a part of the main';[35]
'Cette lumière esclaire la simplicité et la soumission du cœur, mais elle aveugle la vanité et l'eslévation de l'esprit';[36]
(The plan of having doctors to attend all legislators would) 'open a few mouths which are now closed, and close many more which are now open; curb the petulancy of the young, and correct the positiveness of the old, rouse the stupid, and damp the pert'.[37]

Of course the baroque poets, both dramatic and satiric, are full of it:

Damn with faint praise, assent with civil leer,
And, without sneering, teach the rest to sneer.[38]

Climax, which means 'ladder', is the enlargement and elevation of one thought through a graded description of its various aspects, in balanced words, phrases, sentences, or paragraphs rising to a powerful termination. Thus—

'But, my Lords, who is the man that, in addition to these disgraces and mischiefs of our army, has dared
to authorize and associate to our arms the tomahawk and scalping-knife of the savage?
to call into civilized alliance the wild and inhuman savage of the woods?
to delegate to the merciless Indian the defence of disputed rights?
and to wage the horrors of his barbarous war against our brethren?'[39]

And here is an overwhelming address to the atheist, by Dr. Donne:[40]

'I respite thee not till the day of judgement, when I may see thee upon thy knees, upon thy face, begging of the hills that they would fall down and cover thee from the fierce wrath of God, to ask thee then, Is there a God now? I respite thee not till the day of thine own death, when thou shalt have evidence enough that there is a God, though no other evidence but to find a Devil, and evidence enough that there is a heaven, though no other evidence but to feel hell; to ask thee then, Is there a God now? I respite thee but a few hours, but six hours, but till midnight. Wake then; and then, dark, and alone, hear God ask thee then, remember that I asked thee now, Is there a God? and if thou darest, say No.'

Within climax there is one symmetrical device which is so natural and adaptable that it can be used on almost every level of speech without seeming artificial. And yet it was invented by Greek teachers of rhetoric; not all the Romans adopted it or managed it with confidence; but Cicero above all others made it his own; and, although it is not native to the modern European languages, it has now, without leaving the realm of artistic prose, entered the ordinary speech of western nations. This is the tricolon. Tricolon means a unit made up of three parts. The third part in a tricolon used in oratory is usually more emphatic and conclusive than the others. This is the chief device used in Lincoln's Gettysburg Address, and is doubled at its conclusion:

'But, in a larger sense, we cannot dedicate—we cannot consecrate— we cannot hallow this ground.'
'We here highly resolve that these dead shall not have died in vain— that this nation, under God, shall have a new birth of freedom—and that government of the people, by the people, for the people, shall not perish from the earth.'

Although Lincoln himself knew no Cicero, he had learnt this and other beauties of Ciceronian style from studying the prose of the baroque age, when it was perfected in English, in French, and in other tongues.

'Mummy is become merchandise, Mizraim cures wounds, and Pharaoh is sold for balsams.'[41]
'La gloire! Qu'y a-t-il pour le chrétien de plus pernicieux et de plus mortel? quel appât plus dangereux? quelle fumée plus capable de faire tourner les meilleures têtes?'[42]
'The notice which you have been pleased to take of my labours, had it been early, had been kind; but it has been delayed till I am indifferent, and cannot enjoy it; till I am solitary, and cannot impart it; till I am known, and do not want it.'[43]

Such devices (as is evident from the examples quoted) were not used separately but in combination. And there were many more of them. The art lay in combining them aptly. A piece of good baroque prose was planned as carefully and engineered as elaborately, with as many interlocking stresses, as bold a design, and as strong a foundation as a baroque palace or a Bach Mass. And although modern prose is seldom constructed so systematically, these devices are now among its natural instruments. The best writers and speakers use them freely. Audiences remember them. Every American recalls the tricolon in which Roosevelt stated the country's need of broader social assistance:

'one-third of a nation, ill-housed, ill-clad, ill-nourished'.

And, acting by instinct, the popular memory of both Britain and America has condensed Churchill's most famous phrase from its original shape into another immortal tricolon:

'blood, sweat, and tears'.

The debt of English to the King James version of the Bible, and through it to Hebrew literature, is very great; but such phrases as these show that the debt of English and the other western European languages to the classical critics, historians, and orators is much greater. The best modern prose has the suppleness of the Greeks, the weight of Rome.

FICTION

Three famous stories, written in the baroque age, influenced modern literature profoundly, and, at the same time, received and transmitted the influence of certain types of classical fiction, which at first sight seem to be far enough away from them. The three are interconnected by various links of purpose, imitation, and emulation, and can conveniently be examined together. They are:

Telemachus (Télémaque), by François Fénelon (published 1699–1717),
Pamela, by Samuel Richardson (published 1740),
Tom Jones, by Henry Fielding (published 1749).

Briefly, the classical connexions of these books (all best-selling stories in their day) are that Telemachus is a composite of Greek and Latin epic, Greek romance, Greek tragedy, and much else from Greco-Roman literature blended into a continuous and new prose story; Pamela, often called the first purely modern novel, grows partly out of Greek romance and Greek ideals of education; and *Tom Jones* is described by its own author as a comic epic on the model of Homer's extant *Iliad* and the lost burlesque *Margites*. But there is more in it than that. Let us look at the books separately.

Fénelon was an aristocratic bishop, with a fine classical education: he was a better Grecian than most of his contemporaries, and his work shows that he had exquisite taste. In the Battle of the Books he was neutral—largely because he thought there was little to be said on the side of the moderns, and yet felt that the arguments used by or forced on the ancients did little justice to their cause. At the age of thirty-eight he became tutor to the duke of Burgundy, son of the dauphin and second heir to the throne of Louis XIV. According to Saint-Simon, who perhaps exaggerates for the sake of effect, he found him a Hyde and made him a Jekyll. By nature the boy was proud, violent, almost intractable. After Fénelon had dealt with him he was calm, energetic, and genuinely interested in the best of art and conduct. Doubtless most of this was due to Fénelon's subtle and charming character. (Bossuet was tutor to the dauphin, and had much less success—his character being quite as noble, but less winning.) Yet some of the improvement was the result of the care with which Fénelon instilled in his pupil, as easily and pleasantly as possible, the real meaning of history, of culture, and of the well-balanced morality of the Greeks. Bishop though he was, his moral teaching as seen through his books leaned more heavily on Hellenic than on Christian examples. He wrote special schoolbooks for his pupil: first some animal fables, and then a series of *Dialogues of the Dead*, conversations (based on Plato and Lucian) between famous and interesting people on political, moral, and educational themes. Mercury and Charon talk, Achilles interviews Homer, Romulus confronts his virtuous successor Numa.

His best book was ostensibly meant for the duke of Burgundy too; but it reads as though it had a wider educational purpose. This was *Telemachus*, the story of the son of Odysseus. Perhaps it was written in 1695–6. In 1697 Fénelon's tutorship of Burgundy ended. In 1699 four and a half books of his *Telemachus* were published, having apparently been stolen by his copyist and sold without permission to an enterprising publisher. In 1699, because of Fénelon's extreme views on the subject of mysticism, Louis XIV ordered him to be struck off the strength of the duke of Burgundy's household, and confined to his diocese. After this, further parts of his book continued to appear, although the first authorized edition was only published in 1717, by his grand-nephew. It had a phenomenal success. In 1699 alone there were twenty editions of it: 'buyers threw gold pieces at the booksellers'; and it was often imitated.[44]

In form, *Telemachus* is a romance, like the fashionable tales of chivalry, set against vaguely classical backgrounds and decorated by apparently classical names and usages, which were then the height of fashion: for instance, Scudéry's *Clelia*, a book partly descended from d'Urfé's *Astraea*, which we have seen as a combination of pastoral and romance.[45] These romances are fairly direct products of the Greek, or Greco-Oriental, romances which have come down to us from the later Roman empire. With the sources of the stories used by the Greek romancers we did not deal; and indeed their ancestry is now impossible to trace, being chiefly folk-tales orally transmitted, the stories told at caravan-fires and tavern-tables which only rarely, and by good luck, get themselves written down. Still, the romancers did take much of their subsidiary material from higher Greek literature: epic descriptions of storms, battles, shipwrecks and the like, tragic soliloquies and reversals of fortune, rhetorical and elegiac descriptions of processions, works of art, landscapes, and crowd scenes, and many other moving themes. Clearly the authors were educated men. In the same way, but on a much loftier plane and for a higher purpose, Fénelon took over many of the finest scenes and motives from Greco-Roman epic, Greek tragedy, and other fields of classical literature.[46] The actual story of *Telemachus* is parallel to the *Odyssey*, but much fuller. It relates the adventures of the young prince Telemachus during his search for his father. It takes him all over the Mediterranean to even more landfalls than Odysseus himself, so that it rivals not only the *Odyssey* but the *Aeneid* (with the adventurous wanderings of the exiled Aeneas) and the romances of love and travel. It looks backward to the *Comedy* of Dante, which depends on Vergil's *Aeneid* as this depends on the *Odyssey*; it brings in so many episodes copied from non-epic sources that it is also comparable to one of the earliest pastoral romantic stories, Sannazaro's *Arcadia*;[47] and, strangely enough, it was an unconscious ancestor of Joyce's *Ulysses*. The story is told in limpid, harmonious, gently poetic prose, whose chief faults are its intolerable monotony and equally intolerable nobility; yet its invention, its breadth of view, and its well-designed alternation of conversations, descriptions, and adventures are admirable.

Like all Fénelon's works, *Telemachus* was written in order to educate. (His letters to Madame de Maintenon on improving her character, to the young Vidame d'Amiens who asked for advice on how to live virtuously at court, and to other correspondents, are fine educational documents.) But herein lies its chief fault. It educates too obviously. Like Odysseus in the *Odyssey*, the hero Telemachus is accompanied by the goddess of wisdom. Although she is disguised as old Mentor, her presence is much more constant and obtrusive than in the *Odyssey*. She is to Telemachus as Fénelon was to Burgundy. Telemachus is constantly being exposed to moral dangers of every intensity, from the temptation to talk too much about himself to the temptations of lust (his love-affair with Eucharis was so warm that it provoked protests at the time) and of war; while Mentor is always drawing the moral. Mentor also draws morals—or Fénelon draws them for us—whenever the young hero sees a happy nation or visits the kingdom of a wicked monarch. Now, although the *Iliad* and the *Odyssey*, and for that matter the *Aeneid*, are nobly educational works, the lessons they give are nearly always indirect, and so more penetrating and more lasting.[48]

But this frankness was daring at the time the book was published. Fénelon was strongly opposed to many of the chief tendencies of Louis XIV and his court—his love of war, his pride, his weakness for flattery, his sexual laxity, his absolutism, his luxurious extravagance and in particular his building mania, and his neglect of the prosperity of the common people.[49] There are many wicked kings in *Telemachus*, and they nearly all resemble Louis XIV and other baroque monarchs of his type. When Telemachus visits the next world, he finds there are many kings in hell and few in the Elysian fields. Therefore *Telemachus* was, for the young Duke of Burgundy, directly and rather superficially educative: it was designed to make him a different kind of king from Louis. But for its other readers it was indirectly educative, because, by describing luxurious courts and badly run countries long ago in the Bronze

Age, it stigmatized the vices and follies of the baroque kingdoms. It was for this that people bought the book so eagerly—they thought it was a satire on Louis the Great and his court. To some extent it was, although without the humour which is essential to satire. (As early as 1694 Fénelon had written a scathing letter to Louis criticizing his entire régime for its love of war and its mismanagement of the economics of France.) It was because of that interpretation that the book was constantly being republished, and that Fénelon himself never re-entered the royal favour.

In fact, *Telemachus* is the satire on the baroque age which Boileau might have written, and to which he never rose. That kind of satire is not needed now, so that the book is partly dead. Yet it has its own life. It is not merely a disguised reflection of contemporary manners—like Montesquieu's *Persian Letters*, which are far more French than Persian.[50] It makes sense as an adventure-story about Telemachus, and the seventeenth-century personalities come out only now and then in the big episodes—as when the hero is described as hot-tempered and proud, when the original Telemachus, Odysseus' son, was rather quiet and simple. The traditional criticism of the book is that it belongs to a false literary species: prose romance crossed with epic hybridized with instructional manual. But many great books have belonged to false or confused species. The real fault of *Telemachus* is that it is too obvious, and too gentlemanly, and too sweetly equable. Passion is wrong, and emotion maddens: and so Fénelon will not introduce passion and will seldom (except in bad characters) allow the emotions to be roused. And yet passion is sometimes necessary in a book.

Telemachus had a long progeny. Edifying historical romances were written all through the eighteenth and nineteenth centuries on its pattern, and are still appearing. A guide to Greece and Greek history and politics was published in 1787, in a similar fictional form: *Travels of Young Anacharsis in Greece*, by Jean-Jacques Barthélemy, who worked on it for thirty years. It had an enormous success, and helped to deepen the passion for ancient Greece which inspired the generation of the French Revolution. In the great educational expansion of the nineteenth century such books became common. Many scholars of this century were introduced to the manners of ancient Rome through Becker's *Gallus* and to those of ancient Athens through his equally dull and mechanical *Charicles*. But at the same time historical romances, stimulated by the success of Scott, had become a more real and energetic type of fiction; and the offspring of *Telemachus* include *The Last Days of Pompeii, Ben-Hur, I, Claudius,* and Thornton Wilder's recent *The Ides of March*—which, like 'Dares Phrygius', pretends to be a mass of authentic contemporary documents. The past becomes more real as fiction than as fact.

The printer Samuel Richardson published *Pamela, or Virtue Rewarded* anonymously, because the design was so humble, and the style (he thought) so low, that it would make no great impression except among a few quiet lovers of virtue. It was a tremendous success—in England, in sentimental Germany, in France ('Oh Richardson! thou singular genius!' broke forth the impassioned Diderot), and elsewhere. It is sometimes called the first modern novel, but erroneously. The modern novel is not so limited a creation that it can have only one ancestor; and there were many other contemporary character-stories before *Pamela.* Still, *Pamela* made the growing novel more real.

In form it is a series of letters, telling how a young girl resisted all the attempts on her virtue made by a rich, powerful, and unscrupulous social superior in whose house she was a servant; and, despite her humble birth, managed to marry the man who had tried to deceive and seduce her. Thus she acquired the position of lawful wife, 'a reward which often, even in this life, a protecting Providence bestows on goodness', and vindicated *bourgeois* morality against the proud and vicious aristocracy. And Pamela lived long enough to become the mother of the Victorian age, and of its ornaments: Mr. Podsnap, and Mr. Chadband, 'a large yellow man, with a fat smile, and a general appearance of having a good deal of train-oil in his system'.

Contemporary in scene and characters, ahead of its time in form and in morality, what has *Pamela* to do with classical influence? The story is told by poor sweet Pamela herself, a simple maid with no pretensions to learning, scarce indeed to any knowledge except that of virtue, and religion, and the policy of 'Don't let him'. Nevertheless, Richardson her creator knew something of the classics: he knew Homer and Cicero, in translation; he knew Vergil, Horace, Lucan, Juvenal, Ausonius, Prudentius, and Shakespeare's school-author Mantuan.[51] But these are only the external ornaments of culture. What is more fertile and important for his work is the influence of Greek romance. This reached him in two ways.

First, he knew and respected *Telemachus*. Even Pamela herself, bent on self-improvement, is found 'trying to read in the French Telemachus'.[52] The parson, Mr. Williams, says he is reading 'the French Telemachus', which was a sign of both French and classical culture.[53] Further, in Richardson's second novel, *Clarissa*, among the books 'found in the closet' there are 'the following not ill-chosen ones: A Telemachus in French, another in English'.[54] And the general pattern of *Telemachus* and *Pamela* is similar: a young person is exposed to every possible kind of temptation, resists them all, and is rewarded by worldly success and the affection of someone dearly loved but hopelessly distant. Young Telemachus suffers his temptations while making the Grand Tour; Pamela hers while staying at home in her master's house: that is the difference of their sex and rank. The moral purpose which inspires both books is the same.

Then there is a link with Greek romance through Sir Philip Sidney's *Arcadia*.[55] This book had recently been brought up to date, as *Sidney's Arcadia modernized* (1725), and *The Spectator* mentions it as indispensable in the catalogue of a lady's library.[56] Richardson had certainly read it with care. Two of its incidents are echoed in his other novels, *Clarissa Harlowe* and *Sir Charles Grandison*.[57] And the name of his heroine, Pamela, is taken from Sidney's *Arcadia*, where it is the name of the daughter of King Basilius and his Queen Gynecea. By choosing it Richardson no doubt meant to show that, although a rustic, his heroine was really a princess at heart.[58]

The romances of Greece and Rome were still alive in the baroque age: much read and often copied. Fénelon took their pattern, enriched it with much of the finest of classical literature, and, from Greco-Roman epic, gave it an aristocratic moral purpose. Richardson (at second- and third-hand) took the same pattern, kept the excitement and the hairbreadth scapes, and made it the vehicle for the morality of the rising *bourgeoisie*, of which he was himself a pattern.

Henry Fielding was well educated, at Eton, but went to Leyden University instead of Oxford or Cambridge. He was fluent in Latin, French, and Italian, competent in Greek.[59] After beginning his literary career with a translation of part of Juvenal's satire against women (*All the Revenge taken by an Injured Lover*), he went in for the theatre, with some success; and then found his vocation through Richardson's *Pamela*. The book amused him and disgusted him. In 1742 he published a parody of it called *The History of the Adventures of Joseph Andrews*.

Pamela, resisting her master's entreaties and evading his stratagems, at last became his wife. Joseph Andrews (supposed to be her brother) was a servant too, and resisted the seductions of his employer Lady Booby until he at last won the heart of sweet Fanny Andrews. For he proved to be the kidnapped son of a local squire, and Fanny to be the kidnapped sister of Pamela; and they all, including the seductive Lady Booby, lived happily ever after.

Fielding followed this in 1749 with a fine original novel, *Tom Jones, the History of a Foundling*, to which he owes his reputation. The two novels together are milestones in the history of prose fiction. He himself well knew this, and added long disquisitions on the theory which he meant them to exemplify. Their material was thoroughly modern. Their form, he said, was an adaptation of a classical form. They were prose epics. The only features in which they differed from the *Iliad* and the *Aeneid* were, first, that they were in prose; second, that they did not introduce the supernatural; and, third, that instead of being heroic they were funny.[60]

This parallelism Fielding emphasized several times, in digressions which were aimed at readers as scholarly and as much interested in literary theory as Richardson's public was interested in sex, morality, and social success. He drove it home by using quotations from Aristotle and Horace's 'Art of Poetry' at chapterheads, and by inserting frequent parodies of heroic battles, of Homeric similes, and of the epic descriptions of the lapse of time.

It was not merely an empty boast. Fielding was a good classical scholar and widely read. In 1895 Austin Dobson found the catalogue of his library reposing in the British Museum: it is surprisingly large, and contains almost every one of the classics from the greatest to the most obscure.[61] But it is safe to say that, if he had not parodied epic conventions and digressed on the resemblance, very few modern readers would ever have thought his novels were epics. It was at least daring, and perhaps it was pedantic and ridiculous, for the author of a couple of light romantic stories to say he was emulating Homer. Was Fielding justified?

To begin with, it was pointless to claim that his books were written on the pattern of the classical comic epic like the *Margites* attributed to Homer: for we know virtually nothing about the *Margites*, of which only a few words survive, and the only ancient poem which could be called a comic epic is *The Battle of Frogs and Mice*, containing no human characters.

Perhaps Fielding meant that his novels were parodies of epic? They have mock battles, unheroic heroes, ignoble adventures, great aspirations that end in ridiculous catastrophes. Yes, that was in his mind; and yet *Joseph Andrews* began by being a parody, not of a classical epic, but of a recent work of prose fiction. And in *Tom Jones* the mock-heroic episodes are less important than the love-story and the travel-adventures, chance meetings and evasions and unexpected recognitions, which are not epic at all in quality, but belong to another literary type. They are the stuff of *romance*.[62] The main plot of both *Joseph Andrews* and *Tom Jones* turns on a favourite device of Greek romance—the kidnapped child brought up in a low social rank or in ignorance of its parentage, who eventually proves to be well born; and both, like a romance but unlike an epic, culminate in the wedding of two often-separated lovers. These devices appear in the Greek romances like *Daphnis and Chloe*; they recur in the long romantic love-stories of the late Renaissance and the baroque age, *Astraea* and *Clelia* and many others; Fénelon decorated his *Telemachus* with some of their interest and variety; and in *Joseph Andrews* and *Tom Jones* Fielding sometimes parodied them, sometimes used them straightforward, but essentially made them contemporary and real.

Nevertheless, by claiming that his books were epics Fielding did state an important truth, perhaps without fully realizing it. This was that the poetic epic was dying, and that the forces it had once possessed were to flow into the modern novel. The transfusion had begun before Fielding. Cervantes's *Don Quixote* took the fantastic heroic aspirations of epics like *The Madness of Roland* and brought them into contact with real life and prose speech. Fénelon in *Telemachus*, writing the first of many modern stories of growing-up and education, interwove classical epic and romance, and took prose as his vehicle. Fielding explicitly refers to *Telemachus* as an epic comparable to the *Odyssey*;[63] and indeed it is more like an epic than is *Tom Jones*.

So then Fielding saw in theory and felt in practice the two chief classical currents which flowed together to make the modern novel. One of these was Greek romance. The other was Greco-Roman epic. Romance gave the novel its interest in young love, plots full of travel and exciting adventure, chances and changes, disguises and coincidences, its long episodic story-line. In Fielding's day the novel was not yet ready to receive the full force of the epic spirit, but later it became able to contain the bold construction of epic, its large scale, its crowd-scenes, its political and historical profundity, its grand spiritual meanings, and its sense of the hidden mysteries that make human destiny more than its individual adventures and private lives. In the nineteenth century classical romance and classical epic, acting on the modern consciousness, produced *David Copperfield* and *Crime and Punishment*, *Salammbô* and *War and Peace*.

HISTORY

One of the greatest intellectual and artistic achievements of the baroque age was a study of the conflict between the Roman empire and the forces that destroyed it. This was Edward Gibbon's *The Decline and Fall of the Roman Empire*. Gibbon was an Englishman of independent means and poor health, born in 1737, well schooled but mainly self-educated by reading, reading, reading: he himself stated that the year in which he made his greatest intellectual progress was his twelfth. His short stay at Magdalen College, Oxford, was largely wasted.[64] It terminated abruptly when he was converted to Roman Catholicism. His father sent him away to French Switzerland, where he was soon reconverted, and then resumed his self-preparation for the task he dimly foresaw. His first published work was an essay in French (then the main culture-language) on the advantages of classical study. In 1764 he conceived the idea of his great history, which covers more than a thousand years—for the Roman empire did not fall until less than forty years before the discovery of America. Volume 1 appeared in 1776, with enormous success: Gibbon said it was 'on every table and on almost every toilet'. Five more volumes appeared at intervals, the last in 1788; and, after writing an admirably short autobiography, Gibbon died in 1794, expiring simultaneously with the age of baroque.

The Decline and Fall of the Roman Empire is a book of the highest importance. As a symbol of the interpenetration of the Greco-

Roman world and the modern world it is comparable to Milton's *Paradise Lost* or Racine's tragedies, Versailles or St. Paul's Cathedral. Although written by an Englishman, it was an international product. It used the researches of scholars from nearly every country in Europe (particularly the Frenchman Tillemont); it was conceived in Rome; it was written partly in England and partly in Switzerland; its style was a rich fusion of English and Latin, clarified by French (the language in which Gibbon had already started two historical works);[65] its spirit was partly that of the English Whig gentry and partly that of the French and English Enlightenment.

It had two distinguished predecessors. Bossuet, who was tutor to the dauphin, heir to the throne of Louis XIV, wrote for him a *Discourse on Universal History* (1681). This is a chronological summary and synthesis of the histories of the Jews, the Near Eastern empires, the Greeks and Romans, and the invaders and successors of Rome until Charlemagne (A.D. 800), combined with a much longer exposition of God's providence in guiding the course of events towards the establishment of the true faith. Bossuet knew a good deal of history; and he was skilful in combining his facts to produce a single grand picture; but his complete dependence on the Old and New Testaments as the single central unified document of ancient history rendered his work more edifying than reliable. In his concluding chapter he says that all historical facts are the result of God's direct intervention: not only does God decide the event of wars and the fate of empires, but it is God who causes individual men and groups to be lustful or self-controlled, stupid or far-sighted: there is no such thing as chance, nor, apparently, human will or wisdom.[66] This moral is no doubt excellent as a reminder for the heir of an absolute monarch, but changes history into theology.[67]

Fifty years later one of the finest minds of the eighteenth century wrote a much greater book on ancient history. This was Secondat de Montesquieu's *Considerations on the Causes of the Greatness of the Romans and of Their Decadence* (1734). Already known through his *Persian Letters* as a penetrating critic of society and history, and even then preparing his greatest work, *On the Spirit of the Laws*, Montesquieu achieved something in his Roman book which was possible only to the age of reason. In a short, admirably arranged book of limpid clarity and elegant precision, he combined a broad survey of the essential dates, facts, individuals, and institutions of Roman history from the days of Romulus to the Turkish conquests, with a cool, confident, and yet not over-simplified analysis of the moral and social, personal and strategic factors which enlarged, consolidated, and destroyed Rome. It helped to form the work of Gibbon; and indeed, although many of the historical data now need correction and expansion, it is still impossible to read the little work without admiration, and a re-newed confidence in the power of the human mind.

Gibbon's book exceeds one of these two in art, and the other in scope. It could well be described as a culmination of Renaissance scholarship, of the admiration for Greco-Roman art, political wisdom, and humanism that began to vivify the nations of western Europe four hundred years earlier. Looked at from another point of view, it was the end of the age of Rome in modern Europe. After it came the age of Greece.

A majestic book. It begins in the second century of our era, and ends in the fifteenth. It covers not only Rome and Byzantium, but the successor states—the Franks, the Ostrogoths, the Lombards—and the invaders, Tartars, Saracens, Huns, Vandals, many more. A modern admirer notes that on all good critics the work has made the same impression, of great power and superb organization. Walter Bagehot compares it to the march of 'a Roman legion through a troubled country . . . up hill and down hill, through marsh and thicket, through Goth or Parthian . . . an emblem of civiliza-tion'; Sainte-Beuve to 'a great rearguard action, carried out without fire or impetuosity'; and Harrison to 'a Roman triumph, of some Caesar returning, accompanied by all the pomp and cir-cumstance of war: races of all colours and costumes, trophies of barbarous peoples, strange beasts, and the spoil of cities'.[68] It is striking to compare this work, which grasps and sums up so much of ancient history, arranging it in a centuries-long perspective, with one of the earliest little works of art that have come down to us from the very Dark Ages described by Gibbon: the Franks Casket, which compresses all the heroic past into pictures of the founding of Rome, the capture of Jerusalem, the sufferings of a northern hero, and a horse-headed monster from a forgotten legend.[69]

Still, its structure, although magnificent in scale, is not uniform. It could be called incomplete. As Bury points out, the first part, covering rather over five-eighths of the whole, fully describes the period from A.D. 180 to 641, 'from Trajan to Constantine, from Constantine to Heraclius'; while the second, treating 641–1453, is summary and episodic, compressing some long developments into brief surveys and describing certain significant events at disproportionate length. Gibbon justifies this by saying that it would be an 'ungrateful and melancholy task' to describe the last 800 years of the eastern empire in detail—largely because he dislikes both organized Christianity and an elaborate empire, 'a succession of priests, or courtiers'.[70] Here, however, his personal preferences have caused him to distort his subject. It was then a common set of prejudices, but it damaged the truth.

Gibbon's great range would be useless without his analytical power. He had a highly developed sense of intellectual and aesthetic structure. Through this he controlled the enormous and shapeless mass, a thousand processes and a million facts, so that they arranged themselves in large but manageable groups, seventy-one of which made up the entire work, and, uncluttered by appendixes and excursuses and annexes, formed an architectural whole of truly baroque grandeur.

Then there is what has been called 'the immortal affectation of his unique style'. Yet it is not unique. Individuality was not one of the chief aims of seventeenth- and eighteenth-century stylists. It has often been praised, and it is truly praiseworthy as a feat of will-power. The difficulty is that, as the lady in Boileau said of Chapelain's poetry, no one can read it.[71] It is not that Gibbon is too polysyllabic. Nor is he unremittingly solemn—on the contrary, his text is sometimes elegantly witty, and his footnotes, especially for those who are able to penetrate 'the obscurity of a learned language', often scandalously gay. But his sentences are monotonous. Two patterns, with minor variations, are his obsessions. He will say X; and Y. His next sentence will be X; and Y; and Z. Sometimes he will interpose X; but Y. Then, regularly and soporifically as waves on the beach, roll back X; and Y; and Z.[72] The result of reading a few score pages of this is eloquently described by Dickens. After listening to 'Decline and Fall Off the Rooshan Empire', Mr. Boffin was left 'staring with his eyes and mind, and so severely punished that he could hardly wish his literary friend Good-night'.[73] Gibbon overworked the two devices of antithesis and tricolon until they became almost synonymous with the Gibbonian manner. Montesquieu's sentences are more flexible. Before him in England, Donne and Browne were more varied and not less weighty. The two greatest Roman historians themselves would have shrunk from such a limited range of rhythms. Livy is sonorous and dignified in his narration of complex strategic events, breaks into short irregular sentences to relate battles, sieges, conflicts, diplomatic struggles, or disasters, flames into fiery rhetoric when a hero or a villain delivers one of those character-revealing and emotionally moving orations with which he punctuates his action: as a result, he is far more individual, far less expected and monotonous than Gibbon. Tacitus, writing a history of hidden rivalries, complex motivations, treachery, suffering, hatred, and inexplicable folly, made his sentences as obscure, almost as patternless as the events he described. Gibbon thought, perhaps, that he was writing Ciceronian prose; but it was the rolling prose of the perorations only; while in a single speech Cicero covers four or five other methods of expression, rapid, humorous, sharply interrogative, fiercely expostulatory, all untouched by Gibbon. *The Decline and Fall of the Roman Empire* is a perpetual peroration.

The character of Gibbon's style, however, is partly a matter of taste. The objective faults of his book are important and instructive. Two of them were the faults of his age, the third was his own.

Gibbon was more a Roman than a Greek. His Latin was excellent, but he himself says that he did not feel at ease with Greek books: in that he was at one not only with many other distinguished writers, but with the general current of culture since the Renaissance. People often admired Greek literature from a distance, like an Alp, but they were at home in Latin. The effect of this on Gibbon's work was that he misconceived and misrepresented the power of the eastern Roman empire, centring on its capital, Byzantium, and the relations of that empire both to the west and to the barbarians. What made Rome great was that it formed a culture out of its own virtues of energy, discipline, freedom bound by self-made law, with the fertilizing influence of Greek thought, art, science, and literature, and that it communicated that culture far and wide over the world to what had been only barbarian tribes. At its greatest Rome was both Roman and Greek. Although at one extremity the empire was mainly Roman, and at the other almost wholly Greek, yet the two elements interfused at the critical points and were blended throughout. After the division of the empire into two, the western unit was Latin-speaking and the eastern Greek-speaking. Nevertheless, the eastern empire was still Roman in many respects. It called itself Roman, it united military power and civilizing influence, it kept many Greco-Roman cultural traditions alive and developing while the western world was struggling out of a darkness shot with blood and fire. As Bury points out,

'mediaeval historians, concentrating their interest on the rising States of western Europe, often fail to recognize the position held by the later empire (i.e. the Byzantine Roman empire) and its European prestige. Up to the middle of the eleventh century it was in actual strength the first power in Europe, except in the lifetime of Charles the Great, and under the Comneni it was still a power of the first rank. . . . Throughout the whole period, to 1204 (when it was sacked by the Crusaders), Constantinople was the first city in the world. The influence which the Empire exerted upon its neighbours, especially the Slavonic peoples, is the second great role which it fulfilled for Europe.'[74]

Gibbon gave a false impression of the cultural and political importance of the eastern empire, both in comparison with all other European states and as a bulwark against the barbarians. It was through Byzantium that Christianity and Greco-Roman culture first penetrated to the Russians and the Balkan Slav peoples; and it was because of the diplomacy, wealth, organization, and fighting powers of Byzantium that Europe was not far more gravely threatened, perhaps ruined, by savage oriental invasions. The empire had faults, some very grave; they were such as to irritate Gibbon to the point of distorting or obscuring his vision; but they were far less than its virtues and its powers.

The second fault of the book is even more fundamental. When you start to read the history of a long and eminently important process such as the fall of an empire, you expect to be told what cause or combination of causes was responsible for it. And you expect that the causes will be shown operating in various intensities, sometimes accelerated and sometimes held back by conflict or resistance, through the various stages of the process which the historian describes. This you will find in Montesquieu, but not in Gibbon. Coleridge excoriated him for this, in terms characteristically exaggerated:

'And then to call it a History of the Decline and Fall of the Roman Empire! Was there ever a greater misnomer? I protest I do not remember a single philosophical attempt made throughout the work to fathom the causes of the decline or fall of that empire. . . . Gibbon was a man of immense reading; but he had no philosophy.'[75]

On the contrary, you find, scattered here and there through the narrative, a number of different reasons, not interconnected, and sometimes mutually contradictory.

The earliest suggestion we meet is a version of the idea propagated by Gibbon's contemporary Rousseau: savages are strong and virtuous, civilized people are vicious and weak. Thus, in chapter 6, Gibbon contrasts

'the untutored Caledonians [of Ossian's times], glowing with the warm virtues of nature, and the degenerate Romans, polluted with the mean vices of wealth and slavery'.[76]

Very early in his work Gibbon accepts this idea, and implies that the barbarian invasions were a good thing for the world, since (although after a thousand years) they produced modern civilization:

'The giants of the north . . . restored a manly spirit of freedom; and, after the revolution of ten centuries, freedom became the happy parent of taste and science.'[77]

Yet when he turns to describe the internal troubles of the second and later centuries, he concentrates on the excessive power of the army, and in particular of the Italian garrison, the praetorian guards, 'whose licentious fury was the first symptom and cause of the decline of the empire'.[78] At this point he seems to conceive that the empire was broken up from within by the predominating power of the army and the unscrupulousness of the military adventurers who used it. Yet the eastern empire had a powerful army, and did not break up from within. In his second and third volumes Gibbon lays much emphasis on the despotism of Constantine's system, and on faction spirit. In chapter 35 he produces a socio-economic reason—the maldistribution of wealth through bad taxation and the difficulty of financing the vast imperial administration.[79] Finally, having reached chapter 38, he produces 'General Observations on the Fall of the Roman Empire in the West', an essay composed long before, introducing some quite new reasons, and using terms taken from a letter he had written to Hume in 1767.[80] In this he states that the Roman empire 'fell by its own weight'; and, 'instead of inquiring *why* the Roman empire was destroyed, we should rather be surprised that it had subsisted so long'. (Christianity, however, was partly to blame.) This is a much deeper thought, which had already been advanced by Moyle in his *Essay on the Constitution of the Roman Government*, and which reappears on a grand scale in Spengler's *The Decline and Fall of the West*.[81] It is the idea that civilizations, like animals and men, have a natural rhythm of growth, maturity, and decay, beyond which they *cannot* prolong their lives. But, without careful application to the facts and without support from a thorough philosophical discussion, this suggestion is only a confession of failure on the part of the historian. Sometimes Gibbon openly admits his failure to find reasons. For instance, in describing the Gothic invasion of the Ukraine he remarks that its cause 'lies concealed among the various motives which actuate the conduct of unsettled barbarians'.[82] And, when he mentions the formidable plague of 250–65,[83] he does not draw the necessary conclusions which followed from it.

Since Gibbon's day, many general explanations have been offered for the fall of the civilization of Greece and Rome.[84] Rostovtzeff held that the main cause was the hatred which the half-barbarous countrymen serving in the Roman armies felt for the city-folk who fed on them and bled them; but some have thought that he was unconsciously reasoning from the overthrow of the Tsarist government by soviets of peasants and soldiers. Seeck thought the best stock of Rome was killed off by the emperors, leaving only inefficient and cowardly weaklings; and both he and others pointed to the introduction of bad agricultural and financial systems which crushed the free yeomanry out of existence. Clearly, whatever explanation is brought forward must account not only for the fall of the western empire, but for the survival of the eastern empire. It would seem that the men of the west *stopped having new ideas,* while the Byzantines continued to develop new administrative policies, new spiritual activities, new scientific inventions, for many a generation. In the seventh century, for instance, they produced liquid fire and flame-throwers to repel the Arab attack on Constantinople. In Toynbee's phrase, they responded successfully to the challenge of the barbarian attacks, while the western Romans did not. But Gibbon found the actual narration of the vast process so difficult and so complicated that he had no energy left to analyse its causes.

The third fault of the book is its bias against Christianity. It was conceived, he himself tells us, as he sat in the ruins of the Capitol and listened to the barefooted friars singing vespers in the Temple of Jupiter.[85] Even in that brilliant little picture appears the contrast which obsessed him: the contrast between 'a polite and powerful empire' and the half-savage fanatics who refused their allegiance to it, divided it, sapped its energies by teaching 'patience and pusillanimity', and destroyed it. Chapters 15 and 16 are famous as the cleverest and most striking attack on the spirit and the traditions of Christianity which has ever been executed. They pass from apparently respectful narration of the stories told about the early church, through passages of Voltairian irony in which he reproaches the pagan scientists for failing to notice the innumerable prodigies which accompanied the establishment of the faith, to the conclusion in the 'melancholy truth' that 'the Christians . . . have inflicted far greater severities on each other than they had experienced from the zeal of infidels'. These chapters in particular have evoked many counter-attacks ever since they were published.[86] But the same attitude recurs again and again throughout the book: as when Gibbon points out with the hint of a smile that the Christians, who had been so fervent in denouncing the Romans and Greeks for worshipping images, no sooner established their own religion than they filled their churches with pictures and statues, holy icons and holy relics.[87] Even his account of the origins of Mohammedanism is anti-Christian in effect: it shows how close was the parallelism between Islam and Christianity in their early stages, and then emphasizes the fact that Islam (unlike Christianity) rejects all visible portrayals of God and His Apostles.[88] Gibbon's book closes with the famous epigram: 'I have described the triumph of Barbarism and Religion.'[89] It is impossible to read his history without recognizing that he viewed these two forces as equally destructive and equally despicable.

Gibbon's motive for making his history a prolonged attack on Christianity was that—like many great and good men, Montaigne, for instance—he feared and hated religious intolerance. He himself had been a Roman Catholic, and had become a Protestant once more. As a Catholic he had felt some of the rigours of Protestant intolerance. During his reconversion his pastors had no doubt emphasized the attacks on Protestantism carried out by Catholic crusaders and inquisitors. When he lists and expounds the various merits of Roman civilization, the very first he mentions is religious toleration, flowing from 'the mild spirit of antiquity'.[90] When he praises the emperor Julian (called the Apostate), it is because he

'extended to all the inhabitants of the Roman world the benefits of a free and equal toleration; and the only hardship which he inflicted on the Christians was to deprive them of the power of tormenting their fellow-subjects'.[91]

But Gibbon's bias against Christianity led him to falsify history. It caused him to underestimate the achievements and to misconceive the character of the eastern empire, which was both Roman and Christian. It made him skim lightly over the work of Saints Cyril and Methodius and their successors, in civilizing and Christianizing the savage Slavic tribes. The sentence quoted above contains the worst falsification of all. 'The triumph of Barbarism and Religion' is a false description of the fall of the empire. Instead of summing up the entire process, it can at most be a partial description of the troubles in the second and third centuries A.D. But Constantine, the first Christian emperor, gained the throne early in the fourth century. Thenceforward Rome was predominantly, and from 380 completely and officially, Christian. It is true that, before this period, the primitive Christians, firm in their belief that the world was about to end, and despising the obscenities and absurdities of paganism, had withheld allegiance to the emperors, disrupted the imperial administration, and refused to take part in any of the activities of the state. But after Christianity became the official religion, it ceased to be a powerful disruptive force within the Roman world.

The reverse is true. The barbarian invasions and infiltrations were one of the main causes of the fall of the empire. Christianity was one of the main causes of the survival—not indeed of the western empire, but of Greco-Roman civilization in many of its best and most permanently vital aspects. Gibbon may be right in despising the wild ascetics of the Thebaid, the grass-eating anachorets, and the hysterical sectaries of Byzantium;[92] but would he prefer the Tartars, the Turks, the Northmen, and the Huns? The history of nearly every Roman province shows how the successive waves of savages that broke over the walls of the empire were resisted by Christians, and, even when they burst the dikes and flowed in, were at last, through Christian teaching and example, calmed and controlled and civilized. Perhaps it was inevitable for Gibbon in the eighteenth century to believe that Christian fanaticism was one of the most dangerous of all evils, and to despise Christianity for inspiring it. A more complete explanation is that, even if Christian creeds sometimes gave an outlet to the forces of savagery, Christianity was always exercised to repress them or to canalize them. And to us in the twentieth century, who have seen the barbarities of highly organized contemporary pagan peoples and who are likely to see more, Christianity is very clearly a greater thing than Gibbon could understand, one of the greatest constructive social forces in human history.

19

THE TIME OF REVOLUTION

§ 1. INTRODUCTION

IN the second half of the eighteenth century, literature, for ever changing, once more changed its character and methods—this time very decisively. Philosophy and history gave way to fiction. Prose gave way to poetry. Intellectualism gave way to emotion. The ideals of wit, politeness, and self-control were discarded as artificial. People turned to admire sincerity, sensitivity, and self-expression. Fresh literary patterns were developed, and subjects formerly negligible or repulsive became exciting. Because of the new admiration for the Middle Ages—when tales of chivalrous adventure were known as romances[1]—some of the spiritual and aesthetic ideals of the time were named 'romantic'. It is customary now to call it the Romantic Revival. The authors of the period are often known as 'romantic' writers—whether, like Scott, they actually preferred medieval subjects or, like Shelley, cared little for the Gothic past. It has become a cliché of criticism to contrast 'romantic' and 'classical' principles, and to assume that the great poets of that age despised and shunned Greek and Latin literature. This is a misconception which prevents many modern readers from understanding the period.

In fact, the new thought and literature did not turn away from Greek and Latin. It is impossible to believe that the movement which produced Shelley's *Prometheus Unbound*, Keats's *Ode on a Grecian Urn*, Goethe's *Roman Elegies*, Chateaubriand's *The Martyrs*, and the tragedies of Alfieri was anti-classical. On the contrary, most of the great European writers of the epoch 1765–1825 knew much more about classical literature than their predecessors, and were more successful in capturing and reproducing its meaning. Shelley knew more Greek than Pope. Goethe knew more Greek than Klopstock. Leopardi, Hölderlin, Chénier were good scholars. The classics were not neglected during this period. Instead, they were reinterpreted: they were re-read with a different emphasis and deeper understanding.

The element of medievalism and 'romance' in the late eighteenth and early nineteenth centuries was, although striking, relatively

unimportant and superficial. The real moving force of the period
was social, political, religious, aesthetic, and moral *protest*. It was
a time of revolt, and it would be better called the Revolutionary
than the Romantic era. The changes in literature which marked
it were part of a wider spiritual change. Its writers were in rebellion
against conventions, or prejudices, or abuses of power, or limitations of the scope of the human soul. Most of them were political
rebels: so much so that when Wordsworth and Goethe and Alfieri
turned against the French Revolution, they seemed to be deserting
the ideals of their age. The social structure of the baroque period
was disintegrating from within and was being attacked from
without. The influence of aristocracies was being curtailed. The
temporal power of the Roman Catholic church was diminishing.
The tide was setting away from monarchy towards republicanism.
Nevertheless, it would be wrong to consider this as the collapse of
Greco-Roman ideals, the disappearance of a 'classical' age. On the
contrary, in the general movement of revolt, the examples of
Greece and republican Rome were among the most urgent forces.
Ossian was less vital than Plutarch. The revolutionaries believed
themselves to be *more* classical than their opponents, and what they
chiefly attacked was the survival of medieval institutions such as
the feudal privileges of the nobles. Even Napoleon, the revolutionary ruler, was an emperor in the Roman style, with his laurels
and his eagles, as contrasted with Louis, the last of a long procession
of medieval monarchs.

Is it, then, entirely wrong to say that the revolutionary period
was marked by a reaction against the classics? If so, why was such
an erroneous description ever accepted and how has it persisted?
If not, how much truth is there in it?

It was not wholly false. There was, particularly in England,
a reaction against one of the bad effects of classical influence in
literature: the habit of letting the Greek and Roman myths and
the Greek and Roman poets do the work of creation. Instead of
writing something fresh, instead of looking at the world with an
observing eye, instead of producing newer and more subtle echoes
of thought in language, the baroque poets were too often content
to use a classical image, already hackneyed, or to imitate a classical
stylistic device too well known. Instead of describing a moonlit
garden with its nightingales, they would say that the sweet influence
of Diana fell over the groves of the nymphs, who were silent,

listening to the complaint of Philomel. Now, the nymphs, the moon-maiden, and the legend of Philomela are powerful imaginative stimuli, and have been evoking beautiful poetry for nearly 3,000 years.[2] But myths, however beautiful, are not enough to make poetry without fresh imagination; and in the baroque period too many writers were unimaginative copyists. Therefore the reaction which occurred in the revolutionary era was not against the classics as such, but against the lack of imagination characteristic of the baroque age and in particular against the habit of using classical clichés as short-cuts to imaginative expression. This is what Macaulay means when, in his essay on Frederick the Great, he speaks of 'Prometheus and Orpheus, Elysium and Acheron, . . . and all the other frippery, which, like a robe tossed by a proud beauty to her waiting-woman, has long been contemptuously abandoned by genius to mediocrity'.[3] Once the garment of genius, the robe of classical imagery was, for the time, outworn. Its colours were to be revived by greater artists.

Another reason for speaking of the revolutionary period in literature as anti-classical is that some of the emotional and artistic ideals it upheld were opposed to the ideals of Greco-Roman life and literature: at least, to those ideals as interpreted by the men of the seventeenth and early eighteenth centuries. In particular, restraint of emotion was now decried in favour of strong expression of feeling; polished workmanship was held inferior to improvisation and the gush of natural eloquence; and symmetry of the parts within a complete artistic whole was felt to be artificial, unnatural, dead. Poets published unbalanced works like *Faust*, unfinished works like *Childe Harold*, *Hyperion*, *Christabel*, and *Kubla Khan*.

The former ideals had been held in various degrees by the classical authors most admired in the baroque period, and were educed from them as rigid principles by the baroque critics—who then abused the other Greek and Latin writers for not following them. They called Homer vulgar; they called Aeschylus mad. In time, as baroque society became more rigid, the principles became more purely external; many were added which had nothing to do with the classics, but which entered into a general pattern of 'correctness' falsely thought to be derived from the authority of the Greeks and Romans. There is an amusing passage on them in Macaulay's review of Moore's life of Byron. He cites the opinion of some critics that Milton ought not to have put so many similes into the first book of *Paradise Lost*, for there are no similes in the first book of the *Iliad*, and so the first book of an epic ought to be the most unadorned; or that Othello should not be the hero of a tragedy, for a hero ought always to be white. He says he might just as well enact that the number of scenes in every act should be three or some multiple of three; that the number of lines in every scene should be an exact square; that the characters should never be more or fewer than sixteen; and that every thirty-sixth line in heroic couplets should have twelve syllables. Such 'rules'—and many were laid down which were hardly less absurd—were neither necessary nor classical. The word 'classicist', which is not the same as 'classical' but implies an attempt to emulate the classics, suggests itself as a suitable name for them.

The three principles mentioned above were indeed observed by the Greeks and Romans; but within far broader and more sensible limits than the baroque critics admitted. For instance, the expression of emotion was restrained, but only so far as to exclude vulgarity, incoherence, and intolerable physical frankness. The hero could go mad on the stage; he could be dressed as a beggar, or be cast up naked on a strange island; he could even abuse his enemies in 'porter-like language'. Yet, although his manners were not always those of a baroque peer, he could not do things which would degrade humanity: he could weep, but not get drunk; he could go mad, but he would conquer his madness, or die; he would find no sordid escape from this world, our prison. The mistake made by many baroque writers was to believe that the classical authors admired repression or avoidance of emotion. The great authors of the revolutionary period, like the Greeks themselves, felt emotion deeply, but controlled its expression.

There is a further reason for the description of the literature of the revolutionary period as anti-classical. It is that a number of new fields of human experience, outside the scope of classical literature, were now thrown open to poets and their readers. Folk-poetry; peasant life; the Middle Ages and their survivals, ghostly, adventurous, or amorous; wild nature; the mysterious East; political revolutions; the sinister depths of human passion—all these and other motives came surging in on the revolutionary writers. Baroque poets, with all their self-accepted limitations, had usually had too little to write about. Now the revolutionary poets had too much. Most of them cracked under the strain. *Don Juan* was never finished; *The Recluse* was never finished; Goethe had to make titanic efforts to finish *Faust* at the age of eighty; Schiller never managed to produce a book on any classical subject to satisfy himself, and died ill-content with his work; Coleridge, after the first year or two, never finished anything. The baroque period had concentrated chiefly on classical myth and history, human psychology, and certain fundamental philosophical problems; but now vast new fields were opened up. Superficial observers are therefore apt to interpret the revolutionary period as one in which the interest of poets was entirely turned *away* from the classics *towards* something else. But, as their lives show, most of the revolutionary writers loved and understood classical literature better than their predecessors.

We should therefore revise the shallow conception of this period as one of reaction against classical poetry and classical standards. Most conceptions of history, art, or psychology which are based on action-and-reaction are shallow: they are patterns of thought borrowed from physics, and from a physics which is now known to be inadequate. As soon as the sciences completely free themselves from the domination of physics, it is likely that organic chemistry will provide far more illuminating metaphors to describe the activities of the human spirit. History is not like a clock ticking or a pendulum swinging. Instead of viewing this age as one of reaction, let us describe it as one of expansion and exploration.

It could even be called an explosion. The energies it set free were at first uncontrollable. The symbol of the baroque period was a pearl, straining outwards under the pressure of the forces which its smooth but irregular surface contained (p. 289). The revolutionary age was the explosion of the pearl. Its activity was not conflict, and tension, and difficult control, but release. The forces it released, after issuing in startling cruelties, terrible disasters, amazing beauties, and grand spiritual aspirations, reformed in a new shape and became subject to new controls. But the form of the old age was gone for ever.

We can then reach a deeper understanding of the revolutionary era by comparing it with the Renaissance. Like the Renaissance, it was an epoch of rapid and often violent political change, in which long-established structures were quickly broken into fragments; of brilliant and unexpected artistic creations; of fierce conflicts alike between nations, and within societies, and in the souls of individuals; of the discovery of new realms of thought for the spirit to explore; of brilliant men who emerged from obscurity to become world-movers within a few brief ardent years; of proud hope for the future and unbounded trust in the soul of man, often ending in cold despair. Like the Renaissance, it destroyed several systems of thought which had been in existence for centuries and had gradually become less and less vital, more and more meaningless and conventional. Like the Renaissance, it gave the world a fresh group of political and social and aesthetic concepts; like the Renaissance, it was succeeded by a long period of rest and development during which its achievements were assimilated and evaluated. The period which ended in 1914 was to the revolutionary era what the baroque age was to the Renaissance. But, in the revolutionary era as in the Renaissance, one of the great rediscoveries was the world of classical culture.

The two epochs marked two complementary stages in the exploration of antiquity. The Renaissance meant the assimilation of Latin, while the revolutionary era meant a closer approach to Greek. Men of the Renaissance, like Montaigne, would speak of 'the ancients', but in practice think of the Romans; they would quote fifth-rate Latin poets like Silius Italicus freely and first-rate Greek poets like Homer sparsely. This attitude was now reversed. What stimulated Keats was Homer, more than Vergil. Alfieri learnt Greek at fifty. When Shelley and Goethe decided to write great plays, they thought nothing of Seneca, but strove to emulate Aeschylus and Euripides. When the revolutionary poets yearned for an ideal country, it was usually Greece rather than Rome. The time of revolution was the time in which the rococo garlands and rococo cupids copied from Latin adaptations of late Greek art disappeared, and made way for the Elgin Marbles.

Greece was newly discovered by the men of the revolutionary age. What did it mean to them?

First, it meant beauty and nobility in poetry, in art, in philosophy, and in life. For all its worthiness, this sounds an obvious ideal; but we should remember that throughout the preceding age men talked not so much of beauty as of correctness, of *les bienséances*; while nowadays there is a flourishing school of writers and artists which believes that it is not important for works of art to be characterized by beauty and nobility, but rather to be realistically true, or else to have a certain social or political influence on the public. The best examples of the cult of beauty and nobility are the philosophy of Keats, Goethe's life, and Byron's death.

Greece also meant freedom: freedom from perverse and artificial and tyrannical rules. In literature, the poets sighed with relief when they realized that the existence of the Greek tragedians and of Aristotle's little mutilated treatise did not mean that they were bound to write in fixed patterns. This was of course true. What is surprising about the misinterpretation of Aristotle is that it lasted so long and was so rarely criticized as false. The fact probably is that every age gets what it likes out of antiquity. Aristotle became the dictator of correct taste in literature during the baroque period, just as he had been the master of philosophy during the Middle Ages, not because he himself established a system of absolute rules, but because those epochs admired authority more than freedom. This admiration now disappeared, and with it much of the belief in correctness and the false attitude to the 'authority' of the classics.

As applied to morality, the new interpretation of Greco-Roman culture chiefly meant sexual liberty. Thus, Don Juan and his adoring Haidée form

> a group that's quite antique,
> Half-naked, loving, natural, and Greek.[4]

It is not very easy to justify sexual licence from the Greek writers themselves; but revolutionary society made great play with the thin draperies and nude statuary of Greek art. In the early days of the First Republic in France, beauties like Mme Tallien appeared at parties wearing transparent robes, 'like the Graces', and Pauline Bonaparte posed at least half-naked, in a Greek attitude, for Canova. Keats's *Endymion* and Goethe's *Roman Elegies* are good documents for this interpretation of antiquity.

In politics, both Greece and Rome meant freedom from oppression, and in particular republicanism. The Greece of which the revolutionary writers dreamed was either the heroic era, when society was not polluted by exploitation, or the age of the Athenian commonwealth, when liberty raised the Parthenon and opposed Philip. The Rome they admired was not the empire, whose obituary Gibbon had just completed, but the strong, sober, virtuous republic, hater of tyrants. Classical art became a symbol of political liberty and its reflection. The greatest Greek art was produced by the free republic of Athens, therefore tyranny stifled art. This idea was voiced under the Roman emperors by Tacitus (in his *Dialogue on Orators*) and 'Longinus' (*On the Sublime*, 44). It was revived early in the eighteenth century, chiefly by English writers, who, compared with the subjects of a French sun-king, a German princeling, or an Italian tyrant, felt themselves to be as free as air. It was taken up from them by the Germans, the French, and others.[5] The cult of liberty and republicanism as reflected in classical art and literature went very deep, and was manifested in everything from tiny details of interior decoration to great works of art and political institutions which still exist (for instance, the United States Senate). It was emotionally intensified by the fact that both Greece and Italy were then subject to foreign rulers: the Greeks to the barbarous, corrupt, and fiendishly cruel Turks, and the Italians to scarcely less detestable despots, foreign or foreign-dominated. In the eyes of many Europeans the liberation of Greece from the Turks meant an assertion of the virtues of classical civilization over the vices and tyrannies of the modern world.[6] In literature, the noblest voices of this belief are Byron's *The Isles of Greece*, Shelley's *Hellas*, and Hölderlin's *Hyperion*; while the loudest is Hugo's *Les Orientales*.

In religion, the admiration of poets and thinkers for the Greco-Roman world now meant opposition to Christianity. The cult of paganism vindicated had appeared during the Renaissance, even within the church, but had never been very influential. Later, in the Battle of the Books, the first argument of the moderns was that Greek and Roman books written before the revelation of Jesus Christ could not be so good as modern books which were Christian.[7] At that time no defender of the classics ventured to reverse the argument; and indeed many of the 'ancients', like Racine, would not have dreamed of doing so because they were sincere Christians. But now men began to say that Greek and Roman literature, simply because it expressed the noble, free world of paganism, was bound to be better than books produced by the Christian spirit. The Christian God was represented as a tyrant, crueller and more powerful than any Turk. Jesus was imagined as a pale impotent Jew, and His mission as one of suffering and death—the very opposite of the charm and energy of the Olympians.[8] Goethe, after his return from Rome, became a militant pagan. 'It is almost unknown for Goethe to snap and snarl; but there is no other term for the tone he used about Christianity between the years 1788 and 1794', says Prof. Butler, instancing his attacks on Kant's *Religion within the Limits of Pure Reason*.[9] And this was not merely a passing fad. It entered into his soul. It was one of the chief reasons for the difficulty which he found in completing *Faust* and which many readers have felt in appreciating it. The theme of *Faust* is essentially Christian, and medieval at that: sin through great knowledge, the power of the Devil over mankind, regeneration through grace, and the love of woman leading on to heaven. Goethe found this difficult to write because he did not believe in Christianity. His hero never repents of his sins and never appeals to Jesus Christ the Saviour, whose work and personality are virtually ignored throughout the poem. Similarly, the greatest worshipper of Greece among the English revolutionary writers began his career by being sent down from Oxford for publishing *The Necessity of Atheism*.[10] In France, the revolutionaries reconsecrated the cathedral of Our Lady to the goddess of Reason, who was conceived as a classical deity and incarnated in the pretty body of a contemporary actress. We have already seen how Gibbon, certainly not a revolutionary but a near-contemporary of the revolutionaries and imbued with the spirit of Voltaire, viewed the fall of the Greco-Roman world as a tragedy caused by religion and barbarism. Gibbon admired the culture of that world, but he could not worship its gods. Some of the revolutionary writers, however, were quite prepared to do so, and addressed poems to them, not as relics of obsolete mythology, but as eternal rulers of the spirit of man. This cult of classical antiquity as anti-Christian continued throughout the nineteenth century, becoming more rather than less intense, and culminated in the work of Ménard, the poems of Swinburne, and Nietzsche's *Antichrist*.

Allied to the sense of freedom given by Greece was the cult of nature. The northern European world, the present day, the art and poetry of the present and immediate past, came to seem ugly and unnatural. Only Greece and Italy were, or had been, the true realm of nature. Above anyone else, the Greek poets had understood Nature, knowing how to worship her and describe her: the clothes, the manners, the amusements, the arts, the thought, the ethics of the Greeks were not artificial, but satisfied the basic aspirations of the soul. This must be emphasized nowadays, because we have the habit of regarding the classical world as a subject of scholarly research (like Aztec chronology or the habits of the fruit-fly) rather than a deep spiritual satisfaction; and people who do not know Greek and Latin literature sometimes assume that to love it is to subject oneself to an arid and crippling discipline, rather than to learn more about the nature of the world and of beauty. This assumption is confirmed by the common description of the most strictly limited of the baroque poets as 'classical' and by the false belief that, when they adopted the rules of correctness, they were copying the Greeks and Romans. The revolutionary poets knew better than that.

Together with the general revision of standards, the estimates of Greek and Latin poetry changed. The reputation of Homer gained most. He had been attacked as coarse. He was now exalted as natural. Of the three types of literature most admired by the revolutionaries, two were believed to be wholly natural in origin and method, and the third partly so. These were:

folk-poetry: ballads in particular, but folk-songs too (Coleridge's *The Ancient Mariner* and *Christabel*, Schiller's *The Ring of Polycrates*, and hundreds of other revolutionary poems are imitation ballads. It was now that highly charged lyric poems and elaborately self-conscious songs began to be composed in the simple rhythmic and melodic patterns of folk-song);

Homer, 'the blind illiterate minstrel'; and, some distance after him, Pindar and the other Greek lyricists;

the Greek drama, and the freest, noblest Renaissance drama: chiefly Shakespeare and Calderón.

But apart from naturalness in poetry, the men of the revolutionary age admired the naturalness of Greek conduct, in great as in little things. For instance, in 1769 Lessing published a pamphlet called *How the Ancients represented Death*.[11] This was a contrast between the Greek attitude to death and that of the Christian world—particularly during the Middle Ages—as seen in the Danse Macabre,[12] in Brueghel's *Triumph of Death*, in sermons, in poems, in popular belief. Death, said the medieval men, is the King of Terrors; the most frightful of the Four Horsemen of the Apocalypse; the pallid angel who had accused Satan and could never smile thereafter; or, in other interpretations, the very proof of the Devil's power over this world, which but for him would have held a race of immortal and immortally happy beings. But for the Greeks death was as natural a process as birth: mournful, no doubt, but not to be resisted, not to be hated and vainly shunned. Its symbols were not the crowned skeleton, the corpse crawling with maggots, the dust-covered chapfallen skull, but the quiet urn, the marble relief on which the dead and the living clasp hands with an affection too deep and tranquil for any display of lamentation. Among the most beautiful funeral monuments ever created are the fifth- and fourth-century gravestones from Athens, on which young wives and daughters, although dead, are depicted as they were when they lived, immortalized in that lovely serenity which in later ages appears only in statues of the saints and of the Madonna.

Lastly, Greece and Italy and the Greco-Roman world were felt in the revolutionary age to mean escape. They were beautiful lands, musical, ardent, full of the warm South; there was sun, there were mountains, there were blue seas and blue skies and fruit-trees and laughing girls.[13] They meant escape from the sombre north—the escape yearned for by Mignon in Goethe's *Wilhelm Meister* and by Heine's fir-tree which loved the distant palm, the escape achieved by so many sensitive northerners: Keats, Byron, Shelley, Chateaubriand, Landor, Liszt, the Brownings, D. H. Lawrence, and Norman Douglas. It is remarkable, however, that although Greece was a spiritual lodestone, few of the revolutionary thinkers went to it.[14] Most stopped in Italy. Shelley went no farther. Winckelmann was offered a trip to Greece and refused. Goethe felt he ought to go to Greece, but ventured no farther than the once Greek areas of southern Italy. Some of them were afraid of losing themselves, of being swallowed up. But the chief reason for their abstention was the arrogance and corruption of Turkish imperial rule in Greece, the aridity and poverty of the country, and the degradation of much of the population. Something of the conflict between the ideal Hellas imagined by lovers of literature and art, and the real Greece, a poor verminous oppressed Turkish province, can be seen in Chateaubriand's *Journey from Paris to Jerusalem* (1811) and Kinglake's *Eothen* (1844). But the immortal description of early nineteenth-century Greece is in Byron's *Childe Harold's Pilgrimage* (1812). Byron possessed Greece as though she were a woman.

There was something deeper than landscape and lemon-trees in the urge for escape to the Mediterranean. The story of Goethe's first journey south is well known. 'On the third of September at 3 o'clock of the morning, I stole out of Carlsbad; they would not otherwise have let me go.'[15] The odd tone in which this is written (particularly odd for Goethe, who loved revealing things others would have kept secret) shows that it was part of a psychical conflict: 'they' were part of Goethe. His trip to Italy was an escape from that aspect of himself, and from the world which it approved. In Germans this escape is often linked with the most profound hatred for Germany. Goethe, in a poem written during his southern tour, said that it was impossible to write poetry in German.

What did Fate mean to make me? Perhaps the question is too bold:
    out of many a man Fate does not mean to make much.
Yet its intention to make me a poet might have succeeded,
    if this language had not proved an invincible bar.[16]

There is a story that Hölderlin, when his mind was going, talked to some strangers about Greek art, and was asked if he himself were a Greek. He replied 'On the contrary: I am a German.'[17] As for Nietzsche, his hatred and scorn of the Germans almost defied even his eloquence to express.

The escape of the northerners was not only into a world of natural beauty, but into a world of natural art. More than 500 years before, Italy had become the mother of the arts; then, for a time, foreign occupation and the shift of cultural dominance to France had obscured her from the eyes of the rest of the world; and then, in the eighteenth century, her art was rediscovered. Dr. Burney made a musical tour of Italy and found the Italians more truly musical than any other nation in the world, with music which was not confined to opera-houses and salons, but sung in the caffès and fiddled in the streets.[18] Poetry too the Italians loved with a sincere affection: the gondoliers sang stanzas from Ariosto and Tasso, the *improvvisatori* could spout spontaneous poetry so rapidly and so splendidly that even Byron was impressed. And the visitor was surrounded by the Picturesque: Roman ruins, Greek statues, palaces filled with paintings, lovely Renaissance gardens, something beautiful in every street. On his trip to Italy Goethe bought the famous treatise by Palladio (1518–80) in which the principles of architecture are deduced from classical buildings and classical books. It was a revelation to him. He suddenly realized that the essence of great art is harmony. He attempted to become a sculptor himself, he drew a great deal, and he became a better poet. That, or something like that, happened to every visitor to Italy during the time of revolution.[19] From a cold ugly world of intriguing politicians, frowning prelates, and self-satisfied merchants they escaped to a world of art many centuries old and yet for ever young.

We have sketched the principal changes in spiritual and aesthetic ideals and pointed out some of the new interpretations of classical culture which made the revolutionary period. Now let us see the concrete effects of the revolution, with its new influx of Greco-Roman thought, in the literature and symbolism of five great nations: Germany, France, the United States, Britain, and Italy.

§ 2. GERMANY

All nations have had one Renaissance . . . with one single exception, namely, Germany. Germany has had *two* Renaissances: the second occurs about the middle of the eighteenth century, and is linked with such names as Herder, Goethe, Schiller, Lessing, Winckelmann. In it the Greeks predominate, as the Latins did in the first; the national kinship of Germans and Greeks was discovered. That is why the Germans can be Greek as intensely as the English, French, and Italians, right down to this moment, can be Latin. We prefer Homer to Vergil; Thucydides to Livy; Plato to Seneca: that is a fundamental distinction. Instinctively, we think first of Greece, and then of Rome; the men of the first Renaissance and the great civilized nations of the west do just the opposite; and perhaps that goes far to account for the fact that the Germans are so little known and so greatly misunderstood in the world.

PAUL HENSEL[1]

What Hensel says here would be important if it were true. Some of it is true, but much of it is false. Germany did not have two Renaissances, but one. In the fifteenth and sixteenth centuries other countries (though not 'all nations') had both a Renaissance and a religious Reformation. Germany had only a Reformation, whose leader Luther helped to crush out those sparks of the Renaissance flame which did appear at the same time. And the fire did not catch. In other lands the Renaissance meant an immense liberation of intellectual energy, a greatly heightened sense of aesthetic, spiritual, and sensuous beauty, a marked rise in general culture, producing great quantities of books, inventions, and works of art (many quite worthless but some incomparably valuable), and the emergence, from comparatively low social milieux, of a number of indisputable and unpredictable geniuses. If this had occurred in Germany, the sixteenth century would have shown us a German Shakespeare or Milton, a German Tasso or Calderón, a German Rabelais or Montaigne. Instead, we find nothing except a few humanists writing Latin—the most distinguished being Ulrich von Hutten, far less original and creative than his Dutch contemporary Erasmus; a number of vernacular authors doggedly reproducing outworn medieval forms, poorly adapted classical ideas, and folk-patterns, notably the figure Wagner chose as typical of the best in his age, Hans Sachs; and a great cloud of religious writers, mostly sincere enough but devoid of real taste and education. Classical culture always produces its finest effects in the modern world when it penetrates to the ordinary people and encourages a Rabelais to teach himself Greek, puts Chapman's Homer in the hands of Keats, or makes Shakespeare enthusiastic over Plutarch. It was this which did not happen in Germany—partly because the cultural level of the ordinary public was too low, and partly because the class-distinctions of German society kept a gulf fixed between the Latin-reading and writing university men and the outside world. For these and other reasons Germany in the fifteenth and sixteenth centuries had no Renaissance.

During the early part of the baroque period the German states were devastated by the Thirty Years war. Slowly, after that was over, classical ideals and patterns began to filter into Germany—usually not directly from the originals, but indirectly, through imitation of French and English literature, French art and architecture, and Italian music. After Versailles was planned, baroque palaces went up all over Germany; whole baroque towns and city-areas were laid out, as in Dresden, Vienna, Munich, and Düsseldorf; under the creative impetus of the Counter-Reformation many magnificent baroque churches were built in the Catholic south and Austria. The baroque ideals of symmetry, richness, and controlled power had already taken musical form in Italy. Great Austrian and German composers now emerged to develop these ideals still further and enrich them with a graver spiritual content: although the supreme marriage of music and literature could not be achieved by Germans, and was the work of an Austrian and an Italian Jew.[2]

In fact, the influence of baroque classicism produced no German literature of any great importance, and showed itself chiefly in architecture and music. The German Renaissance was 200 years late. It began in the middle of the eighteenth century. It was marked, like the Renaissance in Italy, France, and Britain, by a new, widespread, popular interest in classical culture, by the reflection of that interest in new books written to imitate and outdo the Greeks and Romans, by the foundation or revival of schools and colleges teaching classical literature, history, and philosophy—and, most important of all, by the appearance of great poets and men of letters inspired by classical ideals. This Renaissance in Germany was part of the same revolution of thought which took place in other European countries in the eighteenth century, which founded the American and French republics, and which we shall see working itself out in the literature of France, Italy, and England. The Germans themselves call it the Romantic movement, marked by Storm and Stress.[3] We shall discuss it as part of the general revolutionary trend in literature; but in the history of German letters it is the one and only classical Renaissance.

It began, not with literature, but with the visual arts, particularly sculpture. Its originator was a cobbler's son called Johann Joachim Winckelmann (1717–68) who, with the persistence and penetration of genius, taught himself the essentials of Greco-Roman culture, supplemented them by a mediocre training in the existing German educational institutions, and with incredible suffering learnt the best of Greek literature, Homer, Plato, Sophocles, Herodotus, and Xenophon, by staying up half the night while working during the day as a hack schoolmaster.[4] Then, as librarian to a Saxon nobleman in Dresden, he studied both the elaborately exhibited baroque statuary in the great park and the copies of real Greek and Greco-Roman statues packed away in the store-rooms. With superb taste closer to divination than to knowledge, he evoked the essential qualities of classic art (which were then obscured by baroque affectations) in his first book, *Thoughts on the Imitation of Greek Works in Painting and Sculpture* (1755).[5] This little pamphlet was the beginning of the German Renaissance.

We must not think that meanwhile the rest of Europe was plunged in baroque blindness or Gothic darkness. Continuous progress was being made towards a truer and deeper understanding of Greek culture, although misunderstandings were still common even in such a mind as that of Voltaire. The greatest advances were undoubtedly made by English writers and amateurs of art. Before Winckelmann was born the earl of Shaftesbury (1671–1713) had published a number of fine essays on art and morals which might have been written by a friend of Plato. They taught that our daily life must be shaped according to principles of beauty and harmony, that the aesthetic sense and moral sense are innate, and that both together should guide and ennoble the soul. These ideas flow straight into the books of Winckelmann.[6] A little later, in 1732, a group of English gentlemen founded the Society of Dilettanti (or 'Delighters' in the arts) to explore and appreciate the treasures of classical art. They sent the painter and architect 'Athenian' Stuart and the draughtsman Revett to make a long stay in Athens. The result was a superb work, *The Antiquities of Athens Measured and Delineated* (1762), the first set of accurate reproductions of Athenian architecture. It led to the adoption of Greek architectural style in St. James's Square, thus introducing a fashion which spread throughout northern Europe and into North America.[7] The Dilettanti then dispatched the epigraphist Chandler to explore Greece and what was once Greek Asia. Along with Revett and Pars he produced two magnificent folio volumes of *Antiquities of Ionia* (1769).[8] In the same year the distinguished politician and traveller Robert Wood published the first real attempt to see Homer's life and poetry in its proper historical and geographical setting with his *Essay on the Original Genius and Writings of Homer, with a Comparative View of the Ancient and Present State of the Troade*.[9] These books did more than any others to create the German Renaissance, by moulding the thought of its leaders.[10]

Immediately after publishing his first book Winckelmann went off to Rome to study classical art in more sympathetic surroundings. Italy was full of connoisseurs. If the Italians and Italianate Englishmen like Sir William Hamilton had not been collecting works of ancient art, not even Winckelmann could have studied them. On the contrary, large and well-arranged collections existed long before he arrived in Rome. But he brought a fresh eye to them. He described them in such a way as to elicit from them (even though he knew few of the greatest originals) the fundamental principles of Greek art. He had already summarized its essential qualities as 'a noble simplicity and a quiet grandeur'.[11] These qualities he explained and exemplified in later essays and in his *magnum opus, A History of Art among the Ancients* (1764).[12] This was the first book to treat the history of art—not, as most previous critics did, as a timeless phenomenon or as the history of individual artists, but as 'part of the growth of the human race',[13] or more accurately as a manifestation of the life of the societies which produce it. Winckelmann described the development of ancient art from Egypt through Phoenicia, Persia, and Etruria, to Greece and Rome, connecting that process with the changes in Mediterranean civilization. He also struck out the fundamental method which is now used by all aesthetic historians, and arranged Greek art into *periods*: primitive, classical, late classical, and declining. His next important book, *Unpublished Ancient Monuments* (1767–8),[14] did a valuable service to both art and scholarship by showing that a number of scenes from classical art, mainly reliefs on Roman coffins, were not portrayals of ordinary life but conventional scenes from mythology. Winckelmann had a grasp of perspective comparable to that of Gibbon in history.

Winckelmann's remarkable discoveries, the good taste and intellectual energy which his books embodied, and his example in going straight to one of the classical countries to study instead of getting everything from commentaries and translations, produced a profound effect in Germany. He had the good luck to find in the world of literature an exponent with considerable knowledge and unusual critical sense—Gotthold Ephraim Lessing (1729–81).

Lessing's most distinguished work in this field is his essay on the famous sculptural group, *Laocoon* (1766).

For a German book, *Laocoon* is unusual. It is short, uneven, and brilliant. Something between a Platonic dialogue and an appreciative essay, it is still good reading for those who can follow Lessing's allusions. But it is a puzzle to most modern critics. It is hard nowadays to understand why so much taste and thought were expended on what appears to us to be an inferior and repellent work of art.

Laocoon was a Trojan priest. When his countrymen found the Trojan Horse, apparently a votive statue and really full of concealed Greek soldiers, and proposed to take it into Troy, he warned them that it was probably a trap. He even hurled a spear into its side. He might have persuaded them to leave it outside the walls —but the sea-god Poseidon, who hated Troy and wished it to be destroyed, chose to take the gesture as an insult to his sacred animal the horse. So he sent two huge serpents out of the sea, which, before the eyes of the Trojans, seized and destroyed Laocoon and his two sons.[15] The group shows the priest and his children helpless in the grip and the jaws of the serpents. The father looks up to heaven for the help he will not get, the boys look towards him for the help he cannot give, the snakes enlace them all so cunningly that no escape is possible, neither weapons nor friends are at hand. The group was carved in Rhodes long after the great period of Greek art had ended, about 25 B.C.[16] This date coincides with the Roman interest in tracing back the pre-history of Rome to Troy.[17] And yet the group shows the torture and death of a Trojan priest for violating a statue dedicated to Athena, the most Greek of all goddesses: it would be possible therefore to interpret it as a death-wish for the Romans who descended from Troy and conquered Greece, and thus as anti-Trojan, anti-Roman propaganda comparable to the romance of 'Dares Phrygius'.[18]

Certainly the group is not Greek art at its best. The subject is hideous, for it shows a cruel and unjust death inflicted by a god upon an entire family. The treatment is emotional in the highest extreme: all the figures are undergoing the utmost mental and physical torture. (Later their physical sufferings will be greater; but by then their minds will be less tormentingly alive to the whole situation.) Both to classical Greek taste and to the best taste of modern times the *Laocoon* is a clever monstrosity. Why did Winckelmann, Lessing, Goethe, and many others admire it so deeply?

The first reason is the most obvious. Technically it is a marvellous piece of work. The anatomy is superb; the carving, in spite of the formidable difficulties of the subject, is masterly. On a higher level of technique, viewed purely as a pattern, it is a masterpiece. The figures are beautifully proportioned and balanced. The intricate interplay of all the different limbs and muscles, at so many different angles and elevations, might easily have been a confused mêlée, instead of the harmonious complex which it is. The group as a whole, and each of its figures, fall into a balanced shape as graceful and as various as the triangles formed by the groups in Leonardo's *Last Supper*. And the sculptor's problem of making his work live in three dimensions has been perfectly solved, for the struggling figures lean backwards and forwards and aspire upwards while being held together in a single mass.

Yet this was not what Lessing admired most. He and his contemporaries praised the group chiefly for the qualities which we can scarcely see in it: dignity and restraint. Winckelmann and his followers were never tired of pointing out that the father's lips were just parted in an involuntary groan, whereas, had it not been for the dignity of classical art, he would have been screaming at the top of his voice. He did scream, in Vergil's narrative; but Lessing said he would not scream in marble, because his mouth would have been ugly. This seems to us to leave out the main question: the entire subject is ugly, and the emotional charge in it is excessive. And yet Lessing is correct within broad limits. The figures are suffering, but they are not ungraceful. Five minutes later one of the children will be swollen and the other vomiting blood as the grip of the constrictors tightens; the father's limbs will be twisted out of shape and his face will be losing even the semblance of humanity. At the moment, although agonizing, they are still noble because they are fully human.

Where Lessing was wrong was in treating *Laocoon* as an expression of classical ideals. Tension so extreme as this was never portrayed in Greek art of the great period, when death itself (as Lessing pointed out) was shown in eternal calm. Greek painters would not show the face of Agamemnon at the sacrifice of his daughter; Greek playwrights would not permit Medea to murder her children or Oedipus to blind himself before the audience. The *Laocoon* is a defeat; the highest Greek art preferred to show a victory, however dearly bought. It would not, like Dostoevsky, describe a noble and virtuous man becoming a helpless maniac in the grip of epilepsy.

The truth is that the *Laocoon* is a work of baroque taste. Lessing and Winckelmann were not the first, but almost the last, to admire it. At the very height of the baroque period, in 1667, the Flemish sculptor Van Obstal told the Royal Academy of France, 'Of all the statues which have been preserved, there is not one to equal the *Laocoon*.'[19] One of the major ideals of baroque art is *tension*, the acute polarity between extreme passion and extreme control.[20] It was this tension, rather than the characteristic Greek serenity, which the Academy admired in *Laocoon*, and by which Lessing was still blinded. The closest parallel to the spirit of the *Laocoon* in modern times is the statue of the saint in a seventeenth-century Jesuit church: tall, dignified, draped, comely of shape and handsome of feature, but tormented with aspiration, swirling around in a gale of passion which twists the draperies and bends the body and turns the head sideways and draws the eyes upwards in the last ecstasy of suffering and possession, torn between the dragging earth and the still distant heavens. Nevertheless, although it was part of the taste of a dying age, Winckelmann and Lessing looked at *Laocoon* with a new insight. They taught the world to see it and other Greek statues, not with the cool and sometimes patronizing eye of the Enlightenment, but with the enthusiasm and love which make great criticism, and which were intrinsic elements of the thought of the revolutionary era.

In literary criticism also, Lessing's active mind produced influential new interpretations of classical books and classical principles, particularly in his contributions to *Letters on Modern Literature* and his *Hamburg Dramatic Journal*.[21] We have already pointed out that during the Battle of the Books many supporters of the moderns denounced the classical poets (particularly Homer) for being vulgar, and praised modern literature as more correct in vocabulary and social conduct. In the third phase of the battle Mme Dacier turned this argument against her opponents. They said it was improper for a princess to do the laundry. She replied that Nausicaa was better employed washing her brothers' shirts than wasting her time on cards, and gossip, and other more dangerous occupations, like contemporary ladies of fashion.[22] Lessing now took up the same argument, and used it against the upholders of baroque taste. If we think the Greeks were vulgar and silly, he said, that proves that *we* are vulgar and silly.

But we need not think that in these critical essays Lessing was simply applying Greek principles to contemporary literary criticism. That would have been rather mechanical, even a little narrow. His achievement was broader. The criterion he applied was his own sensitive taste. He began quite early with a defence of Plautus, whom he had translated and was later to imitate.[23] From that he turned to defend the tragedies of Seneca, explaining the real merits which their glaring faults often obscure.[24] Then, after admiring Voltaire for some time, Lessing saw through his shallow tragedies and glib criticisms. Partly because he was on the whole a partisan of the 'moderns' and partly to commend his own epic and dramatic works, Voltaire asserted that French tragedy was superior to Greek tragedy. In 1759 Lessing attacked him both with the blade and with the point, declared that French classicist tragedy was inferior to both Shakespeare and the Greeks, and extended his attack to include, not indeed the unquestioned masterpieces of Racine and Corneille, but Corneille's *Rodogune*, and by implication all the lesser works of the French baroque theatre.[25] Then, some years later, he studied Aristotle's *Poetics*, and gave an interpretation of it which, although now in some respects out of date, was a turning-point in German literary history.[26] Lessing proclaimed that Aristotle did not lay down laws to confine the creative spirit, but offered rules of guidance to make its creative work easier, surer, and finer. During the baroque age many men had felt 'the ancient authors' like a mountainous weight pressing down their minds. Lessing, and those who followed him in the era of revolution, realized that the Greeks could help them to grow.

The movement towards Greek in Germany was hastened by a flood of new translations. Here the chief name was that of Johann Heinrich Voss (1751–1826), professor of classics at Heidelberg, who produced a highly praised version of the *Odyssey* in German hexameters in 1781, following it with versions of the *Iliad*, of Hesiod, of the bucolic poets, and of several Roman writers (Vergil, Horace, Tibullus, and Propertius). They are not great translations, but they were levers to open a heavy door.

At the same time, poets and thinkers were endeavouring to learn Greek, with all the enthusiasm which in other lands had once gripped Renaissance youths beginning to read Latin. Goethe, for example, was started on Greek when he was nine, but gave it up in his adolescence. And then, aged twenty-one, he got a fresh impetus from meeting Johann Gottfried von Herder (1744–1803). Herder, the leader of the Storm and Stress movement, is chiefly known nowadays for his admiration of 'primitive and natural' poetry—ballads, folk-songs, Ossian, and Shakespeare. The fact that he inspired Goethe with a love of Greek shows how mistaken it is to believe in a direct opposition between 'classical' and 'romantic'. He urged Goethe to learn Greek, not to penetrate hidden realms of scholarship, but in order to reach 'truth, feeling, Nature' by reading Homer and Plato in the original.[27] So Goethe started on Homer in 1770; went on to Plato and to Xenophon's *Memoirs* (which give a different view of the life and teaching of Socrates); in 1771 to Theocritus; in 1772 to Pindar (whom he believed to be writing free verse); and by 1773 reached Greek tragedy.[28]

Authors read in order to write. No creative writer can work on his own experience alone; and very often a new book will stimulate an author more than the day-by-day events of his life. But the stronger the stimulus, the harder it is to receive it without being numbed. Exposed to the full power of classical poetry, many promising young writers have either been silenced or become helpless imitators. The German writers of the revolutionary period admitted the power of Greek myth and poetry; but most of them were unable to assimilate it as easily and productively as the simpler influences of folk-song and medieval romance.

Johann Christoph Friedrich Schiller (1759–1805) admired the nobility of Greek philosophy and was deeply impressed by the power of Greek legend. But he produced no large poem on a classical theme. His most ambitious work inspired by Greece was *The Bride of Messina*—an interesting but not wholly successful marriage between a horrific Italian Renaissance plot of incestuous loves and fratricidal hates, with murder and suicide on the stage, and a classically balanced dramatic structure, with several skilfully inlaid adaptations of Greco-Roman themes, and a double chorus composed of retainers. The true successors of this experiment were not the nineteenth-century poetic tragedies but the early operas of Wagner and Verdi. Apart from this, Schiller's love of Greco-Roman culture produced only ballads on Greek folk-tales (such as *The Ring of Polycrates* and *The Cranes of Ibycus*), and odes to hypostatized moral and emotional ideals, partly drawn from Greek thought and modelled on the deified abstractions of the Greek and Roman pantheon. Since Klopstock set the fashion, the German poets had been writing many such lyrics, in the manner of Pindar (as they conceived it) but with all the sentimental idealism of the revolutionary era. Schiller's most famous poem in this vein is his *Ode to Joy*, which Beethoven took as the words for the powerful final movement of the Ninth Symphony:

> Joy, thou lovely spark of godhead!
> Maiden from Elysium![29]

That rapturous lyric had a melancholy counterpart, *The Gods of Greece* (1788). Here is Schiller's most important Hellenic poem.

It is a lament for the dead Greek deities, who have died only because something within the soul of man has died. Once, nature was alive, and the whole world incarnated divinities. Within the tree there was a living dryad. The bird-song in the wildwood was the poignant lament of Philomela. The thing in the sky, which scientists now tell us is a ball of burning gas, was then a golden chariot driven by Helios, calm monarch of the air. The world now, cries Schiller, is nothing but matter. For the Greeks it was matter infused with spirit. Then it meant something; now it means nothing. Then it was both human and humanly divine. Now it is sub-human, an object in physical motion, as dead as the ticking pendulum. It has neither life, nor beauty, nor divinity.

This poem is an open attack on modern science and modern materialism, and an implicit attack on Christianity. The medieval Christian horror of death is contrasted with the calm Greek acceptance of it.[30] Although Schiller does not directly attack the Christian religion, he expresses horror of the Christian world which—unlike the pagan world—lies opaque and dead, without spiritual life. The sorrowful protest of this lyric is echoed in Wordsworth's *The World is too much with Us,*[31] and is deepened and intensified in many poems of the advancing nineteenth century. At the time, many German poetasters published odes intended to answer *The Gods of Greece* and to refute Schiller's complaint, for they felt that he was proclaiming a revolt against some of the deepest values of Christianity, and turning men's eyes away from heaven towards the beauty of this world.[32] They were right: he foretold a war of Greek against Hebrew, of pagan against Christian.

The truest Greek of all the German revolutionary writers was a tragic young man whose career for some time ran parallel to Schiller's—not because he copied Schiller, but because they both felt the same inspiration. This was Friedrich Hölderlin (1770–1802: he lived until 1843, but his life ended in 1802 when he went mad).[33] His first poems echoed Schiller's lyrics very closely, although some of the most important were much more intense and more truly great. It was partly because of this correspondence (which must have seemed rather like plagiarism) and partly because of Hölderlin's extreme other-worldliness, which expressed such unbounded adoration of Greece as to be virtually a death-wish, that the young man was comparatively neglected by both Schiller and Goethe. However, Schiller did help to interest the publishers

in Hölderlin's prose romance *Hyperion*. This is the story of a young
Greek of modern times who is inspired by a strong and noble
master (Adamas, a personification of Schiller) to attempt to recapture the glory of ancient Greece; he fights for Greek independence against the Turks, but fails, and becomes a hermit, dedicated
not to the God of religion but to the divinities of nature. The book
thus combines two of the ideals which ancient Greece symbolized
for Hölderlin's generation. To reach Hellas one might pass through
modern Greece, and struggle to liberate it from tyranny, or one
might cast off society, and find a spiritual home in the Mediterranean landscape, mountains, sea, and sky.

Like most of the German hellenists, Hölderlin attempted a
tragedy. He chose the subject which Matthew Arnold was to treat
later and with more success: *The Death of Empedocles*. It is full of
lofty thought and fine poetry, but, like so many imitative Greek
dramas, it is incomplete. He also wrote translations of Sophocles'
Oedipus and *Antigone*. But the greatest part of his work was lyric
and elegiac: brief poems in a four-line stanza resembling that
which Horace took from the Greeks, elegies in the manner of the
Greek and Roman love-poets, or large odes and hymns like those
of Pindar and the tragedians.[34] Hölderlin understood what men
of earlier generations had not seen: that Greek poetry combines
intense feeling with deliberate objectivity. Because his own
emotions were so acutely sensitive and his life so painful, he found
it all the more difficult to attain this objectivity, and yet all the
more necessary. Even the poems which he wrote when his madness
was approaching him and becoming visible in his words still have
the fundamental nobility of Greece.

The parallel between Hölderlin and Keats is very striking.[35]
Hölderlin was a better classical scholar, Keats a better poet. But
their love for antiquity, particularly for Greece, was similar in
intensity, and in its quality of melancholy tenderness. Hölderlin
had an unhappy love-affair like Keats, but his was far more
wretched. The girl was more sensitive and intelligent than Fanny
Brawne, but was already married, and to a cold business-man
who treated the young poet like a servant. Hölderlin wrote poems
to her under the name of Diotima—the half-mythical priestess
from whom Socrates learned that through love the vision of ideal
beauty and goodness may be attained.[36] Neither Keats nor
Hölderlin admired the robust energy of Aeschylus as a power that

could be assimilated and used to strengthen his own character. Keats was a happier, and, despite his early death, a healthier man. He loved life, and found its finest expression in the grace and nobility of Greece; while Hölderlin loved antiquity because he hated the present day. Keats's Hyperion succeeded, where Hölderlin's failed. But both poets, the melancholy German and the enraptured Englishman, had a tragic consciousness of impending doom. One of them cried:

> When I have fears that I may cease to be
> Before my pen has gleaned my teeming brain . . .

and the other echoed him:

> Only one summer grant me, powerful spirits!
> one autumn, one, to ripen all my songs,
> so that my heart, sated with sweet
> delight, may more willingly die.[37]

Johann Wolfgang von Goethe (1749–1832) acknowledged many powerful influences on his mind: love, travel, science, oriental poetry, the theatre, the court, his poetic friends, folk-poetry. Scarcely any of these was stronger than the influence of Greco-Roman literature. His classical education was limited and uninspiring. Although competent in Latin, he never felt at ease in Greek. When he read a Greek book, he liked to have a translation handy, and often it was only the appearance of a new translation that would turn his attention to a Greek poet.[38] Nevertheless, like nearly all the creative writers of his age, he genuinely loved Greek literature and constantly drew strength from it. It was the eulogies of Herder on Greek poetry, and of Winckelmann's friend and teacher Oeser on Greek art together with Winckelmann's, Lessing's, Blackwell's, and Wood's analyses of Greek aesthetic ideals —which really awakened his interest in the classics;[39] and, with intervals in which other enthusiasms developed other aspects of his versatile character, it remained active and creative in many different stages of his career. Homer was his favourite. He thought about Homer far more than about any other classical author—as much as he thought about the three Athenian tragedians (his next favourites) all together.[40] By the age of twenty-one he was teaching himself to read Homer; and thereafter he read on through most of Greek literature. It meant far more to him than Latin, and gave him the companionship of the immortals throughout his long life.

The ideal world of the past became a reality for him in 1786, when he escaped to Rome. He was overwhelmed not only by its magnificence but by its continuing vitality, especially since he was a young passionate man and found handsome women there. In his *Roman Elegies* he writes that embracing his mistress taught him how to understand sculpture;[41] and it is obvious that having a love-affair with a fiery Roman girl made the love-poems of the classical elegists, and even their sometimes abstruse mythological allusions, immediate and real to him.[42] Previously he had written some imitations of classical poetry on a small scale—for instance, the epigram *Anacreon's Grave* (1785), which Hugo Wolf made into an exquisite song, was inspired by Herder's translations from the Greek Anthology. But now began his long series of imitations, emulations, and evocations of classical literature which, at intervals, continued until the close of his career.

First he took a prose drama on a classical subject which he had already written, and remodelled it in verse. This was *Iphigenia in Tauris*, published in prose in 1779 and in verse in 1787. In its first form it resembled a French classicist tragedy in prose, with five acts, no chorus, and a calm correctitude about the characters. It was based on Euripides' play about Iphigenia among the savages, and was full of imitations of great passages from the Greek dramatists.[43] But in the most important matter of all it was more than an imitation. The morality was modern, almost Christian: a change which Racine had felt bound to introduce into some of the legends he used. Iphigenia escapes, and secures freedom for her brother, not by opposing the savage Tauric prince, nor as in Euripides by tricking him, but by telling him the truth and trusting the better nature which, by her own goodness, she helps to create.[44]

The success of *Iphigenia* was doubtful. Though pure, it seems cold: which Greek tragedy seldom is. But there is no doubt about the success of Goethe's next classicizing work, the *Roman Elegies* (1795). These are poems about love and art in Rome, written in an adaptation of the elegiac couplet used by all ancient writers on such subjects. In form and size, in their preoccupation with passionate love, in their vivid and subtle psychology, and in their frequent allusions to erotic legends, they are directly in the tradition of the Roman elegists. Goethe admired and borrowed from Propertius (Schiller actually called him the German Propertius); he knew Catullus, and he loved Ovid best of all the Roman love-poets. Reminiscences of the work of all three are frequent in the *Roman Elegies*, but so skilfully rehandled and so daringly juxtaposed in new combinations and with new matter that they enhance the originality of the book.[45] The classical echoes in them cannot be called imitations. It would be more accurate to say that they are original poems, produced under three convergent inspirations—Goethe's love-affairs, his aesthetic experiences in Rome, and his reading of the classical elegists. They are (except for one essential factor) extremely beautiful, and are in several ways superior to the Roman elegiac poems he was emulating. For instance, one of the limitations of the Roman elegists is that their poems tend to fall into conventional patterns, no doubt set by the Alexandrian Greeks: the address to the sweetheart's locked door, the poem on the pet animal, &c. One Roman poet after another rehandles these themes, seldom introducing more than minor variations. But Goethe struck out a number of fine new ideas: such as a monologue by an offended mistress, in which we can almost hear the angry tearful Italian girl screaming, and see her stamp on the floor.[46]

The weakness of these poems is their verse-form. German poets had been experimenting for some time with adaptations of classical metres; the famous Friedrich Gottlieb Klopstock (1724–1803) made a great sensation with his first three cantos of *The Messiah* in hexameters (1748), while many other writers had practised the elegiac couplet. Goethe liked this couplet, especially for short poems of a richer texture and lower emotional tone than lyrics. But he never managed to make it as musical as it was in Greek and Latin. Partly this is because of the nature of the German language, which in long-line poetry sounds heavy and involved; but partly it is because Goethe was much too lax in using a difficult metre, which must (as the Romans had discovered after unfortunate early experiments) be used precisely to attain its best nature. Technically, the reason for this is that in Greek and Latin the elegiac metre depends on an alternation of long and short syllables, whereas in modern languages it must depend on an alternation of stressed and unstressed syllables. Now, it is composed of dactyls and spondees, which are fairly easy to find and vary in Greek or Latin, quantitatively used. But a foot corresponding to a spondee in a modern language is quite rare, for it must contain two stressed syllables in succession. Two emphatic monosyllables will produce this effect; but very few dissyllabic words will do so. Therefore the poet writing this metre in German or English tends to use *any* dissyllabic word, leaving it to the reader to slow up the rhythm long enough to maintain the regular march of dactyls and spondees.[47] But this is too much of an effort even for those who have the rhythm of the hexameter in their heads. There are many lines in Goethe's elegies which only classical scholars can read with understanding, and no classical scholar can read with pleasure.

In 1796 Goethe joined Schiller in publishing a collection of several hundred epigrams on contemporary literature, politics, and philosophy. The name, *Xenia*, means 'gifts'. It was taken from the epigrammatist Martial, who has two whole books full of little poems to be attached to gift-parcels; and the spirit was meant to be that of Martial. Some of the poems are trenchant enough to be quoted still. But most of the subjects were ephemeral, and, what is more important, the elegiac rhythm becomes deadly monotonous after the first hundred couplets. Martial would not publish a series of over 300 poems on miscellaneous subjects in roughly the same shape and exactly the same metre: he knew it would be unreadable.

By the French Revolution, and by the daemons of disorder and violence it called up, Goethe was deeply shocked. In a revulsion from it he produced in 1798 a country love-story in nine books, called *Hermann and Dorothea*.[48] The tone is pastoral; the metre is the classical hexameter, freely adapted; the manner is that of the quieter, more conventional aspects of Homer—for example, the straightforward but ennobling description of good simple things such as horses and farm-work, the repeated use of the same epithets for the same characters—

the pastor judicious and noble—[49]

the long speeches, and the leisurely pace of the story. The same kind of poem appears later in British and American literature, with Clough's *The Bothie* and Longfellow's *Evangeline*, both in hexameters. In one of these the subject and in the other the setting is poetic, because distant and strange. But in *Hermann and Dorothea* we are meant to feel that the simple peasant character and the simple small-town surroundings and the simple love-story are in themselves enough to move the imagination. The mood is to be that of contemporary poems like Cowper's *The Task* and Wordsworth's *Peter Bell*. However, the poetic intensity of the work is low, and Goethe has not heightened it by his technique. It begins, for instance, with an almost interminable conversation between the innkeeper, his wife, the local chemist, and the local parson, which is poetic in nothing, nothing but the metre. Such easy narrative and quiet dialogue are intolerable when associated with a style that constantly reminds the reader of the surge and thunder of the *Odyssey*. In music, the parallel is Strauss's *Domestic Symphony*, where the full resources of the orchestra are called in to depict a day and night in the life of a happily married couple, and even the cries of the baby are reproduced. Goethe may have been attempting to blend Homer with the peasant Hesiod and the pastoral Theocritus. Or he may have been misled into believing that, in the simpler descriptive passages of the *Iliad* and *Odyssey*, Homer, as a 'poet of nature', was merely describing exactly what all his audience knew and saw every day: and he himself may therefore have tried to make poetry out of the familiar, the respectable, and the platitudinous.

Hermann and Dorothea is an epic idyll in an adaptation of the Homeric manner. Goethe, who had long admired the Homeric poems, was encouraged to try rivalling them by a book which suggested that Homer had never existed. This was Wolf's *Introduction to Homer*, published in 1795.[50] It was an extremely important work, and determined the direction of much nineteenth-century scholarship.

We have seen how Homer was disliked and misunderstood in the seventeenth and early eighteenth centuries.[51] A decisive step towards the better comprehension of the *Iliad* and the *Odyssey* was made by Wood's *Essay on the Original Genius of Homer*.[52] The nobility and gentry of the baroque era had claimed that the Homeric epics could not be good poetry because Homeric society was in some ways less polished and precise than their own. This was a fault in their historical perspective. Wood, by describing the scenery which Homer knew, and by evoking from the life of the Near East the kind of life he described, primitive but not barbarous, simple but noble, helped to show lovers of poetry what they should really look for when they read the *Iliad*. Translated into German in 1773, the essay had a wide public in Germany, as it did elsewhere. Young Goethe was one of its admirers.

Another admirer was Friedrich August Wolf, who became

professor of classics at Halle in 1783. Like Wood, Wolf set out to put the Homeric poems in their correct historical perspective. But he did not regard them chiefly as works of art. He was interested in their history—and in this he was a successor of such scholars as the great Benedictine, Mabillon, and Bentley, the exploder of 'Phalaris'.[53] He undertook to trace the various stages by which they had been transmitted since they were composed. He pointed out that it was impossible to say there was a single fixed text of the two poems—in the same way as a modern printed book represents, in all its many thousand copies, a single text which (barring accidental errors) is what the author wrote. Instead, there were many different versions of the Homeric poems, varying not much in the main lines, but in many important details; and it was impossible to follow their history back to any time when there was a single text. The farther we go back (he suggested), the less likely it becomes that we could ever reach one poet, Homer, and two solid blocks of poetry called the *Iliad* and the *Odyssey*.

The chief reason for this (according to Wolf) is that writing was virtually unknown at the time when the poems were composed. Twice in the *Iliad* significant marks are mentioned, but in a way more like the runes of the Dark Ages and the heraldry of medieval times than the written books of civilized Greece.[54] The Homeric poems were composed about illiterates, in an illiterate age. (In this argument Wolf acknowledged he was basing his discussion on Wood's essay.[55]) A single epic poem as large as the *Iliad* could neither be composed nor be transmitted without writing.[56] It follows that, until writing was discovered and became widespread in Greece, there was no *Iliad* and no *Odyssey*.

What was there? A collection of 'lays', short enough to be carried in the memory, and to be sung after a feast—as the bards in the Homeric epics sing them: a large collection, in fact an entire tradition, like the ballads of the Middle Ages, 'loose songs' which 'were not collected together in the Form of an Epic Poem, till about 500 years after'.[57] There was no Homer. There were only bards, called 'Homerids' or 'sons of Homer'; and the epics were agglomerations of 'folk-poetry'.[58]

Who then put them together into the form of epics? Pisistratus, the tyrant of Athens (*fl.* 540 B.C.)—or poets and scholars who were working for him.[59] (It is universally agreed that some important job of editing was carried out on Pisistratus' orders, and possibly he initiated the first attempt to make a fixed text of the Homeric poems.)

Wolf did not always go so far as to draw the full conclusions towards which his arguments pointed, but his reasoning was so incisive, subtle, and clear that his readers and followers were bound to conclude

(1) that there had been no epic poet called Homer, but a number of 'rhapsodes' or minstrels working on a far smaller scale, and composing numbers of short poems on the adventures connected with the Trojan war and other events of the heroic age;

(2) that the structure of the two epics was the work of editors, who chose and assembled these short poems after the art of writing had become widespread;

(3) therefore, that it was impossible to cite 'Homer' as a single genius, or to quote any particular line of the Homeric poems as reliable evidence for the thoughts and manners of pre-historic Greece—since it was impossible without intricate research to tell when the line had been written, or interpolated.

This type of analysis was to be practised on most of the classical authors throughout the nineteenth century, and still continues.[60] It had already been initiated in the criticism of the Bible, by eighteenth-century editions of the New Testament which pointed out the important variations in the text of the gospels and epistles; and during the nineteenth century it issued in the dissolution of the Old Testament, under 'higher criticism', into many fragments, and of the gospels into a number of much-edited narratives

On scholars this had a stimulating effect. But literary men found Wolf's book discouraging. It was depressing to think that what they had taken for a pair of great epics was really two groups of small-scale poems, and that individual genius counted for nothing in characterization and planning.

Wolf's theory has now been superseded, although his intelligence and his acumen are recognized.[61] It has been proved that it is quite possible for good poetry on the scale of the *Iliad* and *Odyssey* to be composed without the aid of writing, and to be transmitted faithfully enough from generation to generation. And although it is clear that poems by many different composers were used in the construction of the *Iliad* and *Odyssey*, the work of the poet or poets who built the two epics into their majestic architecture is now called not 'editing' but poetic composition of the highest type.

Goethe was at first encouraged by Wolf's theory. He had felt Homer to be unapproachable; but if there were no Homer, only some smaller talents called 'Homerids', he could endeavour to rival them.[62] And it was in this mind that he wrote *Hermann and Dorothea*. Later, however, as he read the Homeric epics with more and more understanding—and also, no doubt, as he attempted other Homeric poems like his *Achilleis* and continued work on his own large-scale drama, *Faust*—he realized that behind the epics there stood at least one majestic genius; and at last he published a formal retractation of his belief in Wolf's solution of the Homeric problem.[63]

Goethe made other plans to write a classical work in German: Trevelyan's *Goethe and the Greeks* describes the many torsos he left half-finished. He published a number of spirited lyrics in the Pindaric manner;[64] and Greek ideals often appeared in his other work, as in his play *The Natural Daughter*. But he wrote no other important classicizing poem until Part II of *Faust*, which was published after his death.

Faust I, issued nearly a quarter of a century earlier, tells the story of the gifted magician, eternally dissatisfied and yearning like Goethe himself, who tries the pleasures of the senses, culminating in physical love—but without satisfaction. *Faust* II tells how the same man goes through the larger activities of the spirit, art, court-life, war, and others, to find his real fulfilment at last in working for the rest of mankind. The form of the play is wildly unclassical: there are hundreds of characters, stage-effects which are impossible except to a trick camera are constantly demanded, there is no continuity even in the outward appearance of the chief personages, the metre changes incessantly, the acts are virtually independent of one another, and there are dozens of symbolic events which are not only unconnected with each other but excessively obscure by themselves.

However, one of the main episodes is a highly important classical symbol. The friendly fiend, Mephistopheles, shows Faust how to conjure up Helen of Troy. Faust does so, and tries to embrace her, but she disappears with a shock which knocks him senseless. Later Helen herself seeks the help of Faust to keep Menelaus, her wronged husband, from sacrificing her in a ritual of vengeance. Faust now appears in the guise of a medieval noble in a Gothic castle; he saves her and makes her his lady; they have a miraculous son, who leaps gaily about with superhuman strength and agility from the moment of birth, and steals or outdoes all the special gifts of the gods. At last the child Euphorion tries to soar up into heaven in pursuit of beauty, and falls dead like Icarus. His body looks for a moment like 'a well-known form' (that of Lord Byron, we are given to understand), and then it vanishes, and so does Helen.

Helen is clearly a symbol of classical antiquity, and in particular of Greece. What does Goethe mean to tell us by her appearance in *Faust*? The idea that the magician Faust conjured up Helen of Troy and made love to her was part of the original medieval legend; but there it was merely a supreme sensual satisfaction, possession of the world's most beautiful woman. In Goethe's poem the episode has many more complex meanings.

1. Certainly she symbolizes Greece as the home of supreme physical beauty. Other countries have admired beauty together with wealth or power or pleasure or the service of God. None so much as Greece has prized beauty above everything else: beauty in costume, buildings, ornaments, men and women. And Helen, for whom all Greece and the cities of Asia went gladly to war, is the image of perfect beauty.

2. But she means something more than the beauty of woman. The seduction of the lovely but simple Margaret in *Faust* I left Faust profoundly dissatisfied. Helen's beauty transcends that of the loveliest mortal girl and is more permanently enthralling. Faust could not leave her as he left Gretchen. She is spiritually as well as physically desirable. As Gretchen symbolizes sensual passion, so Helen represents aesthetic experience, the higher stage through which Faust's soul must grow towards the highest of all, the experience of power and of altruistic endeavour.

3. In particular, she represents aesthetic experience in its noblest and most complete form—the experience of Greek culture. No doubt other ages and other countries provide nourishment for the sense of beauty, but none so completely as Greek art. When Dante wanted a symbol for the highest influences of classical culture, he chose Vergil, regarding him first as a poet and then as

a thinker.[65] But for Goethe Greek culture does not mean thought. The intellectual genius of Hellas which created science, philosophy, history, political theory, and so many other intellectual systems, is not imaged in Helen of Troy.

4. Part of Helen's charm is her rarity. Faust makes his way to her through a 'classical witches' sabbath'—a phantasmagoria of obscure demons and grotesque monsters assembled from forgotten corners of Greek literature. Their multitudinous ugliness sets off her pure single beauty. It has been suggested that Goethe wanted them to symbolize the vivid powerful scenery and the physical energy which characterize the Mediterranean lands, and which had so much impressed him on his visit to Italy.[66] But there are darker spirits than those of landscape in the sabbath. Perhaps Goethe wished to convey his perception of the fact that the art of the Greeks and the spiritual serenity which marks it were a consciously idealized achievement, rising above a dark and troublous underworld full of terrifying primitive forces: the contrast which Nietzsche was to emphasize, between the raging Bacchantes and the calm Apollo.[67] Goethe also means that Greek culture is difficult. It is aristocratic. Few can reach Helen. Faust himself must put on great state before he can approach her. Even for him she is difficult to attain. She must not be seized as a passive prize: when he grasps her, she vanishes. She must be wooed and won through knightly service.

5. Even then she is a stimulus, not a possession. She may be won, but not kept. The child she gives to Faust is too brilliant to live. And when it dies, she disappears for the second and last time, like Eurydice returning to the world of the dead: only her garments remain, to bear Faust upwards like a cloud into regions he could otherwise never have reached. Goethe means that modern man cannot live in constant close association with the highest beauties of art—although he can and must try to reach them and make them his for a time.

6. Euphorion's name means Energy. He is the result of constant stimulus, and he responds more actively to every challenge until the last is too strong, and kills him. He is aspiration, the ambition of genius, which—when not restrained but called forth by intense experience—climbs higher and higher above the earth and grows more and more wonderful, until, trying to ignore the laws of humanity, it falls to its death. Goethe was thinking of Byron. But

Euphorion could be all the geniuses of that age, who were doomed by their own passionate aspirations to die young. He was born of the difficult but rapturous union of modern man, energetic, adaptable, and a little coarse, with the fine spirit of Greek culture. Therefore he personifies the poets and thinkers of the revolutionary era, their short ardent lives, their violent self-assertions, their insatiable hunger for beauty, and their ambitious philosophies and poems—Byron swimming the Hellespont, Shelley liberating Ireland, Chénier's *Hermes*, Hölderlin's *Empedocles*, Coleridge's Pantisocracy, Goethe's sculpture, and the early deaths which they all challenged or welcomed. Goethe did not believe it was a 'romantic' revival. He thought the real flow of life in it came from Greece.

7. But Goethe speaks as a German. Faust personifies Goethe, and the Germans, and modern man—but modern man stated in German terms. In order to meet Helen of Troy in a guise appropriate to her and to himself, he becomes a medieval Germanic noble; in order to win her, he exhibits the medieval (and German) virtue of martial energy, directing the defensive occupation of Greece by his 'barbarians'—Germans, Goths, Franks, Saxons, and Normans. Goethe means that the Germans, although fascinated by classical culture and eager to master it, felt themselves foreign and half-civilized in face of the Greek spirit, and were unable to have a permanent, sympathetic, productive relationship with it. There is in this symbol an important truth. The Germans feel classical civilization too delicate and too intense to assimilate. Their contact with Greece at its deepest has produced some brilliant Euphorions, but much unhappiness and a deep sense of frustration. Winckelmann and Stefan George were homosexuals; Hölderlin and Nietzsche went mad. The difficulty which Goethe found in finishing *Faust* II resembles the general problem of his compatriots. German critics sometimes talk as though other nations had the Latin heritage, while Germany alone embodied the Greek tradition. The paragraph from Paul Hensel on p. 367 is only one example of this attitude.[68] But the Germans are even farther from Greece than from Rome. Roman ways they acquired over the frontiers and through the church and by osmosis from the Latin lands. The Renaissance scarcely touched them. Their own Renaissance, in the time of revolution, brought them face to face with Greece. Its chief product was Goethe, and his chief product

was *Faust*, the last great poem of the Middle Ages. After a short marriage, Helen vanished, and left Faust to the medieval demon who was his other self.

§ 3. FRANCE AND THE UNITED STATES

These republicans were mostly young fellows who, having been brought up on Cicero at school, had developed a passion for liberty.

CAMILLE DESMOULINS[1]

The French Revolution was a rebirth of the spirit of Greece and Rome. Classical influence on modern life has seldom been so active, so widespread, so clearly marked, and so eagerly accepted. In other European countries at the same time, literature and art were enriched by the new interest in Greek; but in revolutionary France the cult of the classics changed all the arts, invaded social life, moulded political thought, and created monuments for itself in great institutions which are still part of modern life.

This fact is sometimes misinterpreted or overlooked. Assuming that 'classical' means 'imitative' or 'dead', some writers, who have little direct acquaintance with Greek and Latin literature, believe that any recognition of its greatness is reactionary, and therefore bad. They feel that it would be more romantic, that it would fit more neatly into the pattern of action-and-reaction, if the French Revolution had been made by simple farmers, with the Carmagnole on their lips, reacting against corrupt and classicizing nobles. But the truth is that it was made by well-educated middle-class thinkers who took their classical schooling very seriously, and that most of its theories and works were conscious attempts to revive the better world of republican Rome and free Greece.

The chief difference between the thought of France in the time of revolution and that of other countries is that Greece dominated Germany, Italy, and England, while France turned towards Rome. Yet not wholly. The art of revolutionary France was chiefly Greek in origin. Her political thought, her oratory, her symbols and institutions were mainly Roman. (No doubt some of them were originally Greek, but the channel through which they came and the spiritual impetus behind them were Roman.) So, in spite of the barbarities of the Revolution—the guillotines, the mass drownings, the destruction of Christian Gothic art—it did transmit many positive values derived from Greco-Roman civilization. Instead of attempting, like the Russian revolutionaries of 1917, to make a new beginning on a single social and economic theory, or, like the German revolutionaries of 1933, to mould a new European culture on the ethics of the Iron Age, the French revolutionaries built their new world on the civilization of Rome and Greece. Under kindred influences, the American revolutionaries did the same.[2] The results are, among others, that the senior legislative body in the United States, in France, and in most Latin American republics is called the senate—which was the name of the elders' council of the Roman republic; that U.S. senates usually meet in the Capitol—a building named after one of the seven hills of Rome and built on a famous Greco-Roman model; and that, even when the French republic became an empire, the most lasting memorial of its first emperor was the code of laws, logical, business-like, liberal, and universal, which he created on the Roman model to replace the Gothic complexity and irrationality of the laws superseded by the Revolution.

In French art the great representative of this movement is Jacques-Louis David (1748–1825). David combined classical form with revolutionary content, making each strengthen the other. Having won the Prix de Rome in 1775, he underwent the same spiritual revelation in Rome that had already been felt by Winckelmann and was to be experienced by Goethe. Winckelmann's theories on the link between moral grandeur and great simple art had already been expounded in Paris by Diderot, but David took them up more fervently and with a more serious social purpose.[3] Nearly all his pictures breathe a confident energetic spirit of courage in the face of oppression, of heroic or tragic devotion to the cause of humanity, which still produces a powerful effect. His first famous work was *Give Belisarius a Penny* (*Date obolum Belisario*, 1780), which emphasized the ingratitude of monarchs even to the greatest patriots. He then produced a long series of stirring paintings on two types of theme. The manner was always heroic, symmetrical, and vibrant with emotion nobly restrained. The themes were either Greco-Roman (*The Death of Socrates, The Rape of the Sabines*) or revolutionary and Bonapartist (*Marat assassinated, Napoleon pointing the way to Italy*). Both as an artist and as a man, he was one of the chiefs of the Revolution. He was elected to the Convention in 1792, voted for the execution of Louis XVI, became a member of the Committee of Public

Safety and president of the Convention, arranged many great republican festivals, and was appointed painter to the emperor, after Napoleon took that title. His sketch of the widow Capet, Marie-Antoinette, on the way to execution is classically pure in line and fiercely revolutionary in intent: it balances all his heroics with one bitter touch of realistic hate.

In music a similar revolutionary change was initiated by Christoph Willibald Gluck (1714-87). Beginning in an attempt to re-create Greek tragedy,[4] opera had during the baroque period become subject to large numbers of theatrical and even social conventions which had nothing to do with Greco-Roman drama, and which made the operatic stage little more than a show-ground for virtuosi singers. Splendid was the singing, but the dramatic values withered away. Then in 1762 Gluck produced *Orpheus and Eurydice*, and founded modern opera by a return to the principles of Greek drama.[5] He chose a grand simple theme, strengthened the drama by making the characters fewer and more vital, emphasized the role of the chorus, enlarged the orchestra, and abolished most of the baroque ornaments and repetitions in the solos. The character of his work was fully understood by the apostle of Nature, Jean-Jacques Rousseau, who was always one of his partisans and who actually advised on the production of *Alcestis*. (This is another proof that the antithesis *classical)(romantic* is almost meaningless.) Gluck himself thus described his innovations:[6]

'I have tried to reduce music to its real function, that of seconding poetry by intensifying the expression of sentiments and the interest of situations, without interrupting the action by needless ornament.'

But that is too modest. What Gluck almost succeeded in doing was to make a new form of tragedy, based on Greek ideals of emotion and structure, but making the *music* the main vehicle of lyric and tragic feeling. What stopped him was the pettiness of the audiences: they insisted on a happy ending, which weakened and vulgarized the real meaning of the tragic legends he translated into sound.

But it was not merely classical art which the French of this time and spirit admired. Most of the revolutionaries had received a thorough training in classical literature, which formed their minds and suggested a set of symbols to replace those of the monarchic and aristocratic régime. Their education has been described in an interesting book, H. T. Parker's *The Cult of Antiquity and the French Revolutionaries* (Chicago, 1937), which shows many of its effects on their practice. Robespierre and Desmoulins both went to the Collège Louis-le-Grand, concentrating on the classics; Saint-Just and Danton went to similar collèges supported by the religious order of the Oratoire; others, like Marat and Mme Roland, studied the classics privately for their own pleasure and profit. The classical curriculum of the collèges was fairly uniform. It was Latin, not Greek; and its chief authors were Cicero, Vergil, Horace, Livy, Sallust, Ovid, and Tacitus. Analysing the quotations from classical authors in the revolutionaries' newspapers and debates, Professor Parker finds that, with one group of omissions and one important addition, they reflect that curriculum. The poets—no doubt as too frivolous—are omitted. The addition is Plutarch's *Parallel Lives*. Nearly all the other quotations come from these admirable school-books, Cicero's speeches, Sallust's biography of the anti-republican conspirator Catiline, the opening books of Livy's account of the young Roman republic, and Tacitus' savage histories of the emperors.

It was the history of the Greek and Roman republics that gave the French Revolution its strongest moral impulse. The idealized portraits drawn by Plutarch, the heroic adventures related by Livy, made thoughtful men of the eighteenth century feel that they had been born into an age of utter corruption, which ought to be swept utterly away.

The moralist who did most to prepare for the revolution was Jean-Jacques Rousseau (1712–78). True, he did believe that the perfect man was the natural savage of the woods; but neither he nor the revolutionaries could seriously preach the dissolution of the state into primitive anarchy. They hoped rather for its reform, through simplification and purification; and the model which they proposed was the free republic of Rome and the city-states of free Greece. Among the Greek states there was one which shone out in their eyes far more brightly than the others: the kingdom of Sparta, which they conveniently forgot had been a kingdom.

Rousseau himself had no Greek, but he knew Latin.[7] In the original and in translations, he read an amazingly large number of classical authors.[8] But it was Plutarch who most deeply influenced his thought. He began to read the *Parallel Lives* at the age of six, in Amyot's fine translation. He 'knew them off by

heart' when he was eight. He also studied Plutarch's *Moral
Essays*: there is in Neuchâtel Library a commonplace-book with
more than fifty pages of his notes and excerpts from those works,
made while he was writing his *Discourse on Inequality*.[9] In addition to this, his favourite French author was Montaigne—and
Montaigne, as we have seen, was devoted to 'his' Plutarch,[10] so
that it is often impossible to tell whether Rousseau found a particular idea in Plutarch's works or in a citation by Montaigne.

What Rousseau most admired in Plutarch was the description
of the early days of the Roman republic, and, even more, the
description of the laws and virtues of Sparta.

Sparta was one of the most curious anachronisms in history.
Like Prussia, it was 'not a country which had an army, but an
army which had a country'. There were only a few thousand
Spartans, who kept themselves all in a perpetual state of soldierly
alertness, did no work whatever, and lived off the original inhabitants of the country they had conquered. Since these, the
peasants and helots, far outnumbered them, and since they were
further outnumbered by the neighbouring states, they could not
survive and keep power without submitting to the most perfect
military training and discipline, surrendering their wills to the
state, and practising courage, self-sacrifice, soldierly brevity of
speech, and martial resolution, till all these became perfectly
instinctive in every Spartan.

Plato and other philosophers after him believed that this system
was so far superior to the anarchic democracy and individualism of
Athens that it must have been created *en bloc* by a great philosophical legislator. Traditionally, an early Spartan hero called
Lycurgus (who must have been responsible for some important
decisions in the life of his people) was credited with drawing up the
entire code—just as Moses has been believed to be the author of
all the rules observed by orthodox Jews. Plutarch's life of Lycurgus
embodies that belief. It treats him as a great statesman who saw
that the legislator's first duty is to ensure *moral education*. The
fact that the Spartans were economic parasites and bloody
oppressors is scarcely mentioned. Sparta is displayed as a state of
almost perfect virtue, created by a legislative genius.[11]

Rousseau and the other revolutionaries found that this biography, together with Plutarch's other accounts of Spartan virtue,
strengthened their own belief that the innate goodness of man

could be developed by good institutions. Political reform was to be moral reform. In fact, Rousseau seems to have thought that his own mission in life was to become a great moral legislator comparable to the Roman Numa or the Spartan Lycurgus.[12]

In Rousseau's *Discourse on the Sciences and Arts* (1749), which really launched him on his career, and in *The Social Contract* (1762), praise, quite untempered by criticism, is lavished on the Spartan constitution as represented by Plutarch. Its structure is admired: indeed, Rousseau appears to have held that a city-state like Sparta or his own Geneva was the only true democracy.[13] Some of its principles are adopted by Rousseau: for instance, the virtual abolition of private property; and the abolition of subordinate 'associations' within the state, so that 'each citizen might think only his own thoughts: which was indeed the sublime and unique system established by the great Lycurgus'.[14] But more important and more permanent in Rousseau's thought was his admiration for what he believed to be the moral education of Sparta and early Rome. He thought that these states, in shocking contrast to modern European countries, inculcated patriotism, physical vigour, simplicity verging on austerity, democratic equality, and a love of simple agricultural life, instead of hypochondria, luxury, class-distinctions, and the soul-corrupting arts and sciences.[15] It was to Plutarch, and through him to the Greek philosophers from the Cynics back to Plato, that Rousseau owed his revolutionary equation:

a simple, disciplined republic = perfect virtue.[16]

Plutarch's works, particularly his *Parallel Lives*, impressed many other eighteenth-century readers with their moral idealism— which was ultimately the great Greek educational principle, *paideia*.[17] Tragedies were written on the lives of his heroes. New institutions were patterned after those he described. Young men and women thought themselves back into Greece and Rome, and were the better for it. Brissot 'burned to resemble Phocion'. Madame Roland 'wept at not having been born a Spartan or a Roman'.[18] Charlotte Corday, who killed Marat, had been nurtured on the heroic biographies of Plutarch. An important book could be written on Plutarch's creative influence in the eighteenth century:[19] seldom has a philosopher had such a powerful educational and moral effect, at such a remove in space and time.

When the revolutionaries took power they filled France with Roman and Greek symbolism. Some of the best-known symbols of this kind are:

the cap of liberty, modelled on the cap worn in Rome by liberated slaves;

wreaths of laurel, the emblem of immortal fame, used as signs of honour by the republican leaders, and, after them, by Napoleon;

the fasces, symbol of the authority of the republican magistrates;

the eagles, once standards of the Roman legions, and now introduced as regimental insignia in the French army. At Versailles there is a wildly melodramatic picture by David of the young Bonaparte distributing them for the first time to his regimental officers;

the consciously Roman dignity of the portraits and medals representing republican and imperial notables;

the classical simplicity of furniture, costumes, and housedecoration: rococo fussiness was now abandoned for white-and-gold walls, Roman couches, urns, pillars, and Greco-Roman busts; the costumes of the Directoire are a conscious reversion to Greek styles;

official phraseology: Bonaparte became *consul*, and then, by the *senatus consultum* of 18 May 1804 under the authority of the *Tribunate*, he was made *emperor*; similarly the names of the revolutionary months were mostly based on Latin roots—Floréal, Fructidor, Germinal, Messidor, Pluviose;

the new names of streets, towns, and even men, replacing names of medieval or Christian origin. Babeuf publicly renamed himself Gaius Gracchus; the town of Montfort-l'Amaury became Montfort-le-Brutus; in one sector of Paris there were a Rue de Brutus, a Rue de Scaevola, a Rue de Fabius, &c.;[20]

adoration of the personalities of Greek and Roman republican leaders, who virtually replaced the saints of Christendom. A favourite oath of excited orators in the early days of the Revolution was 'I swear on the head of Brutus'.[21]   When the hall of the Convention in the Tuileries was redecorated in 1793, statues of Lycurgus, Solon, Camillus, and Cincinnatus stood around it, their heads shadowed by laurel crowns, like enhaloed saints in a Jesuit church;

Revolutionary and imperial architecture, Roman in conception and design: the Arc de Triomphe, the Panthéon, and the Madeleine (which Napoleon intended to be a Temple of Glory);

inscriptions in the Roman manner: for instance, the sabres of the National Guard were inscribed with a line from the anti-monarchist poet Lucan:

swords were made that none should be a slave;[22]

the dramatic gestures and utterances of revolutionary heroes, nearly always classical in inspiration. Before their fall, Saint-Just and Robespierre cried out that nothing was left for them except—like Socrates—'to drink the hemlock'. In his letter of surrender, Napoleon wrote 'I throw myself, like Themistocles, upon the mercy of the British people': for Themistocles the Athenian statesman had, after leading the Greek war against the Persians, thrown himself when exiled upon the mercy of a foreign power;

the frequent identification of statesmen with heroes of the Roman republic. Thus, among the Girondins, Vergniaud was 'Cicero', Brissot was 'Brutus', and Roland was 'the younger Cato'.

Then, during the Revolution, a new school of French oratory was created. It was modelled on Cicero: for the simple reason that there had never been any political oratory in France, so that there were no French patterns to follow. Besides, as the great orator of an endangered republic, Cicero made the ideal model. In Britain there was a long tradition of noble political rhetoric, and her speakers had found that Cicero's technique was the richest, most adaptable, and most natural for the debates of a free parliament. The best orations of Burke, and Pitt, and Fox, and Sheridan are Ciceronian in almost everything but language. The high standard set by these men, and many of the Latin devices they naturalized, have survived to our own time, to influence many modern speakers who know nothing of Latin and have no idea that they are pupils of Cicero. Similarly, French political oratory realized its true powers during the Revolution, when its makers modelled their speeches on the Cicero they had studied so carefully in school:

that tradition has continued in speeches, editorials, and mani-
festoes, until to-day.

For example, on 29 October 1792 Louvet delivered a violent
attack on a certain Catiline, who (he said) was conspiring against
the Convention as Catiline had conspired against the senate in
Rome; who had a secret agreement with a powerful politician, as
Catiline had had with Caesar; and who intended to seize power
after incendiarism and murder on Catiline's plan had paralysed
the patriotic party. Catiline was no other than Robespierre. The
powerful politician was Danton. And the speech was modelled on
Cicero's Catilinarian orations. The drastic effect of this attack
is shown by the fact that Robespierre asked for a week's adjourn-
ment to prepare his reply. When he delivered his answer, it was
closely patterned on Cicero's speech for Sulla—even to Robespierre's defence of himself against the charge of executing
citizens of the republic, and the comparison of his opponent to a
demagogic tribune. It saved him, for the time.

Again, in one of his most widely read pamphlets, Desmoulins
adapted the famous simile in Cicero's defence of Roscius, where
vigilant prosecutors are compared to the watch-dogs on the
Capitol.[23] The passage struck the public ear; and *aboyeurs*,
'barkers', became the regular nickname for informers during the
Terror. There are many other examples.[24] In fact, one of the
chief difficulties in reading the speeches made during the Revolution is to identify all the politicians who are so freely described as
Catiline, Clodius, and Cicero. The Caesar was still to come.

The Greeks were the inventors of democracy. And in Rome,
although there were more class distinctions than in Athens, the
name of king was detested, and every citizen was free. In remaking
France the revolutionaries therefore went to the examples of
Greece and Rome. The name 'republic' is of course the Latin
phrase *res publica*, 'the commonwealth'. In the legislatures which
formed the First Republic, the Constituent Assembly of 1789–91,
the Legislative Assembly of 1791–2, and the National Convention
of 1792–5, debaters constantly alluded to Greek and Roman
history, because they felt the problems they were facing had
already been faced and solved in Greece and in Rome. And, as
Professor Parker points out, the more radical politicians praised
the ancients more warmly, while the right wing tended to dis-
parage them.[25] Even the public festivals of the Republic, in which

costumes and properties (designed by David) were so often wholly classical, were inspired by those of Sparta. At the end of his career Saint-Just drew up plans to impose on France a Spartan educational and civic discipline, including simple diet, the abolition of private meals in favour of public messes, and the cultivation of Laconic brevity of speech—in fact, he attempted the hopeless, suicidal enterprise of denying the French their cuisine, their wine, and their conversation.[26]

The American revolution also was partly guided by classical ideals. Although it produced few works of literature, its symbols and its institutions were markedly Greco-Roman in inspiration. The Roman origin of *Senate* and *Capitol* has already been mentioned.[27] The title by which Washington is best known, 'Father of his Country', is a translation of *pater patriae*, the honorific name given to several heroes of the Roman state, and with particular distinction to Cicero.[28] The *Federalist* essays (1787–8) by Hamilton, Madison, and Jay, which were largely responsible for creating the present Union out of the early and inefficient Confederation, contain a number of illustrative parallels from Greek and Roman history, with discussion of such Greek attempts at federative government as the Achaean League and the Amphictyonic Council. The Great Seal of the United States bears three quotations in Latin—the famous *e pluribus unum*, 'one (made) out of many';[29] *novus ordo seclorum*, 'a new term of ages', the sentiment expressed in Vergil's Messianic poem and in Shelley's famous revolutionary chorus, 'The world's great age begins anew';[30] and *annuit cœptis*, '(God) has favoured our enterprise', an adaptation of the opening of Vergil's *Georgics*.[31] The city of Cincinnati perpetuates the name of the Roman hero nicknamed 'curly-haired' (= *cincinnatus*) who, at the call of duty, left his plough to lead his country's army, and returned to his plough after his duty was done. The retiring officers of the revolutionary army formed a mutual-aid society and named themselves after him; and, as a compliment to General St. Clair, president of its Pennsylvania branch, the Ohio city took on a Roman name.

Many simpler Greek and Roman names are borne by townships throughout the United States.[32] There were a few before the revolution. Virginia, named for the virgin Queen Elizabeth, is the best known. An estate near the Potomac was named Rome in 1663 by Governor Pope, no doubt because he liked the idea of being called 'Pope, of Rome'. But the flood of classical names was opened, just as in France (p. 396), by the Greco-Roman idealism of the revolution. Even unlearned men writing to the newspapers used to sign themselves Cato, or Publicola, or (following the formidable example of the famous English publicist) Junius. First, in 1789, Vanderheyden's Ferry, New York, was renamed Troy. Probably this was a reminiscence of the old admiration for the gallant Trojans (see p. 54). The first Troy set the pattern for thirty others, in succeeding years. Next, in 1790, a number of settlements in the military tract around Cayuga Lake, New York, had to be named. The committee ran through a classical dictionary, and called them after *heroes*—Aurelius, Camillus, Cato, Cicero (who also appeared under his other name, Tully), Cincinnatus, Fabius, Hannibal, Hector, Lysander the Spartan, Manlius, Marcellus, Romulus, Scipio, Sempronius, Solon, and Ulysses; and *authors*—Homer, Ovid, and Vergil, with three English baroque writers, Dryden, Locke, and Milton. Cincinnati, Ohio, followed in 1790. Seneca, New York, was more complicated: it was a latinization of Sinneken, the Dutch version of the Mohican name of an Iroquois tribe. Utica, New York, was given its name in 1798, in memory of the African town where the great republican Cato killed himself rather than submit to monarchy. In 1800 the inhabitants of an Ohio town were planning to build a college: so they named their town after the first home of learning in the western world, and it became Athens. Next year Athens, Georgia, got its name for the same reason. Many more Greek and Roman names dot the vast map of the United States to remind us that, although the land was at first savage, the civilization which grew up in it was in part derived from Rome and Greece.

That belief was firmly held by the best-known educator of the American revolutionary era, Thomas Jefferson (1743–1826).[33] Throughout his life he was devoted to Greek and Latin literature, which he considered the foundation of all higher culture. He modelled his private life and his country home on the life of a Roman gentleman with a spacious hill-top mansion. The University of Virginia, which he planned, was a re-creation of the linked porticoes, enclosed spaces, and pillared buildings which made up a large Roman villa. To the constant inspiration he drew from Cicero, Horace, and Pliny his visit to France as United States

Minister added new stimulus. In Paris he met David, as well as the equally classical but more reposeful artists Houdon and Wedgwood. At Nîmes in the south, he actually saw and studied Roman buildings: the temple dedicated to Augustus' adoptive sons Gaius and Lucius (it is now known as the Maison Carrée), the Roman gates, and the fine arena. Although he said he preferred the Greek language to Latin, and although the most advanced artists of the late eighteenth century worked on Greek models, Jefferson remained a Roman. The temple of the young Caesars was, under his direction, closely imitated in the Capitol of the state of Virginia. The University of Virginia library is the Roman Pantheon. His own house, which he liked to call Pantops (= 'panorama') and for which he finally chose the name Monticello (= 'little hill'), was in fact a Roman villa like those of Pliny and Cicero. Something of the Roman republic had already been reborn in the symbolism and the idealism of the early United States; and, through Jefferson, its first official buildings were modelled on the mansions, theatres, and temples which Rome had constructed by adding her own power and solidity to the Greek grace.

The greatest French poet of the revolutionary era was André Chénier,[34] born in Constantinople in 1762 of a French father and a Greek mother; well educated at the Collège de Navarre; deeply impressed by a visit to Italy when he was twenty-two; a pupil of David; on the republican side during the Revolution, but repelled by the excesses of the Terror, during which he wrote an ode to Charlotte Corday and a brief for the defence of Louis XVI; arrested in March 1794, and guillotined some three months later, three days before the execution of Robespierre, which would have saved him. His last work, the *Iambics*, was written on tiny slips of paper in microscopic handwriting and smuggled out of his prison; but scarcely any of his poetry was published during his lifetime. His reputation began about a generation after his death, and has risen steadily ever since.

He had a brother, Marie-Joseph Chénier, who was much more prominent at the time, and whose career was both made and blasted by the Revolution. In 1792, despite the counter-manœuvres of the court, he produced a tragedy on the death of Gaius Gracchus —the revolutionary leader of the Roman republic, who, after his brother had been murdered by the forces of reaction, continued to defend the cause of the plebeians against the proud and privileged aristos. It had a huge success: Marie-Joseph became one of the voices of the Revolution. Yet next year the play was banned by the Mountain because it contained the line:

> We seek laws, and not blood.[35]

Then in 1794 he wrote a play on the life of Timoleon—another of Plutarch's heroes, who refused an opportunity to make himself dictator, and retired into private life. This drama was suppressed at the orders of Robespierre.[36] Striking as these events were, and talented though Marie-Joseph was, it is his brother André who now has a permanent place in the literature of the world.

André Chénier may be compared to both Shelley and Keats; but he is inferior to them both in scope. He was essentially a miniaturist, and produced nothing comparable to *Prometheus Unbound* or *Endymion*—although he aimed as high. For ten years he planned a didactic poem, *Hermes*, which was to contain the teaching of the Encyclopaedia in the style of Lucretius; he also wanted to become the modern Homer, with an epic in 12,000 lines on America; but only a few fragments survive.[37] His finest work is undoubtedly his pastoral idylls in the manner of Theocritus.[38] Close to them are his 'elegies' on minor heroic themes (Orpheus, Hylas); and then his love-elegies, modelled on Tibullus, Propertius, and Ovid, which are comparable to Goethe's *Roman Elegies*, surpassing them in intensity of emotion, although hampered by the strictness of French metre.[39] Greek on his mother's side, he was one of the first of the many modern poets who can be called reincarnated Greeks. He knew Greek and Latin literature well, he had delicate taste, and he could transmute effects from the classics into his own poetry with such genuine emotion that the result was far above mere copying. Therefore, for the uninstructed reader, his poems are original evocations of antique scenes; while one who knows Greek and Latin as Chénier himself did sees in them a blend of thoughts, and images, and turns of phrase, taken from a dozen different classical poets but blended into an original composition, partly by the imaginative boldness with which Chénier combines elements that no one before him thought of combining, and partly by his distinguished verse-rhythm and sentence-structure. The tirades of Racine's Greek heroes and heroines, addressing one another as Madame and Seigneur, are often great poetry, but are seldom free from serious anachronisms: so serious that they make the poetry false. But many of Chénier's short poems might be translations from the Greek. They are true. They are re-creations of the eternal aspects of the Hellenic spirit in a modern language, with all the restraint which is the most Greek of poetic virtues. For instance, the lovely little dialogue *Mnazile et Chloé* shows a young couple slipping into a grove separately, each hoping to find the other; they meet, and each says it is nothing but chance; there the poem stops, like a smile on a timid lover's lips. And an evocation of Orpheus ends, with Greek economy, in words which suit Chénier himself:[40]

> Around the demigod the silent princes
> hung on his voice, motionless, listening,
> and listened still when he had ceased to sing.

The second great writer of revolutionary France was a far more complex, far less lovable figure: François-René, vicomte de Chateaubriand (1768–1848), whose adventurous life, titanic pride, startling success, and tragic loneliness make him a fairly close parallel to Lord Byron. He was born and well educated in Brittany, spent a romantic seven months during 1791-2 in the American and Canadian backwoods on a quest for the North-West Passage, lived in poverty from 1794 to 1799 as an émigré in London, but was able to return under Napoleon. Having been converted to Christianity on his mother's death, he wrote *The Genius of Christianity*, a powerful defence of Christian thought, which, published in 1802 just before Napoleon re-established the church, was rewarded with an appointment to the embassy at Rome. But he soon quarrelled with Napoleon, particularly after comparing him to Nero. Like Byron, he toured Greece and the Levant, but his pilgrimage, unlike Byron's, culminated in Palestine. In 1809 he produced a prose epic, *The Martyrs*; he had already written one called *The Natchez* on the French-Indian wars of Louisiana, but was not to publish it complete until twenty years later. He served the Bourbons after their restoration, but quarrelled with them too, and retired into gloomy solitude, working on his *Memoirs from beyond the Tomb*, which were issued in twelve volumes after his death.

The Martyrs, although interesting as a curiosity, is unreadable. It is quite literally an epic in prose. Chateaubriand explains that

Aristotle admits either verse or prose as the vehicle of epic, and cites Fénelon's *Telemachus* as a precedent.[41] The work is an attempt to outdo Fénelon in depth and imagination and Homer and Vergil in Christian nobility. It tells a complicated story of the persecution of the Christians under Diocletian (284–305), ending with the martyrdom of the hero and heroine and the conversion of Constantine to Christianity. It reads like a rather affected translation from Latin into correct but laborious French. Although it has no intrinsic interest, it is a fascinating example of the failure a good writer can make when he chooses the wrong literary pattern. The essential truth which Chateaubriand had grasped was that the day of the verse epic was over. He knew that the grandeur and energy of the epic had now flowed out of it into prose fiction: the epic of the nineteenth century was to be Victor Hugo's *Les Misérables* and Tolstoy's *War and Peace*.[42] But he could not see that, in renouncing the vehicle of verse, a writer must also renounce the smaller stylistic devices which are valid only in poetry: the invocations to the Muse, the conventional epithets, the circumlocutions, the Homeric similes, which, although artificial enough in verse, are sustained by the pulsing rhythm of the hexameter and the rich profusion of the poetic vocabulary, but in prose look like artifice without art.

'Holy Spirit, who madest the vast abyss fertile by covering it with thy wings, it is at this moment that I need thine aid!'[43]

What Chateaubriand intended to be in *The Martyrs* was a greater, a French, a Catholic Milton; what he became was a stilted precursor of *Ben-Hur* and *Quo Vadis?*

On the other hand, *The Genius of Christianity* is a great book. Like most great French books, it possesses few of the literary virtues on which the French pride themselves: brevity, clarity, reasonableness, balance. All the better—for it is a partisan book. It is the strongest possible statement of argument 1 in the Battle of the Books. Thereby it marks the beginning of a Christian reaction against the intellectual paganism of the eighteenth century.[44] Gibbon, we recall, described the fall of the Roman empire as the triumph of barbarism and religion, implicitly equating the two. Chateaubriand now argues that Christianity, properly understood, is far nobler than all the ideals of the pagan world— yes, than even the noblest pagan achievements, in philosophy, in the arts, and in poetry. In its breadth of view, the loftiness of its ideals, and the subtlety and penetration of its analysis, this book marks an epoch in criticism. Milton and Tasso receive their full share of praise, and Dante (so long neglected) is recognized as a master; Racine's dramas are worthily criticized and their fundamentally Christian outlook is explained; there is a great deal of scholarly comment on the Bible, and on the less-known classical authors, with some valuable exegesis of the art and thought of Homer and Vergil. We have all wished that Byron, whose nobility of soul, apparent even behind his bad behaviour and his melodramatic verse, emerged triumphant in his death, had written something not only so striking, but so serious and noble that it would be worthy of his genius. In *The Genius of Christianity* Chateaubriand wrote a work in which the grandeur of his ideals and the sensitivity of his imagination are worthily expressed. It honours him, it justifies the French aristocracy to which he belonged, and it raises the Christian faith far above the pettinesses of most of its attackers and some of its defenders.

The heir of the Revolution

Although he belonged to a later generation, although he lived until nearly the end of the nineteenth century, Victor Hugo (1802–85) was the heir of the Revolution. Among his earliest works were stormy lyrics inspired by the Greek war of freedom against the Turkish oppressors.[45] The climax of his youthful literary career came when he created a revolution in French poetry.

He did this partly by breaking down the strictly limited verse-patterns which had dominated, and crippled, French poets since the opening of the baroque age. But more important and more far-reaching was his extension of the poetic vocabulary. Strange as it seems, it is true that throughout the Revolution and the First Empire poets were forced to avoid many ordinary words, because they were 'low'. Audiences hissed if they heard a word like 'room' or 'handkerchief'. Manuals of correct diction were published, showing that 'spouse' was preferable to 'husband', because the latter signified merely a domestic or sexual relationship, while 'spouse' conveyed the idea of a contract hallowed by society. Poets were forbidden to use the word 'horse'. They were enjoined to replace the word 'negroes' by

mortals blackened by the suns of Guinea.

They were urged not to use 'priest' and 'bell', but to prefer their noble equivalents 'pontiff' and 'bronze'.[46] The most popular translator of the age, Delille, complained that his task was made more difficult by the limitations of the French polite vocabulary. 'In Rome', he said, 'the people was king, and its language shared its nobility; . . . among us, prejudices have debased both words and men, and there are noble expressions and lower-class expressions.'[47] This was not really true of Roman poetry, which was aristocratic enough to eschew large numbers of colloquialisms; but at least in the *Georgics* Vergil could (as Delille could not) use real words for real things, and call the farmer's implement a spade.

Hugo has a spirited poem in which he accepts the charge that he caused a new French Revolution in poetry by breaking down the social distinctions of language. French, he says, was like the state before 1789: words were nobles or commoners, they lived in a fixed caste-system. But I, he cries, I put a red cap on the old dictionary. I called a pig by its name. I stripped the astonished dog of its collar of epithets, and made Maggie the cow fraternize with the heifer Berenice. As if in a revolutionary orgy,

with breasts bare, the nine Muses sang the Carmagnole.[48]

Hugo's relation to classical poetry was strangely affected by his revolutionary character and ideals. The poet he knew best and for long loved best was Vergil. We hear of him translating Vergil at sight, aged nine, at the entrance examination given by his exclusive Madrid school; trying his wings, during his early teens, on poetic versions of *Bucolics*, *Georgics*, and the horror episodes in the *Aeneid*. There is a book on his love of Vergil which shows again and again, almost as sensitively as Lowes does for Coleridge in *The Road to Xanadu*, how a monstrous picture from Vergil like the fight of Hercules and Cacus, or a harmonious echo like the lowing of a homebound herd, lingers and reappears in Hugo's writings as the living product of his own imagination.[49] When he began to feel his strength, in the revolutionary preface to *Cromwell*, he started to call Vergil a copyist, 'the moon of Homer'—an idea repeated in his *William Shakespeare*. Then, when he went into exile under the disguised dictatorship of Napoleon III, he abruptly dropped the rest of his admiration for Vergil. He saw in Vergil only the courtier of the 'tyrant' Augustus. He placed Juvenal and Tacitus, the satirist and the historian who hated the imperial régime, far above him. And yet he could not forget the beauty of Vergil's poetry. In *Interior Voices* he honoured Vergil with a loving tribute, written as by a pupil to his master.[50] As far as he ever solved the contradiction in his own mind, he did so by adoring Vergil simply as a painter of nature; and, ultimately, by deciding that Vergil was a writer of talent, like Racine, rather than a genius, like Homer and Shakespeare. Was he wrong?

Hugo's knowledge of Latin literature was good. But he was prevented from using it fully by his own rebellious nature, and by a revolt which was forced on him in youth. In a brilliant tirade placed early in his book of *Contemplations*, he denounces, scarifies, blasts the pedantic schoolmasters with dirty nails, who ruin both classics and mathematics by making them into forced labour. At school, when he was sixteen, he was looking forward to a day's excursion with the janitor's daughter; his attention wandered; his master jumped on him, making him stay in all Sunday and write out 500 lines of Horace; and, in his lonely attic, he poured out curses on the jailers who distorted Horace, who made Vergil a load for children to drag like oxen, and who

have never had a mistress, or a thought.[51]

This is not the earliest, but it is nearly the strongest expression of the revulsion which bad teachers of the classics have caused by treating the subject as *discipline*. A few years earlier Byron had felt the same hatred, for the same reason.[52] We shall see it growing throughout the nineteenth century, to the point when it almost ruins the study and teaching of classical literature. Of course learning is difficult, but it must not be made repellent: least of all the learning of great languages and of fine poetry. The result on both Byron and Hugo was the same. Involuntarily, they remembered much of what they had learnt: it had become part of them. But, unlike such poets as Dante, and Shakespeare, and Goethe, they refused to go on reading classical literature after leaving school. And, what is most important, they both refused to learn the central classical lesson of aesthetic discipline—how to organize large masses of complex material, how to speak more clearly than a shout. Byron never produced a work as great as his powers promised. Hugo's *Legend of the Ages* is only an Ozymandias group of colossal fragments, and not the epic of mankind.

§ 4. ENGLAND

'We are all Greeks.'

SHELLEY[1]

The lands of Greece and Rome and their civilization were only one of the many excitements under which the English revolutionary writers produced their marvellously varied work; and on each of them that excitement acted in a different way. In order to determine what it did for English literature, we must see what it meant for each of the great poets of that time. But let us take it at its highest intensity. Wordsworth wrote two sonnets on a theme he found in Plutarch:[2] true; still, the poems are bad, and facts like that are not truly revealing. We must rather ask, how did Greece and Rome change the minds of these poets? from the classics, what did they get that was, for them, uniquely valuable?

We think of William Wordsworth as an observer of nature and of natural man. The mountains which ennobled his boyhood and strengthened his manhood (it is inadequate to call him a 'Lake poet': he was a Mountain poet; there have been very few, and he was the greatest), the mountains which in physical nature were the counterpart of the lofty spiritual ideals by which he lived; the lakes in which he swam and on which he skated and rowed (always surrounded by the dominating mountains), the lakes which symbolized the soft gracious influence of his sister and his wife; the trees and flowers, the fields, the men and women who worked the land and wandered over it, that visible proof of the world's divinity,

the infinite magnificence of heaven;[3]

his own enraptured soul that saw the best and truest in all these; and the great spirit which pervades them and is their life—these made his poetry. Surely the Greeks and Romans can have had little meaning for such a poet?

Then his style is remarkably free from imitation and reminiscence. Although he admired Milton more than any other poet, his conception of poetic diction and of the use of allusion in poetry is diametrically opposed to Milton's. Another of the revolutionary poets described the ideal of poetic creation in the phrase 'load every rift with ore'.[4] Although this is too intense an image to fit

Wordsworth's calm poetry, it does emphasize the fact that for all these poets writing was a natural process, and the poet's mind like the rich earth full of inestimable wealth effortlessly produced by the creative powers of nature. For Milton, poetry was not native ore, but a difficult piece of craftsmanship made from metal twice and thrice refined, worked by earlier artists, and by himself remoulded and set with even more finely cut jewels. But Wordsworth seldom used the words of any other poets, even of those he loved best.

Lastly, one of Wordsworth's special contributions to literature consisted in a departure from classical tradition. He created a new pastoral. Of all the Greco-Roman clichés, the thinnest, the most easily abused, and the least vital had been that of Arcadian poetry and art. It became particularly nauseating when cultivated by the French court, with their own peasantry living on tree-bark and nettle-soup just outside the gates. Wordsworth perceived new beauties in country life, and for Strephon and Phyllis substituted a fresh range of symbols which meant more, and owed nothing to Greek and Latin tradition.

In view of all this, what, if anything, did Wordsworth take from the classics? What did they mean to him?

They meant spiritual nobility. He did not, except in his less fortunate works, imitate their words and methods. But he had a good university education, knew a considerable amount of Latin and a little Greek, read an increasing amount of both Latin (in original and translation) and Greek (in translation) as he grew older, and learnt much of the deeper meaning of the classics from Coleridge's conversation.[5] His dependence on Roman history and Greco-Roman philosophy, as well as his general affection for classical literature, has been well explained by Miss Jane Worthington in *Wordsworth's Reading of Roman Prose*. The ideals he derived from the classics affected his poetry and his thought in three main ways.

First, it was Roman history, vitalized by the French Revolution, that made Wordsworth 'a great political poet'.[6] After a period as a Godwinian anarchist, he came to believe that one of the most important objects of human effort is national independence. And he always felt that political power was worse than useless, both wicked and doomed, if it were not associated with morality. Miss Worthington points out that the Roman historians, unlike

many modern historians, always emphasize the indissoluble connexion between private virtue and public security and prosperity.
(This is part of the long and noble tradition of *paideia*,[7] which
made it impossible for a Greek or Roman to write a worthy book
merely to record facts, without any intention of bettering his
readers' souls.) But the Roman historians meant nothing to
Wordsworth until he saw their teaching applied in the beginnings
of the French Revolution, and, in conversation with a French
officer, felt its emotional impact. In *The Prelude*, 9. 288–430, he
described Beaupuy's personality, paid tribute to his idealism, and
explained its profound educational influence on him by comparing
it to that of Plato upon Dion of Syracuse—one of the great
examples of *paideia* in politics.[8] The chief results of this in Wordsworth's poetry are his patriotic sonnets (*Poems dedicated to
National Independence and Liberty*), which stress the close link
between politics, intellectual and artistic culture—

> Milton, thou should'st be living at this hour![9]

—and morality:

> by the soul
> Only, the nations shall be great and free.[10]

The second great classical influence on Wordsworth was Greek
philosophy. He seems not to have read the Greek Stoics (apart
from Epictetus, who belongs to the Roman period), but he knew
a great deal of the Roman Stoics, particularly that difficult author
Seneca. The effect of this was to strengthen his belief in the unity
of God, man, and the external world. Man (the Stoics held) is a
part of the physical world, and the world is a manifestation of God.
Again and again in Wordsworth's poems this is most beautifully
expressed in terms of the grandeur of nature.

> I have felt
> A presence that disturbs me with the joy
> Of elevated thoughts; a sense sublime
> Of something far more deeply interfused,
> Whose dwelling is the light of setting suns,
> And the round ocean and the living air,
> And the blue sky, and in the mind of man:
> A motion and a spirit, that impels
> All thinking things, all objects of all thought,
> And rolls through all things.[11]

And once, in a fragment which he never published,[12] he says that

> all beings live with god, themselves
> Are god, existing in the mighty whole. . . .

His thought here is not that the world is divine because it is beautiful (which is a Platonic idea), but that it is divine because it is alive. Because it lives and is supreme, all-embracing, it is God. In his attitude to moral obligations also, Wordsworth was a Stoic. They should be accepted as natural, not struggled against or questioned, their fulfilment not justified by external praise or endangered by external blame, but recognized as part of the universal process. Virtue, for the Stoic, means living according to nature; and a good action is complete once it has been willed— whether it succeeds or not is unimportant, the essential thing being the harmony of man's will with the spirit of the universe. Two of Wordsworth's most famous poems on moral subjects express this belief: *Character of the Happy Warrior* and the *Ode to Duty*; both were written in 1805, and the latter is prefaced by a motto from Seneca to stress its Stoical inspiration. Duty as an end in itself is a Stoical concept. In *The Excursion* other aspects of Stoicism reappear: especially in book 4, where Wordsworth describes the wise man as perfectly free (one of the Stoic 'paradoxes') and, quoting eight lines from Samuel Daniel, identifies two of them as a translation from a little-known passage in Seneca.[13] In *The Excursion* he is turning more and more away from Stoicism towards Christianity. Nevertheless, he is one of the few great modern Stoic poets: and none has summed up the Stoic philosophy better than Wordsworth in his identification of duty with the deepest laws of physical nature:[14]

> Thou dost preserve the stars from wrong;
> And the most ancient heavens, through Thee, are fresh and strong.

But his finest poem is not Stoical: it is Platonic. This is the ode, *Intimations of Immortality from Reminiscences of Early Childhood*, written at a turning-point of his own life, and, despite its fundamental emphasis on eternal life, implying a lament for his own approaching spiritual death. The ode is a great question, and a great answer. It asks why the poet himself no longer feels the exulting beauty and joy experienced by nature, and animals, and children; and it replies that children enter the world from heaven and still remember how they lived there: heaven 'lies about them in their infancy'. Children and their joy in nature are therefore a proof that the soul is immortal. The adult sees only 'the light of common day', and has no knowledge of eternity except the

> obstinate questionings
> Of sense and outward things . . .
> those first affections,
> Those shadowy recollections

which are a lasting remembrance of heaven. This is the doctrine which Plato expressed through Socrates, in the theory of Ideas known perfectly in heaven before our birth, and 'recollected' under proper stimulus in the world. Plato stresses its intellectual side: knowledge is recollection of heavenly knowledge. Wordsworth stresses its emotional and imaginative side: joy in nature is recollection of heavenly happiness. But the doctrine is the same, and no doubt it was that great Platonist, Samuel Taylor Coleridge, who imparted it to him.[15]

And fundamentally, Wordsworth was a classic in his attitude to emotion. The Greeks believed that it was wise to control it, in order to avoid the madness of passion; and, in art, that it could be more perfectly expressed in restrained terms. In an otherwise unlikeable poem on a Greek legend, *Laodamia*, Wordsworth expresses the first belief with noble emphasis:

> The Gods approve
> The depth, and not the tumult, of the soul.

And he himself both felt and practised the second rule: for his ideal of poetry was 'emotion recollected *in tranquillity*'.[16]

George Gordon Byron, Lord Byron, would have been contemptuous if anyone had called him a classicist; and yet he died in Greece, for Greece. He would have been even more scornful if he had been labelled a romantic: his first considerable poem (*English Bards and Scotch Reviewers*) contained a savage attack on romantic writers like Scott and praise of the classicist Pope; and yet his life was romantic, and his death a strange, quixotic, essentially un-Greek gesture. Goethe symbolized him in Euphorion, the child of medieval energy and classical beauty, whose ambitions and senses were too intense to allow him to live on this earth.[17] The symbol is not unjust: Byron was a strong young man who loved strong sensations and exciting beauties. He appreciated Greco-Roman culture best in its most immediate and most vital forms. Would it be true, then, to say that he hated classical culture as seen through books, and enjoyed only its concrete visible relics, the Italian and Greek lands, their buildings and statues, their men and their beautiful women? Certainly he protested with alarming violence against Lord Elgin's removal of the famous marbles from the Parthenon to the British Museum, one of his reasons being that they looked better and more natural where they were.[18]

But that explanation would be a false antithesis. He did know a great deal of classical literature. He remembered it again and again in his Mediterranean tour, quoted it aptly and sincerely, and added notes to *Childe Harold's Pilgrimage* connecting the scenes he had witnessed with the great passages they had recalled to him.[19] He thought the writers of his own time were as vulgar and silly, compared with Pope and the Greeks and Romans, as slums and Gothic castles compared with the Parthenon.[20]

Yet there is a famous passage in his autobiographical *Pilgrimage* which shows that there was a conflict within him about his attitude to the classics: a mingled attraction and repulsion. Travelling through Italy, he sees the snow-capped mountain Soracte, which inspired Horace with the beginning of a famous and beautiful ode.[21] Unexpectedly, he checks the rein of his galloping imagination. He says: 'Others may quote Horace if they like: but I could not:

I abhorred

Too much, to conquer for the Poet's sake,
The drilled dull lesson, forced down word by word
In my repugnant youth, with pleasure to record
Aught that recalls the daily drug which turned
My sickening memory; and, though Time hath taught
My mind to meditate what it then learned,
Yet such the fixed inveteracy wrought
By the impatience of my early thought,
That, with the freshness wearing out before
My mind could relish what it might have sought,
If free to choose, I cannot now restore
Its health—but what it then detested, still abhor.'[22]

In this, as in other aspects of his character, Byron announced the age to which we ourselves belong. He did not hate Greek and

Latin literature, or Greek and Latin ideals. Only a few lines later, he breaks out into a splendid dirge over Rome, crying

> Alas, for Earth, for never shall we see
> That brightness in her eye she bore when Rome was free!

Nevertheless, psychical blocks created by bad teaching kept Byron from taking the full influence of classical culture into himself, and profiting from it. Hundreds of thousands of Byrons, since his day, have rejected Greek and Latin literature because its preliminary discipline was made hateful to them; and therefore, they have sometimes rejected even the necessary disciplines of art and thought. We have seen Hugo rebelling in the same way, not against Latin, but against hateful teachers of Latin.[23] Swinburne was similarly affected.[24] Byron loathed the drudgery of learning Latin grammar and vocabulary in order to approach the poetry; and although, in his note, he pays a compliment to his master at Harrow, he says the *system* of making little boys learn Horace by heart was wrong. And it is evident that schoolmasters were then starting to believe that it was *more* important for their pupils to learn syntax and scansion than to grasp and respond to the poetry they were studying. The age of gerund-grinding had begun.[25] Perhaps even that would not have mattered if, after the preliminaries, Byron's teachers had explained something of the real greatness of Greco-Latin literature. But evidently they did not. They stopped at the 'drilled dull lesson'.

What was the result? Byron himself admired the formality, the restraint, and the intellectual power of classical poetry, and those qualities as reproduced in English baroque literature. Yet he himself wrote frenetic and often formless poetry, that suffers from its own love for the limitless. It is clear that he was never shown the greatest achievements of classical literature, that his teachers led him to think most of it was like Horace—cool, sane, limited in scope, and rather middle-aged. If he had read as much of the best as Shelley, he would have been a far greater poet than he was, with more pride in his mission and more real understanding of the tradition which he was helping to transform.

And he had a strangely mixed, almost embarrassed attitude to classical literature. It has been pointed out that he was often happier when parodying Greek mythology than when writing seriously about it;[26] and yet whenever a figure of legend became palpably beautiful (like the Medici Venus) or nobly human (like Prometheus) he threw his whole soul into admiration.[27] He could comprehend books as books, but never love them fully. The countries where the books were written, and the ideals which still survived there—especially those that suited his own character: political liberty, admiration of sensuous beauty, scorn of minor conventions, yes, and aristocratic hauteur—these, with the men and women who embodied them, he loved. From one point of view Byron's career was a protest against the assumption that we can learn about Greece and Rome by reading books. No one could call the man anti-classical who swam the Hellespont to rival Leander, who wrote an ode on the isles of Greece to evoke liberty in the name of Sappho, who imaged himself as Prometheus chained to the rock and vulture-haunted, and who, again and again, in burning poems and at last in his own self-sacrifice, repeated that the ideals of Greece were alive, were nobler than those of our own materialistic existence, and were worth dying for.

John Keats was the Shakespeare of the revolutionary period: in his stimulating but incomplete education, in his undistinguished descent and early poverty, in his determination to write poetry, in his tremendous productivity, in his essential originality, and in the rich fertility with which his mind developed themes taken from classical literature and legend. The exuberant sensuousness of *Endymion* is closely akin to that of *Venus and Adonis*; and the grandeur of *Hyperion* foreshadows something which would have equalled *Antony and Cleopatra*. The schooling of the two poets was not very different, although Keats was much more of a book-man. Like Shakespeare, he learnt Latin but no Greek at school, and, like Shakespeare, he got a great deal from translations of Greek later. Keats, however, knew more Latin, and by the age of fourteen had made his own translation of the whole *Aeneid* into English prose: an interesting act, which shows both that he realized the value of classical poetry for himself, that he disliked the existing translations, and that he was not yet sure of his own style. But it was Greek poetry that really moved him, although, 'standing aloof in giant ignorance',[28] he could not read the language. His friend Cowden Clarke, son of the headmaster of his school at Enfield, gave him the run of his library with the translations it contained: it was after a night spent in Clarke's study that Keats wrote his first great poem, *On first looking into Chapman's Homer.* (He had already read Pope's version, which made no impression on him.) At first it scarcely mattered that he could not read the originals: for he was building his own style out of the best of English poetry, and the stories and imagery he could get, as Shakespeare got them, through translations. He found renderings of Hesiod, Apollonius Rhodius, and other little-known poets in a collection called *The Works of the English Poets from Chaucer to Cowper*: which contained a fifteenth-century poem by Alain Chartier called *La Belle Dame sans mercie*.[29] Keats even used classical dictionaries: Lemprière, Tooke, and Spence—who in spite of their refined prose style give the myths quite vividly—were among his favourite reading in his last year at school. Like Shakespeare, he learnt much classical mythology at second hand, from authors who had studied the originals and used Greek and Latin material in work he admired. The legend of *Lamia*, for instance, he took from Burton; but Burton took it from Philostratus' life of the miracle-working fakir Apollonius of Tyana. Keats's favourite English author was Spenser, and Spenser was deeply read in the classics.

The gods, the goddesses, the nymphs and Titans, and the men and women of Greece were made more real to him by Greek sculpture. At first he studied reproductions, in Spence's valuable *Polymetis*. And then, as by Chapman's Homer, a new world was thrown open to him by the Elgin Marbles. He was taken to see them in 1817 by the painter Haydon, to whom he sent two sonnets which acknowledge their own incoherence but express the same overpowering ecstasy as his poem on the discovery of Homer.[30] 'He went again and again to see the Elgin Marbles, and would sit for an hour or more at a time beside them rapt in revery. On one such occasion Severn came upon the young poet, with eyes shining so brightly and face so lit up by some visionary rapture, that he stole quietly away.'[31]

This rapture was the work, not of imitation, but of creation. The graceful figures in *Endymion* and the Titanic majesty of the divinities in *Hyperion* were inspired by the Elgin Marbles; yet it is impossible to say that Keats described any one figure or group. Rather it was the grandeur and the repose of the Parthenon sculptures which tranquillized his burning imagination and gave his poetry a larger scope. Henceforward magnificent statuesque scenes occur at intervals in his longer poems, to serve as points of rest in the bewildering flow of imagery and colour. Similarly, his *Ode on a Grecian Urn*, although it exquisitely evokes the delicate grace and the vivid reality of Greek vases, is not a description of any particular vase. It blends motives from at least two—a calm religious rite, and an ecstatic dance with 'men or gods' in pursuit of maidens loath. These are the two central elements in his own life, his quest for tranquillity and his consuming passion. Many different sources have been suggested for the single urn which Keats imagined;[32] but what he created was a unique fusion of his own mortal genius with the immortality of Greece.

In spite of his incomparable imagination, the gaps in Keats's classical knowledge injured his poetry. He knew little of philosophy: and so, in his longer poems, the gorgeous descriptions sometimes seem to be, not the imaginative efflorescence of clear original thinking, but decorations concealing the commonplace. Like Shakespeare in his youth, he lacked the sense of tragedy. And he did not grasp the large structural principles governing Greek poetry. Shelley, who understood more about the architecture of classical literature, built his own poems far better because of that understanding; and every reader of Keats regrets that, as soon as he goes beyond a simple story like *The Pot of Basil*, or a brief lyric, he becomes diffuse, vague, and sometimes incomprehensible. The severest judgement that could fairly be levelled against *Endymion* is that its structure lacks the clarity which illuminates even the most complex and imaginative Greek poems.

What Greek poetry and art meant to Keats he himself has told us: they meant beauty. They meant the highest manifestations of physical beauty, in women, in sea and sky and mountain and forest, in flower-laden earth and winding grottoes, in noble statues and immortal paintings, and they meant the spiritual beauty of friendship, love, and the kind emotions, of imagination, and above all, of poetry. These two aspects of beauty were, for Keats, indissolubly connected. Physical beauty was the expression of spiritual beauty. Love, imaginative ardour, poetry, were the response to physical beauty. And yet physical beauty is limited and temporary. Spiritual beauty is eternal. Unless they are linked together like body and spirit, one and perhaps both are meaningless. A moment, whatever passion fills it, is only a bursting bubble unless it is eternalized by the spirit. Keats had learnt that from the Greeks.

Physical beauty exists only as a symbol of spiritual beauty, and as a way to it. Like Endymion, it is always searching and always in danger of death until it is transfigured by the kiss of an immortal. Like the lovers on the Grecian urn, it is transient and immemorable unless it is made permanent by art and imagination. All things in this world die; only their beauty can become immortal. Keats says beauty is truth, and truth is an eternal reality.

If Keats was the Shakespeare of this nineteenth-century Renaissance, its Milton was Shelley. Not Wordsworth, greatly though he admired Milton's patriotism and moral nobility; but Shelley, the poet of grand cosmological visions, of conflicts between eternal spirits of evil and spirits of good; the scholar who like Milton read and re-read the classics until phrases, images, ideas, characters, scenes, entire conceptions from them became part of his own thought; the critic who, like Milton, had a thorough grasp of the principles of classical form, which served not to repress but to guide his luxuriant imagination. In many things the two poets would have been profoundly unsympathetic to each other, but in many others they were closely akin. The author of *Samson Agonistes* and *Paradise Lost* would have admired *Prometheus Unbound*; and Shelley joined the author of *Lycidas* when he wrote a Greek pastoral lament for the dead Keats.

Shelley was the result of an excellent classical education, acting on a unique personality in a stirring age. He was a tremendous reader. His friend Hogg says that at Oxford he often read sixteen hours a day. He read at meals—not while he ate, but while the food grew cold. He read walking about the streets and fields. He read in bed as long as the candle lasted, and sometimes all night. Not only that: he read the best books again and again. 'It would be a curious problem', Hogg remarks, 'to calculate how often he read the whole' of Homer. And he read his favourites aloud to his friends, sometimes translating as he went. He was only thirty when he died, but he had read much more widely and intensively in Greek literature than many professional scholars.

After starting Latin with a tutor at seven or eight, he got an admirable schooling at Eton, far better than Harrow could give the rebellious Byron. He may have been unhappy among the boys, but the masters trained him well. We hear that he wrote good Latin verses, recited one of Cicero's speeches against Catiline on speech-day, tried his prentice hand on poetic translations of Vergil,[33] and certainly remembered enough of Ovid's *Metamorphoses* to borrow the charming name Ianthe for *Queen Mab* and for his baby daughter.[34] Oxford seems to have carried him on from Latin to Greek, not very thoroughly—he read Plato in translation only—but certainly in such a way as to encourage him to go on to the originals. The rest of his short life he spent on completing this education.

Whatever Shelley loved came out in his poetry: although not always directly, yet always clearly. It is easy to determine the classical authors whom he loved best.[35]

First, Homer, whom he read through year after year. In 1818 he translated seven of the 'Homeric' hymns into English verse.

Next, the Greek tragedians. Aeschylus, whom he preferred far above the others, now at last returned to his rightful place in literature. As early as 1809 Shelley was quoting him;[36] he translated *Prometheus Bound* to Byron in 1816 and to Medwin in 1820–1. Aeschylus is in fact an overpoweringly great poet, whose wings beat too strongly and soar too high for any but a bold spirit to follow. Shelley admired his eloquence—the complex rhythms of his choruses, his long bravura descriptions, the skill and daring with which he forms new words to express the almost inexpressible; the profound and complex spiritual meanings carried by his tragedies; and the grand imagination which produced those vast plots and superhuman characters. Shelley's own *Hellas* was 'a sort of imitation of *The Persians*' of Aeschylus;[37] while in *Prometheus Unbound* he wrote for Aeschylus' *Prometheus Bound* a sequel which actually surpassed the Greek poet in nobility, if not in depth of thought.

When he was drowned, or murdered, he was reading Sophocles.[38] He preferred the Oedipus dramas, which he specifically mentions in his preface to *The Cenci*, and *Antigone*, whose heroine resembles Beatrice.

For Euripides, whom he must have felt to be cynical and negative, he cared less; but he translated Euripides' *Cyclops*, the only complete satyr-play in existence.

In prose his favourite author was Plato, who would have liked him as a pupil. Shelley translated *The Symposium* in 1818, and later *Ion*, *Menexenus*, parts of *The Republic*, and two of Plato's love-poems. There have been other Platonists in English literature; Milton himself was one;[39] but Shelley was the most understanding. Two long prose essays were directly inspired by his Platonic studies: *A Discourse of the Manners of the Ancients relative to the Subject of Love* by *The Symposium*, and *A Defence of Poetry* by Plato's attack on poetry in *The Republic*. In the latter, he says that Plato was 'essentially a poet' because of the splendour of his imagery and the brilliance of his language; he overlooked only the fact that Plato was also a dramatist. Philosophical ideas derived from Plato coloured all his thought. Like Wordsworth, he was impressed by the fine idea that the immortality of the soul can be proved by the child's recollections of his antenatal life in heaven. (Shelley took the word *ante-natal* from its inventor Godwin.) And the doctrine of *The Symposium* that sexual love can be made a path towards the perception of eternal beauty and goodness appeared both in his life and in his poetry. *Epipsychidion* is a rhapsody on Platonic themes.

Theocritus and the other bucolic poets he knew and in part translated. Before written history began, the Greeks in Asia celebrated an annual rite dedicated to mourning the dead summer; they sang songs for it, and personified it as a beloved youth cut off in the flower of his strength and beauty. Sometimes the youth was called Adonis: the legend told of Venus' love for him and of his untimely death.[40] The dirge they sang for him was later taken up by the pastoral poets, who wrote of shepherds and nymphs mourning for a fair youth who died too soon. For the pastoralist Bion, a friend wrote such a lament; and many other poets elaborated the same pattern, none more eloquently than Milton in *Lycidas*. And now, when Keats was cut off in his springtime, Shelley took the beautiful old form to make a threnody for him, changing the name of Adonis to the more melodious Adonais. The same two-thousand-year-old themes reappear in Shelley's dirge, and yet they are changed so as to become real for Keats.[41] Instead of calling him an actual shepherd with Arcadian sheep, Shelley speaks of

> the quick Dreams . . .
> Who were his flocks, whom near the living streams
> Of his young spirit he fed.[42]

Adonis was wounded to death by a wild boar in the mountains, and his mourners sadly reproached him for his daring. So Shelley asks:

Why didst thou leave the trodden paths of men
Too soon, and with weak hands though mighty heart
Dare the unpastured dragon in his den?

The dragon that Keats faced, and the poison which (like Bion) he drank, were the reviewers and their deliberately deadly malice.[43] Then, for a time, the brilliant imagination of the comic poet Aristophanes fascinated Shelley.[44] His greatest failure, *Oedipus Tyrannus or Swellfoot the Tyrant*, was an attempt at an Aristophanic farce-comedy based on the scandalous affair of Queen Caroline. The chorus, suggested to him by the comical noises of a herd of pigs that passed his window, is a 'swinish multitude', parallel to Aristophanes' choruses of frogs, wasps, and birds; but the satiric intention is too ungenerous and crude to make the play comparable with Aristophanes, and the form of Attic comedy was impossible to resuscitate.

Shelley's favourite Latin poet was the young Stoic Lucan.[45] After reading the first four books of the *Civil War*, he wrote to Hogg that it was a 'poem of wonderful genius, and transcending Virgil'.[46] Later, in *A Defence of Poetry*, he said Lucan was a 'mock-bird' rather than a real poet. For all that, he admired Lucan's perfervid rhetoric, his hatred of tyrants, some aspects of his Stoicism (for instance, the idea that the soul of man originates from the divine fire[47]), and his deeply poetic power of imagining macabre scenes and beings. One of the most famous of these evocations is Lucan's description of the snakes that attacked Cato's legions in the African desert, inflicting not one but many different kinds of death.[48] Their victims shrivelled away or burst into flames, swelled up out of human semblance, or melted into liquid matter. . . . These snakes have impressed many poets· Dante brought the scene into *Inferno*, 24, Milton into his own hell.[49] Shelley often mentions the monsters with their monstrous names in *The Revolt of Islam* and *Prometheus Unbound*.[50] The awful figure of Demogorgon in *Prometheus Unbound* apparently originated from Lucan also;[51] and Lucan himself appears in *Adonais*, to mourn Keats as another inheritor of unfulfilled renown.[52]

His friend Medwin said that Shelley's atheism began at school, when he read Pliny's chapters on the gods, in the *Natural History*, and the poem of Lucretius, who as an Epicurean believed the gods had nothing to do with the world.[53] The epigraph of *Queen Mab* is from Lucretius: otherwise there is little trace of his influence in Shelley.

Vergil, with his pessimistic belief in the inevitability of war and his praise of empire, could mean little to Shelley except as a nature poet. But once at least their two spirits met. In the most famous of his smaller poems, written at the end of the atrocious civil wars, Vergil prophesied that the birth of a miraculous baby would bring in a new era of peace and of life according to nature.[54] The thousand-year pattern of history, starting again in the Golden Age, would unroll itself once more: the Argonauts would sail again and there would be a second Trojan war. But he did not pursue the idea of perpetual repetition, and lingered rather on the theme of perpetual peace, unlaborious earth, and oarless sea.[55] This ideal was repeated by Shelley in the last chorus of *Hellas*:

> The world's great age begins anew,
>   The golden years return,
> The earth doth like a snake renew
>   Her winter weeds outworn.

But, in the spirit of Vergil, he corrected his master's inconsistency, crying:

> Oh, write no more the tale of Troy,
>   If earth Death's scroll must be! . . .
> Oh, cease! must hate and death return?
>   Cease! must men kill and die?

Vivid as Shelley's imagination was, he could never have created the superb scenery and majestic figures of his mature poems unless he had studied Greco-Roman sculpture and architecture, and unless he had lived in Rome.[56] In his preface to *Prometheus Unbound* he says it was largely written among the ruins of Rome. Two generations earlier Gibbon had imagined *The Decline and Fall of the Roman Empire* while sitting among those same ruins. Yet that was a book of clear-sighted resignation and autumnal regret. Shelley's drama was composed under the inspiration of 'the vigorous awakening spring in that divinest climate, and the new life with which it drenches the spirits even to intoxication'. The contrast epitomizes the difference between the two eras. Gibbon sits among the ruins and looks backward towards the past. Shelley finds in the ruins an inspiration for the future; his poetry is a rebirth of beauty from the magnificent fragments of that immortal yesterday which is eternally reborn.

For Shelley, the most important gift of the Greek spirit was freedom. The Greeks practised genuine freedom of religion. Although Socrates was executed on a charge including heresy, that was at a time of extreme political and spiritual strain; and Athens was far less affected by religious persecutions than all modern states have been: one of the chief reasons for Shelley's admiration of that great religious poet, Aeschylus, was that he wrote a tragedy whose hero defies the tyrant, God. Political freedom was the watchword of Athenian democracy, and another of the greatest achievements of Greek civilization. As the combined Greek states had resisted enslavement by the ancient Persians, so Shelley hoped they would cast off the despotism of the modern Turks—and that all similar despotisms throughout the modern world would be shattered for ever. Sexual freedom also, beyond the limits set by

> that great sect,
> Whose doctrine is, that each one should select
> Out of the crowd a mistress or a friend,[57]

was assumed by some of the speakers in Plato's dialogues and practised by Shelley, in spite of its melancholy results. Finally, all these freedoms were expressions of that central Greek principle, the freedom of thought: which is based on the belief that man's nature is, in itself, capable of the best. Shelley was like the Greeks in saying *Yes* to nature: even to human nature.

Yet the Greeks meant to him much more than models to copy or rivals to emulate. Thus, he scarcely ever imitated Homer, and yet read him year after year. From Homer, as from the other great classical writers, he took an influence too large to trace in any one of his writings. Just as he preferred to write in a tower overlooking the Mediterranean Sea, or among the flowers and arches of the Colosseum, or with the mountains of northern Italy before his eyes, so his constant study of the Greeks gave him examples of greatness and companions in nobility.

§ 5. ITALY

> Alas, in agony is conceived and born
> the song of Italy.
>   LEOPARDI[1]

The ferment of revolutionary reading and thinking was stirring the states of Italy. But there the corruption of the late baroque age had sunk more deeply. Morality, intellect, even will-power were drugged by the division of the nation and its subjection to corrupt oligarchies and petty tyrants. Therefore it was more difficult for young writers to make their way towards the light. Those who did fight their way up and out usually suffered terribly while doing so. Their lives were torn with agonizing conflicts. They died in gloomy or despairing silence. Their work is unlike the serene lyricism of Keats and Chénier; it has none of the optimism of Shelley and Goethe; it has not the sombre Mazeppa energy of Byron. It is profoundly pessimistic. It is a cry from the abyss. But even that cry is music.

We hear it in three voices: tragic, elegiac, and lyric.

Count Vittorio Alfieri was born of an old, noble, and wealthy family in 1749, neglected by his relatives, and atrociously ill educated. Although he was obviously talented and hungry for spiritual food, he was starved. He did not even know Tuscan, the literary language of Italy—only French, and a local Piedmontese dialect. Plato says that a brilliant character always suffers the worst corruption if misdirected;[2] and Alfieri was so corrupted. As soon as he became his own master he plunged into dissipation, which still was not enough to discharge his volcanic energies. He rode swift horses; he fought duels; he had burning love-affairs; he travelled with demoniac restlessness throughout Europe, from country to country, from Scotland to Russia, from Norway to Portugal. . . .

In his twenties he began to educate himself—not planning his future, but merely feeding his starved mind with Montesquieu and Helvétius and Rousseau and Voltaire. Through them he met Plutarch. He read the *Parallel Lives* all through four or five times. Here, for the first time, his imagination found subjects worthy of itself to work upon. In his fascinating autobiography he says that, as he read, he would leap to his feet with admiration for such men as Caesar, Brutus, and Cato, and then weep at his own misery in being a subject of a tyrannical government.[3] His mind was finally set in its right track by his reading of Montaigne (where he chafed at not understanding the Latin and Greek quotations) and by the educational and poetic encouragement given him by a wise Italian abbé, whom he called 'a Montaigne in the flesh'.

In 1775 he wrote his first tragedy, *Cleopatra*. It was performed, and warmly applauded. Yet he knew it was inadequate. He had not said what he had in him to say. We can see why. He had no models to work on, but the tragedies of Metastasio and Racine (through which he could only distantly feel the force of Greco-Roman drama) and the artificial and basically false tragedies of Voltaire. He could read no Greek; and he knew scarcely anything of the central tradition of literature, to which tragedy belongs. Yet he divined it. He started a course of severe self-education, taking a vow never again to speak or write French, studying Latin and Tuscan, and working at his tragedies with all his characteristic driving speed and energy.

The rest of his life was stirringly dramatic—his elopement with Prince Charlie's wife, his renunciation of his estates in the king of Sardinia's territories as the price of freedom from the king's police, his publication of satires pouring scorn on kings, nobles, middle class, and commoners, his escape from the French revolutionary Terror,[4] his savage lampoons called *The Gaul-hater* (*Misogallo*) on the invading troops of Napoleon, his learning Greek when nearly fifty, his foundation of a knightly Order of Homer. . . . It was indeed more variously dramatic than his tragedies.

He produced twenty-two in all.[5] They were far the best tragedies ever composed in Italian, and marked a new high level in his country's dramatic literature. They deal with important and interesting historical subjects, ranging from Agamemnon to Lorenzo de' Medici, from Saul to Mary Queen of Scots; the characters are clearly drawn and the emotions boldly differentiated; the medium is blank verse, energetic and sometimes harsh, but firmly controlled. Byron, who in many ways resembles Alfieri, often gives us the feeling that his eloquence has broken into a wild gallop and run away with him. Sometimes he even lashes it on. Alfieri rides a steed quite as violent; it is black and tireless; but he has a tight grip on its reins.

His tragedies have been accused of being undramatic. Some of them are: despite their nobility, these are his less satisfactory works. Two different reasons account for this. One is Alfieri's own resolution to preserve the unity of action by cutting out all episodes and sub-plots—not as a gesture of subservience to Aristotle, but in order to concentrate on heroism. The other is the habit common to nearly all the writers of the revolutionary era: he makes long speeches on important ideals—patriotism, tyranny, filial love—and substitutes these for action. The essence of drama is change. Yet in 1780 the utterance of a bold speech on tyranny was so novel that, even if it did not advance the plot, it seemed to be dramatic.

Still, Alfieri wrote some fine plays: for instance, *Myrrha*, a powerful variation on the Oedipus theme, in which a girl falls hopelessly in love with her own father;[6] *Merope*, a tense intrigue in which (quite credibly) a mother almost orders her own son executed;[7] and a superb *Saul*, showing the struggle between violent madness and wise sanity, both within the spirit of the king himself, and in the conflict between the influence of his daughter, his son, and his successor David, and the power of his evil minister, Abner.

The chief importance of Alfieri's tragedies is that they put a revolutionary message into a classical form. Two-thirds of his plays are on themes from Greco-Roman history and legend.[8] All are in a pattern which he assimilated as closely as he could to that of classical tragedy. Nearly all contain bold denunciations of tyranny, gallant eulogies of freedom. Sometimes the heroes are too whitely good, and the despots too blackly evil; but not always; and in truth the frontier between tyranny and heroism *is* the frontier between black and white, between bad and good. The purity of his tragic form enhances the power of Alfieri's social protest, in which he is a precursor of Shelley.

The form in which he wrote was derived indirectly from Greek and Roman tragedy. But the tragedies which he knew best were those of Racine and Voltaire. Of all the ancient poets, he was closest to Seneca; yet he did not study him as carefully as the Renaissance playwrights did. Formally, what he did was to simplify and dignify baroque tragedy into something more truly classical.

The content of Alfieri's message is bold and simple: *down with tyranny!* Tyranny is power exercised for the sake of its possessor. Usually one man makes himself a tyranny; but a family, a group, or a class—even the working class—can be a tyrant.[9] In this belief he had predecessors in Montesquieu and Helvétius, and a close ally in André Chénier.[10] Before Alfieri published his treatise *On the Prince and Literature* (1786), he read it to Chénier, who expressed similar ideals next year in his own *Essay on the Perfection and Decadence of Literature* and his idyll *Liberty*.[11] Both Chénier and Alfieri equated liberty and literature. Without liberty, they held, virtue was impossible; and without virtue, great writers could not exist. Alfieri's own violent imperious character made him feel for the tyrant—which he himself might easily have been —both interest and hatred. Relentless will; terrifying cruelty, exercised even against his own family; serpentine treachery—these are the tyrant's qualities.[12] Among his subjects they breed abject fear, unprincipled treachery, a corrupt reverence for money, and the abolition of all standards of morality;[13] in some, a gloomy melancholy begotten of the certainty that a full free life is impossible, and in heroes, a determined revolt, all the more resolute if it is doomed. In that resolution Alfieri summed up the best of his own revolutionary era, and at the same time re-created the spirit of classical tragedy.

Alfieri's dramas had many imitators—some, like Vincenzo Monti (the Italian Southey), more successful in their day than Alfieri himself. The best poet among them was the Venetian Ugo Foscolo, who was born in the Greek island of Zante in 1778, and was to die an exile in London in 1827. Unimportant though his plays were in contrast with his other work, they resounded with the same revolutionary and nationalist ardour as those of his master. But like so many others, Foscolo was cruelly disappointed by the greatest of all revolutionists, Napoleon Bonaparte. Everyone knows how Napoleon at first appeared as the liberator of oppressed nations, the destroyer of tyrants; and then as the leader of French nationalist aggression; and lastly as the betrayer of republicanism, the assassin of liberty, the emperor of the French and almost of all Europe. Everyone knows how Beethoven dedicated his 'Heroic' Symphony to the liberator, and then, when he heard of Napoleon's new dynastic plans, tore off the dedicatory page and inscribed the work 'to the *memory* of a great man'. Everyone knows how Wordsworth, after hailing the rising sun of liberty—

Bliss was it in that dawn to be alive,
But to be young was very heaven—[14]

saw it darkened by the tempests of ambition and war. From Poland to Spain, the same disillusionment sickened the youth of the whole continent.

Foscolo fought as a volunteer in Napoleon's armies. In 1797 he saluted him in an *Ode to Bonaparte the Liberator*. A few weeks later Napoleon sold the territory of Foscolo's homeland, Venice, to Austria, by the treaty of Campo Formio. The ensuing despair of Foscolo's generation was immortalized in a novel of unhappy love, mental agony, and suicide, *The Last Letters of Iacopo Ortis*— an extension of Goethe's *Sorrows of Werther* beyond individualism into patriotism.

Foscolo was a competent classical scholar. Like Chénier, he heard modern Greek spoken around him in his childhood; like Chénier, he went on to study ancient Greek with taste and erudition.[15] Graceful echoes of Greek and Roman poetry can be heard even in his slighter personal lyrics.[16] His greatest poem, however, is not a chord of echoes, but a complete and vital interpenetration of the ancient and modern worlds; an assertion that history is one of the values we live by; a claim that the past is not dead while it inspires the present; a warning that the present is dead if it forgets its past. This is his famous elegy *On Tombs*.

In 1806 the new revolutionary government issued an order designed to introduce equality and fraternity among the dead. It enjoined that all bodies without exception should be buried in a public cemetery, under tombstones of exactly the same size, with inscriptions censored and 'co-ordinated' by the local authorities. Foscolo might have viewed this as a piece of petty tyranny, and denounced it in a bitter satire. If he had, his poem would scarcely have survived longer than the ordinance which provoked it. Instead, he meditated on the whole context of the order, until he reached the broadest and most deeply human meaning of the custom of burial. Tombs are built (he reflected) and gravestones are carved with names and titles, as a symbol of the continuing life of the dead in the minds of those who survive. They should not bear images of woe and dismal skeletons;[17] they should be among evergreen trees, green as a deathless memory, or in gardens outside the city as they are in Britain. Above all, the tombs where great men lie are a focus of national life, and an encouragement to greatness among the living. It would be shameful for Parini[18] to lie beside some criminal; and the Holy Cross church in Florence, which holds the graves of Machiavelli, of Michelangelo, of Galileo, yes, and now of Alfieri, is one of the greatest sanctuaries of Italy. So it has always been. Across the Aegean Sea lie tombs which the Muses love to haunt. A blind man once wandered among these tombs, and they told him their story, and with his

song he did homage to the shades that lived there. That song made
Hector of Troy famous

> wherever men revere and mourn the blood
> shed for the fatherland, while still the sun
> illumines the misfortunes of mankind.[19]

In form this fine poem is a descendant of the Greco-Roman
elegy. Its modern ancestors are the English eighteenth-century
elegiac meditations: Blair's *The Grave*, Young's *Night Thoughts*,
Gray's *Elegy written in a Country Churchyard*; and their successors
in France, the reflective poems of Legouvé and Delille. It is
tempting to see *On Tombs* as a letter, rather than an elegy: it is
in blank verse, and is addressed to the poet Pindemonte, who replied
in an *Epistle*. But the Roman poets also addressed elegies to
sympathetic friends, and the deeply imaginative and emotional
tone of the poem makes it an elegy—one of the noblest and broadest
in literature.

Its thought begins with the poet's own day, and moves back
through the history of Italy's greatness to the source of the central
stream in European culture: the Trojan war and the poems of
Homer. As a meditation on the fact that time becomes eternity, it
is therefore a descendant of Dante's *Comedy*. But it is a pagan
poem, not a Christian poem.[20] Foscolo does not speak of the
Christian doctrine of death and eternal life. He knows that it is
possible to think of graves as reminders of mortality; but he
believes that to do this is almost as inadequate as to demand that
all graves should be equal and indistinguishable. That is to deny
much of the highest of which humanity is capable. The present
contains the past and lives by it. Tombs, like poems, are a record
of past greatness and a stimulus to future achievement. The
Muses both remember and inspire.

Although Foscolo's elegy was a protest against a decree of the
revolutionary government, he himself was none the less a poet of
revolution: for he was calling on the Italians to break away from
their ignoble lassitude, and to make themselves a new nation,
worthy of the magnificent past which linked them with Roman
gravity and Greek heroism.

Count Giacomo Leopardi (1798–1837), the saddest lyric poet of
Italy, grew up in a loveless provincial home where his only friends

were books. Like Fénelon and Gibbon, he educated himself by devouring his father's library. Unlike them both, he ruined his health by excessive study. This, with his loneliness and his mother's neglect, permanently darkened his soul. Before he was twenty, he made himself a distinguished Greek scholar.[21] At fifteen, he composed a history of astronomy. At sixteen, he wrote a translation of two works by the sixth-century historian Hesychius, with a biographical essay; a Latin commentary, with notes and emendations, on Porphyry's life of the Neoplatonist philosopher Plotinus; and a Latin commentary on several important rhetoricians of the imperial period.[22] At seventeen he produced an *Essay on the Popular Errors of the Ancients*. By the age of twenty he had written more works of scholarship than some modern professors do in their entire lives. But he did not feel himself physically and mentally strong enough to embark on a long career of research; and he found that hardly anyone in Italy cared for scholarship. Restless like Alfieri, but far less vigorous, and shackled by dependence on his parents, he travelled (after being set free) from city to city, finding no one to talk to except an occasional foreign savant like Niebuhr, or, rarely, an Italian littérateur like Giordani.[23] His own poetry has many poignant images of loneliness and homelessness: the solitary sparrow; the wandering shepherd on the plains of Asia; the broom growing alone on the slopes of a volcano. And his lyrics are full of questions—urgent and sad questions which no one hears, and which are never answered.

Like so many of the poets we have studied, Leopardi began writing by translating classical authors, and then by trying to rival them. At seventeen he translated the poems of Moschus and the little mock epic, *The Battle of Frogs and Mice*.[24] At eighteen he ventured on an experimental translation of part of the *Odyssey*. This was his first published work. It was received with cold indifference or sarcastic laughter.[25]

Early in 1817, aspiring higher, he issued translations of a *Hymn to Neptune* and two anonymous odes 'from the Greek', with illustrative notes. There was no such hymn; there were no such odes. Leopardi invented them. In his notes he said the author of the hymn was *not* Simonides or Myro—in fact, it looks like the work of a talented pupil of Callimachus. The short odes—which are characteristically addressed *To Love* and *To the Moon*—

Leopardi said he 'would gladly ascribe to Anacreon'. The publication of these innocent forgeries marked an important turning-point in his life. He already felt he could at least equal the scholars of his own time. Now he set out to equal the poets of Greece, in preparation for his own work in the same field, lyric poetry. Just in the same way fifty years before, another unhappy boy called Chatterton had produced original poems of remarkable merit, and disguised them as relics of the past he admired.

As he came to manhood, Leopardi made the same breaks as his contemporary Shelley and other young poets of his epoch. He gave up Christianity, and became a free-thinker, with an emotional preference for the Greek divinities.[26] He became, for a brief time, a social reformer, opposed to the forces of conservatism and repression. And he sympathized with the growing movement of nationalism—not merely as resistance to foreign aggrandizement, but as a positive revival of the intelligence, the eloquence, and the historical sense of the Italians. In his first original poems, three important and closely linked lyrics, he evoked different aspects of the new renaissance he hoped for. These were *To Italy*, *On the monument of Dante*, and *To Angelo Mai after his Discovery of Cicero's 'On the Commonwealth'*.[27] The thought of these lyrics was closely akin to that of Foscolo's elegy on tombs. They lamented the decay and ruin of Italy, her moral disintegration, the loss of that courage and resolution which she ought to have inherited from ancient Rome, and the misdirected heroism which led her young volunteers to fight in Russia with Napoleon rather than in their own land for liberty. They reminded Italians of the nobility of Dante, 'the unconquered enemy of Fortune', the sweet melancholy of Petrarch, the exploratory courage of Columbus, the imagination of Ariosto, the infelicity of melodious Tasso, and, last, the proud energy of Alfieri.[28] They said, and repeated, that men cannot live by the present alone, for the present alone, without becoming as dull and cowardly as a ruminating beast. Heroism is built on history. Modern men should think shame to be less heroic than Leonidas and his few Spartans, facing the overwhelming power of Persia.[29]

But disillusionment came upon Leopardi, as upon other reformers. Added to his loneliness, his ill health, the coldness and stinginess of his family, and his unhappiness in love, it brought him to a depth of despair more profound than anything we have seen among the poets of his time. He reached the clear-eyed hopeless agony of De Quincey's *Our Lady of Darkness*:

'She droops not; and her eyes rising so high *might* be hidden by distance. But, being what they are, they cannot be hidden; through the treble veil of crape which she wears, the fierce light of a blazing misery, that rests not for matins or for vespers, for noon of day or noon of night, for ebbing or for flowing tide, may be read from the very ground.'[30]

In its name he pronounced that life was meaningless; or, if it had a meaning, that it was cruel. The ideal of progress was a silly delusion. Love itself was an experience so overpowering that it must end in its twin brother, death.[31] Once, brooding on this, he recalled the Greek poetess Sappho, who in one legend had killed herself for love: he pictured her standing on the moonlit precipice, reflecting on her implacable sufferings and the agonizing death of her hopes, and then hurling herself into the nothingness which is freedom.[32] No other revolutionary poet expressed such abysmal despair, although many (Byron, Heine, Hölderlin) felt it. In Leopardi it turned into the objective judgement that life, in this world, is hopeless. He has often been viewed as a precursor of the philosopher of pessimism, Schopenhauer. Through Schopenhauer the line leads from Leopardi to Nietzsche; while as a poet he is the ancestor of James Thomson (*The City of Dreadful Night*) and Charles Baudelaire.[33]

As Leopardi matured, his pessimism grew into something approaching a complete philosophy, which he expounded in his *Short Works on Morals*[34]—a series of brief dialogues in the manner of Lucian. But Lucian's dialogues have a mocking smile, sometimes slightly twisted. Leopardi's have a grin like a skull. There are conversations between an embalmer and his mummies; between Death and Fashion; between a lonely Icelander and Nature—not mother Nature, but stepmother Nature, indifferent or cruel. There is a long discussion on suicide, between the Neoplatonists Plotinus and Porphyry, and another on the longing for death which Leopardi so often felt: he himself appears in it, under the sombre name of Tristan. The note of ghastly humour which returns again and again like a facial tic is that which we find in the tales of Poe and Hoffmann, in some of the prose poems of Baudelaire, and in the life and personality of the demoniac Paganini. The philosophy of the dialogues is Leopardi's own materialist conception of life.

The world is only a ball of earth and steam, he tells us, and we men are only like the animals and insects, the trees and fishes, which it has produced. Why then, he continues, are we tortured with emotions like hope and love? with aspirations like fame and immortality? Why are we alive at all? All our activities, our life itself, are as purposeless as the dance of gnats in the summer air, and less beautiful, and more painful. This might have been true of Leopardi himself, had he not written his exquisite lyrics.

Leopardi's thought is so much his own that we can scarcely lay a finger on any part of his work and say 'This is classical, that is modern, this again comes from his reading in the Renaissance'. It has all passed through the furnace of his own mind and been transformed there.[35] In form his dialogues are Greek. His poems, on the other hand, are free variants of the long-stanza Italian lyrics (*canzoni*) which developed out of folk-song and were used by dozens of poets after Petrarch set the model. Their language has fairly frequent latinisms, which give it austere dignity rather than the appearance of affectation.[36] There are important references to Greek and Roman myth and history, which Leopardi connects closely with modern life as example and inspiration. There are also several echoes of classical thought, sometimes direct quotations: as when, in his fine poem *On an Ancient Grave-relief*, he reflects:

> Never to see the light
> would, I believe, be best—

taking both thought and words from a tragedy of Sophocles.[37] *Sappho's Last Song* is on the same situation as Ovid's *Letter of Sappho to Phaon*, although it is far less brilliant and more sincere;[38] and the pathetic *Dream*, in which the dead girl whom he had loved at a distance appears to him, restates the theme of one of Propertius' finest elegies, which reached him through Petrarch's *Triumph of Death*.[39]

His closest links in classical literature are with Lucretius the Epicurean, who believed that creation and the life of man were a pure accident, having no significance beyond itself; that nature was neither kindly nor hostile to us, but indifferent; and that the only sensible purpose of living was to attain, through well-spaced and well-chosen pleasures and an intelligent understanding of the universe, a calm and reassured happiness. Like Lucretius,

Leopardi is a materialist; like him, he admires the charm of the Greek deities, although he knows that they have really no effective connexion with our world;[40] like him, he looks at human excitements and efforts with astonished pity, as we do at an ant-hill struck by a falling apple.[41] But—here is the fundamental difference not only between Leopardi and Lucretius, but between many modern poets and nearly all Greco-Roman poets—the conclusion which Leopardi draws is that life, because of its futility, is a cruel agony where death is welcome; and the conclusion of Lucretius is that life, if properly understood and managed, is still liveable. Even Greek tragedy does not mean that life is hopeless; but that, at its most terrible, it still contains nobility and beauty. Perhaps because of the sickness which afflicted both Leopardi's body and his soul, he was never able to fight through to this truth. At least, not consciously. Yet, as an artist, he grasped it. His chief debt to classical poetry and his truest claim to equal the great lyric poets is that he sees his tragic subjects with sculptural clarity, and describes them with that combination of deep passion and perfect aesthetic control which we recognize as Greek.

§ 6. CONCLUSION

It is right that our survey of the revolutionary generations should end with Leopardi, in mortal sickness and despair. So many writers of that time died sadly young, like Keats; were killed, like Chénier; went mad, like Hölderlin; or (quite as significantly) suffered the death of their imagination, survived by their bodies, their reputations, and their interminable flow of words. The revolutionary era was a brief meteoric blaze, illumining the whole sky, burning away neglected relics, casting unreally dark shadows, lighting up beauties long unperceived, and ending in what looked like sombre gloom but was really the light of common day. We have already compared it to the comet-like brilliance of the Renaissance. Yet, like the Renaissance, it did not end abruptly. While some of the new forces it released were checked, and others were diverted, many flowed on into the century which succeeded it: and one of these was the deeper understanding of Greco-Roman art, literature, and thought.

It has been impossible to discuss all the currents which rushed into the literature of this era. Some of them are now difficult to admire, such as Orientalism, and Ossian with his one-stringed harp. Others have grown to be dangerously powerful. Nationalism, the cult of the Folk, has produced new and valuable differentiations in modern thought, and has helped to eradicate many intolerable oppressions. But human civilization, which is a higher ideal than national civilizations, is now in danger of being destroyed by them. Those who believe it is more important to appreciate *American* novels, *English* poetry, *French* criticism, *German* philosophy,[1] *Russian* music, *Bolivian* science, *Tibetan* theology, than to admire and improve the thought of humanity as a whole (or as a few large interrelated and co-operative wholes) are quite capable of reducing mankind to a mass of mutually unintelligible and hostile tribes.

It has also been impossible to discuss, even to name, all the writers and artists who, partially under Greek and Roman inspiration, contributed to the revolutionary era. Some of those neglected are highly interesting: for instance, the Austrian dramatist Grillparzer (1791–1872), who made his name with a trilogy on the Argonauts, and wrote a fine series of lyrics expressing the disillusionment of his time, with a title suggested by the elegies of the exiled Ovid, *Laments from the Black Sea*.[2] Some belong to nations which stood rather on the edge of the main stream, and which therefore reproduced in their own languages inspirations which first awakened elsewhere. Such were the Polish poets Casimir Brodzinski and Kajetan Kozmian, who put the spirit of the Polish country-side into Theocritean idylls and Vergilian georgics; and Zygmunt Krasinski, who wrote a drama, *Irydion*, on the revolt of Greece against the Romans—as Hölderlin wrote of his Hyperion rebelling against the Turks. Some also are less richly creative writers than Goethe, Chateaubriand, Keats, and others we have discussed.[3] Some—for reasons which varied with each individual—deliberately turned away from Greek and Roman influence, although they often felt its power. Horace came in for much mistaken hatred in France, as the supposed instigator of Boileau and the purveyor of literary rules.[4] And the apocalyptic Blake, while constantly using Greek sculpture as models and inspirations for his drawings, cried 'The Classics! it is the Classics, and not Goths nor Monks, that Desolate Europe with Wars!'— a sentence which has very little meaning except as a contradiction of Gibbon.[5]

A creative era is one in which a large number of powerful

spiritual forces flow together, strengthening, renewing, and en-
riching one another. Such an era was the time of revolution. It
has been shown that it was not anti-classical, but more deeply
penetrated with the classical spirit than the age preceding it.
Among all the energies that made it, the current of Greek and
Roman culture was only one; but it was very powerful, very varied,
very fertile. It moved young writers and thinkers to strive for
political freedom; religious liberty; aesthetic perfection; beauty,
sensuous and spiritual; beauty in an external nature which was
not dead or animally alive, but inhabited by spirits of superhuman
strength and loveliness. For some, it provided an escape from the
hateful world of materialism and oppression—and this, we shall
see, it continued to provide throughout the nineteenth century.
Some were inspired by it to emulate the ideal of a balanced
psychical and physical life which sings in Greek poetry and shines
out from the Greek statues. And some, the greatest, took from their
studies of antiquity a deeper sense of one of the central truths in
human life—the fact that civilization is a continuous achievement.

20

PARNASSUS AND ANTICHRIST

IN one of his most famous poems, Wordsworth accuses his contemporaries of killing their own souls. They think of nothing,
he says, but making money and spending it; and in exchange for
money they have given away their hardened and worthless hearts.
They cannot feel the grandeur of nature: of the moonlit sea, the
winds, the calm. In a sudden fit of exaltation he shouts that he
would rather be a pagan, believing in the divinities of Greece—
for the Greeks not only felt the beauty of the external world, but
peopled it with spirits.

> So might I, standing on this pleasant lea, . . .
> Have sight of Proteus rising from the sea;
> Or hear old Triton blow his wreathèd horn.

This poem was written in 1806.[1] It was one of many attacks on
contemporary materialism delivered by the revolutionary poets.
Other abuses of the human spirit stirred them to protest also:
religious oppression, arid social convention, survivals of feudalism.
But after they died, the generations of writers who succeeded them
saw the forces of rebellion divide and dwindle, and, with the
growth of nineteenth-century capital and industry, the power of
materialism increase. They saw also, or thought they saw, that
Christianity, once the champion of the poor and oppressed, was
becoming the stronghold of money, social privilege, and the timid
or sordid tricks by which they are acquired and kept. The
nineteenth century was a great time for money-making, but for
thinkers, poets, and artists, for men who loved nature and
humanity, it was hell.

Materially also the nineteenth century was ugly. The sky had
become dark with smoke; the air was thick with factory-fog and
rasped by the roar and chatter of machinery. Within a few years,
smiling valleys were turned into acres of slums, quiet moors were
ripped open, green fields were buried under barren slag. Drawings
of interiors, pictures of the homes of the rich (even of such
artists as Wagner and Zola), photographs of streets and crowds,
show us scenes of appalling hideousness. Millions of repulsive

buildings and towns, brick churches and 'dark Satanic mills', constructed in that period, still afflict our eyes.

The result was that most of the great nineteenth-century writers hated and despised the world in which they lived. Again and again they said so, in poetry, in criticism, in prose fiction, and in philosophy. Other ages have provoked revolt among artists, but it is difficult to think of any other period in which so many talented authors have so unanimously detested their entire surroundings and the ideals of the people among whom they were forced to exist. Perhaps the twelfth-century satirists and student tramps hated their own times as much, but who else?

Many poets of the nineteenth century felt it was impossible to write anything beautiful about the life they saw around them. They cried:

> Mist clogs the sunshine.
> Smoky dwarf houses
> Hem me round everywhere;
> A vague dejection
> Weighs down my soul.²

They turned away in disgust from the industrial cities which were growing up around them, from the vulgar books, paintings, and plays which delighted their contemporaries, and from the materialist ideals which they thought dominated the age. They looked to other lands and other ages, beautiful in themselves and made lovelier by distance. And often they turned towards Rome and Greece. Often—not always. There were other regions full of beauty and energy to which they could escape. Gauguin went to Tahiti. Rimbaud went to Java, and then to east Africa. Pierre Loti and others went to the Orient. De Quincey and Baudelaire went to the artificial paradise of drugs. Many went back to the romantic Middle Ages. But none of these provided such a large, consistent, and satisfying refuge as the culture of Greece and Rome.

Nineteenth-century writers admired this culture for two chief reasons: because it was beautiful, and because it was not Christian. They saw their own civilization as squalid and greedy; they praised the Greeks and Romans as noble and spiritual. They felt contemporary Christianity to be mean, ugly, and repressive; they admired the cults of antiquity as free, strong, and graceful. Looking at the soot-laden sky, pierced by factory chimneys and neo-Gothic steeples, they exclaimed:

> Great God! I'd rather be
> A Pagan suckled in a creed outworn.[3]

There are, then, two types of classicizing art and thought in the nineteenth century, which can be distinguished by two symbolic names: Parnassus and Antichrist. Both attitudes sometimes appear in the same writer, and even in the same book. But usually they are distinguishable; and they differ so deeply in intention and result that they should be separately discussed.

PARNASSUS

Unworldly aesthetes and intellectuals are often said to live in an ivory tower.[4] It is a fine phrase, but Parnassus is a better symbol for the nineteenth-century idealism which loved Greco-Roman culture. The name was given by a group of French poets to the periodical in which, between 1866 and 1876, they published their work: *Le Parnasse contemporain*, or *The Modern Parnassus*. Parnassus is the mountain inhabited by the Muses—who are not goddesses of poetry alone, but patrons of history, philosophy, science, drama, in fact of everything in civilization that is above material concerns. Parnassus is a mountain: far away from cities, part of wild nature, above the world; loftier, more beautiful, stronger, more real than a tower of ivory. And it is not a mountain of Hebrew or Christian legend, 'the secret top of Oreb, or of Sinai',[5] nor a medieval stronghold like Tintagel, nor a friendly peak in modern lands.[6] It is a remote mountain in Greece. The French gave its name to the hill where the universities, the art, and the thought of Paris are assembled. It is Montparnasse, which stands in perpetual opposition to the hill on the more modern (and materialistic) right bank, crowned by the Christian church of Sacré-Cœur and bearing the medieval name of Martyrs' Mount. Although the word 'Parnassian' has been kept for the relatively small group of French poets who joined in publishing the magazine mentioned above, the symbol is too broadly useful to be confined to them; and many of the ideals in which they believed were shared by poets in other countries.[7] We may therefore call the whole movement to assert the beauty of Greek and Latin aesthetic ideals, in opposition to those of the nineteenth century, Parnassian.

Much of its energy was, as we have said, devoted to opposing materialism. But it was a complex movement, and, like most important spiritual events, cannot adequately be described as 'reaction'. Looked at from another point of view, it was an expression of dislike for the romantic ideals which grew exuberant and extravagant after the age of revolution. Many of the Parnassians felt that, if a mill-owning millionaire was disgusting, a Byronic corsair was ridiculous; and that a modern corrugated-iron chapel was no more repulsive than a medieval cathedral full of hideous gargoyles and exaggerated saints. Therefore some of the Parnassian writers despised romanticism for distorting life, as they despised industrialism for degrading it. What they maintained was (they believed) neither reaction nor escapism, but a group of positive aesthetic and spiritual ideals, which, discovered in Greece, were the foundation of all civilization worthy of the name, and were eternally true.

The first Parnassian ideal which claims attention is *emotional control*. Although its expression is restrained, the emotion of Greek poetry is none the less real and intense. But it is more genuine, more central, than violent expressions of extravagant feeling; it is usually more beautiful; and even at its wildest it does not degrade human dignity. For example, three of Victor Hugo's novels deal with love—its idealism, the gulfs which separate lover and beloved, and the renunciation which in great love rises above desire. The characters he chooses to symbolize these aspects of love are a hideous deaf hunchback in love with a homeless gipsy, a nobleman kidnapped in childhood and mutilated into a perpetual grinning mask, but beloved by a blind girl, and a workman who, after carrying out single-handed a technical feat of superhuman strength and skill to win a girl, finds that she loves someone else, and commits suicide by sitting in a rock chair to be covered by the tide, while she sails past him with her husband.[8] Dramatic ideas, these, and expressed with tremendous vigour; unforgettable; but unreal.

From such exaggerations of desire and suffering, Parnassian restraint was a relief. Edgar Allan Poe, although himself a wildly romantic writer, once felt that relief. In his lyric *To Helen*, addressed to the girl whose name and face image the perfection of Greek beauty, he said that her serene loveliness had brought him home, a

weary way-worn wanderer, . . .
On desperate seas long wont to roam.

He had been on the romantic adventure. He had felt the visionary magic

> Of perilous seas, in faery lands forlorn.[9]

But after those wild visions, he found gentle beauty and a sense of repose in

> the glory that was Greece,
> And the grandeur that was Rome.

The contrast between the frenetic emotionalism of such poets as Swinburne and the serenity which produces saner thought and better poetry was put by Matthew Arnold (1822–88) in a fine poem called *Bacchanalia; or, The New Age*. He describes an evening, after a hot summer day, with the perfume of the flowers coming out and the stars rising slowly; and then, suddenly, an irruption of wild maenads rioting through the quiet sheaves and tearing out the flowers from the hedge. He asks the shepherd (who is himself or any kindred poet) why he does not join the revel, pipe for the dance:

> Glow not their shoulders smooth?
> Melt not their eyes?
> Is not, on cheeks like those,
> Lovely the flush?—

But the shepherd answers:

> Ah, so the quiet was!
> So was the hush!

The same ideal was summed up by the leader of the French Parnassian group, Charles-Marie-René Leconte de Lisle (1818–94), in the word *impassibility*. Similarly, in criticism, the latinist Désiré Nisard (1806–88) wrote a brilliant essay on the later Latin poets, charging Hugo and his followers with being degenerate writers and distorting the standards of literature, as Lucan and Statius had done in the decadence of Rome.[10] And in Italy, Giosuè Carducci (1835–1907), although a revolutionary liberal and an admirer of Goethe and Hugo, denounced the 'romantic' attitude to life. In *Classicism and Romanticism*[11] he compares classicism to the rich strong life-giving sun, and romanticism to the morbid moon, which ripens neither flower nor fruit, but looks down with most pleasure on graveyards and on skulls less white than its own dead face. (It is difficult not to remember Leopardi's many poems written in the white glare of the moon, that planet of love and death.) In painting, the same ideals of restraint, conveyed likewise in Greco-Roman symbols, were expressed by David's pupil Ingres, and by the tranquil visions of Puvis de Chavannes. Ingres's *Apotheosis of Homer* proclaims the idealism of Greek thought and Greek art; but it mirrors only half of the Hellenic spirit. The other half appears in his superb nude, *The Spring*, which shows a Greek nymph brought close to us by modern tenderness and realism. Her dawning smile, and the little flowers at her feet, make her (like Botticelli's Venus) something more than a copy of an antique model, and exemplify once more the inextinguishable vitality of Greek myth.

Although Greco-Roman poetry laid down no absolute laws of poetic structure, yet its control of form, and its avoidance of the extravagant, vague, and unbalanced, are impressive ideals. Therefore the Parnassians admired and practised *severity of form*. They felt that Victor Hugo and other writers of his type were deliberately cultivating length, incoherence, and eccentricity. Hugo would write a poem with lines three syllables long, or fill chapter after chapter of a novel with lectures on natural history and meditations about God; he and his followers would never use one word if ten would do as well. In order not to make these extreme errors, the Parnassians cultivated precision, clarity, and patterns which were regular and traditional rather than novel or extravagant.

In this field the most impressive of their works is *The Trophies*—a single book of sonnets, perfectly regular and rigidly controlled, by José-Maria de Heredia (1842–1905).[12] Beginning with the earliest legends of Greece, and passing through Rome to the Middle Ages and the Renaissance, it freezes the whole of western European history in a series of vividly coloured and dazzlingly bright crystals, each of exactly the same form and each showing some heroic enterprise or moment of beauty at its extremest intensity. Thus, one sonnet sums up the love, the luxury, and the catastrophe of Antony and Cleopatra by describing one embrace in which Antony, gazing deep into Cleopatra's blue eyes flecked with gold, sees

a whole vast sea, with routed ships in flight.[13]

This one book was like the great single works on which classical poets spent a lifetime, working with what we now think of as a scientist's self-forgetfulness to cut out the inessential and the false. It made Heredia a member of the Academy, and, in an even greater sense, an immortal.

His contemporary Carducci had, some years earlier, published a collection of *Barbarian Odes*, in the manner of Horace, on Greek and Italian themes.[14] The rhythms are a curious adaptation of Horace's metres, not as Horace himself sang them, but as they would be spoken by someone reading with the stress-accent of late Latin and modern Italian.[15] The benefit of using difficult metres of that type, modelled on rigid forms in which great poetry has already been written, is that it compels the poet to combine intensity of feeling and economy of language with extreme clarity of thought. In Carducci's first poem—reminiscent of Horace's

> I hate the vulgar mob, and fence it off—[16]

he compares ordinary poetry with a prostitute, and the complex forms he himself strives to master with a nymph caught on the mountains by a faun, and all the lovelier because she is so difficult to subdue and resists so passionately.[17]

This time, however, the admirers of Greek and Roman art did not make the baroque mistake of educing any 'rules' from their models. The Parnassians saw that the essence of classical form is not the use of traditional laws, but the acceptance of discipline, not the slavish copying of a pattern, but the subordination of personal fancies to a supra-personal tradition. Théophile Gautier (1811–72) stated this in a fine poem whose form is none the less austere because it is not classical in origin:[18]

> No false restraints put on!
> Yet, to walk steadily,
> Muse, you must don
> a narrow buskin high.

(The buskin was the thick-soled boot worn by Greek tragic actors to increase their height: hence the symbol of tragedy, and of high poetic standards.)

The same poem ends with a statement of the ruling ideal of the Parnassians—one which was not confined to France by any means, nor even to literature, but spread to every western country and to all the arts. This is that *beauty is an independent value.*

It was not a new idea. But it was proclaimed with great fervour
by the Parnassians, because its falsity was either assumed by their
opponents without argument, or preached in those tones of unctu-
ous self-assurance which are so familiar in the nineteenth century.
It was a defiance of the materialists, who thought that food,
lodging, and medicine were all that man needed, or who, themselves
rich, enjoyed nothing but the parade of riches—like Mr. Podsnap
in *Our Mutual Friend*; a defiance of the realists, particularly of
writers who appeared to enjoy describing *bourgeois* materialism
and poverty-stricken squalor; and, above all, a defiance of the
moral and religious propagandists like Mr. Pecksniff in *Martin
Chuzzlewit*, who held that no art was good unless it taught an
improving lesson, and vice versa. Against such people, Gautier
wrote:

> All passes. Art alone
> has immortality.
> The bust of stone
> outlives the stone city.[19]

Leconte de Lisle, who began as an idealist with hopes of social
reform, but was soured by the 1848 defeat of liberalism, put the
doctrine in a sentence which distinguishes it from the ideal of
Keats. Keats had identified truth and beauty. Leconte de Lisle
said: 'The Beautiful is not the servant of the True.'[20]

However, the most famous expression of the doctrine is the
phrase *Art for art's sake*. Victor Hugo said he invented it, but
Hugo was never quite as original as he thought.[21] It was, it seems,
an infiltration into England and France of the idea worked out by
Kant and his philosophical successors, that there is an aesthetic
sense by which we appreciate the beautiful—a sense quite independent of our moral judgement, independent of our intellect. If
that is true, it follows that the artist works through this special
sense, and that it is quite irrelevant to introduce moral or intellectual standards into the appreciation of a work of art. Kant said
works of art had 'purposefulness without purpose',[22] by which he
meant that they seemed to have been created to serve some special
end; yet they had no clearly defined function like a chair or a
machine: rather, they were like a flower. In the same way, Picasso,
when asked what one of his pictures meant, is said to have replied
'What does a tree mean?' In England the doctrine was proclaimed
by A. C. Swinburne (1837–1909), an ardent admirer of Gautier;

and then set in elaborately jewelled phrases by Walter Pater (1839–94), whose *Studies in the History of the Renaissance* became the young Parnassians' breviary.[23]

Although many of its devotees were admirers of the classics, it should be noted that this is not a classical doctrine. The Greeks and Romans did not believe that art was divorced from morality. On the contrary, their literature was profoundly moral in intention —except for a few minor types such as mime and epigram; and their great sculptures were expressions of spiritual as well as physical ideals.[24] It was rather (like the mysticism of the Pre-Raphaelites) a revolt against the Victorian attitude that literature must be edifying—an attitude often combined with supreme indifference to good taste and beauty.[25]

It is a dangerous belief. '*All art*', wrote Pater, '*constantly aspires towards the condition of music*':[26] for in music, matter has merged entirely into form; a piece of music has no meaning other than its own beauty. But literature is not music. It deals with people, and people are moral agents: therefore it is impossible to write about human thoughts and human actions without, consciously or unconsciously, raising moral problems and answering them.

And it is a very short step from declaring that art is non-moral to making it immoral. Those who say literature has nothing to do with ethical standards often mean that they wish it to reject *current* ethical standards, and by implication to teach different ones. In Huysmans's famous novel about the aesthete who lives alone to devote himself to a life of pure beauty, composing symphonies of perfume and reading a few obscure and perfect authors, the hero initiates the corruption of a boy of sixteen, so that, when he is sufficiently corrupted, he will murder his disgustingly *bourgeois* father.[27] This act is presented, not as a deliberately vicious deed, but as morally colourless, another episode in des Esseintes's search for interesting sensations, or at most an ironical comment on the stupid world which believes marriage and the family worth preserving. But in fact Huysmans knew that it was evil; and in later books his heroes, the projection of himself, sank lower still —until they felt the conviction of sin, and, like Huysmans, began to remake their lives through religion. Similarly, two British writers whose devotion to Greek ideals was very marked both maintained the Parnassian doctrine that art has nothing to do with morality; but both in fact used their art to teach a new moral code, chiefly in sexual matters. One was Swinburne. The other was the pupil of Pater and the admirer of Huysmans, Oscar Wilde (1856–1900).[28] Swinburne's considerable scholarship and amazing technical skill only emphasized the fact that his Greeks led a life far more purposefully devoted to sexual ecstasy than the real men and women of classical Greece; and while Wilde ostensibly admired Greece as the home of beauty at its purest and passion at its most intense, we know from repeated hints in his work as well as from the ruin of his career that—like his friend Gide—he also loved Greece for the homosexuality which was practised there, although never (at least in Athens) accepted as morally indifferent.

All these principles seem to be restrictions and negations. Did Parnassus mean anything positive?

If there is something actively valuable in Greek and Roman culture, surely the Parnassian writers should have brought it out. Most of them were deeply read classical scholars. While still a boy, Alfred Tennyson (1809–92) was taught by his father to recite all Horace's odes by heart: although he hated this 'overdose', he learned Horace's difficult art of placing words, and came to respect the quiet inimitable artist. He himself was surely the English Vergil; and the address *To Virgil* which he wrote as a mature poet is among the finest tributes ever paid by any artist to his predecessor. For Arnold and Swinburne, reading Greek and writing poetry were interdependent activities.[29] Walter Savage Landor (1775–1864) wrote Latin poetry as freely as English. Having begun his career by publishing a collection of English and Latin poetry, together with an essay (in Latin) supporting the practice of writing Latin verse—a tradition in which he was the successor of many bilingual poets as distinguished as Milton and Dante—he continued to write in both languages, and said 'I am sometimes at a loss for an English word, for a Latin never'.[30] Robert Browning (1812–89) read Greek and Latin as energetically as he read Italian and French and other vernaculars, and has left translations from three Greek dramas.[31] Giosuè Carducci was a professor of literature, and ranged with fine freedom from medieval to classical and back to modern prose and poetry. Leconte de Lisle was 'mediocre in Greek' when he graduated, but worked at it, discussed it, gave up much of his life to it, and published translations of the *Iliad*, the *Odyssey*, and other classical poems which inflamed his younger readers with his own adoration of the Hellenic world.[32]

Why did these poets write so much about the world of Rome and Greece? Were they merely escapists? defeatists?

Partly, yes. But not wholly; and scarcely more than poets always have been. The past is never dead. It exists continuously in the minds of thinkers and men of imagination. We tend to-day to think too much of the immediate and ever-changing present, which, because its dangers are so urgent, presses upon us, but which, because it is so hard to see clearly, is scarcely a fit subject for poetry. *Most* poets throughout the world, from Homer to this moment, have sung of ages earlier than their own, and other worlds. Shakespeare blended the past and the present. Ariosto and Vergil, Milton and Racine, expressed their ideals more clearly and nobly at a heroic distance.

There were several different reasons for the re-creation of the classical past by the Parnassians of the nineteenth century.

Compared with the chimney-pots, the hideous furniture, the dreary cities, the ruined landscapes, and the drab clothes of the nineteenth century, Greece and Rome were physically beautiful. Their beauty stimulated the imagination of poets, evoking the graceful and eloquent language which was choked by the squalid present. Their beauty lay not only in soft Venus de Milo curves, but in intense colours and strong vivid forms. The heir of Keats liked the softer charm, and sang:

> A land of streams! some, like a downward smoke,
> Slow-dropping veils of thinnest lawn, did go;
> And some thro' wavering lights and shadows broke,
> Rolling a slumbrous sheet of foam below.[33]

Browning preferred a complex vigour not unlike his own:

> And no ignoble presence! On the bulge
> Of the clear baldness,—all his head one brow,—
> True, the veins swelled, blue network, and there surged
> A red from cheek to temple,—then retired
> As if the dark-leaved chaplet damped a flame,—
> Was never nursed by temperance or health.
> But huge the eyeballs rolled back native fire
> Imperiously triumphant: nostrils wide
> Waited their incense.[34]

But neither these poets nor the others limited their imaginations to the Greco-Roman past: which shows that it was not a pedantic classicizing fad, as it often became in the baroque age. Tennyson, the modern Vergil, spent most of his effort on re-creating the medieval legends of Arthur. Browning's largest single work is a reconstruction of a seventeenth-century murder case. Others wrote serial reconstructions of great moments throughout history. Heredia's *Trophies* begin in the twilight of Greek prehistory, with Hercules fighting the monstrous lion, move through Greece to Rome, then past the Middle Ages into the Renaissance, out to the Spanish empire in America, thence to Egypt, Islam, Japan, and other distant, beautiful realms of the fancy. His master Leconte de Lisle was the leader of the French Parnassians, and is sometimes thought of now as having been a complete hellenist, a reincarnated Greek. But his *Antique Poems* begin with evocations of Hindu legend before they pass on to Greece; and he followed them by *Barbarian Poems*, in which he painted picture after vivid picture of biblical antiquity, Phoenician, Scandinavian, and Celtic history, medieval life, and modern times.[35] Landor himself, the Greek Englishman, ranged over a great part of history in his most important work, the *Imaginary Conversations*, as well as in his dramas and dramatic scenes.

This movement into the past was, then, not confined to those writers who had a nostalgia for Greece and Rome. It was part of a new sense of history and legend, spreading and deepening in the nineteenth century. The historical perspective that had been partly created by Gibbon, by Winckelmann, by Wood and Wolf, by Niebuhr, was now shared by many of the public. Hundreds of new history books were written. Vast historical paintings were produced. Directors of plays on historical subjects took elaborate care to make costumes, and properties, and gestures, authentic and correct. (The great operas of this period—Wagner's, Verdi's, Strauss's, Puccini's, and those of the Russians—were all, with minor exceptions, historical and legendary.) For the first time, authors of romantic stories about the past began to aim at ever closer accuracy of reconstruction. As an astronomer photographs the rays of light impinging on the earth from a star which may have died a million years ago, so nineteenth-century writers and artists, using imagination, scholarship, and aesthetic tact, placed the modern reader under the sunlight and among the people of many a distant land and century.

The Parnassian poets also felt that their own age was morally base. They turned to the world of Greece and Rome because it was nobler. Whereas everyone around them was occupied with making money and spending it, with winning a social position and maintaining it, they themselves found that in the Hellenic legends they could write of young love, or the desire for fame, or the rapid passing of youth, without introducing any of the sordid motives flaunted by their own contemporaries.

It has been well said that the Parnassian movement and the 'art for art's sake' theories in France cannot be understood unless as a refuge from the disillusionment caused by the failure of the Second Republic.[36] It was largely for this reason that Leconte de Lisle turned away from the ruined present, to inhabit a world of tranquil Greek beauty and vivid antique barbarism. Landor had not been so disappointed, but he had the same sovereign contempt for contemporary standards of power, wealth, and happiness. Seldom he mentions them, and with bitter scorn:

> Curse on that chief across the narrow sea,
> Who drives whole herds and flocks innumerable,
> And whose huge presses groan with oil and wine
> Year after year, yet fain would carry off
> The crying kid, and strangle it for crying.[37]

Nineteenth-century writers also felt that the universal emotions could be expressed more clearly and intensely by classical than by contemporary figures. From this point of view, Tennyson's *Ulysses* is a typical Parnassian poem: a bold statement of the ideals of energy, indomitable will, and exploratory adventure, without any thought of such powerful Victorian motives as profit or self-sacrifice.[38]

In particular, utterances of sexual passion could be frank, and yet graceful and eloquent, in a Greco-Roman setting. Thus Tennyson's *Lucretius* is a very daring picture of extreme sexual tension, with fantasies taken both from Lucretius' own poem and from Tennyson's psychical insight. After the flaring atom-streams that rush before the eyes of the maddened poet, and the rainstorms of blood which fall on the earth to produce girls dancing round him in narrowing circles, several strong images of love and death are fused in this immortal picture:

> Then, then, from utter gloom stood out the breasts,
> The breasts of Helen, and hoveringly a sword

> Now over and now under, now direct,
> Pointed itself to pierce, but sank down shamed
> At all that beauty; and as I stared, a fire,
> The fire that left a roofless Ilion,
> Shot out of them, and scorch'd me that I woke.

In Browning's *Fifine at the Fair*, written after his wife died, Helen also appears as an ideal but almost irresistible temptation, while his *Pan and Luna* is a franker dream than anything Tennyson dared to print. Leconte de Lisle's *Antique Poems* are noticeably, and Banville's classicizing lyrics overwhelmingly, concerned with erotic themes. And although many stories and poems were written in the nineteenth century about women deceived and deserted, in few did the woman speak as eloquently, and in very few as boldly, as Tennyson's Oenone. In spite of the cumulative power of Tolstoy's *Anna Karenina*, for example, and the pathos of Anna's suicide, her final monologue—

'We are drawn apart by life, and I make his unhappiness, and he mine, and there's no altering him or me. Every attempt has been made, the screw has come unscrewed. Oh, a beggar-woman with a baby. She thinks I'm sorry for her. . . .'[39]

—is weak and unconvincing compared with the torrent of noble imagery in *Oenone*:

> O death, death, death, thou ever-floating cloud,
> There are enough unhappy on this earth,
> Pass by the happy souls, that love to live . . .
> Thou weighest heavy on the heart within,
> Weigh heavy on my eyelids: let me die.

One of the main reasons for using Greco-Roman characters and settings is now, as it has always been, their impersonality. Problems that torment the poet himself can be expressed more clearly, and perhaps their tension will be relieved, if they are transferred to figures both distant and noble. The best example is Arnold's *Empedocles on Etna*. In this Faustian drama a philosopher-poet, troubled by his own thoughts, tormented by the pressure of world problems, saddened by the slow death of his imagination, waits for the ever rarer moment when he feels at one with the universe, and then unites himself with it and destroys the petty troubles of the self, by leaping into the crater of a volcano. Meanwhile a calm young musician, thought-free, sings the praise of poetry and melody, within hearing but out of sight, far below the barren mountain-shoulders and the fiery lava, among cool streams and green trees. This was Arnold's own problem. These were Arnold's two selves, the thinker and the singer. That was Arnold's own wish for a fuller life, or death. Had Arnold written it openly about himself, it would have been embarrassing, perhaps ridiculous, and certainly more limited in its effect. By situating the conflict in a distant ideal time, he made it comprehensible and sympathetic to thousands of readers who have felt something of it themselves, and can identify themselves more easily with a vague, legendary, universal figure like Empedocles than with an individual like Matthew Arnold himself.

Yet the great Greek and Roman figures are not really devoid of personality. They are more than plastic dolls. They are people, not dimmer but more intensely alive than most of ourselves. The beautiful Helen, the martyred Socrates—around these immortal beings cluster a crowd of stories, ideas, pictures, suggestions, desires and admirations, symbolic meanings, private dreams. Their very names stir the imagination. Therefore a writer who uses them often finds that he is being used by them—that they awake in him visions he had not tried to see, that his readers trace significances he scarcely hoped to create.

But this evocative quality of mythical figures has its dangers. One is that an audience ignorant of their names and natures will miss their meaning. Readers who, by diverse nationality or by inadequate schooling, stand outside the tradition of western culture may recognize the names of Solomon and Hercules and Nero—but the innumerable associations which cling to those names and make those personalities will be lost to them. The other danger is that authors in search of new subjects may choose obscure and tedious myths which stir neither their own imaginations nor those of their readers. To avoid that, the Greeks (and Seneca) usually kept to a few dozen legends which were widely known and had many overtones of meaning.

This was one of the dooms which afflicted the classical dramas of the Parnassians. Swinburne was not interested in Atalanta, and still less in Erechtheus (whoever *he* was). Arnold admired Empedocles, as Tennyson admired Lucretius; but he cared nothing for Merope.[40] He had to write a long preface explaining the story, and its previous treatments, and his reasons for choosing it; but its very style, so dull and dutiful compared with his lectures *On translating Homer*, shows that the whole thing was a boring task for him. As he himself wrote, 'no man can do his best with a subject which does not penetrate him.' Yet in these very plays the choruses, where Arnold and Swinburne could let their imaginations fly free, are interesting poetry: they alone have survived.

Two souls, and a deeply personal problem, appeared in Browning's largest and strangest poem on a classical theme. *Balaustion's Adventure* is an enormous monologue by a young Greek poetess.[41] She tells how she arrived in Sicily soon after the defeat and enslavement of the Athenian army; and how she saved herself and vindicated Athens by remembering a play by Euripides. The Sicilians were hungry for poetry, but, the war intervening, had been cut off. Balaustion (her name means Wild-pomegranate-flower) recites the entire drama in the theatre of Syracuse, cutting a few dull patches and interspersing such brilliantly vivid descriptions that, as we read or listen, the actors appear before our very eyes. So, Hercules strides in

> Happy, as always; something grave, perhaps
> The great vein-cordage on the fret-worked front,
> Black-swollen, beaded yet with battle-dew
> The yellow hair o' the hero!—his big frame
> A-quiver with each muscle sinking back
> Into the sleepy smooth it leaped from late.
> Under the great guard of one arm, there leant
> A shrouded something, live and woman-like,
> Propped by the heartbeats 'neath the lion-coat.

The play itself is the not-quite-tragedy of *Alcestis*, which reverses the tale of Orpheus and Eurydice. Queen Alcestis volunteered to die instead of her husband, Admetus. He lamented her, but lost her. Hercules, however, conquered Death and brought Alcestis back to her husband, now doubly embarrassed. Browning's young poetess gives this story, told cynically by Euripides, a kindly interpretation. Then, after reaching its end, she retells it once more, giving it an even kinder meaning. Evidently Browning is trying to face and solve the problem of the husband who feels unworthy of his wife and has lost her. Long afterwards, in a less successful poem, he thought of himself—still tied down to earth and flesh—as a swimmer buoyed up by the water and yet sinking deep in it, while a butterfly (symbol of the soul and inhabitant of the air) floated above him, watching his heavy body imitating flight.[42] In Balaustion's second version of the Alcestis myth the dead wife returns to her husband because, having become his very soul, she cannot die while he lives. This was close indeed to Browning's own love-story. He himself (like Hercules) had once pulled Elizabeth Barrett out of a grave, and after she died her spirit lived on within him. A quatrain of her poetry appears as the epigraph for the whole *Adventure*, and is quoted towards the end; and surely, as well as being Alcestis, she is Balaustion herself, the lyric girl who loved Euripides.

It was not, then, wholly a desire for escape that led so many nineteenth-century writers to use classical themes. Some of them did detest their own contemporaries. Some did, like Huysmans's hero and like Baudelaire, attempt to shut themselves away in a private artificial paradise. But Greco-Roman subjects and figures were creatively used by many others who wished to create beautiful images and music as an offset to modern materialism and ugliness, and who felt bound to speak more clearly, more *permanently*, about their own problems and the problems of our civilization.

ANTICHRIST

Christianity was hated and despised by many of the most ardent lovers of the classics during the nineteenth century. In this the revolutionary poets—Shelley, Hölderlin, and others –showed the way; but their successors were more energetic and rancorous. They loved paganism for everything that was not Christian in it. They hated Christianity because it was not Greco-Roman, or was a perversion of Greco-Roman ideals. This conflict included some of the same issues and revived many of the same arguments as appeared in that other war between past and present, the Battle of the Books.[43] But this time it was less of a declared war between open enemies, and yet the opponents were farther apart. Seldom speaking out directly, the pagans delivered their attacks in apparently innocuous stories, escapist poems, and professedly objective histories.

The chief arguments which lay behind the work of the anti-Christians were three in number. Although they were often confused, they can be best considered separately.

1. *Christianity is not part of the European tradition; it is oriental, and therefore barbarous and repulsive.*

This attitude is usually connected with half-acknowledged anti-Judaism. It appears in the famous *Prayer on the Acropolis* by the eminent orientalist Ernest Renan (1823–1892).[44] The prayer is an address to Athene, patroness of Athens, as goddess of truth, wisdom, and beauty, the supreme and central divinity of the world. In it Renan speaks of Christianity as 'a foreign cult, which came from the Syrians of Palestine', and of the apostle Paul as 'an ugly little Jew, speaking the Greek of the Syrians'. Renan's chief work, *The Origins of Christianity*, had much to do with the rise of religious scepticism in the nineteenth century: although it treats Jesus himself with reverence as a remarkable man, and his followers with the admiration due to men who achieved the impossible, it emphasizes the idea that they were Jews, and that they were part of an Asiatic tradition.

A similar attitude appears in Anatole France (1844–1924), an early admirer of the great Parnassian Leconte de Lisle.[45] In a famous short story, *The Governor of Judea*,[46] he presents Pontius Pilate as an elderly official in retirement, taking the waters in great luxury at Baiae. Discussing his career with a friend, Pilate expresses the most biting scorn and hatred for the Jews as a cruel and uncivilized tribe of fanatics. His friend recalls being in love with a beautiful red-haired Jewess, who lived in a vile underworld of 'soldiers, mountebanks, and publicans'; she was a barbaric but wonderfully voluptuous dancer; but she disappeared and took up with the followers of a young Galilaean miracle-worker.

'He called himself Jesus the Nazarene, and he was crucified for some crime. Pontius, do you remember the man?'
Pontius Pilate frowned. . . . After some moments of silence:
'Jesus?' he murmured. 'Jesus the Nazarene? I do not recall him.'

The story is nonsense, of course. The execution of Jesus was a striking event in Judea, accompanied by serious disorders, and certainly made a strong impression on Pilate. No Roman official could forget having been forced to make a gesture as striking (and as un-Roman) as washing his hands in public self-exculpation. But France's distortion of the facts is characteristic of this interpretation of Christianity: that its founder and his first followers were poor Jews from villages and slums, too obscure for a cultured

Roman to remember. The same feeling inspired France's *Thaïs*, a contrast between the lovely, civilized, Epicurean courtesan of Alexandria, and the barbarous, fanatical, Christian monk of the desert who converted her, leading her to place her talents and her beauty at the service of God, but who, by the exaggerated violence of his own cult, was driven after contact with her from the extreme of purity to the extreme of sin. It is traceable also in Oscar Wilde's *Salomé*, where the disputing Jews are grotesque (Strauss emphasized their grotesqueness when he added music to the play), St. John the Baptist an appalling figure like a Hindu ascetic, and the atmosphere of the entire play perverse, oriental, and evil.

2. *Christianity means repression, paganism means liberty.*

We have already seen this belief in Shelley. It was given vigorous expression by Giosuè Carducci, who began his career with a passion for liberalism, and a violent hatred for those who opposed the liberation and unification of Italy. Among the forces of oppression he thought the worst was the Roman Catholic church, and its head, Pius IX, whom he attacked again and again.[47] He had an Italian predecessor, Alfieri;[48] but went far beyond him. His most famous manifesto is his hymn *To Satan* (written in 1863, published in 1865). This is quite unlike Baudelaire's *Litanies of Satan*, the invocation to the patron of the wretched; indeed, Baudelaire much disliked the neo-pagans. It is a hymn to the spirit of progress—whom Carducci calls Satan because he believes that progress and the free life of the human spirit have always been opposed by the Roman Catholic church. He praises Satan as the god who ruled the happy pagan worlds of Ahriman in Persia, Astarte in Asia Minor, Venus and Adonis in Lebanon and Cyprus; as the patron of the witch and the alchemist—those forerunners of science—in the Middle Ages; as the consoler sending wretched Héloïse visions of the beauty described by Vergil and Horace, whom, even behind nunnery walls, she could not forget; as the inspirer of the great reformers, Arnold of Brescia, Wycliffe, Huss, Savonarola, Luther; and now as the victorious leader of science, riding through the world on the chariot of fire which has conquered Jehovah. This chariot is the locomotive.[49] In a larger sense it is the image of modern scientific progress, which raises man above the limits of time and place, and which, Carducci believed, would free him from the policemen who controlled thought.

Another remarkable anti-Christian poem by Carducci is *By the Springs of Clitumnus*, the Umbrian stream known to the Roman poets. The clear river still flows down from the Apennines. The peasants still dip the struggling sheep in it, and water the great white oxen. This is the river that saw the fall of Umbria's power, and of Etruria, and then the rise of Rome. It saw the invasion of Hannibal, when Rome suffered and triumphed. But Rome now triumphs no longer, since a red-haired Galilaean ascended the Capitol and told her to take up the Cross. The nymphs fled, shrieking. Black-clad monks came; they made a desert, and called it the kingdom of God. From this desert Carducci calls on the spirit of Rome, reincarnated in that of modern industrial progress, to rise and free mankind.

In France, Leconte de Lisle produced a *Popular History of Christianity*, which was a savage philippic against the church and its corruptions—blood-thirsty inquisitors, greedy popes, terrifying superstitions. A thousand years of Greco-Roman paganism, he implied, had produced no atrocities to compare with the burning of heretic Christians, no such abuses of the human spirit. Twice he wrote the tragic story of Hypatia, the beautiful Alexandrian girl whose soul, nourished on the Neoplatonic philosophy, was as beautiful as her body. She was stripped naked by a Christian mob, flayed alive with sharp shells, and then burnt. You, priestess and incarnation of beauty (cried Leconte de Lisle),

were struck and cursed by the vile Galilaean.[50]

Leconte de Lisle's friend Louis Ménard (1822–1901) not only preferred Greek to Christian morality but justified Greek religion —which to others seems a confused though sometimes beautiful congeries of disparate superstitions, poetic myths, and half-understood barbarian survivals—as being a truer philosophical picture of the universe. In *Hellenic Polytheism* and other books he asserted that polytheism represented an orderly cosmos, where the forces of nature, fully developed, unite to produce harmony. That is a peaceful republic. Christian monotheism, where all is subject to one supreme God, is, he said, a monarchy with all the vices of absolute power. The Greek cosmos embodied the rule of law, according to Ménard, and the rule of Jehovah was the rule of force. And, he went on, look at the book of Genesis, in which work is imposed on mankind as a punishment. Compare that with the healthier and more natural attitude of the Greeks, who believed that their gods invented agriculture, the cultivation of the vine, and other useful arts in order to benefit mankind. Ménard was more than an interesting old eccentric: he has been described as 'a scholar among poets—and perhaps a poet among scholars'.[51]

In particular, some nineteenth-century writers detested Christianity because of its restrictions on sexual liberty, and admired Greco-Roman paganism because (they believed) love in Greece was free and unashamed. On one side is the pale Galilaean, preaching fasts and virginity. On the other is a wild wood with two lovers:

> And soft as lips that laugh and hide
> The laughing leaves of the trees divide
> And screen from seeing and leave in sight
> The god pursuing, the maiden hid.
> The ivy falls with the Bacchanal's hair
> Over her eyebrows hiding her eyes;
> The wild vine slipping down leaves bare
> The bright breast shortening into sighs . . .[52]

Beautiful poetry, beautiful dreaming: especially in a Victorian world of heavy clothes and cumbrous conventions. But the theory from which it flowed did in fact credit the Greeks with far more sexual licence than they admitted or admired—except in a few cosmopolitan cities like Alexandria. Sometimes it distorted the facts of history by confusing Hellenism with Orientalism.

Here the great sinner—how he would have welcomed the title!—is Pierre Louÿs (1870–1925), a vicious but talented writer.[53] He did not learn Greek at school, and, having read a poor translation of Homer, disliked even the *Iliad* and *Odyssey* until he found Leconte de Lisle's version. 'It was a revelation': he went on to read all Leconte de Lisle's translations, and then, at eighteen, began to learn Greek seriously. Strange how many modern poets have learnt Latin without enthusiasm at school, and then, under a more vital impetus, have taught themselves the Greek language or literature in adolescence: Keats, Shelley, Goethe, many more. Louÿs always revered Leconte de Lisle for teaching him to think of classical Greece as the ideal home of the human body and spirit; and Louis Ménard, whom he called 'a great pagan, a saintly man' and imitated in his story *A New Pleasure*. At twenty-three Louÿs produced the first French translation of the exquisite epigrams of the Syrian-Greek poet Meleager, at twenty-four a rendering of Lucian's *Courtesans' Conversations*, and at twenty-five the book which made his name. This was *The Songs of Bilitis*, a collection of prose poems supposed to be translated from a Greek manuscript found in a tomb. It gives, in a form which is a cross between a diary and a volume of Hellenistic epigrams, the autobiography of a peasant girl of ancient Greece who, after the death of her first love, became a member of Sappho's circle of Lesbian lovers and poetesses, and then, just as naturally and happily, a temple-prostitute in Cyprus. Gide (to whom the first edition was dedicated) says Bilitis was modelled on Mériem ben Atala, an Arabian girl Louÿs met in Biskra; the landscapes are remembered from Louÿs's tours in north Africa and Egypt; the open-eyed frankness of the poems on homosexuality and prostitution is not Greek but oriental.[54] It is strange, so long after 'Dares the Phrygian', to see another romancer using the same device of the 'MS. found in a tomb' to carry a modern invention.[55] But this time it found a detective to expose it and a real hellenist to show its falsity. The great Ulrich von Wilamowitz-Moellendorff, professor of Greek at Berlin, knew perfectly well that *The Songs of Bilitis* were made 'out of whole cloth' by a young modern author; but, because Louÿs had pretended they were translations from an authentic Greek manuscript, fell upon him like a hawk on a rabbit. His review, in ten closely printed pages, brushes aside Louÿs's amateur scholarship, and even the anachronisms, to concentrate on the crucial faults of the book: that oriental passions and extravagances are attributed to the self-disciplined Greeks, and that a homosexual lust is represented as the moving force of Sappho's art. A woman who led a life like Bilitis, he concludes, *could* not have written great poems; and it is a complete falsification of the Greek ideals to think they aimed at producing such art or such people.[56]

Louÿs once wrote a poem saying that, when all the other Greek divinities died, only the goddess of love survived.[57] The year after *Bilitis* he dedicated a romantic novel to her more extreme avatars. *Aphrodite* was published at his own expense in early April 1896, and became an immediate best-seller, reaching its twenty-sixth edition in June. (Still very popular, it has attracted some outstandingly repulsive illustrators.) It is a story of Alexandria in the first century before Christ, the heroine a courtesan, the hero a sculptor even more sought after and not less bored with love. Only

her indifference attracts him; after she promises herself and he
dreams of possessing her (in a scene largely composed of quotations
from the Song of Solomon), he loses interest again, to regain it
only when she has been cruelly executed for blasphemously posing
as Aphrodite in the goddess's stolen regalia. Using her corpse as
a model, he carves his masterpiece.

The immediate literary ancestors of this odd book were France's
Thais, Mérimée's *Carmen* ('if you do not love me, I love you'),
and Flaubert's *Salammbô*. In structure it was based on Greek
tragedy, having five 'acts' with a *peripeteia*, or sudden reversal, at
the end of the fourth; it was filled with details imitated or quoted
from certain regions of Greek literature. But it was not a picture
of Greek life. Its heroine was a Syrian prostitute (there are
pointed allusions to Jewry as a half-barbarous Asiatic outpost), its
scene the polyglot megapolis of Alexandria (which was then no
more Greek than modern New Orleans is French or Rio de
Janeiro Portuguese), its goddess a divinity far more terrible and
Asiatic than the smiling spirit born of Aegean sea-foam, and its
morality, though striking, unlike all we know of Greece through
its greatest poetry and philosophy. Every age finds what it wants
in the classics. Evidently what Louÿs and his readers wanted was
not the clear water of Ilissus, beside which Socrates talked to young
Phaedrus of passion and the mastery of reason, but a draught from
the turbid Nile.

3. *Christianity is timid and feeble, paganism is strong and intense.*

The theory was put with great violence by another of the
Germans who were destroyed by their love for Greece. Friedrich
Wilhelm Nietzsche (1844–1900) went to the best German classical
school, Pforta, with Wilamowitz-Moellendorff; became professor
at Basle before he was twenty-five; and in 1872 produced a theory
of the origin of Greek tragedy which—bitterly attacked by
Wilamowitz—was historically false but contained some psychological truth.[58] He held that the essence of Greek art was misrepresented as calm, impassive, statuesque. It grew, he believed,
out of a tension between the wild forces represented by Dionysus,
god of the dithyrambic frenzy, cruel and uncivilizable, which roves
the forests and mountains, and the spirit of Apollo, god of light,
beauty, healing, and art. It was the result of the artistic sense
working, not on a neutral material, but on savage subconscious

urges. So Greek art is not cool and white and lifeless, a Greek play not a lofty, formalized, intellectual exercise: they are the products of violent conflict, and represent not serene repose but a hard-earned victory.

Nietzsche admired Greek art for its intensity; its difficulty; its aristocratic quality. He despised Christianity because he thought it weak, easy, and vulgar. Aeschylus, the eagle of poetry, was one of his heroes. Another Greek, who wrote at an earlier stage in history, during the class-wars of the sixth century, interested Nietzsche deeply and helped to form his dislike for Christian moral ideals. This was Theognis, who called his fellow oligarchs 'good' and the commoners 'bad'—or, as we still say, with a reminiscence of feudal distinctions, 'gentle men' and 'villains'.[59] Like Theognis, Nietzsche held that only the moral values of the powerful few were worthy of respect. He loathed Christianity as the 'morality of slaves' and of 'herd-animals'. He thought that *Blessed are the peacemakers* meant *Don't fight for your rights*; that *Blessed are the meek* meant *Lie down when you are challenged* (*and feel happy because your conqueror will be damned in the next world*). The gospel of loving one's neighbour seemed to Nietzsche—as Socrates' definitions of justice seemed to the demagogue and the propagandist[60]—to be a trick to get the few strong, clever, energetic, brave men, who care nothing for others and who can rule the world, to submit to namby-pamby rules designed to cripple their talents and reduce their natural superiority. And he described Christianity as a Jewish stratagem of revenge on the Romans and on the whole world:

'To smash the strong, to make great hopes sickly, to cast suspicion on the happy enjoyment of beauty, to bend all independence, virility, conquest, mastery, all instincts that are peculiar to the highest and most successful type of man, into uncertainty, troubles of conscience, disruption of the self, in fact to convert all love for earthly things and for the domination of the earth into hatred for the earth and earthly things —*that* was what the Church made its task.'[61]

'The Jews—a people "born for slavery", as Tacitus and the entire ancient world would say, "the chosen people among the peoples", as they themselves say and believe—the Jews have carried out a masterly reversal of values . . . their prophets have confused "rich", "godless", "bad", "violent", "sensuous" all together, and for the first time have stamped the word "world" as a shameful expression. In this transformation of values . . . lies the significance of the Jewish people: with it begins the *slave-revolt in morality*.'[62]

And yet it is possible to find, among the extremely unsystematic utterances of Nietzsche on the conflict of Christianity and paganism, evidence that he saw deeper than that. He knew that Socrates was one of the first to criticize a morality of instinct and tradition which had long been, but in a changing world could not continue to be, sufficient unto itself; and that in that sense Socrates the stonemason was one of the forerunners of the Galilaean carpenter.[63]

Nietzsche once spoke of Flaubert as a 'decent citizen' who tormented himself by bitterly enjoying the stupidity of the middle class.[64] But Nietzsche cultivated the aristocratic foible of admiring his ancestors and hating his peers. Like him, Gustave Flaubert (1821–80) detested nineteenth-century morality, despised contemporary Christianity as unfit for intelligent people,[65] and said that the world had passed through three stages, the last being the lowest: paganism, Christianity, and skunkery, his own age being ruled by the skunks.[66] His chief complaint against the era of skunkery was its pettiness. No one could live a genuine, full life. Everyone was the slave of second-rate delusions, whether created by himself (as the provincial doctor's wife invented dreams of romance) or delivered by the newspapers and other garbage-factories.[67] Flaubert did not write poetry; but he felt the ugliness of his century as acutely as a Tennyson or a Gautier. Sometimes he would dissect it in a coldly realistic novel; and sometimes he would reconstruct the world of the past, where, instead of bogus romances, there were fiery passions and ardent asceticisms, instead of the middle class with top-hat and bank-book there were warriors and barbarians and saints, instead of Louis Napoleon there were St. Anthony and Hamilcar. *Salammbô*, one of the greatest historical novels in the world, is not about Greece, nor about Rome, but about the rival culture of Carthage. That modern Brueghel, *The Temptation of St. Anthony*, is about an early Christian hermit in Egypt. The sources from which Flaubert drew his material for both books are Greek and Latin, but the subjects lie on or over the frontiers of the classical world. Like Louÿs, he was guided towards his counter-assertion of values superior to those of the modern world by reading classical literature. Pater quotes a letter in which Flaubert says he is re-reading the *Aeneid*, with its phrases haunting him like unforgettable melodies.[68] But like Louÿs he could not, or would not, describe the highest states of Greco-Roman

civilization as a contrast to the life he lived and hated. The
books he wrote on the past were ferociously cruel, and, compared
with both Greek and modern ideals, perverse in an oriental way.
Flaubert's hatred of his own vulgar age pushed him (like Nietzsche)
into admiration for the extreme opposite: he did not falsify it, but
constructed it from materials which he found in Carthage and the
Thebaid, on the further extreme of the calmer, richer, better-
balanced world of Greece and Rome.

But Christianity, in spite of this opposition, was still a vital
force. Many nineteenth-century writers admired the simple faith,
the moral purity, the energy and courage of the early Christians.
They thought the poems and novels which represented the pagan
world as a heaven on earth were false in fact and morally dangerous.
Confident that the gospel was saving the world, they set out to
show that, when it was first preached, it had met with even more
bitter opposition from an age even more corrupt and brutal.
Chateaubriand put this point of view in *The Martyrs*, whose form
and ill-chosen style kept it from reaching a very wide public.[69]
But the rise of prose fiction encouraged the production of a number
of popular novels based on classical documents and describing the
conflict between Christian and pagan ideals in the Roman empire.
They were not all well written—they were on a far lower aesthetic
level than Swinburne's poems and the rest of the pagan opposition:
but they had an immense circulation and influence. In particular,
they established the belief that Rome fell because it was an
immoral pagan empire. This is now widely believed, and the fact
that both the western and the eastern empires fell long after they
had officially become Christian is ignored.

The best known of these novels are:

The Last Days of Pompeii (1834), by E. G. E. L. Bulwer-Lytton,
later Lord Lytton (1803–73), a melodramatic description of
the struggle of Christianity and paganism emphasized by the
symbolic destruction of a wicked pagan city.

Hypatia (1853), by Charles Kingsley (1819–75), a more complex story of the conflict between the northern barbarians,
the effete pagans of Greece and Rome, their higher ideals
as represented by the beautiful girl-philosopher of Alexandria, earnest and noble Christians like St. Augustine, and
the cruel intolerance of the Christian mob that lynched

Hypatia.[70] Kingsley sub-titled the book *New Foes with an Old Face*, feeling that the murder of Hypatia sprang from the root of religious intolerance, which he thought was sending out new shoots in his day.

Ben-Hur (1880), by Lewis Wallace (1827–1905), who served as a major-general in the Northern army during the Civil War, and saved Washington from the Confederate advance. His book, in exciting and often memorable scenes, dramatizes the interaction of Romans, Jews, and Christians during the lifetime of Jesus. The hero is a Jewish nobleman condemned to the galleys on the charge of attempting to murder a Roman official. His life as a galley-slave, his shipwreck and escape, the healing of his mother and sister from leprosy, and above all the famous chariot-race against his Roman friend and enemy, are among the most vivid descriptions of the ancient world ever published.

Quo Vadis? (1896), by the eminent Polish novelist Henryk Sienkiewicz (1846–1916), is a laboriously detailed account of the penetration of Rome by Christianity during the reign of Nero and the ministry of Peter and Paul, ending with bloodcurdling descriptions of the Neronian persecutions—which gain fervour from Sienkiewicz's hatred for the German and Russian persecutors of Poland. The story is really a patriotic manifesto, in which, despite frightful sufferings, the small community of early Christians vindicating itself against the oppressions of a vast and powerful empire expresses the admiration and hope which Sienkiewicz felt for his own Poland. The correspondence is rather over-emphasized by the fact that the heroine is a Christian princess from the area of northern Europe which later became Poland.[71] Authentic historical documents are followed—although not always quite accurately; there are acute character-sketches of St. Peter, Nero, and Petronius;[72] but the plot, which culminates with a gigantic Pole killing a huge German aurochs in the arena with his bare hands in order to free the princess tied naked to its horns, is really too sensational.

Much of the interest in these books came from their vivid historical detail, which was a product of the broader and deeper knowledge of ancient history made available by nineteenth-century research.[73] Fénelon's *Telemachus* owed part of its popularity to the same interest, at an earlier stage, which later made *The Travels of Young Anacharsis in Greece* a continuous best-seller for generations.[74] Even in the prosaic heart of Macaulay, his Scottish blood and the romantic ballad-fervour blended with Niebuhr's theory that the chief early Roman historical records were folk-poems about great events: the result was his stirring *Lays of Ancient Rome*;[75] and school libraries are still full of text-books disguised as fiction, like Becker's *Gallus*, whose fault is that they have too much matter and too little art.

The Christian novels, however, owed more of their influence to the fact that they countered the rationalist criticism of biblical tradition which began with David Strauss's *Life of Jesus* and grew to a tall and shaky structure of hypothesis throughout the nineteenth century. It is impossible to believe in Christianity without accepting its traditions with faith as well as with reason. Therefore the purely rational type of criticism, which sometimes treated the gospel and the growth of the faith purely as 'a product, like sugar or vitriol', was in effect anti-Christian. Against that, these novels showed the establishment of Christianity as the deliberate intervention of God to save a spiritually dying world. After the revolutionary pangs which brought the nineteenth century to birth, this interpretation was, to many, very welcome.

Finally, as we have shown in outline, pagan ethics and pagan ideals were being defended by some of the most eminent poets, philosophers, and novelists of the day, and the morality of nineteenth-century Christianity was being attacked directly and by implication. As a counter-attack, these novelists now produced pro-Christian stories which revived Argument 1 of the Battle of the Books—in a new form, with a stronger foundation of fact.[76] Their counter-propaganda had an effect still very active to-day. It was another of the many conflicts, which are also confluences, between the spirit of Christendom and the spirit (through which it reached us) of Greece and Rome.

There is one other novel which deserves deeper attention, since it is in a different category from the rest. This is Walter Pater's *Marius the Epicurean* (1885). It is a study of the process of Christian conversion, not through passion or miracle, but through reflection. Its hero is a thoughtful young Roman noble, living in the age of the Antonines—which Gibbon and others believed to be the highest point ever reached by human existence on this planet. At first the warm paganism of the household gods and the spirits of the farm is enough for him. The deaths of his mother and of a close friend, a sceptic, plunge him into doubt. He becomes an Epicurean. Then, after meeting and admiring Marcus Aurelius, he rises to Stoicism. From Stoicism he penetrates deeper into the realm of the spirit. He is about to become a Christian when he is arrested (at a Christian meeting), and dies for the faith to which he does not yet belong. Like Vergil, like many noble pagans, he has become a soul worthy of Christ.

This deeply poetic book has far less action and personal interest than the others we have described, but much more understanding of the best in both paganism and Christianity. It shows the long difficult process of conversion as it occurred in many thoughtful souls of the late Roman empire, and as it was repeated in many no less troubled spirits of the nineteenth century. And, instead of showing the great historical change from Greece and Rome to Christendom as a war, in which one side was victorious and the other crushed out of existence, it makes us see the long interpenetration by which the highest elements of Greek and Roman spiritual life were taken up and transformed in Christianity.

21

A CENTURY OF SCHOLARSHIP

'Time to taste life,' another would have said,
  'Up with the curtain!'
This man said rather, 'Actual life comes next?
  Patience a moment!
Grant I have mastered learning's crabbed text,
  Still there's the comment.'

BROWNING[1]

D URING the century which succeeded the revolutionary era and
closed with the First World War, classical knowledge increased both in distribution and in depth. More was known about
Greece and Rome than ever before; and more people learnt something about Greece and Rome than ever before. But the two
graphs of increase did not coincide. During the first fifty or sixty
years they ran roughly parallel. After that, one began to turn down,
while the other kept on going up—more slowly, perhaps, but still
continuously until 1914.

Throughout the century scholars were discovering more and
more about Greco-Roman antiquity, and the growing sum of
knowledge was being tabulated and made more and more available.
By 1914 the library of the average professional classicist was ten
times larger, and the books at his disposal in his college library
fifty times more numerous, than those which his predecessor in
1814 could command.

Meanwhile the distribution of classical knowledge at first increased; and then fell off. In the first sixty or seventy years of the
nineteenth century the existing schools and universities grew
bigger; many new ones were founded, private, and religious, and
state-supported; more boys and even girls were encouraged to
attend; a new seriousness of educational purpose made itself felt.
Classical education gained a great impetus from the striking advances in Greek and Latin scholarship which were being achieved,
and also from the inspiration of widely admired authors whose
classical knowledge was part of their reputation: Goethe, Chateaubriand, Tennyson. However, towards the eighteen-eighties the
classics began to lose their hitherto undisputed primacy in education. Other subjects—particularly the physical sciences—were
called upon to supply the demand for experimentalists and techni-

cians. New disciplines introduced in universities began to compete for attention: political philosophy, economics, psychology. Modern languages were taught more widely, as avenues to both culture and commerce. It became obviously impracticable to teach Greek and Latin to the huge numbers of children now entering public schools every year. The general increase in material prosperity which marked the nineteenth century out from nearly all other eras in human history encouraged a widespread demand for schooling which was 'practical', which would train boys and girls first and foremost to make things and earn money. For all these reasons the teaching of classics in schools and universities fell off in the two generations preceding the first war. The process had another, perhaps less apparent cause, which will be discussed later in this chapter.

At the beginning of the nineteenth century one man could sit in a library and master the whole of classical knowledge. He would have had to be exceptionally gifted, with health, talent, money, good training, and what the Greeks called 'brazen bowels'; but he could have done it. Mr. Gibbon, who spent much time and effort outside the subject, still mastered a great deal of it; while Bentley and Porson, Mabillon and Niebuhr, came very close to complete coverage. But at the end of the period no one man could possibly have known all that was to be known about Greece and Rome. The best he could hope for was to understand the fundamentals, to follow the main channels along which research was moving, and to be at home in a number of fields chosen by himself as illuminating the rest of classical antiquity. (One of the differences between a good and a bad scholar is that one specializes in topics which complement each other, and together light up most of the general area of his interest, while the other works on peripheral and unrelated provinces, like the frontier administrator who tries without success to understand the central problems of an empire.) It was not merely that the sum of things known about Greek and Roman civilization had become too large, that there were too many books for one man to read. Classical knowledge had been developed, rapidly and intensively, along dozens of divergent lines, too varied and specialized for anybody to master them all, and for any but the most gifted and industrious of scholars to survey in a single lifetime.

The increase and intensification of classical knowledge in the nineteenth century were due partly to the closer contact of scholars with social and political life, partly to the use of modern industrial techniques, but chiefly to the application of the methods of physical science to what had until then been regarded as a field midway between art and philosophy. For instance:

1. *New branches of knowledge were developed through the application of the direct exploratory methods of experimental science.*

Archaeology had existed for centuries, chiefly for artistic ends. It now acquired new meaning with the work of Heinrich Schliemann (1822–90), a retired business-man who discovered and excavated the sites of Troy in 1873 and Mycenae in 1876. He had predecessors; and he committed many errors; yet by applying the decisive and practical principles of the explorer to an open field of scholarship, he literally made history.

Scarcely any modern man had seen papyri until after the middle of the nineteenth century. Papyri are pieces of the Egyptian paper made from slices of giant bamboo-like reeds: they were the usual Greek and Roman writing-material until after A.D. 100. The oldest documents previously known to have survived from antiquity were written on vellum, incised in clay, or carved and painted on stone. But in the eighteenth century a number of rolls of papyrus, badly charred and almost unreadable, were recovered from the ruins of Herculaneum, the sister city of Pompeii. Next, a few rolls, more or less intact, were discovered in Egypt, and passed from hand to hand until they reached European collections. And then expeditions went out to Egypt, explored the sites of former Greek settlements and other likely areas, and began to bring back loads of papyri which had been preserved in the dry sands. Some were literary, but most were financial, legal, and personal documents straight from the hand of the writer. To read and interpret them became a new branch of classical scholarship.

Anthropology, linguistics, comparative religion, and other departments of knowledge, although not wholly new, were now founded as practical sciences, enlarged, and developed in the special field of classics.

2. *Established branches of classical knowledge were revised and elaborated by the application of scientific method.*

The history of the Greco-Roman world was critically analysed— in the same way as the traditions of Christianity, the records of

Egypt, Babylonia, and primitive Europe, and the whole of medieval and modern history were now scrutinized, not from the pulpit or the writing-desk, but under the microscope. Classical literature also was subjected to clinically detailed examination. The manuscripts of the Greek and Latin authors, the literary patterns in which they wrote, the affiliations between individuals and schools, and the vocabulary, sources, and content of single authors were all studied in hitherto unparalleled detail. Greek and Roman literature and history were reinterpreted in the light of the methods and results of other branches of study. Our knowledge of Homer was enlarged not only by the study of the epics of other peoples—the Finns, the Anglo-Saxons, the Indians—but by the discovery of some of the cities mentioned in the *Iliad* and *Odyssey*, and of weapons, ornaments, and utensils comparable with those used by Homer's people. The origins of Greek drama were illuminated by anthropological parallels and reconstructions. (The only trouble with this was that it sometimes relegated the conscious arts of Greece and Rome to a less important place than they deserved: for instance, the art of rhetoric, highly developed in antiquity, was neglected.)

3. *The scattered facts in many fields of classical knowledge were now completed, centralized, and made readily available.*

Just as Johnson's *Dictionary*, made in the baroque period, was succeeded in the nineteenth century by the *Oxford English Dictionary*, so the smaller classical handbooks of earlier times were now replaced by great reference manuals written by many hands and aiming at absolute completeness: dictionaries—Liddell and Scott's Greek lexicon, the *Thesaurus Linguae Latinae*; encyclopaedias—Daremberg and Saglio's *Dictionnaire des antiquités classiques*, the enormous Pauly–Wissowa–Kroll *Real-Encyclopädie der classischen Altertumswissenschaft*. All the known Greek inscriptions in the world were collected in the *Corpus Inscriptionum Graecarum*, familiarly known as the *CIG*, and all the Latin ones in the *CIL*. Large, detailed, comprehensive histories of Greek and Roman religion, political development, literature, fine art, &c., were compiled, often by many authors and in many volumes.

4. *Mass-production methods were used to make classical books available to a wide public.*

Long series of classical texts in a standard format were published, with the ultimate aim of covering all classical literature: the set issued by Teubner of Leipzig was the largest, and next, far behind, the Oxford Classical Texts, and the Didot series in France.

The university presses began publishing a vast variety of scholarly works on 'everything knowable', the mass of which is one of the finest intellectual monuments of the nineteenth century.

Educational publishers produced series of annotated editions for schools and colleges. Nothing like these had been issued since the Renaissance except—significant parallel—the collection of standard texts with Latin prose versions and notes, now known as the Delphin series, because they were designed *ad usum serenissimi Delphini*, for the use of His Serene Highness the Dolphin, or Dauphin of France. The best in this line are the Teubner school series in Germany and the red Macmillans in Britain.

Lists of standard translations of Greek and Latin classics began to be published. A great deal of harm was done here by hack word-by-word translations made to help dullards and ill-taught schoolboys. The Bohn series (parodied by Kipling and Graves in *Horace's Fifth Book of Odes*) helped to kill the interest of many intelligent boys in classical literature by making it appear both ugly and stupid. It has now been replaced by the very unequal Loeb series, which contains some 200 authors. France has the Budé collection (named after Guillaume Budé, the scholarly friend of Rabelais), often useful but sometimes unreliable.

5. *The technique of specialization developed by nineteenth-century science and industry was applied to research in classical scholarship, as to every other branch of learning.*

An almost inconceivable number of articles, papers, essays, pamphlets, dissertations, treatises, and theses on small areas of knowledge, particular aspects of individual authors, single blocks of facts selected from a larger range, new theories, unknown personalities, unguessed connexions and unobserved parallels and untraced derivations, was now produced—partly under the orders of professors who were building up their own subjects, partly to gain the doctorate for their authors, partly to win promotion out of an obscure post,[2] but also often from the disinterested belief that any objective contribution to knowledge, however small, was valuable.

Periodicals were founded, to collect the results of research which might otherwise remain unpublished, or like so many dissertations be lost in the limbo of limited editions; and, presumably, to organize the study of certain fields of classical knowledge which deserved exploration. The collected product of the most important of these journals now fills many bookshelves and contains a vast amount of valuable information. Such are *Hermes, Philologus,* the *Rheinisches Museum, The Classical Quarterly, The American Journal of Philology, La Revue de Philologie, Mnemosyne,* and the *Neue Jahrbücher für das klassische Altertum.*

6. *And to join all these activities together, societies were founded* throughout Europe and America: to meet and talk, to correspond and criticize, to discuss problems of common interest, and in general to encourage scholarship in the classics. All this activity was growing into an international exploration of truth, a 'federation of the world', but it was halted and crippled by the First World War, and, after an attempt at recovery, still further damaged by the Second.

Whether those days of free exchange of knowledge between men of learning in all countries will return within the next few centuries seems doubtful. Stanley Casson (killed in 1944) used to say that the present generation reminded him of one of the latest Roman poets, Sidonius Apollinaris—a Gallic noble who became bishop of Clermont. Sidonius spent some years (A.D. 461–67) living in retirement in France, visiting his friends and writing letters to a large circle of correspondents. The letters, which are bright and interesting, somehow survived the many centuries of savagery, massacre, gang-rule, and primitivism which followed his death. The odd thing is that Sidonius did not foresee those centuries, or anything like them: at least, not while he was writing his letters. Every now and then he mentioned that a woman had been carried off by outlaws and sold,[3] or described a half-civilized northern barbarian potentate who was more powerful than any Roman. But he did not understand that the barbarians and the outlaws were going to become more and more numerous and powerful; that the rich civilized cities were going to be attacked and destroyed in repeated wars and invasions; that the trade-routes would be broken, and remain broken for centuries; that the map was not rearranging its colours, but breaking up into isolated fragments; that law, and science, and philosophy, and cultivated codes of behaviour, and of course the treasures of literature and art which he himself loved, were about to dissolve, most of them apparently for ever, some to survive in gross transformations half-understood, some to be preserved in monasteries like the relics of miracle-working saints, and the rest to lie in tombs and pits like dormant seeds, to become alive only when they were restored to the light, hundreds of years later.

Are these shadows on so many of our horizons the outriders of another long night, like that which was closing in upon Sidonius? We cannot yet tell. But modern scholars must regret that they have to work during a time when, instead of that generous supra-national comradeship which helped to build the learning and culture of the sixteenth and nineteenth centuries, it is becoming more and more difficult to exchange opinions across the world, to bring from distant countries books where new and vital points of view are freely expressed, to carry on many-sided correspondences with far-off scholars and encounter no difficulties other than those involved in the common search for truth, and to feel oneself part of a world-wide structure of art and learning, greater than all the things that divide mankind: nationalities and creeds, fear and hate.

There were three special fields in which the new forces in classical scholarship affected literature (and, through literature, society) during the nineteenth century and the opening of the twentieth century. These were *history, translation*, and *education*. The third is by all odds the most important.

The history of the Greco-Roman world was rewritten by the scholars of the nineteenth century. The job is still unfinished, but it had been carried well forward by 1914.

The modern method of dealing with Greek and Roman history, and indeed all history, was introduced by a German-descended Dane who became professor at Berlin: Barthold Georg Niebuhr (1776–1831).[4] Although the outlines and many of the details of ancient history were already known, or believed to be known, Niebuhr revalued them by insisting on the distinction between first-hand and second-hand information, and by evolving methods of filling in the gaps. Many of his principles were fundamentally the same as those governing the work of the baroque scholars, but he applied them more rigorously, energetically, and imaginatively. Through his teaching, scholars grew accustomed to the idea that it is unsafe to trust any historian who writes long after the events he describes; and that, when such a historian is the only authority available, we should not swallow all he says, but rather try to penetrate through his writings to the sources which he used. For instance, our main authority for the history of early Rome is Livy. But Livy was as remote from Tarquin and Horatius as we are from the wars of the Roses. Therefore we must try to discover what sort of authentic contemporary evidence he had for the stories he related, in fact, how much he really knew about early Rome. Niebuhr conjectured that the main evidence he used was ballads handed down from old times by word of mouth. If this were true, obviously Livy's account of the period would be far less reliable than it appears, it would be melodramatic and biased and over-simplified.

A brilliant imaginative attempt to reconstruct these ballads was made by Macaulay in the *Lays of Ancient Rome*: his preface gives a useful summary of Niebuhr's theory, although most of us skip its measured prose in our eagerness to reach the irresistible gallop of

> He reeled, and on Herminius
> He leaned one breathing-space;
> Then, like a wild cat mad with wounds,
> Sprang right at Astur's face.

The only difficulty is that there is hardly any evidence that such ballads ever existed. Niebuhr belonged to the Time of Revolution; and as such he admired the unspoilt peasantry, which he felt *ought* to have a folk-poetry far more beautiful than anything produced in later times by professional poets.[5]

(Macaulay rightly stresses the fact that the principle was not new, but had been revived and energized by Niebuhr.[6] It was given additional weight by Leopold Ranke (1795–1886), who stated the ideal of the nineteenth-century historian in the phrase 'to show what really happened'.[7] Ranke was not a classical but a modern historian, and he himself said that in writing his famous *Criticism of Modern Historians* he was not thinking of Niebuhr. Yet he had

Niebuhr's bust in the place of honour in his study; and (as Mommsen said) 'all historians are Niebuhr's pupils'.)[8]

But if we cannot find any contemporary evidence, if all our books are late and imaginative, how can we discover what really happened? By inference, Niebuhr replies. Social forces do not emerge unexpectedly and disappear quickly. They leave long-lasting results. From the results we can infer the character and interaction of the forces, even though no eyewitness has left us a description of them. And we can strengthen our inferences from parallels elsewhere. Thus, Niebuhr was able to explain several complex problems in the economic history of early Rome from his own knowledge of the Danish and north German peasantry and his own experience as an expert in public finance. For another of his principles was the concept of social evolution, applied to classical antiquity. Nations, according to this theory, grow and change just as human beings do in the course of a lifetime. It is possible, therefore, for a historian who understands the regular stages of that development to work back (with the help of parallels observed in the life-history of other nations) from the known facts in the later development of a people, to reconstruct an earlier stage for which there is no direct evidence. A. J. Toynbee's *A Study of History* contains a brilliant application of this principle on a much larger scale; and in the nineteenth century Niebuhr's work helped, in England, to produce Grote's *History of Greece*, Arnold's *History of Rome*, and Macaulay's *History of England*.

The greatest classical historian of the nineteenth century was Theodor Mommsen (1817–1903). He published three volumes of his *Roman History* in 1854–6, covering the rise and fall of the republic. Then he stopped. He never went on to write the history of the empire—although, thirty years later, he produced a brilliant description of the provinces under imperial rule. This arrest is peculiar, all the more peculiar because Mommsen lived so long and wrote so much. He produced uniquely valuable treatises on the Roman coinage and Roman criminal law. His *Roman Constitutional Law* has been called 'the greatest historical treatise on political institutions ever written'.[9] And it was he who edited the huge *Corpus of Latin Inscriptions*—a task which demanded as much energy and organizing ability as building a transcontinental railway, to say nothing of the unrivalled knowledge Mommsen brought to bear on it.

Many attempts have been made to explain why his history of Rome was left incomplete. Fueter, the historian of historians, suggested that Mommsen refrained from writing about the empire because (a) he had no interest in the personal history of the emperors, and (b) he did not want merely to rewrite Tacitus and Suetonius.[10] This is clearly an inadequate explanation, for there is much more in the Roman empire than Tacitus, Suetonius, and the personal history of the emperors: and Mommsen knew that.

Mr. Toynbee begins his *Study of History* with a discussion of the invasion of modern historical thought by techniques and ways of thinking derived from the industrial system. He takes Mommsen as an illustration of this. He says that after Mommsen had written his history of the republic, 'he became almost ashamed of it and turned his magnificent energy and ability into other channels'.[11] Those other channels, Mr. Toynbee suggests, were the collection of the 'raw materials' of history and the work of superintending their 'manufacture', as a plant foreman superintends the construction of a series of motor-cars; and in this, Mr. Toynbee concludes, Mommsen was yielding to the spiritual pressures of industrialization.[12] This may be true. Part of it probably is. But it does not explain the abrupt break in Mommsen's work on Roman history, the difference in tone between its beginning and its continuance.

President Butler of Columbia University mentions the Mommsen problem in his reminiscences. He writes that he himself

'heard Mommsen say, at one of Zeller's Sunday evening gatherings, that the reason why he had never continued his *Römische Geschichte* through the imperial period was that he had never been able to make up his mind as to what it was that brought about the collapse of the Roman Empire and the downfall of Roman civilisation.'[13]

This looks like a deeper explanation, and perhaps brings us closer to the truth. Was Roman history a question which Mommsen could not answer? Yet he had answered the question of the Roman republic with sovereign confidence and brilliance. Why could he not answer the question of the empire? Did he feel that the empire could not be explained by the republic? or, perhaps, did he come to think that his own explanation of the republic was wrong?

Mommsen's *Roman History* is the only scholarly work in which he allowed his personal emotions to appear, and his personal judgements to stand on the same level as objective statements of fact. It is powerfully, sometimes violently, written, with far more emphasis on politics than on all other aspects of Roman civilization. Modern parallels are constantly drawn, in the manner to which Spengler has accustomed us since. The younger Cato appears as Don Quixote. The Roman aristocrats look like German Junkers. Pompey is a stupid sergeant-major; and Cicero is a flabby journalist, a shifty lawyer without principles or strength of character. Julius Caesar—whom other historians have seen as a political crook who ruined his country out of personal ambition— Caesar is superman, the ideal Roman. Energy, passion, a sense of immediacy boil through the book.

Now, Mommsen was not only a scholar but a politician. He was deeply involved in the revolution of 1848, and had to leave his post to avoid reprisals. It is clear, then, that his *Roman History* was sparked by his own experience of the 1848 débâcle. He could not admire the weak liberals. He loathed the feudal landowners of Germany. The working classes he felt to be passive, not active. What could he admire, then? The man of action, the master-spirit who would dominate the weaklings and break the stiff-necked and mould the passive and make a single powerful Reich. He wished for such a man in Germany: a Bismarck. He wrote that such a man had been the salvation of Rome: Caesar.

Why then did he not go on, and write the history of the empire? Was it not because he felt that, after all, the empire had been a failure? If Caesar and Caesarism were right for Rome, then Mommsen would have had to show that the Roman empire was happier, more virtuous, and more powerful than the Roman republic. And this he could not do. He did in fact describe the provinces, because they were actually happier under the imperial régime. In his *Roman Constitutional Law* he advanced the theory that the rule of Augustus was a 'dyarchy'—a division of power with the senate rather than a monarchy—and that the emperor's powers flowed out of the Roman republican constitution. This looks like an attempt to justify the rule of the emperors in a way which *cannot* be harmonized with the complaints of those Romans who actually lived under it. Any history of the Roman empire must face the problem of absolutism, and of the various forms of resistance to it: the senatorial and Stoic opposition, the military revolts, and the very important opposition of the Christians. Mommsen could not face this problem because he shrank from applying to the German empire, then just coming to its birth, the conclusions to which his answer must lead.

Instead, he spent much of his enormous energy on describing one of the greatest achievements of the Roman genius, which was begun by the republic and carried to completion by the emperors— Roman law. Posterity will always be grateful to him for the power and penetration which he used to expound this vast and important subject. But, if law is one of the pillars of Roman spiritual greatness, humane culture is another. It is regrettable, therefore, that Mommsen was misled by the political aspirations of his own time and place into making a radically false estimate of the man who, more than all others, transmitted Greco-Roman philosophical and literary thought to the modern world. The early empire is not only Augustus; it is Vergil. And in the last generation of the republic, and for the future of the world, the work of Caesar was no more vital than the work of Cicero.[14]

Another spiritual descendant of Niebuhr, but as patriotic a Frenchman as Mommsen was a German, was Numa-Denys Fustel de Coulanges (1830–89). Just as Ranke made his reputation by going behind the historians to the archives and reading the actual reports of the Venetian ambassadors, so Fustel de Coulanges demanded evidence, in the shape of a Greek or Roman document, for any assertion made about ancient history. His favourite question was 'Avez-vous un texte?' and he boasted of being the only man who had read every Latin text from the sixth century B.C. to the tenth century of the Christian era.[15] Where Mommsen emphasized the role of political institutions and individual statesmen in making history, Fustel regarded them both as less important than the social facts of which they were expressions and results. In the book which made his name, *The Ancient City*, he worked out the theory that religion was the determinant factor in moulding the institutions which are the framework of politics, and hence of history. He showed how, as little local deities became inadequate and disappeared, the small states that worshipped them lost their identities, merging into larger nation-states; and how, as the nation-states (Rome in particular) adopted more cosmopolitan, more universal deities, a world-religion, like the sun rising as the stars go out, at last occupied the whole firmament. Toynbee would say that the universal religion was the work of the internal proletariat, a phenomenon parallel to the universal state which was the later Roman empire; but Fustel held that Christianity, by overthrowing the old cults, destroyed Greco-Roman society and established Christendom on its ruins.

He then went on to spend his life on a political history of France during the period when it was ceasing to be fully Roman: *History of the Political Institutions of Ancient France*. The main purpose of this work was to confute a number of modern historians by proving that Roman Gaul was not conquered, not crushed and transformed, by Germanic tribes in the Frankish, Visigothic, and Burgundian invasions of the fifth century A.D.; that the language, law, religion, and social structure of Gaul were consequently not germanized; that the theory of 'German virtues' regenerating the decadent French was—however pleasing to the emotions of Germans—false to the facts; and that it was quite untrue to say that the French nobility was descended from conquering Germans and the vassals and peasants from conquered Gauls—a theory which would represent the French Revolution as one of the latest battles in a struggle which had begun more than a thousand years before. This question had been argued in the eighteenth century, by Dubos against Boulainvilliers, but had gained new importance with the rise of nineteenth-century nationalist feeling.[16] Fustel's interpretation of the invasions took long to penetrate and was bitterly attacked, but is now widely accepted, and not in France alone.

The last of these great men, and the first of the modern super-historians who survey the whole universe of the past (to which the present generation is attached, like a new and not particularly significant asteroid), was Eduard Meyer (1855–1930), a scholar qualified by a knowledge not only of Greek and Latin but of their more abstruse dialects, and of Hebrew, Arabic, Sanskrit, and Egyptian. He wrote the first useful history of Egypt; an invaluable account of the economic development of the ancient world; and an unfinished *History of the Ancient World*—which he could never complete because it was constantly being revised as fresh discoveries were made. Meyer's special contribution to history was a combination of the ideas of Gibbon and Niebuhr—that, although nations develop severally, they are all parts of a common process, the history of human civilization. Thus, it is impossible to understand Greece without knowing the history of the other Mediterranean peoples. Isolated views are distorted. This is now widely recognized—in politics, in science, in comparative literature, in aesthetic history, in the history of religion. Meyer much admired Oswald Spengler (1880–1936), the author of *The Decline and Fall of the West*; and it is the modern universal historians like Spengler and Toynbee who are his real successors.[17]

Many *translations of classical books* were made during the nineteenth and early twentieth centuries; and a number of new theories of translation were put into practice. There were some brilliant results. But the total effect was unsatisfying.

Translation is a difficult art. The translator must be a good scholar in a foreign language—or else have access to the results of good scholarship, together with an unerring flair for divining what is right and useful among them. And he must in his own language be an extremely good writer. It is hard enough to set one's own thoughts on paper in prose, still harder in poetry; but setting down the thoughts of another man who thought in another tongue means that, although one is spared the pangs of creation, one suffers the keenest tortures in finding the right words and choosing the right order for them. Now, during this period the difficult art of translation did not progress so far or so surely as other branches of classical learning and of general literature. Before we discuss the reasons for this, let us survey the field. It will be best to examine the English translators, who are better known to most readers of this book, and who are typical of the general trends in European translation.

The most interesting documents on the subject in English are Matthew Arnold's lectures *On translating Homer* and his essay *On translating Homer. Last words* (1861–2). Both were aimed at an erudite and affected verse translation of the *Iliad* published in 1856 by the eccentric professor F. W. Newman, and in particular at the assumptions in Newman's preface.[18] It was a common practice for Victorian critics to attach a general discussion to a particular criticism; but although Arnold at first broadened his treatment of the subject by bringing in Chapman, Pope, Cowper, and other translators of Homer, he eventually fell into rather trivial disputation with Newman, which blurred the general outline of the problem and lowered the tone he had intended to maintain. Nor did he assist his criticism by including some lumbering and irregular hexameters of his own design and manufacture. But the chief merit of his criticism is that it emphasizes, clearly and un-forgettably, the fact that Homer is a poet, a great and noble poet.

The revival of interest in folk-poetry, which was part of the movement of thought in the revolutionary era, had greatly changed the general estimate of Homer. Pope saw him as a court poet in a rather primitive court. Many (though not all) of Pope's successors saw him as Homer the Rhymer, and translated him into the jaunty metre and quaint old-fashioned language of the ballads. Newman's preface and the manner of his translation made him an excellent representative of this school, for, by recoiling from the polished ice of the baroque translators, he had fallen among the hedges and ditches of the ballad-mongers. He writes:

'The style of Homer himself is direct, popular, forcible, quaint, flowing, garrulous, abounding with formulas, redundant in particles and affirmatory interjections. . . . In all these respects it is similar to the old English ballad. . . . The moral qualities of Homer's style being like to those of the English ballad, we need a metre of the same genius. It must be fundamentally musical and popular. Only those metres which, by the very possession of these qualities, are liable to degenerate into doggerel, are suitable to reproduce the ancient Epic. . . . I ought to be quaint; I ought not to be grotesque.'[19]

This preface is followed by a glossary of his own quaint words: *behight* (= stipulate), *bragly* (= braw, proudly fine), *gramsome* (= direful), *sithence* (= ever since), and so forth. And then off he pelts into twenty-four books of ballad metre, modelled on

> She kissed his cheek, she kamed his hair,
>   As oft she did before, O,
> She drank the red blood frae him ran,
>   On the dowie houms o' Yarrow.

But only a very strong-willed Victorian could have refused to see, before he ever reached the Battle at the Ships, that Homer's rich vocabulary, spacious descriptions, and flowing rhetoric could not be crushed into that little ditty-measure. The result was the painful incongruity which Arnold denounced:

> Beneath the car the axle,
> And the broad rims orbicular, with gore of men were pelted.[20]

Arnold's criticism of this translation had two results. The first was that he destroyed the false parallel between Homer and the ballads. This he did by destroying Newman's translation, but in passing he also attacked Maginn's *Homeric Ballads* and Macaulay's *Lays of Ancient Rome*.[21] The second was that, by putting Homer on a level with Dante and Milton, by discussing their grandeurs as being unlike but comparable, by defining the difference between Shakespeare's rapid power and the serenity of Homer, by introducing illuminating comparisons with the moderns, Wordsworth, Longfellow, and Tennyson, and by maintaining almost throughout a tone of unmistakable, unaffected love for great poetry with all its various possibilities, he raised Homeric criticism out of the morass of pedantry, conjecture, dissection, and tastelessness into which it had been sinking. His lectures were an implicit protest against the scholarly attitudes to Homer which had become prevalent throughout Europe and America—that the *Iliad* and *Odyssey* were remarkable collections of facts about the Bronze and early Iron Ages; that they were monuments of Homeric grammar (which of course is so interesting because of its differences from Attic grammar); that they were fascinating relics of the Aeolic dialect; or anything except the essential fact that they were, and remain, great poems, among the greatest in the whole world.

For all that, there were mistakes and overstatements in Arnold's criticism, while Newman had a certain amount of right on his side.[22] And the crucial problem was not fully argued out by either of them. Yet it is fundamental. It recurs whenever the time comes for a new translation of a great classic to be made. Arnold begins by saying that every translator of Homer should remember, and in his version show, that Homer is (1) rapid, (2) plain and direct in language, (3) plain and direct in thought, and (4) noble. He goes on to show how various English translations of Homer have failed through missing one or other of these qualities. Most readers would agree with him on the first, and third, and fourth. But the crux of his argument with Newman was the second. For Homer is often the very reverse of plain and direct in language, and seems undeniably obscure and odd. This raises a radical question of taste, closely connected with difficult problems of scholarship, which both Arnold and Newman ought to have analysed in detail. Here is an outline of the difficulty.

Homer uses words which no other Greek poet ever employs; he is very free with strange verbal forms and combinations of particles and metrical tricks and relics of obsolete letters and combinations of disparate dialects and unintelligible ejaculations. Some of his phrases look really unnatural and distorted. The Greeks themselves found it difficult to explain such parts of his language. Scholars argued—not about its fine shades, but about its real meanings. Erudite allusive poets (like Apollonius) embedded fragments of it in their own poetry: still not quite understanding it, but hoping that it would produce the right effect, like Chatterton and Browning with *slug-horn* and Spenser with *derring-do*. It is a splendidly flexible and sonorous language, but it is odd and difficult.

Nevertheless, Homer's thought is direct and plain.

This phenomenon is not so hard to understand if we look at the subject-matter of the *Iliad*. The characters, and their motives, and the lines of the story, are direct and plain. But the settings, the accessories, are odd and difficult: weapons, strategy, customs— it is not that they are remote from us, like the customs of *Beowulf*, but that they are difficult in another way, apparently through confusion and incompatibility. (Even the life which we see through the windows of Homer's similes is different from the life led by his characters.) Now, suppose a great poet had blended many traditions which he had received as vehicles of great poetry or of great poetic material—phrases, transitional formulas, ennobling adjectives; and passages of narrative and description, attached to famous names and polished by the work of generations of craftsmen. Suppose that sometimes these traditions were conflicting, because they came from different places and times, or through different channels. Suppose, again, that the poet himself did not always intellectually understand all the phrases and descriptions, but felt them to be valuable because they were the setting of noble events, the very habit of great men as they lived. And finally, suppose that such a poet had lived towards the end of a long succession of invasions, migrations, and destructions, in which customs and language had suffered many changes, some surviving, some only dimly remembered, and others swept away, while the ideals of heroism and beauty and noble poetry had remained—not surviving with the skin of the teeth, but illumined and intensified. Such a poet might be Homer, and his poetry might look like the *Iliad* and the *Odyssey*.

The problem then is how to convey, in English verse, the extremely complex impression which we receive when reading

Homer. The narrative is swift, the rhetoric sweeps us on grandly and surely, the scope and depth of the whole poem are so vast that they bear witness to the magnificence of the spirit which conceived and worked it out. But, for all its splendour, the language is sometimes odd and obscure, and details of the descriptions are hard to comprehend. That is the difficulty of translating the epics.

Arnold, who confined himself to three lectures and one article, and Newman, in his long rebuttal, did not examine this question fully. They approached it from different sides. Newman had the best of it in Greek, because he did emphasize and prove the strangeness of Homer's language, which makes it quite impossible for us to call it 'eminently plain and direct'. But he omitted one essential fact—apparently because he was incapable of seeing it. That was the fact which Arnold saw; and Arnold had the best of it in English. The fact is that, even when Homer's language seems odd, it is always beautiful: vividly decorative, or curiously memorable, or rich and melodious in sound, or all together. What was wrong with Newman's version, and with his principles, was that he omitted beauty. Arnold had taste; Newman had none. *Dappergreaved Achaeans*, alone, would damn him.

But there was another aspect of the problem, which Newman raised in his preface and Arnold dismissed in his first lecture, but which is not irrelevant. Should a translator try to reproduce the effect Homer's poetry produced on its Greek audiences? If Homer seemed difficult to them, should the English translation be made to seem difficult to English readers? Arnold said the question was meaningless, 'for this simple reason, that we cannot possibly tell *how* the *Iliad* "affected its natural hearers" '. This is, however, not quite true. We have enough evidence, even apart from the philological facts given by Newman in his *Reply*, to know that the *Iliad* struck the classical Greeks as odd and antique, and that some of its nobility consisted for them in that impression of oddity and antiquity. (Of course, the men for whom Homer himself sang, steeped in epic poetry as they must have been, no doubt understood and felt it as deeply as he himself did.) On the other hand, we must never forget that the classical Greeks learnt Homer in childhood, and were constantly quoting and hearing Homer throughout their lives. Therefore, although his language sounded unlike anything else, they found it quite *familiar*: even if they missed the exact meaning or found the words peculiarly shaped, they felt what the poetry meant.

There is a modern parallel for this. For many generations the English and Scots have been reading the King James version of the Bible at school and Sunday-school; they have been hearing it at least once a week read aloud and expounded in church; it has been quoted again and again; many of its phrases have passed into the English language. Most of it is quite familiar; and yet it is not all understood. Who knows what *anathema* means, or its expansion *Anathema Maran-atha*?[23] What is *the mark of the beast*, and who are *the poor in spirit*?[24] Even the hyperbole which I used a few paragraphs ago, *escape with the skin of the teeth*, is very strange as soon as one looks closely at it.[25] But all these and many other such phrases were familiar to educated English-speaking people throughout the nineteenth century, and were used with a perception of most of their meaning and all of their force which was a good substitute for intellectual comprehension. That was the sort of perception which, thanks to education and familiarity, the classical Greeks had when dealing with Homer's language. That is one of the reasons why his poetry has been called the Bible of Greece.

The question how Homer struck the classical Greek audiences who loved him so much is then neither insoluble nor irrelevant. The suggested parallel of the English Bible (although omitting Homer's magnificent verse and much of his sonority) offers a solution to the problem of finding a style. The *Iliad* and *Odyssey* might be translated into the strong, vivid, dignified, often melodious, often strange and archaic and yet familiar and welcome prose of the Authorized Version. Arnold himself, towards the end of his third lecture, attempted a translation of part of *Iliad* 6, justified his choice of words by citing the Bible, and recommended Homeric translators to take Cruden's *Concordance to the Holy Scriptures* for a guide in difficulties of language.

This also was the solution adopted by the most influential English translator of Homer in the late nineteenth century. Andrew Lang (1844-1912) was not a classical scholar, and often lamented his relative ignorance of Greek; but he had a vast knowledge of the heroic ages of the world and their poetry, and he had admirable taste. His *Homer and the Epic*, in refuting the niggling criticism which had led scholars to dissect the two poems into collections of ill-assorted 'lays' put together by what Wilamowitz called a 'botcher', was common sense raised to the point of brilliance. In collaboration with more exact classicists he produced versions of the *Odyssey* (with S. H. Butcher) in 1879 and the *Iliad* (with Walter Leaf and Ernest Myers) in 1883. They became very popular. Their style was stately without being inflated, and, through use of the vocabulary and syntax of the King James translators, contrived to be almost as varied and strange, almost as intelligible and noble, as Homer. But they are in prose: a fatal defect. To read a prose translation of Homer, however skilful, is like hearing a single pianist, however gifted, playing a version of Beethoven's Ninth Symphony.

Matthew Arnold himself apparently felt the failure of the hexameter translations with which he experimented in his lectures. He made no more attempts to translate Homer. But in two heroic poems which he published in 1853 and 1855 he had already tried to embody in English verse some of what he thought the most important Homeric excellences. The poems are epic fragments, what the Greeks called *epyllia*. They have lived longer than his imitation of Sophocles, *Merope*, because they are much more than imitations. In some ways they are not heroic at all, and neither has a Greek theme: *Balder Dead* comes from Norse, and *Sohrab and Rustum* from Persian legend. These two fine pieces contain something of the nobility of Homer, some though not all of his aristocratic formalism, much of his strong simplicity; the half-primitive quality of his scenes and characters—tribal armies, warrior chiefs in single combat, hero-like gods and godlike heroes, the primacy of the deed over word and thought, the supernatural and the human closely intertwined; a few close adaptations of great passages from Homer and Vergil;[26] several important structural elements, such as the stately speeches, great crowd-scenes, conventional epithets, and, most of all, similes drawn from nature and elaborated for the sake of their own beauty. Milton had already used this splendid device (although not often enough), and so had other modern heroic poets. Arnold, who loved nature deeply, brought in many spacious nature-images comparable to those of Homer. Comparable sometimes in nobility, for the simile of the lonely eagle[27] is as great as all but the greatest of Homer; comparable in vividness—the cardinal difficulty of the modern epic writer, which Arnold solved by choosing similitudes clearly imaginable by us, vivid and evocative, and yet appropriate to the oriental and northern subjects of his poems;[28] but not comparable in strength, for most of them, very revealingly, reflect fear, or grief, or helplessness.[29]

But in the main the spirit and the style of Arnold's two poems are not Homeric. They are Homer twice removed. The style is eminently plain and direct, much more so than Homer's. Sometimes verse after verse, clause after clause, begins with *And*: which is a biblical rather than a Homeric habit. The syntax is straightforward, with none of Homer's quirks, although often it has his long-sustained roll. The vocabulary is far simpler than Homer's in variety and splendour. And the verse-rhythm, compared with Homer's, is calm and monotonous. If you spend a summer day in a highland glen, the air around you will be warm and perfumed, and the breeze will blow on you, lightly at noon, strongly at dawn and evening, nearly always from one direction. If you climb the mountain and spend the day on the top, the winds of heaven will attack you, jostle you, caress you, confuse you, threaten and excite and exalt you, but never leave you feeling that you are more powerful than they. If they cared, they could crush you. Arnold is the breeze in the valley. Homer is the air among the peaks.

But what readers of Arnold miss most is the spirit of energy and daring which fills the *Iliad* and *Odyssey*. His images, although beautiful, are melancholy. The theme of his poems is the tragic and useless death of a young hero, the doom by which each man kills the thing he loves. Mourning, the decline of greatness, the waste of promise—these are the central thoughts. This penetrating pessimism, with the slower pace and tenderer imagery, makes it clear that Arnold was inspired not by Homer but by a man much more like himself, the melancholy, sensitive, overburdened Vergil. In *Sohrab and Rustum* some would hold that he actually surpassed Vergil—particularly in the superb close, which is more than, but seems to have grown out of, an epic simile. As Rustum is left alone with his dead son in the gathering night, the scene darkens and grows smaller, and we find ourselves following, not any human struggle, but the majestic river Oxus which flows past the battlefield, and away from it towards the north, itself to meet conflict and to waste strength and beauty among the deserts, until at last, like a hero reaching triumph through agony, it finds its

> luminous home of waters . . . bright
> And tranquil, from whose floor the new-bath'd stars
> Emerge, and shine upon the Aral Sea.

After Arnold there were few successful attempts to turn Homer into English verse. Tennyson emphasized Arnold's failure, in a note in the 1863 *Cornhill*, saying that it had 'gone far to prove the impossibility' of using hexameters in English: he himself held that blank verse was the only appropriate English metre, and he showed it by adding a fine rendering of *Iliad*, 8. 542–65, which Arnold had discussed and partly translated into prose in his first lecture. Of course, Tennyson's Arthurian poems contained many 'faint Homeric echoes'.[30] But, like Arnold, he modelled his own heroic style more on Vergil than on Homer—and indeed he conceived his duty towards the Prince Consort, when he presented

King Arthur, like a modern gentleman,

as similar to that of Vergil towards Octavian Augustus.[31]

Through his *Lectures* Arnold had abolished the conception that Homer was a ballad-monger. In Lang's translations Homer appeared stately, slow-paced, solemn. Towards the end of the nineteenth century Samuel Butler (1835–1902) brought his sharp convention-hating intelligence to the problem. He began by pointing out that the epics were sometimes deliberately funny. In a short lecture, *The Humour of Homer* (1892), he suggested that the heroic prowess of the Greeks in the *Iliad* was so overdone that the poem was probably written by someone with Trojan sympathies, who exaggerated in order to poke fun at the conquerors; and he emphasized what has been agreed by scholars, that the gods are presented as 'human, all too human', to the point of being ridiculous—for instance, in the scene where Hera fascinates her husband Zeus, father of gods and men, and diverts his attention from the Trojan war to a much more urgent matter. The effect of this approach was to humanize the epics, to break their frame of convention and allow them to be criticized as ancestors of the modern novel. Butler continued this process in *The Authoress of the Odyssey* (1897), where he contended, largely by arguments of the 'no man could have written this' type, that the *Odyssey* was written by Nausicaa, the young princess of *Od.* 6, that she lived in Trapani in western Sicily, about 1050 B.C., and that she chose to make the poem a feminine counterblast to the masculine *Iliad*. Butler even knew how she wrote it—'with a sharply pointed style of hardened bronze . . . on plates of lead'.[32] Although Butler's

criticism lacked historical perspective, it carried farther the movement to discredit the theory preached by Wolf and taken up by
dozens of German scholars (p. 384), that the epics were assem-
blages of 'lays'. Butler not only made the *Odyssey* the work of one
person, but, from the difficulties and incongruities smelt out by the
Wolf-pack, reconstructed a fallible human authoress.

Butler published prose translations of the *Iliad* in 1898 and the
Odyssey in 1900. As he said in chapter 1 of *The Authoress of the
Odyssey*, he felt that the Butcher and Lang translation showed
'a benevolent leaning towards Wardour Street', where the bogus
antiques are sold; and that he himself preferred Tottenham Court
Road, where the goods are plain, cheap, and up to date. The result
was that his translations lacked the metre, most of the stylistic
conventions, the rich vocabulary, the flexible syntax, and the
sonority of the original. They still contained what he considered
the essentials—plot, characterization, and speeches. It was probably a useful action on Butler's part to create an easily readable
prose translation, for the period when he wrote was inclined to
enjoy prose fiction and to respect, but ignore, poetry; and the
Odyssey was meant to be enjoyed. Still, it is a pity that no poet
arose to give us the whole, rather than half a loaf.

T. E. Lawrence (1888–1935) followed Butler part of the way in
another prose translation of the *Odyssey*, published under his new
name of Shaw in 1932. He too felt that the poem was one single
story told by one single writer intimately familiar with the *Iliad*
and better acquainted with books and home-life than with action
and danger; for him, though, the author was not a young princess
but an elderly bookworm, 'as muddled an antiquary as Walter
Scott'.[33] The style of his translation was an unsatisfactory attempt
to render in prose some of the effect of those conventional turns of
speech which are essential parts of the Homeric verse—like the
bars that punctuate and support a stained-glass window. Butler
accused earlier translators of leaning towards the sham antique.
Lawrence said the author of the *Odyssey* himself was a sham
antique. This assumed knowledge far greater than any human
being possesses, yea, even six scholars of these degenerate days
could not raise such an hypothesis. The result was what we should
expect from *Seven Pillars of Wisdom*: energetic and swift sentences
and paragraphs, with a vocabulary affected and often ('Lady mine,
hitherto we have both travailed exhaustively')[34] ludicrously false.

In fact there are only two major ways of accounting for the incongruities and incomprehensibilities of the *Iliad* and the *Odyssey*. One is to say that the poems grew up of disparate and more or less independent materials, which were attracted together because they belonged to the same large tradition, but which were never built into a single structure by any intelligent creator. This is the Wolf theory. The other is stated on p. 482 above; and to it adhere Butler and Lawrence, although they much underrate the power of tradition over an early author, and make the epic poets improbably self-conscious. The best illustration can be drawn from another art. The Gothic cathedrals are masses of disparate and often incongruous material. Sometimes their original plan was never completed, sometimes it was altered so as to give the same building two different kinds of tower, and nearly always the older simplicity was overlaid, but not concealed, by later elaborations. And yet almost every one of these great buildings had a master-plan, and sometimes a single man or group as master-builder. The plan is grand, and evident, and dominating, while the incongruities usually come from a wish to combine subtler expressions of that plan with the reverence for tradition which is an essential element in early, perhaps in all, great art.

The difficulty remains unsolved: the difficulty of finding a suitable style in which to translate *into poetry* not only Homer but the other masterpieces which are concealed from modern readers by old-fashioned or inadequate versions. Professor Gilbert Murray has translated many of the Greek tragedies and some of Aristophanes into a late nineteenth-century style which owes much to Swinburne and something to William Morris. His translations, for all their charm, lack the strength of the Greek; and nowadays their style, instead of allowing us to see the original clearly, appears as an addition and distortion. T. S. Eliot has attacked them in an essay of disagreeable, but explicable, violence,[35] and it seems clear that future translations of classical books must, in order to reach the public that needs them, master and expand the new poetic style which Eliot has done most to develop.

But the difficulty goes deeper than the choice of a style. Throughout the nineteenth century we can trace a conflict, in the matter of translation, between scholarship and literature, between knowledge and taste. The most interesting and vital ideas on translation have come from the amateurs—Arnold, Lang, Butler,

Lawrence. The professors, like Newman and Wilamowitz, have a killing touch.[36] Murray's were far the best of a long line of translations by classical scholars, most of which were dull and some excruciatingly bad. Many of these give readers the impression that their authors hate their own literature and know nothing about it, for they write in a language neither modern, nor beautiful, nor even real. This conflict is an expression of a deep-seated illness in the culture of the nineteenth and twentieth centuries. The illness is even more clearly manifest in the problem of education and in *the decline of classical studies.*

'As a boy I had the common experience of fifty years ago—teachers whose sole object was to spoonfeed classes, not with the classics but with syntax and prosody . . . with the result that we loathed Xenophon and his ten thousand, Homer was an abomination, while Livy and Cicero were names and tasks. . . . My experience was that of thousands, yet, as I remember, we were athirst for good literature. . . . What a tragedy to climb Parnassus in a fog!'

That is Sir William Osler's description of his classical education at a Canadian school in 1866.[37] He was a clever energetic boy, full of life and curiosity, ready to be absorbed in anything interesting. However, his headmaster managed to disgust him with classical literature, by setting him work which 'consisted largely in the committing to memory of countless lines of Homer and Virgil, read with the aid of Schrevelius' lexicon and Ross's grammar, in which the definitions were in Greek and Latin respectively'. Meanwhile another master, who had a real love for science, took the boys for fascinating field-trips, talked to them about fossils and the formation of the earth's crust, and showed them marvels through the microscope. The result was that young Osler plunged into science, and became a brilliant doctor. At an early age he was appointed the first professor of medicine at Johns Hopkins University, which he left only to become Regius Professor of Medicine at Oxford. Throughout his life he admired classical literature and classical scholars—in particular, two great men of the Renaissance who were both physicians and humanists, Browne and Linacre.[38] He built up a fine classical library. He was never tired of warning his students that the natural sciences, including medicine, were only half the material of education, and that great literature (the classics of Greece and Rome being the greatest) was the more important part. But, while he did not wish his career other than it had been, he never ceased to regret that, through bad and perverse teaching, he had been denied the full understanding of the classics.

Osler was one of many distinguished men of the nineteenth century who found that bad teaching stifled even the readiest youthful impulse to love good literature. Here is a description of the classical work at Columbia College in New York, in 1879, written by Nicholas Murray Butler, who later became president of Columbia and for decades occupied the first place among American educators:[39]

'The teaching of the classics in those days was almost wholly of that dry-as-dust type which has pretty near killed classical study in the United States. Professor Drisler, who was then the Jay Professor (of Greek), was a man of remarkable elevation of character and of mind as well as a sound and thorough scholar. He was, however, so given to insistence upon the minutest details of grammar that our eyes were kept closely fixed on the ground and we hardly ever caught any glimpse of the beauty and larger significance of the great works upon which we were engaged. For example, I recall that during the first term of the sophomore [= second] year we were to read with Dr. Drisler the *Medea* of Euripides and that when the term came to an end we had completed but 246 lines. In other words, we never came to know what the *Medea* was all about or to see either the significance of the story or the quality of its literary art. . . . In Latin Professor Charles Short was a pedant if ever there was one. . . . Whether he was dealing with Horace, with Juvenal, or with Tacitus, he was always attending to the less important matters which the study of these authors suggested.'

In another great American college a few years later the same dismal condition is recorded by a young man who later became one of the best loved teachers of literature in all America. Describing Yale in 1883-4, William Lyon Phelps says:

'Most of our classrooms were dull and the teaching purely mechanical; a curse hung over the Faculty, a blight on the art of teaching. Many professors were merely hearers of prepared recitations; they never showed any living interest, either in the studies or in the students. I remember we had Homer three hours a week during the entire year. The instructor never changed the monotonous routine, never made a remark, but simply called on individuals to recite or to scan, said "That will do", put down a mark; so that in the last recitation in June, after a whole college year of this intolerable classroom drudgery, I was surprised to hear him say, and again without any emphasis, "The poems of Homer arc the greatest that have ever proceeded from the mind of man, class is dismissed," and we went out into the sunshine.'[40]

From a British public school at the same period we can hear the same dry bones rattling; and once again it is not a hostile critic who rattles them, but an original writer who later worked in Greece and loved Greek literature for its own sake: E. F. Benson on Marlborough:

'. . . How dismal was the system, which, expunging all human interest and beauty from a subject that is instinct with humanity and loveliness, taught a language [Greek], and that the most flexible of all human tongues, as if it had been a series of algebraical formulae. How willingly would those dry irregularities have been learned if the imagination had first been kindled. . . . But at the time when I was learning Greek, the methods of tutors resembled that of those who, by making their pupils chop up dry faggots of wood, hoped to teach them what was the nature of the trees that once the wind made murmurous on the hillsides of Attica.'[41]

Many more examples of this phenomenon could be quoted from the biographies—not of dullards, nor of 'practical' business men, nor of erratic discipline-hating artists, nor of men devoted from boyhood to scientific research, but of genuine lovers of classical culture. Clearly something went profoundly wrong with the study of the classics in the nineteenth century.

At the opening of this chapter we said that the available knowledge of Greece and Rome increased steadily throughout the century that ended in 1914. Yet during that same period the distribution of classical knowledge, after an initial rise, fell away. Fewer boys and girls learnt Greek and Latin at school. Fewer students chose classical courses at the university. Direct attacks were made on the teaching of Latin and Greek in public schools, and they were usually successful. The regulations prescribing Latin as a necessary qualification for admittance to a university were relaxed or abandoned. The general familiarity with Greek and Latin poetry, philosophy, and history dwindled, so that, while in the first part of the nineteenth century it would have been quite natural for a debater in Parliament to cite Vergil and for a journalist writing a leading article to introduce illustrations from Greek history, by the end of the century that would have been regarded as pedantry or affectation, and would have had little or no other effect on the public. The tide which had been rising until about 1870 or 1880 now faltered, stopped, and began to ebb more and more rapidly. Some thought that this was a sign of Progress. Others concluded that a new age of mass vulgarity and 'Gothic ignorance', like that described by Pope at the end of the *Dunciad*, was setting in. In any case, it was a large and complex event, which is still difficult to see in proper perspective.

Like all complex events, the decline of public interest in classical studies had a number of different causes. Some of these had nothing to do with classical culture, others were only indirectly connected with it, others again were actually part of the changing process of classical learning.

To some extent, it was due quite naturally to the rapid advance of science, industrialism, and international trade. That created new subjects, which appeared to have a better right to be taught in schools and universities: chemistry, physics, economics, modern languages, psychology, political philosophy. By asserting their rights, these subjects forced the classics to occupy less of the school day, and took away many of the good classical students.

Another reason was the introduction of universal education. Latin and Greek are fairly difficult languages, and it is quite as impractical to teach them to the whole school population as to train every pupil to paint or play the violin. In a few countries, at certain periods, Latin has been taught in all the schools; but either those schools did not serve the whole population, or else (as in Scotland) the public had an exceptional respect for education, not because of its reward in money, but because of its spiritual prestige, because educated men were the real aristocracy. But democracy as it advances usually turns against such *élites*. The subjects taught and respected in schools are the subjects which everyone can assimilate. A contributory factor is that schooling under a democracy seems to get to work later and later, and to spend the early years teaching only the fundamentals. Difficult things like languages are left till later. But of course the best way to learn Greek and Latin is to begin at nine or so, when the mind is so flexible that anything prints it without an effort, and the essential memory-work can be got quickly over, in time to let the boy understand and appreciate Greek and Latin literature when he reaches the appreciative age.

But certainly one of the chief reasons was that the classics were

badly taught. Of course, there have always been lazy and un-
interested teachers, like Gibbon's tutor Waldegrave of Magdalen:

'My tutor . . . proposed that we should read every morning, from ten
to eleven, the comedies of Terence. The sum of my improvement in the
University of Oxford is confined to three or four Latin plays; and even
the study of an elegant classic, which might have been illustrated by a
comparison of the ancient and modern theatres, was reduced to a dry
and literal interpretation of the author's text.'[42]

Dry and literal, because Waldegrave did not care enough either for
the subject or for the pupil to bother about treating the comedies
as works of art. Eventually Gibbon gave up even these tutorial
hours, since they 'appeared equally devoid of profit and pleasure'.
His tutor paid no attention whatever.

Yet that was not the kind of bad teaching that disgusted Osler
and Butler, Phelps and Benson, and so many others in the nineteenth century. Their masters were seldom indolent. The trouble
with them was quite different. We have already seen it at work,
and observed the violent reaction it produced, in Byron (p. 413 f.).
and Hugo (p. 407). Potentially they were good pupils. Byron says
himself that he was idle, but not slow.[43] He remembered a great
deal of classical literature, badly taught though it was. Hugo, too,
had an active mind, greedy for good books; but his appetite was
choked. The same thing happened to thousands of others. Their
complaint was always the same. It was that classical literature was
spoilt by being taught with an over-emphasis on precision—and
particularly on grammatical usage and syntactical explanation,
what Butler called 'insistence on the minutest details' and Osler
'dry husks'. It can be summed up in the admirable story about the
headmaster who introduced his pupils to one of the greatest of
Greek tragedies by saying:

'Boys, this term you are to have the privilege of reading the *Oedipus
Coloneus* of Sophocles, a veritable treasure-house of grammatical
peculiarities.'[44]

To discuss why teachers of the classics should have been increasingly guilty of these errors during the nineteenth century
would require a volume. Partly it was caused by the strengthening
of the examination system; partly by the multiplication of rich
scholarships and prizes to be won by 'good examinees' for displays of memory and accuracy; partly by a change in the ideals of

classical study, which we shall discuss later; and very largely by the ethos of the nineteenth century itself, which admired Discipline, and System, and Flogging, and Hard Work, and Facts. Dickens satirized that sort of teaching in *Hard Times*—he called one of the chapters 'Murdering the innocents'—and although his Mr. Gradgrind and the coldly factual schoolmaster Mr. McChoakumchild were more interested in science than in the classics, they were examples of a widespread Victorian attitude to all education: that it ought to be exact, difficult, and pleasureless. *Discipline* was its method, and its ultimate aim. Now, it is impossible to teach Latin and Greek without precision: grammar and syntax are essential parts of the study of the languages; but it is necessary to give the young something more besides. Everyone who knows children knows that they will work with amazing precision and attention to detail on something that interests them—making a code, or drawing a map, or learning the names of aircraft and stars. But the detail must be a means, and not an end in itself; and any teacher who attempts to drive in the detail for its own sake, or for the sake of 'discipline', will find his work difficult and its results hateful.

University teaching of the classics was sometimes injured by another fact. As research progressed farther and farther, many university teachers became specialists in abstruse branches of Greco-Roman history, literature, philology, and kindred subjects. Sometimes they carried specialization so far that they lost touch with their pupils. At Oxford and Cambridge this was discouraged by the tutorial system, which is based on the constant contact of minds between dons and undergraduates. The result was that the standard of teaching in these universities was exceptionally high throughout the century: from them came few complaints like those quoted above; in fact, the dons usually felt it their duty to sacrifice research to teaching, if both could not be carried on. But in the great universities of the Continent and the United States it was not uncommon to find a professor whose lectures were unintelligible or repulsive to all but his best students, because his intellectual life was spent in an atmosphere too rarefied for most of them to breathe.

But the worst kind of bad teaching had a different cause. This was the belief that the study of Greek and Latin was a *science*, and nothing but a science. To us now this appears an obvious exaggeration. Clearly the scientific virtues of accuracy, organization, objectivity, and clarity must be used in classical research as in any other kind of study. Clearly the methods of applied science can usefully be employed in many areas of Greco-Roman literature and history. But the subject-matter of classical study is not wholly, or even chiefly, objective facts comparable to the material of geology. Much of it, and much of the best of it, is art; and art must be studied with taste and imagination as well as with cameras and callipers. Much of it is history, and historical research involves moral judgement, while historical writing entails aesthetic choice. However, the nineteenth-century classical scholars, led by the Germans (who are more noted for their industry than for their taste), resolved that their duty was to be scientific. This resolution did much to ruin the teaching of the subject.

It is well exemplified in the paradoxical life of A. E. Housman. He was a fine poet, and a sensitive, though limited, critic of letters. But his chief work in the classics consisted of trying to establish the original text of Propertius, Juvenal, Lucan, and Manilius—that is, of removing the mistakes and unintelligibilities introduced into their poems by ignorant copyists and medieval scholars. Difficult and necessary as this is, it is ultimately a glorified form of proof-reading. And he did not care particularly for these four poets, or said he did not. (Actually, the sensitive love-poet, the cruel satirist, the ranting Stoic, and the scholarly recluse did appeal to certain sides of his character.) He said he chose them because they presented difficult problems. In his inaugural lecture at London University he declared that classical scholarship had no justification whatever, except that in its way—in one of many possible ways—it satisfied man's desire for knowledge. Not for useful knowledge: the information it provided was no more applicable to daily life than the discoveries of astronomy. Not for spiritual enlightenment: we need not hope through it to 'transform and beautify our inner nature' (he said)—because, although classical literature does sharpen the faculty of appreciating what is excellent, most people do not possess such a faculty, and are spiritually deaf and blind. We study the classics, therefore, only because the desire for knowledge is innate in us. Housman did not explain in detail why anyone should choose to study Greek and Latin literature rather than the Calypso songs of Trinidad and the hymns of the Tibetan monasteries (which would also provide intricate subjects of study); but, in a rapid sentence or two (noticeably less clear than the usual acid-tipped needle-stab with which he made the points he was sure of), he said it was a matter of personal preference. Would he have refused to admit that the writings of the Greeks and Romans are, objectively and universally, more beautiful? that they are more relevant to us, who are at some removes their spiritual descendants?[45]

One incident which illustrates this attitude is both pathetic and comic. Housman used to lecture on Horace's lyrics, concentrating on the text, syntax, and prosody, adding 'just so much commentary as was necessary for the interpretation of the passage under discussion',[46] never looking at his pupils, and never mentioning the essentials of the poetry. But—

'one morning in May, 1914, when the trees in Cambridge were covered with blossom, he reached . . . the seventh ode in the fourth book of Horace. . . . This ode he dissected with the usual display of brilliance, wit, and sarcasm. Then for the first time in two years he looked up at us, and in quite a different voice said: "I should like to spend the last few minutes considering this ode simply as poetry." Our previous experience of Professor Housman would have made us sure that he would regard such a proceeding as beneath contempt. He read the ode aloud with deep emotion, first in Latin and then in an English translation of his own (now the fifth in More Poems). "That," he said hurriedly, almost like a man betraying a secret, "I regard as the most beautiful poem in ancient literature," and walked quickly out of the room.'[47]

One of the men who watched this said, 'I was afraid the old fellow was going to cry.' He was. In part, because of the extreme sensitivity which made it uncomfortable for him even to recall certain lines of poetry while he was shaving, because his skin bristled and turned the razor's edge; but in part also because of his embarrassment at feeling that he had permitted personal emotion to escape, and invade what he held should be nothing but an objective field of thought, sterile as ice, bright as an operating-table.

This belief that the study and teaching of the classical literatures ought to be purely and scientifically objective has spoilt many a teacher and many, many good pupils. It was largely responsible for the recession in public interest in the classics during the latter half of the nineteenth century. Put broadly, it has meant that classical scholars feel more obliged to extend knowledge than to disseminate it. The gap between the scholar and the public, which in the Renaissance and in the revolutionary era was bridged by a constant interflow of teaching and questioning and propaganda and imitation and translation and emulation, has now widened to a gulf. Earlier in this chapter we discussed some of the translations of classical poetry made during the last hundred years, and pointed out that on the whole they were unsatisfactory. That fact is another aspect of the lack of communication between scholars and the public. Few scholars think it worth while to translate the books they read: and, if they do so, they are apt to choose a woefully old-fashioned style which, instead of interesting and stimulating a non-classical reader, repels him. Non-specialists who wish to try their hand at translating and adapting often find that the work of the specialists has built an impenetrable zariba of thorns around the beauty they are seeking.

The actual writing of scholarly books on classical subjects is seldom good, and is sometimes deliberately repulsive. For this the Germans are chiefly to blame. They have always found it hard to write good prose; in the name of science, they have cultivated difficulty and gracelessness. Mommsen is actually reputed to have said 'In spite of his beautiful style, Renan was a true scholar'.[48] A very good example is provided by the huge German encyclopaedia of classical learning, Pauly–Wissowa–Kroll's *Real-Encyclopädie der classischen Altertumswissenschaft*. It contains a monumental amount of valuable information, fully and carefully analysed. But it is, even for scholars, painful to read. The sentences are clogged with parentheses and citations and cross-references, the language is thick and technical, and even the format, close type in double column, is repellent. I never use it without thinking of Lemprière's classical dictionary, a single volume, far less scholarly and far better written, which, in his last years at school, was the favourite reading of John Keats.

Even the format of most classical books is ugly. The essential Teubner series, containing practically every Greek and Latin work, with Latin prefaces and a list of manuscript variations and conjectures, is hideous. The Oxford Classical Texts and the Budé series are better, but they scarcely attract the reader. Why is it that one can buy an edition of Donne or Goethe which is a pleasure to handle, and can hardly find a Juvenal or Euripides which does not look like a medical text-book?[49]

The false parallel with science caused many more errors and exaggerations in classical study. One odd one was the habit of *Quellenforschung*, the search for sources, which began as a legitimate inquiry into the material used by a poet, historian, or philosopher, and was pushed to the absurd point at which it was assumed that everything in a poem, even such a poem as the *Aeneid*, was derived from earlier writers. It is a typical scientific assumption that everything can be explained by synthesis, but it omits the essential artistic fact of creation.[50]

The scientific approach, as well as the expansion of knowledge, has also been responsible for the fragmentation of classical study. For several decades the majority of scholars have preferred writing small studies of single authors, of separate aspects of single authors, of tiny areas of social and literary history, of topics obscure and peripheral and unexplored. Meanwhile, much remains to be done on the great central subjects. There has been a widespread belief, not without foundation, that scholars actually chose to write on subjects which were safe because so few people knew anything about them. In Germany the custom was invented of awarding doctoral degrees only to students who had produced a piece of 'original research'. Because of the close relation between American and German universities in the latter part of the nineteenth century, the habit spread to the United States, where it now rages unchecked. Hundreds of Ph.D. candidates every year produce dissertations on subjects which often interest neither themselves nor anyone else; and which the doctors seldom re-explore in the light of their later, more mature knowledge. The defence usually offered for this practice is that each of the dissertations is like a single brick, which helps to build the great edifice of scholarship. The image is true enough as far as it goes; but the terrain is getting more and more littered with scattered heaps of bricks which are manufactured and tipped out without any plan whatever, unless it be to cover every inch of exposed ground. As they accumulate, the task of scholarship becomes not less but more difficult. And meanwhile, those looking in from outside see no cathedral arising, and very few builders have appeared. For brick-making does not produce architects.

It is, then, the fundamental fault of modern classical scholarship that it has cultivated research more than interpretation, that it has been more interested in the acquisition than in the dissemination of knowledge, that it has denied or disdained the relevance of its work in the contemporary world, and that it has encouraged the public neglect of which it now complains. The scholar has a responsibility to society—not less, but greater, than that of the labourer and the business man. His first duty is to know the truth, and his second is to make it known. For classical scholarship is one of the main channels through which the uniquely valuable influence of the culture of Greece and Rome, still living and fertile, still incalculably stimulating, can be communicated to the modern world—the world that it has already, not once but twice and thrice and oftener, saved from the repeated attacks of materialism and barbarism.

22

THE SYMBOLIST POETS AND JAMES JOYCE

THERE is an important group of modern poets who may be called symbolists.[1] They believe that single events and individual persons are petty, transient, unimportant;[2] that they cannot be made into subjects worthy of art unless they are shown to be symbols of eternal truths. This in itself is a Greek idea. Plato taught that every thing in the world was merely a poor copy of its perfect pattern in heaven, and that it could not be understood except by those who knew that pattern.[3] Plato meant philosophers. The symbolists, on the other hand, would say that only imaginative artists could see high significance in trivial daily things. No doubt that is their own conception: they are not conscious Platonists. Yet many of the most memorable symbols which compose their vision of life come from the rich imaginative world of Greek myth.

They have not written much, but their books have been very influential. Many contemporary poets are now engaged on intensifying and elaborating their discoveries. Their leaders, and their most notable works inspired by Greek legend, are:

Stéphane Mallarmé (1842–98):
> *Herodias* (1869)
> *The Afternoon of a Faun* (1876);

his friend Paul-Ambroise Valéry (1871–1945):
> *The Young Fate* (1917)
> *Fragments of 'Narcissus'* (1922)
> *The Pythian Prophetess* (1922);

Ezra Pound (born 1885):
> *Personae of Ezra Pound* (collected 1917)
> *Cantos* (1933–47);

his friend T. S. Eliot (born 1888):
> *Prufrock and other observations* (1917)
> *Ara Vos Prec* (1920)
> *The Waste Land* (1922)
> *Sweeney Agonistes* (1932).

Together with these we may consider one prose-writer. His style and his aims differ from theirs in many respects; yet he is

linked with them by his use of Greek legend, and by sharing several other important techniques and attitudes. This is
James Joyce (1882–1941):
> A Portrait of the Artist as a Young Man (1916)
> Ulysses (1922).

The influence of Greek and Roman culture on the symbolist poets is often overlooked because their method is not like that of the classical writers. They leave much to the imagination. But do the Greek poets also not leave much to the imagination? Yes, but the Greeks state the essentials, and allow the hearer to supply the details. The symbolist poets do not state the essentials. Instead, they describe the details, which, although not central, are so vivid as to haunt the mind.

This is the technique of Debussy and Ravel in music, of Monet and Whistler in painting. Such artists leave as much as possible to the imagination of the beholder, who thus becomes an artist himself, for he must help to create the poem, or the musical impression, or the picture which is adumbrated for him. The impressionist artists and writers intend this. They believe that most people are unable or unwilling to contribute any effort to the appreciation of beauty. They believe also—and here again Plato would have recognized them as his pupils—that the most important truths and beauties are too lofty or too fragile to be described. But they deny —and here they are un-Greek—that the essential truths can be approached more and more closely by systematic thought. On the contrary, they think that, just as the best way to see a faint star is to look to one side of it, so the best way to reach a profound or beautiful idea is to grasp a detail which, although apparently peripheral and even irrelevant, still carries the mind inevitably to the bright centre. This conception is Chinese and Japanese, and was encouraged by the growing admiration for Far Eastern art in the later decades of the nineteenth century. Whistler, who was a close friend of Mallarmé, collected Japanese pictures and emulated the elusiveness of oriental art; among Pound's best poems are several groups of translations from early Chinese lyrics; and Mallarmé, in one of his most decisive announcements of his own ideals,[4] asserts that he

> will discard the greedy art of a cruel
> country, and . . .
> copy the limpid, sensitive Chinese

in painting, upon frail porcelain, a few lines which merely evoke evening, a crescent moon, and a lake gazing upwards like an azure eye. The carefully irregular metres and cryptic allusions of Eliot and Pound, the distilled and compressed thought of Valéry, the evasive dreamlike fancies of Mallarmé, are all produced by the extreme sensitivity and subtle psychological awareness which are characteristic of many modern poets. They are also a deliberate retreat from the intrusive, the obvious, and the vulgar, towards privacy and remoteness, towards the difficulty of the ideal. This reaction is a fact of great importance for the social function of modern literature. It is largely oriental in inspiration. Certainly it is not, in the central sense, classical.

Nor are these poets classical in their form, in their logic. It is not that their works are vague. They are precise enough in describing the particular details which the reader is to notice. Mallarmé tells us how many reeds he would paint beside the lake. Pound presents phonetic transcripts of American and English dialects in his *Cantos*. (Joyce, too, is scrupulously exact in reporting and echoing every noise heard in a bar, every advertisement glimpsed in a shop-window.) But what they state is the detail. The central thought, and the articulation of the detail with the central thought, are left for the reader to work out. And the transitions from one impression to another are made with the bewildering rapidity and irregularity of a dream, so that even the details appear evasive, evanescent. The logical sequence of such writing is, therefore, extremely obscure, and is sometimes shaped not by the laws of thought so much as by some private excitements of the writer. To say that these authors have not a classical sense of form does not mean that they do not use external patterns created by the Greeks. (As a matter of fact, they sometimes do.) It means that they eschew symmetry, continuity, smoothness, harmony, and logic, in favour of abrupt, unforeseeable, apparently arbitrary transitions (not only between sections of one passage but between sentences and phrases), a general pattern which resembles an unrehearsed monologue or a random conversation rather than any regular progression of well-balanced ideas, and a deliberate avoidance or concealment of the intellectual substructure of the whole.

If you look at one of Claude Monet's pictures, you will first of all see a mass of delectable colours. As you gaze, it assembles itself into a play of different lights on the façade of a building—or is it a wood, or a cloud? No, it is a large church. It is a cathedral. Step closer. There is nothing now except blurs of blue and gold and opalescent rose. Step back and look again. It is the great door of Rouen Cathedral, with the two towers rising above it. Such an impressionist picture is clearer than impressionist poetry, because it is bound to a recognizable scene with a structure not dictated by the painter's fancy but imposed on him. And yet, in Monet's cathedral, what we see is sunlight. The architecture is only an arrangement of surfaces on which light reacts; and the massive stones that rise into arch and column, the precise carving and disposition of the statuary, the complex interplay of weight, thrust, mass within the structure, are all melted into a rainbow.

All these writers have endeavoured to use classical patterns, as though they felt the need of some form to guide them. But the results have usually been distorted or fragmentary. Eliot, for instance, has published 'fragments of an Aristophanic melodrama' called by the mock-tragic title *Sweeney Agonistes.* Apparently he intended to develop the contrast between the squalor of to-day and the nobility of the classical past, so far as to create a mock tragedy in which the characters were typical American and British vulgarians like Sweeney and Doris, the dialogue the blatant empty jabbering of pubs and parties (intensified by an occasional sentence of startling brutality), the lyrics a series of nightmare jazz choruses, but the form that of the purest and most symmetrical classicism. However, he has never finished it. In *Herodias* Mallarmé created three fragments of a miniature Greek drama, but he could not finish that either. Valéry's *Fragments of 'Narcissus'* also are incomplete in form, though not in thought.

Joyce's *Ulysses* shows with particular clarity how these writers, though wishing to be free, yet find themselves bound to adopt some externally suggested form, which is often classical in origin. To hold the vast discharge of reminiscence and description which Joyce wanted to use in evoking Dublin life, he had to find some large, firm mould. If he had not, the whole thing might have been as shapeless as its last chapter, Mrs. Bloom's drowsy interior monologue, the single sentence which runs for forty pages, or its successor *Finnegans Wake*, which is a nebula of dream-particles held together only by the magnetism of association. He therefore chose to model it on Homer's *Odyssey*, to which he added the unities of time and place. The main plot resembles that of the *Odyssey*: a resourceful middle-aged wanderer makes his way through trials and temptations towards his home, wife, and son, while a young man sets out into life, which tests and educates him as he makes his way towards his lost father. The climax is the scene in which, after long separate wanderings, the two meet at last. The wandering Jew, Bloom, saves the student Stephen Dedalus from a drunken row into which he is driven by hysterical memories of his refusal to worship God at his mother's death-bed; the two go home to Bloom's house. Stephen's own family has not given him a home, Bloom's wife is unfaithful, and his little boy is dead. Now the bereaved father has found the orphaned son.

But many readers could go through *Ulysses* without realizing that it was patterned on the *Odyssey*. The original manuscript had quotations from Homer as chapter-headings; but Joyce removed them before publication.[5] The title *Ulysses*[6] is an indication; but it is obscured by Joyce's own pseudonym. He calls his young self Dedalus; and there is no tradition of any link between Ulysses and the craftsman Daedalus. Even a reader who had seen a general resemblance to the *Odyssey* would surely not observe that every chapter in *Ulysses*, almost all the characters who appear for more than a moment, and many of the inanimate things they use are designed to be parallel to elements in the *Odyssey*. For instance, the four women of Odysseus' wanderings reappear in *Ulysses*. The secret nymph Calypso is the typist Clifford, who corresponds with Bloom but remains invisible; the young princess Nausicaa is the adolescent Gerty MacDowell, towards whom he directs lewd thoughts on the sea-shore; Circe, who turns men into beasts, is the keeper of the brothel where he meets young Dedalus; and the faithful wife Penelope is his faithless wife Molly. The Cave of the Winds is imaged by a Dublin newspaper-office; the giant Polyphemus is a coarse violent insular Irishman; Odysseus' burning log is Bloom's cigar; and so on. Most of these parallels are too obscure to be recognizable without the work of the scholiasts who knew Joyce and apparently received the clues from his own lips.[7] Many of them are so distorted as to be meaningless. For example, the clever hero Odysseus got his crew out of the power of Polyphemus by making him drunk, sharpening and heating a tree-trunk, and burning out the giant's one eye. Bloom's cigar plays no such part in the plot, and the correspondence of the two burning sticks is therefore a piece of supererogatory elaboration

The parallelism between details of *Ulysses* and the *Odyssey* is close but artistically pointless. What Joyce wanted from the epic was its structural plan, and that, except in the barest outline, he failed to take. The plot of the *Odyssey* has, with justice, been admired by most of its readers. With superb skill and yet with apparently effortless ease Homer solves the problems of bringing Odysseus and his son Telemachus closer and closer together in their quest without letting them meet until just before the climax, of telling all the previous adventures of Odysseus' long wanderings so as to prepare for his single-handed heroism at the end, of maintaining and increasing the suspense from episode to episode, of providing a satisfying final resolution, and of concentrating the reader's attention upon the main figures throughout. But Joyce has rearranged the incidents of the epic into eighteen sections which have a far looser connecting structure, and most of which are united only by that weakest of bonds, coincidence. For pages and pages he reports events only because they happened to occur in Dublin on the 16th of June 1904. Had he not been determined to observe the unity of time, he might have reported everything that occurred on the 15th too, and made the book twice as long. The same criticism applies to the plot, and to the treatment of the characters. The *Odyssey* is the story of a quest: father and son search for each other (although really Odysseus is not looking for Telemachus but trying to regain his home and his wife). *Ulysses* is not the story of a quest. Bloom and Dedalus merely wander through Dublin, unguided by any single purpose. They do not know each other and belong to dissimilar worlds. When they meet, Dedalus is too drunk to understand what has happened; he, not Ulysses-Bloom, occupies the centre of attention throughout; and their chance association can never grow into a real father-son relationship. Thus, the climax of the book is that Dedalus rejects his true mother and is found by a false father. This rambling inconclusive story-line is responsible for much of the disappointment *Ulysses* causes to its readers. For the rest, Joyce's lack of selectivity can be blamed. The book begins by centring attention on 'stately, plump Buck Mulligan', who drops out of sight after a few chapters;[8] it continues through brilliantly vivid descriptions of unimportant people and things; and then, after an unreadable chapter in the form of question-and-answer, meant to represent the gradual focusing of the mind after a bout of drunkenness, ends with a vast irrelevant monologue by Mrs. Bloom, who has never appeared and is almost as unknown to us as she is to Dedalus.

Joyce and the symbolist poets are, then, too sensitive or too wilful to accept the creative discipline of classical forms. But they admire and use the creations of classical legend. Greek myths play a more important part in the symbolism of these poets than any other material (except nature-imagery), and are all the more powerful because they are, though not childish, apparently unreasonable.

First, they all employ Greek mythical figures to symbolize certain spiritual attitudes: to make them permanently intelligible and yet vividly real—all the more real because they are distant from the vulgar, violent, accidental, transitory Here-and-Now. Mallarmé was convinced, and perhaps the others too believe in part, that only the ideal is valuable, and that the ideal is life purged of its inessential attributes by art, or by death. (The first words of his epitaph on Poe describe the poet, now immortal, as

changed by eternity into Himself at last.)[9]

So, to take a complex personal emotion and to embody it in a symbolic figure of legend is to immortalize it, to make it art.

The most famous of these symbolic figures is the Faun in Mallarmé's *The Afternoon of a Faun.* Mallarmé himself calls the poem an eclogue, so that it is one of the latest in the long succession of pastoral poems which begins with Theocritus.[10] Half dream and half music, it is the monologue of a faun half Caliban and half Ariel. He has captured two nymphs; they have escaped; he dreams of them, wonders if the brief incomplete embrace was itself a dream, dreams of capturing others . . . perhaps Venus herself . . . sacrilege . . . he sleeps in the noonday heat, to dream again. The Faun symbolizes man's erotic dreams of women, dreams which are composed not only of animal desire but of reverence for fragile and delicate beauty, and of aspiration towards an ideal all the more desirable because it is elusive or dangerous. Hairy, horned, goat-like in lust is the Faun; but he is also a musician and a poet: a dreamer. Without the dreams, his desires would be merely bestial; without the desires, his dreams would be empty. Mallarmé had the good fortune to have his work translated into music by Claude Debussy,[11] whose *Prelude to the Afternoon of a Faun* follows the dream as sensitively, as caressingly, as the Faun's flute evokes the line of a white back.

The princess Herodias in Mallarmé's *Herodias* is the antithesis of the Faun. Young, lovely, virginal as the moon, she is a symbol of the proud pure beauty which repels everything that can violate it—from the touch of her old nurse to the savagery of lions, from the perfumes which would drown her immaculate hair to the thought of the lover whom the perfumes might bring nearer. She loves 'the horror of virginity', which she defends, throughout a dialogue with her cringing caressing nurse, in tones as sharp and metallic as the Faun's were warm and musky. And yet she protests too much. She knows it. In her last speech she accuses herself of lying, and foresees her childhood, which is her maidenhood, breaking apart like cold bright stones through which are thrust the irresistible stalks of growth.[12]

After a few experiments and a long silence, Mallarmé's admirer and pupil Valéry produced in 1917 a poem which combined many of the themes of *The Afternoon of a Faun* and *Herodias*, while outdoing them both in obscurity.[13] This is *The Young Fate* (*La Jeune Parque*), a monologue in some 500 lines.[14] *Parque* is in Latin *Parca*, one of the three Fates; but the doubt and ignorance and passionate excitement of the speaker show that she is not, or not yet, one of the three inexorable spirits who live in the world of eternity, for ever spinning, measuring, and cutting the threads of human life. Still, she is a creature of Greco-Roman inspiration, adoring the sun and recoiling from a serpent whom she calls Thyrsus (the Bacchic symbol of passion). The poem describes, in a flow of iridescent metaphors mixed with tinsel eccentricities,[15] the questioning, anxiety, despair, excitement, orgasm, remorse, and calm fulfilment experienced by a young woman, or spirit, at a crisis of her life. She passes from one group of states to another, its opposite and enemy: from sleep (after a dream of a snake by which she was 'known more than wounded') to waking, from calm to fear, from impassibility to tenderness, from unreflective activity to thought, from ignorance to self-knowledge, from simplicity to complexity, from winter to spring, from virginity to dreams of love and fears of motherhood, from troubled night (filled with reminiscence of sunbright thoughtless day) to a terrifying dawn when the very earth underfoot moves and threatens to lapse into sea, and then at last to the welcome and richer day. She symbolizes not only the passage of a girl into womanhood, but the pangs of the soul confronted with the choice of examining itself or simply living, the rewarding agony of the ideal when it is forced to become part of reality; and much else. Valéry has combined these tensions into one living figure who, speaking at the moment of her most difficult choice and change, is rightly called a young Fate.

In a broken monologue called *Fragments of 'Narcissus'*, far less precious in imagery and more skilful in sound, Valéry used the figure of Narcissus, who died for love of his own beauty mirrored in a forest pool, to symbolize the self which is happiest away from others, contemplating and adoring 'the inexhaustible I'.[16] As Narcissus bends lower and lower to embrace his dear image, as he touches and breaks the liquid mirror and enters the dark eyes which grow closer and closer to him, he reaches the last ecstasy of self-annulling self-absorption.

Much of the imagery in these poems is sexual; and although Valéry's commentators and Valéry himself have usually written as though his chief problem were that of the mind divided between the external and internal worlds of contemplation, his poetry also expresses a horror of sexual love as a power which dominates, uses, and humiliates the independent self. The young Fate and Narcissus both prefer calmer satisfactions. Narcissus abandons himself entirely to himself. The Fate finds that her own love for herself awakes a hidden serpent. A third poem, *The Pythian Prophetess*, completes the trilogy.[17] Here Valéry presents the horrors and the agonies of a woman mastered by a power which is within her and yet is not herself, under the figure of the priestess who could prophesy only when possessed by Apollo. Chiefly, the poem symbolizes the pangs of the artist who finds himself forced, at the cost of his own peace and independence, to utter the words dictated by the creative spirit; but the sexual undertones which make it complementary to *Narcissus* are unmistakable, and increase its power.

Joyce also used symbolic and mythical figures to describe himself as a young man. He called himself Stephen Dedalus: Stephen because he owed his education to University College by St. Stephen's Green, and Dedalus after the mythical inventor.[18] Exiled from Athens, and kept in the island of Crete by King

Minos, Daedalus made wings of wax and feathers, taught himself and his son Icarus to fly, and escaped through the air.[19] Joyce felt this myth very deeply. The last words of the diary which concludes *A Portrait of the Artist* are an invocation to the 'old father, old artificer' to help him in leaving Dublin and launching himself on the unknown, while its epigraph is a quotation from one of Ovid's versions of the legend.[20] Daedalus was the explorer of 'unknown arts' whom he wished to emulate. To conceive *Ulysses* and perhaps *Finnegans Wake* in Dublin was for him the equivalent of Daedalus' inventions. And not only in novelty, but in nature: for Daedalus was both the constructor of the labyrinth, to which Joyce's two vast books are comparable in secrecy and intricacy, and also the maker of wings on which to escape from an island prison. Joyce's wings were the talent that took him out of Dublin, and the imagination that raised him, for a time at least, above the sordid daily world.

As well as Greek mythical figures, these five writers use Greek stories. Through them they interpret important spiritual experiences, beliefs, aspirations. This is one of the original purposes for which myths are created. It is because men are wicked and because natural catastrophes resemble the acts of an avenging god that people tell the story of the Flood, in Babylonia, Judea, and Greece. It is because purity is felt to increase a fighter's strength that men make the legends of Samson and Galahad. Every nation has such stories, many of them as silly, as terrifying or disgusting, as unintelligible or as haunting as dreams, which they are.[21] The Greeks have the greatest store of clear, memorable, beautiful myths. Far from being dead, they are still alive and fertile in our mind.

One of these stories appears as early as the *Odyssey*. The hero Odysseus is carried far from his homeward way by storms and disasters. At the advice of the sorceress Circe, he visits the world of the dead in order to ask the seer Tiresias his best route home. It is a grim ordeal, but, for the clever determined Odysseus, not an overwhelming one. He carries out the right rituals, interviews the right ghost, pays his devoirs to his mother and friends, and, after the appearance of several great personages of the past, withdraws discreetly.[22]

Other Greek heroes visited the underworld—Heracles and

Theseus by force, Orpheus by art; but no great poem on their adventures has survived, although the Orpheus legend has become part of world literature. In Latin the myth was taken up by Vergil, who gave it a deeper meaning. His hero Aeneas, exiled and landless, visits the underworld, guided by the immortal Sibyl and carrying as a symbol of immortality the golden bough.[23] From his dead father he learns how to reach and establish his future home, and is shown a limbo of heroes still unborn, in which the mighty Romans who are to be his heirs, in a Rome yet uncreated, pass in all their majesty before his eyes.

Obviously the myth means many things; but one of its chief meanings is that the brave man must conquer death, or go through hell, before he finds his home. In the early and medieval Christian church Christ himself was represented as having spent three days in hell after his crucifixion and before his resurrection, exercising his kingly power by delivering some prisoners and triumphing over the devils. There is no mention of this in the gospels: it was not part of the original story of Jesus, and was an adaptation of the legend of the hero's successful journey through the world of death. Then another great poet took up the tale. Exiled for ever from his own home, wandering like Odysseus and Aeneas among strange men and cities, Dante wrote a poem in which he himself, guided by Vergil, passed through hell in order to make his way to his home in heaven, where like Penelope his lost love Beatrice awaited him.

One of the modern symbolists has used this myth in poetry. Ezra Pound's largest poem bears the provisional title *Cantos*, which acknowledges a debt to Dante. It begins with a vigorous and partly unintelligible version of the Homeric account of Odysseus' visit to hell,[24] and goes on to several scenes in which figures whom Pound hates, such as capitalists, warmongers, and journalists, are put into obscene and hideous Dantesque hells. Yeats asserted that the other motive of the *Cantos* was transformation, and that Pound was inspired by Ovid's *Metamorphoses*,[25] but I cannot see much effect of this influence in the poem, except for a few references to the characters of Ovid's myths.

Joyce's *Ulysses* is the next large treatment of the legend. But Joyce makes the visit to hell relatively unimportant. According to his scholiast,[26] Paddy Dignam's funeral in the rat-haunted cemetery is the parallel to Odysseus' visit to the world of death. The witches' sabbath at the end of section 2, the drunken dream in which Dedalus passes through nighttown, and which gives all its readers the impression of being beset by devils meaner but not less evil than Dante's, is said to correspond to Odysseus' visit to Circe.[27] Despite that official version, we feel that in this chapter Joyce is really describing hell, the hell he foresaw in *A Portrait of the Artist*,[28] the hell whose descending circles are poverty, drunkenness, and lust.

Most artists have used myths to ennoble contemporary life. Louis XIV was portrayed by his court painters among the Olympian gods. Below the world's hugest skyscrapers America's genius for invention and America's titanic energy are imaged by the figures of Prometheus and Atlas. But the symbolists sometimes use Greek myths (that is, the stories as distinct from the figures) to degrade life: to show, by contrast with the heroism or beauty of classical legend, how sordid the men and women of to-day have made themselves. That is the chief purpose of the epic parallel in *Ulysses*. It contrasts the strong, noble, statuesque past with the nasty, poor, brutish present, in which everything is dirt and humiliation, even sexual love, even the courage of combat (Dedalus is knocked helpless and just saved from a thrashing), even the dignity of renunciation (when his mother's beseeching ghost appears to him, Dedalus yells out the crudest of obscenities). *Ulysses* is not mock-heroic like *Tom Jones*, but anti-heroic.[29] No one who has read it can doubt its power. It has been called an explosion in a cesspool. The commonest criticism of it is that its filth is exaggerated; but few of those who offer this criticism have spent the first twenty years of their lives in a large industrial city. The truth is not that the filth is exaggerated, but that it is not balanced by the gaiety, vigour, and native wholesomeness which are part of man's life, even in Dublins and even in slums; and that it underestimates the power of chance, even in squalid surroundings, to provide moments of fun and pauses of beauty. Its model, the *Odyssey*, is better balanced. The *Odyssey* is not all a heroic narrative. In the baroque age it was despised for its vulgar realism.[30] Its hero wears no plumes and has no quarterings. He loses his armour, his men, his ships, and his treasure, and is cast naked on a strange island where princesses do their own washing. When he reaches home he has to live in a swineherd's hut and cringe like a beggar in order to get near his own house. No one recognizes him in his home, except his old dog, which greets him and dies of joy among its lice. Is the death of a verminous old dog on a dunghill not the nadir of squalor? No. The last gesture of Argus was one of self-forgetting nobility, and he remains a heroic figure in our hearts, while the phantom of Bloom's lost son, in an Eton suit with diamond and ruby buttons and an ivory cane, is deliberately and effectively cheap, vulgar, and repellent.[31]

Less filthily, more beautifully, but no less despairingly, T. S. Eliot has used Greek legend to cast a pure but revealing light on the meanness of modern life. The poets of the Renaissance used Greco-Roman myth and history as a noble background to dignify the heroic deeds they described.[32] Eliot does the opposite. When the Renaissance poet compared his hero to Hector or his heroine to Helen, he made them more brave and more beautiful. By comparing Sweeney leaving a pick-up girl to Theseus deserting his mistress Ariadne, Eliot shows the modern infidelity to be vile—because the world which tolerates it is ignoble, coarse, repetitious, and complacent, and because even the actors lack that style which, in a heroic era, elevates a crime into a tragedy.[33]

Sweeney is one of the figures Eliot has created to typify certain tendencies he sees in our world. By his name, Sweeney should be the descendant of Irish peasant immigrants to America; he may have crossed Eliot's path in Boston, where his kin seized power from the gloved hands of the late George Apley and other Brahmins;[34] he is a tough, hairy, somatotonic cave-man with no regard for the feelings of others, a liking for low associations, and a talent for making offensive gestures. In *Sweeney among the Nightingales* he sits carelessly over his coffee after a meal in an inn, chatting with the prostitutes who shared it: he feels confident and euphoric. Royal and triumphant, King Agamemnon was murdered by his wife after a banquet; and the nightingales sang then as they are singing now. Eliot's immediate purpose in mentioning Agamemnon is to bring out the full horror of the situation. Until the last stanza, he is merely describing a taproom scene, suspicious, even sinister, but not murderous, something out of Stephen Dedalus' night-town. But as soon as Agamemnon's cry ('ah, I am struck a death-blow, deep within!') is evoked, the room darkens, the faces change, the sunset looks like blood on the floor. There is also a deeper purpose: to accentuate by contrast the sordidness of to-day, when even our crimes are vulgar.[35] The last stanza says that the nightingales, after the murder of Agamemnon,

> let their liquid siftings fall
> To stain the stiff dishonoured shroud.

This sentence is Eliot's own addition to the legend. With its revoltingly skilful sound-effect, it fuses into one image the contrasting ideas of beauty and squalor which dominate the poem.

They say that every composer has his favourite instrument; and, less credibly, that all his music can be distilled into one pet phrase. Certainly a great deal of Eliot's poetry grows out of the contrast between the brutal materialism of to-day and the frail life of the spirit which is bound to suffer in conflict with it, although it will survive, maimed or transfigured. This contrast appears in a crude form in *Sweeney among the Nightingales*. It is refined in *The Waste Land*, 2. Philomela was kidnapped, raped, imprisoned, and mutilated by her sister's husband Tereus; her tongue was torn out; but she wove her story into tapestry, sent the dumb but speaking work of art to her sister Procne, and joined her in a revenge so horrible that they all ceased to be human and changed into birds— Procne to the swallow, and Philomela to the nightingale which, although invisible and imprisoned in the night, still sings for ever of passion and of pain. This myth made one of the first poems in any European language when it re-entered literature from Ovid in an old French adaptation.[36] It lived through centuries of song ('Philomel with melody'), grew dull in the baroque age, and revived for the poets falsely called 'romantic'—

> Swallow, my sister, O sister swallow[37]

—to sing again, not less poignantly, above the waste land of the twentieth century.

The poet is both bird and prophet. In both incarnations he is opposed to force, brutality, materialism, lovelessness. There is another figure in Eliot's poetry, more complex than the nightingale, which symbolizes that opposition. This is Tiresias, the Greek prophet whom Eliot calls the most important personage in *The Waste Land*.[38] Tiresias appears in some very strange legends. He warned Oedipus of his unbelievable doom; and it was to find him that Odysseus ventured into the world of the dead. But before that he had been changed into a woman for seven years and then back into a man, so that he had experienced love from both the man's and the woman's point of view. Because he declared that women have more pleasure in it than men, and thereby decided against Juno in a dispute with her husband Jupiter, the indignant goddess struck him blind; but Jupiter compensated this by giving him the power of prophecy.[39]

Tiresias has several meanings in Eliot's poetry. In a way, he is Eliot. For Eliot in writing his early poems imagined himself to be feminine in weakness and delicacy, in contrast with the masculine violence which rules the world. In 1917 he personified himself as Mr. Prufrock—a name composed of *prude* and *frock*, the same two elements, hypersensitivity and femininity. In *The Waste Land* Mr. Prufrock becomes Tiresias,

> old man with wrinkled dugs,[40]

and identifies himself not with the enterprising man who takes, but with the defenceless woman who is taken:

> I Tiresias have foresuffered all
> Enacted on this same divan or bed.[41]

Defenceless because of his femininity, Tiresias is also helpless because he is blind. In Sophocles' *Oedipus* he is led on stage by the hand, tapping his way with a stick, groping and dependent as Oedipus himself is to become scarcely two hours later. And yet, although blind, he is a seer. Blind to the ordinary daylight, he can see into the darkness. His blindness is the cause and condition of his power of second sight. For Eliot he symbolizes the fact that those who understand the world most deeply, the poets and thinkers who have the inward eye, are blind and helpless in practical daily life; and that they gain the rare gift at the cost of the common sense.

Finally, Tiresias is old. His age makes him wise, but it also makes him impotent. The world which surrounds him is full of young violent unfeeling men like Sweeney, who know nothing of the past and see nothing of the future. Like Tiresias, Eliot has many centuries of antiquity present to his mind; as he broods on them, they help him to bear the blows of the present; but they make him old and weak. Elsewhere, in a less successful image, he compares himself to an aged eagle,[42] the far-sighted bird. The theme recurs in the epigraph to *The Waste Land*:

'I myself saw the Sibyl at Cumae, hanging up in a bottle, and when the kids said to her "Sibyl, what do you want?" she answered "I want to die".'

This is an odd piece of folk-lore.[43] The Sibyl was a prophetess who had a life-span of a thousand years, but without eternal youth, so that she gradually wasted away into nothing but a bodiless prophetic voice. It was she who guided Aeneas through the world of death. When Trimalchio saw her in the bottle, she had perhaps been changed into a grasshopper, dry, thin, but shrill. She combines the chief meanings that Eliot finds in Tiresias: she is female, she is weak, she is so old that she longs for death, but she is a seer.

We have discussed the use of Greek legend in the work of the symbolists, both to supply symbolic figures and as a source of immortal stories. The classical world has another function for the symbolist writers, which is less important, which it shares with other worlds of thought, but which must still be mentioned. This is to provide a decorative background of metaphor and allusion. Images, beautiful but frail, almost too small to be called symbols, are drawn from it. When Mallarmé looks at the glass of champagne in which he is to toast poetry and fellow poets, he sees the froth changed into the foam of magic seas, in which there is a glimpse of the white flanks of the Sirens.[44] When Eliot thinks of the splendour and brutality of military power, he images it in the eagles and trumpets of Rome.[45]
These writers are extremely sensitive to artistic beauty—beauty made by men, as distinct from natural beauty. Wordsworth found strength and consolation in the memory of a host of golden daffodils. But for Eliot, half a dozen quotations from poetry are the fragments he has shored against his ruins. They come at the end of *The Waste Land*, heaped together hastily, almost despairingly.[46] One is a phrase from the late Latin poem that haunted Marius the Epicurean, *The Vigil of Venus*,[47] which evokes (in the rhythm of Swinburne) the swallow, sister of the nightingale. So also, part 4 of *The Waste Land*—which is concerned with the theme of Death by Water—is an evocation of the many epitaphs on drowned sailors in the Greek Anthology.[48] This is highly specialized art. The masses cannot be expected to understand it. It would be stupendous if they could. Ezra Pound once cried:

> The thought of what America would be like
> If the classics had a wide circulation
> Troubles my sleep.[49]

But most of this group believe that the mass-man is Sweeney, who cannot hear the nightingales.

The debt of these writers to Greco-Roman literature is difficult to assess. Naturally. The symbolists are elusive poets, and Joyce is a cryptic novelist. Their methods tend to disguise and transform all the material that passes through their minds, until nothing is left but a hint, a nuance, a grotesque, a parodic reminiscence, a phrase repeated in a dream, a poignant echo. They do not care to explain. They never shout. They speak gently to those who wish to hear. Pound was bitterly attacked and derided for publishing the following poem:[50]

PAPYRUS

Spring . . .
Too long . . .
Gongula . . .

But hardly any of his critics cared to understand the title and listen for its suggestions. Yet they are clear, and boldly imaginative. Searching through the ruins of what were once Greek-speaking villages in Egypt, scholars have found many heaps of papyri miraculously preserved for fifteen or twenty centuries (see p. 468). Most of the writings on these papyri are not literary: they are letters, or school exercises, or tax-sheets. But occasionally we find poems or prose pieces by famous authors. Sometimes these are works which vanished in the Dark Ages and had been given up for lost. Sometimes they are merely fragments—yet precious, like the hand or head which is all that remains of a lost masterpiece of sculpture. A few words on a torn sheet of papyrus may be all that we can recover of a great poem; but they speak in the accents of immortality.

Now, the word *Gongula* occurs twice in poems by the exquisite Greek lyricist Sappho.[51] It was the name of one of Sappho's pupils. We know scarcely anything about her, except that she was dear to Sappho. What Pound has done in this poem, therefore, is to write four words containing something of Sappho's own feeling for nature, something of her passionate yearning, and the name of one of those she loved. He has created a fragment of a poem which Sappho herself might have written.

This technique shows how infinitely adaptable classical material can become. A few decades earlier, poets like Heredia and Landor were composing poems on Greek themes in which every detail was as firm as marble, as clear as sculpture. The technique changed. The Parnassians were succeeded by Mallarmé—just as Ingres and Puvis de Chavannes were succeeded by Seurat and Monet, with their vague outlines and shimmering deceptive colours. Yet Greek and Roman themes stirred the imaginations of both these very different groups of poets, and with each of them grew into new and valuable poetry.

As well as cultivating the technique of elusiveness, these writers approach the Greco-Roman world in a different way from their predecessors. They are not scholars. Compared with Shelley, for instance, or Milton, or Goethe, they are amateurs. They range rather more widely, and do not dive so deep. Joyce calls himself only 'a shy guest at the feast of the world's culture':[52] he appears to have had a fair amount of Latin and not much Greek; however, in his Jesuit school and his Roman Catholic college he was given a certain amount of critical insight into classical literature. Mallarmé and Valéry had a good French education, which still gives intelligent boys a wider acquaintance with literature than that of any other country; but the chief interest of each was in a non-classical field. Eliot, who went to Harvard and Oxford, was president of the Classical Association in 1941: however, he disclaims any specialist knowledge of Greek and Latin. Pound is a brilliant smatterer, with a remarkable gift for extracting vivid pictures from partly understood poems in Latin, Greek, Italian, Provençal, and miscellaneous dialects.[53]

But these writers believe it is impossible to conquer a central truth by a central invasion. Therefore, they do not think of Greek and Latin literature as a discipline to train the mind, or as a storehouse of wisdom. They find in it, first, an excitement of the imagination, and, together with that, an aesthetic consolation against the stresses, dangers, and vulgarities of life. Other symbolist poets have found these outlets elsewhere: Yeats in Celtic mythology, in occultism, in Hindu mysticism; Rilke in his private treasure-stock of remembered pictures, statues, noble lives, and visions. This little group itself has other excitements and consolations—Eliot in mystical Christianity, for example—but those it derives from Greece and Rome are among its most intense.

We have shown how myths and legendary figures acted as

stimuli on these five writers. To read their work is to be convinced that they also loved the classics as consolation. This is one of the chief subjects of *The Waste Land*. Our present life (Eliot believes) is brutal, hard to understand. Its cruelties and problems, if we are conscious of them, *must* be looked at and made endurable—not through any philosophical theories or plans of political action (which are all inadequate)—but through the frames of noble legends, through mystical words which haunt the mind, through beautiful phrases of poetry, graceful sounds of music, pictures themselves beyond intellectual understanding:

> Inexplicable splendour of Ionian white and gold . . .
> The peal of bells
> White towers
>   Weialala leia
>   Wallala leialala.[54]

Through this poem and others of Eliot's, we hear the voice of the nightingale, which is a cry of eternal pain, transformed into music. The transformation was the work of the Greek spirit, which has provided for these five, as for other less-known poets of their generation, both comfort in facing the vileness of life, and stimulus to soar, although wounded, above it.

THE REINTERPRETATION OF THE MYTHS

AT the present time the most interesting development of classical influence in modern thought and literature is the reinterpretation and revitalization of the Greek myths. This is going on in two different fields, and apparently in two different directions. One is almost wholly literary, and mainly dramatic. The other has produced a great deal of literature indirectly, and will produce more, but is primarily psychological and philosophical.

For century after century men have been captivated by the Greek legends, have told them in different ways, elaborating some and neglecting others, have sought different beauties and values in them, and, when they gave them conscious interpretations, have educed from them many different kinds of truth. However, there are three main principles on which the myths can be interpreted. One is to say that they describe single *historical facts*. The second is to take them as symbols of permanent *philosophical truths*. The third is to hold that they are reflections of *natural processes*, eternally recurring.

Many of the myths are about human beings, and gods in human shape: so they need hardly be changed to be interpreted as accounts of historical events. This kind of interpretation began in Greece itself, with Euhemeros (*fl.* 300 B.C.). He explained all the legends —divine, human, and semi-human—as being ennobled versions of the exploits of real warriors and chiefs long ago, who had been changed into gods by their admiring tribes. (The technique of rationalizing myth as the reflection of history is called, after him, euhemerism.[1]) And indeed, an essential part of Greco-Roman religious and political thought was the idea that men, by showing superhuman excellence, could become gods. The most famous example was Hercules, who made his way to heaven through his twelve labours and his heroic death. There were also Bacchus, and Castor and Pollux, and Aesculapius; then Aeneas, and Romulus. Alexander the Great was treated as a god during his lifetime. After his example it was not too difficult to deify dead emperors (not all, but those who had done great services for mankind) and to worship Caesar as the Saviour and the Prince of Peace.[2]

Again, some Christian writers have believed that the legends about pagan divinities were really stories about the devils who went to and fro upon the earth before the revelation of Jesus Christ.[3] This is the interpretation given by Milton. In *Paradise Regained* Satan reproaches Belial for suggesting that the best way to tempt Jesus would be to 'set women in his eye and in his walk'; and he implies that the 'sons of God', who the Bible says 'went in unto the daughters of men',[4] were Belial and his companions masquerading as the Greek deities:

> Have we not seen, or by relation heard,
> In courts and regal chambers how thou lurk'st,
> In wood or grove, by mossy fountain-side,
> In valley or green meadow, to waylay
> Some beauty rare, Calisto, Clymene,
> Daphne, or Semele, Antiopa,
> Or Amymone, Syrinx, many more,
> Too long—then lay'st thy scapes on names adored,
> Apollo, Neptune, Jupiter, or Pan,
> Satyr, or Faun, or Silvan?[5]

Then some scholars hold that the warrior heroes, Achilles, Agamemnon, Ajax, and their peers, were personifications of warring tribes, and that their victories and deaths represented the conquests of one clan or another during the great migrations. Historians of religion think that many of the myths in which a god is associated with an inferior personage commemorate religious revolutions, in which the cult of one deity was replaced by that of another. For example, if a divinity usually known in human shape is described as occasionally transforming himself into an animal, or killing an animal, or being accompanied by an animal, that would mean that the worship of the animal was abolished, replaced by the worship of the anthropomorphic god, and only dimly remembered. Finally, many legends are believed to record great inventions or advances in civilization: the 'culture-hero' Dionysus or Bacchus represents the discovery of wine, Triptolemus and Hiawatha the discovery of agriculture, the Argonauts the exploration of the unknown seas east of the Mediterranean, the Golden Fleece the wealth of the Black Sea trade-route, and Prometheus the discovery of fire, metal, and the handicrafts on which civilization is built.

In the nineteenth century there was a school which taught that the myths were not echoes of single events, but cryptic representations of profound philosophical truths. This school began in Germany, with G. F. Creuzer's *The Symbolism and Mythology of the Ancient Peoples* (1810–12), but it had a wider influence in France.[6] Creuzer's book was translated and expanded into a ten-volume treatise by the French scholar J. D. Guigniaut as *The Religions of Antiquity, considered principally in their Symbolic and Mythological Forms* (1825–51); and many other such books were produced in France during the forties, fifties, and sixties. The most notable was *Hellenic Polytheism*, by the brilliant Louis Ménard. It was through him and his pupil Leconte de Lisle that Greek legends, instead of being merely pretty rococo decorations, became, for the French Parnassians, grand and beautiful expressions of profound truths.[7] Strange to see how the symbolic interpretation of legends which was carried out so thoroughly in the Middle Ages with *Ovid Moralized*[8] reappears in France five hundred years later, but now without its Christian colouring.

Myths have also been thought to be symbols of important processes, either in the external world or in the soul. Max Müller (1823–1900), the German naturalized Englishman who was one of the founders of comparative philology, held that nearly all the myths symbolized the grandest phenomenon in the physical universe: the passage of the sun through the heavens every day and through the twelve signs of the zodiac every year. Thus, he interpreted almost every hero, from Hercules and his twelve labours and his flaming death to Arthur and his round table and his twelve knights, as a sun-myth. This theory went back long before him, at least as far as C. F. Dupuis (1742–1809), who declared that Jesus was really the sun and his twelve disciples the signs of the zodiac. It is not now generally accepted. One of the books which helped to explode Dupuis's version of it was a very amusing essay by J. B. Pérès, *How Napoleon never existed* (1835), which proves that Napoleon Bonaparte—whose name means 'certainly Apollo, from the good region' of the East—was really the sun, and that his twelve active marshals were the Ram, the Bull, the Heavenly Twins. . . .

A large group of myths has been associated (notably by Sir J. G. Frazer in *The Golden Bough*) with the processes of reproduction, sexual and agricultural, and with the connexion made between these two processes in the primitive mind. Such were the myths of Demeter and Persephone in the Mysteries; such were the legends of Venus and Adonis, Attis and Cybele, Isis and Osiris. There is something of this in the Christmas story too. For there is no evidence in the Bible that Jesus was born in December; but it seems right that the infant Saviour should be born about the winter solstice, to bring new life to a world apparently cold and dead. Our rejoicing round the Christmas-tree is a relic of a pagan winter ritual which used the evergreen as a symbol of the longed-for resurrection, to come in the spring-time.

Psychologists now regard myths as expressions of permanent but unacknowledged psychical attitudes and forces. This interpretation was launched by Sigmund Freud (1856–1939). He pointed to the many parallels between famous and widespread legends and the symbols which occur in dreams to represent (under an acceptable disguise) powerful instinctive drives.[9] Accordingly, he gave a Greek legendary name to the most powerful of all, the son's love of his mother and jealousy of his father. He called this, after the tragedy of the royal house of Thebes, the Oedipus complex. The parallel attitude, in which the daughter loves her father and is jealous of her mother, he named the Electra complex, because it recalls the tragedy of the princess who hated her proud cruel mother Clytemnestra. And the self-adoration and self-absorption which may make a man or woman dead to the whole external world were first and most graphically found in the mythical youth who died for love of his reflection in a pool; so, after Narcissus, the neurosis is called narcissism.

Freud's suggestions are now being elaborated by C. G. Jung (born 1875), particularly in his *Psychology and Religion*, *Psychology and the Unconscious*, and *Integration of the Personality*, as well as in the periodical *Eranos* which he sponsors. The essence of this interpretation of the myths is that they are symbols of the desires and passions which all mankind feels but does not acknowledge. Girls wish to be surpassingly beautiful and to marry the richest, noblest, handsomest man in the world, who will find them in spite of the neglect and hostility of their family and their surroundings. They relieve the tension of this desire by saying that it has already come true, by re-telling or re-reading the story, and by identifying themselves with its heroine Cinderella. Boys wish to be the only object of their mothers' love and to expel all their competitors, of whom father is the chief. They do so by telling the story of a gallant young man who, as part of his adventurous career, kills an unknown old man who turns out to be his father, and marries a beautiful queen who turns out to be his mother. Oedipus, Cinderella, Psyche, Helen of Troy, Don Juan, Aladdin or Gyges, David the slayer of Goliath or Jack-the-giant-killer, Sindbad or Ulysses, Hercules or Samson—all these characters are not so much historical individuals as projections of the wishes, passions, and hopes of all mankind. The great legends, and even the great symbols, such as the mystic flower, and the mystic numbers three, seven, and twelve, keep recurring throughout human history and human literature, not only in Europe but all over the world. They are constantly being remodelled. They emerge again and again as superstitions, or foundations of great creeds, or universal patterns of art and ritual. Jung calls them 'archetypes of the collective unconscious': patterns in which the soul of every man develops, because of the humanity he shares with every other man. Every married couple dreams of having a child which will be—not imperfect, not even ordinary, but superb, the solver of all problems, good, strong, wise, heroic. This dream becomes the myth of the miraculous baby.[10] And, in the deepest sense, the dream is true. Every baby is a miracle.

According to Jung, it is because of this universality that the great legends can be attributed to no one author, and can be rewritten again and again without losing their power. The work done on them by many generations of taletellers and listeners is truly 'collective'. They represent the inmost thoughts and feelings of the human race, and therefore they are—within human standards —immortal.

We must not, however, think that all legends are saccharine wish-fulfilments. Certainly the Greek myths are not. There is need of a book which will analyse them, tracing the manifold relations which link them to the myths of other nations and to the more conscious art of the Greeks, and explaining how they differ from other groups of legends. One essential difference is that many of them are tragic: the stories of Narcissus, Arachne, Syrinx, Phaethon, Oedipus himself. They knew, the wise Greeks, that the realization of the extreme wishes of mankind usually leads to tragedy. Cinderella lives happily ever after. But Oedipus blinds himself and goes into exile. Hercules, with his own body changed to an instrument of torture, burns himself to death.

Meanwhile, in literature, work of remarkable vitality has been produced by a number of modern authors who have been retelling Greek myths as plays or stories—occasionally giving them a modern setting, but more frequently retaining the ancient milieu and characters. Oddly enough, few of them actually treat the myths as symbols of the unconscious, or seem as familiar with psychological research as Joyce in *Finnegans Wake*. On the contrary, they prefer to use the legends as the Greek poets did, making them carry moral and political significance for a contemporary audience.

Although this movement has outposts in several other countries, its base is in modern France, and its activities there are by far the most fertile and interesting. Its chief is André Gide (born 1869), who began as long ago as 1899 with *Philoctetes* and *Prometheus drops his Chains*, followed by a play on the Gyges legend, *King Candaules* (published 1901). He then turned to other methods of presenting the problems that obsess him; but his work continued to presuppose a classical education in his readers (for example, in the Vergilian allusions of his 'Platonic dialogues' justifying homosexuality, *Corydon*, 1924), and he has always considered himself to be a classicist in style.[11] In 1931 he returned to Greece with a terse and shocking drama on the Theban legend, *Oedipus*; and his latest is a prose tale in the form of autobiography, *Theseus* (1946), embodying some material from his unfinished *Considerations on Greek Mythology*.

There can be little doubt that Gide was led to become a neo-Hellenic writer by the example of Oscar Wilde, himself a disciple of Pater and a good classical scholar.[12] He admired Wilde for two chief reasons. Wilde was an artist, with a lofty conception of the artist's place in society, and a technique which curiously blended sensuality and restraint; and he was a homosexual, with the courage of his perversions. In his essay *Oscar Wilde* Gide describes how, when he was only twenty-two, he first met and was fascinated by Wilde. In his marvellously attractive voice, with his exquisite choice of words, Wilde told fanciful story after story; and then, drawing young Gide aside, he told him a special tale of two strange lovers. It was a variation on the legend of Narcissus, who died for love of his own image in the water: Wilde said that the water had loved Narcissus dearly, because it could see its own beauty reflected in his eyes. This, the first utterance of Wilde that Gide records, not only prefigures their relationship, but symbolizes certain common essentials in their characters: overmastering love of sensuous beauty, homosexual passion, and cold self-sufficiency.

In the chronology of Gide's early works the classical influence exerted by Wilde reappears. In 1891 and thereafter Wilde told Gide the sequel to the legend of Narcissus, with many other variants on the Greek myths; in 1899 Gide produced *Prometheus drops his Chains*, a sequel to the legend of Prometheus. In 1893 Wilde published *Salomé*, dramatizing an oriental story from the fringes of the Greek world, in a style of classical restraint; in 1901 Gide published *King Candaules*, dramatizing an oriental story from the fringes of the Greek world, in a style of classical restraint. Both plays deal with sinister distortions of sexual passion, and both authors have added a still more sinister twist to the original plot. And surely Wilde's *Dorian Gray* (1891) is the elder brother of Gide's *Immoralist* (1902)? There is much in Gide which was not in Wilde; and there was something in Wilde which found no echo in Gide. Yet the two had many characteristics in common, including their strangest and their strongest. The rest of the story is hinted at in Gide's *Mopsus* and told in *If the Seed die not*.

A few dramas on Greek mythical themes were produced in Germany before and during the First World War. Among them were Hugo von Hofmannsthal's *Electra* (1903), a play of outrageous violence, later set to psychopathic music by Strauss; Franz Werfel's *Trojan Women* (1914), a tragedy of war in which the heroine is Hecuba, who suffers all the agonies of defeat and yet has the courage to survive; and a melodramatic *Antigone* (1917) by Walter Hasenclever, in which the tyrant Creon and his marshal bear an obvious resemblance to Wilhelm II and Ludendorff.[13]

In America a considerable impression was made by Eugene O'Neill's *Mourning becomes Electra* (1931), in which the family relationships, most of the incidents, and some of the moral issues of the tragedy of Agamemnon are restated in terms of nineteenth-century New England; but narrowed by a coarse insistence on the theme of sexual repression, and by the omission of the greater religious and moral problems faced by Aeschylus in the *Oresteia*.[14]

Sex is also the leading motive of the recent adaptations of *Medea* made in America by Robinson Jeffers and in France by Jean Anouilh. Euripides knew well, when he wrote the tragedy, that much of Medea's criminal frenzy was due to Jason's rejection of her love and the prospect of endless sexual starvation which she faced. But he knew there was more in it than that. He knew that it would lessen Medea's tragic grandeur if, instead of being a great lady spurned, an exile beggared, a comrade deceived, and a proud woman humbled, she were shown mainly as a half-savage girl writhing in the frustration of lust. Anouilh makes little more of her than that: she appears as a foul-mouthed Russian gipsy, and, instead of escaping in sombre triumph at the end, burns in her own caravan like the subject of a cheap *crime passionnel*. Jeffers's Medea is a woman of more stature. (Jeffers is a shamefully neglected poet: none of his creations lacks a memorable grandeur.) But since one of his chief themes is the daemonic power of the sexual impulse, and its close link with the urge to kill, he presents Medea mainly as a beautiful woman changed into a fury by the distortion of that impulse.[15]

Doomed heroism is the theme of two other adaptations of Greek myth. One is the tragedy *Icarus* (1927) by the young Italian poet Lauro de Bosis.[16] It shows Icarus and his father Daedalus as heroes of thought, the discoverers of iron, the first men to fly through the air. They personify the creative mind of man, and its greatest works—knowledge and poetry. It is a fine conception, expressed in some eloquent speeches and lyrics.[17] Unfortunately the plot—which makes Icarus fall from the sky after he has refused the love of Queen Pasiphae, who calls on her father (the Sun) to punish him—is a relatively meaningless intrigue, unworthy of the poet's ideals. De Bosis ended his own life with a lofty idealistic gesture. He was an opponent of Mussolini. After working underground for some time, he bought an aircraft, flew over Rome scattering anti-fascist leaflets, and, like his own Icarus, soared up again to his death.

Then the contemporary philosopher Albert Camus has embodied his belief that life is 'absurd' in several tales and plays and in a group of essays called *The Myth of Sisyphus*.[18] After trying to outwit the gods and conquer death, Sisyphus was sent to hell and condemned to push a huge stone up a mountain: an endless punishment, because the stone always rolled down again when it reached the top. Although many of us lead similar lives here and now, Camus says we are not tragic or heroic because we are not aware that our tasks are hopeless—that life itself is absurd. To realize that, and to rise above it, is the true victory. 'The struggle towards the summits is enough in itself to fill a man's heart. We must conceive Sisyphus as happy.' This is not so new as Camus thinks. It is the very voice of Byron to his own proud Titanic kinsman, Prometheus:[19]

> Like thee, Man is in part divine,
>   A troubled stream from a pure source;
> And Man in portions can foresee
> His own funereal destiny;
> His wretchedness, and his resistance,
> And his sad unallied existence:
> To which his Spirit may oppose
> Itself—an equal to all woes—
>   And a firm will, and a deep sense,
> Which even in torture can descry
>   Its own concentered recompense,
> Triumphant where it dares defy,
> And making Death a Victory.

Prometheus was the chief inspiration of a Swiss mystic, who carried out the most powerful single transformation of Greek myth in modern times. Although he won the Nobel Prize in 1919, Carl Spitteler is still almost unknown outside central Europe.[20] Yet he is a remarkable poet. Born in 1845, he studied for the church, but abandoned it. He made his own religion. After spending eight years as a tutor in Russia, he returned, and published a strange book called *Prometheus and Epimetheus* (1880–1).

Prometheus and Epimetheus was a cloudily complex elaboration of the ancient myth of the two brothers, Foresight and Hindsight, Vision and Repentance: one wise, unselfish, eternally progressing, and eternally suffering; the other simple, grasping at wealth without reflection, greedily accepting the perfect woman Pandora although her dowry contained all the troubles of mankind. One is a martyr to his own independence, the other a victim of his own complaisance. They are two aspects of the human soul. In the poetry of the revolutionary era Prometheus—the creator, the enemy of God, the crucified martyr—was a favourite hero.[21] In Spitteler's book, however, both brothers hold the stage. They occupy a world in which Greek legends are curiously interwoven with Christian and Gnostic supernatural notions and Spitteler's own mysticism, a world ruled not directly by God but by an angel. The angel offers its viceroyalty to Prometheus, who refuses, in order to keep the liberty of his soul. But Epimetheus accepts. He becomes rich, powerful, and unsuccessful. He fails to guard the angel's three children (Myth, Hiero, and Messiah) from the attacks of the evil spirit Behemoth. His brother Prometheus is recalled from beggary and exile, and saves the kingdom of the world, which the brothers then leave to the Messiah.

This book, published under a pen-name, was a failure. It was too big for the Swiss critics like Keller; it was soon overshadowed by another work written in the same apocalyptic vein and quasi-biblical prose, but with more violence and assurance—Nietzsche's *Thus spake Zarathustra*;[22] and it was too hard to understand without prolonged study. Reading complex allegories is like solving cryptograms—you must feel fairly certain that there is some message before you start. Few were sure of *Prometheus and Epimetheus*.

Twenty years later Spitteler wrote an epic, *Olympian Spring* (1900–6, revised 1910). This is a magnificent story in bold spacious six-beat rhyming couplets, telling how the Olympian dynasty of gods, at the summons of Fate, emerged from a long sleep in the underworld, climbed Mount Olympus (passing the dethroned chivalry of Kronos riding down), competed for the kingship and for Hera's hand, and then, with their natures and relations defined, wandered freely throughout the world, in full exercise of all their daemonic powers—until at last the happiness of heaven began to break up, and with it the rule of Zeus. He created Heracles, and sent him down to save suffering mankind.

These two works, together with *Prometheus the Sufferer*, a revised and reinterpreted version of the first, give Spitteler his claim to fame. *Prometheus and Epimetheus* has many remarkable qualities. *Olympian Spring*, for which he was awarded the Nobel Prize, is clearly the greater work of art.

Both are allegories. They are tales of visible and physical conflict between superhuman beings, but they image a number of conflicts between the spiritual forces of the human world. Yet, like *The Faerie Queene*, they tell their stories so vividly and make their characters, though strange, so real that our pleasure in them is not limited to understanding their deeper meanings. And, like all powerful symbolic artists, Spitteler creates images and incidents which we remember apparently for their own sake, and which, as we look at them, become slowly translucent, allowing us to penetrate into film after film, layer after layer of significance, all contained and vitalized within them.

There is no space in this book to discuss what all the meanings are. Some are obvious. The new gods, making their way up to Olympus, and competing for primacy, and acquiring their full strength, and dispersing in manifold activities over the world, symbolize the growth of the human spirit through childhood to energetic unreflective youth, and the difficulties, conflicts, and sufferings of developing into manhood. They remind us also how strangely a nation, or a race, or an empire, or a civilization appears out of darkness, how happy is its springtime of energy, how surely its death is fated, and how it may survive if, instead of dominating others, it sends out a saviour to them. Many other meanings are buried far deeper within the poems. But even a first reading will give anyone who loves poetry a number of scenes to haunt him quite as constantly as the symbolic scenes in *Faust*: Prometheus retreating into exile with his lion and his dog; the catastrophic rush of Kronos into ruin, like a giant fir-tree felled on a mountainside and hurtling down, leaving only a late echo of its fall.

Most of Spitteler's mythical figures are Greek in origin.[23] His fundamental pessimism, his judgement that life is beautiful but bad, stems partly from Schopenhauer through Burckhardt, and is partly pure Greek. Nietzsche too, thinking independently along the same lines, evoked a similar pessimism from his study of Greek art. However, Spitteler's characters are Swiss, and indeed German, in execution. They suffer and fight, fear and hate, more than the gods of Hellas. Monsters, not like the Python that Apollo slew but as dangerous as Fenris-Wolf, threaten them. Their Olympus is not the serene peak floating heaven-high over the Aegean: it is a meadow-shouldered Alp and a thunder-wrapped and lightning-blazing Valhalla. Hebe herself, bringing the new gods the food of immortality, leaps and yodels like an Alpine cowgirl in a dirndl.[24] Nevertheless, Spitteler's feeling for the Alps is finely conveyed. We said that Wordsworth was one of the few mountain-poets: Spitteler is another, scarcely less great.

It is hard to liken him to other artists. In music, he is akin to

Bruckner, with his long unhurried pace and simple nobility; to
Strauss, with his love of the mountains and of heroic strife; and to
Wagner, in his immense conceptions and his primitive sense of
doom. In literature there is no one quite like him, for he combines
the lofty grandeur of Landor with the religious mysticism and the
driving energy of Nietzsche. The painter most like him is his
Swiss contemporary Arnold Böcklin.[25]
But Spitteler was more than a nineteenth-century artist. He
was like a natural force. The world he inhabited was the world
which we enter when, far up on the ridge of a mountain, miles
from any road or town, we feel a new rhythm of life beating
slowly, ponderously, through us; the torrent roars far below, the
glens re-echo it, the wind shouts in our ears, the peaks all around
are not still, but seem to be heaving and straining in a thousand-
year-long struggle, clouds ten miles wide gallop under a heaven-
broad arch, forests and glaciers march and countermarch in
eternal war, and the whole universe is a realm of aeonian conflicts,
slow and mighty, which human pygmies cannot fully understand,
but must revere.

In recent years there have been many more retellings of the
Greek legends, in poetry, prose, and drama: too many to mention
here. (Those in English and American poetry are fully and sensitively discussed by Professor Douglas Bush in the later chapters
of his *Mythology and the Romantic Tradition in English Poetry*.)
The most interesting single group, however, is the neo-Hellenic
dramas produced by the modern French playwrights. We have
indicated André Gide as the leader of this movement in France.
Not all the dramatists mentioned can be called disciples of his,
yet they have all adopted many of his attitudes to myth, transforming and sometimes distorting the legends in the same way as he
does; and they share something of his basic spiritual outlook. His
work can therefore be considered along with theirs. His most
important books on Greek legendary themes have been listed. Of
the others, these are the chief:

Jean Cocteau's *Antigone* (1922), *Orpheus* (1926), and *The
Infernal Machine* (1934);
Jean Giraudoux's *Amphitryon 38* (1929), *The Trojan War will
not take place* (1935), and *Electra* (1937);

Jean Anouilh's *Eurydice* (1941), *Antigone* (1942), and *Medea* (1946);

Jean-Paul Sartre's *The Flies* (1943).

Before we consider these plays in detail, we might ask why so many modern playwrights have gone to Greek mythology for their plots. There are several different answers.

First, they are in search of themes which can be treated with strong simplicity—themes which have enough authority to stand up without masses of realistic or 'impressionist' detail to make them convincing. The same tendency is exemplified in contemporary music by Stravinsky's *Oedipus Rex* and Satie's *Gymnopédies*, and even better in art by the paintings of Chirico and the sculptures of Maillol.

Then these themes are not only simple in outline, but profoundly suggestive in content—and it is here that the neo-Hellenic dramatists join hands with the psychologists, for they know that every great myth carries a deep significance for the men of every age, including our own. Thus, under the German occupation, by rehandling the legends of Antigone and Orestes, Anouilh and Sartre were able to deal with the problem of resistance to an unjust but apparently irresistible authority, not only more safely but much more broadly than if they had invented a contemporary plot. And similarly, because one element of tragedy is the audience's foreknowledge of the coming disaster, there was a deeply tragic quality in Giraudoux's play showing all the efforts and sacrifices made by statesmen on both sides to avoid the Trojan war, which was forced on them by the passionate folly of mobs and demagogues. Since his play was produced in 1935, it was not only a Greek but a contemporary tragedy.

Also, since the French intellectuals are always defending themselves against the Olympians, Gide and Cocteau and the others find a certain relief in humanizing, debunking, and even vulgarizing some of the formidable old traditions. By bringing the myths nearer to humanity they make them more real. On the other hand, they also find the myths to be inexhaustible sources of poetry. One of the gravest defects of modern drama is that it lacks imaginative power. It is quick, clever, sometimes thoughtful, always realistic. But the great dramas of the world do not stay on the ground. They leave it and become poetry. Because of the modern world's emphasis on material power and possessions it is extremely difficult to write a contemporary play which will rise, at its noblest moments, into poetry; but contemporary problems, treated as versions of Greek myths, can be worked out to solutions which are poetic, whether the poetry is that of fantasy or that of tragic heroism.

In form, the plays are restrained without being rigidly classical. Except for Cocteau's *The Infernal Machine*, they observe the unities of time and place closely but unobtrusively, and all maintain the indispensable unity of action. They are all in completely modern prose, which in Cocteau and Giraudoux often mounts into poetic imagery, and in both these two and the others often descends into vulgarity and slang. The chorus of Greek tragedy appears only vestigially: a few women talking flat prose in Gide's *Oedipus*, a single commentator (like the Chorus of *Henry V*) in Anouilh's *Antigone* and Cocteau's *Antigone* (where Cocteau himself took the role at the first performance).[26]

The plots are almost always the same in outline as the myths on which they are based. They could scarcely be different. It would be ridiculous to write a play proving that Julius Caesar was not assassinated, or that Troy was never captured and burnt. What can be done, though, is to take the story of Caesar's murder or the fall of Troy, and give it new implications, explain the facts in an odd and interesting way, cast strange lights on the characters involved, and, by remodelling values, motives, and results, to emphasize the infinite uncertainty and complexity of human life. Euripides was the master of this art in Greece: he specialized in dramatizing little-known legends, such as the story that the gods kept Helen in Egypt and sent a beautiful ghost to Troy instead. We have already seen how a romancer of the late empire not only contrived to distort the fall of Troy into a stab-in-the-back defeat, but imposed his fiction on generations of medieval poets.[27] Every writer who attempts to create anything on a basis of myth must add, or subtract, or alter.[28]

One distinguished French novelist has destroyed, or inverted, a very famous legend—not because he dislikes Greek and Roman poetry but because he prefers nature to statuesque heroism. This is the Provençal writer Jean Giono, who tells us in his autobiography that the discovery of Vergil was a revelation as blinding for him as a religious conversion. He has written several works designed to recapture in prose the pastoral and animistic richness he feels in classical literature. In his *Birth of the Odyssey* (1938) he tells the story of the return of Odysseus, situates it in a fertile country-side more like southern France than barren Ithaca, and reduces the hero himself to a nervous and ageing liar, who invents the stories about the Cyclops, and Scylla and Charybdis, and so forth, merely in order to account for the years he spent *en route* living with bewitching women like Circe, and to compensate for his shabbiness and timidity as he approaches his home. His yarns are picked up by a blind old guitarist, who makes them into new ballads and sings them round the country-side.

The details of this story are carefully calculated to be anti-heroic. For instance, Odysseus is terribly afraid of Antinous, the strong young athlete with whom Penelope has been living in adultery; but, getting into an argument, he hits Antinous by accident, puts him to flight, chases him, and sees him caught in a landslide that throws him mutilated into the sea. Hence the tale that Odysseus killed all the suitors of Penelope. Instead of the faithful old dog Argus, a pet magpie recognizes the returning Odysseus; but, to avoid being detected by Antinous, he crushes it to death. In one version of the legend he was killed unwittingly by his own son—not Telemachus, but Circe's child Telegonus. But Giono's book ends with the rebellious Telemachus preparing to murder his father in cold blood. Although the story is ingenious and the descriptions vivid, the inversion of the heroic saga of Odysseus is pretty artificial. Such an unsubtle and pacific character would never even have regained his home, far less fought successfully through ten years of war at Troy.

Apart from this one instance, the modern French taletellers and playwrights keep the outlines of the legends; but they rehandle them in such a way as to bring out unexpected truths. For instance, there is not much authority for believing that Hector and Odysseus made a concerted effort to avert the Trojan war by negotiation, but were forced into it by unknown hotheads; yet it is certainly plausible that the two cautious heroes should have planned for peace rather than for war. And although Giraudoux, in inventing a blustering militarist and an excited propagandist to precipitate the conflict, has created characters more appropriate to modern Germany and France than to Bronze Age Greece, the anachronism does not vitiate the main truth he is conveying.

Anouilh's *Eurydice* is unlike most of the others, because it is entirely modern in setting and yet almost unintelligible without knowledge of the myth. The story is that Eurydice, wife of the master musician Orpheus, died suddenly; that he, by the power of his music, gained entrance to the world of the dead and was allowed to bring Eurydice back—on condition that he would not look at her before they reached the living world; that he forgot his promise, lost her for ever, and wandered about in despair until he was torn to pieces by the savage maenads of Thrace. In Anouilh's play Orpheus is a café violinist who meets a touring actress in a railway station and falls in love with her, but loses her when he insists on questioning her about her previous lovers. She is given back to him by a mysterious Monsieur Henri (who would be quite meaningless if he were not understood as part of the Greek myth) on condition that he shall not look her in the face until morning. But he asks her again for the whole truth, and stares her in the face, and loses her again in death. His failure is a symbol of the fact (worked out in such detail by Proust) that a lover cannot keep from trying to find out everything about his sweetheart's life, even if it will kill their love.

In Gide's *Prometheus drops his Chains* Prometheus has left his crag; but he still keeps his eagle as a pet, and feeds it on his own vitals. Why? Because he likes to see it looking handsome; and because he, like each of us, enjoys having a private eagle, not hanging round his neck like a dead albatross, but loving him and living on his heart's blood. And Gide's *Oedipus*—in which one of Oedipus' sons writes a book closely corresponding to works by two of Gide's disciples,[29] and where the Sphinx is only the monstrous enigma of life, intimidating every youth, but ready to disappear as soon as the youth answers its riddle with the word MAN (that is, by asserting that human nature creates its own standards)—surely this play, in which everyone is corrupt but proud, is a reflex of Gide himself and of the corrupt but proud children of his spirit. Of all these neo-Hellenic works, Giraudoux's *Amphitryon 38* is the richest in its power of revealing unexpected truths about great subjects: the love of husband and wife, the power of any woman over any man (even a god in man's disguise), and the relation of man and the gods.

All these playwrights are good psychologists; and they have all discovered new and yet credible motives for the actions recorded in mythical tradition. In the autobiography of Theseus Gide says that when Ariadne gave him a thread to guide him back out of the monster-haunted labyrinth she was really trying to attach him to herself; that this was why he later abandoned her on a desert island; and that, when he 'forgot' to mount the white sails which would tell his father he was safe (thus indirectly causing his father's suicide and his own accession to the throne), he did not really forget, any more than he forgot Ariadne on Naxos. In the same book Oedipus says that he put out his eyes, not to punish himself, but to punish them for not seeing what they ought to have seen. Creon is usually the typical harsh tyrant; but in Anouilh's *Antigone* he explains very coolly and patiently that, so far from being cruel, he is merely an administrator of law and order and efficient government, an ideal nobler than any individual's private code of morals. Yes, and after the tragedy, after Antigone has hanged herself, after Creon's own son has denounced him and killed himself, after his own wife has cut her throat, he only sighs heavily and goes off to do his duty by presiding at a cabinet meeting: a death as complete as that of the others. The most striking reinterpretation of motives, though not the deepest, is in Cocteau's *The Infernal Machine*, where the Sphinx, although a deity vastly more powerful than the arrogant young Oedipus, tells him her secret because he has charmed the human part of her, but, as Nemesis, looks on with pity at the fulfilment of his burning ambition, the ambition favoured by the gods: that he shall supplant his father, and win the kingdom, and marry his mother, and, after the fuse has burnt down to the explosive, be shattered in the ruins of his own strength. 'They kill us for their sport.'

André Gide stands apart from all the others as an inventor of repulsive new episodes and vicious motives. For more than two thousand years men have rehearsed the awful history of the Labdacids; but Gide was the first to suggest that the sons born of Oedipus' unknowing incest were deliberately (and not without success) trying to seduce their sisters.[30] The story of Candaules and Gyges, as told by Herodotus (and retold by Gautier), is spicy enough: the king is so proud of his wife's beauty that he hides his vizier Gyges in the bedroom to watch her undressing. But Gide makes the king, in a phenomenal access of generosity, leave the room and tell Gyges to substitute for him that night.[31] Theseus, in the legend, carried off both Ariadne and her sister Phaedra. But

Gide says that he told Ariadne he had taken a fancy to her young *brother*, that she connived at her brother's corruption, and that Phaedra was then smuggled aboard in the disguise of the disappointed boy.[32] Bad taste on Gide's level, like Nero's poetry or Gaudi's architecture, is as difficult to achieve as good taste, and is at least as rare. Theseus is not the most attractive of mythical champions, but Gide gives him that peculiarly cynical type of sexual immorality which most of Gide's heroes carry as proudly as an oriflamme. 'I never like leaving a desire unsatisfied,' he says as he turns from one sister to another, 'it is unhealthy.'[33] Even Ariadne's scarf, which lovers of poetry have always known as a pathetic token of her betrayal and her loneliness, the scarf with which Ovid says she waft her love to come again to Naxos—

> as to remind you that I was forgotten,
> to a long branch I bound my veil of white—[34]

Gide has succeeded, consciously or unconsciously, in dirtying even that slight thing. In his story it blows off Ariadne's head, and is picked up by Theseus, who at once, and publicly, wraps it around him as a loin-cloth.[35]

All these authors are eager to keep their plays from being remote, archaic, unreal. Therefore, although they do not deliberately put anachronisms on the stage, they make the language as modern as they can, and frequently lapse into vulgarities of detail and expression. In Giraudoux's *Electra* an angry wife talks of having to light her husband's cigars and filter his coffee.[36] Helen of Troy, like a modern Frenchwoman, says Paris may desert her for a while 'to play bowls or fish for eels'.[37] In Sophocles' *Antigone* there is a sentry who reports Antigone's crime to Creon in comparatively blunt and simple language; but in Anouilh's *Antigone* there are several sentries, and they accentuate the lonely virginal idealism of the heroine by very coarse conversations about getting drunk and going to a brothel. In Cocteau's *Orpheus* the poet is torn to pieces because he submits in a poetry competition the oracular phrase *Madame Eurydice Reviendra Des Enfers*, the initial letters of which form the commonest French obscenity. Gide (except in his early *Philoctetes*) tries deliberately to be banal, because he thinks heroics are false while banality is real. One example will be enough. After Oedipus discovers his sin and rushes out to blind himself, Gide makes the chorus remain on stage. Instead of

keeping silence or chanting a song of pity and terror, it breaks out
into infuriatingly trivial comments:

'It's all just a family affair: nothing to do with us.... He's made his
bed, and now he's got to lie in it.'[38]

In spite of such eccentricities the best of these plays are very
fine, and even the worst of them contain striking and memorable
thoughts. Tragedy must rise above the realities of every day, upon
the wings of imagination and emotion. The great tragedians have
known this necessity, and have used many means of fulfilling it:
vivid descriptions like the beacon-speech in Aeschylus' *Agamemnon*;
striking stage-pictures like the storm in *King Lear* and the sleeping
Furies in *The Eumenides*; symbols like the crimson carpet in
Agamemnon, the jester's skull in *Hamlet*, the hand-washing in
Macbeth; metrical richness, both dramatic and lyrical; physical
suffering like that of Prometheus, Philoctetes, Orestes, Othello,
Gloucester, Phèdre; and, above all, supernatural appearances—
omens, divinities, spirits of health or goblins damned. Yielding
to the decline in taste and the contraction of imagination, most
modern playwrights do not even attempt such bold effects: or, if
ever, do so awkwardly and unconvincingly. However, the French
neo-Hellenic dramatists, stimulated by the example of their
predecessors and strengthened by the myths which they are using
(or: which are using them), employ several of these effects to
ennoble their work.

A powerful new symbol for the sense of guilt which is basically
weakness and cowardice was created by Sartre in *The Flies*, when
he showed the blood-guilty city of Argos infested with a plague
of fat black blowflies, and the Furies themselves threatening
Orestes in the shape of monstrous blood-sucking flies. Flies
annoy, and weaken, and in swarms even terrify, but they rarely
kill. With energy and decision, by killing some and driving others
away and ignoring the rest, one can survive. *The Flies* was produced when France was occupied by the Germans. Again, in
Cocteau's *The Infernal Machine*, Jocasta, the pitiful, nervous, but
still beautiful queen, enters leading Tiresias, the blind seer who
foresees her tragedy. Her scarf trails behind her, and Tiresias
treads on it. She cries: 'I am surrounded by things that hate me!
This scarf has been choking me all day. It hooks on to branches,
it rolls itself round chariot-axles, and now you tread on it....

It's terrifying! It will kill me.' That is the scarf with which she hangs herself; and in the last scene she appears (visible only to the blinded eyes of Oedipus) with it bound around her neck. In the same play the wedding of Oedipus and his mother is treated with masterly tact and imagination. The couple, left alone in the bridal chamber, are exhausted by the coronation ceremonies, the long procession, the heavy robes: they move and live half-asleep in an uneasy dream. Oedipus falls asleep just as he has thrown himself down to rest, across the marriage-bed, his tired head lolling over the foot of it. And his head rests on the empty cradle (once his own) which Jocasta kept in memory of the child she lost; and then, as he sleeps, she rocks the cradle.

The authority of legend makes it easier for a playwright to introduce the supernatural in a mythical play than in a contemporary drama. The French dramatists are not as a rule content with imitating the traditional appearances of supernatural beings in Greek drama. They prefer to give their creations new forms. The flies of Sartre are one such creation. The Furies also appear in Giraudoux's *Electra*: as little girls who gradually grow into maidens and then into tall powerful women, while the revenge of Orestes approaches its maturity. In the same play, a vulture is seen in the last act, at first floating very high above the head of the doomed Aegisthus, and then gradually, gradually planing lower. Cocteau's *Orpheus* is really a surrealist extravaganza, clever but silly. However, it contains one impressive deity: Death. Neither a crowned skeleton nor a winged angel, she appears as a beautiful impassive young woman, who puts on a surgeon's white coat and mask, and, while Eurydice, her patient, is dying, directs the manipulation of machines as intricate and terrifying as those of modern hospitals. No horseman, no reaper could be so effective for to-day. But the most impressive of all these figures is the Sphinx in Cocteau's *The Infernal Machine*. At first only a girl whom young Oedipus meets on the road, she changes into a winged monster, half-woman, half-lioness; and the proud Oedipus falls before her, bewitched and aghast.

Much might be said of the eloquence of Giraudoux, who wrote exquisite prose, and whose characters talk in flashingly vivid images, following the French dramatic tradition of *raisonnement*, disquisitions on abstract themes. If anything, his characters do discuss too much. But Giraudoux and Cocteau are the only two of these writers whose style reaches real eloquence at great moments. One example will suffice. When Oedipus falls before the Sphinx, he is paralysed. He shouts 'I *will* resist!' And she replies:

'It is useless to close your eyes, to turn your head away. My power does not lie in my gaze nor in my song. When I act, I am defter than a blind man's fingers, swifter than a gladiator's net, subtler than the lightning, stiffer than a charioteer, heavier than a cow, more dutiful than a schoolboy wrinkling his brows over a sum, more rigged and sailed and anchored and balanced than a ship, more incorruptible than a judge, greedier than the insects, bloodier than the birds, more nocturnal than an egg, more ingenious than an Asiatic torturer, more deceitful than the heart, more supple than the hand of a cheat, more fateful than the stars, more diligent than the snake as it moistens its prey with saliva; I can secrete and produce and abandon and wind and ravel and unravel so that when I will these knots of mine they are tied, and when I think them they are tightened or loosened; so delicate that you cannot grasp them, so pliant that you feel them like a creeping poison, so hard that if I let them slip they would maim you, so taut that a bow could draw a note of divine anguish from the bond between us; clamped like the sea, like the pillar, like the rose, thewed like the octopus, complicated like the mechanism of a dream, invisible above all else, invisible and majestic like the blood in the veins of a statue, a thread binding you in the multiple swirls and twists of a stream of honey falling into a cup of honey.'[39]

We opened this discussion by asking why these playwrights chose Greek legends for their subjects. The central answer is that the myths are permanent. They deal with the greatest of all problems, the problems which do not change, because men and women do not change. They deal with love; with war; with sin; with tyranny; with courage; with fate: and all in some way or other deal with the relation of man to those divine powers which are sometimes felt to be irrational, sometimes to be cruel, and sometimes, alas, to be just.

24

CONCLUSION

WE have come a long way. We have traced the river of Greek and Roman influence in literature from its first mingling with the life of modern Europe, among the forests and wildernesses of the Dark Ages, through the softer landscapes of the Middle Ages, which it helped to enrich and adorn, into the tremendous fertility of the Renaissance, a hot summerland of bright flowers and clustering fruit; then past that, flowing along a bed now carefully controlled, lined with marble and watched by statues, through the baroque era; then bursting out again in new and unexpected courses with the age of revolution—sometimes meandering with a mazy motion through the rich fancies of a young poet in love, sometimes, with a melodious roar, breaking down old traditions and surging high against the very temples of Christianity itself; then, in new channels, flowing strongly and graciously through the literature of the nineteenth century and into that of the twentieth, right on into our own time, when modern psychologists and playwrights look with admiration and with awe at the immortal figures of faun and hero, nymph and god, borne along in its eternal stream.

We have not been able to follow all its wanderings, to trace all its varied currents, or to do more than indicate a few of its many effluents. It would have been attractive to explore some of the countries lying a little beyond its main course: to look, for instance, at the fantastic lyrics of the Spaniard Góngora, to examine the famous but forgotten *Adonis* of the Italian baroque poet Marini, or to admire the Homeric tragedy and the fine odes of Ronsard's Polish admirer Kochanowski. Many modern authors, too, must be omitted, because, although they felt the power of Greco-Roman influence, they expressed it less creatively or more eccentrically than their contemporaries. In England, one might point to Robert Bridges; in America, to the imagist H. D.; in Germany, to Stefan George.

It would have been interesting, again, to follow the course of Greek and Roman philosophical thought through the life of modern Europe and America, showing how much Voltaire owed to it, how it moulded the mind of the medieval church, how the logic and metaphysics of the Greeks have become part of the intellectual equipment without which no western man can reason. Or it would have been a novel and valuable approach to history, to show how many great men have modelled their lives and actions on the classical heroes of whom they read when they were young. Charles the Twelfth thought he was Alexander. Jefferson wished to be Cicero. Napoleon made himself Caesar.

Nor have we been able to mention the many thinkers and artists of the modern world who, although they wrote little or nothing showing the direct influence of the classics, still found that classical literature was of immense value to them as a challenge and a stimulus. Within the nineteenth century, for example, we might think of a German composer, an American poet, and a Russian novelist, of whom this is true.

Wagner, when composing *The Ring of the Nibelungs*, used to spend all morning working at his music. After luncheon he sat in the garden and read Greek tragedies—because he felt that no other literature would maintain him at the same lofty pitch of energy and passion. Not only that, but he evidently conceived his operas to be modern parallels to the Greek tragedies. Like Aeschylus' *Oresteia*, *The Ring* is called a trilogy (with a prelude), while the gods and heroic deeds and the sense of tragic brooding fate in the four operas are clearly inspired by the majestic figures of Greek drama.[1]

Whitman called the Muses to come away from Greece and Ionia. His own poetry was boldly untraditional in pattern and feeling. Yet his friend Thoreau recalls that he loved to ride up and down Broadway on a bus, sitting beside the driver just above the horses, with his hair and beard flying in the wind, declaiming Homer at the top of his voice.[2] In fact, he must have looked rather like Homer, who would have heard him with a smile of friendship.

Tolstoy began to learn Greek at forty-two. After he could read it, he wrote to his friend Fet: 'I have become convinced that of all that human language has produced truly and simply beautiful, I knew nothing'; he taught it, on a novel but effective system of his own, to his children; and he finally uttered his conviction that 'without a knowledge of Greek there is no education'.[3]

Or consider education itself. One of the main achievements of the work of civilization which has been going on for the last twelve or fifteen centuries has been to teach more and more people more and more thoroughly. Until late last century the core of that education was Latin, and sometimes Greek, poetry and prose. It would be tempting to write a good history of education in terms of the classical curriculum, and to include tributes to the many fine teachers who have proved their genius by producing, with the aid of Greco-Roman literature, many brilliant poets and constructive thinkers. The largest single group of such teachers would be the Jesuits, whose pupils include Molière, Descartes, Tasso, Voltaire, Calderón, Montesquieu, Corneille, Buffon, Diderot, Goldoni, Bossuet, Lesage, Chiabrera, and Joyce. Next to them would come the wonderful teachers of the Renaissance, from the Scot Buchanan to the Italian Ficino, from Dorat to Erasmus. And close to them would be the group we tend to forget, although we should remember them with admiration and affection. These are the fathers who introduced their sons to the great books and the beautiful languages of Greece and Rome, who awakened their interest, and helped them over the dry sands and stubborn fences, and studied along with them, until often the sons became famous men whom we admire as though they had produced themselves out of nothing. It was for this, more than for their physical existence, that Pitt and Casaubon, Browning and Montaigne, were grateful to their fathers.[4] That is true fatherhood, not only to beget the body but to help in making the mind of your son.

However, the subject of this book is literature. It has been necessary, therefore, to omit everything which does not bear directly upon it. Philosophy, art, education, and other works of the Greco-Roman spirit have been mentioned only in so far as they contributed immediately to modern western literature.

No one would claim that the stream which we have been following is the only one in the majestic flow of literature. There are many other currents. Chief of all is the personal experience of each writer—not only his emotional life, but the political calms or storms through which he lives, his success or failure in the task of making money, the city or court or country-side in which he has his home, the friends and enemies he makes, the works of art he admires, the religion he practises or neglects. Another powerful current is the course of history, which with wars and dynasties and revolutions can make or break the aesthetic patterns of a whole generation of artists. Still another is the imagination of the ordinary people of each nation: those who make the ghost-stories and the songs, the dances, jokes, and proverbs, the fables and ballads, which are so often literature themselves, and are always one of the vital forces in literature. Still, the current flowing out of Greece and Rome has always been a strong one, always productive, and often central. How strong and how productive it has been, this book has endeavoured to show. It can also be proved negatively: imagine that all the books, plays, and poems, in all the European languages, which were written under direct inspiration from the classics, should be destroyed. Not only would nearly all the best work disappear—Dante's *Comedy*, Shakespeare's tragedies, much of the finest nineteenth-century poetry—but several complete areas of European literature would drop out of sight entirely, like cities swallowed up in an earthquake, leaving nothing behind but a few flowers growing on the edge of the chasm, here a tale of chivalry and there a little love-song, here a book of letters and there a farce.

That fact is often underestimated or ignored because of a mistake made by many modern thinkers. The mistake is to believe that the past is dead. When they are asked how far back they would place this death, they give various answers. Some say 1776, others 1848, others 1917; many say the beginning of the Christian era. All agree that something of the past is still alive, but they differ in defining how much. They are misled by a false analogy between the physical death of individual men and the passage of events into history. Men die, but mankind lives continuously. No historical fact is dead if it is still actively producing results: for its life is in the mind of humanity.

Take two simple examples. Languages are meant to be read and spoken. They are methods of conveying thought through words, whether the words are uttered or written. As long as they continue to convey thoughts, they are not dead. Therefore Latin and Greek, which are still conveying new thoughts to new readers, are not dead languages. The instance of Hebrew, which survived the drums and tramplings of seven conquests as a language which was read but seldom spoken, shows how mistaken it is to think of unspoken tongues as dead. The only dead languages are those which no one now either speaks or reads, like Etruscan and Cretan.

Again, one of the fundamental facts in European civilization was the establishment of the Roman empire, followed by its division into Greek-speaking and Latin-speaking sections. The fact continues to be active and vital. Through a continuous chain of causes and effects it has produced the present political division between east and west in Europe—a division now affecting all the rest of the world—and the long-standing religious schism between the Greek (and Slavic) Orthodox church and the Roman Catholic church. We cannot live as though this fact had ceased to exist. But we can live better by understanding it. We can, for instance, stop thinking of Russia as an Asiatic nation, when in fact it is a European society which was partly civilized by the Greek part of the Roman empire, and then (under the Tartars) isolated and arrested. Its true relationships are European. It received few fertilizing currents from the East. For centuries it was part of the stream which flowed from Greece and Rome through Byzantium; and its earliest known rulers were Scandinavian northmen who eventually found their way to Byzantium not round the Mediterranean sea-lanes but through the vast Russian rivers. Then that connexion was cut. But Poland, so like Russia in racial stock and language, received the stream through Rome and continued to be enriched by it, while Russia, although clinging to its Byzantine-Christian religion and its Greek-Slavic letters, was otherwise isolated. All these events, however distant, are facts which still exist and affect our lives. To understand them is to help in solving the problems which they raise.

But here, literature is our concern; and literature passes into the background even less rapidly, and changes under pressure even less radically, than historical facts. Every book from which you can get new interests and ideas is alive, although it was written many centuries ago. To realize that is to open a broader universe to your own mind. The difference between an educated man and an uneducated man is that the uneducated man lives only for the moment, reading his newspaper and watching the latest moving-picture, while the educated man lives in a far wider present, that vital eternity in which the psalms of David and the plays of Shakespeare, the epistles of Paul and the dialogues of Plato, speak with the same charm and power that made them immortal the instant they were written.

The purpose of this book has been to correct that error as applied to literature, by showing that the history of much of the best poetry and prose written in western countries is a continuous stream flowing from its source in Greece to the present day, and that that stream is one current in the continuous spiritual life of western man. From another point of view this could be looked at as a continuous process of education. Greco-Roman civilization did not die with the fall of the empire. It taught us. It helped to civilize us. Its lessons differed at different times.

At first, our vernacular literatures went to it, like children to their mother, for stories. It told us myths and legends, and we repeated them: the fall of Troy, the tale of Sir Hector and Lady Helen and Sir Aeneas, the adventures of Caesar and Pompey, the weird stories of Midas and Philomel, the loves of Pyramus and Thisbe.

Then, as the nations began to grow, it taught them language— giving them words which would be more than a practical tool for daily life and become vehicles for thought—and taught them philosophical ideas on which to exercise their expanding minds. These were its chief gifts in the Middle Ages.

In the Renaissance it taught them two new lessons. It gave them the patterns of literature in which to express the new ideas which came flooding in: tragedy and comedy, ode and essay and elegy, epic and satire. And it showed them, exemplified in the bodies of its statues and the minds of its writers, a new ideal of individual life lived at its highest intensity for its own sake, 'humanism' ennobled by the consciousness of its own best powers.

The nations matured. They became aware of themselves not only as groups but as parts of Europe and as heirs of history. They penetrated farther back into their own ancestry, rediscovering and re-creating the past to serve as a frame for their own thoughts. Now it taught them political lessons: the Roman ideal *republic*, the Greek creation *democracy*, were realized again.

In this latest stage of the growth of our literature, we have turned again to listen to the legends. This is part of our deeper exploration of the human mind. Like a man who remembers a tale told him in his childhood and realizes that it has profound significance, we are now retelling the Greek myths, finding that they are often the only illumination of many dark places of the soul, and drawing from them a hundred meanings which are vital for ourselves.

Throughout the whole process, two fundamental facts have continued to exist and affect it. One of these is the conflict between

Christianity and Greco-Roman paganism. From one point of view, this is the conflict between two views of the past: should it be totally rejected, or should it be accepted and transformed for our use? In that form we saw the conflict in the Battle of the Books. From another point of view, it is the conflict between the view that the world and human nature are totally bad, depraved beyond human redemption, and the view that both contain much good which can be bettered. The condemnation of human nature by ascetic Christians has often provoked an equally violent counter-condemnation by those who felt that human nature was basically good, and who admired the Greeks and Romans for eliciting the best from it. In this conflict, truth does not lie wholly with one side or with the other. It rests with those who have taken the best of paganism and transformed it by the admixture of the highest of Christian thought.

The other fact is the nature of civilization itself. Many of us misunderstand it. We live in a materialistic world. Most of us think incessantly about making money, or about gaining power—expressed in material terms—for one group or one nation, or about redistributing wealth between classes, countries, or continents. Nevertheless, civilization is not chiefly concerned with money, or power, or possessions. It is concerned with the human mind. The richest state in the world, or a world-society of unlimited wealth and comfort, even although every single one of its members had all the food and clothing and machines and material possessions he could possibly use, would still not be a civilization. It would be what Plato called 'a city of swine', eating, drinking, mating, and sleeping until they died.[5]

The Greeks were keen business-men. The Romans built a vast empire of tremendous power and wealth. But if they had done no more than that, they would be as dead as the Assyrians. They are still alive, and working through us, because they realized that civilization means education. *Civilization is the life of the mind.* Naturally it cannot exist without material security, physical health, and properly distributed wealth. But these are not ends. They are means. Their ultimate objective is the good life of the mind. It is through the mind that we are truly human. The rest, the games and the food and the shelter and the fighting, we share with the animals.

Civilization means education—not only for children but for men and women throughout their lives. One of the most varied and interesting methods of such education is literature. Greece knew that dramas and songs, tales and histories, are not only amusements for a moment but, because of their continuously fertile content, permanent possessions for the mind. This was the discovery of the Greeks. They were not very rich, or very powerful. Egypt was richer. Persia was far more powerful. But the Greeks were civilized, because they *thought*.

They taught this to the Romans. Rome knew much which the Greeks never learned or acquired too late. Rome quieted the warring savages, and built the roads and harbours and bridges and irrigation-systems, and made the laws. That too is civilization. But after that, what? The Greeks replied 'Bread for the soul', and gave it.

The spiritual food which they received from the Greeks was passed on by the Romans to the whole of western Europe. It was purified and strengthened by Christianity, which as it grew brought in still more nourishment from the Greek spirit. Then the Roman empire was overthrown, first in the west and later in the east. Nothing survives of its material wealth and its power. But the spiritual force of Greece and Rome survives. It conquered the barbarian conquerors, and then civilized them. It helped to make us.

The true relation between the modern world and the classical world is the same, on a larger scale, as the relation between Rome and Greece. It is an educational relationship. Rome was wealthy and powerful. Much of its wealth and power was used for sensual pleasures—drink and the races, parties and yachts, expensive furniture and gorgeous clothes. But, taught by Greece, many Romans also used the wealth and power of their state to make possible, for everyone who could read then and thereafter, a stronger and more sensitive life of the mind. Now we remember them. Some tremendous conquerors we know, and some tyrants: Caesar, and Nero, and—who was it who beat Hannibal? The millionaires we have forgotten, except as ridiculous figures who had dishes of nightingales' tongues and heated gold swimming-pools. But those we still know and admire are the men (whether rich or poor) who used their brains: the self-made lawyer who, after reaching the top of his profession and holding the highest state offices, made himself a persuasive voice for much of the most difficult Greco-Roman philosophy; the farm-boy who, putting the whole Roman destiny into a heroic Greek shape, inspired Dante and Milton and Tennyson and Hugo and many others; the slave's son from the barren south whose thrifty father sent him to Greece, and who returned to write, first satires on the greedy rich, and then songs of temperate happiness and deeply based patriotism, which have amused, charmed, and strengthened hundreds of thousands of modern men. These are Cicero, Vergil, Horace. In Greece we remember Homer, Plato, Sophocles, Aristotle, while the rich and powerful and luxurious and ambitious have ceased to exist. Only thought and art live.

Rome grew powerful through her military and political genius; and then, from Greece, she learnt to live the life of the mind. We have grown powerful through our scientific and industrial genius. The only way in which we can justify that power, use it for our own lasting benefit, and contribute something permanent to the development of the human race, is to understand and spread a system of noble spiritual ideals. Some of these we ourselves are working out. Many others we derive from Christianity. And many—in art and philosophy and literature—we have received from Greco-Roman civilization, as a priceless legacy. The real duty of man is not to extend his power or multiply his wealth beyond his needs, but to enrich and enjoy his only imperishable possession: his soul.

BRIEF BIBLIOGRAPHY

THERE is, as far as I know, no single book which gives even in outline a survey of the whole field of Greek and Roman influence on modern literature. It has been partly covered by three series of publications, which, although they contain many useful facts, are very unevenly written and organized. These are:

Das Erbe der Alten, in two groups, both published at Leipzig: the first, in ten volumes (ed. O. Crusius, O. Immisch, and T. Zielinski), from 1910 to 1924, the second, in twenty-six volumes (ed. O. Immisch), from 1919 to 1936;

Our Debt to Greece and Rome, forty-four volumes (ed. G. D. Hadzsits and D. M. Robinson) issued first in Boston and later in New York between 1922 and 1935;

Vorträge der Bibliothek Warburg (ed. F. Saxl, Leipzig, 1923–32) and other publications of the Bibliothek Warburg, an organization which was created in order to foster research in the influence of Greek and Roman culture on the modern world, and which has been continuing its work, after moving in 1934 to London, under the name of the Warburg Institute.

The most useful books and articles which I have met with when working on special sections of the field are mentioned in the notes on individual chapters. See in particular note 51 on chapter 5 (Chaucer), the introductory note on chapter 6 (Translation in the Renaissance), the introductory note on chapter 11 (Shakespeare's Classics), and note 1 on chapter 14 (The Battle of the Books).

Besides these, the following are among the most valuable single works.

1. C. BAILEY (ed.), *The Legacy of Rome* (Oxford, 1923).

Essays on the various parts of our civilization—law, political organization, &c.—which have been formed or influenced by Rome. Well written and edited.

2. F. BALDENSPERGER and W. P. FRIEDRICH, *Bibliography of Comparative Literature* (University of N. Carolina Studies in Comparative Literature, Chapel Hill, 1950).

Book 2, Parts 2, 3, and 4, and Book 3, Part 2, compose the newest and best available bibliography of Greek and Roman influence on modern literature.

3. K. BORINSKI, *Die Antike in Poetik und Kunsttheorie von Ausgang des klassischen Altertums bis auf Goethe und Wilhelm von Humboldt* (Das Erbe der Alten, 9 and 10, Leipzig, 1914 and 1924).

A history of the influence of classical ideas and examples in developing modern critical standards: brilliantly written, almost too tightly packed with material.

4 H. BROWN, *A Bibliography of Classical Influence on English Literature* (Harvard Studies in Philology, 18 (Cambridge, Mass., 1935), 7-46).
A valuable list of books and articles.

5. D. BUSH, *Mythology and the Renaissance Tradition in English Poetry* (Minneapolis and London, 1932).

A survey of the manifold appearances of Greco-Roman myths in English poetry (excluding drama) during the Renaissance: an indispensable work, written with fine taste and extensive knowledge.

6. D. BUSH, *Mythology and the Romantic Tradition in English Poetry* (Harvard Studies in English, 18, Cambridge, Mass., 1937).

A similar survey beginning in the eighteenth century and running down almost to the present day. This book is quite as gracefully written as its predecessor, but labours a little under the effort of covering *all* the poets who fall within the period and the pattern. Still, it is nearly always a pleasure and a profit to read.

7. C. L. CHOLEVIUS, *Geschichte der deutschen Poesie nach ihren antiken Elementen* (2 volumes, Leipzig, 1854 and 1856).

This is the most complete book known to me which deals with classical influence on any area of modern literature. Its scope is even broader than its title, for it discusses not only German poetry but German criticism and philosophy, analyses German prose dramas and novels, and gives some biographical information about German authors. Although immensely long (1,283 closely printed pages), it is clearly and spaciously written. Like many books of its time it oversimplifies complex characters and movements by dissolving them into two opposing factors called 'romantic' and 'classical'. It suffers also from a nationalist point of view which makes its author underestimate the debt of German to other European literatures, and sometimes spend an unconscionable amount of space on relatively unimportant writers merely because they happen to be the chief figures in a barren period. (Thus, he has more on Bodmer's epic about the Flood, the *Noachid*, than on Goethe's *Roman Elegies* or the entire career of Hölderlin.) But it is an important work both for students of German literature and for those interested in the continuing vitality of Greco-Roman influence.

8. G. S. GORDON (ed.), *English Literature and the Classics* (Oxford, 1912).

A collection of essays, originally designed as lectures by experts in separate areas of this field. Scrappy and uneven, it contains a few useful articles (for instance, Owen on 'Ovid and romance') and some disappointingly superficial pieces; there is no attempt at integrating them into a comprehensive outline.

9. O. GRUPPE, *Geschichte der klassischen Mythologie und Religions-geschichte während des Mittelalters im Abendland und während der Neuzeit* (supplementary volume of the *Ausführliches Lexikon der griechischen und römischen Mythologie*, edited by W. H. Roscher; Leipzig, 1921).

This book describes the different views of Greco-Roman mythology held by the Europeans of the Dark and Middle Ages, the Renaissance, the baroque period, and modern times. Although it pays some attention to the handbooks of mythology on which many poets and artists fed their imagination, and mentions a few of the modern works of art which have re-created classical legends, its chief emphasis is upon the successive theories which thinkers have devised to explain the origin and meaning of the myths. In treating them Gruppe gives certain eighteenth-century and nineteenth-century writers more, and the medieval and Renaissance scholars much less space than they deserve; but, because of its continuity, scope, and analytical penetration, his book is a valuable groundwork for further study of the subject.

10. O. IMMISCH, *Das Nachleben der Antike* (Das Erbe der Alten, new series, 1; Leipzig, 1919).

A short book developed out of a series of war-time lectures. It is interestingly written, and contains some useful information, but suffers from trying to resist the attacks of German modernists and nationalists on classical education, by proving that German life and language were largely built on Latin and Greek foundations, rather than to explain what types of Greek and Roman influence are still potent in European thought.

11. W. JAEGER, *Paideia: the Ideals of Greek Culture* (3 volumes, translated by G. Highet, Oxford and New York, 1939–44).

The word *paideia* means both 'civilization' and 'education'. The Greeks differed from other nations in this: they believed that men progressed in civilization, not by gaining power or wealth, but by educating themselves. Their great books—tragedies, epics, histories, speeches, philosophical works—are great because they were designed to educate their readers; and that is why we still profit from reading them. Professor Jaeger works out this thesis in detail, for all the best books in Greek literature from Homer to Demosthenes. A masterly work, full of deeply fruitful ideas.

12. SIR R. LIVINGSTONE (ed.), *The Legacy of Greece* (Oxford, 1921).

Essays on the immortal forces of Greek culture—art, philosophy, literature, medical science, and many others—showing how they continue to be relevant to our own life. A companion to no. 1 in this list; well written and full of material.

13. R. NEWALD, *Nachleben der Antike 1920–1929* and *Nachleben der Antike* (*Jahresberichte über die Fortschritte der klassischen Altertums-wissenschaft* 232. 3. 1–122 and Supplementband 250. 1–144, Leipzig 1931 and 1935).

Bursian's *Jahresberichte* is a periodical which prints elaborately detailed bibliographical and critical surveys of various fields of classical scholarship, each survey covering a period of ten to twenty years and linking up with an earlier article. These are the first it has published on the survivals of Greek and Roman culture in the modern world. They are very full and careful, and deal not only with literature but with other realms of thought, such as law and religion. Together, they are intended to list the books and articles that appeared between 1920 and 1930, and to lead into the Warburg bibliographies (see no. 24).

14. F. O. NOLTE, *German Literature and the Classics: a Bibliographical Guide* (Harvard Studies in Philology, 18 (Cambridge, Mass., 1935), 125–63).

Another useful bibliography on the same plan as no. 4.

15. L. PETIT DE JULLEVILLE (ed.), *Histoire de la langue et de la littérature française* (8 volumes, Paris, 1896–9¹ and 1908–12²).

This is an admirably written and very comprehensive history of French literature, now rather out of date on disputed points, but indispensable as a groundwork. Although it does not bear centrally on this subject, I have cited it so often in the notes that it should be listed here.

16. H. PEYRE, *L'Influence des littératures antiques sur la littérature française moderne: état des travaux* (Yale Romanic Studies, 19, New Haven, 1941).

A sensitively written survey of the recent books and articles on this subject so far as it concerns French. Much more than a bibliography, it points out the gaps which still exist and makes many stimulating suggestions for books which need to be written.

17. F. E. PIERCE, 'The Hellenic Current in English Nineteenth-century Poetry' (*Journal of English and Germanic Philology*, 16 (1917), 103–35).

A first-rate article, succinct but complete.

18. J. E. SANDYS, *A History of Classical Scholarship* (3 volumes, Cambridge, 1903–8).

The most complete and best balanced account of the subject in existence. It traces the progress of Greek and Latin studies from their beginnings in Greece and Rome (where many of the methods and materials of modern philology were worked out), through the Middle Ages and Renaissance down to our own time. Its style is necessarily dry, but now and then becomes surprisingly sympathetic. Its chief weakness is that it pays far more attention to the biographies of individual scholars than to the large central trends which are more important in the history of scholarship.

19. E. STEMPLINGER, 'Die Befruchtung der Weltliteratur durch die Antike' (*Germanisch-romanische Monatsschrift*, 2 (1910), 529–42).

A bibliographical survey of five or six important areas of the subject, with suggestions for further work: contains some books which I have not seen mentioned elsewhere.

20. J. A. K. THOMSON, *The Classical Background of English Literature* (London, 1948).

This work came out while I was finishing the revision of the present book: I thought it would be better not to read it, in order to avoid any suspicion of plagiarism. But the reputation of its author and the pleasure I have gained from his earlier books assure me that it will be worth reading.

21. T. G. TUCKER, *The Foreign Debt of English Literature* (London, 1907).

A well-informed work emphasizing the interpenetration of all the western literatures. It suffers a little from the author's determination to explain all about the literature of each nation before going into its influence on English, but it is useful for undergraduates.

22. G. VOIGT, *Die Wiederbelebung des classischen Alterthums* (Berlin, 1880–1²).

This fine old book is still a mine of information for those who are beginning to study the Renaissance, particularly about the gradual rediscovery of the achievements of the Greek and Latin genius.

23. *Vom Altertum zur Gegenwart* (no editor's name, introduction by E. Norden and A. Giesecke-Teubner, Leipzig and Berlin, 1921²).

A collection of twenty-nine essays, mostly about 10 pages long, on almost every conceivable aspect of the relationship between the Greco-Roman world and our own. Some of them are very good, some quite useless; a number are spoilt by being little more than counter-propaganda directed against nationalist, socialist, and 'progressive' proposals for changes in the German educational system; and the emphasis of the whole is on the relatively narrow field of German literature and society rather than on the whole European and American civilization which has roots in Greece and Rome. A two-page index, no notes.

24. The Warburg Institute, *A Bibliography of the Survival of the Classics 1931–3* (2 volumes, London, 1934).

A superb collection of names of books and articles over a remarkably wide range, with full bibliographical information and critical summaries of each item.

25. T. ZIELINSKI, *Cicero im Wandel der Jahrhunderte* (Leipzig, 1912³).

A history of Cicero's influence in the modern world, originally written to counter Mommsen's attack on his character and neglect of his permanent significance. Like everything Zielinski wrote, it is brilliantly original and packed with unusual information—although it is very thin on the Middle Ages, and stops at the end of the eighteenth century. Quotations in this book are from its third edition: there was a fourth in 1929, but the text remained virtually unchanged. Often Zielinski rises to genuine eloquence, as in these paragraphs from his concluding pages:

'Anyone who has had the pleasure of travelling along one of those great roads which have long been among the chief highways of the human race—the roads which run northwards and westwards from the plain of Lombardy through the Alps—will always remember his experiences. He has felt the very pulse-beat of world history. All the ages have left their memories behind them: here a Roman watch-tower built for the wars of Marcus Aurelius, there a knightly castle recalling a Hohenstaufen's visit to the strange land across the mountains; this gorge speaks of Hannibal, this dam of Napoleon, this bridge of Suvorov; that lake was ennobled by an epigram of Catullus, yonder valley by a terzina of Dante, this view by a page in Goethe's diary; on this rock, like a strayed bird, the memory of Tristan and Isolde with their grievous love once alighted.

'Every reader of Cicero will have a similar experience, if he has a sense of history; and that experience alone is enough—even if the caricaturists are right in all they say—to give him thoughts and feelings of incomparable depth. This phase of Cicero's was locked by Jerome in his heart, in spite of his dream vow; with that, Diderot endeavoured to destroy the "superstition" of posterity. That thought charmed Petrarch; by this, in the midst of tormenting doubts, the mind of Luther was "much and deeply moved". Here is the pearl that Bossuet set in the gold of his style; there the steel out of which a Jacobin forged his dagger. This sentence won a delicate worldly laugh from the pretty admirers of the patriarch of Ferney; and that moved the terrorized judges of Louis XVI to tears. It is a unique and unforgettable pleasure; but one must not be afraid of the effort it takes, for it cannot be denied that it is easier to walk over certain other paths than to travel the Roman road.'

Notes on I. INTRODUCTION

1. Latin was the regular language for the debates of the legislatures of Hungary until 1840 (Toynbee, *A Study of History*, Oxford, 1939, 5. 496 n.) and of Poland until later. The last considerable English poet who wrote Latin as well as English verse was Walter Savage Landor, who died in 1864 (see p. 446).

2. It is strange to visit towns in former Roman provinces—say, in Turkey or north Africa—and find that nobody can read or write except an occasional merchant and official, while large Greek and Roman inscriptions surviving from the empire have been built into farm-house walls or used as foundation-stones. Expeditions have found papyrus copies of Homer, Demosthenes, and Plato, fragments of what were once useful libraries, buried under remote Egyptian villages on the fringe of the Sahara desert, now inhabited by illiterate peasants. See C. H. Roberts, 'The Greek Papyri', in *The Legacy of Egypt* (ed. S. R. K. Glanville, Oxford, 1942), especially 265–6.

3. The story of Hamlet is told in Saxo Grammaticus. For the runes, see Saxo, 3. 6. 16: 'proficiscuntur cum eo bini Fengonis satellites, litteras ligno insculptas (nam id celebre quondam genus chartarum erat) secum gestantes.' On Bellerophon see *Il.* 6. 168–70.

4. There is a fine Anglo-Saxon poem, *The Ruin*, on the remains of Roman Bath, written by someone who did not know who had built the noble halls which now lay in destruction, but admired them and felt the pathos of their death.

5. As early as the third century B.C. the Jewish scriptures were being turned into Greek for the use of Jews in Egypt who could not understand Hebrew. This is the version called the Septuagint, which means 'seventy', from the story that it was made by seventy-two rabbis (see c. 6, n. 1, p. 594). S. Lieberman, *Greek in Jewish Palestine* (New York, 1942), has brought out the great penetrative power of the Greek language even into Rabbinical teaching in Palestine itself.

6. The dialects and languages of the western part of the empire did not entirely disappear for many generations; and we do not know the stages of their disappearance. Some few, like Basque, survived in remote corners. But the essential fact is that they were backwaters or underground streams, while the main river of civilization flowed through Latin. Meillet puts it well in his *Esquisse d'une histoire de la langue latine* (3rd ed., Paris, 1933), 230:

'Les trouvailles de la Graufesenque ont montré que, au Iᵉʳ siècle de l'ère chrétienne, la langue d'un atelier de potiers du Sud de la France était encore le gaulois: rien de [plus] imprévu. Encore au IIIᵉ et au IVᵉ siècle, on sait que le gaulois subsistait dans les campagnes. . . . Tout moyen fait défaut pour déterminer quand, au fond des campagnes d'Etrurie, le dernier paysan a parlé l'étrusque; quand, dans les vallées de l'Apennin, le dernier paysan d'Ombrie a parlé l'ombrien; quand, au pied des Alpes, le dernier paysan de Ligurie a parlé le ligure. Un seul fait est sûr: toutes ces langues sont mortes; à partir du

moment où se répand le latin, on n'entend plus parler d'aucune; elles se sont
éteintes obscurément comme s'est éteint en Prusse, au xvie siècle, le dernier
sujet parlant prussien, comme s'est éteint, sur les bords de l'Elbe, le polabe au
xviiie siècle, sans qu'on sache quand est mort le dernier sujet parlant polabe,
comme s'éteint, comme vient de s'éteindre sans doute, en Poméranie, le dernier
sujet parlant slovince.'

7. Caesar, when he saw Brutus attacking him, is reported to have said
'You too, my boy?'—καὶ σύ, τέκνον; (Suet. D. Iul. 82. 2). Many of the
court jokes recorded by Suetonius are in conversational Greek; Martial
and Juvenal both complain that Roman ladies used affectionate Greek
phrases in public, as a modern English-speaking girl might say *chéri*; and
there is an odd letter from Augustus to his wife which begins in Latin and
slips into Greek and then back into Latin, two or three times in the same
sentence (Suet. D. Claud. 4).

8. The alphabet used by Russians and other Slavic peoples is called
Cyrillic after its reputed inventor, St. Cyril (827–69), the missionary to
the Slavs, who based it on Greek as pronounced in his day, and invented
extra letters for Slavic sounds unparalleled in Greek. On the civilizing
power of Byzantine Christianity and culture among the eastern Slavs see
S. H. Cross, 'The Results of the Conversion of the Slavs from Byzan-
tium', in *Annuaire de l'Institut de Philologie et d'Histoire Orientales et
Slaves*, 7 (1939–44). On the dissension of the empires and the sack of
Constantinople see Gibbon, *Decline and Fall of the Roman Empire*, c. 60.
Cf. also Stanisław Kosciałkowski, 'Rome and Byzantium in the Culture of
Mediaeval Europe', in *The Bulletin of the Polish Institute of Arts and
Sciences in America*, 4 (1945–6), which emphasizes the power and magni-
ficence of Byzantium as a world-capital.

9. On the extinction of Greek in western Europe, see P. Courcelle, *Les
Lettres grecques en occident de Macrobe à Cassiodore* (Paris, 1943); M. Roger,
L'Enseignement des lettres classiques d'Ausone à Alcuin (Paris, 1905); and
G. R. Stephens, *The Knowledge of Greek in England in the Middle Ages*
(Philadelphia, 1933). Knowledge of Greek disappeared from the provinces of Spain, Britain, and Africa during the fifth century (Courcelle,
390). It was very hard for St. Augustine to learn Greek in Africa early in
that century, and then the province was cut off by the Vandal invasions
(Courcelle, 193 f., 205 f.). The often-repeated assertion that Greek
culture survived in Ireland during this period is very difficult to accept or
substantiate: see Roger, 268 f.; Courcelle, 390, and n. 2 on that page. It
lived on in Gaul until the sixth century (Courcelle, 246 f.). In Italy itself,
the tradition of Greek culture was first broken by the invasions of Alaric
(beginning in A.D. 400), revived under the Ostrogoths with Boethius and
Symmachus (on whom see p. 41 f.), and then died about the end of the
sixth century. The Bible, however, had been translated into Latin in
good time—first about the end of the second century A.D., in the version
called the *Itala*, used by St. Augustine, and then, by the Balkan saint
Jerome with the help of Jewish scholars, towards the end of the fourth
century. His rendering is now known as the Vulgate, the *uolgata lectio* or
'popular edition'. It did not win general acceptance at first, but the

influence of Pope Gregory the Great (590–604) helped to make it what it now is, the official Bible of the Roman Catholic church. (It is strange to think that the very word 'testament', in the titles Old Testament and New Testament, is a mistranslation of the Greek διαθήκη = 'agreement' or 'covenant'.) During the late Middle Ages, in the twelfth and thirteenth centuries, a few scholars appear who have acquired a knowledge of Greek, such as Robert Grosseteste and Roger Bacon (see S. H. Thomson, *The Writings of Robert Grosseteste, Bishop of Lincoln*, Cambridge, 1940); but the tradition of Greek learning was not re-established in the west until Boccaccio's time. On the relation between ancient and modern Greek and the quarrel between the popularizers and classicizers in modern Greek, see A. J. Toynbee, *A Study of History* (Oxford, 1939), 6. 68 f. On the Arabian intermediaries of classical thought, see R. Walzer, 'Arabic Transmission of Greek Thought to Mediaeval Europe', in *The Bulletin of the John Rylands Library*, 29 (1945), 1. 160–83.

10. Latin died as a national language during the barbarian conquests of the sixth and seventh centuries A.D. Childebert I made France Frankish in 536; Sisebut and Swinthila made Spain Visigothic in 612–29; Rothari conquered the last Roman parts of Lombardy in 650. These changes were marked by the codification of the conquerors' laws (e.g. the Langobardic code in 643) and the composition of histories written from their point of view (e.g. Gregory of Tours's *History of the Franks*). Books and documents from the sixth, seventh, and eighth centuries show that even written Latin was breaking up and melting away. Manuscripts are full of shocking mistakes in grammar and even in spelling. Mass-books show that the priests who used them scarcely understood their ritual language. A deed of gift by Childebert I, dated to 528, has phrases like *pro nos, per locis*; and *ille, ipse, unus* now come to be used as articles. Gregory of Tours, himself a bishop, constantly apologizes for the bad Latin he writes, and says that most of his contemporaries can understand a rustic talking patois but not a professor discussing philosophy; while Pope Gregory the Great bluntly says that he does not care if he makes barbarous mistakes in language. Glossaries now begin to be produced, not explaining difficult words, but explaining ordinary Latin words by simpler or more 'rustic' words. And one of the surest symptoms of the onset of the Dark Ages now appears—the spread of illiteracy. From the fifth century onwards, people begin to sign with an X, which means 'I cannot read or write, but I am a Christian'. On the entire subject see G. Gröber, 'Sprachquellen und Wortquellen des lateinischen Wörterbuchs', in *Archiv für lateinische Lexicographie*, 1. 35 f., and F. Lot, 'A quelle époque a-t-on cessé de parler latin?', in *Archivum Latinitatis medii aevi*, 6 (1931), 97 f.

Meanwhile, the birth of the modern languages of western Europe was long delayed by the superiority of Latin as a written medium, by the authority and convenience of church Latin and legal Latin, and— probably most of all—by the unsettled political conditions of the Dark Ages, which made it difficult for any one local dialect to conquer its competitors. In French, the oldest document is the Oaths of Strasbourg

(A.D. 842); but when Roger Bacon was travelling in France in 1260, he found that many of the inhabitants could not understand one another's dialects. The earliest literary documents in the language that flowed as the main stream into modern French date from the tenth century, and the first long poem is *Alexis, c.* 1040. In 1520 the king ordered that the official language should be French, which then ousted Latin in deeds and documents. The oldest document in Italian is a short cantilena dated to about 1150. Dante's magnificent work fixed the literary language as the Florentine dialect, in a form which continues with little change to-day, although other Italian dialects are still spoken and even printed. The growth of Spanish was retarded by the Moorish invasion and occupation. The first documents in something like modern Spanish date from the tenth century: the first great work of literature is *El cantar del mio Cid*, which shows in its very title the Arabic influence (Cid = the Arabic *Sayyid*, 'lord') and is dated about 1140. Castilian became the official language of Spain under Ferdinand III (1217–52), and even invaded Italy along with the Spanish forces: it has left traces in modern Italian. German dialects were for long in confused competition, so that no single literary language was worked out. Also, Latin seems to have been used for cultural purposes much more exclusively than in western countries, with less contact between educated men and the ordinary people. German is used in deeds from the middle of the thirteenth century. Modern German is usually dated from Luther's translation of the Bible (1522–34); but his opponents in the Catholic states, and certain groups who spoke other dialects, refused to accept standardization, so that unification of the German language did not come until the eighteenth and nineteenth centuries. The dialect Luther actually chose was that used by the chancery of the duke of Saxony.

11. Some of the Christian propagandists, like Lactantius and Minucius Felix, wrote elegant classical Latin. Others, such as Tertullian and Cyprian, are deliberately non-classical: although they did not write 'vulgar' Latin, they used a new revolutionary language to fit their new and revolutionary subject-matter. But the majority of the writers of the early church simplify both their vocabulary and their syntax when they are addressing the general public.

12. The largest and most important part of Petronius' *Satirica* was discovered as late as 1650 in the little Dalmatian port of Trogir—or perhaps rediscovered, after having already been found during the Renaissance, stolen from its owner, hidden, and lost (see A. C. Clark in *The Classical Review*, 22 (1908), 178 f.).

13. Vergil, *Buc.* 4, on which poem see pp. 72, 422, 524. Cf. E. Norden, *Die Geburt des Kindes* (Leipzig, 1924), on the entire theme.

14. Aug. *Conf.* 3. 4. On the influence of Cicero in the early Christian church, see E. Zielinski, *Cicero im Wandel der Jahrhunderte* (Leipzig, 1912³), cc. 7 and 8. A. J. Toynbee, *A Study of History*, 5. 583 n., even conjectures that the description of the communistic practices of the early Christians in Acts iv. 32–5 is exaggerated, and is ultimately based on Plato, *Republic*, 5. 462c.

15. The vital period for the synthesis of Greco-Roman philosophy and Christian thought was the fourth century. Then it was that Christians like Augustine and Jerome, by taking over what they could use of the tradition of Greco-Roman culture, and giving it a new life from their own source of spiritual energy, far surpassed their pagan contemporaries in depth and power. This synthesis continued, in spite of opposition, to exert its creative influence throughout the Dark and Middle Ages. On the *naïveté* of the Christian writers, Professor Werner Jaeger of Harvard writes me: 'The love of simplicity in the Church Fathers is often only a traditional Christian attitude, and the sophisticated style in which they actually write proves that it is a concession which they had to make, just as nowadays even the most fastidious aesthete starts with a bow to the "common man".' See also Prof. Jaeger's Aquinas lecture, *Humanism and Theology* (Marquette University, Milwaukee, Wis., 1943), 23–4.

16. This rule is often called *ecclesia uiuit lege Romana*. O. Cassola, in *La recezione del diritto civile nel diritto canonico* (Tortona, 1941), p. 5, suggests that the phrase is first adumbrated in the *Lex Ribuaria*, tit. 58. 1:

> et episcopus archidiacono iubeat, ut ei tabulas secundum legem Romanam, quam ecclesia uiuit, scribere faciunt.

On this subject see also H. O. Taylor, *The Classical Heritage of the Middle Ages* (New York, 1911³), and P. Hinschius, 'Geschichte und Quellen des kanonischen Rechts', in von Holtzendorff's *Encycl. der Rechtswissenschaft* (Berlin, 1890⁵), v. 1. The existence of Roman law in Italy was continuous throughout the Dark Ages. Its study revived during the Middle Ages and the church began to systematize it. In the eleventh century the famous Florentine manuscript of Justinian's *Digest* (the sixth-century codification of Roman imperial law) was discovered and had a fructifying influence on the legal system of the church. The Bolognese monk Gratian finished the codification of canon law about A.D. 1140: see Le Bras, 'Canon Law', in *The Legacy of the Middle Ages* (ed. C. G. Crump, Oxford, 1926).

17. Pliny, *Ep. ad Traianum*, 96.

18. Spengler, *Der Untergang des Abendlandes*, 2. 7. 7.

19. It should not be forgotten that, after the split between the empires, the Roman empire lived on in the east, centred on Constantinople, for nearly a thousand years after the fall of the western empire. E. Bach, 'Imperium Romanum', in *Classica et Mediaevalia*, 8 (1945), 1–2, shows that even in the twelfth century the Byzantine emperor still considered himself the sole legitimate ruler of the world, the heir of Rome. J. B. Bury, in the *Encyclopaedia Britannica* (1946), s.v. 'Later Roman Empire', points out that modern diplomacy is another survival from Rome, having been continued in the Byzantine empire and transmitted through it to the Venetian republic, and thence to the west; but surely the Roman Catholic church also preserved much of the Roman diplomatic tradition. It should also be remembered that the Christian church, like the empire, split into an eastern and a western section. The Greek Orthodox church can therefore claim to be a spiritual heir of the Roman empire, comparable to the Roman Catholic church; but it has been gravely weakened in the past

500 years by the fact that first Constantinople and then Moscow have been taken over by non-Christian governments.

20. There is an excellent description of the Franks Casket, with a picture, in E. V. K. Dobbie's edition of *The Anglo-Saxon Minor Poems* (New York, 1942), preface, p. cxxv f. (By the way, the object which Weland is giving to Beadohild is surely the cup with which he drugged her.) See also W. P. Ker, *Epic and Romance* (London, 1922²), 48 f., and *The Cambridge History of English Literature*, 1. c. 2, p. 13.

21. It is almost superfluous to recommend Miss Helen Waddell's stimulating book, *The Wandering Scholars* (London, 1934⁷).

22. For a discussion of Gombo, see E. L. Tinker's 'Gombo: the Creole Dialect of Louisiana' (*Proceedings of the American Antiquarian Society*, April 1935). There are lots of charming songs and fables, some satires, and many fine recipes in Gombo, but hardly anything else.

23. This is why the Chinese use Mandarin officially: there are so many provincial dialects in that vast country which are mutually unintelligible that some vehicle is needed to carry the *whole* of Chinese culture.

24. See J. A. Symonds, *The Renaissance in Italy*, and in particular c. 2 of his volume, *The Revival of Learning*.

25. This makes a curious parallel to the earlier introduction of Greek into Italy in the second century B.C. It came in then through the same two channels: (1) Roman generals brought back vast quantities of Greek objects of art from the wars; and (2) three Athenian professors who were visiting Rome as envoys (Critolaus, Diogenes, and Carneades) gave lectures while waiting for the Senate's decision on their plea, and thus created an immediate demand for more Greek knowledge in Rome.

26. Gibbon, *The Decline and Fall of the Roman Empire*, c. 66.

27. As early as 1494 Lascaris printed an edition of the Greek Anthology all in capitals, 'imitated from inscriptions', but the example was rarely followed.

28. Gibbon, *The Decline and Fall of the Roman Empire*, c. 66.

29. J. A. Symonds, *The Revival of Learning*, c. 2.

30. Shakespeare, *Macbeth*, 2, 2. 62–4.

31. Lincoln modelled his oratory largely on the English prose of the baroque age, and it is full of Ciceronian cadences and structural devices derived through the baroque writers from Greek and Latin: for instance, the triple arrangement, or tricolon, which appears so often in the Gettysburg Address:

> 'we cannot dedicate—we cannot consecrate—we cannot hallow this ground'.
> 'government of the people, by the people, for the people.'

Lincoln blends this very skilfully with the equally Ciceronian device of antithesis:

> 'living and dead . . . add or detract . . . long remember—never forget . . . died in vain—new birth of freedom.'

Most of these devices have become so much the general property of modern western nations that it is a surprise to be reminded that they are

Greek and Roman artifices which we had to learn with difficulty and practise with care, or to find modern books written by uneducated people, in which they are used seldom and with difficulty. For a more detailed discussion of this subject, see c. 18, p. 330 f.

Notes on 2. THE DARK AGES: ENGLISH LITERATURE

1. See R. W. Chambers, *Beowulf* (Cambridge, 1932[2]), 3, with his quotation from Gregory of Tours, *Hist. Franc.* 110; H. M. Chadwick, in *The Cambridge History of English Literature* (ed. A. W. Ward and A. R. Waller, Cambridge, 1920), 1. 3; C. W. Kennedy, *The Earliest English Poetry* (New York, 1943), 54 and 78 f.; and W. W. Lawrence, *Beowulf and Epic Tradition* (Cambridge, Mass., 1930), c. 2. On the Geatas in particular see the discussions in Chambers, 2–12 and 333–45.

2. Bodvar Biarki, who may have been the prototype of Beowulf, won fame by killing a monstrous great bear. Another view is that Beowulf himself was the son of a bear, a bear-like spirit: hence his riddling name, 'bee-wolf', since the bear is death to bees. If this is true, he reaches even farther back in history, to the point where man is just emerging from the animal world. See Chambers (cited in n. 1), 365 f., and Rhys Carpenter, *Folk tale, Fiction, and Saga in the Homeric Epics* (Sather Classical Lectures, 20, Berkeley, Cal., 1946).

3. *Iliad*, 6. 179–83.

4. For the sake of brevity the account in the text has been simplified. Strictly we should distinguish between different types of short heroic poems, since it is probable that only formal lays, and not songs and ballads of heroism, grew into the full stature of epic. See C. M. Bowra, *Tradition and Design in the Iliad* (Oxford, 1930), c. 2, and A. J. Toynbee, *A Study of History* (Oxford, 1939), 5. 296 f.

5. *Beowulf*, 1063–1159.

6. *Beowulf*, 2200–10, 2397–509.

7. *Beowulf*, 1–52, the funeral of that mysterious monarch Scyld Scefing.

8. *Beowulf*, 853–1159.

9. *Beowulf*, 2892–3075.

10. This judgement depends partly upon taste, but partly too on objective facts. Homer, for instance, has proportionately a much wider vocabulary, many more types of sentence-structure, far subtler varieties of metre, and a more delicate sense of language than the author of *Beowulf*, without being less powerful in scenes of conflict. No doubt this is because there was a longer tradition of composition behind him, and a larger range of dialects and poetic styles from which he made his language (see pp. 481–2). But it is quite wrong to believe that one cannot praise *Beowulf* if one admires the *Iliad*. *Beowulf* contains much fine and memorable poetry, and has often been unfairly criticized: for example by Taine, who writes:

'On ne peut traduire ces idées fichées en travers, qui déconcertent toute l'économie de notre style moderne. Souvent on ne les entend pas; les articles, les particules, tous les moyens d'éclaircir la pensée, de marquer les attaches des termes, d'assembler les idées en un corps régulier, tous les artifices de la raison et de la logique sont supprimés. La passion mugit ici comme une énorme bête informe, et puis c'est tout.' (*Histoire de la littérature anglaise*, Paris, 1905¹², I. 5.)

The critics have recently been criticized by Mr. J. R. Hulbert, '*Beowulf* and the Classical Epic' (*Modern Philology*, 44 (1946–7), 2. 65–75). He defends the plan of the poem—packed as it is with digressions sometimes obscurely told and abruptly introduced—by suggesting that the poet was using the allusive, associative method of such sophisticated writers as Browning and Conrad. This is possible, but, considering the simplicity of Old English society and thought, scarcely probable. Mr. Hulbert is right in saying that the style of *Beowulf* is strong and impressive, but he has been misled by Matthew Arnold into thinking that Homer's style is 'prosaic'. In fact, it is as rich, strong, and poetic in both simplicity and elaboration as that of Shakespeare's tragedies. (On this point also see p. 481 f.) The truth is that *Beowulf*, like the life it describes, belongs to a more primitive stage of history than Homer. Judging from their fragments, the early epics of the fighting Romans, such as Nacvius' *Punic War*, must have looked a little like *Beowulf*. Nacvius' poem is lost, but *Beowulf* has been miraculously preserved, like the shields and helmets and drinking-horns which are still found in the Scandinavian peat-bogs, to be treasured both as rare historical relics and as true works of art.

11. In recent years there have been several studies of possible classical influence on *Beowulf*, and in particular of the supposed influence of Vergil. The following are the main arguments:

(*a*) We could scarcely 'explain the existence of such a broadly constructed epic poem without the model of Vergil' (F. Klaeber, 'Aeneis und Beowulf', in *Archiv für das Studium der neueren Sprachen und Literaturen*, n.s. 26 (1911), 40 f. and 339 f.). This means that no Anglo-Saxon poet was capable of conceiving a large-scale poem from his own imagination and from the earlier heroic Anglo-Saxon poems he had learnt in his youth. That is an assumption which by its nature cannot be proved, and is improbable. Large heroic poems have been composed in a number of countries outside any possible Vergilian influence (we shall soon be dealing with *The Song of Roland*, whose author or authors obviously knew no Latin), and the Anglo-Saxon poets have no lack of originality and boldness. What they did lack was the finer taste which would have allowed the composer of *Beowulf* to construct his epic more graciously and richly and symmetrically. If he had really known the *Aeneid*, *Beowulf* would have been better built. In addition, as Klaeber himself admits, there is hardly anything in common between the general plan of the *Aeneid* and the general plan of *Beowulf*.

(*b*) A number of incidents in the *Aeneid* and in *Beowulf* are similar. (Klaeber gives a list; there are others in T. B. Haber, *A Comparison of the 'Aeneid' and the 'Beowulf'*, Princeton, 1931.) Some of these parallels are ludicrously far-fetched: for instance,

{ Beowulf lands in Denmark and is interrogated by coastguards.
{ Aeneas lands in Libya and is interrogated by his mother Venus in disguise.

Others are genuine resemblances, as when both heroes tell of their past exploits, at a royal banquet. These resemblances, however, prove not that one poet copied the other, but that the scenes and customs they described were similar: which we know to be true. In order to show that *Beowulf* copied the *Aeneid* in describing a hero's feast or funeral we should have to prove that the Anglo-Saxons had no such customs of their own. But we know that they, and their predecessors in Europe, had a culture very similar to that of the Homeric Greeks and Trojans. (See H. M. Chadwick, *The Heroic Age*, cc. 15–19.) It is therefore more probable that the author of *Beowulf* described customs practised or known through tradition among his own people than that he borrowed from an account in a book written in an alien language and a different national tradition.

(*c*) Some of the descriptions of nature in the *Aeneid* and *Beowulf* are similar. (Thus, C. W. Kennedy, *The Earliest English Poetry*, 92–7, suggests that the description of the haunted tarn where Grendel lives, *Beowulf*, 1357–76, is imitated from Vergil's *Aeneid*, 7. 563–71.) It is possible that the poet of *Beowulf* copied such descriptions from Vergil, but it is highly improbable. First, because there was a much larger and handier reservoir of poetic description on which he could draw: the existing Old English poetry, which must have been far greater in volume than the few fragments which have survived to modern times. Mr. Kennedy himself points out on pp. 180–2 how the poet of *Exodus* inserted incongruous conventional descriptions of battle and blood-stained water into his account of Pharaoh pursuing the Hebrews into the Red Sea; and Mr. Rhys Carpenter, in *Folk tale, Fiction, and Saga in the Homeric Epics*, 6–9, reminds us how full a collection of stereotyped descriptions and phrases oral poets possess and transmit. Then, secondly, the Anglo-Saxon poets, if they did not use traditional descriptions in their own tongue, were well able to evoke the scenery of the gloomy north without borrowing details from an Italian poet. The splendid descriptions of the sea in many Old English poems, and the fine elegiac account of Roman ruins in *The Ruin*, are evidence for their powers of original observation.

(*d*) Turns of phrase in the *Aeneid* and *Beowulf* are similar, e.g. *swīgedon ealle* (*B*. 1699) and *conticuere omnes* (*A*. 2. 1); *wordhord onlēac* (*B*. 259) and *effundit pectore uoces* (*A*. 5. 482). (T. B. Haber, op. cit. in note *b*, 31 f.) My knowledge of Anglo-Saxon does not permit me to offer a useful opinion on this point; but from translations, the parallels look like coincidences of fairly obvious imagery (e.g. 'tossed on the waves of care') and the like, rather than imitations. And certainly the differences in language which can be observed are far more striking than the resemblances.

(*e*) Vergil's *Aeneid* was well known in northern Britain, and 'would surely have appealed to a poet versed in Germanic traditions' (Lawrence, *Beowulf and Epic Tradition*, 284–5). This argument is usually pushed much too far, and should be balanced by the following qualifications:

(1) Priestly scholars knew Vergil during the Dark Ages in Britain, but they did not write long secular heroic poems in the vernacular. Aldhelm is reported to have sung vernacular songs to attract people to hear the

gospel, but he was only making a one-way bridge over a gulf he would not cross. The greatest of these scholars, Alcuin, wrote a letter to a British bishop expressly decrying the taste for poems of heroic legend (Chadwick, *The Heroic Age*, 41 f.) and calling a hero like Beowulf a damned pagan.

(2) We do not hear, and it is difficult to imagine, that professional bards, like the maker of *Beowulf*, already steeped in their native tradition of heroic poetry, were enabled to learn enough Latin to study the *Aeneid*. In the Dark Ages, and for centuries afterwards, the way to learn Latin was to start with the Latin Bible. But the knowledge of the Bible shown in *Beowulf* is so extremely thin and vague that the poet can hardly have been able to read the Vulgate directly. Bede himself knew the Bible and the church fathers far better than Vergil, and Vergil was the only classical author he knew first-hand (M. L. W. Laistner, 'Bede as a Classical and a Patristic Scholar', *Transactions of the Royal Historical Society*, series 4, vol. 16, 73 f.). How then could a bard who barely knew the opening chapters of Genesis be so familiar with the difficult *Aeneid* as to imitate it in detail and in general plan? There is a parallel to this in the first appearance of the Trojan story in French medieval literature. Benoît de Sainte-Maure, who put the legends into French poetry, took them not from the *Aeneid* or the Latin *Iliad* but from a short romance in prose which was far easier to read; and even then he did not follow it carefully. See p. 53.

(3) When at last the two traditions, of Latin and of Anglo-Saxon poetry, blended, the results were grand. The blending begins with Cædmon, and goes on through the later poems attributed to him, through Cynewulf, to *The Dream of the Rood* and *Phoenix*. But all such poetry, although it uses the Anglo-Saxon poetic conventions, is religious in content as well as purpose. Anyone who at that time learnt enough Latin to understand the *Aeneid* would be dedicated to the service of God, and would not write a poem on monsters overcome in bloody battles, not by the power of the spirit but by strength of arm and magical weapons.

(4) In general, the sort of imaginative stimulus experienced by sensitive modern writers after reading a moving book is not likely to occur in primitive poets. As we see from *Phoenix*, when they copy a book, they copy it carefully and obviously. But they do not write poetry of their own containing 'reminiscences' of classical poetry. That road leads not to Grendel's cave, but to Xanadu.

12. Lady Gregory, *Gods and Fighting Men* (London, 1910), 2. 11. 4.

13. See H. M. Chadwick, *The Heroic Age* (Cambridge, 1912), 47–8. F. A. Blackburn, 'The Christian Coloring in the *Beowulf*' (*PMLA*, 12, n.s. 5 (1897), 205–25), analyses the passages which show acquaintance with certain elementary Christian doctrines, and shows that they could (and probably must) have been added after the poem assumed virtually its present shape as a pagan epic. For instance, the numerous mentions of God could be replaced by *Wyrd*, 'fate', without in the slightest altering the meaning; and sometimes *Wyrd* has been allowed to remain in such passages.

14. *Beowulf*, 107 f., 1261 f. (Cain and Abel): *orcnēas* in 112 is variously translated 'sea-monsters', and 'hellish things', from the Latin root of *Orcus*. The Flood appears in 1688–93.

15. A. J. Toynbee, *A Study of History* (Oxford, 1939), 5. 610 f.

16. This is the point of view expounded by J. B. Bury in *The Invasion of Europe by the Barbarians* (London, 1928): see also p. 478 of this book on Fustel de Coulanges.

17. There is a fine example of this, reported by a Roman historian, from an earlier but similar era. After Hannibal had crossed the Alps, he determined to give his exhausted troops new courage for their first battle with the Romans in Italy. So, as a living example of the gallantry that despises death, he brought out some of the wild Alpine tribesmen (evidently Celts) whom he had captured *en route*. He offered them the chance of winning their liberty by fighting duels, the victor to be set free. They accepted gladly, seizing the weapons and dancing a highland fling, *cum sui moris tripudiis*. And then, during the fighting, the spectators expressed just as much admiration for the loser, if he died well, as for the winner: 'ut non uincentium magis quam bene morientium fortuna laudaretur' (Livy, 21. 42).

18. Hige sceal þe heardra, heorte þe cenre,
    mod sceal þe mare, þe ure maegen lytlað   (*Maldon*, 312–13).

19. Bede's phrase *quasi mundum animal ruminando* implies a charmingly naïve comparison of the meditative cowhand, chewing the cud of scripture in the byre, to his own cattle.

20. Bede calls them *doctores* and *multi doctiores uiri*. It is often assumed that Cædmon was attached to Whitby Abbey when he began to make poetry. See, for instance, Stopford Brooke, *English Literature from the Beginning to the Norman Conquest* (London, 1898), 127: 'Cædmon . . . was attached in a secular habit to the monastery—one of its dependants.' Similarly A. Brandl, in Paul's *Grundriss der germanischen Philologie* (Strassburg, 1908), 2. 1. 1027: 'Cædmon . . . lebte zunächst als Laie in einer Klostergemeinschaft usw.'; E. E. Wardale, *Chapters on Old English Literature* (London, 1935), 112; and many others. This assumption is not justified by Bede's story, which in fact points in the other direction. According to Bede, Cædmon was a farmhand, with a cottage of his own. When he got the gift of song, he told the foreman of the farm and he was taken to the abbess. Obviously the foreman said 'This looks like God's work, we must ask Abbess Hilda', and took Cædmon up to the abbey. Now, it is not stated that the farm on which Cædmon and the foreman worked was, or was not, attached to the abbey. But if Cædmon had already been a member of Whitby community, Bede would almost certainly have said that he had already been an earnest hearer of the Word, a humble worker on the abbey estates who listened to the preaching and pondered it deeply in his heart, and other things of the kind. This is the argument from silence; but it is less dangerous than the assumption that there was only *one* farm-foreman near Whitby, and that he and his men were employed by the abbey.

21. See D. Masson, *The Life of John Milton*, 6 (New York, 1946), 557, n. 1; other literature on the subject is listed by C. W. Kennedy (cited in n. 1), 163.

22. *Hymn to Apollo*, 172.

23. The poem on Christ is in three parts. Only the second part (440–866) is signed by Cynewulf, and there are marked differences between the three sections in manner and matter. The original is Gregory, *Homiliae in euangelia*, 2. 29 (Migne, *Patrol. Lat.* 76. 1213–19).

24. On the source of *Juliana* see J. M. Garnett, 'The Latin and the Anglo-Saxon *Juliana*' (*PMLA*, 14, n.s. 7 (1899), 279–98). Juliana died about A.D. 309. Cynewulf was paraphrasing a life of her similar to those now in *The Acts of the Saints*, but the actual biography he used is lost.

25. Rune letter-names are all nouns; but I could not find a modern name whose letters could all, like *bee*, serve as nouns.

26. For this point, and a sympathetic sketch of Cynewulf's work, see K. Sisam's Gollancz Lecture in *The Proceedings of the British Academy*, 1932.

27. The opening is *hwæt!*, the traditional cry by which the bard called his listeners' attention, and the 'young hero', *geong Hæled*, is in line 39.

28. Lactantius, *De aue phoenice*. The myth of the phoenix is ultimately a product of Egyptian animal-worship, and probably arose from the observation of strange migratory birds. It reached the Greek world through Herodotus' description of Egypt (2. 73, possibly from Hecataeus). On its rich symbolism see J. Hubaux and M. Leroy, *Le Mythe du phónix dans les littératures grecque et latine* (Paris, 1939).

29. Ambrose, *Hexaemeron*, 5. 23. 79–80, is the original of *Phoenix*, 443 f. Job xxix. 18 is quoted and paraphrased in 546 69.

30. For instance, lines 15–20 of Lactantius' poem are from Vergil, *Aen*. 6. 274 81; 21–5 from Homer, *Od*. 4. 566–7, plus *Od*. 6. 43–5, plus Lucretius, 3. 18–23.

31. *Phoenix*, 9–12, tr. J. D. Spaeth, *Old English Poetry* (Princeton, 1922).

32. Lactantius, *De aue phoenice*, 161–6:

> A fortunatae sortis fatique uolucrem
> cui de se nasci praestitit ipse deus!
> femina sit, uel mas, seu neutrum, seu sit utrumque,
> felix quae Veneris foedera nulla colit!
> mors illi Venus est, sola est in morte uoluptas:
> ut possit nasci, appetit ante mori.

33. See W. P. Ker, *Epic and Romance* (London, 1922²), 2. 4 f., and appendix, note A.

34. Lactantius, *De aue phoenice*, 11–14:

> Cum Phaethonteis flagrasset ab ignibus axis,
> ille locus flammis inuiolatus erat;
> et cum diluuium mersisset fluctibus orbem,
> Deucalioneas exsuperauit aquas.

35. *Phoenix*, 38–46, tr. Spaeth (cited in n. 31).

36. *Phoenix*, 52, tr. Spaeth (n. 31).

37. *Phoenix*, 675–7, tr. Spaeth (n. 31). There is a poem on the Incarnation in this same odd blend of Latin and Anglo-Saxon: see J. S. Westlake in *The Cambridge History of English Literature* (Cambridge, 1920), 1. 7. 146–7. Childish as it is, it has a certain charm; but, what is more important, it shows (like Ælfric's schoolbooks) a high degree of interpenetration between Latin and Old English, many centuries before other European nations ventured to bring the vernacular speech into contact with the learned language.

38. See A. J. Toynbee, *A Study of History*, 2. 322–40 and 421–33. There is a much more detailed study by L. Gougaud, *Christianity in Celtic Lands* (tr. from author's manuscript by M. Joynt, London, 1932): see especially 185 f. Mr. Gougaud tends to minimize the conflict, saying (213) that the British church was 'a little aloof' but not 'separatist and independent'. Others might think the differences went deeper. The British church is often called the Irish church, and sometimes, more correctly, the Celtic church. Established in Britain before the fall of the Roman empire, as a part of the original Roman Christendom, it was largely submerged by the Saxon invasions of England. After them it continued its existence in the northern and western areas (including Brittany). Gildas was a typical member of it. From Wales and Ireland it worked back into Scotland and Saxon England, sometimes competing with the Roman missionaries who later made their way up from the south, and then meeting them head-on at the synod of Whitby. But its tradition was quite continuous, so that it should really be called the church of Britain. On p. 240 f. Mr. Gougaud asks where the Irish got their knowledge of classical culture. From south Wales? through Alexandrian or Byzantine missionaries? through refugees from Gaul? He concludes, with arguments which seem convincing, that the Irish got their culture and their interest in Christianity from the original British church, which had 'imbibed a certain amount of Latin culture' as the church of one of the provinces of the Christian Roman empire; and that they then started Latin schools to help in the understanding of the scriptures and the Latin writings of the church fathers.

39. See L. Gougaud, *Christianity in Celtic Lands*, 185 f. P. F. Jones, 'The Gregorian Mission and English Education', in *Speculum*, 3 (1928), 335 f., shows that Augustine's mission was not educational but purely religious. The essential thing was to convert the new Saxon pagans first, and then teach them. Only after his mission had done its work could Theodore and Hadrian start their school. The fact that Augustine often wrote to Rome to consult Gregory on points that now appear quite trivial shows how closely he was supervised by the pope. It might be added that it shows a striking resemblance to the administrative methods of the Roman empire. When Pliny the younger was sent out to regulate the finances of the province of Bithynia, he wrote back to submit every problem slightly above his level to the emperor Trajan, with just the same meticulous precision.

40. Bede, *Hist. eccl.* 4. 1; M. Roger, *L'Enseignement des lettres classiques d'Ausone à Alcuin* (Paris, 1905), 286 f. This school, however, did not

establish any solid and lasting tradition of Greek scholarship in England at the time. During the Dark Ages and the early Middle Ages, Greek books were very rare in England, and men who could read them still rarer: see the useful thesis by G. R. Stephens, *The Knowledge of Greek in England in the Middle Ages* (Philadelphia, 1933).

41. Roger (cited in n. 40), 261 and 288–303.

42. See M. L. W. Laistner, 'Bede as a Classical and a Patristic Scholar', in *The Transactions of the Royal Historical Society*, series 4, v. 16, 69 f.

43. M. L. W. Laistner (cited in n. 42) has shown that Bede's purely classical learning was practically confined to Vergil and Pliny's *Natural History*. Other authors (with a few exceptions, p. 74) he quoted from citations of their works made by grammarians—in fact, from the Reader's Digest type of collection which was one of the favourite approaches to the classics throughout the Dark and Middle Ages well into the Renaissance. But his first-hand knowledge of the Christian poets like Prudentius, and of the fathers (especially Jerome), was enormous. See also Mr. Laistner's 'The Library of the Venerable Bede', in *Bede, His Life, Times, and Writings*, ed. A. H. Thompson (Oxford, 1935).

44. See W. Levison, 'Bede as Historian', in *Bede, His Life, Times, and Writings* (cited in n. 43). This brilliant article suggests that Bede was drawn towards history by his interest in two convergent subjects: chronology and hagiography.

45. Dante put him in heaven among other great teachers, including his own admired master St. Thomas Aquinas (*Paradiso*, 10).

46. On Johannes Scotus Erigena or Eriugena, see L. Gougaud, *Christianity in Celtic Lands* (cited in n. 38), 302 f.; C. R. S. Harris, 'Philosophy', in *The Legacy of the Middle Ages* (ed. C. G. Crump, Oxford, 1926); P. Kletler, *Johannes Eriugena* (Leipzig, 1931); and M. L. W. Laistner, *Thought and Letters in Western Europe 500–900 A.D.* (New York, 1931), 197 f.

47. This entry is for A.D. 839. Quotations from the *Anglo-Saxon Chronicle* are taken from R. K. Ingram's 'Everyman' translation. On the phrase 'from the pirates' country , my colleague Professor E. V. K. Dobbie informs me that the text reads *of Heredalande*, which is a place-name, and which has been identified with a region near Hardanger in Norway.

48. On their fate see W. Levison, *England and the Continent in the Eighth Century* (Oxford, 1946) and H. Waddell, *The Wandering Scholars* (London, 1934⁷), 2. 5.

49. See Gougaud (cited in n. 38), 395.

50. Alfred, preface to the *Hierdeboc*.

51. Gregory himself speaks of his book as the *Regula pastoralis* (*Ep.* 5. 49 Migne). In English studies it is often called *Cura pastoralis*.

52. So P. G. Thomas in *The Cambridge History of English Literature* (Cambridge, 1920), 1. 6.

53. Boethius set out to bridge the widening gap between Greek and Latin culture by translating books on all the sciences which prepare the mind for philosophy, then all the works of Aristotle on logic, ethics, and

physics, and then all the works of Plato. His comparatively early death prevented him from realizing more than a small part of this grand design. Nevertheless he became, through his surviving translations, one of the founders of the educational system known as the *quadrivium*, and was revered by nearly every medieval educator (e.g. Sigebert, *De scriptoribus ecclesiasticis*, 37; Migne, *Patrol. Lat.* 160. 555). His translations covered music, arithmetic, geometry, and Aristotelian logic. On his importance as a translator see P. Courcelle, *Les Lettres grecques en Occident de Macrobe à Cassiodore* (Paris, 1943), 260–78.

54. *De consolatione philosophiae*. There are a handy edition by Adrianus a Forti Scuto and G. D. Smith (London, 1925) and ample bibliographies in Courcelle (cited in n. 53) and H. R. Patch, *The Tradition of Boethius* (New York, 1935).

55. The Menippean form was introduced to Latin literature by Varro in the first century B.C., and, after long disuse, popularized again by the philosopher Martianus Capella in another work which became a foundation-stone of medieval education, *The Marriage of Philology and Mercury*: this was written not long before Boethius' own day.

56. Much of the prose looks like deliberate imitation of Cicero: the clausulae, for instance, are consistently Ciceronian. The verse interludes, providing moments of calm and lyricism after long passages of dialogue, fulfil something of the same artistic and emotional function as the choruses in Seneca.

57. Boeth. *Cons. Phil.* 4. 7: 'omnis enim (fortuna) quae uidetur aspera nisi aut exercet aut corrigit punit.'

58. See the close analysis of Boethius' sources by P. Courcelle (cited in n. 53), 278-300. I have seen only an abstract of the same author's thesis, *La 'Consolation' de Boèce: ses sources et son interprétation par les commentateurs latins du IXe au XIIIe siècle* (Paris, École nationale des Chartes, 1934). In both works M. Courcelle shows how deeply Boethius' thought is penetrated with Neoplatonism, and suggests that he learnt both Greek and philosophy at Alexandria, as a pupil of Ammonius.

59. Kant, *Critique of Practical Reason*, ad fin.

60. George Meredith, *Lucifer in Starlight*.

61. Boeth. *Cons. Phil.* 4. 4:

'Nullane animarum supplicia post defunctum morte corpus relinquis?' 'Et magna quidem,' inquit, 'quorum alia poenali acerbitate, alia uero purgatoria clementia exerceri puto.'

Courcelle (cited in n. 53) offers on pp. 300–4 what looks like an acceptable solution of the problem of Boethius' Christianity by suggesting that he was endeavouring to produce a reconciliation and synthesis between Neoplatonism and the Christian faith.

62. See W. Jaeger, *Paideia*, 3 (New York, 1944), c. 1, especially p. 30 f.

63. For accounts of Boethius' enormous influence in the Dark Ages and the Middle Ages, see M. Manitius, *Geschichte der lateinischen Literatur des Mittelalters*, 1 (Munich, 1911), 33–5, and H. R. Patch, *The Tradition of Boethius* (New York, 1935), with its very full notes and bibliography.

Boethius' book was one of the great best-sellers, almost greater than Vergil. Copies of it were made all over western Europe, and are listed in library catalogues of monasteries from Durham to Cremona. Something like 400 manuscripts still exist. No other book, except the Bible, was so much translated in the Middle Ages. It was put into English by Alfred about 900, by Chaucer about 1380 (two translations that enriched not only English thought but the English language), by Queen Elizabeth herself, and by others less well known. There is a fragment of a Provençal poetic paraphrase of it dated as early as the tenth century. Jean de Meun, whom we shall meet in a later chapter, turned it into French prose about 1300, and there was a translation attributed to Charles of Orleans before 1422. In the fourteenth century the Franciscan monk Alberto of Florence turned it into Italian, the Dominican Antonio Ginebreda into Catalan, and the Byzantine Maximus Planudes into Greek. A German translation was produced by Notker Labeo about 1000 (see II. Naumann, *Notkers Boethius: Untersuchungen über Quellen und Stil*, Strassburg, 1913). Finally, Boethius is quoted again and again in the Middle Ages. Particularly noble echoes occur in Dante, who calls Boethius *l'anima santa*, and puts him in Paradise beside the Venerable Bede (*Paradiso*, 10. 125). For instance,

> nessun maggior dolore
> Che ricordarsi del tempo felice
> Nella miseria; e ciò sa il tuo dottore (*Inf.* 5. 121–3)

is usually thought to be an echo of *Cons. Phil.* 2. 4. 1:

'in omni aduersitate fortunae infelicissimum est genus infortunii fuisse felicem.'

(It has, however, been thought that the phrase 'your teacher' might better apply to Vergil, in which case the words could be an allusion to *Aeneid*, 2. 3:

> Infandum, regina, iubes renouare dolorem.)

Another such echo is the beautiful close of the entire *Commedia*:

> L'amor, che move il sole e l'altre stelle.

This was inspired by Boethius, *Cons. Phil.* 2. 8:

> O felix hominum genus,
> si uestros animos amor
> quo caelum regitur regat!

—a noble utterance, which Dante quoted again in *De mon.* 1. 9. 25–8. The fourth chapter of Mr. Patch's book cited at the beginning of this note surveys the work of many of the medieval authors who echoed and imitated Boethius, and lists some of the countless prisoners who found consolation in reading him. Even the mercurial Casanova was given a copy by the prison doctor, and was grateful, saying: 'Je vous en suis bien obligé; il vaut mieux que Sénèque; il me fera du bien' (*Mémoires*, ed. R. Vèze, Paris, 1926, 4. 196–7).

64. Boethius, *Cons. Phil.* 2. 7: 'sed materiam gerendis rebus optauimus quo ne uirtus tacita consenesceret.'

65. Alfred's translation, c. 17, translated and edited by W. J. Sedgefield (Oxford, 1900), who observes that Alfred's words might have been suggested by a commentary on the passage in Boethius. See H. R. Patch (cited in n. 63), 48–54, for a survey of Alfred's translation.

66. For example, Boethius (3. 4) says:

'Quo fit ut indignemur eas (dignitates) saepe nequissimis hominibus contigisse, unde Catullus licet in curuli Nonium sedentem strumam tamen appellat.'

This is an allusion to Catullus' epigram against an upstart politician (52):

> Quid est, Catulle? quid moraris emori?
> sella in curuli struma Nonius sedet.

But Alfred knows nothing of Catullus' poetry, and cannot understand either the abusive nickname *struma* ('wen' or 'carbuncle', as we now call an offensive man a 'blister') or the curule chair of office used by the higher Roman magistrates. So he writes:

'Hence the wise Catulus long ago became angry and heaped insult and disgrace on the rich Nonius, because he met him seated in a gorgeous carriage. For it was a strict custom among the Romans at that time that only the most respectable people should sit in such carriages. Catulus despised the man because he knew he was very ignorant and dissolute; so without more ado he spat upon him. Now, Catulus was a Roman chief and a man of great intelligence, and he would certainly not have insulted the man so gravely, had the latter not been rich and powerful.' (Alfred's translation, c. 27, tr. Sedgefield (adapted), Oxford, 1900.)

Homer is mentioned and quoted in Boethius (*Cons. Phil.* 5. 2, with a pretty adaptation of a Homeric phrase); but Alfred (metr. 30) makes the allusion naïve and vague:

> In the East Omerus   among the Greeks
> was in that country   in songs most cunning,
> of Firgilius also   friend and teacher,
> of that famed maker   best of masters.

Alfred's inadequate knowledge of Roman customs, language, history, and geography comes out also in his translation of Orosius, which is full of names. Miss Ann Kirkman ('Proper Names in the Old English Orosius', *Modern Language Review*, 25 (1930), 1–22 and 140–51) has shown that, out of the 700 proper names, 490 are misspelt, and are often spelt differently each time they appear. Persons are called by the names of places, and vice versa. The difficulty was apparently increased by the fact that the scribe was not copying by eye, but taking dictation, so that he wrote things like Plicinius (for P. Licinius) and Pelopensium (for Peloponnensium). Since surnames were not known in Anglo-Saxon England, Alfred himself at first could not understand the system by which the Romans had three names each. He began by using only the first of the three. Later he used the first and second as though they were alternatives:

> Fabio Maximo quintum Decio Mure quartum consulibus   (136. 32)
> 'Cwintus was a consul, with another name Decius.'

But later (143. 35) he understood the system, and he had it right by the time he went on to translate Boethius.

67. Alfred mentions the priests with reference only to Gregory's *Regula pastoralis*, but he must have had assistance with the other books. It was Bishop Asser who wrote the famous biography of Alfred.

68. See the *Anglo-Saxon Chronicle* for A.D. 854, 883, 888, and 889.

69. On the history of the Lindisfarne Gospels, see the British Museum's *Guide to a Select Exhibition of Cottonian Manuscripts* (London, 1931).

70. Ireland too maintained high cultural standards until the Vikings began to attack it in 795. It was their devastations that caused the dispersal of the Irish scholars, and retarded Irish culture behind the rest of western Europe. See H. Waddell, *The Wandering Scholars* (London, 1934[7]), 2. 5.

Notes on 3. THE MIDDLE AGES: FRENCH LITERATURE

1. C. Lenient, *La Satire en France au moyen âge* (Paris, 1893), 28, quoting Muratori's *History of Bologna*.

2. The unholy trinity appears in *Roland*, 2696–7. H. Grégoire has suggested that these deities were introduced in order that the monotheistic Moslems could be presented as idolatrous pagans, as part of the propaganda for the First Crusade. See his essay 'Des dieux Cahu, Baraton, Tervagant' in *Annuaire de l'Institut de Philologie et d'Histoire Orientales et Slaves*, 7 (1939–44), where he derives Tervagant (in one of its readings Trivigant) from Trivia, the epithet of Diana of the Crossroads —because it is the name given to the Syrian Ashtoreth in an early Latin version of 1 Kings xi. 5–7. Others believe the name is derived from that of a Celtic divinity.

3. *Roland*, 1391–2:

> L'encanteür ki ja fut en enfer:
> Par artimal l'i cundoist Jupiter.

This mysterious word is interpreted as coming from *arte mathematica* ('mathematic art', a common synonym for astrology and magic), but might simply come from *arte mala*, 'evil art'.

4. *Roland*, 2615–16:

> Ço'st l'amiraill, le viel d'antiquitét,
> Tut survesquiet e Virgilie e Omer.

5. Most of these long medieval poems and stories bear the name *roman*. Most of them deal with chivalrous adventure and fighting, courtly love, or the marvellous, or some or all of these together. These are subjects which for over a century now have been called 'romantic'. Specialists in the period, however, distinguish:

(*a*) romances—tales of Arthurian, Roman, Greek, and Trojan adventure in which most of the characters are human beings;

(*b*) *chansons de geste*—'adventure poems' mainly about Charlemagne and his circle;

(*c*) allegories such as *Le Roman de la Rose* (see p. 62 f.) in which most of the characters are abstractions.

6. See C. H. Haskins, *The Renaissance of the Twelfth Century* (Cambridge, 1939); Hastings Rashdall, 'The Mediaeval Universities', in *The Cambridge Mediaeval History*, 6. 17; and J. E. Sandys, *A History of Classical Scholarship*, 1. 527 f., who shows, for instance, that Aristotle's logic had hitherto been imperfectly known (through Boethius' translations of the *Categories* and the *De interpretatione*), but that the other three parts of the *Organon* became known between 1128 and 1159, and the *Physics* and *Metaphysics* about 1200.

7. It really contains some horrible Latin. For instance, *ruere_* = fall dead; *audiuit quia* = heard that; *nec destitit nisi* (+subjunctive) = and continued until . . . .

8. Dares, 44: 'ruerunt ex Argiuis, sicut acta diurna indicant quae Dares descripsit, hominum milia DCCCLXXXVI'. Cf. Dares, 12 init.

9. For a pleasant survey of these books, see E. H. Haight, *Essays on the Greek Romances* (New York, 1943) and *More Essays on Greek Romances* (New York, 1945). Erwin Rohde's *Der griechische Roman und seine Vorläufer* (Leipzig, 1914³) is rather old, but still very valuable. The survival of the romances in modern literature is discussed in c. 9 of this book, p. 166 f.; see also pp. 341, 343.

The idea of correcting Homer's version of the Trojan war was not new. Philosophers had often objected to his character-drawing and his theology (e.g. Plato, *Rep.* 2. 377 *d* f.). Historians criticized his conception of the size and importance of the conflict (e.g. Thucydides, 1. 10). Scholars pointed out inappropriate phrases, gestures, and incidents: so Zoilus the critic was nicknamed the Scourge of Homer for his pitiless dissection of the epics. Creative authors wrote books based on the many traditions about the war which Homer did not use. For instance, Euripides wrote a melodrama, *Helen*, on the idea that the gods sent only a phantom Helen to Troy, to trick the combatants into senseless slaughter (which Euripides thought was the real meaning of all war), while they hid the real Helen in Egypt. Vergil's *Aeneid*, with its anti-Greek tendency, radically altered the emphasis of the *Iliad* and the *Odyssey*. But the idea of writing a completely new account of the Trojan war, to replace Homer, was boldly original.

'Dares the Phrygian' and 'Dictys the Cretan' produced the most thorough attempts at such a substitute, but the most interesting and apparently the best written was a book by their near contemporary Philostratus. This was the man who wrote a life of the miracle-working sage Apollonius of Tyana, to compete with the growing tradition of Jesus Christ and his miracles, his wisdom, and his holiness. Comparable to this is his dialogue, *Heroicus*, in which a Phoenician merchant, storm-stayed in the Dardanelles, talks to a farmer who has a vineyard on the peninsula opposite the site of Troy. The farmer tells him that his land is protected by the ghost of Protesilaus, the first Greek soldier to be killed on the Trojan beachhead. The merchant finds this hard to believe. But the farmer assures him that Protesilaus often appears, larger than life, talks to him, and tells him all about the Trojan war. (Remember, this is not 'in ancient Greece': Philostratus is writing about A.D. 215, when the

Trojan war was a prehistoric legend well over a thousand years old.) The farmer goes on to give a first-hand account of the war, as received from Protesilaus, who took part in the preparations for it and saw it all as a ghost. The entire story, we are told, was distorted by the wily Odysseus, who, after murdering the brilliant inventor Palamedes, persuaded Homer to alter the incidents of the war, leaving out Palamedes and glorifying Odysseus himself. The farmer also gives 'the true version' of many other important events. For instance, how was Achilles killed? He fell in love with the Trojan princess Polyxena (who escorted Priam to ransom Hector's corpse), and promised to raise the siege of Troy in return for her hand. On the wedding-day he went alone to the temple, and was murdered by a Trojan ambush. Polyxena fled to the Greek camp and there killed herself. But after death (Philostratus goes on) Achilles became the husband of Helen, the bravest man with the most beautiful woman, and they live together in perpetual immortality on the specially created island of Leuké in the Black Sea.

This is substantially the same story as that told by 'Dares' and 'Dictys'. It is tempting to conjecture that the brilliant Philostratus first outlined it, creating the ideas of Achilles' romantic love-death and of a complete, authentic, *eyewitness* account of the Trojan war; and that 'Dares' and 'Dictys' then filled it out with variations and some rather mechanical supplements. However, H. Grentrup, in *De Heroici Philostratei fabularum fontibus* (Münster, 1914), following K. Münscher, *Philologus*, suppl. 10 (1907), 504 f., has shown that Philostratus wrote his book about 215, to please the emperor Caracalla (who thought himself a new Achilles, as Charles XII of Sweden thought himself a new Alexander), while the Greek manuscript of 'Dictys' was written some years earlier.

A well-written analysis of the *Heroicus* by E. J. Bourquin will be found in the *Annuaire de l'Association pour l'Encouragement des Études Grecques en France*, 18 (1884), 97–141. M. Bourquin points out that one of the purposes of the work was to propagandize for paganism by opposing the miraculous deeds of the Homeric heroes, living an eternal life near their tombs, to those of Christian saints. An important predecessor of the *Heroicus* was the speech called Τρωικός by Dio of Prusa (on which see Grentrup, c. 5). F. Huhn and E. Bethe in *Hermes*, 52 (1917), 616 f. suggest that the purpose of the *Heroicus* is to justify Homer against the new anti-Homeric history by 'Dictys'; but this is surely over-simplifying the relationship of these complex works.

10. Dares, 41: 'Antenor et Aeneas noctu ad portam praesto fuerunt, Neoptolemum susceperunt, exercitui portam reserauerunt, lumen ostenderunt, fugam praesidio sibi suisque ut sit prouiderunt' (a sentence which gives a good idea of Dares' crisp military style). On the departure of Aeneas, see 43: 'Agamemnon iratus Aeneae quod Polyxenam absconderat eum cum suis protinus de patria excedere iubet. Aeneas cum suis omnibus proficiscitur.'

11. Dares, 13 fin.: 'Briseidam formosam, non alta statura, candidam, capillo flauo et molli, superciliis iunctis, oculis uenustis, corpore aequali, blandam, affabilem, uerecundam, animo simplici, piam.' Philostratus'

Heroicus contains many 'eyewitness' descriptions of the Trojan heroes—on which see Grentrup (cited in n. 9), c. 8.

12. For instance, it is odd that, in the version of 'Dares' which we now have (than which what could be shorter?), there is a detailed description of Briseida (n. 11), although she plays no part in the story as given there. But my colleague Professor Roger Loomis writes me: 'In view of the very free and original handling which Benoît shows in other respects, it seems probable that he invented the Troilus–Briseida affair.' For a discussion of floating medieval traditions about the Trojan war independent of 'Dares' and 'Dictys', see E. B. Atwood, 'The Rawlinson *Excidium Troiae*', in *Speculum*, 9 (1934), 379–404.

13. See p. 458. It is delightful to find that there are still unwary readers who can be caught by the ingenious authors of 'Dares' and 'Dictys'. The latest known to me is Mr. J. P. Harland, who in an essay, 'The Date of the Hellenic Alphabet' (*Studies in Philology*, 42 (1945), 417), repeats the story of the discovery of the 'Dictys' book, 'written on linden-bark', and suggests that it was in 'Minoan linear script', which was not deciphered until 1953.

14. B. P. Grenfell, A. S. Hunt, and J. G. Smyly, *The Tebtunis Papyri* (University of California Publications: Graeco-Roman Archaeology), 2 (London, 1907), 9 f., say that the Greek 'Dictys' cannot be later than A.D. 200; but give no factual reason for this assertion. (It is datable to the same period as the accounts on the reverse, which were written in 206.) For a transcription and discussion see M. Ihm in *Hermes*, 44 (1909), 1 f.

15. Dictys, 5. 17: '(Aeneas) deuenit ad mare Hadriaticum multas interim gentes barbaras praeuectus. ibi cum his qui secum nauiguerant ciuitatem condit appellatam Corcyram Melaenam.'

16. Benoît came from Sainte-Maure in Touraine. We do not know whether he attended the Benedictine school of Saint-Maur-sur-Loire, some distance away, or not. There is a handy account of Benoît in H. O. Taylor, *The Mediaeval Mind* (London, 1930⁴), 2.253 f.

17. The little *Ilias Latina*, known throughout the Middle Ages, was a potted version 1,070 lines long, of which more than half were devoted to books 1–5 of the *Iliad*. It was written in the first century A.D., perhaps by Silius Italicus.

18. For this point, see F. N. Warren, 'On the Latin Sources of *Thèbes* and *Énéas*', in *PMLA*, n.s. 9 (1901), 375–87.

19. T. Hodgkin, *Italy and Her Invaders* (Oxford, 1892–1916), 3. 294.

20. See G. S. Gordon, 'The Trojans in England', in *Essays and Studies by Members of the English Association*, 9 (1924), and D. Bush, *Mythology and the Renaissance Tradition in English Poetry* (Cambridge, Mass., 1937), 39–41. It seems probable that the proud Order of the Golden Fleece was named after a similar belief, that its holders could date their nobility back to Jason and the Argonauts. As early as the end of the Roman republic the learned Varro compiled a book *De familiis Troianis*, tracing the Trojan ancestry of the great Roman clans.

21. Quoted by J. C. Collins, *Greek Influence on English Poetry* (London, 1910), 47–8.

22. Sidney, *Apologie for Poetry* (ed. A. Feuillerat, Cambridge, 1923), 16.

23. Jonson, *Every Man in His Humour*, 4. 4; Dekker, *The Shoemaker's Holiday*, 5. 5. There are many more examples in P. Stapfer, *Shakespeare and Classical Antiquity* (tr. E. J. Carey, London, 1880).

24. For instance, it was translated and expanded in Holland by Scher Dieregotgaf and Jacob van Maerlant; it reached Germany in the early-thirteenth-century *Liet von Troye* of Herbort von Fritslar and in an unfinished poem (1287) by Konrad von Würzburg.

25. *Historia destructionis Troiae*, ed. N. E. Griffin (Cambridge, Mass., 1936).

26. Italian by Filippo Ceffi (1324); French by Raoul Lefèvre (1464); German in 1392, Danish in 1623, Icelandic in 1607, and Czech in 1468. There is a metrical version of Guido by an unknown author in a Laud MS. at Oxford, a very early Scots alliterative version (ed. Panton and Donaldson for the Early English Text Society), another Scots version attributed to Barbour, and a Troye-Boke by Chaucer's Benedictine pupil, Lydgate (1420).

27. This is itself an odd distortion of the original story. In Homer there are two girls taken captive by the Achaeans. One is Chryseis, who is given back to her father. The other is Briseis, whom Agamemnon takes away from Achilles, thus causing the Wrath. The basis of the story and its distortions is the beautiful captive, or hostage, who is desired by one or more of her captors and passes from one to the other.

28. Even in Homer (*Il.* 4. 88 f.) Pandarus is treacherous.

29. See E. Faral, *Recherches sur les sources latines des contes et romans courtois du moyen âge* (Paris, 1913), 63 f.

30. Cf. F. N. Warren (cited in n. 18). In this connexion there is an interesting article on 'Lucan in the Middle Ages' by J. Crosland in *The Modern Language Review*, 1930. The author points out that, although an epic poet, Lucan was often classified as a historian and philosopher in the Middle Ages; that books based on his poem, such as *Li hystoire de Julius Caesar* by Jehan de Tuim, are among the earliest books on ancient history in vernacular French; and that British authors (such as Geoffrey of Monmouth and Richard of Cirencester) liked to quote *Bell. ciu.* 2. 572—

territa quaesitis ostendit terga Britannis

describing Caesar's defeat in Britain, while French chroniclers magnified his exploits so as to glorify their Latin ancestors. Since Lucan was more spectacular than Vergil, he was more often imitated in old French heroic poetry.

As the sense of history developed, and classical scholarship improved, attempts were made to compose real historical accounts of Rome and the past in vernacular French. The two earliest of these deserve attention, although they lie rather outside the scope of this chapter.

(1) The *Histoire ancienne jusqu'à César* is the earliest attempt at writing a universal history in a modern language. Beginning with the creation of the world, it synthesizes sacred and profane history, to produce a complete general survey of the past. Much of it is based on Orosius; the

Trojan section comes from 'Dares'; other sources include Vergil and Valerius' epitome of the Alexander story; it breaks off while describing Caesar's Gallic wars. It was apparently written between 1223 and 1230 for the Châtelain Roger of Lille.

(2) *Li fet des Romains compilé ensemble de Saluste et de Suetoine et de Lucan*, usually known as *Les Faits des Romains*, is really a biography of Julius Caesar, drawn not only from the three authors mentioned but from Caesar's own commentaries and their continuations; glosses in manuscripts (particularly on Lucan); Isidore's *Etymologies*, Josephus' *Jewish War*, Augustine's *City of God*, the Bible, Geoffrey of Monmouth, and the romances of Thebes and Alexander. What we have is, according to the prologue, the first volume of a compilation which was intended to cover the reigns of the first twelve Caesars down to Domitian. It was written in or near Paris before 1250, and translated into Italian in 1313. Brunetto Latini used it for his *Treasure*. Paul Meyer calls its author a cross between a Renaissance humanist and a medieval minstrel: for although he followed his sources carefully, he improvised many insertions of his own which are absolutely medieval in tone. For instance, he made the battle of Pharsalus into a medieval conflict, where *ot mainte bele jouste fete et maint bel cop feru, dont Lucans ne parle pas* (p. 146d): knights called Galeran and Aufamien did marvellous deeds, and Pompey and Caesar wounded each other in single combat. And he gave a pen-portrait of Cleopatra (p. 175b-c) which was modelled on those of 'Dares'. There is a good edition by L. F. Flutre and K. Sneyders de Vogel (2 vols., Paris and Groningen, undated), in which volume 2 gives a detailed analysis of the sources. On both these works see the introductory essay by Paul Meyer in *Romania*, 14 (1885), 1-81.

31. For a general survey see A. Ausfeld, *Der griechische Alexanderroman* (ed. W. Kroll, Leipzig, 1907). The Arch-priest Leo's version has been edited by F. Pfister (Heidelberg, 1913).

32. Shakespeare, *Othello*, 1. 3. 144 f.

33. See J. Bédier in L. Petit de Julleville's *Histoire de la langue et de la littérature française*, 2. 76 f. The Aristotle group appears, for instance, at Lyons and St.-Valéry-en-Caux. G. Sarton, 'Aristotle and Phyllis', in *Isis* 14 (1930), 8-19, traces the oriental origins of the story, and suggests that as it appears in the Middle Ages it reflects the protest of the priesthood against the veneration felt for the pagan thinker Aristotle.

34. This vassalage of the lover to his mistress was called *domnei*: see the examples of the use of this word in K. Bartsch's *Chrestomathie provençale* (6th ed., revised by E. Koschwitz, Marburg, 1904). But it should be remembered that, although doubtless feudal in its origin, this conception was strengthened by the example of the Latin love-elegists, who all call their mistresses *dominae*, and practise or advise complete subjection to the will of the beloved. (This appears first in Cat. 68. 68 and 156, and then becomes frequent: see Tib. 1. 1. 46 and 2. 4.)

35. For detailed discussions of the nature and expressions of romantic love, or (as it is more properly called in the Middle Ages) 'courtly' love,

see C. S. Lewis, *The Allegory of Love* (Oxford, 1936), J. J. Parry's introduction and commentary to Andreas Capellanus's *De arte honeste amandi* (New York, 1941), and A. J. Denomy's brilliantly learned 'Inquiry into the Origins of Courtly Love' (*Mediaeval Studies*, 6 (1944), 175–260). Father Denomy considers that the chief intellectual currents which flowed together to create the concept were (*a*) Neoplatonic mysticism, which taught that the soul struggles to rise above the body, above matter, towards union with the Good, which is apprehended and desired through its beauty; (*b*) the Albigensian heresy, with its doctrine that spirit and matter belonged to two different worlds, and its consequent teaching of extreme asceticism; and (*c*) Arabic mysticism and philosophy, some of which originated from Plato. But what he does not prove (p. 257) is that the troubadours who fixed and developed the concept had anything but the vaguest notions of the first and third of these regions of thought. On pp. 188–93 he disallows the theory that Christian mysticism had some influence on courtly love, although he agrees that there are superficial resemblances between the two; and in note 2 on p. 193 he asserts that the cult of the Virgin had nothing whatever in common with the concept— on the ground that Christians, obeying an extension of the injunction of Jesus to St. John (John xix. 26–7), love Mary as their own mother. Still, it is a little difficult to believe that the artists who created and the worshippers who revered the statues of young, beautiful, attractively dressed maidens as part of the cult of Mary were all thinking of the Virgin as they did of their own mothers, and in no other way.

36. Ovid was at last civilizing the Goths. See Manitius's list of quotations and echoes from Ovid in medieval Latin poets and scholars, *Philologus*, suppl. 7 (1899). Traube (*Vorlesungen und Abhandlungen*, Munich, 1909–20, 2. 113) called the twelfth and thirteenth centuries the *aetas Ouidiana*.

37. Dante, *Inf.* 4. 88 f.

38. See pp. 602–3.

39. Ov. *Am.* 3. 4. 17: *nitimur in uetitum semper cupimusque negata.*

40. Ov. *A.A.* 1. 233 f. I owe these quotations to E. K. Rand's charming little book, *Ovid and His Influence* (Boston, 1925), 132–3; see also H. Waddell, *The Wandering Scholars* (London, 1934⁷), cc. 5 and 9.

41. Lecta sunt in medium,   quasi evangelium,
praecepta Ovidii,   doctoris egregii:
lectrix tam propitii   fuit evangelii
Eva de Danubrio,   potens in officio
artis amatoriae,   ut affirmant aliae   (ll. 25–9).

This Council of Remiremont is mentioned by H. Waddell in *The Wandering Scholars* (London, 1934⁷), c. 9. The text of the poem, edited by G. Waitz, is in *Zeitschrift für deutsches Altertum*, 7 (1849), 160–7. I have not seen W. Meyer, *Das Liebesconcil in Remiremont* (1914).

42. Ov. *Met.* 4. 55–166. See especially 4. 53:
haec quoniam uolgaris fabula non est.

G. Hart, *Ursprung und Verbreitung der Pyramus- und Thisbe-Sage* (Passau, 1889–91), does not attempt to trace the story back beyond Ovid, but outlines its widespread influence in modern literature. The French *Piramus* is discussed by L. Constans in L. Petit de Julleville's *Histoire de la langue et de la littérature française*, 1. 244.

43. Ov. *Met.* 6. 424–674.

44. *Philomena*, a translation and expansion of the original, is said to be by Chrétien de Troyes (Bush, *Mythology and the Renaissance Tradition in English Poetry* (Minneapolis and London, 1932), 13. The story is mentioned in Homer, *Od.* 19. 518 f.

45. *Titus Andronicus*, 4. 1. 45 f.

46. W. P. Ker, *Epic and Romance* (London, 1922²), Appendix, gives the extract; I add the sources of the songs which the popular troubadour would know, to show how many of them are Ovidian:

Qui volc ausir diverses comtes	
de reis, de marques, e de comtes,	
auzir ne poc tan can si volc;	
anc null' aurella non lai colc,	
quar l'us comtet de PRIAMUS,	The tale of Troy.
e l'autre diz de PIRAMUS;	Ovid's *Metamorphoses*, 4.
l'us contet de la bell' ELENA	The tale of Troy, and Ov. *Heroides*, 17.
com PARIS l'enquer, pois l'anmena;	,, ,,
l'autre comtava d'ULIXES,	The tale of Troy.
l'autre d'ECTOR et d'ACHILLES;	,,
l'autre comtava d'ENEAS	The tale of Aeneas.
et de DIDO consi remas	,,
per lui dolenta e mesquina;	,,
l'autre comtava de LAVINA	,,
con fes lo breu el cairel traire	,,
a la gaita de l'auzor caire;	The tale of Thebes.
l'us contet d'APOLLONICES	(Polynices, Tydeus, Eteocles.)
de TIDEU e d'ETIDIOCLES;	Apollonius of Tyre (a late Greek
l'autre comtava d'APOLLOINE	romance).
comsi retenc Tyr de Sidoine;	The tale of Alexander.
l'us comtet del Rei ALEXANDRI,	Ovid's *Heroides*, 18.
l'autre d'ERO et de LEANDRI;	The tale of Thebes, and Ov. *Meta-*
l'us dis de CATMUS quan fugi	*morphoses*, 3.
et de TEBAS con las basti;	Ovid's *Metamorphoses*, 7.
l'autre comtava de JASON	,,
e del dragon que non hac son;	Ovid's *Metamorphoses*, 9.
l'us comtet d'ALCIDE sa forsa,	
l'autre con tornet en sa forsa	Ovid's *Heroides*, 2.
PHILLIS per amor DEMOPHON;	
l'us dis com neguet en la fon	Ovid's *Metamorphoses*, 3.
lo belz N ꞏRCIS quan s'i miret;	Ovid's *Metamorphoses*, 10.
l'us dis de PLUTO con emblet	,,
sa bella moillier ad ORPHEU. . . .	

Then follow a few biblical myths; a number from the Arthurian cycle; several tales from the history of early France (among which comes Lucifer and how he fell), and finally:

l'us dis lo vers de Marcabru,   (A troubadour.)
l'autre comtet con DEDALUS   Ovid's *Metamorphoses*, 8.
saup ben volar, et d'ICARUS   ,,
co neguet per sa leujaria.   ,,
Cascus dis lo mieil que sabia.

                            Flamenca, 617–706.

47. See *Ovide moralisé*, ed. C. de Boer (Amsterdam, 1915). This editor observes that the main sources of the author's explanatory comments are: the Bible, Ovid's *Heroides* and *Fasti*, Statius, and the mythographers Hyginus and Fulgentius.

48. *Ovide moralisé*, 3. 1853 f.:

> Narcisus florete devint.
> Florete quel? Tele dont dist
> Li Psalmistres c'au main florist,
> Au soir est cheoite et fletrie.   (1886–9)

In Petit de Julleville's *History of French Literature* (1. 248) the moral of the story of Apollo and Daphne is quoted:

'Daphne, daughter of a river and cold by temperament, represents virginity; she is changed into a laurel, which like virginity is perpetually green and bears no fruit. She represents the Virgin Mary, loved by him who is the true sun; and when Apollo crowns himself with the laurel, he represents God putting on the body of her whom he made his mother.'

There is a useful summary of the whole movement of allegorizing Ovid, with details of other works of this kind, by L. K. Born, 'Ovid and Allegory', in *Speculum*, 9 (1934), 362–79.

49. *Roman de la Rose*, 9–10 (Langlois):

> ançois escrist l'avision
> qui avint au roi Scipion.

50. Hence the popularity, in this period, of stories in which the lovers die after one night together, or even die just before their first embrace. A beautiful modern use of the symbolism of the rose, in a rococo setting, is *Der Rosenkavalier*, by Hugo von Hofmannsthal and Richard Strauss.

51. See p. 41 f.

52. E. Langlois, *Origines et sources du roman de la Rose*, 136 f.

53. The sermon in lines 4837 f. = (?) Chaucer, *Romaunt of the Rose*, fragment B 5403 f.

54. *Roman de la Rose*, 5036 f.:

> ce peut l'en bien des clers enquerre
> qui Boece de Confort lisent,
> e les sentences qui là gisent;
> don granz biens aus genz lais ferait
> qui bien le leur translaterait.

On Jean de Meun's translation see H. R. Patch, *The Tradition of Boethius* (New York, 1935), 63.

55. *Roman de la Rose*, 37–8 (cf. the echo in 22605–6 (Marteau)):

> Ce est li Romanz de la Rose
> où l'art d'amors est toute enclose.

56. *Roman de la Rose*, 12740–14546.

57. Ov. *A.A.* 2. 279:

> ipse licet uenias Musis comitatus, Homere,
> si nihil attuleris, ibis, Homere, foras.

58. *Roman de la Rose*, 13617–20:

> D'amer povre ome ne li chaille,
> qu'il n'est riens que povres on vaille;
> se c'iert Ovides ou Homers,
> ne vaudroit-il pas deus gomers.

59. C. Lenient, *La Satire en France au moyen âge* (Paris, 1893[4]), 115 f.

60. Quoted by L. Thuasne, *Le Roman de la Rose* (Paris, 1929), 66.

61. Medieval literary theory paid little or no heed to the problem of finding the proper plan and proportion for a large work. See, for instance, E. Faral, *Les Arts poétiques du XIIe et XIIIe siècle* (Bibliothèque de l'École des Hautes Études, 238, Paris, 1924), 59–60. Only two of the theorists examined by M. Faral even mention the question. One of them, Geoffroi de Vinsauf, merely discusses how to attach the main body of the work to the beginning. The other, Jean de Garlande, says that a work should be composed of 'exordium, narration, petition, confirmation, refutation, and conclusion'—which is, of course, the plan of a Greco-Roman legal speech, taken from some handbook, and has nothing whatever to do with writing poetry or imaginative prose. M. Faral goes on to say, with justice: 'A la vérité, la composition n'a pas été le souci dominant des écrivains du moyen âge. Beaucoup de romans, et des plus réputés, manquent totalement d'unité et de proportions. On se l'explique si l'on considère qu'ils n'ont pas été faits, en général, pour soutenir l'examen d'un public qui lisait et pouvait commodément juger de l'ensemble, mais pour être entendus par des auditeurs auxquels on les lisait épisode par épisode.'

62. *Roman de la Rose*, 13263–4:

> Mil essemples dire en savraie
> mais trop grant conte à faire avraie.

63. See W. Jaeger, *Paideia* (Oxford, 1939), i. 2 fin.

64. *Roman de la Rose*, 1439–1510 = Ov. *Met.* 3. 339–510. *Echo, une haute dame* appears in 1444.

65. Pygmalion is in Ov. *Met.* 10. 243–97 = *Roman de la Rose*, 20817–1183. Dido and Aeneas appear in 13174–210, and Verginia in 5589–658.

66. Juvenal is actually quoted in 8709 f., 8737 f., and 9142 f. Jean also quotes the authority of Theophrastus in 'his book hight Aureole'. No such work existed in his time, and none by that name had ever existed. But there was a book by Theophrastus, which was one of the first to give philosophical reasons against marriage, and which formed part of the tradition of misogynistic writing to which Juvenal 6 belonged. It was known to the men of the Middle Ages because Jerome, writing in the same tradition, quoted it and called it an *aureolus liber*, 'worth its weight in gold'

(*Adu. Iouin.* 1. 47). See F. Bock, 'Aristoteles Theophrastus Seneca de matrimonio' (*Leipziger Studien*, 19. 1899), and J. van Wageningen, 'Seneca et Iuuenalis' (*Mnemosyne*, n.s. 45 (1917), 417 f.), for discussions of the transmission of these misogynistic ideas.

67. Ov. *Met*. 1. 89–112.

68. L. Thuasne, *Le Roman de la Rose* (n. 60), 27. Lorris could not have known Gallus, whose work was lost. Either he had seen the bogus poems passing under Gallus' name or he had copied it out of a list of love-poets.

69. For these sources, see E. Langlois, *Origines et sources du roman de la Rose* (Paris, 1891).

70. The text of Gerson's counterblast is given by L. Thuasne (n. 60), 53 f.

Notes on 4. DANTE AND PAGAN ANTIQUITY

1. See *Inf*. 16. 128, 21. 2. As for the adjective 'divine', that was not added by Dante, and has nothing to do with the vision of God in the *Paradiso*, but—according to Scartazzini (*Dante-Handbuch*, Leipzig, 1892, 413)—came into use about the middle of the sixteenth century, and was carried over from the conventional phrase applied to a supremely great writer, 'divine poet'.

2. *Letter to Can Grande*, 10. Dante knows something of the meaning of the word *tragedy*, but he gets it essentially wrong. It means 'goat-song'. He explains that this is because it is smelly, like a he-goat:

dicitur propter hoc a *tragos*, quod est hircus, et *oda*, quasi cantus hircinus, id est foetidus ad modum hirci, ut patet per Senecam in suis tragoediis.

He has heard of the function of tragedy, which is to inspire terror and pity; and he is trying to square this with the literal etymology of the word, through the equation: billy-goat = smelly = repulsive = tragic.

3. *Inf*. 20. 113.

4. Scartazzini, *Dante-Handbuch* (Leipzig, 1892), 413; and see p. 577, n. 30.

5. The key passage on Dante's earlier view of this problem is *De vulgari eloquentia*, 2. 4, where he distinguishes the *vulgare illustre*, the *vulgare mediocre*, and the *vulgare humile*, and says:

si tragice canenda videntur, tunc assumendum est vulgare illustre, et per consequens cantionem oportet ligare.

He goes on to say that the subjects of such *canzoni* are Salus, Amor, and Virtus. On the other hand, his statement in the Letter is far simpler:

remissus est modus (Comoediae) et humilis, quia loquutio vulgaris, in qua et mulierculae communicant.

Either this means that Dante thought women talked in the same style as that in which he was writing the *Paradiso*—which seems absurd; or else he had dropped the distinction between the three different Italian styles and was now contrasting the Italian language, which could be used by anybody (even by unlettered women—whence the half-tender, half-contemptuous diminutive), with the Latin language, in which he was writing his *Letter*, and which could be employed only by scholars and gentlemen. It was not for writing a low Italian style instead of a lofty one, but for writing Italian instead of Latin, that he was reproached by Giovanni di Virgilio; and he answered that charge in a Latin 'eclogue' modelled on Vergil, to show that he was, in spite of using Italian for the *Comedy*, a man of culture.

6. The Vision of Er, in the tenth book of Plato's *Republic*, is only one of many Greco-Roman treatments of this majestic theme, on which see p. 510 f. of this book. The earliest-known such Christian work is the series of Visions of Wettin, put into a thousand-line Latin poem in A.D. 827 by Walafrid Strabo. There are some interesting early Irish ones, in particular the Vision of Adamnan and the Vision of Tundale.

7. *Purg.* 21 ; and see *Purg.* 22. 64–73, where Statius explains that it was Vergil's 'Messianic' poem which turned him towards Christianity.

8. On Vergil's reputation as a Christian see Comparetti, *Vergil in the Middle Ages* (tr. E. F. M. Benecke, London, 1895), especially c. 7.

9. Aug. *Ep.* 137. 12, quoted by Comparetti (note 8).

10. See, among many others, E. Norden, *Die Geburt des Kindes* (Leipzig, 1924), and the psychological interpretation by C. G. Jung, *Das göttliche Kind* (Amsterdam, 1941).

11. For the grateful worship given by the subjects of the Roman empire to men like Pompey and Octavian who freed them from war, see the summary in A. J. Toynbee, *A Study of History* (Oxford, 1939), 5. 648 f., and the classical poems and modern treatises quoted in his notes on the passage.

12. In a pathetic letter to Octavian, he himself said he must have been mad to undertake the poem:

tanta incohata res est ut paene uitio mentis tantum opus ingressus mihi uidear (Macrob. *Sat.* 1. 24. 11).

With this compare the numerous expressions of painful though rewarding effort throughout the *Aeneid*:

tantae molis erat Romanam condere gentem (1. 33)
attollens humero famamque et fata nepotum (8. 731).

It is well known that he wanted to destroy the poem when he died: it would be limiting our view of his genius too closely to believe that this, and his expression of despair to Octavian, were due only to his sense of the difficulty of mastering all the complex material he used.

13. This misspelling began at a very early date, perhaps because of Vergil's nickname Parthenias, 'Miss Purity'. (For a similar reason, Milton at Cambridge was known as the Lady of Christ's.) In the Middle Ages the name was taken to refer to Vergil's powers as a magician, because *uirga* means *wand*.

14. See p. 486.

15. See *Inf.* 2. 13–27.

16. *Inf.* 34. 61–7.

17. Verg. *Georg.* 2. 136–76.

18. *Purg.* 6. 76 f.

19. *Inf.* 27. 26–7, 28. 71.

20. There are many examples of this: see any index to the poem, s.v. 'Latino'. The whole topic is well discussed by J. Bryce, 'Some Thoughts on Dante' and J. W. Mackail, 'The Italy of Rome and Vergil', in *Dante; Essays in commemoration 1321–1921* (London, 1921).

21. *Inf.* 4. 131 f.: *il maestro di color che sanno*.

22. *Inf.* 1. 86–7:

tu se' solo colui, da cu' io tolsi
lo bello stile che m'ha fatto onore.

23. *Aen.* 3. 29–30:

mihi frigidus horror
membra quatit gelidusque coit formidine sanguis.

24. *Inf.* 13. 44–5:

io lasciai la cima
cadere, e stetti come l'uom che teme.

25. *Purg.* 24. 57: *dolce stil novo*. The lyric quoted by Bonagiunta is the first in Dante's *Vita Nuova*.

26. In one way Dante's lyrics were a development from Provençal love-poetry, in another, a reaction against it. They were still much closer to the troubadours (one of whom, Arnaut Daniel, is highly praised by Dante in *Purg.* 26) than to any classical poetic style. For discussions see L. Azzolina, *Il 'dolce stil nuovo'* (Palermo, 1903), V. Rossi, *Il 'dolce stil novo'* (Florence, 1905), and F. Figurelli, *Il dolce stil novo* (Naples, 1933).

27. 'In its arrangement of rhymes that manner of Dante had, as it were, the form of a *serventese'* —Antonio da Tempo in *Summa artis rithimici* (1332), quoted and translated by E. G. Gardner, 'Dante as Literary Critic', in *Dante; Essays in commemoration 1321–1921* (London, 1921).

28. *Inf.* 10. 62–3.

29. *Inf.* 1. 83–4.

30. A strong objection to this view is that, when Dante told Vergil he had taken his beautiful style from Vergil's poetry, he was only at the beginning of his journey through the universe of hell, purgatory, and paradise, not at its end; and therefore he could not be referring to the style of the *Comedy*, which was yet to be written. Nevertheless, in *Inf.* 4, Dante is presented by Vergil to Homer, Horace, Ovid, and Lucan, the 'lords of highest song', and they honour him by making him a sixth in their company. This honour could not have been given to Dante for his lyrics. In the world of Time, the *Comedy* is unwritten until the experiences described in it are over; but in the world of Eternity, to which Vergil and those others belong, it is already written, and Dante is honoured for it. In the same world of Eternity, Dante is Vergil's pupil, and the style of the *Comedy* can be said (even at its temporal opening) to be taken from Vergil's book.

31. In his *Studies in Dante* (1st series, Oxford, 1896), Moore points

out one of the most subtle and poignant tributes ever paid by one artist to another. How is Vergil to leave Dante, after bringing him close to the beloved vision of Beatrice? Shall Dante bid a sad farewell to the master and friend who cannot accompany him up towards the sight of God, and who must live in desire without hope? No. After the poets have passed through purgatory, a glorious procession comes to meet them. Out of a cloud of flowers cast by angels, like the sun from mists, dawns Dante's lady Beatrice. Like a child to its mother, Dante turns to Vergil, to say 'I recognize the traces of the old flame': the very words in which Vergil's own lovelorn Dido spoke of her irresistible passion (Verg. *Aen.* 4. 23). But Vergil has vanished. And then, in a triad of lines, Dante repeats his name yearningly and lovingly three times:

> ma Virgilio n'avea lasciati scemi
> di sè, Virgilio dolcissimo patre,
> Virgilio a cui per mia salute die' mi   (*Purg.* 30. 49-52).

He places the name in exactly the same spot of each line as, in telling how Orpheus lamented for his beloved, torn from him to return to the dead, Vergil himself had placed the sadly repeated name:

> tum quoque, marmorea caput a ceruice reuolsum
> gurgite cum medio portans Oeagrius Hebrus
> uolueret, 'Eurydicen' uox ipsa et frigida lingua
> 'a miseram Eurydicen' anima fugiente uocabat,
> 'Eurydicen' toto referebant flumine ripae   (*Georg.* 4. 523-7).

Everything is in the echo: admiration, sorrow, eternal love.

32. The primary division of hell is into three groups of sins: incontinence, violence, and deceit. Aristotle's division was also into three: incontinence (uncontrolled desires), bestiality (perverted desires), and vice (the abuse of reason): ἀκρασία, θηριότης, and κακία (*Eth. Nic.* 7. 1145^{a}16). This distinction really goes back to Plato's division of the soul into three parts, that which desires, that which is spirited and energetic, and that which thinks. The sin of uncontrolled desire is incontinence. Plato would recognize violence as the sin of the 'spirited element'. The perversion of reason is worst, because it is the corruption of our highest part, the mind. See K. Witte's *Essays on Dante* (tr. C. M. Lawrence and G. H. Wicksteed, Boston, 1898), and W. H. V. Reade's *The Moral System of Dante's Inferno* (Oxford, 1909), for the many complex details growing out of, and often obscuring, this general scheme.

33. Charon, *Inf.* 3. 82 f.; Minos, *Inf.* 5. 4 f.; Cerberus, *Inf.* 6. 13 f.; Harpies, *Inf.* 13. 10 f.; Centaurs, *Inf.* 12. 55 f. The principal medieval demons are Malacoda and his squad, *Inf.* 21.

34. *Inf.* 5. 4-12.

35. *Purg.* 12. 34-45. Moore, *Studies in Dante* (1st series, Oxford, 1896), has pointed out these instances.

36. Although the anti-monarchist Cato was Lucan's hero, Dante was probably influenced, in making him the guardian of purgatory (*Purg.* 1. 31 f.), by the scene in Vergil's heaven:

> secretosque pios, his dantem iura Catonem (*Aen.* 8. 670).

37. *Inf.* 2. 32.

38. This is in *Purg.* 30. 19–21. The two greetings come from Matt. xxi. 9, and *Aeneid* 6. 884.

39. *Inf.* 5. 82: *quali colombe dal disio chiamate.*

40. *Aen.* 6. 202–3: *sedibus optatis.*

41. On the beauty of reminiscence, see p. 156 f.

42. Thus, the dead warrior resurrected by a witch (*Bell. Ciu.* 6. 413 f.) is strangely alluded to in *Inf.* 9. 22 f.; the African snakes, imitated by so many other modern poets from *Bell. Ciu.* 9. 700 f., in *Inf.* 24. 82 f.; and Amyclas (*Bell. Ciu.* 5. 504 f.) in *Par.* 11. 67 f.

43. *Conv.* 2. 13. The moral essays of Cicero referred to are *Cato* (*de senectute*), *Laelius* (*de amicitia*), *De finibus*, and *De officiis.*

44. *Inf.* 26. 52 f. = Stat. *Theb.* 12. 429 f.

45. *Purg.* 22. 13 f. and Juv. 7. 82 f.

Notes on 5. TOWARDS THE RENAISSANCE

1. His legal name was Francesco di Petracco, which is only a diminutive form of Peter. He latinized it in order to make it more than a little local nickname, and to attach it to the main tradition of culture. Later, in the full Renaissance, many scholars translated their entire names into Greek or Latin for the same purpose: for instance, Philip Schwarzerd became Melanchthon (the Greek for 'black earth' = Schwarzerd).

2. Dante and other leaders of the White party, among whom was Petrarch's father, were charged with corruption in office and with offences against the Guelph party, supported by the pope. They were exiled by a decree of 27 January 1302.

3. Petrarch, *Fam.* 21. 15, tr. by J. H. Robinson and H. W. Rolfe, in *Petrarch, the First Modern Scholar* (New York and London, 1914²).

4. Petrarch, *Rer. mem.* 427, for which see Robinson and Rolfe (cited in n. 3), 175 and note:

'moribus parumper (?) contumacior et oratione liberior quam delicatis et fastidiosis aetatis nostrae principum auribus atque oculis acceptum fuit'.

5. G. Voigt, *Die Wiederbelebung des classischen Alterthums* (Berlin, 1880–1²), 1. 118 f.

6. Ov. *Trist.* 4. 10. 51: *Vergilium uidi tantum.*

7. Another modern parallel is the quantity of valuable unpublished music which is known to exist, but which is inaccessible even to music-lovers: for example, most of the delightful symphonies of Haydn, much of the work of Lully, and the later piano compositions of Scriabin.

8. One of the speeches was the *Pro Archia* (Sandys, *A History of Classical Scholarship*, Cambridge, 1908, 2. 7 and note). For the story, see Voigt (cited in n. 5), 1. 38 f., and P. de Nolhac, *Pétrarque et l'humanisme* (Paris, 1907), 1. 41.

9. For Salutati, see p. 18. On Petrarch's discovery of Cicero's letters (*Ad Att., Ad Brut., Ad Q. fr.*) see Voigt (cited in n. 5), 1. 43 f., and Sandys, ibid.

10. See E. Zielinski, *Cicero im Wandel der Jahrhunderte* (Leipzig, 1912³), 26 f., for a discussion of Cicero's influence, through Petrarch, on the ideal of humanism. There is an admirable essay on the same topic in W. Rüegg's *Cicero und der Humanismus* (Zürich, 1946).

11. Petrarch, *Fam.* 24. 3; Sandys (cited in n. 8), 2. 7.

12. Petrarch determined, in return for a house, to bequeath his library to the republic of Venice. It would have become the first public library in western Europe since the destruction of the Roman empire; but he was not in Venice when he died, so it was broken up. See P. de Nolhac, *Pétrarque et l'humanisme* (Paris, 1907), 1. 13, 78–81, and 87 f.

13. Petrarch's imitation of Vergil did not include echoes of Vergil's own words, because he aimed at being an entirely original poet in Latin: he actually altered a line in his *Eclogues* to root out a Vergilian reminiscence. But the matter and much of the manner of Vergil he did imitate, and in his *Letters* he quotes Vergil scores of times (P. de Nolhac (cited in n. 8), 1. 123, n. 2).

14. Dante, *Inf.* 4. 89: *Orazio satiro.* Petrarch quotes Horace oftener than any other Latin poet except Vergil: we have the very text he used (P. de Nolhac (cited in n. 8), 1. 181).

15. Petrarch, *Fam.* 24. 8—quoted by Voigt (cited in n. 5), 1. 44 f., and discussed by de Nolhac (cited in n. 8), 2. 16 f., who shows that Petrarch's manuscript of Livy lacked book 33. On Petrarch's knowledge of Roman history in general, see de Nolhac, c. 6.

16. Sandys, *A History of Classical Scholarship* (cited in n. 8), 2. 8, and see de Nolhac (cited in n. 8) on Petrarch's romantic passion for Greek.

17. Still, Petrarch was far from understanding the true relationship between the Greek and Roman cultures: he put Plato below Cicero as a philosopher. See de Nolhac (cited in n. 8), 1. 214 and 2. 127 f.

18. P. de Nolhac (cited in n. 8), 2. 166–7. The last actual words Petrarch wrote were part of a biography of Caesar (de Nolhac, 1. 85).

19. Sandys (cited in n. 8), 2. 10; de Nolhac (n. 8), 2. 147 f.; Voigt (n. 5), 1. 80 f.

20. P. de Nolhac (n. 8), 2. 189 f.

21. Petrarch, *De ignorantia*, 1151; Voigt (cited in n. 5), 1. 94.

22. The main source of the *Africa* is Livy, whom Petrarch sometimes transcribes almost verbatim, as in his account of the death of Lucretia. The style, vocabulary, and rhythm are modelled on Vergil and Vergil's imitator Statius. Over forty years after Petrarch died, a real Latin epic on the same subject and in the same style was discovered—the *Punica* of Silius Italicus (A.D. 26–101), which Petrarch had never heard of. The best that can be said of Petrarch's *Africa* is that it is better than the *Punica*. L. Pingaud, *De poemate F. Petrarchae cui titulus est Africa* (Paris, 1872), conjectures that the gap after book 4 represents a lacuna of three books, and that the whole poem was meant to contain twelve books like the *Aeneid*. On Ronsard's *Franciade*, see p. 144.

23. See p. 41 f. For a summary of the *Secret*, with extracts in English, see Robinson and Rolfe (cited in n. 3), c. 7. Those who are interested in Petrarch's Latin writings should begin with his *Rerum memorandarum*

libri, which give a conspectus of his tastes and knowledge. There is an admirable edition by G. Billanovich (Florence, 1943—XXI).

24. See Liszt, *Années de Pèlerinage: 2ᵉ Année: 'Italie'*.

25. Dante, *Purg.* 29, especially 106 f.

26. On the deeper significance of the laureateship, and the connexion between the ideals of Petrarch and Rienzo, see K. Burdach, *Rienzo und die geistige Wandlung seiner Zeit* (part 1 of the *Briefwechsel des Cola di Rienzo*, ed. K. Burdach and P. Piur, in the series Vom Mittelalter zur Reformation: Forschungen zur Geschichte der deutschen Bildung, ed. K. Burdach, Berlin, 1913–28). Passages of particular interest are: p. 31, giving the pope's charge of paganism against Rienzo; 75 f. on the idyllic renewal of the youth of Rome; 321 f. and 384 f. on Frederick II; and 504 f. on the coronation of Petrarch as a model for that of Rienzo. Petrarch's changing views of Rienzo's policy and character have been traced through a selection of his letters, translated and annotated, by M. E. Cosenza, *Francesco Petrarca and the Revolution of Cola di Rienzo* (Chicago, 1913).

27. It is often said that the first italic printing-type was modelled on Petrarch's handwriting. (So, for instance, J. E. Sandys, *A History of Classical Scholarship*, Cambridge, 1908, 2. 99.) This is a mistake: it comes from a misreading of the preface to the Aldine Petrarch of 1501, where it is stated that the *text* was based on a manuscript in the poet's own hand (see A. F. Johnson, *Printing Types*, London, 1934, 126–7). In actual fact, Petrarch wrote a Gothic *bastarda*. Aldus's type derived from the neo-Caroline script of the humanists, which, in its cursive form, did not differ in essential structure from that of Niccolò Niccoli. On this, see James Wardrop in *Signature*, n.s. 2 (1946), 12.

28. The *Teseida* has 9,896 lines, like the *Aeneid*, if one stanza (3. 69) is omitted with some manuscripts; but R. A. Pratt, 'Chaucer's Use of the *Teseida*' (*PMLA*, 62 (1947), 3. 599), implies that this is an uncritical excision. Voigt, *Die Wiederbelebung des classischen Alterthums* (Berlin, 1880–1²), 1. 165, says that the story about Boccaccio's sitting at Vergil's tomb comes from Filippo Villani, not from Boccaccio himself.

29. The chief classical source is Statius' *Thebaid*. Boccaccio used an annotated edition, and published his own *Teseida* with similar annotations (so Pratt, cited in n. 28). He also used Dante's *Comedy*, and drew much material from the medieval *Roman de Thèbes* (on which see p. 56). J. Schmitt, *La Théséide de Boccace et la Théséide grecque* (Bibliothèque de l'École des Hautes Études, 92, Paris, 1892, 279–345), disproves the theory that Boccaccio was using a translation of a Greek romance now lost.

30. See p. 52.

31. Verg. *Aen.* 3. 588 f.; Ov. *Met.* 14. 160 f.

32. On the use of heroic examples, see p. 67 f.

33. *Fiammetta*, bk. 3 med.

34. *Fiammetta*, bk. 4 fin. and med.

35. *Fiammetta*, bk. 1; cf. *Le Roman de la Rose* fin.

36. This passage is quoted from and translated by J. E. Sandys, *A History of Classical Scholarship* (Cambridge, 1908), 2. 13. It comes from

the lectures of Boccaccio's pupil Benvenuto on Dante: the particular passage which Benvenuto was explaining was St. Benedict's denunciation of the corruption of the monasteries (*Parad.* 22. 73 f.).

37. On *The Romance of the Rose* see p. 62 f.

38. Chaucer also took some material from Joseph of Exeter's *Bellum Troianum* (D. Bush, *Mythology and the Renaissance Tradition in English Poetry*, Minneapolis and London, 1932, 8). *Troilus and Criseyde* has nearly 3,000 lines more than *Il Filostrato*, and less than one-third of its material is directly borrowed from Boccaccio (B. A. Wise, *The Influence of Statius upon Chaucer*, Baltimore, 1911, 4). For an analysis of the changes Chaucer introduced, see C. S. Lewis, 'What Chaucer really did to *Il Filostrato*', in *Essays and Studies by Members of the English Association*, 17 (1932), 56–75.

39. Chaucer used the *Teseida* not only in the Knight's Tale, but in *Anelida and Arcite, Troilus and Criseyde*, and several other poems: it meant a great deal to him. See R. A. Pratt, 'Chaucer's Use of the *Teseida*' (*PMLA*, 62 (1947), 3. 598–621).

40. *The Clerk's Prologue*, 26–33.

41. *The Tale of the Wife of Bath*, 1125–30 = Dante, *Purg.* 7. 121–4.

42. J. L. Lowes, 'Chaucer and Dante', in *Modern Philology*, 1915, 1916, 1917, points out such resemblances as:

> *The Parliament of Fowls*, 141 f. and *Parad.* 4 init.;
> *The Parliament of Fowls*, 288 f. and *Inf.* 5. 58–69, plus Bocc. *Tes.* 7. 62;
> *Troilus*, 2. 22–5 and *Conv.* 2. 14. 83 f., plus Horace, 'Art of Poetry', 70–1.

Note also the resemblance of the general plan of *The Parliament of Fowls* to Dante's *Inferno*: e.g. the Roman guide, and the inscription on the gate (127 f. = *Inf.* 3. 1 f.). The eagle in *The House of Fame* is clearly inspired by the heavenly eagle in *Paradiso*, 18 f. And several of Chaucer's most fervent prayers are adapted from Dante: *The Second Nun's Tale*, 36 f. = *Parad.* 33. 1–6, and the final prayer in *Troilus* (5. 267) = *Parad.* 14. 28–30.

43. *Introduction to the Man of Law's Prologue*, 92.

44. *Anelida and Arcite*, 21.

45. Hor. *Ep.* 1. 2. 1–2:

> Troiani belli scriptorem, Maxime Lolli,
> dum tu declamas Romae, Praeneste relegi.

46. See an excellent article by G. L. Kittredge, 'Chaucer's Lollius', in *Harvard Studies in Classical Philology*, 28 (1917), 27–137. Confusion worse confounded has been introduced by the authoress of a recent book on Chaucer (M. Chute, *Geoffrey Chaucer of England*, New York, 1946, 166 n.), who, after quoting the two lines of Horace, translated them:

'While you are preaching oratory in Rome, Maximus Lollius, I have been reading Praeneste (i.e., Homer), the writer of the Trojan war.'

If a modern writer could believe that the holiday town of Praeneste was another name for Homer, it must have been easy for a medieval writer, with fewer resources at his command, to believe that Lollius was a little-known but accomplished historian.

47. *The House of Fame*, 1464–8.

48. E. A. Poe, *The Gold Bug*, init.

49. *The Monk's Prologue*, 3161–9, 83 f. It is most unlikely that by *exametron* Chaucer could have meant the six-foot metre (iambic trimeter) used by Seneca, since hardly anyone was able to scan Seneca's tragedies until well into the Renaissance. See also *Troilus and Criseyde*, 5. 1786, where, addressing his poem, he says:

> Go, litel book, go litel myn tragedie

to join Vergil and other epic writers.

50. Here are some other mistakes of the same type:

(a) And Thetis, Chorus, Triton, and they alle (*LGW*, 8. 2422).

> Et senior Glauci *chorus* Inousque Palaemon
> Tritonesque citi Phorcique exercitus omnis;
> laeua tenent Thetis et Melite Panopeaque uirgo (Verg. *Aen.* 5. 823–5).

(b) And hir yonge son Iulo
And eek Ascanius also (*HF*, 177–8).

Iulus was the other name of Ascanius; one of the essential points about Vergil's story of Aeneas was that, through this boy Ascanius-Iulus, Aeneas was the ancestor of the Julian family, to which Octavian Augustus belonged.

(c) And Marcia that lost her skin (*HF*, 1229).

Marcia is the Roman name of a woman; Marsyas, who was flaycd, was a male Greek satyr.

(d) And on hir feet wexen saugh I
Partriches winges redely (*HF*, 1391–2).

Chaucer apparently mistook *pernicibus alis* in Verg. *Aen.* 4. 180 for *perdicibus*, 'partridges'; but he got it right later, in *Troilus and Criseyde*: see E. Nitchie, *Vergil and the English Poets* (New York, 1919), 57.

51. See H. M. Ayres, 'Chaucer and Seneca', in *The Romanic Review*, 1919; B. L. Jefferson, *Chaucer and the Consolation of Philosophy of Boethius* (Princeton, 1917); J. Koch, 'Chaucers Belesenheit in den römischen Klassikern', in *Englische Studien*, 1923, 8–84; T. R. Lounsbury, *Studies in Chaucer* (New York, 1892), 2. 250 f.; E. Nitchie, cited in n. 50 d; S. G. Owen, 'Ovid and Romance', in *English Literature and the Classics* (ed. G. S. Gordon, Oxford, 1912); R. K. Root, *The Poetry of Chaucer* (Boston, 1906); H. Schinnerl, *Die Belesenheit Chaucers in der Bibel und der antiken Literatur* (Munich, 1923), of which I have seen only a summary; E. F. Shannon, 'Chaucer and Lucan's *Pharsalia*' (*Modern Philology*, 16 (1919), 12. 113–18), and *Chaucer and the Roman Poets* (Harvard Studies in Comparative Literature, 7, Cambridge, Mass., 1929); W. W. Skeat's large edition of Chaucer (Oxford, 1894–1900); and B. A. Wise, *The Influence of Statius upon Chaucer* (Baltimore, 1911). I owe much to all these scholars.

52. Dryden, Preface to *Fables, Ancient and Modern*.

53. *Introduction to the Man of Law's Prologue*, 47 f. *The Manciple's Tale* of the crow is from Ovid, *Met*. 2. 531 f. Koch (cited in n. 51) gives many examples of Chaucer's borrowings from the *Metamorphoses*, book by book, which make it clear that Chaucer knew all books 1–8 and 11, something of books 9, 10, 12, 13, 14, and apparently nothing of book 15 (if he did know it, he never used it). His favourite books were 4, 6, 8, and 11 (Koch, 68).

54. *The House of Fame*, 379 f. The *Heroides* summarized are, in order, *Ep*. 2, 3, 5, 6, 12, 9, 10, and 7.

55. So Shannon (cited in n. 51).

56. *LGW*, 1680 f. = Ov. *Fast*. 2. 685 f.

57. *The Wife of Bath's Prologue*, 680; *The Book of the Duchess*, 568.

58. His favourite books were 1, 2, and 4. There is little proof that he read books 7–12 except the brief summary in *HF*, 451–67 (Koch (cited in n. 51), 44–52). It does not appear that he read the *Bucolics* and the *Georgics*. The Prioress's motto *Amor vincit omnia* (Prol. 162) is not from *Buc*. 10. 69, but from St. Augustine, quoted by Vincent of Beauvais (n. 73).

59. In Vergil (*Aen*. 4. 328–9), Dido says sadly that she has no 'little Aeneas'. Ovid (*Her*. 7. 133 f.) alters this, and makes her say that she may be pregnant. This is in line with his general attack on the Vergilian characterization of Aeneas, who, for Ovid, is a 'traitour'.

60. B. L. Jefferson has shown this in his book cited in n. 51; see also H. R. Patch, *The Tradition of Boethius* (New York, 1935), 66–72.

61. *Troilus and Criseyde*, 4. 958–1078 and *The Nun's Priest's Tale*, B. 4420–40.

62. Plato, *Rep*. 6. 496.

63. Chaucer mentions Boethius in *The Nun's Priest's Tale*, B. 4484, as one that 'can singe', which might be a reference to his *De musica*; and the line in *The House of Fame*, 765,

Soun is noght but air y-broken

probably comes from the same book through a Reader's Digest.

64. *Troilus and Criseyde*, 2. 100–8. His episcopal Grace is the seer Amphiaraus.

65. *Troilus and Criseyde*, 5. 1480 f. Wise (op. cit. in n. 51) points out that all the patent references of Chaucer to the Theban saga in *Troilus*, except 5. 932–7, are in parts of the poem not adapted from *Il Filostrato*, so that Chaucer used the Latin original.

66. M. A. Pratt, 'Chaucer's Claudian', in *Speculum*, 22 (1947), 419 f., suggests that Chaucer found Claudian's *De raptu Proserpinae, Laus Serenae*, and the prologue to *De VI cons. Honorii* (mistakenly set before *De rapt. Pros.*) in one of the medieval Latin anthologies used as school-books and called *Libri Catoniani*. On these see M. Boas, 'De librorum Catonianorum historia atque compositione', in *Mnemosyne*, n.s. 42 (1914), 17–46, who conjectures they were built up in the ninth century (as part of the Carolingian Renaissance?). Named after the 'dicta Catonis' with which they began, they contained several short second-rate poems

such as the *Ilias Latina* (dropped in the twelfth century) and Statius' *Achilleid*. For Chaucer's references to Claudian, see *The House of Fame*, 1507 f. and *The Merchant's Tale*, E. 2227 f. Petrarch, however, knew Claudian well.

67. The *Dream* is mentioned again in *The Nun's Priest's Tale*, B 4313–14.

68. *The Tale of the Wife of Bath*, 1184: the sentiment is quoted from Seneca, *Ep.* 2. 5, who got it ultimately from Epicurus.

69. See the discussion by Professor H. M. Ayres (op. cit. in n. 51). Pandarus' arguments in *Troilus and Criseyde*, 1, are largely taken from Seneca's epistles, the authorship being concealed under phrases like 'as writen clerkes wyse': for instance,

1. 687 = Sen. *Ep.* 3. 4;	1. 891 = Sen. *Ep.* 2. 1;
1. 704 = Sen. *Ep.* 99. 26;	1. 960 = Sen. *Ep.* 2. 2.

The Pardoner's Tale, too, is full of Seneca (especially *Epp.* 83, 95, and 114: see lines 513 16 and 534 48); and the discussion of slavery in *The Parson's Tale*, 1. 761 f. comes from Sen. *Ep.* 47.

70. On Valerius Flaccus see Shannon (cited in n. 51), 340–55.

71. Poggio found the manuscript on his famous expedition to St. Gallen: see J. E. Sandys, *A History of Classical Scholarship* (Cambridge, 1908), 2. 27 and notes. Petrarch did not know Valerius Flaccus (P. de Nolhac, *Pétrarque et l'humanisme*, Paris, 1907, 1. 193).

72. *Troilus and Criseyde*, 4. 197–201 = Juv. 10. 2–4, with a direct quotation ('cloud of errour' = *erroris nebula*). *The Tale of the Wife of Bath*, 1192–4 = Juv. 10. 22.

73. For instance, Boccaccio, 2. 2, gives the name of Hypermnestra's husband (Lynceus) as Linus (dat.); and so Chaucer in *LGW*, 2569, calls him Lino. Adriane (in *HF*, 407) comes from Adriana in Boccaccio, 10. 49. Chaucer mentions Vincentius Bellovacensis' *Speculum historiale* in *LGW*, 307:

> What Vincent, in his Storial Mirour?

On these two books and others which Chaucer used less, see Koch (op. cit. in n. 51), 70–8.

Notes on 6. THE RENAISSANCE: TRANSLATION

INTRODUCTORY NOTE. Among the authorities used for this chapter are:

A. Bartels, *Geschichte der deutschen Literatur* (Leipzig, 1905⁴).

A. H. Becker, *Loys Le Roy de Coutances* (Paris, 1896).

R. Bunker, *A Bibliographical Study of the Greek Works and Translations published in France during the Renaissance: the Decade 1540–1550* (New York, 1939).

C. H. Conley, *The First English Translators of the Classics* (New Haven, 1927).

L. Cooper and A. Gudeman, *A Bibliography of the Poetics of Aristotle* (Cornell Studies in English, 11, New Haven and London, 1928).

W. J. Entwistle, *The Spanish Language* (London, 1936).

J. Fitzmaurice-Kelly, *A History of Spanish Literature* (New York, 1920).

F. M. K. Foster, *English Translations from the Greek* (New York, 1918).

K. Goedeke, *Grundriss zur Geschichte der deutschen Dichtung* (Dresden, 1884–6²).

E. Hernández García, *Gramática histórica de la lengua española* (Orense, 1938).

R. Huchon, *Histoire de la langue anglaise* (Paris, 1923–30).

A. Hulubei, 'Virgile en France au XVIᵉ siècle' (*Revue du seizième siècle*, 18 (1931), 1–77).

B. L. Jefferson, *Chaucer and the Consolation of Philosophy of Boethius* (Princeton, 1917).

O. Jespersen, *Growth and Structure of the English Language* (Oxford, 1935⁸).

H. B. Lathrop, *Translations from the Classics into English from Caxton to Chapman (1477–1620)* (University of Wisconsin Studies in Language and Literature, 35, Madison, Wis., 1933).

H. R. Palmer, *List of English Editions and Translations of Greek and Latin Classics printed before 1641* (London, 1911).

J. E. Sandys, *A History of Classical Scholarship* (Cambridge, 1903–8).

R. K. Spaulding, *How Spanish grew* (Berkeley and Los Angeles, 1943).

L. S. Thompson, 'German Translations of the Classics between 1450 and 1550' (*Journal of English and Germanic Philology*, 42 (1943), 343–63).

A. A. Tilley, *The Literature of the French Renaissance* (Cambridge, 1904).

F. Vogt and M. Koch, *Geschichte der deutschen Literatur* (Leipzig, 1926⁴).

G. Voigt, *Die Wiederbelebung des classischen Alterthums* (Berlin, 1880–1²).

K. von Reinhardstoettner, *Plautus. Spätere Bearbeitungen plautinischer Lustspiele* (Leipzig, 1886).

L. M. Watt, *Douglas's Aeneid* (Cambridge, 1920).

C. Whibley, 'Translators', in *The Cambridge History of English Literature* (Cambridge, 1919), 4. 1.

B. Wiese and E. Percopo, *Geschichte der italienischen Litteratur* (Leipzig, 1899).

A. M. Woodward, 'Greek History at the Renaissance' (*The Journal of Hellenic Studies*, 63 (1943), 1–14)

and the contributors to volumes 2 and 3 of L. Petit de Julleville's *Histoire de la langue et de la littérature française* (Paris, 1896–9).

1. The story is given in great detail in the 'Letter of Aristeas'. There were 72 rabbis—apparently 6 from each tribe—and they completed the work in 72 days, under the auspices of Ptolemy Philadelphus. But it is now believed that the translations of the Hebrew scriptures into Greek were made piecemeal and gradually put together, and that the letter is a propagandistic forgery constructed long after the translations were finished. Probably it was written between 145 and 100 B.C. in order to give authority to a new, revised, 'official' version of the Jewish law in Greek. However,

the story was long accepted, and has given us the name Septuagint (= 'seventy') for the Greek version of the Old Testament. On the Septuagint and the 'Letter of Aristeas' see Christ–Schmid–Stählin's *Geschichte der griechischen Litteratur* (Munich, 1920⁶), 2. 1. 542 f. and 619 f., and P. E. Kahle, *The Cairo Geniza* (The Schweich Lectures of the British Academy, 1941, London, 1947), 132–79.

2. For instance, it was Livius who established the now well-known correspondences between Greek and Roman deities: Venus = Aphrodite, Jupiter = Zeus, and so on. When Homer called on the Muses, Livius substituted the native Italian spirits of song, the Camenae; but their personality was too faint to survive.

3. See p. 5. Thus, Cicero practised public speaking in Greek; Horace began his career as a poet by writing in Greek; Cicero's friend Atticus actually gave up Rome and went to live in Athens, whence his nickname.

4. Quoted by F. Brunot in L. Petit de Julleville (cited in introductory note), 2. 542.

5. This interesting man was one of the first important French translators, and turned the *Ethics* and *Politics* of Aristotle into French in 1370–1, from the Latin versions made about 1280 by William of Moerbeke and others. He was also one of the earliest scientific economists: he began his career with a treatise on the theory of money (*De origine, natura, jure, et mutationibus monetarum*). Apparently it was he who introduced, among many other words, *poète* and *poème* into French. On his work and that of his contemporaries in France, see Voigt (cited in introductory note), 2. 341 f.

6. Quoted by F. Brunot in L. Petit de Julleville (cited in introductory note), 2. 541.

7. Rabelais, 2. 6, translated by F. Urquhart. The student's bad French is good enough Latin. For instance, 'by vele and rames' (*par vèles et rames*) is Cicero's *uelis remisque* = 'with sails and oars' = 'at full speed'. To this same kind of pedantry no less a man than Milton fell victim: see pp. 160–1, 609–11.

8. This point is stressed by B. L. Jefferson (cited in introductory note).

9. So W. J. Sedgefield, in the preface to his translation of Alfred's *Boethius* (Oxford, 1900).

10. So O. Immisch, *Das Nachleben der Antike* (Das Erbe der Alten, n.s. 1, Leipzig, 1919), 26.

11. For details see L. S. Thompson (cited in introductory note). Mr. Thompson points out that most of the translations published in German were done by second-rate men like Boner, who knew no Greek. Goedeke (cited in introductory note), 2. 317, agrees, but emphasizes the valuable influence of the German translations of Greek and Roman history made during the Renaissance in bringing Germany closer to the traditions of western Europe. On the limitations of Spanish humanism, there is a valuable article by O. H. Green, 'A Critical Survey of Scholarship in the Field of Spanish Renaissance Literature 1914–44' (*Studies in Philology*, 44 (1947), 2), which points out that the main force of the new

scholarship in Spain flowed into religion, rather than scholarship or literature.

12. The Latin version was by Pier Candido Decembri. See K. Vollmöller, 'Eine unbekannte altspanische Übersetzung der Ilias', in *Studien zur Litteraturgeschichte Michael Bernays gewidmet* (Hamburg, 1893), 233–49, who gives specimens. Juan de Mena had produced a translation of the *Iliad*, but it was the Latin *Iliad*, a verse epitome from the first century A.D.

13. The *Imtheachta Æniasa* has been edited by the Rev. G. Calder (London, 1907): E. Nitchie, *Vergil and the English Poets* (New York, 1919), 80, n. 8.

14. See H. J. Molinier, *Octovien de Saint-Gelays* (Rodez, 1910), for details of his work and his too short life. His translation of the *Aeneid* is described and discussed by A. Hulubei (cited in introductory note): it was presented to Louis XII in 1500, and printed in 1509.

15. There is a useful analysis of Douglas's work in L. M. Watt's book, cited in the introductory note to this chapter. How slowly and with what difficulty it attained its real poetic reputation has been shown by J. A. W. Bennett, 'The Early Fame of Gavin Douglas's *Eneados*' (*Modern Language Notes*, 61 (1946), 83–8). It is important to notice that Douglas savagely attacked Caxton for perpetuating the false traditions put about by 'Dares', and thus showed himself, in spite of the crudities of his translation, to be completely in touch with Renaissance thought.

16. On Lucan as a historian see p. 577.

17. For this point see C. Schlayer, *Spuren Lukans in der spanischen Dichtung* (Heidelberg, 1927), 68 f. It is a curious example of the power of classical influence, for although Jauregui himself preferred the pellucid sweetness of Tasso's *Amyntas* (of which he had produced a fine translation), he was mastered, against his own will, by the burning intensity of Lucan's style.

18. See p. 62.

19. See p. 205.

20. For Montaigne's tribute, see his *Essays*, 2. 10. Other references to Plutarch's tremendous influence on French thought will be found on pp. 191, 393–5, and 402.

21. Details on p. 210 f.

22. The story, with references, will be found in Sandys' *A History of Classical Scholarship* (Cambridge, 1908), 2. 180.

23. Jean-Antoine de Baïf's *Antigone* was written well before 1573. On these two versions, see M. Delcourt, *Étude sur les traductions des tragiques grecs et latins en France depuis la Renaissance* (Mémoires de l'Académie Royale de Belgique, Classe des lettres et des sciences morales et politiques, 19. 4, Brussels, 1925), 26–33 and 71–81.

24. The French *Hecuba*, published anonymously, was long believed to be by Lazare de Baïf, because it bore the motto *Rerum vices*, held by a branch of his family; but it has been shown that it was Bochetel's, and indeed it is in a completely different style from Baïf's *Electra*. See

M. Delcourt (cited in n. 23), 34–6, and the authors there quoted.
25. Only a fragment of Ronsard's *Plutus* translation remains. The tradition that he made a complete one has been doubted, on the ground that (in view of the contemporary interest in the play) the whole thing would have been preserved. See M. Delcourt, *La Tradition des comiques anciens en France avant Molière* (Bibliothèque de la Faculté de Philosophie et Lettres de l'Université de Liége, 59, 1934), 75 f. But in her earlier work (cited in n. 23) she accepts the story, and in fact confirms it by observing that such translations (e.g. Dorat's *Prometheus Bound*) were often made for a small group and not printed. On this subject she cites R. Sturel's 'Essai sur les traductions du théâtre grec en français avant 1550' (*Revue d'histoire littéraire de la France*, 20 (1913), 269–96 and 637–66), which discusses the manuscript translations still extant.

26. On the relation between this translation and *The Comedy of Errors* see p. 624 f.

27. On these, see W. Creizenach's *Geschichte des neueren Dramas* (Halle, 1918²), 2. 1. 201 f. and 560 f.

28. See H. J. Molinier (cited in n. 14), 241 f., on this translation.

29. On the aims and methods of these translators, and the changes they introduced, see H. B. Charlton, *The Senecan Tradition in Renaissance Tragedy* (Manchester, reissued 1946), pp. cliii–clviii; and there are some remarks of interest in F. R. Amos, *Early Theories of Translation* (New York, 1920), 111 f.

30. On Dolce's versions and the stage translations in Italian, see Creizenach (cited in n. 27), 2. 1. 353 f. and 381 f. On the French translations see M. Delcourt (cited in n. 23), 85–115. Jean de la Péruse's *Médée* (before 1555) was apparently an adaptation rather than a translation.

31. The parallel between Philip of Spain and the empire-building Philip of Macedon was close. Centuries later we shall see the same orator's speeches being used as warning propaganda against the imperialistic aggression of Napoleon: see p. 328.

32. H. B. Lathrop (cited in introductory note) says on p. 41 that this translation by Elyot was the first made in English directly from the Greek original. The educational importance of the speeches *Nicocles* and *To Nicocles* is discussed by W. Jaeger in *Paideia*, 3 (New York, 1944), o. 4.

33. For details see L. S. Thompson, cited in the introductory note to this chapter.

34. On *Ovide moralisé* see p. 62. Guillaume's exposition of the sacred significance of the miracle of the bees, in *Georgics*, 4, must seem either comic or blasphemous to anyone who does not understand something of medieval thought: it is given in A. Hulubei's article, cited in the introductory note.

35. See p. 245. The influence of Horace in Spain has been magnificently treated by M. Menéndez y Pelayo, *Horacio en España* (Madrid, 1885²).

36. On the lyrics of Horace see c. 12, p. 225 f. Some of the many modern versions are described by E. Stemplinger, *Das Fortleben der horazischen Lyrik seit der Renaissance* (Leipzig, 1906); by the same author in his

Horaz im Urteil der Jahrhunderte (Das Erbe der Alten, n.s. 5, Leipzig, 1921); and by G. Showerman, *Horace and His Influence* (Boston, 1922).

37. For this suggestion see H. B. Lathrop (cited in introductory note), 219-20.

Notes on 7. THE RENAISSANCE: DRAMA

1. See pp. 71, 97, 134-5.

2. *Hamlet*, 2. 2. 424 f.

3. That was the greatest contribution of classical drama to modern drama. It has been interesting to watch the gradual self-education of the films (largely through experiment, but to a considerable extent also by tutelage from the stage and by criticism) from the early crudity when they produced nothing but farces, serial melodramas, and spectacles, towards something like a real understanding of the power of drama.

4. See E. Rigal in L. Petit de Julleville's *Histoire de la langue et de la littérature française*, 3. 264.

5. R. Garnett and E. Gosse (*English Literature, an Illustrated Record*, New York, 1935², 1. 168) sum up the situation: 'Instead of bringing the theatre to the audience, it had become necessary to bring the audience to the theatre.' The first public theatre in Britain was The Theatre, built in London in 1576.

6. For a reproduction of De Witt's sketch, and his comments, see Allardyce Nicoll, *The Development of the Theatre* (London, 1927), 121 f.

7. Allardyce Nicoll, *The Development of the Theatre* (London, 1927), 88 f. See also K. Borinski, *Die Antike in Poetik und Kunsttheorie* (Das Erbe der Alten, 10, Leipzig, 1924, 2. 65 f., who shows how the theatre-designers of the Renaissance adopted plans from Vitruvius in order to achieve the full resonance for which the Greek and Roman theatres were famous. The end-product of this is the modern opera-house.

8. Such were Politian's *Orfeo*, in ottava and other lyric metres; Correggio's *Cefalo* in ottava, Boiardo's *Timone* in terzini.

9. T. S. Eliot, 'Seneca in Elizabethan Translation' (in *Selected Essays*, New York, 1932), 69 f., suggests that English blank verse was designed as the closest attainable equivalent to the metre of Seneca; but it was probably inspired in the first instance by Italian experiments.

10. For instance, B. Marti, 'Seneca's Tragedies, a New Interpretation', in *Transactions of the American Philological Association*, 1945, suggests that they were dramatized moral lessons, intended not for acting but for reading. My own belief is that most of them were written to be performed in Nero's private theatre (*domestica scaena*, Tac. *Ann.* 15. 39), sometimes with the stage-struck young emperor playing the lead. I hope to develop this view in a forthcoming paper.

11. *Hamlet*, 2. 2. 424 f., quoted on p. 128.

12. Horace did not think of it as an 'art of poetry', but as a letter to the younger Roman writers, represented by the addressees, the brothers Piso: he meant it to have a restraining, educative effect on amateur poets.

13. See p. 120 f. J. W. Cunliffe, *The Influence of Seneca on Elizabethan Tragedy* (London and New York, 1893), 9 f., points out, what should never be forgotten, that in England 'the knowledge of Greek tragedy was confined to a very small circle', and that only Seneca was widely known.

14. J. Plattard, *L'Œuvre de Rabelais* (Paris, 1910), 175. Rabelais preferred Lucian; but Lucian took some of his ideas from Aristophanes, so that there was an indirect contact between the two kindred geniuses.

15. It was Nicolaus Cusanus who discovered them for Poggio, and they are now in the Vatican Library: see Sandys, *A History of Classical Scholarship*, 2 (Cambridge, 1908), 34.

16. The tyrant was also known in medieval drama: he was King Herod. Some of Herod's ruthlessness passed into the tyrants of the Renaissance stage, who were made still more diabolical by reminiscences of the teachings of Machiavelli.

17. Lodge, *Wits Miserie and the Worlds Madness* (1596).

18. Marlowe, *Tamburlaine the Great*, 2. 2. 4. 103 f.

19. On *La Deffence et illustration de la langue francoyse* see p. 231 f. Jodelle, who produced the first modern French tragedy and comedy, was a member of the Pléiade with Du Bellay.

20. See Moore's comparison of *Eccerinis* and *The Comedy* in his *Studies in Dante, Third Series* (Oxford, 1903), 363 f. The text is in L. A. Muratori, *Rerum Italicarum scriptores*, 10 (Milan, 1727), 785–800. There is a sensational first act in which Ezzelino's mother reveals (to his delight) that he was begotten on her by the Devil; but the rest is mostly messengers' speeches.

21. In an examination of the Latin dramas written by Jesuit teachers and produced in the Ordensschule at Posen between 1599 and 1627, their strong debt to Seneca is emphasized: this is *Tragoediae sacrae: Materialien und Beiträge zur Geschichte der polnisch-lateinischen Jesuitendramatik der Frühzeit*, by Adolf Stender-Petersen (Acta et commentationes Universitatis Tartuensis, Tartu, 1931, 25. 1).

22. J. S. Kennard, *The Italian Theatre* (New York, 1932), 1. 6. 129, n. 2.

23. Politian, who became professor of Greek and Latin in Florence, was only 17 when he wrote *Orfeo*, and he completed it in two days. There is a useful translation of it and of Tasso's *Aminta*, with an introductory essay on the pastoral (Oxford, 1931) by L. E. Lord.

24. J. S. Kennard, *The Italian Theatre* (New York, 1932), 1. 105 f., explains the debt of Renaissance Italian comedy to Plautus and Terence in some detail; see also W. Creizenach, *Geschichte des neueren Dramas*, 2 (Halle, 1918²), 1. 250 f.

25. A recent analysis of the dramatic weaknesses of *Sofonisba* appeared in *The South Atlantic Quarterly*, 26. 1 (1947), 93–108: 'The Genesis of Neo-Classical Tragedy', by E. Roditi. He points out that Trissino, knowing that tragedy ought to inspire pity and terror, apparently thought this meant his characters ought to display these emotions in order to make the audience feel them. On Trissino's equally dull epic, see p. 146.

26. See the admirable description of Cinthio's work and reputation by

H. B. Charlton, *The Senecan Tradition in Renaissance Tragedy* (Manchester, reissued 1946), p. lxxii f.; see also W. Creizenach (cited in n. 24), 2. 1. 367 f.

27. 'Françaisement chanter la grecque tragédie', said Ronsard. There is a good criticism of *Cléopâtre captive* in A. Tilley's *Literature of the French Renaissance* (Cambridge, 1904), 2. 72 f.

28. On the legendary connexion between Troy and modern European countries see p. 54.

29. The name Thersites means Audacious: it is from the same root as *thrasonical* (*As You Like It*, 5. 2. 35). He is the only common soldier mentioned by name in the *Iliad*, and his attempt to present the views of the 'other ranks' is shown as a ridiculous and disgusting piece of effrontery, rightly punished by the wise prince Odysseus (*Il.* 2. 211 f.). Shakespeare's Thersites is—except for his 'railing'—barely recognizable. In the farce of *Thersites* the hero is a braggart soldier who gets the god Mulciber (= Vulcan) to make him a suit of divine armour: evidently a reminiscence of the arms of Achilles in *Iliad* 18 and those of Aeneas in *Aeneid* 8; but he is not invulnerable, being beaten and disgraced like Thersites in the *Iliad*. This is a very early example of the degrading parody of epic themes.

30. The 'parasite', who attached himself to the rich, and bought his dinners by his wit, mendacity, and flattery, was a Greek, not a Roman type, and was foreign even to the audiences of Plautus. Much of the plot and dialogue in *Ralph Roister Doister* is original; but Merrygreek's flattery of Ralph, comparing him to great heroes, telling of his mighty deeds, and making him believe all the women love him, comes from Plautus' *Miles gloriosus*. Compare, for instance, *Ralph Roister Doister*, 1. 2. 114 f., with *Miles gloriosus*, 1. 1. 58 f. and 4. 2; *Ralph Roister Doister*, 1. 4. 66 f. (the Deed of the Elephant), with *Miles gloriosus*, 1. 1. 25 f.

31. Spanish influence on French baroque drama, however, was considerable—as the very title of *Le Cid* would show. On Lope's classical knowledge see R. Schevill, *The Dramatic Art of Lope de Vega* (Berkeley, Cal., 1918), 67 f.: he had the elements of Greek, much Latin, fluent Italian, and some French. What he chiefly took from the classics was (a) mythology, and (b) philosophical ideas, some from Plutarch's *Moralia* and some from Neoplatonism.

32. Allardyce Nicoll, *The Development of the Theatre* (London, 1927), c. 7, section vi.

33. Milton, *Comus*, 494 f.

34. Milton, *Comus*, 463–75 = Plato, *Phaedo*, 81b1–d4 (see H. Agar, *Milton and Plato*, Princeton, 1928, 39–41).

35. There is a well-written survey in W. W. Greg's *Pastoral Poetry and Pastoral Drama* (London, 1906).

36. See p. 163 f. on Vergil's Arcadia.

37. 'Bucolica eo successu edidit ut in scaena quoque per cantores crebro pronuntiarentur' (Donatus' life, ed. Brummer, 90). There is a vaguer reference to this in Tac. *Dial.* 13, and a very strange one, involving Cytheris (the Lycoris of *Buc.* 10) as diseuse, in Serv. *Comm. ad Buc.* 6. 11.

38. This is the legend Vergil uses in *Georg.* 4. 453 f. Ovid deliberately altered it in *Met.* 10. 8 f. K. Vossler, 'Die Antike in der Bühnendichtung der Romanen' (*Vorträge der Bibliothek Warburg*, 1927-8, Leipzig, 1930), 225 f., suggests that *Orfeo* was a synthesis of bucolic poetry on the classical model with the religious pageants known as *sacre rappresentazioni*, but his arguments are not very convincing. He does, however, bring out the connexion between the early pastoral drama and the pastoral scenes in religious plays of the late Middle Ages, and the relevance of the French lyrical love-episodes with a pastoral setting, called *pastourelles*. (On these see W. P. Jones, *The Pastourelle* (Cambridge, Mass., 1931).)

39. For a summary see Greg (cited in n. 35), 174-5.

40. The comparison to music is Symonds's, and the other I owe to Greg (cited in n. 35), who develops them both in a finely written paragraph on his p. 192. Delibes' charming ballet *Sylvia* is based on *Amyntas*.

41. For this theory see W. Creizenach, *Geschichte des neueren Dramas*, 1 (Halle, 1911²), 380 f.; Allardyce Nicoll, *Masks, Mimes, and Miracles* (London, 1931); and K. Vossler (cited in n. 38), 241 and note 2.

42. Ovid, *Met.* 1. 438-567. Summaries of both *Dafne* and *Euridice*, with musical analyses and quotations, are given by D. J. Grout, in *A Short History of Opera* (New York, 1947), 1, c. 5. Mr. Grout says that *Dafne*, written in 1594, was first performed with Marco da Gagliano's music in 1608. Wiese and Percopo (*Geschichte der italienischen Litteratur*, Leipzig, 1899, 138) give 1594 as the date for the earlier performance of *Dafne*, with music by Peri and Caccini.

43. This was the νόμος Πυθικός, composed by Sacadas, who flourished in 580 B.C. It was still being played by virtuosi 600 years after his death.

44. Quoted from E. J. Dent, 'The Baroque Opera', in *The Musical Antiquary* for January 1910: a valuable article.

45. The book referred to is J. E. Spingarn's *A History of Literary Criticism in the Renaissance* (New York, 1899), and the reference to Aristotle is *Poet.* 1451ᵃ 32. See also K. Borinski, *Die Antike in Poetik und Kunsttheorie* (Das Erbe der Alten, 9, Leipzig, 1914), 1. 215 f. and 219 f., who shows that Aristotle's influence on the stage began, very tenuously, about 1492, and emphasizes the paradox that, as Aristotle's authority as a moralist and philosopher fell, his prestige as a literary critic rose. But in the Middle Ages and the early Renaissance the *Poetics* was too hard for most critics to read.

46. Ar. *Poet.* 1449ᵇ 12 f.

Notes on 8. THE RENAISSANCE: EPIC

1. Ronsard wrote that his inspiration was destroyed by the death of Charles IX—who had urged him to undertake the poem, and even chosen the disastrous metre. But in fact he was relieved from an intolerable compulsion. He intended twenty-four books, sketched fourteen, but left only four (some 6,000 lines). It is interesting to watch him trying to be Greek, and being Roman in spite of himself—just as in his Odes, where he wishes

to be Pindar and returns towards Horace (see p. 247 f.). In his preface to
La Franciade he wrote:

'J'ay patronné mon œuvre plustost sur la naïve facilité d'Homere que sur la
curieuse diligence de Virgile'

(was he thinking of *curiosa felicitas*, the phrase Petronius used of Horace,
in *Sat.* 118. 5 ?)—and yet he took relatively little from Homer, and a great
deal, down to single words, from Vergil. Cf. P. Lange, *Ronsards Franciade
und ihr Verhältnis zu Vergils Aeneide* (Würzen, 1887), who gives pages of
verbal correspondences. Lange points out that the chief device Ronsard
did borrow from Homer was the wide-eyed step-by-step account of a
single operation, such as a chariot loading or a fleet putting to sea: this
makes the description sound incomparably natural and vivid. The actual
subject of *La Franciade*, the legend of the survival of the Trojan prince
Francus as ancestor of the French, was a product of the decaying Roman
empire and of the contact between the barbarians and classical mythology,
like Theodoric's Trojan ancestry (see p. 54); it first appeared in Fredegar
during the seventh century. Ronsard got it out of the *Illustrations des
Gaules et Singularitez de Troye*, by Jean Lemaire de Belges (1509–13),
and had already used it in his Odes (1. 1 and 3. 1). For other aspects of
the myth see H. Gillot, *La Querelle des anciens et des modernes en France*
(Paris, 1914), 131 f.

2. *Os Lusíadas* is in ten cantos, and uses the stanza made famous by
Ariosto: eight 11-syllable lines rhyming ABABABCC—called *ottava
rima*. Lusus was the mythical ancestor of the Portuguese, whose land the
Romans knew as Lusitania.

3. The metre of *La Araucana* also is Ariosto's (n. 2). The subject of
the poem is extremely interesting, and some of the episodes are very
moving; but Ercilla's narrative style sometimes becomes painfully prosaic.
Here is a stanza from canto 9, as translated (not unworthily) by C. M.
Lancaster and P. T. Manchester (*The Araucaniad*, Nashville, Tenn.,
1945):

> Lord, I gleaned this information
> From the lips of many authors.
> On the 23rd of April,
> Eight days hence, four years exactly
> It will be, since in that army
> Such a miracle they pondered,
> Fourteen hundred men well counted
> In the year of 1550.

As for the structure of the poem, Ercilla tried to make it a well-built whole,
but failed because he wanted to get everything in. It should really end
with the death of the formidable Indian chief Caupolicán, but it tails off
into Ercilla's own autobiography and a discourse on the Spanish attempt
to conquer Portugal. The strongest classical influence on it is that of
Lucan, whom Spanish epic poets of the Renaissance admired because he
was himself a Spaniard and had a certain proud violence in his style which
they found sympathetic. Some of the adaptations Ercilla made from
Lucan have been pointed out by C. Schlayer, *Spuren Lukans in der*

spanischen Dichtung (Heidelberg, 1927), W. Strohmeyer, *Studie über die Araukana* (Bonn, 1929), and G. Highet, 'Classical Echoes in *La Araucana*' (*Modern Language Notes*, 62 (1947), 329–31).

4. Cervantes, *Don Quixote*, 1. 6.

5. *Orlando Furioso* has forty-six cantos, arranged in stanzas of hendecasyllabic lines rhyming ABABABCC (n. 2). Roland was actually on the staff of Charlemagne, but that emperor with his wars against the pagans is often confused with his grandfather Charles Martel, who turned the tide of Islamic aggression with his victory at Tours in A.D. 732.

6. *Orlando Furioso*, 34. 83:

> E fu da l'altre conosciuta, quando
> Avea scritto di fuor: Senno d'Orlando.

7. *The Faerie Queene* is in a more complex stanza than Ariosto's: eight decasyllabic lines with a closing alexandrine, rhyming ABABBCBCC. Spenser, in his introductory letter to Raleigh, told him it was meant to embody the best of Homer, Vergil, Ariosto, and Tasso. There is a useful list of the classical authors whom Spenser knew in W. Riedner, *Spensers Belesenheit* (Münchener Beiträge, 38, Leipzig, 1908), but it should be balanced by the indications given in H. G. Lotspeich, *Classical Mythology in the Poetry of Edmund Spenser* (Princeton Studies in English, 9, Princeton, 1932), who points out that Spenser depended heavily on two manuals of mythology, Boccaccio's *Genealogia deorum* and the *Mythologiae* of Natalis Comes, using their comments and quotations freely. Still, considering his age and occupations, he was a considerable scholar. He knew Homer well, and Plato (*Apol.*, *Gorg.*, *Phaedo*, *Phaedrus*, *Rep.*, *Symp.*, *Tim.*), and Aristotle, and some Plutarch; he knew Hesiod's *Theogony* and a little Herodotus, but (despite his friend E. K.'s boasts) only one or two works each of Theocritus, Bion, Moschus, and Lucian. (On the pastoral poets see M. Y. Hughes, 'Spenser and the Greek Pastoral Triad', *Studies in Philology*, 20 (1923), 184–215.) He was more widely read in Latin: he knew Vergil very well (Riedner, 68–90, gives a remarkable list of his debts to the *Aeneid*) and Ovid's *Metamorphoses* equally well; Horace's letters, odes, and epodes; Caesar; Cicero's *Tusculan Discussions* and *On the Orator*; Lucretius (the opening Invocation is adapted in *FQ*, 4. 10. 44 f.); Pliny's *Natural History*; and, less certainly, Persius, Lucan, and Juvenal.

8. *Gerusalemme Liberata* uses the same metre as Ariosto, and runs to twenty cantos. The version Tasso issued after alteration was called *Gerusalemme Conquistata*: it was heavily 'corrected' so as to place more emphasis on the Christian elements in the poem and to make it less romantic, more classical.

9. Gibbon, *The Decline and Fall of the Roman Empire*, c. 58.

10. This was the attack which Boethius was suspected of inviting: see p. 41. The title of the poem varies slightly; I take the version which appears in the Verona edition of Trissino's works, published in 1729.

11. See p. 136, and n. 25 on p. 599.

12. A remarkable didactic poem of an earlier period should not be overlooked: *La Sepmaine*, or *La Création du Monde*, by the Gascon

Guillaume de Salluste, Sieur du Bartas (1544–90), which was published in 1578 and had a great success. It tells, in seven books of alexandrine couplets, the story of the creation, in language which is occasionally affected but often sublime. The theme is taken from Genesis i–ii, but is vastly expanded by the use of Greco-Roman poetry, science, and philosophy, and of contemporary scientific knowledge. Du Bartas and Tasso are Milton's two most important predecessors.

13. In his letter to Raleigh, Spenser said he planned *The Faerie Queene* in twelve books because, according to Aristotle, there were twelve moral virtues, each of which he intended to exemplify in his poem. But Aristotle offered no such cut-and-dried scheme of the virtues. This is a typical example of the Renaissance and baroque habit of considering as laws what the Greeks meant as suggestions, and of forcing symmetry even on material which should be left flexible. See J. Jusserand, *A Literary History of the English People* (New York, 1926³), 2. 479 n., who traces the error through Spenser's friend Bryskett to the Italian humanists Piccolomini and Cinthio. From another point of view this schematism was Spenser's attempt to introduce classical design into a typically loose episodic story like Ariosto's: see M. Y. Hughes, *Virgil and Spenser* (University of California Publications in English, 2. 3, Berkeley, Cal., 1929), 322–32. The schematism was helped by the fact that twelve was a mystical number, embodied in the disciples of Jesus, and that the *Aeneid* was in twelve books. *Paradise Lost* was originally in ten books, but was rearranged into twelve in 1674.

14. The myth has been revived in our own day by the South African poet Roy Campbell, who has published a book of poems containing something of the same rebellious violence that appears in Camoens's conception of the giant made mountain, and has entitled it *Adamastor*. (It was issued in London in 1930: see in particular the poem *Rounding the Cape*.) The reference is *Os Lusíadas*, 5.

15. Ercilla, *La Araucana*, 23.

16. For many of these things there are parallels in Greek legend: the winged horse Pegasus is like the hippogriff, the ring of Gyges made him invisible, &c. But none of the great classical epics makes such supernatural properties essential in its plot.

17. In *The Faerie Queene*, 1. 1. 37 f., the wicked hermit Archimago invokes Hecate and Gorgon, and sends a sprite to Morpheus for a false dream. The sprite leaves through the ivory door, which appears in Vergil (*Aeneid*, 6. 894–9). There are some valuable remarks on Spenser's descriptions of hell and their debt to Vergil, in M. Y. Hughes's *Virgil and Spenser* (University of California Publications in English, 2. 3, Berkeley, 1929), 371 f.

18. Tasso, *Gerusalemme Liberata*, 8. 60. The image is suggested by the terrible vision of Bertran de Born in Dante, *Inf.* 28. 118 f. Cf. Ariosto, *Orlando Furioso*, 18. 26 f.; and Vergil, *Aen.* 7. 323 f.

19. Circe is in Homer, *Od.* 10; Acrasia in Spenser, *The Faerie Queene*, 2. 12; Armida in Tasso, *Gerusalemme Liberata*, 10. 65 f. It is a favourite trick of Ovid's, and a very effective one, to describe a metamorphosis step

by step, making it not an abrupt Arabian Nights transformation, but a comprehensible, easily visualized, and therefore credible development.

20. Milton, *Paradise Lost*, 11. 244.

21. Milton, *Paradise Lost*, 5. 285, a reminiscence of Mercury landing on Mount Atlas (Verg. *Aen.* 4. 252):

hic primum paribus nitens Cyllenius alis
constitit.

Shakespeare was thinking of the same fine picture when he wrote

A station like the herald Mercury
New-lighted on a heaven-kissing hill (*Hamlet*, 3. 4. 58 9).

There is an even more complete fusion of pagan deities and Christian spirits in Trissino's *La Italia liberata da Gotti*, which contains angels called Gradivo (— Gradivus — Mars, book 12 ·

l'Angel Gradivo, che *dal cielo*
Scese per ajutar la genta Gotta),

Palladio (a derivative of Pallas Athene, book 2 and *passim*), Nemesio (a derivative of Nemesis, book 20), and Erminio (a derivative of Hermes, book 23 and *passim*). The ubiquitous Onerio (book 1 and *passim*) appears to be an angelic form of the dream, *"Oνειρος*, sent by Zeus to Agamemnon in *Iliad*, 2 init.

22. Tasso, *Gerusalemme Liberata*, 7. 92. So also the guardian angel heals Godfrey's wound not only by giving it the same treatment as Venus gave her son Aeneas, but actually by exhibiting the same herb (*Gerusalemme Liberata*, 11. 72 f. = *Aeneid*, 12. 411 f.).

23. Milton, *Paradise Lost*, 1. 732 f. (Mulciber = Vulcan) and *Paradise Regained*, 2. 149 f. (on which see p. 521). There is an admirable discussion of Milton's double attitude to classical mythology in C. G. Osgood's *The Classical Mythology of Milton's Poems* (Yale Studies in English, 8, New York, 1900), pp. xlvi–li.

24. See O. H. Moore, 'The Infernal Council' (*Modern Philology*, 16 (1918), 169–93), and M. Hammond, 'Concilia deorum from Homer through Milton' (*Studies in Philology*, 30 (1933), 1 16). It is impossible to imagine the fiends portrayed by Hieronimus Bosch and Pieter Brueghel as holding a stately council in the halls of Pandemonium, but it is easy enough to think of Milton's devils as Olympians overthrown.

25. Milton, *Paradise Lost*, 6, especially 637 f. The devils fall for nine days—the figure suggested by Hesiod, *Theog.* 722.

26. Milton, *Paradise Lost*, 4. 990 f. — Hom. *Il.* 8. 69–77 and 22. 209–13 = Verg. *Aen.* 12. 725–7.

27. Genesis i. 26–7.

28. Milton, *Paradise Lost*, 2. 351 f. = Verg. *Aen.* 10. 115, with a fine sound-effect of thunder:

totum nutu tremefecit Olympum.

The idea recurs also in Tasso, *Gerusalemme Liberata*, 13. 74 (as observed by C. M. Bowra, *From Virgil to Milton*, London, 1945, 148–9). There are several Homeric models.

29. Ariosto, *Orlando Furioso*, 46. 80–96. Similarly, the net of the giant Aligoran in 15. 56 f. was the identical net made by Vulcan to entrap Mars and Venus, then stolen by Mercury to catch Chloris the flower-goddess, then kept in the temple of Anubis at Canopus, and finally stolen by Aligoran, who lived near Cairo. And in *The Faerie Queene*, 3. 2. 25, Arthegall is seen wearing a splendid suit of armour inscribed

'Achilles' arms, which Arthegall did win'

—a notion adopted from Ariosto's *Orlando Furioso*, 30, where Ruggiero wins the arms of Hector.

30. Camoens, *Os Lusíadas*, 2. 45 f.
31. Spenser, *The Faerie Queene*, 3. 9. 33–51.
32. Milton, *Paradise Lost*, 1. 196 f.
33. Ercilla, *La Araucana*, 3 and 7.
34. Ariosto, *Orlando Furioso*, 18. 64, and 18. 65. 6:

Orazio sol contra Toscana tutta.

35. Ercilla, *La Araucana*, 2.
36. Camoens, *Os Lusíadas*, 9.
37. Spenser, *The Faerie Queene*, 1. 1. 6.
38. Milton, *Paradise Lost*, 4. 266 f.; for discussions, see D. Bush, *Mythology and the Renaissance Tradition in English Poetry* (Minneapolis and London, 1932), 278–86, and W. Empson, *Some Versions of Pastoral* (London, 1935), 172 f.
39. Milton, *Paradise Lost*, 1. 713 f. It is possible, however, that Milton was thinking of St. Peter's in Rome!
40. Tasso, *Gerusalemme Liberata*, 16. 2–7, inspired by Verg. *Aen.* 1. 455 f. and 6. 14–33.
41. Spenser, *The Faerie Queene*, 1. 2. 30 = Tasso, *Gerusalemme Liberata*, 13. 40 f. = Ariosto, *Orlando Furioso*, 6. 28–9 = Dante, *Inferno*, 13. 28 f. = Vergil, *Aen.* 3. 22–48. The incident also occurs in different forms in Boccaccio's *Filocolo*, but Ariosto probably took it from Dante: see P. Rajna, *Le fonti dell' Orlando Furioso* (Florence, 1900²), 169–70.
42. Tasso, *Gerusalemme Liberata*, 17. 66 f. = Verg. *Aen.* 8. 626–731 (inspired by Homer, *Il.* 18); and Tasso, *Gerusalemme Liberata*, 18. 92–6, inspired by Homer, *Il.* 5 and 21, and by the tremendous climax of the fall of Troy in Vergil, *Aen.* 2. 589–623:

apparent dirae facies, inimicaque Troiae
numina magna deum.

43. Ercilla, *La Araucana*, 23, and Camoens, *Os Lusíadas*, 10: inspired by Verg. *Aen.* 6. 756–887.
44. Ariosto, *Orlando Furioso*, 3. 16–59 (on which see P. Rajna, cited in n. 41, 133 f.); Spenser, *The Faerie Queene*, 3. 3. 21–49; Milton, *Paradise Lost*, 5. 563–7. 640, 11. 423–12. 551.
45. Ariosto, *Orlando Furioso*, 17. 45 f. = Hom. *Od.* 9. 413 f.
46. Ariosto, *Orlando Furioso*, 10. 92 f. = Ov. *Met.* 4. 663–752.

47. Ariosto, *Orlando Furioso*, 46. 101 f. = Verg. *Aen.* 12. 681 f.
48. Verg. *Aen.* 12. 951–2:

> Ast illi soluontur frigore membra
> uitaque cum gemitu fugit indignata sub umbras.

49. Ariosto, *Orlando Furioso*, 46. 140:

> Alle squallide ripe d'Acheronte,
> Sciolta dal corpo più freddo che giaccio,
> Bestemmiando fuggì l'almà sdegnosa,
> Che fù sì altiera al mondo e sì orgogliosa.

Notice that the pagan is not sent to hell, where Dante and the author of *La Chanson de Roland* would certainly have put him, but to the classical underworld.

50. *Roland*, 1015:

> Paien unt tort e chrestiens unt dreit.

51. Tasso, *Gerusalemme Liberata*, 2. 89 f. = Livy, 21. 18.
52. Ariosto, *Orlando Furioso*, 17. 11 = Verg. *Aen.* 2. 471–5. Cf. Tasso, *Gerusalemme Liberata*, 7. 55 = Verg. *Georg.* 3. 229 f. (the angry bull); Tasso, *Gerusalemme Liberata*, 9. 75, the escaped stallion = Hom. *Il.* 6. 506 f. R. E. N. Dodge, 'Spenser's Imitations from Ariosto', in *PMLA*, 1897, 151–204, shows how Spenser will take quite small images from Ariosto and reproduce them, usually more vividly.
53. Ercilla, *La Araucana*, 3.
54. Milton, *Paradise Lost*, 2. 636 f. The mountain simile is in *Paradise Lost*, 4. 987:

> Like Teneriffe or Atlas, unremoved

and probably comes from Vergil, *Aen.* 12. 701–3, where Aeneas (also ready to fight) is said to be

> quantus Athos, aut quantus Eryx, aut ipse coruscis
> cum fremit ilicibus quantus gaudetque niuali
> uertice se attollens pater Appenninus ad auras.

It is also like Tasso, *Gerusalemme Liberata*, 9. 31.
55. Penthesilea is mentioned in Verg. *Aen.* 1. 491, and appeared in many minor epics. Camilla appears in *Aen.* 7. 803 f. and 11. 532 f. Ariosto's predecessor Boiardo had introduced another beautiful virago in his *Orlando Innamorato*: Marfisa, who plays some part in Ariosto's poem too. Something of Hippolyta's tough independence was retained by Shakespeare in *A Midsummer-Night's Dream*, 4. 1. 118 f., where she sounds like a fox-hunting English girl from the Shires—although her discord is more musical, her thunder sweeter.
56. Tasso, *Gerusalemme Liberata*, 12. 23–37. Heliodorus, *Aethiopica* (on which see pp. 164–5): the queen there looked at Apollo's statue; in Tasso she looked at a picture of St. George: the children of both were white, and Clorinda aspired towards Christianity. On the river, Vergil, *Aen.* 11. 547–66. Camilla was vowed to Diana by her father, as Clorinda was vowed

to St. George by her mother. On the type, see Pio Rajna, *Le fonti dell'*
Orlando Furioso (Florence, 1900²), 45 f.

57. Dante, *Inf.* 2. 7 f., 32. 10 f.; *Purg.* 1. 7 f., 29. 37 f. (where Helicon
is a spring instead of a mountain); *Par.* 1. 13 f. (where Apollo is invoked
with an appeal to his own exploits), 2. 8, 18. 82 f.

58. Tasso, *Gerusalemme Liberata*, 1. 2:

> O Musa, tu che di caduchi allori
> Non circondi la fronte in Elicona,
> Ma su nel Cielo infra i beati cori
> Hai di stelle immortali aurea corona. . . .

It has been suggested that Tasso here means the Virgin Mary. For a less
formal invocation see 6. 39.

59. Milton, *Paradise Lost*, 9. 13 f.; cf. 1. 1–16, 7. 1–39, and *Paradise
Regained*, 1. 8–17. Ultimately Milton's inspiration is the Third Person
of the Trinity.

60. Milton, *Paradise Lost*, 1. 84 f.

61. Vergil, *Aen.* 2. 274 f.:

> Ei mihi, qualis erat, quantum mutatus ab illo
> Hectore qui redit exuuias indutus Achilli!

62. Eliot, *The Waste Land*, 2. 77 f. = Shakespeare, *Antony and Cleopatra*, 2. 2. 199 f.

63. Tasso, *Gerusalemme Liberata*, 2. 86:

> Noi morirem, ma non morremo inulti.

Verg. *Aen.* 4. 659–60:

> 'moriemur inultae!
> sed moriamur,' ait.

Tasso has introduced other reminiscences of Dido, more appropriately
this time, in the parting of Armida and Rinaldo (*G.L.* 16. 36 f.). See, for
instance, 16. 57:

> Nè te Sofia produsse, e non sei nato
> De l'Azio sangue tu: te l'onda insana
> Del mar produsse e il Caucaso gelato,
> E le mamme allattar di tigre ircana.

And compare Verg. *Aen.* 4. 365 f.:

> Nec tibi diua parens, generis nec Dardanus auctor,
> perfide, sed duris genuit te cautibus horrens
> Caucasus Hyrcanaeque admorunt ubera tigres.

64. Aubrey Bell, *Luis de Camoes* (Hispanic Notes and Monographs:
Portuguese Series, 4, Oxford, 1923), 92.

65. Milton, *Paradise Lost*, 10. 312–13.

66. Milton, *Paradise Lost*, 1. 266.

67. Milton, *Paradise Lost*, 11. 668–9: the speaker was probably Enoch
(Gen. v. 24).

68. Milton, *Paradise Lost*, 6. 83–4 = Verg. *Aen.* 7. 789 f. (the shield of Turnus):

> At leuem clipeum sublatis cornibus Io
> auro insignibat, iam saetis obsita, iam bos,
> argumentum ingens.

69. Milton, *Paradise Lost*, 12. 2–3.

70. Milton, *Paradise Lost*, 2. 151 f. Translate it into Latin, and it is perfectly straightforward: *sit hoc bonum* or *licet hoc bonum sit* = 'assuming that this is good'.

Here are some further examples of Milton's grecisms and latinisms, for many of which I am indebted to F. Buff, *Miltons Paradise Lost in seinem Verhältnisse zur Aeneide, Ilias und Odyssee* (Hof, 1904), and E. Des Essarts, *De ueterum poetarum tum Graeciae tum Romae apud Miltonem imitatione* (Paris, 1871). All quotations are from *Paradise Lost* unless otherwise signalized.

(a) Words used with their Latin root-meaning rather than their current English meaning:

Frighted the reign of Chaos and Old Night	(1. 543)
(*regna* = 'kingdom')	
What remains him?	(2. 443)
(*manere* = both 'remain' and 'await')	
On the rough edge of battle	(6. 108)
(*acies* = 'edge' of a blade, and thence 'battle-line')	
By tincture or reflection they augment	
Their small peculiar	(7. 367–8)
(*peculium* = 'private property')	
Obvious to dispute	(8. 158)
(*obuius* = 'exposed to')	
Lest that too heavenly form, pretended	
To hellish falsehood, snare them	(10. 872–3)
(*praetentus* = 'placed in front of', 'screening')	
And with our niglis the air	
Frequenting	(10. 1069 90)
(*frequentare* = 'to crowd').	

(b) Many such words and phrases are direct quotations of phrases from the Greek and Latin poets, and the un-English use of a word is meant to serve as an echo to recall the original:

Where pain of unextinguishable fire	
Must exercise us	(2. 88–9)
ergo exercentur poenis ('they are driven, or vexed, by punishments')	
	(Verg. *Aen.* 6. 739)
Him round	
A globe of fiery Seraphim enclosed	(2. 511–12)
globus ille uirum densissimus urget ('a thick crowd of men presses hard')	
	(Verg. *Aen.* 10. 373)

Or hear'st thou rather pure Ethereal stream   (3. 7)
seu Iane libentius audis ('or do you more gladly hear the name Janus?'—an
affectation, and a reminiscence of another language, even in Latin)
                                                    (Hor. *Serm.* 2. 6. 20)

   Reign for ever, and assume
Thy merits   (3. 318-19)
sume superbiam/quaesitam meritis ('put on the pride earned by your merit')
                                                    (Hor. *Carm.* 3. 30. 14)

  Perhaps asleep, secure of harm   (4. 791)
(i.e. not 'safe', but 'careless', as in Verg. *Aen.* 1. 350)

   Their flowing cups
With pleasant liquors crowned   (5. 444-5)
crateras magnos statuunt et uina coronant ('they set up great wine-bowls and
crown them with wine'—i.e. 'fill them brim-full', ultimately from Homer,
Il. 1. 470, 8. 232, &c.)

Things not revealed, which the invisible King,
Only omniscient, hath suppressed in night   (7. 122-3)
prudens futuri temporis exitum/caliginosa nocte premit deus ('God in his wisdom
covers future events in misty night')   (Hor. *Carm.* 3. 29. 29-30)

   No need that thou
Should'st propagate, already infinite,
And through all numbers absolute, though One   (8. 419-21)
omnibus numeris absolutus ('perfect in every element')
                                                    (Pliny, *Ep.* 9. 38)

Something like this phrase occurs in Cicero, who calls the universe

  perfectum expletumque omnibus suis numeris et partibus.
       (*De natura deorum* 2. 13. 37)

Ultimately it comes from Greek philosophy, where πάντες ἀριθμοί means
something like 'all the parts' of a whole. By the time it has passed through
Latin and reached Milton it is practically unintelligible.

  So glistered the dire Snake, and into fraud
  Led Eve.   (9. 643-4)
Quis deus in fraudem, quae dura potentia nostri/egit? ('What god, what hard
power of ours, led him into harm?')   (Verg. *Aen.* 10. 72-3)

(*c*) Latinisms and grecisms in syntax:

   Never, since created Man   (1. 573)
 (= 'since the creation of Man')

Me miserable!   (4. 73)
(from *me miserum!*)

Proud, art thou met?   (6. 131)
(= *O superbe* . . .)

A glimpse of light, conveyed so far
Down to this habitable   (8. 156-7)
(a neuter adjective serving as a noun)

 The lawless tyrant, who denies
To know their God, or message to regard   (12. 173-4)
(= 'refuses', *denegat*).

It should be noticed that one of the most striking of Milton's stylistic devices, the adjective-noun-adjective phrase, as in

The Eternal King Omnipotent   (6. 227),

is more Italian than Greek or Latin: *caro figlio adorato*.

The Latin and Greek influences on Milton's style introduced an element of distortion which belongs to the baroque age rather than to the Renaissance, and links him with Góngora in Spain, Marini in Italy. Juan de Jauregui, who had begun by writing poetry as smooth as *L'Allegro*, found that he was forced, when translating Lucan into Spanish, to write in a Gongoristic style (see p. 116) for very much the same reasons. Thus, when Milton speaks of 'the pure marble air' (*Paradise Lost*, 3. 564) he means 'gleaming as brightly as marble', and he is thinking of ἅλα μαρμαρέην in *Iliad*, 14. 273 and *marmoreo sub aequore* in *Aeneid*, 6. 729, but he has gone beyond both Homer and Vergil into the realm of baroque conceits.

Notes on 9. THE RENAISSANCE: PASTORAL AND ROMANCE

1. Did Theocritus invent pastoral poetry as we know it? Apparently he did. The evidence is re-examined by R. Reitzenstein, *Epigramm und Skolion* (Giessen, 1893), and H. Wendel, *Arkadien im Umkreis bukolischer Dichtung in der Antike und in der französischen Literatur* (Giessener Beiträge zur romanischen Philologie, Giessen 1933), together with many others. There were Arcadian poets—such as Anyte of Tegea (fl. 290 B.C.) —and there were poets who wrote of the pleasures of country life and invoked Pan. But there is no sign that anyone before Theocritus produced the characteristic blend of pastoral life with natural poetry and music, seen as the utterance of singing herdsmen and rustic lovers.

2. Theocritus' poems are called *idylls*: a word of obscure origin and meaning. It is thought to be short for εἰδύλλιον βουκολικόν, εἰδύλλιον being a diminutive of εἶδος, and meaning 'a little individual poem.'

3. Vergil did not call them 'eclogues', which is a name invented (it would seem) by the critics of the later empire; they used *ecloga*, 'selection', to mean one poem selected from the ten *Bucolics*.

4. See Pausanias, 7 and 8; and L. R. Farnell, *Cults of the Greek States* (Oxford, 1909), 5.

5. B. Snell's essay on this subject in *Die Entdeckung des Geistes* (Hamburg, 1946) cites E. Kapp's suggestion that Arcadia became the ideal land of music because of a passage in the historian Polybius (4. 20–1). Himself an Arcadian by origin, Polybius, after narrating an atrocity committed in Arcadia, inserted a long apologia, explaining that the Arcadians were really highly civilized and had national musical training and musical competitions—except for the one community where the atrocity took place. But this passage can scarcely be relevant to the creation of the ideal Arcadia: because Polybius emphasized, not the wildness and rusticity of the music of his country, but its highly developed culture. He wrote not of shepherds warbling their native wood-notes wild, but of elaborate

performances by trained choruses singing difficult modern music by Philoxenus and Timotheus. He wanted to prove that Arcadia was not 'natural' but highly civilized. Also, the probability that a young poet like Vergil, writing about a lovelorn elegist, would base his fantasy on a comparatively obscure passage in a comparatively dry author is much less than that Vergil thought of Pan, *deus Arcadiae* (*Buc.* 10. 26). Bucolic poetry was invented by Pan, with his pan-pipes: see Reitzenstein (cited in n. 1), 249–53.

6. I owe much in this section to a well-written book about these strange stories: S. L. Wolff's *Greek Romances in Elizabethan Prose Fiction* (New York, 1912). See also W. W. Greg's *Pastoral Poetry and Pastoral Drama* (London, 1906), E. H. Haight's *Essays on the Greek Romances* (New York, 1943) and *More Essays on Greek Romances* (New York, 1945), and F. A. Todd's *Some Ancient Novels* (Oxford, 1940). The central book on the subject is Erwin Rohde's *Der griechische Roman und seine Vorläufer* (Leipzig, 1914³). The word *romance* is used both for the stories of chivalrous adventure which became popular in the twelfth century (c. 3), for these Greek tales, and for modern stories in which adventure is more important than character-drawing. Strictly, this is loose and inaccurate, but it can perhaps be excused by the general contemporary use of the word *romantic* to cover nearly all the chief elements in all these three types of fiction.

7. On 'Dares' and 'Dictys' see p. 51 f.

8. A. J. Toynbee, *A Study of History* (Oxford, 1939), 6. 363, n. 7, comments on the fact that when the angels announced the birth of Jesus (Luke ii) and when the Greek Muses related the birth and descent of the Hellenic gods (Hesiod, *Theog.* init.), the hearers they chose were 'shepherds abiding in the field'—because, Mr. Toynbee suggests, shepherds and not townspeople have guileless and simple hearts fit to receive such a revelation.

9. On *Robin et Marion* see W. W. Greg, *Pastoral Poetry and Pastoral Drama* (London, 1906), 63–5; on the *pastourelles*, W. P. Jones, *The Pastourelle* (Cambridge, Mass., 1931).

10. Sannazaro, *Arcadia* (ed. M. Scherillo, Turin, 1888), *prosa*, 11. 308 = Homer, *Il.* 23. 724.

11. 'Le manuel le plus complet de pastoralisme qu'il soit possible d'imaginer'—H. Genouy, *L'"Arcadia" de Sidney dans ses rapports avec l'"Arcadia" de Sannazaro et la 'Diana' de Montemayor* (Montpellier, 1928), 53.

12. Cervantes, *Don Quixote*, 2. 67; the book-burning is in 1. 6.

13. See pp. 91–3.

14. Others of this type published about the same time are Greene's *Menaphon*, which, with its multiple disguises, kidnappings, and shipwrecks, stems straight from the Greek romances; and Lodge's *Rosalynde*, which gave Shakespeare much material for *As You Like It*, and which was ultimately based on the saga of the English pastoral hero Robin Hood.

15. See Genouy (cited in n. 11), 109 f.

16. See Genouy (cited in n. 11), 174 f., for details.

17. For the link between Sidney's book and the eighteenth-century novel, see c. 18, p. 341.

18. *Love's Labour's Lost*, 4. 2. 96 f.

19. Ce ne sont pas bergers d'une maison champestre
Qui menent pour salaire aux champs les brebis paistre,
Mais de haute famille et de race d'ayeux.
(*Eclogue* 1, first speech.)
H. Wendel (cited in n. 1) examines on p. 50 f. Ronsard's debt to the classical bucolic writers; and on the whole subject see A. Hulubei, *L'Églogue en France au xvie siècle* (Paris, 1938).

20. See M. Y. Hughes, 'Spenser and the Greek Pastoral Triad' (*Studies in Philology*, 20 (1923), 184–215), and the same scholar's *Virgil and Spenser* (University of California publications in English, 2. 3, Berkeley, Cal., 1929). Mr. Hughes emphasizes the scholarship of Baïf, and holds him really responsible for creating French pastoral poetry on a firm classical foundation.

21. These quotations are from *The Passionate Shepherd to His Love*, which appeared in *England's Helicon* (1600), and is ascribed to Marlowe.

22. Gallus, *Buc.* 10; Varius, *Buc.* 9. 35; Bavius and Maevius, *Buc.* 3. 90.

23. *Buc.* 1. 43 f.; cf. *Buc.* 9. 2 f.

24. For the echoes of Greek pastoral in these poems, see *L'Allegro*, 81–90; *Il Penseroso*, 131–8.

25. *Lycidas* 119 f.

26. *Paradise Lost*, 4. 192–3. The most extreme example of pastoral-ecclesiastical satire in English is probably Quarles's *Shepherds' Oracles* (1646), on which see Greg's *Pastoral Poetry and Pastoral Drama* (London, 1906), 118–19.

27. On *Adonais* see also pp. 420–1. It is a touching example of the continuity of poetic tradition that Keats should have had a vision of Lycidas only a few years before his death, in the 'cathedral of the sea', Staffa. See his poem written there during his tour of Scotland.

28. See p. 139.

29. See pp. 135–6.

30. On these pieces see Greg, *Pastoral Poetry and Pastoral Drama* (London, 1906), 170 f. and his Appendix I.

31. Details on *Il sacrifizio* in Greg, *Pastoral Poetry and Pastoral Drama* (London, 1906), 174 5.

32. On *Les Ombres* see A. Tilley, *The Literature of the French Renaissance* (Cambridge, 1904), 2. 115 f.

33. Their Italian names are *Aminta* and *Il pastor fido*. Some of the innumerable imitations are described by K. Olschki, *Guarinis 'Pastor fido' in Deutschland* (Leipzig, 1908).

34. H. Smith, 'Pastoral Influence in the English Drama' (*PMLA*, 12 (n.s. 5), 1897, 355–460), discusses the subject at length.

35. See *As You Like It*, 2. 1. 21 f.

36. See p. 139. There is an admirable treatment of *Comus* in D. Bush's *Mythology and the Renaissance Tradition in English Poetry* (Minneapolis and London, 1932), 264 f.

37. See p. 141, and P. H. Láng, *Music in Western Civilization* (New York, 1941), 337 f.

38. P. H. Láng (cited in n. 37), 347.

39. H. Hauvette, *Littérature italienne* (Paris, 1924⁶), 322: 'un long bêlement retentit des Alpes à la Sicile'.

40. The history of the society was begun by I. Carini, *L'Arcadia dal 1690 al 1890* (v. 1, Rome, 1891). There is a fine evocation of Arcadia in c. 1 of Vernon Lee's *Studies of the Eighteenth Century in Italy* (London, 1907²), marred only by a little too much of the 'now it is all gone, but how quaint it was' attitude.

41. *L'après-midi d'un faune* is discussed on p. 507 f.

42. This is *Die Bekehrte*, no. 27 in Wolf's *Goethe-Lieder*.

Additional note

The famous phrase *Et in Arcadia ego* is often misquoted as *Et ego in Arcadia* (e.g. by Goethe, Schiller, and Nietzsche) and mistranslated as 'I too have lived in Arcady'. It occurs first in a painting by Barbieri (called 'Guercino') showing two Arcadian shepherds coming upon a tomb, surmounted by a rat-gnawed skull. The theme was copied by Poussin in a fine painting now at Chatsworth, and in a more famous one in the Louvre. The phrase means 'Even in Arcadia I (*Death*) am found.' Its medieval ancestor is the meeting of the Three Dead Men and the Three Living Men, which is connected with the Danse Macabré by J. Huizinga, *The Waning of the Middle Ages* (London, 1937), 129 f. There is no trace of the phrase in classical literature, and it was probably coined in the Renaissance. Its meaning and background are discussed by E. Panofsky in *Philosophy and History: Essays presented to Ernst Cassirer* (Oxford, 1936), 223 f. and *Gazette des beaux arts*, 1938; W. Weisbach in *Die Antike*, 6, and *Gazette des beaux arts*, 1937; and H. Wendel (cited in n. 1), 72 f.

Notes on 10. RABELAIS AND MONTAIGNE

Rabelais

For the study of Rabelais in relation to his sources and his milieu, Jean Plattard's *L'Œuvre de Rabelais* (Paris, 1910) is of prime importance.

1. J. H. de Groot, *The Shakespeares and 'The Old Faith'* (New York, 1946), makes out a good case for the theory that John Shakespeare, the father, remained a Roman Catholic in secret and that William gave more sympathy to Catholicism than to Protestantism. Still, religion plays a markedly small part in the thought of such men as Hamlet, Macbeth, and Othello.

2. See Plattard, c. 5.

3. On the other hand, Rabelais is almost the only doctor who has ever managed to make medical descriptions funny. See, for instance, the wounds inflicted by Friar John (1. 44), the lecture of Rondibilis (3. 31), and the anatomical description of Shrovetide (4. 30 f.), taken from a

description of unnatural monsters, *Gigantes*, by the Italian humanist Celio Calcagnini (Plattard, 162–5, 297 f.).

4. The devil appears and speaks in the mystery of Saint Louis, described by L. Petit de Julleville, *Histoire du théâtre en France: les mystères* (Paris, 1906⁶), 2. 527 f. For the spelling, see the critical edition of Rabelais by A. Lefranc, J. Boulenger, H. Clouzot, P. Dorveaux, J. Plattard, and L. Sainéan (Paris, 1912–31), v. 3, pp. xv and xvii.

5. N. H. Clement, 'The Influence of the Arthurian Romances on the Five Books of Rabelais' (*University of California Publications in Modern Philology*, 12, Berkeley, Cal., 1925–6, 147–257), describes the book as 'a burlesque imitation of the French medieval romances, but particularly of the romances of the Round Table'—1 and 2 parodying the Arthurian romances in general, and 3–5 the Grail quest. This is doubtless true, but we must not forget the giant powers and giant appetites of Rabelais's heroes, which come from Pulci and from the medieval tales of marvels like the *Cronicques*. For a very detailed and careful analysis of the relation between Rabelais and the popular giant-stories which started him off, see M. Françon, 'Sur la genèse de "Pantagruel"', *PMLA*, 62 (1947), 1. 45–61.

6. For Ponocrates see 1. 23, Anagnostes 1. 23, Gymnast 1. 18 and 1. 35, Philotimus 1. 18, Picrochole 1. 26.

7. Thelema is in 1. 52, its motto in 1. 57.

8. The Dipsodes are in 2. 23, the Amaurots and Utopia in 2. 2, Epistemon first in 2. 5, and Panurge first in 2. 9.

9. On Vittorino dei Ramboldini (1378–1446), called Vittorino da Feltre, and his magnificent educational career, see J. E. Sandys, *A History of Classical Scholarship*, 2. 53 f.

10. Plattard, 54 f. and 300.

11. Bédier and Hazard, *Histoire illustrée de la littérature française*, 164.

12. H. Schoenfeld, 'Rabelais and Erasmus' (*PMLA*, n.s. 1 (1893)), has pointed out that many of Erasmus's beliefs reappeared in those of his junior Rabelais, who had something of the same kind of life. The *Adages* are full of satirical remarks against women, monks, jurists, ceremonies, the temporal power of the popes, vanity, and anti-humanist forces generally, very much as the books of Rabelais are. Le Duchat has shown that Erasmus's *Echo* was copied by Rabelais in Panurge's discussion of marriage in 3. 9 f.; and Birch-Hirschfeld conjectured that a letter, expressing the deepest indebtedness to an instructor, and written by Rabelais in 1532 while he was working on *Pantagruel*, was in fact addressed to Erasmus.

13. See 2. 8. In spite of his professed admiration for Plato, Rabelais makes few direct quotations from the dialogues, and gets most of his knowledge of Platonic doctrines from Erasmus's *Adages* and by osmosis out of the surrounding humanist atmosphere (Plattard, 225).

14. 1. 33: the debate comes from the interview between Cineas and Pyrrhus given in Plutarch's life of Pyrrhus (c. 14), plus Lucian's *The Ship* (or *Wishes*): Plattard, 207–8.

15. 2. 30, from Lucian's *Menippus*: Plattard, 208 f.

16. Trouillogan is modelled on Pyrrho, as depicted in Lucian's *Sale of Lives* (itself modelled on a lost satire of Menippus'): Plattard, 212 f.

There are a few more incidents which Rabelais has taken directly from Lucian, generally improving them and giving them more vigour.

17. Preface to *Pantagruel*, tr. Urquhart.

Montaigne

The essential book on Montaigne for our purposes is P. Villey's *Les Sources et l'évolution des essais de Montaigne* (Paris, 1908). There is a good modern translation with very useful notes, partly based on Villey, by J. Zeitlin (New York, 1934–6).

18. *Essays*, 1. 25: *Of the institution and education of children: to the Lady Diana of Foix.*

19. *Essays*, 1. 25, Florio's translation, adapted.

20. George Buchanan and Marc-Antoine Muret were among the greatest teachers of the Renaissance. On Buchanan see J. E. Sandys, *A History of Classical Scholarship* (Cambridge, 1908), 2. 243–6; on the even more remarkable career of Muret, 2. 148–52.

21. The words are from one of the inscriptions Montaigne put up in his study, and apparently come from Epicurus (fr. LVIII Bailey).

22. P. Villey, quoted in the introductory note above; see also P. Hensel, 'Montaigne und die Antike' (*Vorträge der Bibliothek Warburg 1925–6* (Leipzig, 1928), 67–94). In 'La Bibliothèque de Montaigne' (*Revue d'histoire littéraire de la France*, 2 (1895), 313–71) P. Bonnefon gives a list of the extant books known to have belonged to Montaigne (9 Greek, 35 Latin, 13 Italian, 2 Spanish, and 17 French), with a transcription of the Greek and Latin sentences which he inscribed on the ceiling of his tower-study. On the various editions of the *Essays* see J. Bédier and P. Hazard, *Histoire de la littérature française illustrée* (Paris, 1923–4), 1. 204: they say that the 1588 edition was 'a fifth edition (the fourth which we know)', and give a large photograph of a page from the *Essays* covered with Montaigne's own handwritten additions in a positively Proustian intricacy.

23. *Essays*, 2. 10: *Of Books.*

24. For a discussion of the question whether Montaigne really knew Greek or not, see Börje Knös, 'Les Citations grecques de Montaigne', in *Eranos*, 44 (1946), 460–83. Montaigne, in *Essays*, 1. 25 and 2. 4, said he knew none; and he liked using translations where possible. Nevertheless, he quoted Greek, he understood what his quotations meant, and he had Greek quotations inscribed on his ceiling. Mr. Knös concludes that Montaigne knew some Greek (having come under the hellenizing influence of Turnebus and Lambinus at Toulouse) but did not want to appear scholarly to the point of pedantry.

25. A. D. Menut, 'Montaigne and the "Nicomachean Ethics" ' (*Modern Philology*, 31. 3 (1934), 225–42), gives a list of 27 references in Montaigne's *Essays* to the *Nicomachean Ethics* (a list more complete than Villey's), and indicates a number of important areas of indirect contact, where Montaigne's thought coincides with that of Aristotle not only because he has learnt Aristotelian principles from intermediary authors but because he has arrived independently at the same point of view.

26. C. H. Hay, in *Montaigne lecteur et imitateur de Sénèque* (Poitiers, 1938), emphasizes the preference of Montaigne for Seneca's style and thought over those of Cicero. (On that point see also p. 323 f.) On p. 167 f. Dr. Hay examines Montaigne's essay *De la solitude*, finding that it is largely built on Senecan ideas, and that its peroration is a pastiche of sentences translated directly from Seneca.

27. Villey (quoted in introductory note), 215.

28. On Montaigne's debt to Seneca and Plutarch, see his own assertions in 1. 25 and 2. 32. Shakespeare is known to have read the *Essays* with interest and affection (see J. M. Robertson, *Montaigne and Shakspere*, London, 1897), so that some of Montaigne's classical learning certainly reached him through these channels also, commended by the charm of their style.

29. On this point see a good essay by G. S. Gordon, 'Theophrastus and His Imitators', in *English Literature and the Classics* (ed. Gordon, Oxford, 1912).

30. Horace, *Serm.* 2. 1. 32 f.: the votive picture of a shipwreck or some other accident always showed every detail with naïve clarity, as modern offerings of the same kind still do.

31. Ramus, a slightly older contemporary of Montaigne, got his doctorate in 1536 by maintaining the thesis that all Aristotle's doctrines were false: *quaecumque ab Aristotele dicta essent commentitia esse.* (On him, see H. Gillot, *La Querelle des anciens et des modernes en France*, Paris, 1914, 56 f., who compares Montaigne's *Que sçais-je?* with the thesis of Sanchez: *Quod nihil scitur.*)

Notes on 11. SHAKESPEARE'S CLASSICS

There are many good books and articles on this subject. The following will be found particularly helpful:

P. Alexander, *Shakespeare's Life and Art* (London, 1939).

H. R. D. Anders, *Shakespeare's Books* (Schriften der deutschen Shakespeare-Gesellschaft, 1, Berlin, 1904).

A. L. Attwater, 'Shakespeare's Sources', in *A Companion to Shakespeare Studies*, ed. H. Granville-Barker and G. B. Harrison (New York, 1934).

T. W. Baldwin, *William Shakspere's Small Latine and Lesse Greeke* (Urbana, Ill., 1944).

D. Bush, *Mythology and the Renaissance Tradition in English Poetry* (Minneapolis and London, 1932).

J. W. Cunliffe, *The Influence of Seneca on Elizabethan Tragedy* (London, 1893).

T. S. Eliot, 'Shakespeare and the Stoicism of Seneca' and 'Seneca in Elizabethan Translation', in *Selected Essays 1917–1932* (New York, 1932).

J. Engel, 'Die Spuren Senecas in Shaksperes Dramen' (*Preussische Jahrbücher*, 112 (1903), 60–81).

E. I. Fripp, 'Shakespeare's Use of Ovid's *Metamorphoses*', in his *Shakespeare Studies, Biographical and Literary* (London, 1930).

E. I. Fripp, *Shakespeare, Man and Artist* (London, 1938).

S. Lee, *A Life of William Shakespeare* (New York, 1925⁴).

F. L. Lucas, *Seneca and Elizabethan Tragedy* (Cambridge, 1922).

M. W. MacCallum, *Shakespeare's Roman Plays and their Background* (London, 1910).

S. G. Owen, 'Ovid and Romance', in *English Literature and the Classics* (ed. G. S. Gordon, Oxford, 1912).

L. Rick, 'Shakespeare und Ovid', in *Jahrbuch der deutschen Shakespeare-Gesellschaft*, 55 (1919), 35–53.

R. K. Root, *Classical Mythology in Shakespeare* (New York, 1903).

W. W. Skeat, *Shakespeare's Plutarch* (London, 1875).

P. Stapfer, *Shakespeare and Classical Antiquity* (tr. E. J. Carey, London, 1880). Other works on the theme are mentioned in these notes.

1. *The Rape of Lucrece* narrates the crime which caused the expulsion of the kings; *Coriolanus, Julius Caesar*, and *Antony and Cleopatra* concern the republic; *Cymbeline* the early and *Titus Andronicus* the late empire. W. Dibelius, 'Zur Stoffgeschichte des *Titus Andronikus*' (*Jahrbuch der deutschen Shakespeare-Gesellschaft*, 48 (1912), 1–12), suggests that the scene is really Byzantium, that Titus Andronicus is the violent Byzantine emperor who reigned from 1183 to 1185, and that Tamora is Thamar of Georgia (1184–1220), the unidentifiable Demetrius being a Dmitri. See also 'The Story of Isaac and Andronicus' by E. H. McNeal, in *Speculum*, 9 (1934), 324–9. This tells how the emperor Andronicus was tortured to death with frightful barbarity, and explains how the story could have reached England via the army of Richard I: it appears in the chronicle of Benedict of Peterborough. The setting of *Cymbeline* is partly Roman, partly vague early-British; but the play really concerns Rome much less than the subject which long haunted Shakespeare's mind, the conflict between English honesty and Italian treachery: see 3. 2. 4, 5. 5. 197 f., 5. 5. 211.

2. One of these, *The Comedy of Errors*, is an adaptation of two Roman adaptations of Greek plays (see pp. 214, 624–5). One is from Athenian history (*Timon of Athens, c.* 407 B.C.). Three are set in the prehistoric past of myth (*Venus and Adonis, Troilus and Cressida, A Midsummer-Night's Dream*); and one, *Pericles*, is a retelling of a late Greek romance. (On these romances see p. 163 f.)

3. See p. 4.

4. *Hamlet*, 5. 2. 29 f.

5. *Hamlet*, 2. 2. 350 f.

6. Two of the Italian plays take place in Venice and the Venetian empire (*Othello* and *The Merchant*); two in Verona (*Romeo and Juliet* and *The Two Gentlemen*); one in Messina (*Much Ado about Nothing*); one in Sicily (*The Winter's Tale*); and one in Padua (*The Taming of the Shrew*).

7. In Lodge's *Rosalynde*, from which Shakespeare took the basis of *As You Like It*, the setting was the forest of Ardenne in north-eastern

France, pastoralized and idyllized. By changing its name Shakespeare moved it to England near his own home: his mother's name was Mary Arden. H. Smith, 'Pastoral Influence in the English Drama' (*PMLA*, 12 (n.s. 5), 1897, 378 f.), shows how greatly Shakespeare reduced the conventional pastoral colouring in adapting Lodge's story, and how much more real and homely he made it.

8. *Troilus and Cressida*, 4. 2. 31.

9. *Cymbeline*, 2. 3. 21 f.

10. *The Winter's Tale*, 4. 3. 120 f.

11. *Hamlet*, 3. 4. 55 f.; and see p. 605.

12. *The Merchant of Venice*, 5. 1. 9 f.

13. *Henry V*, 2. 3. 9.

14. *2 Henry IV*, 3. 2. 300 f.

15. *King Lear*, 3. 4. 185; cf. Browning's *Childe Roland to the Dark Tower came*.

16. See Stapfer, *Shakespeare and Classical Antiquity* (cited in introductory note), 223, and Attwater (introductory note), 233-5. Ajax in *Troilus and Cressida* is made not only stupid, but vain—'covetous of praise, self-affected'. Homer's Ajax is not at all like that. R. K. Root (cited in introductory note) shows on p. 36 f. that this part of Ajax's character comes from Ovid (*Met*. 13), where Ajax competes with Ulysses for the weapons of Achilles, and is presented, both in his own speech and in that of his rival, as ridiculously conceited.

17. *Troilus and Cressida*, 2. 2. 166.

18. *Troilus and Cressida*, 1. 1. 81. The seven-day week did not exist in Greece.

19. *The Comedy of Errors*, 5. 1.

20. Nashe, preface to Greene's *Menaphon*.

21. C. Spurgeon, *Shakespeare's Imagery* (New York, 1935). See especially pp. 13, 19-20, 44-5, and Chart V.

22. *As You Like It*, 3. 3. 7 f.

23. *Romeo and Juliet*, 3. 2. 1 f. The myth of Phaethon is in Ovid, *Metamorphoses*, 1. 748-2. 332; 'waggoner' is the Elizabethan translator Golding's word for the young charioteer, and no doubt Shakespeare remembered it. (See Root—cited in the introductory note—97.)

24. The phrase comes from Jonson's commendatory verses in the First Folio. J. E. Spingarn, *Literary Criticism in the Renaissance* (New York, 1899), 89 n., suggests that Jonson was quoting a phrase from Minturno, *Arte poetica*, 158: *poco del latino e pochissimo del greco*. On the entire subject of Shakespeare's education see Mr. T. W. Baldwin's valuable book cited in the introductory note.

25. There are only a few striking nouns, like *cacodemon* (*Richard III*, 1. 3. 144), *anthropophagi* (*Othello*, also 1. 3. 144), and *misanthropos* (*Timon of Athens*, 4. 3. 53), which last comes from a footnote in North's Plutarch, is mispronounced, and is carefully explained.

26. The Welsh-spoken schoolmaster in *The Merry Wives* is apparently modelled on Thomas Jenkins, Shakespeare's own Latin master at Stratford (see Baldwin and Fripp, cited in the introductory note). John Aubrey

reports a tradition from William Beeston's mouth that Shakespeare himself was 'in his younger years a schoolmaster in the country'.

27. See *Pantagruel*, 2. 6, and p. 108.

28. *Love's Labour's Lost*, 4. 3. 342 f.

29. See p. 156 f.

30. *The Tempest*, 1. 2. 167.

31. *The Merchant of Venice*, 5. 1. 60 f.; cf. Plato, *Rep.* 10. 617 *b*.

32. Baldwin (cited in introductory note), 2. 418 f. R. K. Root (introductory note) has shown that the overwhelming majority of Shakespeare's mythological allusions come directly from Ovid, and the remainder, with few exceptions, from Vergil. 'In other words, a man familiar with these two authors, and with no others, would be able to make all the mythological allusions contained in the undisputed works of Shakespeare, barring some few exceptions.' Mr. Root also points out that, as Shakespeare matured, he almost gave up using mythology, and that he returned to it in later life, giving it much deeper meanings.

33. Meres, *Palladis Tamia: Wits Treasury*, 280.

34. 'The first heir of my invention' (Dedication to *Venus and Adonis*).

35. In Ovid's tale of Venus and Adonis (*Met.* 10. 519–59 and 705–39), Adonis is not cold and reluctant as Shakespeare makes him. Shakespeare took his froward resistance to love from Ovid's story of Hermaphroditus and Salmacis in *Met.* 4. 285–388. The two stories coalesce completely in *The Passionate Pilgrim*, 6, where Adonis bounces into a brook, and Venus cries 'O Jove, why was not I a flood?'—for Salmacis bounced in after her beloved, the two joined, and both became a flood. See D. Bush (cited in introductory note), 139 f., for a detailed analysis of the treatment of Adonis; and R. K. Root (introductory note), 31–3, for the proof that Shakespeare's description of the raging boar (*Venus and Adonis*) comes from a different passage of Ovid, *Met.* 8. 284–6, probably in Golding's version.

36. Ov. *Am.* 1. 15. 35–6.

37. The story of Lucretia is in Livy, 1. 57–9, and Ovid, *Fasti*, 2. 721–852. Since no English translation of the *Fasti* appeared until 1640, and since Shakespeare adapts phrases from the poem, he apparently knew the original. (See Owen—cited in the introductory note—Fripp (ditto), 1. 363 f., and Bush (ditto), 149 f.)

38. *The Taming of the Shrew*, 3. 1. 26 f. The quotation is from Ovid, *Heroides*, 1. 33–4. Penelope writes to Ulysses that the other heroes have all returned home, and are now telling their battles over again, sketching the terrain on the table, and saying

> Here flowed the Simois; here is Sigeum;
> here was old Priam's lofty citadel.

39. *Titus Andronicus*, 4. 3. 4 = Ov. *Met.* 1. 150; *3 Henry VI*, 1. 3. 48 = Ov. *Her.* 2. 66.

40. Ov. *Met.* 1. 395 (Pyrrha), 3. 173 (Diana), 6. 346 (Latona), 14. 382 and 438 (Circe). Anders (see introductory note), 22, points out that the name Titania is not in Golding's version of the *Metamorphoses*, so that

Shakespeare, with his delicate ear, must have remembered it from the original Latin.

41. T. S. Eliot, *The Classics and the Man of Letters* (London and New York, 1943). Mr. Eliot's whole discussion of the classical tradition in Shakespeare's and Milton's education is well worth reading.

42. The original is Ov. *Met.* 15. 181 f.:

> ut unda impellitur unda
> urgeturque prior ueniente urgetque priorem,
> tempora sic fugiunt pariter pariterque sequuntur
> et noua sunt semper.

Shakespeare's 'sequent' may be a sign that he had looked at the original. In Ovid the waves are the separate waves of a river, the Greek philosophers' image for permanence in change. Shakespeare makes them the waves of the sea on the shore, because British rivers seldom have waves, and because he is thinking of the sea-image in Sonnet 64. (See S. G. Owen, cited in introductory note.)

43. Ov. *Met.* 15. 75 f., especially 165 f.: ultimately from Heraclitus.

44. Tranio, in *The Taming of the Shrew*, 1. 1. 29 f.

45. *Romeo and Juliet*, 2. 2. 92 f. = Ovid, *A. A.* 1. 633; but see Root (cited in introductory note), 82, for the suggestion that this idea may have reached Shakespeare through Boiardo's *Orlando innamorato*, 1. 22. 45.

46. *The Taming of the Shrew*, 4. 2. 8.

47. Shakespeare's source here was Ovid, *Her.* 7, the letter of Dido: there is at least one straight quotation:

> What says the married woman? You may go?
> Would she had never given you leave to come!
>   *(Antony and Cleopatra*, 1. 3. 20–1).
> Sed iubet ire deus. Vellem uetuisset adire!   *(Her.* 7. 139).

And in 4. 12. 53 Shakespeare makes Antony explicitly compare himself and Cleopatra with Aeneas and Dido. For this and other interesting parallels see T. Zielinski, 'Marginalien' (*Philologus*, 64 (n.F. 18), 1905, 1 f.), who points out that Cleopatra, like Dido in *Her.* 7. 133 f., hints at being pregnant: see *Antony and Cleopatra*, 1. 3. 89–95.

48. *The Tempest*, 5. 1. 33–50. The tiny fairies of the seashore and the glade, brothers to Pease-blossom, Cobweb, and Mustard-seed, are here reminiscences of Ariel's gentler kinsman Puck rather than assistants in Prospero's prodigious magic. Doubtless they were suggested to Shakespeare, not by the content of the invocation, but by Golding's word *elves*.

49. *Macbeth*, 4. 1. 4 f.

50. Ov. *Met.* 7. 262 f.

51. *Macbeth*, 3. 5. 23–4.

52. Ov. *Met.* 3. 206 f.

53. *M.N.D.* 4. 1. 118 f. See also *The Merry Wives*, 2. 1. 120:

> Like Sir Actaeon he, with Ringwood at thy heels

—where Ringwood is the dog-name Golding substituted for Ovid's Hylactor, Barker. (See Root, cited in introductory note, 30.) The following passages also are worth comparing:

A Midsummer-Night's Dream, 1. 1. 170, and Ov. *Met.* 1. 470, a parallel which suggests that the difficult line 172 in Hermia's speech refers to the arrow, and ought to be placed before 171;
As You Like It, 3. 3. 10 f., and Ov. *Met.* 8. 626–30;
The Winter's Tale, 4. 3. 116 f., and Ov. *Met.* 5. 391 f.

54. e.g. *As You Like It*, 3. 3. 7 f. (quoted on p. 199), and *L.L.L.* 4. 2. 128, both containing Latin puns.

55. e.g. *Cymbeline*, 2. 2. 44 f., and *Titus Andronicus*, 4. 1. 42 f.

56. *A Midsummer-Night's Dream*, 5. 1. 129 f.

57. *The Winter's Tale*, 5. 3. 21 f. Fripp, *Shakespeare, Man and Artist* (London, 1938), 1. 102–14, has a detailed and sensitive discussion of Shakespeare's love for Ovid. He also points out (1. 597, n. 4) that Shakespeare, who sympathized with Montaigne in so much, resembled him in his early admiration of the *Metamorphoses*. (See p. 186.)

58. *Titus Andronicus*, 2. 1. 133 f. = Sen. *Phaedra*, 1180, garbled; 4. 1. 81–2 = Sen. *Phaedra*, 671–2, with a textual variation that would occur only to a latinist. The latter passage is directly imitated in Jonson's *Catiline*, 3. 4. 1–2, and adapted in Tourneur's *The Revenger's Tragedy*, 4. 2.

59. This subject has been treated in detail by J. W. Cunliffe and F. L. Lucas, whose books are cited in the introductory note.

60. *Hamlet*, 5. 2. 232 f.; *Macbeth*, 5. 5. 19. f.

61. *Timon of Athens*, 4. 1, 4. 3.

62. *King Lear*, 4. 1. 36 f.

63. See Cunliffe (quoted in introductory note), 25 f., who refers to Seneca, *Phaedra*, 978 f.:

> Res humanas ordine nullo
> Fortuna regit sparsitque manu
> munera caeca, peiora fouens;
> uincit sanctos dira libido,
> fraus sublimi regnat in aula.

64. e.g. in Webster's *The Duchess of Malfi* (5. 3 fin., 5. 5 fin.).

65. *Hamlet*, 5. 1. 245 f.

66. *1 Henry IV*, 1. 3. 130 f.

67. *Timon of Athens*, 4. 3. 178 f.

68. See pp. 132–3.

69. So Cunliffe (cited in introductory note), 16–17, and T. S. Eliot, in his essay 'Seneca in Elizabethan Translation' (*Selected Essays 1917–1932*, New York, 1932).

70. See *Richard III*, 1. 2. 68 f., 4. 4. 344 f., and compare Eliot (cited in n. 69), 72 f., and Lucas (introductory note), 119 f.

71. Cunliffe (cited in introductory note) gives details on 68 f.

72. Sen. *Phaedra*, 715 f., in the same scene which contains Hippolytus' cry to heaven for vengeance, cited in note 58:

> Quis eluet me Tanais aut quae barbaris
> Maeotis undis Pontico incumbens mari?
> non ipse toto magnus Oceano pater
> tantum expiarit sceleris.

73. Sen. *Herc. Fur.* 1323 f., ending

> haerebit altum facinus.

74. *Macbeth*, 2. 2. 61 f., 5. 1. 56. Murder is constantly imaged as a blood-stain in this play: see 2. 2. 47 f., 2. 3. 118–23, 5. 1 throughout, and hints such as 4. 1. 123 and 4. 3. 40–1.

75. Sen. *Herc. Fur.* 1258 61.

76. *Macbeth*, 5. 3. 22 f.

77. Sen. *Herc. Fur.* 1261–2.

78. *Macbeth*, 5. 3. 40.

79. *Macbeth*, 1. 7. 7 f. = Sen. *Herc. Fur.* 735–6:

> quod quisque fecit patitur: auctorem scelus
> repetit suoque premitur exemplo nocens.

Macbeth, 4. 3. 209 f. = Sen. *Phaedra*, 607, a favourite line with the Elizabethans:

> curae leues loquuntur, ingentes stupent.

A parallel between the invocations of Lady Macbeth (*Macbeth*, 1. 5. 41 f.) and Medea (Sen. *Medea*, 1–55, especially 9–15 and 40–50) has been noticed, but is less convincing. But it seems clear that the long series of phrases in praise of sleep (*Macbeth*, 2. 2. 37 f.) was suggested by Seneca, *Herc. Fur.* 1065 f.; and still more reminiscences are given by Engel, whose essay is quoted in the introductory note to this chapter.

80. See p. 393 f.

81. In the final scene of *Timon of Athens* (5. 4. 70 f.) Alcibiades reads out what is supposed to be an epitaph written for Timon by himself and engraved on his tomb:

> Here lies a wretched corse, of wretched soul bereft:
> Seek not my name; a plague consume you wicked caitiffs left!
> Here lie I, Timon; who, alive, all living men did hate:
> Pass by, and curse thy fill; but pass, and stay not here thy gait.

Obviously this is not one poem but two. A glance at Plutarch shows that he gives two different epitaphs written at different times (one by Callimachus, one attributed to Timon himself) and mutually incompatible. But Shakespeare, careless of the incongruity, runs the two together.

82. Shakespeare's father was a whittawer, who processed leather for the manufacture of gloves, purses, parchment, &c. As trades went, this was doubtless dignified and lucrative; but in its social opportunities it was far below the professions and the landed gentry. As for the school at Stratford, it was efficient enough, but it was not St. Paul's, or Winchester, or Eton.

83. *Julius Caesar*, 2. 1. 61–5.

84. Before this, Shakespeare knew Seneca, had copied him in *Richard III*, and, if *Titus Andronicus* be his or partly his, had tried his prentice hand at writing Senecan tragedy; but it was only after he married the manner of Seneca to the matter of Plutarch that he created great tragedy.

85. Shakespeare's use of North's Plutarch has been treated eloquently and in detail by M. W. MacCallum, whose book is cited in the introductory

note. See also Skeat's reprint of the text, mentioned there. Skeat points out that many of the names of secondary characters in Shakespeare's other dramas come from Plutarch—Marcellus, Lysander, and perhaps Demetrius (but see note 1). W. Warde Fowler has a useful essay on *Julius Caesar* in his *Roman Essays and Interpretations* (Oxford, 1920).

86. *Julius Caesar*, 1. 2. 191 f.

87. *Julius Caesar*, 2. 2. 37 f. H. M. Ayres, in 'Shakespeare's *Julius Caesar* in the Light of some other Versions' (*PMLA*, n.s. 18 (1910), 183–227), points out that during the Renaissance the dramatic conception of Caesar's character had, in default of a model in classical tragedy, been distorted to resemble that of the braggart Hercules in Seneca (e.g. in Marc-Antoine Muret's Latin tragedy on Caesar), and that the passages in Shakespeare's play where Caesar struts and brags are affected by the hybristic heroes of Seneca and their copies in contemporary drama.

88. *Antony and Cleopatra*, 2. 2. 194 f. See also p. 157.

89. The question whether Shakespeare used a translation of Plautus when writing *The Comedy of Errors* has been much vexed. It seems to me to have been given more importance than it deserves: for if Shakespeare could read *Amphitruo* in Latin, he could surely read *Menaechmi*, and no one has undertaken to show that a translation of *Amphitruo* was available. However, these are some of the main facts:

(a) *The Comedy of Errors* was written and produced between 1589 and 1593, when France was 'making war against her heir', Henri IV (see 3. 2. 127–8). The joke would be obscure before August 1589 and out of date after 1593.

(b) The only known Elizabethan translation of Plautus' *Menaechmi* was published by Creede in 1595 and attributed to W. W., who may have been William Warner. The publisher in his foreword says that W. W. had translated several plays of Plautus 'for the use and delight of his private friends, who in Plautus owne words are not able to understand them', and that he himself had prevailed on W. W. to publish this one. If this is true, the translation had been circulating in manuscript. If Shakespeare was one of W. W.'s friends, he could have seen it. But it seems more probable that (as has been suggested) the success of *The Comedy of Errors* prompted W. W. to publish his version.

(c) A comparison of *The Comedy of Errors* with W. W.'s translation shows that the two do not coincide. Several important characters and dramatic roles are different, and although people in similar situations say similar things in both plays, Shakespeare's characters do not echo W. W.'s words. The presumption is therefore heavily against Shakespeare's use of W. W. (See the detailed comparison by H. Isaac, 'Shakespeares Comedy of Errors und die Menächmen des Plautus', *Archiv für das Studium der neueren Sprachen und Litteraturen*, 70 (1883), 1–28.)

(d) On New Year's Day 1576–7, the 'children of Powles' produced something called *The Historie of Error* at Hampton Court. The boys of St. Paul's School were good latinists (as they still are) and this could have been an adaptation of *Menaechmi*, just as *Ralph Roister Doister* was an adaptation of themes from *Miles gloriosus*. If it was, Shakespeare could have seen and used it. But we do not know that it was, or that he ever saw it.

(e) M. Labinski, *Shakespeares Komödie der Irrungen* (Breslau, 1934), suggests that Shakespeare might have used an Italian adaptation of Plautus: for the names of Dromio and Adriana and Luciana, and the characters of the goldsmith Angelo and the merchant Balthazar, are contemporary Italian. But no adaptation very like his play has been found.

To the fact that Shakespeare read *Amphitruo* in the original should be added the fact that he also knew a third comedy by Plautus, the *Mostellaria*. In *The Taming of the Shrew* the names of the servants Tranio and Grumio come from the *Mostellaria*; and so also do some incidents, and the character of Tranio—who, as in Plautus, is made his young master's guardian, but instead turns him into merry ways (see his speech in 1. 1. 29 f.).

90. Several studies of Shakespeare's technique in *The Comedy of Errors* have shown that, in taking over the stories of Plautus' *Menaechmi* and *Amphitruo*, he was not hindered by any difficulty in understanding Latin, but felt quite free to alter and transform, as one feels free only when one has a firm grip on one's material. These articles emphasize, among others, the fact that he purified and ennobled the play by making the courtesan less prominent and the loving wife Adriana more real and human. See, in particular, E. Gill's 'A Comparison of the Characters in *The Comedy of Errors* with those in the *Menaechmi*' (*Texas University Studies in English*, 5 (1925), 79–95), the same author's very careful essay 'The Plot-structure of *The Comedy of Errors* in Relation to its Sources' (*Texas University Studies in English*, 10 (1930), 13–65), and M. Labinski's *Shakespeares Komödie der Irrungen* (Breslau, 1934). There are some suggestive remarks in V. G. Whitaker's 'Shakespeare's Use of his Sources' (*Philological Quarterly*, 20 (1941), esp. 380 f.). G. B. Parks, in 'Shakespeare's Map for "The Comedy of Errors"' (*Journal of English and Germanic Philology*, 39 (1940), 93–7), shows that, when Shakespeare wanted to find some other locale than the relatively unknown Epidamnus (where Plautus put the *Menaechmi*), he looked up the index of the great atlas of Ortelius of Antwerp, and there, beside Epidamnus, found Ephesus. He then moved the locale to Ephesus, which every modern reader knows from the sensational episode in the Acts of the Apostles; and he rearranged the journey of the chief characters very intelligently to fit the change. He also brought in Epidaurus, which appears in the index just after Epidamnus: see 1. 1. 93. Only one verbal reminiscence of Plautus' plays seems to have been pointed out in *The Comedy of Errors*—a small one at that: *The Comedy of Errors*, 3. 1. 80 = *Amphitruo*, 1048.

91. *1 Henry IV*, 2. 1. 104; *Much Ado about Nothing*, 4. 1. 21–2; and especially *The Merry Wives of Windsor*, 4. 1.

92. For instance, a servant in Terence (*Eun.* 1. 1. 29) tells his master that, since he has been captured by love, his only resort is to ransom himself as cheaply as possible:

> quid agas? nisi ut te redimas captum quam queas minumo.

Colet and Lily abbreviated this into one line, no doubt to illustrate the idiom of *quam* with the superlative (='as . . . as possible'); and in that form Tranio quotes it to his master (*The Taming of the Shrew*, 1. 1. 166):

> If love have touched you, nought remains but so:
> Redime te captum, quam queas minimo.

And although *Titus Andronicus* is shaky evidence for Shakespeare's practice, there is a most amusing illustration of this method of quotation in it. The villains are sent certain weapons bearing the inscription:

> Integer vitae scelerisque purus
> Non eget Mauri iaculis neque arcu (Horace, *Carm.* 1. 22).
> An innocent unstained with crime
> will need no Moorish spears nor bow.

When Demetrius reads this out, Chiron observes:

> O! 'tis a verse in Horace; I know it well;
> I read it in the grammar long ago. (*Titus Andronicus*, 4. 2. 20).

93. *L.L.L.* 4. 2. 96 f.
94. *Hamlet*, 5. 1. 260 f.
95. Persius, 1. 38–9:

> Nunc non e tumulo fortunataque fauilla
> nascentur uiolae?

96. Baldwin, *William Shakspere's Small Latine and Lesse Greeke*, 1. 649.

97. *The Comedy of Errors*, 1. 1. 31 = Verg. *Aen.* 2. 3:

> Infandum, regina, iubes renouare dolorem.

Other Vergilian reminiscences include:
The Tempest, 4. 1. 101–2 = Verg. *Aen.* 1. 46 blended with 1. 405;
the stage direction in *The Tempest*, 3. 3. 53 = Verg. *Aen.* 3. 219 f.:
'claps his wings' being a translation of *magnis quatiunt clangoribus alas*, 3. 226;
the saffron wings of Iris in *The Tempest*, 4. 1. 78 = Verg. *Aen.* 4. 700–2 (perhaps through Phaer's translation: see Root, *Classical Mythology in Shakespeare*, 77);
the herald Mercury in *Hamlet*, 3. 4. 58 = Verg. *Aen.* 4. 246–53 (Root, 85);
and a neat pun in *2 Henry VI*, 2. 1. 24 = Verg. *Aen.* 1. 11, where *caelestibus*, 'heavenly', is taken as though it meant 'clerical'.

98. *2 Hen. VI*, 4. 7. 65 = Caesar, *B. G.* 5. 14. 1:

'ex eis omnibus longe sunt humanissimi qui Cantium incolunt'; of these (the southern British) the inhabitants of Kent are far the most civilized.

99. See E. I. Fripp, *Shakespeare, Man and Artist*, 96 f.
100. *Julius Caesar*, 5. 3. 94 f.
101. Lucan, *Bell. Ciu.* 1. 2–3. The probability that Shakespeare is echoing Lucan is strengthened by the oddity of the phrase 'turns our

swords *in* our own proper entrails', which looks like a remembered mistranslation of the Latin:

> populumque potentem
> *in* sua uictrici conuersum uiscera dextra.

102. *Hamlet*, 2. 2. 200 f.

103. Nevertheless, Shakespeare's knowledge of Juvenal's satire is obviously very vague: if he had read it, he would certainly have remembered it vividly. The brilliant detail 'thick amber and plum-tree gum' is not in Juvenal (who would have admired it), and the rest of Hamlet's speech is only a faint reflection of the poem. The satire is sometimes called *The Vanity of Human Wishes*, and was adapted in English by Johnson under that title. Theobald and others have detected a reminiscence of its powerful opening lines in Menecrates' warning to the ambitious Pompey (*Antony and Cleopatra*, 2. 1. 5–8):

> We, ignorant of ourselves,
> Beg often our own harms, which the wise powers
> Deny us for our good; so find we profit
> By losing of our prayers.

For a larger treatment of Shakespeare's satirical purposes and methods, see O. J. Campbell, *Comicall Satyre and Shakespeare's 'Troilus and Cressida'* (San Marino, Cal., 1938), and his *Shakespeare's Satire* (New York and London, 1943).

Notes on 12. LYRIC POETRY

1. 2 Samuel vi. 14 f.

2. 'Lyric' means 'music for the lyre'. The Greeks usually spoke of 'melic' poetry, from *melos* = 'song', the word we know from 'melody'.

3. For a chronological account of his long and magnificent career, traced through the poems produced at its various stages, see U. von Wilamowitz-Moellendorff, *Pindaros* (Berlin, 1922), and G. Norwood's beautifully written *Pindar* (Sather Classical Lectures, 1945, Berkeley, Cal., 1945).

4. When the verses are longer than can be sung or danced in a single sweep, they are divisible again into phrases (*kola*) which correspond in their turn.

5. Hor. *Carm.* 4. 2. 5–8. It is a mistake, however, to believe that Horace thought Pindar's odes were written in 'free verse'. The patternless rhythms are strictly limited, by Horace's logical division, to the dithyrambs: see lines 10–24. E. Fraenkel, 'Das Pindargedicht des Horaz' (*Sitzungsberichte der Heidelberger Akademie der Wissenschaften*, 1932–3), has a valuable discussion of the poem.

6. See pp. 271–2 for the story of a French lady who refused to believe her husband's literal translation of Pindar's first Olympian ode.

7. Quoted from Racan's *Vie de Malherbe* by A. Croiset, *La Poésie de Pindare et les lois du lyrisme grec* (Paris, 1895³), 449.

8. Boileau, *Art poétique*, 2. 72.

9. Norwood, *Pindar* (quoted in n. 3), 98 f. On p. 51 f. of his *Pindar, a Poet of Eternal Ideas* (Baltimore, 1936), Prof. D. M. Robinson suggests that Pindar was the first poet to develop one of the most famous images in the world, the Wheel of Fortune (*Ol.* 2. 35 f.). The suggestion is taken up by Prof. Norwood on p. 253 f.

10. Hor. *Carm.* 4. 2. He never attempted to copy Pindar's astonishing metres or his sumptuous vocabulary; but he did use a number of Pindar's themes: for instance, in *Carm.* 1. 12 init., 3. 4, and the important victory ode 4. 4. On the whole subject see E. Fraenkel, cited in n. 5, P. Rummel, *Horatius quid de Pindaro iudicauerit* (Rawitsch, 1892), and E. Harms, *Horaz in seinen Beziehungen zu Pindar* (Marburg, 1936).

11. According to the *Encyclopaedia Britannica* (1946), s.v., our swan is the *Cygnus olor*, which can only hiss, and the legend that the swan sings comes from the voice of the migrant whooper swan (*Cygnus musicus*), which has an American cousin, the trumpeter swan.

12. Gray, *The Progress of Poesy*; and not he alone.

13. Yet if Horace thought he was a bee in contrast to the swan-like Pindar, he also thought that he himself was a swan in comparison with ordinary men (*Carm.* 2. 20, 4. 3. 19 f.). I cannot follow L. P. Wilkinson (*Horace and his Lyric Poetry*, Cambridge, 1945, 62) in believing that Horace was overcome by the giggles in the middle of *Carm.* 2. 20, and then became serious again to finish the poem. A poet like Horace does not lose control in the middle of a lyric, nor publish a half-comical poem in such an important place as the end of an entire book. The poem is a failure, not because Horace could not restrain his sense of humour, but because six brief tight Alcaic stanzas do not give him enough room to make his metamorphosis imaginatively convincing. In a short poem you can say that you have built a monument, but scarcely that you are turning into a large bird.

14. See p. 418 f.

15. A long book could be written on the false antithesis 'classical)(romantic'. Other remarks on the subject will be found on pp. 355 f., 375, 390 of this work. There is an exuberant attack on the distinction in Victor Hugo's 1824 preface to *Odes et ballades*:

'Il [i.e. Hugo] répudie tous ces termes de convention que les partis se rejettent réciproquement comme des ballons vides, signes sans signification, expressions sans expression, mots vagues que chacun définit au besoin de ses haines ou de ses préjugés, et qui ne servent de raisons qu'à ceux qui n'en ont pas. Pour lui, il ignore profondément ce que c'est que le genre classique et que le genre romantique.... Le *beau* dans Shakespeare est tout aussi classique (si *classique* signifie digne d'être étudié) que le *beau* dans Racine; et le *faux* dans Voltaire est tout aussi romantique (si *romantique* veut dire mauvais) que le *faux* dans Calderon.'

See Henri Peyre's valuable discussion of the idea of Classicism with his extensive bibliography: *Le Classicisme français* (New York, 1942).

16. Bergk, *Poetae lyrici Graeci* (Leipzig, 1878–82⁴), 3, p. 315, no. 31:

μεσονυκτίοις ποθ᾽ ὥραις,
στρέφεθ᾽ ἡνίκ᾽ Ἄρκτος ἤδη
κατὰ χεῖρα τὴν Βοώτου . . .

Did Poe know this poem, and diabolize it in *The Raven*? The theme is the same: a supernatural being enters a lonely man's room at midnight, and, refusing to leave, dominates his life.

17. Unfortunately the scope of this book will not permit a discussion of the modern epigram, nor of the different influences exercised upon it by Martial and by the Greek epigrammatists.

18. There are two admirably thorough studies of the subject by James Hutton, *The Greek Anthology in Italy*, and *The Greek Anthology in France and in the Latin Writers of the Netherlands to the Year 1800* (Cornell University Press, Ithaca, N.Y., 1935 and 1946). See also *Classical Influence upon the Tribe of Ben*, by K. A. McEuen (Cedar Rapids, Iowa, 1939), cc. 7 and 8.

19. Cat. 85:

> Odi et amo. Quare id faciam fortasse requiris.
> Nescio, sed fieri sentio et excrucior.

20. Cat. 2 and 3, two of the most famous poems on a favourite theme—the lover's identification of himself with a pet animal which his mistress caresses. The colloquialism of the language in these hendecasyllabic poems is very important, and is sometimes overlooked: it shows, among other things, that they were posing as improvisations.

21. Details in *Orazio nella letteratura mondiale* (Istituto di studi romani, Rome, 1936—XIV).

22. *Carm.* 4. 2: pp. 225–6 above.

23. Alamanni was then living in exile at the French court. Laumonier believes, apparently with justice, that Ronsard did not study or imitate Alamanni's Pindarics in any important degree (see his *Ronsard poète lyrique*, Paris, 1923², 344 n. 1 and 704–6). It is sometimes said that the choruses in Trissino's tragedy *Sofonisba* (on which see p. 136) are 'in agreement with Pindaric practice' (R. Shafer, *The English Ode to 1660*, Princeton, 1918, 60 f.); but they are not called odes, nor divided into sections called strophe, antistrophe, and epode. Even if Trissino was trying to write a Greek chorus in *Sofonisba*, he is much more likely to have been thinking of the tragic choruses, which were also triadic, than of Pindar. The poems look to me just like Trissino's ordinary *canzoni*. See also P. de Nolhac, *Ronsard et l'humanisme* (Paris, 1921), 45 f.

24.　　　　　 Le premier de France
　　　　　　 J'ay pindarizé　(*Odes*, 2. 2. 36–7; cf. 1. 4 fin.).

25. See pp. 94, 145.

26. This friend has been identified by de Nolhac as Claudio Duchi (see Laumonier, *Ronsard poète lyrique* (cited in n. 23), 5–6, and H. Chamard, *Histoire de la Pléiade*, Paris, 1939–40, 1. 72). Strange, and a little ungenerous, that Ronsard never mentions him.

27. For testimonies to Dorat's teaching, see Ronsard's ode to him (*Odes*, 1. 13); H. Chamard (cited in n. 26), 1, c. 2; P. de Nolhac (cited in n. 23), cc. 6–7; J. E. Sandys, *A History of Classical Scholarship* (Cambridge, 1908), 2. 186–8. His name was sometimes spelt D'Aurat and latinized as

Auratus, but more usually Dorat. (He had given up the family name Dinemandi: Dorat was supposed to be the name of his ancestors.) E. Gandar, *Ronsard considéré comme imitateur d'Homère et de Pindare* (Metz, 1854), 80 f., points out that there was no tradition of Pindaric learning and no complete French edition of Pindar when Ronsard started his reading in Greek, so that Dorat both explained the difficult language and showed his pupils the beauties of the poetry in Pindar's odes. On this see also Chamard (cited in n. 26), i. 338 f.

28. There was a group of poets in Alexandria in the third century B.C. who were called the Pleiad after the constellation. (Alexandrian critics and those who admired them liked to group greatnesses in sevens.) Ronsard knew a good deal about Alexandrian poetry (he copied Callimachus in his *Hymns*), and he was probably thinking of this group when he transferred the name to his own clique. Binet gives their names as: Dorat, Ronsard, Du Bellay, Baïf, Belleau, Jodelle, and Tyard (Chamard, cited in n. 26, v. 1, c. 5).

29. The title in the first edition is *La Deffence, et Illustration de la Langue Francoyse*. The word *illustration* might simply mean 'explanation' —i.e. an elucidation of the powers and the future of the language. But in fact it means 'glorification' or 'ennoblement'. It contains two ideas:

(*a*) a method of making the French language noble and respected;

(*b*) a proof that the French language is genuinely noble. Du Bellay was chiefly thinking of the former, as is shown by the synonyms he uses for *illustration*, and by such sentences as this about the French language:

'Je ne te puis mieux persuader d'y ecrire, qu'en te montrant le moyen de l'*enrichir et illustrer*, qui est l'imitation des Grecz et Romains'   (2. 2. 191–2).

But the two meanings were connected. He believed that to enrich the French language was the way to increase its prestige. On the book see Chamard (cited in n. 26), i. 4.

30. 1552 old style = 1553. See p. 137, also Chamard (cited in n. 26), 2. 11.

31. Cf. Ronsard, *Odes*, i. 22 (*A sa lyre*):

Je pillay Thebe, et saccageay la Pouille,
T'enrichissant de leur belle despouille.

There is a youthful boldness about this metaphor; but a sensitive Roman might think there was also an unfortunate touch of atavistic barbarism. Horace could have written an amusing epode on the young Gauls staggering homewards with their shoulders bent beneath their loot—sacks full of sculptural heads and limbs, bales of pictures cut up into small neat squares.

32. 'Sur toutes choses prens garde que ce genre de poëme soit eloigné du vulgaire, enrichy et illustré de motz propres et epithetes non oysifz, orné de graves sentences, et varié de toutes manieres de couleurs et ornementz poëtiques, non comme un *Laissez la verde couleur*, *Amour avecques Psyches*, *O combien est heureuse*, et autres telz ouvraiges, mieux dignes d'estre nommez Chansons vulgaires qu'Odes ou Vers liriques.'

(Du Bellay, *Deffence* 2. 4, quoted and annotated by Laumonier (see n. 23), introd. xxi.) The amusing thing is that the second of these pieces is itself on a classical theme, and comes from an anthology of poems entitled *Lament of Venus on the Death of Fair Adonis*. But the objection to it was that it was too folksy and not classical enough.

33. Du Bellay does not say this explicitly, nor could he, since Dorat composed much Latin and Greek poetry; but it is a necessary implication.

34. See Laumonier (cited in n. 23), introd. xv, xx f., xxix, xxxi f., and 706 f.

35. I. Silver, 'Ronsard and Du Bellay on their Pindaric Collaboration' (*Romanic Review*, 33 (1942), 1–25), shows that Du Bellay tried his hand quite as soon as Ronsard, if not before; and, after finding himself unequal to the task, relinquished priority to Ronsard. At some time their teacher Dorat wrote Pindaric odes in Latin, as an Italian humanist had done (see Chamard, cited in n. 26, 1. 339). It seems most probable that he wrote these first, and that his pupils then set out to emulate them in French. (Details in P. de Nolhac, cited in n. 23, 44–52.) In a preparatory article, 'Did Du Bellay know Pindar?' (*PMLA*, 56 (1941), 1007–19), Mr. Silver showed with practical certainty that he did. Du Bellay's *Ode au Prince de Melphe*, although Pindaric in its loftiness, criticizes Pindar as obscure and rambling.

36. Ronsard's tremendous ode to Michel de L'Hospital, 1. 10, in 24 triads, was evidently designed to outdo the longest of Pindar's odes, *Pyth*. 4, with its 13 triads.

37. *Odes*, 1. 1–7 and 9–15 are in the Pindaric *A–Z–P* pattern. *Odes*, 1. 8 is often described as 'monostrophic' and treated as an imitation of such odes as Pindar, *Ol*. 11 (so Laumonier, cited in n. 23, 298). Its theme, its metre, and its opening, however, show that it is not Pindaric but Horatian, a development of the epilogue to Horace's third book, *Carm*. 3. 30, which it exactly equals in length and shape.

38. *Carm*. 4. 2. 1–4 (p. 225 f.); cf. Ronsard, *Odes*, 1. 11, ep. 4:

> Par une cheute subite
> Encor je n'ay fait nommer
> Du nom de Ronsard la mer,
> Bien que Pindare j'imite.

39. Laumonier (cited in n. 23), 399, quotes a particularly tough passage from *Odes*, 2. 13:

> Ah! que maudite soit l'asnesse,
> Laquelle pour trouver de l'eau,
> Au serpent donna la jeunesse,
> Qui tous les ans change de peau!
> Jeunesse que le populaire
> De Jupiter avoit receu
> Pour loyer de n'avoir sceu taire
> Le secret larrecin du feu.

The myth is terribly obscure (it comes from Nicander, *Theriaca*, 343 f.); but the wording is quite clear. Laumonier thinks that when Boileau reproached Ronsard for 'talking Greek and Latin in French' he was criticizing not his language but his use of mythical names and periphrases (see his p. 407, and 316 f., 395 f.).

40. Pindar, *Pyth.* 9. 28 f.

41. See p. 144.

42.   Horace harpeur Latin,
        Estant fils d'un libertin,
        Basse et lente avoit l'audace;
        Non pas moy de franche race,
        Dont la Muse enfle les sons
        De plus courageuse haleine   (*Odes* 1. 11, epod. 4).

43. On Ronsard's Anacreontic poems see Chamard (cited in n. 26), 2. 56–70. It was on the model of Anacreon—though helped by the little neo-Latin love-lyrics of Joannes Secundus and the like—that he created the miniature ode, or odelette.

44. For Ronsard's metrical innovations see Laumonier (cited in n. 23), 639 f. Chamard (n. 26), 1. 373–4, emphasizes the fact that Ronsard's Pindaric odes had many admirers and imitators from 1551 until about 1660.

45. 'Thebanos modos fidibus Hetruscis/adaptare primus docuit:/Cycnum Dircaeum/audacibus, sed non deciduis pennis sequutus/Ligustico Mari/nomen aeternum dedit.' (Epitaph in v. 1 of the Milan edition of 1807, p. xxxv.)

46. For details, see F. Neri, *Il Chiabrera e la Pléiade francese* (Turin, 1920).

47. This is the pattern of the fifth of his poems on Tuscan naval victories, no. 72 in the *Canzoni eroiche*. A few Pindaric poems also occur in his *Canzoni sacre*.

48. *L.L.L.* 4. 3. 99.

49. *As You Like It*, 3. 2. 382–6.

50. Cf. notes 24, 31 above.

51. For the analysis of Southern's poems, for quotations from them, and for much other information in this section, I am indebted to R. Shafer's *The English Ode to 1660* (Princeton, 1918). In Ode 1 (epode 2) Southern speaks of

        the great Prophets,
        Or Theban, or Calaborois,

and in strophe 2 he orders the Muses to stand up and sing

        A newe dittie Calaborois,
        To the Iban harpe Thebanois.

'Calaborois' is his stupid miscopying and misunderstanding of Ronsard's *calabrois*, 'Calabrian', applied to Horace, who came from south Italy.

52. On this poem see Shafer (n. 51), 92 f., and G. N. Shuster, *The English Ode from Milton to Keats* (New York, 1940), 67. On Milton's copy of Pindar see Robinson (cited in n. 9), 26 f.

53. See Shafer (n. 51), 96 f. Mr. Shafer also points to the invocation of Pindar at the opening of Jonson's *Ode to James Earl of Desmond*.

54. Pope, *Imitations of Horace, Ep. 2. 1. 75 f.* The epic was a *Davideis*, which, by a significant coincidence, Cowley abandoned at the very point (after finishing four books) where Ronsard dropped *The Franciad* (see p. 144).

55. Details in Shafer (n. 51), 128 f., who cites Milton's *On Time* and *At a Solemn Music*, Vaughan's *Resurrection and Immortality*, *The Holy Communion*, and *Affliction*, and numerous poems by Crashaw, who was a close friend of Cowley: for instance, *Prayer, an Ode*. See also Shuster (cited in n. 52), c. 4. It has often been said (apparently on Gosse's authority) that Cowley did not understand the triadic form of Pindar's odes, and that Congreve attacked him for his ignorance. A. H. Nethercot, 'The Relation of Cowley's "Pindarics" to Pindar's Odes' (*Modern Philology*, 19 (1921–2), 107 f.), explains that these are misapprehensions: as early as 1675 Milton's nephew Phillips was pointing out that the 'Pindaric' ode as Cowley practised it was much freer than Pindar's own patterns. Congreve's *Discourse on the Pindarique Ode* (1705) really asserted that free verse in the manner of Cowley was improper, and that even rhapsodical odes had their laws.

56. See p. 227.

57. Milton, *At a Solemn Music*.

58. See D. J. Grout, *A Short History of Opera* (New York, 1947), i. 11, on English opera of this period. In i. 14 Mr. Grout gives a superb sketch of the technical powers of the singing virtuosi of this period. For many of the facts on this branch of the subject I am indebted to G. N. Shuster (cited in n. 52), 132 f.

59. R. M. Myers, 'Neo-classical Criticism of the Ode for Music', in *PMLA*, 62 (1947), 2. 399–421. Pope's *Ode on St. Cecilia's Day, 1708* is a good example of the kind of thing.

60.   Quelle docte et sainte ivresse
                        Aujourd'hui me fait la loi?

Docte means 'poetically learned', 'wise in the secrets of the Muses'. This is the opening of Boileau's ode on the capture of Namur—a neat little piece in stanzas of ten short lines each, which is as far from Pindar as the Tuileries gardens from the forests and glens and mountains of Greece. There is a brilliant parody of it by Prior, which is actually a better poem.

61. At most it might be conceded that the baroque Pindaric-writers were genuinely moved by the idea of lofty rank. Unfortunately this is a subject which fails to excite us now; and even at the time, these poets often failed to communicate their emotion because they chose to do so by the use of ridiculous exaggerations. For instance, at the beginning of the Namur ode Boileau tells the winds to keep silent, because he is about to speak of Louis XIV. Such stuff was being written all over Europe. Turn to Portugal, and you find Antonio Dinys da Cruz e Silva combining light metres and grandiose hyperboles: he calls King José a more excellent monarch than Cyrus, Alexander, and Trajan (*Odes*, 30. 7). During this period real emotion is more often found in the poets who imitate Horace: see p. 249 f.

62. From Young's *Imperium pelagi*, quoted by D. B. Wyndham Lewis and C. Lee, in *The Stuffed Owl* (London, 1930), 62: a lovable collection of bad poetry.

63. So Shuster (cited in n. 52), 137. Mr. Shuster helps to account for the disappointing character of this poem by emphasizing Dryden's debt to Cowley in it.

64. Horace's more obviously moral works, the *Satires* and *Letters*, were much preferred in the Dark Ages and Middle Ages. Dante, for instance, knew him as a satirist (see p. 84). He was called *ethicus*, and quoted scores of times in Reader's Digest collections. The eighth-century *Exempla diuersorum auctorum* cites him seventy-four times and Brunetto Latini's *Li livres dou tresor* (*c.* 1260) sixty times. His lyrics were seldom read. Hugo of Trimberg (d. 1313), a schoolmaster living near Bamberg, is typical in that he knew them but distrusted them; in his *Registrum auctorum* (2. 66) he says:

> Sequitur Horatius, prudens et discretus,
> Vitiorum emulus, firmus et mansuetus,
> Qui tres libros etiam fecit principales,
> Duosque dictaverat minus usuales,
> Epodon videlicet et librum odarum,
> Quos nostris temporibus credo valere parum.

For details, see E. Stemplinger, *Horaz im Urteil der Jahrhunderte* (Das Erbe der Alten, 2nd series, 5, Leipzig, 1921), and the articles by J. Marouzeau and L. Pietrobono in *Orazio nella letteratura mondiale* (cited in n. 21).

65. See L. Pietrobono, *Orazio nella letteratura mondiale* (cited in n. 21), 118 f. On Landino see J. E. Sandys, *A History of Classical Scholarship* (Cambridge, 1908), 2. 81 f.; on Politian see pp. 135–6, 599 of this book.

66. Details in C. Riba's article on Spanish Horatians, in *Orazio nella letteratura mondiale* (n. 21), 195 f. The most famous of Garcilaso's poems in this vein is Canción 5, *La Flor de Gnido*, developed from Horace, *Carm.* 1. 8, with graceful luxuriance.

67. See A. Coster, *Fernando de Herrera* (Paris, 1908), 283 f., and R. M. Beach, *Was Fernando de Herrera a Greek Scholar?* (Philadelphia, 1908).

68. This is Canción 3 in Coster's edition, addressed to Don Juan after the rising of the Moriscos in 1571 (not after Lepanto). Herrera's lyrical pattern is the canción, made up of eleven-syllable lines mixed with shorter lines at the poet's own choice: all stanzas echoing the pattern set by the first in each poem. The models are Horace, *Carm.* 3. 4 and 4. 4.

69. 'Se me cayeron como de entre las manos estas obrecillas', quoted by C. Riba in *Orazio nella letteratura mondiale* (cited in n. 21), 198, n. 13.

70. Verg. *Aen.* 8. 31–67; Hor. *Carm.* 1. 15.

71. Luis de León, *¡Que descansada vida!* and Garcilaso's second Eclogue come from Horace, *Epod.* 2:

> Beatus ille qui procul negotiis
> ut prisca gens mortalium . . . .

The poem had already been echoed by the Marques de Santillana, and was adapted later by Lope de Vega (see G. Showerman, *Horace and His Influence* (Boston, 1922), 118).

72. P. Laumonier (cited in n. 23), 25, n. 2.

73. On Chiabrera see pp. 235–6.

74. For a more detailed account of this problem see L. P. Wilkinson (cited in n. 13), 169 f.

75. The attempt was made in Italian by Claudio Tolomei in his *Versi e regole della nuova poesia toscana* (1539). In English there are several notorious letters on the subject by Gabriel Harvey, who says he is revising English prosody and setting precedents for all future poets, as Ennius did in Latin. (The letters are supposed to be addressed to Spenser; still, J. W. Bennett, 'Spenser and Gabriel Harvey's "Letter Book"' (*Modern Philology*, 29 (1931–2), 163–86), gives reasons for thinking them a literary fiction.) In France the leader of the movement now best known was J. A. de Baïf, but Du Bellay, Ronsard, and d'Aubigné were all associated with it in one way or another. There is a recent dissertation on the subject, *French Verse in Classical Metres, and the Music to which it was set, of the Last Quarter of the Sixteenth Century*, by D. P. Walker (Oxford, 1947), of which I have seen only a summary. See also E. Egger, *L'Hellénisme en France* (Paris, 1869), Leçon 10, and H. Chamard (cited in n. 26), 4. 133 f.

76. See p. 381.

77. On Carducci, see also p. 443.

78. Details in Laumonier (cited in n. 23), 662–3.

79. *Odes*, 1. 11, epode 4.

80. Laumonier (cited in n. 23), 5 f.

81. Laumonier (cited in n. 23), 41 f., and Chamard (n. 26), 1. 9, give details.

82. *Odes*, 1. 22, 2. 1.

83. On this change in Ronsard's mind see Laumonier (cited in n. 23), 113 f., 123, 137, 161 f., and particularly 170–4. J. Hutton, in *The Greek Anthology in France and in the Latin Writers of the Netherlands to the Year 1800* (Ithaca, N.Y., 1946), 350 f., shows that there are no direct echoes in Ronsard from the Anthology before 1553. Then the *Folastries* contain seventeen translations from it. After that, he continues to allude to it, translate it, and imitate it, working his way slowly but steadily through the entire collection. A number of the sonnets in the 1578 edition of his *Works* are deeply indebted to the Anthology. Ronsard's interest in Catullus was awakened in 1552 by Muret's lectures; and his *Folastries* contain a number of echoes. But I cannot feel that he understood Catullus, and a piece like the *Gayeté*, 'Jaquet aime autant sa Robine . . .', is merely vulgar when compared to its original, Catullus 45.

84. 'Je me rendi familier d'Horace, contrefaisant sa naïve douceur, dés le méme tens que Cl. Marot (seule lumiere en ses ans de la vulgaire poësie) se travailloit à la poursuite de son Psautier.'

85. Laumonier, 625–6. But see P. de Nolhac (cited in n. 23), 61 f., for a charming account of a poetic and scholarly picnic at Arcueil where

Dorat presided over his pupils, and recited to them a neat Horatian ode in Latin, on the spring by which they had been drinking:

O fons Arculii sidere purior . . . .

As many of Ronsard's lighter odes show (5. 15, 5. 16), much of his pleasure in drinking came from the company of poetic friends: see also de Nolhac's pages 237–9.

86. On the quotation in *Titus Andronicus* see p. 626. When Shakespeare cried

Not marble, nor the gilded monuments
Of princes, shall outlive this powerful rhyme

(Sonnet 55), he was echoing Horace (*Carm.* 3. 30). But had he seen the poem at school, or heard it quoted by friends, or even glimpsed Ronsard's eighth ode:

Ne pilier, ne terme Dorique
d'histoires vieillies decoré . . . ?

87. See K. A. McEuen (cited in n. 18) on the entire subject; also R. Shafer (cited in n. 23), 99–103. On Herrick there are some notes by M. J. Ruggles, 'Horace and Herrick' (*The Classical Journal*, 31 (1935–6), 223–34), and further remarks, with some excellent parallels, by G. W. Regenos, 'The Influence of Horace upon Robert Herrick' (*The Philological Quarterly*, 26 (1947), 3. 268–84).

88. Hor. *Carm.* 1. 5. Milton remembered this picture when, in *Paradise Lost*, 4. 771 f., he described Adam and Eve in their bower:

These, lulled by nightingales, embracing slept,
And on their naked limbs the flowery roof
Showered roses.

89. See p. 159 f.

90. Hor. *Carm.* 1. 16: *O matre pulchra filia pulchrior*, echoed in Milton's twentieth sonnet.

91. From Sonnet 11, inspired by Hor. *Carm.* 1. 2. 18–20:

sinistra
labitur ripa Ioue non probante u-
xorius amnis.

92. This subject is well developed in an essay by J. H. Finley, Jr., 'Milton and Horace' (*Harvard Studies in Classical Philology*, 48 (Cambridge, Mass., 1937), 29–73).

93. For England there is a handy treatise on the subject by C. Goad, *Horace in the English Literature of the Eighteenth Century* (Yale Studies in English, 58, New Haven, 1918).

94. Later, Swinburne's *Ode on the Proclamation of the French Republic* begins with six consecutive strophes, then six antistrophes, followed by a lonely epode. Used like this, the terms are almost meaningless.

95. There is an interesting discussion of the subject in E. Maass's *Goethe und die Antike* (Berlin, 1912), c. 10.

96. Among these are *Mahomets Gesang*, *Wanderers Sturmlied* (which actually invokes Pindar), *Prometheus*, *Das Göttliche*, *Ganymed*, and *Grenzen der Menschheit*. The resemblance between the free verse of such poems as *Grenzen der Menschheit* and Arnold's lyrics in *Empedocles on Etna* is very striking.

97. For a detailed analysis, see F. Beissner, *Hölderlins Übersetzungen aus dem griechischen* (Stuttgart, 1933), E. Lachmann, *Hölderlins Hymnen* (Frankfurt a/M., 1937), and G. Zuntz, *Über Hölderlins Pindar-Übersetzung* (Marburg, 1928). Hölderlin's translations covered about half the *Olympians* and nearly all the *Pythians*, but he often did not complete his rendering of the ode on which he was working, whether from lassitude or from the difficulty of the task. For more on Goethe and Hölderlin see pp. 379 f., 377 f.

98. *Odes*, 5. 12, however, is a handsome little Horatian lyric.

99. There is a detailed, but not very satisfactory, study of the subject for England by M. R. Thayer, *The Influence of Horace on the Chief English Poets of the Nineteenth Century* (Cornell Studies in English, 2, Yale University Press, New Haven, 1916).

100. Gray's *Hymn to Adversity* should also be mentioned. It was inspired by Horace's ode to Fortune (*Carm.* 1. 35), and helped to inspire Wordsworth's *Ode to Duty* (on which see p. 411); but it is comparatively unsuccessful as a poem. Horace introduced far fewer Personifications, and those he did introduce were made alive, by having solidly real actions and appurtenances: *albo Fides uelata panno*; Necessity carrying heavy nails, and wedges, and molten lead.

101.   My heart aches, and a drowsy numbness pains
        My sense, as though of hemlock I had drunk,
        Or emptied some dull opiate to the drains
        One minute past, and Lethe-wards had sunk. . . .

        Mollis inertia cur tantam diffuderit imis
            obliuionem sensibus,
        pocula Lethaeos ut si ducentia somnos
            arente fauce traxerim . . .   (Hor. *Epod.* 14. 1–4)

This unmistakable transference was first spotted by Sir G. Greenwood, in his *Lee, Shakespeare, and a Tertium Quid* (London, 1923), 139. It was then beautifully elaborated by Mr. Edmund Blunden, who compares the first words of Horace's next poem:

        Nox erat, et caelo fulgebat Luna sereno
            inter minora sidera.

with the fourth stanza of the Nightingale ode:

        And haply the Queen-Moon is on her throne,
            Clustered around by all her starry Fays.

Finally, he points to the closing words:

        Was it a vision, or a waking dream?
        Fled is that music:—Do I wake or sleep?

with the resemblance to Horace s

> Auditis, an me ludit amabilis
> insania?   (*Carm.* 3. 4. 5–6)

These reminiscences, he says very convincingly, would justify us in
believing that Keats had his Horace in his hand when he sat down in the
garden on that evening, and presently began to write. (See his 'Keats and
his Predecessors', *London Mercury*, 20 (1929), 289 f.)

102. Quoted by D. S. Savage, 'The Americanism of Hart Crane'
(*Horizon*, 5 (1942), May).

103. 'O damn anything that's low, I cannot bear it' (Goldsmith, *She
Stoops to Conquer*, 1. 2). The same feeling was neatly put by the French
surrealist Croniamental:

> Luth
> Zut!

(Quoted in R. G. Cadou's *Testament d'Apollinaire* (Paris, 1945), 168.)
Hatred of baroque pretentiosity and the feeling that the ode-writers
aspired too high produced many parodic odes in the eighteenth and nineteenth centuries. Wolcot, for instance, wrote commonsensical but vulgar
poems on current affairs, called them odes, and took the pseudonym Peter
Pindar. But some of the parodies are delightful: for instance, Calverley's
Sapphic on tobacco:

> Sweet, when the morn is gray;
> Sweet, when they've cleared away
> Lunch; at the close of day
> Possibly sweetest.

And doubtless it was the founding of the Royal Society for the Prevention
of Cruelty to Animals (1824) which inspired the great ode *To an Expiring
Frog*:

> Can I view thee panting, lying
> On thy stomach, without sighing;
> Can I unmoved see thee dying
> On a log,
> Expiring frog!

This ode was repeated by Mrs. Leo Hunter, in character ('in character!'
said Mr. Pickwick) as Minerva.

Notes on 13. TRANSITION

1. One important cultural date which ought to be remembered along
with such things as the foundation of the Académie in France and the
Royal Society in Britain is the publication of many of the greatest Latin
classics in a single series of sixty-four uniform volumes, with renderings in
Latin prose, illustrations, and explanatory notes by the best living French
scholars. This is the famous Delphin edition, produced under the

patronage of Louis XIV *ad usum serenissimi Delphini*, for the use of the dauphin. It was proposed in 1672 by the Comte de Montausier, major-domo to the dauphin, and the dauphin's tutors Bossuet and Huet, and most of it was produced between 1674 and 1698. It was attractively pro-duced and carefully expurgated; the vocabulary indexes are occasionally still useful.

2. The word for high school in French is *lycée*, named after Aristotle's college, the Lyceum, in the same way as American and British schools are often named after Plato's college, the Academy. The German word is *gymnasium*, after the place where Socrates taught. The word *school* is the Greek σχολή, through the Latin *schola*: it means 'leisure', as opposed to the serious daily work which an adult does.

3. See p. 466 f.

4. Wordsworth, *The Prelude*, 11. 108–9.

5. There are vivid, though brief, descriptions of this disaster, taken from contemporary accounts, in J. E. Sandys, *A History of Classical Scholarship* (Cambridge, 1908), 2, and J. A. Symonds, *The Renaissance in Italy: the Revival of Learning*, c. 7. The Roman Academy, founded in the mid-fifteenth century by the distinguished teacher and humanist Pom-ponius Laetus, was ruined: its head saw nearly all his fine collection of manuscripts and antiquities looted and destroyed. Paolo Giovio lost his only copy of part of the first ten books of his ambitious *History of Rome*, and, at the end of his collection of biographies, lamented that the Germans had 'robbed exhausted Greece and slumbering Italy of the ornaments of peace, learning, and the arts'. Scholars everywhere wrote to each other that the light of the world had perished.

6. 'Of the foremost scholars of France in the sixteenth century, Turnebus died some years before the eventful date of St. Bartholomew; Ramus perished in the massacre, Lambinus died of fright, while Hotman and Doneau fled to Geneva, never to return. Joseph Justus Scaliger withdrew to the same city. . . . Isaac Casaubon was born at Geneva of Huguenot parents, who had fled from Gascony. At the age of nine he could speak and write Latin. He was learning Greek from his father, with Isocrates, *Ad Demonicum*, as a textbook, when the news of the massacre of St. Bartholomew's drove them to the hills, where the lessons in Greek were continued in a cave in Dauphiné.' (Sandys, cited in n. 5, 2. 199 and 2. 204, quoting A. A. Tilley, *The Literature of the French Renaissance*, Cambridge, 1904.) Casaubon was later pressed to become a Catholic, so urgently that he left France for England, where he studied until his too early death.

7. The scholar and poet, Aonio Paleario (1504–70), denounced the Index as 'a dagger drawn from the scabbard to assassinate literature', and lamented that because of it 'the study of the liberal arts was deserted, the young men wantoned in idleness and wandered about the public squares'. He died a martyr's death in Rome in 1570. (Sandys, cited in n. 5, 2. 155.)

8. See Allardyce Nicoll, *The Development of the Theatre* (London, 1927), c. 9.

Notes on 14. THE BATTLE OF THE BOOKS

1. A number of good books and essays have been written on this subject. I am particularly indebted to:

F. Brunetière, *L'Évolution des genres dans l'histoire de la littérature* (Paris, 1924), Quatrième leçon.

A. E. Burlingame, *The Battle of the Books in its Historical Setting* (New York, 1920).

J. B. Bury, *The Idea of Progress* (London, 1920), cc. 4 and 5.

A. F. B. Clark, *Boileau and the French Classical Critics in England* (Bibliothèque de la Revue de littérature comparée, 19, Paris, 1925).

G. Finsler, *Homer in der Neuzeit von Dante bis Goethe* (Leipzig, 1912).

H. Gillot, *La Querelle des anciens et des modernes en France* (Paris, 1914).

R. F. Jones, 'The Background of the *Battle of the Books*' (*Washington University Studies, Humanistic Series*, 7. 2, St. Louis, 1920, 99–162).

R. F. Jones, *Ancients and Moderns* (Washington University Studies, New Series, Language and Literature, 6, St. Louis, 1936).

H. Rigault, *Histoire de la querelle des anciens et des modernes*, v. 1 of his *Œuvres complètes* (Paris, 1859).

A. A. Tilley, *The Decline of the Age of Louis XIV* (Cambridge, 1929), c. 10.

C. H. C. Wright, *French Classicism* (Harvard Studies in Romance Languages, 4, Cambridge, Mass., 1920).

2. *Paradise Regained*, 4. 331 f. This is a very ancient doctrine in the Christian church, and appears as early as the second century. Justin Martyr asserted that all pagan philosophy and poetry was really stolen from the Hebrews; and he was followed by Tatian, Theophilus of Antioch, Clement of Alexandria, Tertullian, Origen, even St. Jerome.

3. See p. 608, and Chapter 8, p. 155 f. On the opposition to the use of pagan machinery in Christian poems, see A. F. B. Clark (cited in n. 1), especially 308 f.

4. A. E. Housman, *A Shropshire Lad*, 31.

5. The counter-argument about forgotten crafts appeared very early in this dispute. There is an interesting account of a discussion held in 1637, and reported (as part of a general cultural programme) by Renaudot, the founder of the *Gazette de France*. The subject proposed was: *S'il y a eu de plus grands hommes en quelqu'vn des siécles precédens qu'en cettui-ci?* Five speakers took part, and although the arguments were not always as clearly cut as later debaters made them the four chief points were covered. One of the speakers, however, went beyond the counter-argument mentioned on p. 266, and attempted to show that the Romans equalled the moderns in science, because they had invented such things as malleable glass (Pliny, *N.H.* 36. 195; Petron. *Sat.* 51). Sir William Temple overplayed this particular argument, and made it absurd. For the discussion in question, see L. M. Richardson, 'The "Conférences" of Théophraste Renaudot' (*Modern Language Notes*, 48 (1933), 312–16).

6. A history of this phrase is given by F. E. Guyer, 'The Dwarf on the Giant's Shoulders' (*Modern Language Notes*, 45 (1930), 398–402). It was

apparently coined by Bernard of Chartres (although others have associated it with Roger of Blois), and passed by his pupils William of Conches and Richard l'Évêque to John of Salisbury, who used it in his *Metalogicus*. It was current through the Renaissance, and appears in such odd places as Montaigne (*Essays*, 3. 13), d'Urfé's preface to *Sylvanire*, and Burton's *Anatomy of Melancholy*—where it is attributed to Didacus Stella, an author obscure enough to delight even Burton.

7. The scientists in particular liked this argument. Bacon uses it; Descartes's thought presupposes it; and there is a fine statement of it in Pascal's *Fragment d'un traité du vide*:

'Les hommes sont aujourd'hui en quelque sorte dans le même état où se trouveraient les anciens philosophes, s'ils pouvaient avoir vieilli jusqu'à présent, en ajoutant aux connaissances qu'ils avaient celles que leurs études auraient pu leur acquérir à la faveur de tant de siècles. De là vient que, par une prérogative particulière, non seulement chacun des hommes s'avance de jour en jour dans les sciences, mais que tous les hommes y font un continuel progrès, à mesure que l'univers vieillit, parce que la même chose arrive dans la succession des hommes que dans les âges différents d'un particulier. De sorte que toute la suite des hommes, pendant le cours de tant de siècles, doit être considérée comme un même homme qui subsiste toujours et qui apprend continuellement; d'où l'on voit avec combien d'injustice nous respectons l'antiquité dans sa philosophie: car, comme la vieillesse est l'âge le plus distant de l'enfance, qui ne voit que la vieillesse dans cet homme universel ne doit pas être cherchée dans les temps proches de sa naissance, mais dans ceux qui en sont les plus éloignés? Ceux que nous appelons anciens étaient véritablement nouveaux en toutes choses et formaient l'enfance des hommes proprement; et comme nous avons joint à leurs connaissances l'expérience des siècles qui les ont suivis, c'est en nous que l'on peut trouver cette antiquité que nous révérons dans les autres.'

8. Sometimes this argument was carried one stage farther, and the conclusion was drawn that we are now in the old age of civilization, that it is wise but enfeebled, and that it is approaching its death. This idea became so popular in the early seventeenth century that it was set as the subject for the philosophical disputation at Cambridge in 1628. The respondent, whose duty it was to argue against it, called upon Milton for help; Milton answered with a vigorous attack on the belief in the senility of the universe, his Latin poem *Naturam non pati senium*. See V. Harris, *All Coherence Gone* (Chicago, 1950).

9. *La nature est immuable* (quoted by Rigault (cited in n. 1), 192). This point had already been made by Du Bellay in his *Deffence*, and supported by Ronsard: see Gillot (cited in n. 1), 45.

10. Plato, *Rep.* 2. 377*b* f.

11. See J. L. Gerig and G. L. van Roosbroeck, 'Unpublished Letters of Pierre Bayle' (section 10), *The Romanic Review*, 24 (1933), 211.

12. Quoted by Brunetière (cited in n. 1), 123.

13. Homer, *Od.* 6. 71 f. Perrault, fourth dialogue, quoted by Rigault (cited in n. 1), 211 f.; also in the preface to the parody *Les Murs de Troye ou l'origine du burlesque*, which he wrote with his brother Claude (Finsler, cited in n. 1, 179).

14. Chesterfield, *Letters*, 1734 (1750), iv, 1610, quoted by D. Bush,

Mythology and the Romantic Tradition in English Poetry (Harvard Studies in English, 18, Cambridge, Mass., 1937), 6.

15. This revulsion from the use of the names of ordinary objects is one of the central characteristics of the taste of the baroque age. Ladies and gentlemen simply could not bear unladylike and ungentlemanly words— i.e. working-class words. They were 'low', not because they were obscene, but because they carried the connotations of working with one's hands. We shall meet this feeling again (see pp. 299 f., 318 f.); meanwhile, here are three quotations to illustrate it:

'Ces mots de veaux et de vaches ne sont point choquants dans le grec, comme ils le sont en notre langue, qui ne veut presque rien souffrir.' (Racine, *Remarques sur l'Odyssée d'Homère*, 10. 410 f.)

'Nous trouvons de la bizarrerie en des façons de parler, qui seroient ridicules en François, si on les traduisoit mot à mot. Nous trouvons de grandes bassesses dans les termes de chaudrons et de marmites, dans le sang, dans les graisses, dans les intestins et autres parties des Animaux parce que tout cela n'est plus que dans nos cuisines et dans nos boucheries, et que ces choses nous font bondir le cœur.' (Le Bossu, *Traité du poème épique*, 6. 8, quoted by Gillot (cited in n. 1), 188–9.)

'On est bien plus délicat qu'on ne l'estoit même du temps d'Auguste. On veut que tout soit remply de bon et de beau, et qu'il n'y ait rien de bas. Pourroit-on souffrir que je fisse certaines comparaisons comme Virgile qui compare Amatas furieux à un sabot, ou à une toupie que les enfants font aller dans quelque galerie; ou quand il compare une fureur à une eau qui bout dans un chaudron? ou quand il compare un esprit agité à une eau qui est aussi dans un chaudron, dans laquelle la lumière du soleil semble trembler et est agitée, et par répercussion frappe de tous côtés et les murailles et les planches d'une salle? Ces comparaisons portent l'esprit à des choses basses. . . . Maintenant, on ne veut rien que de fort noble et de fort beau.' (Desmarets de Saint-Sorlin's letter to his brother Rolland, quoted in Gillot (cited in n. 1), 505.)

The attacks on Homer's bad taste began as early as 1561, when Julius Caesar Scaliger, who adored Vergil, published his *Poetice*, containing dozens of bitter denunciations of the crude and silly behaviour of the Homeric gods and heroes. Details and quotations will be found in Finsler, 135 f., and Gillot, 70 f. (both cited in n. 1). Some of the classical poets were denounced at this period as being genuinely obscene, as indeed they are. Bayle described Juvenal's satires as *égouts de saleté*, and therefore inferior to Boileau's; he called Martial and Catullus *des esprits grossiers et rustiques*, inferior to La Fontaine. (See Gerig and van Roosbroeck, cited in n. 11.) This argument, however, was much less often used, since it was relevant only to the minor genres of classical literature.

16. Hom. *Il.* 11. 558 f. Racine, who knew more about Homer than any man of his time, wrote a very judicious letter to Boileau on this passage. Boileau had thought of defending Homer by saying that 'donkey' was really a very noble expression in Greek. Racine says, 'J'ai fait réflexion aussi qu'au lieu de dire que le mot d'âne est en grec un mot très-noble, vous pourriez vous contenter de dire que c'est un mot qui n'a rien de bas, et qui est comme celui de cerf, de cheval, de brebis, etc. Ce *très-noble* me paroît un peu trop fort' (letter 125, 1693).

17. Hom. *Od.* 17. 297 f.

18. 'Quella maniera di guerreggiare usata dagli antichi, i conviti, le cerimonie, e l'altre usanze di quel remotissimo secolo pajono alcuna volta a' nostri uomini nojose, e rincrescevoli, anzi che no, come avviene ad alcuni idioti, che leggono i divinissimi libri d'Omero trasportati in altra lingua. E di ciò in buona parte è cagione l'antichità de' costumi, la quale da coloro, che hanno avvezzo il gusto alla gentilezza, e al decoro da questa, è schivata come cosa vieta, e rancida' (Tasso, *Discorsi del poema eroico* (*Opere*, ed. G. Rosini, Pisa, 1823, v. 12), 2, pp. 46–7).

19. Tacitus, *Ann.* 1. 65: 'amissa per quae egeritur humus aut exciditur caespes'. Nero's *deuerticula* (which correspond to what Suetonius called *popinae* in *Nero* 26. 1) appear in *Ann.* 13. 25.

20. 'Quel ton! quel effroyable ton! ah, Madame, quel dommage que le Saint Esprit eût aussi peu de goût!'—quoted by Lytton Strachey in 'Madame du Deffand' (*Books and Characters*, New York, 1922). One would rather translate *ton* by 'style'—but that has come to mean literary style, whereas the Maréchale meant the entire social tone of the biblical world.

21. On the feminine influence in seventeenth-century taste, see Gillot (cited in n. 1), 349 f.

22. Quoted by Lytton Strachey, in 'Racine' (*Books and Characters*, New York, 1922). In this passage Strachey discusses Racine's use of such periphrases: for instance, where Roxane, calling for bowstrings to strangle her lover, says:

> Qu'ils viennent préparer ces nœuds infortunés
> Par qui de ses pareils les jours sont terminés.

Strachey gives two reasons to justify this kind of thing. One is that 'the things of sense—physical objects and details—. . . must be kept out of the picture at all hazards . . . so that the entire attention may be fixed upon the central and dominating features of the composition—the spiritual states of the characters'; and he then compares the periphrasis to 'the hastily dashed-in column and curtain in the background of a portrait'. But the comparison will not stand scrutiny, for it was actually more difficult for Racine to devise such periphrases than to write down the simple words which they replaced; nor will the reason, for the spiritual states of characters are often most clearly and memorably shown, and the audience's attention most closely fixed upon them, when they are made vivid by the introduction of the things of sense. The last scene of *Lear*, the sleep-walking scene in *Macbeth*, are examples. Strachey's other reason is that sometimes Racine manages to make such a circumlocution convey the confusion in the minds of his characters—which proves that he was a fine artist, but not that the rule was aesthetically useful. It would have been better to acknowledge that the rule was imposed, not by aesthetic purism, but by social censorship; to deplore it; and to show how Racine contrived to circumvent and overcome its limitations.

23. 'Les neuf Muses, seins nus, chantaient la Carmagnole.' (Hugo, *Les Contemplations*, 1. 7: *Réponse à un acte d'accusation*; on this subject see p. 405 f.)

24. Dante, *De vulgari eloquio*, mentioned on p. 71 f.

25. See p. 231 f. on the *Deffence et illustration de la langue francoyse*. The French nationalist aspect of the modernist attack in the Battle of the Books is brought out by Gillot (cited in n. 1), 37 f. Many of the moderns felt that it was a struggle between Latin, the international language, and French, which, having ceased to be a dialect, was now asserting itself as a culture-language; and one of the hottest engagements was fought over the question whether an inscription in memory of Louis XIII should be written in Latin or French. (This was the occasion on which Desmarets de Saint-Sorlin (p. 278 f.) published his *Comparaison de la langue et de la poésie française avec la grecque et la latine* (1670).) Another argument sometimes put up by the 'moderns' in France was that French was the ideal speech, far superior in beauty and expressiveness to Latin or any other language, just as France was the perfect country, endowed with every variety of wealth and grace. This thesis, although scarcely worth objective examination, has reappeared in other countries from time to time; we can still hear it to-day, and no doubt to-morrow also.

26. On this see Rigault (cited in n. 1), 159 f.

27. Quoted from R. F. Jones, 'The Background of the *Battle of the Books*' (cited in n. 1), 117; see the same essay, 102 f., on Bacon's increasingly aggressive attitude. The medieval reverence for Aristotle's philosophy was the chief target of this attack, so that many of the 'ancients' joined the modernists in it. Boileau wrote an *Arrêt burlesque* in 1671 to deride the professors who had attempted to procure legislation forbidding the dissemination of Descartes's philosophy and supporting Aristotelian scholasticism. F. Morrison, in 'A Note on *The Battle of the Books*' (*Philological Quarterly*, 13 (1934), 4. 16–20), points out that Swift might have seen that parody before writing his own.

28. Molière, *Le Misanthrope* 1. 2:

> *Alceste*: Ce style figuré, dont on fait vanité,
> Sort du bon caractère et de la vérité:
> Ce n'est que jeu de mots, qu'affectation pure,
> Et ce n'est point ainsi que parle la nature.
> Le méchant goût du siècle, en cela, me fait peur.
> Nos pères, tous grossiers, l'avoient beaucoup meilleur,
> Et je prise bien moins tout ce que l'on admire,
> Qu'une vieille chanson que je m'en vais vous dire:
> > Si le Roi m'avoit donné
> > Paris, sa grand' ville,
> > Et qu'il me fallût quitter
> > L'amour de ma mie,
> > Je dirois au roi Henri:
> > 'Reprenez votre Paris:
> > J'aime mieux ma mie, au gué!
> > J'aime mieux ma mie.'

29. *Éliante*: L'amour, pour l'ordinaire, est peu fait à ces lois,
Et l'on voit les amants vanter toujours leur choix ...

= Lucretius, *De rerum natura*, 4. 1153 f.

30. See Tilley (cited in n. 1), 338 f.; Rigault (n. 1), c. 5; Finsler (n. 1), 191 f.

31. *Pensieri diversi*: the ninth and tenth books contain the arguments which are relevant to the battle. According to Finsler (cited in n. 1), 85 f., it had already appeared in 1601 under the name of *Quistioni filosofiche*. Finsler has a useful discussion of the book, and of another Italian work which carried similar ideas, Paolo Beni's *Comparazione di Torquato Tasso con Omero e Virgilio* (1607). True, the connexion between Tassoni and the French 'moderns' is not very close; but Pierre Perrault published a translation of *La Secchia rapita* in 1678, and used the preface to aim modernist propaganda against Boileau.

32. Boileau, *Art poétique*, 3. 193 f. Finsler (cited in n. 1), 160 f., discusses the epics of Desmarets.

33. This is the *Délices de l'esprit* (1658), which uses arguments 1 and 2, with particular reference to progress in architecture.

34.   Viens défendre, Perrault, la France qui t'appelle;
        Viens combattre avec moi cette troupe rebelle:
        Ce ramas d'ennemis, qui, faibles et mutins,
        Préfèrent à nos chants les ouvrages latins.

(Quoted by Rigault (cited in n. 1), who is the author of the comparison with Hamilcar on p. 279.)

35. These appear as Epigrams 22–8 in Boileau's works. The savages are the Hurons of North America and the Topinambous of Brazil.

36. De Callières's *Histoire poétique de la guerre nouvellement déclarée entre les Anciens et les Modernes* (1688) is summarized by Finsler (cited in n. 1), 186–9, and its model, a battle of pedants and philosophers by Furetière, is described. See also Rigault (cited in n. 1), c. 13.

37. On the 'modernist' arguments in Bayle's *Dictionnaire philosophique* see Finsler (cited in n. 1), 198 f., and Rigault (n. 1), 250 f.

38. Rigault (cited in n. 1), book 2, c. 1: 'L'Angleterre, selon son habitude en toutes choses, nous a pris un peu plus qu'elle ne nous a donné.' A fuller analysis of St. Évremond's attitude to the dispute will be found in Gillot (cited in n. 1), 407–14.

39. On 'Dares' and 'Dictys' see p. 51 f.

40. So J. E. Sandys, *A History of Classical Scholarship* (Cambridge, 1908), 2. 405. See his pp. 401–10 for a sympathetic account of Bentley; there is also a good life by Sir Richard Jebb, and a finely written essay by De Quincey.

41. Pope, *The Dunciad*, 4. 203–74.

42. So Housman, *The Classical Review*, 34 (1920), 110: no doubt partly in irony.

43. *Paradise Lost*, 1. 63.

44. There is a charming essay on 'Milton and Bentley' in Virginia Woolf's *The Common Reader* (London and New York, 1925), and a dazzling analysis of Bentley's emendations of Milton in William Empson's *Some Versions of Pastoral* (London, 1935), 149–91.

45. See Swift's *Apology* (in *The Prose Works of Jonathan Swift*, ed.

H. Davis, Oxford, 1939), pp. 7–8, and the editor's introduction, xxix, with literature there cited.

46. Swift let the tone of epic parody run over into the fable: thus, the spider lives in a terrible fortress, like a giant of romance; there is an unmistakable allusion to the efforts of Homeric heroes in the description of the struggles of the bee ('Thrice he endeavoured to force his passage, and thrice the centre shook'); and the spider thought they meant 'that nature was approaching to her final dissolution; or else, that Beelzebub with all his legions was come. . . .'

47. On Horace and the bee, see p. 226, and n. 13 on p. 628.

48. On Swift's Pindaric odes, see H. Davis's introduction to the edition cited in n. 45, pp. xi–xv.

49. The wit of Bentley's opponents is well described by C. J. Horne, 'The Phalaris Controversy' (*The Review of English Studies*, 1946, 289–303).

50. Reference in n. 41.

51. Nevertheless, there were some good ideas in Houdar de la Motte's preliminary *Discours sur Homère*: see Finsler (cited in n. 1), 214 f.

Notes on 15. A NOTE ON BAROQUE

1. The derivation of 'baroque' given in the text is that which was long accepted, and is found, for example, in the *Oxford English Dictionary*. It was originated by Ménage in his *Dictionnaire étymologique* in 1650, and taken up in 1755 by Winckelmann in his *Sendschreiben*. But another derivation has been proposed by K. Borinski, in *Die Antike in Poetik und Kunsttheorie*, v. 1, *Mittelalter, Renaissance, Barock* (Das Erbe der Alten, 9, Leipzig, 1914)—to whom I owe the references to Ménage and Winckelmann—and Benedetto Croce, in *Storia dell' età barocca* (Scritti di storia letteraria e politica, 23, Bari, 1929). They derive the word from *baroco*, the mnemonic label for a type of syllogism which was used to support far-fetched arguments. Phrases like *argomento in baroco* were, they point out, gradually extended until people spoke of *discorsi barocchi*, 'extravagant disquisitions', and the word came to mean 'extremely sharp-witted', 'weirdly elaborate'. Borinski traces this meaning back to Baltasar Gracián, and connects it with the intellectually extreme conceits, which were fashionable in the Renaissance but became a rage in the age that succeeded it. It would, therefore, be pretty close to the use of 'metaphysical' in seventeenth-century literature.

This derivation, although its context is intellectual, rather than aesthetic like that given in the text, still carries much of the same fundamental meaning of *strain*. It means that reason dominates, but has been pushed to a remote extreme, almost out of balance. That meaning also harmonizes with the description of baroque tension given in the text of this chapter, for the idea of baroque is not single and monolithic, but dual: either 'beauty almost breaking outward from the sphere', or 'intelligence pushed by fancy to a bizarre extreme'.

The word at first had a pejorative sense very close to 'grotesque': on its

German contexts see J. Mark, 'The Uses of the Term "baroque"' (*Modern Language Review*, 33 (1938), 547–63). It has only recently been extended to include all the grand and formal art and thought of the seventeenth and early eighteenth centuries. There is a good analysis of some of its chief implications in W. Weisbach's *Der Barock als Kunst der Gegenreformation* (Berlin, 1921). No study of the subject would be complete without the superb article on the history of the term and its rapid expansion during the last thirty years by René Wellek, 'The Concept of Baroque in Literary Scholarship' (*The Journal of Aesthetics and Art Criticism*, 5 (1946), 2. 77–109). In the same issue there are useful articles by W. Stechow, 'Definitions of the Baroque in the Visual Arts', and R. Daniells, 'English Baroque and Deliberate Obscurity'.

But the intellectual understanding of the term is useless without aesthetic and emotional appreciation. This can be got only from listening to the music, seeing the plays, walking round the noble and gracious buildings, studying the paintings, and reading the prose of the period both for its content and for its style. Sacheverell Sitwell's exquisitely written books will stir any reader's imagination: *Southern Baroque Art* (London, 1924), *German Baroque Art* (London, 1927), *Spanish Baroque Art* (London, 1931). For other works on the subject, see Mr. Wellek's rich bibliography.

2. Macaulay, *The History of England from the Accession of James II*, c. 7, init. Saint-Simon's portrait of the Duc de Bourgogne (on whom see p. 336 f.) gives the same impression of forcible restraint exercised upon violent passions:

'Mgr le duc de Bourgogne étoit né avec un naturel à faire trembler. Il étoit fougueux jusqu'à vouloir briser ses pendules, lorsqu'elles sonnoient l'heure qui l'appeloit à ce qu'il ne vouloit pas, et jusqu'à s'emporter de la plus étrange manière contre la pluie, quand elle s'opposoit à ce qu'il vouloit faire. . . . D'ailleurs, un goût ardent le portoit à tout ce qui est défendu au corps et à l'esprit. . . . Tout ce qui est plaisir, il l'aimoit avec une passion violente, et tout cela avec plus d'orgueil et de hauteur qu'on ne peut exprimer. . . . Le prodige est qu'en très-peu de temps la dévotion et la grâce en firent un autre homme, et changèrent tant et de si redoutables défauts en vertus parfaitement contraires. . . . La violence qu'il s'étoit faite sur tant de défauts et tous véhéments, ce désir de perfection . . . le faisoit excéder dans le contre-pied de ses défauts, et lui inspiroit une autorité qu'il outroit en tout.'

In fact, one of the principal ideals of the baroque era was the Clement Monarch, the man who, like Augustus, combined vast power with superhuman kindness and self-restraint. He appears in many plays and political treatises, and has been apotheosized by Mozart in *La clemenza di Tito* and *Die Entführung aus dem Serail*.

3. The famous eunuch Farinelli, one of the greatest singers who ever lived, could execute a cadenza on one syllable of a song, which covered two octaves and ran to 155 notes ending with a long trill. There is a transcription of such a masterpiece on p. 195 of vol. 1 of D. J. Grout's *A Short History of Opera* (New York, 1947).

4. See H. Peyre's study of the concept, *Le Classicisme français* (New

York, 1942): he observes that English can, while French cannot, use 'classicism' and 'classicizing' to connote extreme formalism going beyond anything deducible from Greek and Roman literature.

Notes on 16. BAROQUE TRAGEDY

1. See C. Müller, *Die Phädra Racine's, eine Quellenstudie* (Leipzig, 1936).
2. On this book see p. 164. Shakespeare knew it too, through Underdown's translation. His Duke, in *Twelfth Night*, 5. 1. 121 f., refers to one of its exciting incidents:

> Why should I not, had I the heart to do it,
> Like to the Egyptian thief at point of death,
> Kill that I love?

The close relation between Heliodorus' romance and *Phèdre* is demonstrated by G. May, 'Contribution à l'étude des sources grecques de *Phèdre*', *Modern Language Quarterly*, 8 (1947), 228–34; there are echoes in *Andromaque* and other plays too.

3. On Milton and the Greeks there is a good monograph by W. R. Parker, *Milton's Debt to Greek Tragedy in 'Samson Agonistes'* (Baltimore, 1937). Mr. Parker points out that it is impossible to assess Milton's precise debt to any one of the three tragedians, because he so completely assimilated what he learned from them. According to Milton's daughter Euripides was his favourite; certainly he often quotes Euripides in his non-dramatic writings. Aeschylus, however, evidently supplied the model for Samson, and also for the technique which keeps one actor alone on the stage through nearly half the play. In other things—the role of the chorus, the use of irony, the nature of the denouement—Mr. Parker believes Milton chiefly followed Sophocles.

4. On the size of the theatre audience in seventeenth-century Paris there is an estimate in H. C. Lancaster's monumental *History of French Dramatic Literature in the Seventeenth Century* (Baltimore and Paris, 1929–42), which has recently been criticized by J. Lough in *French Studies*, 1 (April 1947), 2. Mr. Lough quotes Voltaire's remark in 1733 that there were less than 4,000 people in Paris who went constantly to the theatre; and he estimates the regular public of the Comédie Française at 10,000 to 17,000.

5. *Hamlet*, 3. 4. 212.

6.   Nay, but to live
> In the rank sweat of an enseamed bed,
> Stewed in corruption, honeying and making love
> Over the nasty sty!
>   O, speak to me no more.   (*Hamlet*, 3. 4. 91 f.)

7. *Macbeth*, 1. 5. 51 f.; *The Rambler*, 26 Oct. 1751.
8. See p. 272, and note 15 on p. 642.
9. Aesch. *Agamemnon*, 109 f.

10. Et Pâris, couronnant son insolente flamme,
     Retiendra sans péril la sœur de votre femme?
     (Racine, *Iphigénie*, I. 2.)

11. Racine, *Iphigénie*, 2. 4.

12. For a sketch of the origin of these 'laws', see p. 142 f.; and consult C. H. C. Wright, *French Classicism* (Harvard Studies in Romance Languages, 4, Cambridge, Mass., 1920), cc. 8 and 9.

13. H. Peyre, 'Les Règles', in *Le Classicisme français* (New York, 1942), 91–103.

Notes on 17. SATIRE

1. There has recently been an attempt to derive *satura* from the Etruscan *satir* (= 'speech'), but it is more probable that it comes from *satur*, 'full', the derivation which is alluded to in Livy's *impletas modis saturas* (7. 2) and Juvenal's *nostri farrago libelli* (1. 86). 'Farce', which comes from the Low Latin *farsa*, 'stuffing', is a similar word.

2. On Horace's lyrics, see p. 225 f.

3. The manuscripts call this work the *Ludus de morte Claudi*, but it is usually thought to be the same as the *Apocolocyntosis* which Dio says Seneca wrote to amuse Nero's court. 'Pumpkin' in the title corresponds to the Latin *cucurbita*, slang for 'fool': the point therefore is that the process of deification, instead of making a real god of Claudius, made a fool of him. The British parallel is Byron's *Vision of Judgment*, which satirizes Southey's apotheosis of George III.

4. The title is *Satirica* or *Satyrica*, not *Satiricon*, which is a genitive plural depending on *libri*. On the purpose of this work and its relation to the character of its author, see G. Highet, 'Petronius the Moralist', in *Transactions of the American Philological Association*, 72 (1941), 176–94.

5. For this point see p. 66 f.

6. *Brief life is here our portion* and *For thee, O dear, dear country* also come from Bernard's poem, of which there is a fine edition by H. C. Hoskier (London, 1929). See also T. Wright's *The Anglo-Latin Satirical Poets and Epigrammatists of the Twelfth Century* (London, 1872) for other works of this type, a particularly interesting one being the *Architrenius* of John de Hauteville (fl. 1184).

7. Juvenal, 10. 81.

8. Juvenal, 6. 660–1.

9. Housman, *A Shropshire Lad*, 48.

10. Juvenal, 1. 79. Swift's epitaph: HIC DEPOSITVM EST CORPVS JONATHAN SWIFT, S.T.P., VBI SAEVA INDIGNATIO VLTERIVS COR LACERARE NEQVIT.

11. Here is a specimen of Abraham's style, in the form of a brilliant antiphonal parody of Psalm cx. He says that many when they are singing vespers are thinking of the evening's gambling, like this:

DIXIT DOMINUS DOMINO MEO	heut gehen wir zum Herrn Leo
SEDE A DEXTRIS MEIS	heut werde ich gewinnen, das ist gewiss
DONEC PONAM INIMICOS TUOS	gestern hab ich verspilt drey Mass
SCABELLUM PEDUM TUORUM	heut wird sich das Glück kehren um
VIRGAM VIRTUTIS TUAE	was gilts ich werd haben figuri tre....

(*Judas der Erzschelm*, 3. 103.)

See Hugo Mareta, *Ueber 'Judas der Erzschelm' von Abraham a Sancta Clara* (no date, no place, *circa* 1875); Theodor von Karajan, *Abraham a Sancta Clara* (Vienna, 1867); K. Bertsche, *Abraham a Sancta Clara* (Munich, 1922²). I could scarcely find any of Abraham's works in the bookshops of ten German cities in 1945–6. The Vienna Akademie der Wissenschaften is issuing his works from the original manuscript: volume 3 appeared in 1945; but they are very difficult to come by.

12. Much of Casaubon's invaluable commentary is now embodied in Conington's commentary on Persius, and Dryden took over a great deal of his essay on satire for the *Discourse concerning Satire* with which he prefaced his translation of Juvenal.

13. There is a good verse translation, introduction, and commentary (containing a useful bibliography, and illustrated with the original woodcuts) by E. H. Zeydel (New York, 1944).

14. Brant's friend Locher made a Latin translation of the work as *Stultifera nauis* (1497), and included (with Brant's help) a conspectus of its sources, which has been worked over by modern scholars. Mr. Zeydel (n. 13) gives Brant's chief Latin sources as: the Vulgate, Ovid, the *Appendix Vergiliana*, Juvenal, Terence, Seneca; he also knew something of Catullus, Cicero, Persius, and Boethius; and he had read Plutarch's essay *On the Education of Children*, Xenophon, and Homer, apparently in Latin translations.

15. A. K. Foxwell, *A Study of Sir Thomas Wyatt's Poems* (London, 1911), observes in c. 11 that 'very little classical influence' is to be traced in these satires; but the reminiscences of Juvenal and others are pretty clear. The first, for instance, begins with a variation of Horace's fable of the town mouse and the country mouse (Hor. *Serm.* 2. 6); the second has a good adaptation of Juvenal's tremendous sneer:

> quid Romae faciam? mentiri nescio . . . (3. 41 f.).

Details will be found in R. M. Alden, *The Rise of Formal Satire in England under Classical Influence* (Philadelphia, 1899), 52 f.

16. See R. M. Alden (cited in n. 15), 67 f.

17. The story is in Alden (cited in n. 15), 98 f.

18. For an interesting development of the suggestion that the satiric spirit, its direct outlet choked by this ban, flowed into drama, see O. J. Campbell's *Comicall Satyre and Shakespeare's 'Troilus and Cressida'* (San Marino, Cal., 1938).

19. See p. 183 f.

20. See F. Giroux, *La Composition de la Satire Ménippée* (Laon, 1904).

21. As often with emulators of classical patterns during the Renaissance, priority is difficult to decide. According to L. Petit de Julleville, in his *Histoire de la langue et de la littérature française*, 4. 30 f., Vauquelin de la Fresnaye published his satires in 1605, but Régnier's had been circulating in manuscript before that.

22. 　　　　Or c'est un grand chemin jadis assez frayé
　　　　Qui des rimeurs françois ne fut oncq' essayé:
　　　　Suivant les pas d'Horace, entrant en la carrière,
　　　　Je trouve des humeurs de diverse manière. 　　(*Sat.* 14.)

23. These five leading elements in Régnier's work are distinguished by
L. Petit de Julleville in his chapter on Régnier, referred to in n. 21.

24.   Je n'entends point le cours du ciel ni des planètes,
        Je ne sais deviner les affaires secrètes.   (*Sat.* 3.)

Compare Juvenal, 3. 42–7:

                        Motus
astrorum ignoro; funus promittere patris
nec uolo nec possum; ranarum uiscera numquam
inspexi; ferre ad nuptam quae mittit adulter,
quae mandat, norint alii: me nemo ministro
fur erit. . . .

Courtiers particularly liked this satire: Wyat had already used it; see note
15.

25. 'Du siècle les mignons, fils de la poule blanche' (*Sat.* 3); cf.
Juvenal, 13. 141:

               gallinae filius albae.

(Were the white hen's eggs the best in the farmyard, or was she simply a
favourite because of her colour?) Among Régnier's satires 3 is inspired
by Juvenal, 3; 7 by Lucretius, 4. 1134 f. and Ovid, *Am.* 2. 4; 8 by Horace,
1. 9, with verbatim quotations; 12 more or less by Horace, 1. 4; 13 by
Ovid, *Am.* 1. 8 and Prop. 4. 5, with quotations from other poems; and
15 by Horace, 2. 3. Many other quotations are easily identifiable: for
instance, Petronius, *Satirica*, 127 f., turns up in *Sat.* 11.

26.   Il faut suivre un sentier qui soit moins rebatu,
        Et, conduit d'Apollon, recognoistre la trace
        Du libre Juvénal; trop discret est Horace
        Pour un homme picqué. . . .   (*Sat.* 2, init.)

27.   Devant moy justement on plante un grand potage
        D'où les mousches à jeun se sauvoient à la nage.   (*Sat.* 10.)

28.   Ainsi dedans la tête
        Voyoit-on clairement au travers de ses os
        Ce dont sa fantaisie animoit ses propos.   (*Sat.* 11.)

Probably either Régnier or his Italian model knew the coarser version of
this idea in *Priapea*, 32. 5-6, about the thin girl

        cuius uiscera non aperta Tuscus
        per pellem poterit uidere haruspex.

29.   Trois dents de mort pliez en du parchemin vierge.   (*Sat.* 11.)

30. Satire 13, about the religious bawd, comes partly from contemporary
life, partly from Ovid (*Am.* 1. 8), partly from Propertius, 4. 5, and partly
from the *Roman de la Rose*, which in its turn (see p. 66 f.) took something
from Juvenal, 6.

31. Dryden himself was responsible for satires 1, 3, 6, 10, and 16.

32. This is Juvenal's fourth satire. There is also a Greek mock-heroic
satire, a Battle of the Philosophers, called Σίλλοι, 'Sneers', by Timon of
Phlius (fl. 280 B.C.), of which considerable fragments remain; but it is
unlikely that Dryden knew them.

33. A. F. B. Clark, in his *Boileau and the French Classical Critics in England* (Bibliothèque de la Revue de Littérature Comparée, 19, Paris, 1925), 153–5, suggests that *La secchia rapita* is not the ancestor of Boileau's *Lutrin* and Pope's *Rape of the Lock*, because (*a*) it is longer, and (*b*) it is really quite a serious poem with burlesque exaggerations. Nevertheless, the subject of all three poems is the same: a tremendous conflict over nothing. The fact that in Tassoni's poem the conflict is a real war, while in Boileau's it is an ecclesiastical dispute and in Pope's a social feud, is not an essential difference, but a change in style from Renaissance to baroque and rococo. (Even in *La secchia rapita* the war is not a serious, nearly contemporary war, but a tussle between two little city-states hundreds of years earlier, whose champions are fools.) And Boileau himself, in *Le Lutrin*, 4, invokes the muse who inspired Tassoni; while Pope's title is an obvious allusion to Tassoni's title as translated by Ozell. The real difference between the poems is that *La secchia rapita* is a parody of Renaissance chivalric epic, and in particular of *The Liberation of Jerusalem* (Tassoni *v.* Tasso), while the other two are parodies of the purely classical epic; but that difference is not enough to make the satires belong to different types. In *The Rape of the Lock* some beautiful parodies of Pope's own translation of Homer have recently been pointed out by W. Frost. See '*The Rape of the Lock* and Pope's Homer' (*Modern Language Quarterly*, 8 (1947), 3. 342–54). Mr. Frost suggests that, although the translation appeared later than *The Rape*, some of the most notable lines in it already existed in Pope's mind or in manuscript when he was writing his satire.

34. For some remarks on the relation of *The Dunciad* to classical satire, see G. Highet, '*The Dunciad*', in *The Modern Language Review*, 36 (1941), 3. 320–43.

35. There is a good analysis of the relation between originals and adaptations by J. W. Tupper, 'A Study of Pope's *Imitations of Horace*', in *PMLA*, 15 (1900), 181–215. The real difference (as we should expect) is that Pope adds far more of his own personal friendships and hatreds, makes many passages more vividly real than their originals by introducing much contemporary detail, and, on the whole, expands rather than contracts his borrowings.

36. The debt of English baroque satire to Roman originals should never be assessed without reference to its almost equally considerable debt to Boileau. Thus, Juvenal begins satire 10 with a world-sweeping glance:

> Omnibus in terris, quae sunt a Gadibus usque
> Auroram et Gangen. . . .

Johnson's variation on this is justly famous:

> Let observation, with extensive view,
> Survey mankind from China to Peru.

Yet the best thing in that comes from Boileau (*Satire* 8, init.):

> De tous les animaux qui s'élèvent dans l'air,
> Qui marchent sur la terre ou nagent dans la mer,
> De Paris au Pérou, du Japon jusqu'à Rome,
> Le plus sot animal, à mon avis, c'est l'homme.

37. Juvenal, 1. 127 f., gives the idea of describing the entire course of the day:

> Ipse dies pulchro distinguitur ordine rerum. . . .

Persius, 3, begins with a spoilt and lazy young man waking up late in the morning, and goes on with a long apostrophe to him, as Parini's poem does. These reminiscences do not diminish the admirable originality of *Il giorno*.

38. Boileau, letter to Racine, 7 October 1692.

39. Pope, *The Dunciad*, 4. 551–4.

40. Boileau, *Satire* 8. 29–39.

41. Dryden, *Absalom and Achitophel*, 1. 108–15.

42. Boileau, *Art poétique*, 2. 175–8.

43. D. Mornet, *Nicolas Boileau* (Paris, 1942), 101 f. On p. 57 Mr. Mornet points out that Régnier's satires were reissued several times after his death, but that from 1641 onwards each successive edition was cleaned up a little more.

44. See p. 272.

45. Boileau, *Satire* 6. 37–8 and 6. 94; Juvenal, 3. 292–5.

46. Dryden, *Absalom and Achitophel*, 2. 464–5.

47. Pope, *Epistle to Dr. Arbuthnot*, 309–10.

48. Persius, 3. 34; Dante, *Inf*. 7. 117 f., with a good sound-effect.

49. Boileau, *Satire* 10. 195–200.

50. Juvenal, 6. 461–4, 471–3:

> Interea foeda aspectu ridendaque multo
> pane tumet facies, aut pinguia Poppaeana
> spirat, et hinc miseri uiscantur labra mariti.
> Ad moechum ueniunt lota cute. . . .
> Sed quae mutatis inducitur atque fouetur
> tot medicaminibus coctaeque siliginis offas
> accipit et madidae, facies dicetur an ulcus?

Swift's *On a Young Nymph going to Bed* is far worse than this.

51. Régnier, *Satire* 3. 82; Juvenal, 13, 105.

52. Boileau, *Satire* 12, *L'Équivoque*.

53. A useful proof of this limitation of scope is to count the persons actually mentioned in one of Boileau's satires, and to compare the number with those mentioned in its Roman original or in a Roman satire of similar size. For instance, in his eighth satire, which is 308 lines long, Boileau mentions

> seven living men
> six recently dead
> eight historical figures, from Aesop to Calvin.

In Juvenal, 8, approximately the same length, there are

> twenty-three living people
> twenty-five historical figures;

and in Horace, *Serm*. 2. 3, with 326 lines altogether, we find

> thirty living people
> twenty-four dead characters.

Pope usually errs in the other direction, and puts in a bewildering assortment of characters. In Boileau the tendency to turn the eyes away from real life developed so far that in his last satire, *L'Équivoque*, on the important subject of Jesuitry, there are no living men at all, only four who had died within recent memory, and eight historical characters, or waxworks.

54. Pope, *Epistle to Dr. Arbuthnot*, 203.

55. Boileau, *Épître* 10, ad fin.

Notes on 18. BAROQUE PROSE

1. This was Scudéry's *Clélie*.

2. In this section I am much indebted to the brilliant essays of Professor M. W. Croll. See in particular his '"Attic Prose" in the Seventeenth Century', in *Studies in Philology*, 18 (1921), 2. 79-128; 'Muret and the History of "Attic" Prose', in *PMLA*, 39 (1924), 254-309; and 'The Baroque Style in Prose', in *Studies in English Philology . . . in honour of Frederick Klaeber* (Minneapolis, 1929), 427-56. Professor Croll prefers to use the phrase 'baroque style' for only one of the two rival schools of prose which flourished in the late sixteenth, the seventeenth, and the eighteenth centuries: the 'anti-Ciceronian' school. That is, of course, his right; but I cannot help thinking that baroque architecture and music, highly decorated, full of complex symmetries and counterbalancing variations on a fundamentally simple design, have more in common with the elaborations of Ciceronianism, and that either a style like Johnson's should be called pure baroque or the term should be extended to cover both styles.

3. On Asianism and Atticism, see E. Norden, *Die antike Kunstprosa* (Leipzig, 1898), 1. 251-99; and Wilamowitz's remarkable essay 'Asianismus und Atticismus' in *Hermes*, 35 (1900), 1-52. Cicero's *Brutus* and *Orator* show his side of the controversy: true to his guiding principle, he endeavoured to show that his own style embodied the essentials of both schools.

4. The distinction is made by Professor M. W. Croll, 'The Baroque Style in Prose' (cited in n. 2), 431 f. It is important to grasp the difference in the origins of the two styles. The *période coupée*, the 'curt manner', was consciously modelled on Seneca. The 'loose manner' was not really modelled closely on any classical author, but was built up from the double wish (a) not to be formal like Cicero, and (b) to reflect the flexibility and the occasional inconsequence and vagueness of the processes of thought.

5. Burton, *The Anatomy of Melancholy*, partition 1, section 2, member 2, subsection 6, med. (London edition, 1924, p. 161).

6. Donne, Sermon 34 (St. Paul's, Whitsunday 1623).

7. There is an able introduction to this subject, with a good bibliography, 'The First Political Commentary on Tacitus', by A. Momigliano, in *The Journal of Roman Studies*, 37 (1947), 91-101.

8. This incident is quoted by J. E. Sandys in his edition of the first *Philippic* and the *Olynthiacs* (London, 1897), preface, p. ix f.

9. Demosthenic passages occur in Pitt's speeches on the motion for augmenting the national force in case of invasion (18 Oct. 1796), on the

general defence bill (2 June 1801), and on the volunteer regulation bill (27 Feb. 1804).· These references, and the fact about Niebuhr, are given by J. E. Sandys (quoted in n. 8). On a similar use of Demosthenes' speeches against Philip at an earlier date, see p. 122.

10. See T. Zielinski, *Cicero im Wandel der Jahrhunderte* (Leipzig, 1912³), 247 and note. Speaking through Memmius, Voltaire heaps praises on Cicero's book *On Moral Duties*. Memmius was the patron of the philosopher-poet Lucretius.

11. Voltaire, *Commentaire sur le livre 'Des Délits et des peines'* (1766), c. 22.

12. Juvenal, 8. 124: *spoliatis arma supersunt*; quoted from Burke's speech on Conciliation with the Colonies, 22 March 1775.

13. On the use of classical citations in epic, see p. 156 f.

14. Browne, *The Garden of Cyrus*, 5. 12.

15. Vergil, *Georg.* 1. 250–1:

> Nosque ubi primus equis Oriens adflauit anhelis
> illic sera rubens accendit lumina Vesper.

The account is taken from J. E. Sandys, *A History of Classical Scholarship* (Cambridge, 1908), 2. 433 f.

16. Faydit, quoted by A. Hurel, *Les Orateurs sacrés à la cour de Louis XIV* (Paris, 1872), 1. 335 n. In an essay written to advise a young orator Bossuet says that his aim was to combine St. John Chrysostom and St. Augustine: 'ce que j'ai appris du style, je le tiens des livres latins et un peu des grecs; de Platon, d'Isocrate, et de Démosthène, dont j'ai lu aussi quelque chose . . . de Cicéron, surtout de ses livres . . . mais aussi de ses discours, avec choix . . . enfin Tite-Live, Salluste, Térence.' He says it is to them he owes his style 'tourné et figuré', and advises learning one's own language first, and then studying the literatures of other countries, 'surtout la latine, dont le génie n'est pas éloigné de celui de la nôtre, ou plutôt est tout le même'. (Quoted by A. Rebelliau in Petit de Julleville's *Histoire de la langue et de la littérature française*, 5. 5.)

17. *Chair angélisée* is quoted by F. Brunetière, *Bossuet* (Paris, 1914²), 31, from the sermon on the First Assumption, section 2. The other words are given by F. Brunot in L. Petit de Julleville's *Histoire de la langue et de la littérature française*, 5. 795 f.

18. There are long lists of Johnson's favourite words of Latin origin in H. Schmidt, *Der Prosastil Samuel Johnson's* (Marburg, 1905), 4 f. A study of their nature, which shows that the heaviness of his style is due to the fact that they are predominantly intellectual in content, has been made by Z. E. Chandler, *An Analysis of the Stylistic Technique of Addison, Johnson, Hazlitt, and Pater* (University of Iowa Humanistic Studies, 4. 3, Iowa City, 1928).

19. Boswell, *Life of Johnson* (Oxford ed., 1924), 2. 569.

20. See G. Guillaumie, *J. L. Guez de Balzac et la prose française* (Paris, 1927), 132 f. Balzac attacked the use of such words as *onguent* and *auspices* ('c'est parler latin en français'), and reproached even Richelieu for calling someone a *pétulant exagérateur*. He himself, nevertheless, used

words like *vécordie*, *helluon*, and *remore* (= *retard*): which shows, not that his standards were uneven, but that the plague of pedantic latinisms was very widespread. His real name, by the way, was Guez; Balzac was the name of a property in his mother's dowry, and he added it in order to appear noble.

21. Browne, *Urn Burial*, c. 5.
22. Johnson, *Life of Savage.*
23. Browne, *Letter to a Friend.*
24. Bossuet, *Sur l'honneur du monde*, 2.
25. Milton, *Areopagitica.*
26. Bossuet, *Sur la justice*, 3.
27. Bacon, *Of Studies.*
28. Donne, Sermon 66 (29 Jan. 1625/6).
29. Pope, *Letter to a Noble Lord.*
30. Lincoln, *Gettysburg Address.*
31. Bourdaloue, *La Misère de notre condition.* (He went on, after this heaping up of separate terms, to work out each separately. See F. Brunetière, 'L'Éloquence de Bourdaloue', in *Études critiques sur l'histoire de la littérature française*, huitième série (Paris, 1907), 151 f.)
32. Joyce, *A Portrait of the Artist as a Young Man*, c. 3 init. (London, 1928, p. 133 f.).
33. Bourdaloue, *Sur le royaume de Dieu* (14th Sunday after Pentecost). See M. F. Hitz, *Die Redekunst in Bourdaloues Predigt* (Munich, 1936), 44.
34. 'Trouvez-moi, je vous en défie, dans quelque poète et dans quelque livre qu'il vous plaira, une belle chose qui ne soit pas une image ou une antithèse.' (Voltaire, quoted by Guillaumie (cited in n. 20), 444.) Antithesis ran mad in a comparatively early elaboration of English prose style —Euphuism. The precise origin of this curious set of mannerisms has not yet been determined. However, in an article called 'The Immediate Source of Euphuism' (*PMLA*, 53 (1938), 3. 678–86), W. Ringler gives reason for believing that Lyly and the others got it from the brilliant and celebrated Latin lectures of John Rainolds, of Corpus Christi College, Oxford, whose effects they set out to reproduce in English. The next question is, if this is true, where did Rainolds get it? Mr. Ringler thinks he modelled his style on 'St. Augustine and Gregory Nazianzen'—which seems rather hard to believe—and on the teaching of the anti-Ciceronian humanist Vives. Now Vives himself was at Corpus from 1523 to 1525, and gave two remarkable courses of lectures (Sandys, *A History of Classical Scholarship*, Cambridge, 1908, 2. 214–15): he was a friend of Erasmus, another opponent of the imitation of Cicero, and was a superb teacher. If we consider that Euphuism is (*a*) highly formal and artificial, (*b*) carefully symmetrical, (*c*) highly alliterative, (*d*) excessively learned, and (*e*) not Ciceronian, we might conjecture that it was an English reflection of a newly created type of Latin style, worked out by a humanist like Vives who wished to achieve as much intricacy and artistry as Cicero without using Cicero's own patterns. (The speeches of Isocrates, whom Vives would no doubt know, combine alliteration and assonance and antithesis rather like Euphuism, although more moderately.)

35. Donne, *Devotions*, 17.

36. Balzac, *Socr. disc.* 11, quoted by Guillaumie (cited in n. 20). M. Guillaumie, on p. 461 f., shows how Balzac gave French prose a new and smoother harmony, by cultivating symmetry of all kinds: antithesis, grammatical parallelisms, balanced rhythms, blended sounds. Balzac formed his style partly by his own excellent taste, partly by his admirable training in Latin (received from a Jesuit teacher, Garasse), and partly by the refining influence of the Italian orators and prose-writers, working both in Italian and in Latin. 'Fusion harmonieuse du génie latin et du goût français, tel nous apparaîtra l'art de Balzac', says M. Guillaumie on p. 111. In view of this it is unfortunate that M. Guillaumie should have written a long book on Balzac, dominated by the idea that it is a mistake for talented students to learn Latin: he calls the education which Balzac himself believed largely responsible for his talent 'ce préjugé si tenace et . . . si funeste' (26), and says it gave him 'la fausse illusion d'avoir pénétré dans la pensée intime et l'âme véritable des anciens' (77). Yet the rest of the book is devoted to proving how much Balzac profited from this injurious system.

37. Swift, *A Voyage to Laputa*, c. 6.

38. Pope, *Epistle to Dr. Arbuthnot*, 201–2.

39. Pitt on the war with the American colonies (*On the Motion for an Address to the Throne*, 18 Nov. 1777).

40. Donne, Sermon 48 (25 Jan. 1628/9).

41. Browne, *Urn Burial*, c. 5.

42. Bossuet, *Oraison funèbre d'Henriette d'Angleterre*.

43. Johnson, *Letter to Lord Chesterfield*. From a later age there is a famous and beautiful tricolon in Landor's *Aesop and Rhodope*:

'Laodameia died; Helen died; Leda, the beloved of Jupiter, went before.'

44. 'On jetait des louis d'or à la tête des libraires' (Brunetière, *Histoire de la littérature française classique* (Paris, 1904), 2. 4. 2). On the popularity of the book abroad, see A. Eckhardt, 'Télémaque en Hongrie' (*Revue des études hongroises*, 4 (1926), 166 f.); H. G. Martin, *Fénelon en Hollande* (Amsterdam, 1928); and G. Maugain, *Documenti bibliografici e critici per la storia della fortuna del Fénelon in Italia* (Bibliothèque de l'Institut français de Florence, 1. 1, Paris, 1910).

45. On *Astrée* see p. 170.

46. Thus, book 12 contains a potted version of Sophocles' tragedies *Philoctetes* and *Trachiniae*; and book 9, in which Mentor calms a group of savages by the power of speech, takes up the opening theme of Cicero's *De inuentione*. Zielinski, *Cicero im Wandel der Jahrhunderte* (Leipzig, 1912³), 321–2, says that this ideal continued to be potent in the days of the French Revolution, apparently through Fénelon's evocation of it: 'die Schaufenster der Buchläden boten gern das Bild des beredten Greises, der mit seinem Wort die aufgeregte Menge bezaubert.' There is a short list of Fénelon's borrowings from the classics in P. Janet, *Fénelon* (Paris, 1892), 123 f., and fuller information in L. Boulve, *De l'hellénisme chez Fénelon* (Paris, 1897).

47. On *Arcadia* see p. 167.

48. On the educational content of Homer's epics see W. Jaeger, *Paideia*, 1 (Oxford, 1939), c. 3.

49. For an expansion of this, see A. Tilley, *The Decline of the Age of Louis XIV* (Cambridge, 1929), c. 8.

50. See Brunetière (cited in n. 44).

51. Details in E. Poetzsche, *Samuel Richardsons Belesenheit* (Kieler Studien zur englischen Philologie, n.F. 4, Kiel, 1908).

52. Richardson, *Pamela* (Oxford, 1929 edition), 3, letter 18, p. 93.

53. Richardson, *Pamela* (Oxford, 1929 edition), 2, p. 55.

54. Richardson, *Clarissa* (Oxford, 1930 edition), 3, letter 59, p. 318. The next batch of lighter books consisted of 'Steele's, Rowe's, and Shakespeare's Plays'.

55. On Sidney's *Arcadia* see pp. 169–70.

56. See M. Gassmeyer, *Samuel Richardson's 'Pamela', ihre Quellen und ihr Einfluss auf die englische Literatur* (Leipzig, 1890), 11 f.

57. So S. L. Wolff, in *Greek Romances in Elizabethan Prose Fiction* (New York, 1912), 463 n. If there are references in *Pamela* to the content of *Arcadia*, I have been unable to trace them.

58. Richardson got the pronunciation wrong. In Sidney it was Paméla, as is shown by one of the lyrics where it appears as 'Philóclea ánd Paméla swéet': probably meant to be *Πάμμηλα* (cf. *εὔμηλος*), 'rich in flocks of sheep'. Richardson made his heroine mispronounce her own name in *Verses on My Going Away* (letter 31), where she scanned it Pámela, as everyone does nowadays. Fielding sneered at this immediately in his parody *Joseph Andrews*: 'they had a daughter of a very strange name, Pamĕla, or Pamēla; some pronounced it one way, and some the other' (4. 12).

59.   Tuscan and French are in my head,
Latin I write, and Greek—I read.
(Fielding, *Letter to Walpole*, 1730).

60. See *Tom Jones*, bk. 8, c. 1, on the 'marvellous'; and the preface to *Joseph Andrews* on the ridiculous in epic.

61. A. Dobson, *Eighteenth-century Vignettes* (London, 1896), 3. 163 f.

62. On the Greek romances see p. 163 f.

63. 'Thus the Telemachus of the Archbishop of Cambray appears to me of the epic kind, as well as the Odyssey of Homer; indeed it is much fairer and more reasonable to give it a name common with that species from which it differs only in a single instance, than to confound it with those which it resembles in no other—such as those voluminous works, commonly called Romances, namely, Clelia, Cleopatra, Astraea, Cassandra, the Grand Cyrus, and innumerable others, which contain, as I apprehend, very little instruction or entertainment'—Fielding, *Joseph Andrews*, preface, init. Fielding then confuses confusion, by going on in the next sentence to talk of his own work as a comic romance, and defining a comic romance as a comic epic poem in prose. This shows that he dimly

recognized the presence of both elements in his book—only felt that epic was more vigorous and manly, and disliked romances as artificial and unreal.

64. On Gibbon's Oxford days, see p. 494.

65. See A. J. Toynbee, *A Study of History* (Oxford, 1939), 5. 506 n. and 5. 643–5 on Gibbon's choice of English as the vehicle of his great work, which Mr. Toynbee attributes to the victory of Britain in the Seven Years war. (He also has an interesting mention of the influence of Gibbon's style on the young Abraham Lincoln.)

66. Bossuet, *Discours sur l'histoire universelle*, 3. 8 init.: 'Dieu tient du plus haut des cieux les resnes de tous les royaumes; il a tous les cœurs en sa main: tantost il retient les passions, tantost il leur lasche la bride, et par là il remuë tout le genre humain. . . . Il connoist la sagesse humaine toûjours courte par quelque endroit; il l'éclaire, il étend ses veûës, et puis il l'abandonne à ses ignorances; il l'aveugle, il la précipite, il la confond par elle-mesme. . . . Ne parlons plus de hazard ni de fortune, ou parlons-en seulement comme d'un nom dont nous couvrons nostre ignorance. Ce qui est hazard à l'égard de nos conseils incertains est un dessein concerté dans un conseil plus haut'—a remark which chimes with the teaching of Boethius in his last book (p. 42).

67. See R. G. Collingwood's remarks in *The Idea of History* (Oxford, 1946), 117 f. on the general character of Christian historiography.

68. These quotations are from Black, *The Art of History* (New York and London, 1926), 144 f., who refers to Bagehot, *Literary Studies*, 1. 226; Sainte-Beuve, *Causeries du lundi*, 8. 456, and Harrison, 'The Centenary of Gibbon', in *Memories and Thoughts*.

69. See p. 10.

70. Montesquieu also tailed off towards the end. See Gibbon's explanation of his change of plan (with an explicit quotation of Montesquieu's final phrase) at the beginning of his c. 48.

71.   Puis, d'une main encor plus fine et plus habile,
      Pèse sans passion Chapelain et Virgile;
      Remarque en ce dernier beaucoup de pauvretés,
      Mais pourtant confessant qu'il a quelques beautés,
      Ne trouve en Chapelain, quoi qu'ait dit la satire,
      Autre défaut sinon qu'on ne le saurait lire.
                          (Boileau, *Satire* 10. 453–8).

72. Here is a characteristic succession of these simple sentence-patterns, from c. 55, p. 518 of the Everyman edition, vol. 5:

'But the saints were deaf or inexorable; and the torrent rolled forwards, till it was stopped by the extreme land of Calabria. A composition was offered and accepted for the head of each Italian subject; and ten bushels of silver were poured forth in the Turkish camp. But falsehood is the natural antagonist of violence; and the robbers were defrauded both in the numbers of the assessment and the standard of the metal. On the side of the East the Hungarians were opposed in doubtful conflict by the equal arms of the Bulgarians, whose faith forbade an alliance with the pagans, and whose situation formed the barrier of the Byzantine empire. The barrier was overturned; the emperor of Constantinople beheld the waving banners of the Turks; and one of their boldest warriors presumed to strike a battle-axe into the golden gate. The arts and treasures of the Greeks diverted the assault; but the Hungarians might boast in their retreat that they had imposed a tribute on the spirit of Bulgaria and the majesty of the Caesars. The remote and rapid operations of the same campaign appear to magnify the power and numbers of the Turks; but their courage is most deserving of praise, since a light troop of three or four hundred horse would often attempt and execute the most daring inroads to the gates of Thessalonica and Constantinople. At this disastrous era of the ninth and tenth centuries, Europe was afflicted by a triple scourge from the North, the East, and the South: the Norman, the Hungarian, and the Saracen sometimes trod the same ground of desolation; and these savage foes might have been compared by Homer to the two lions growling over the carcase of a mangled stag.'

73. Dickens, *Our Mutual Friend*, c. 5.

74. J. B. Bury, in *Encyclopaedia Britannica*, s.v. 'Roman Empire, Later'.

75. Coleridge, *Table Talk*, 15 Aug. 1833.

76. Gibbon, *The Decline and Fall of the Roman Empire*, c. 6 init. (Everyman edition, 1. 126). Yet contrast his remark at the beginning of c. 9 (Everyman edition, 1. 213): 'a state of ignorance and poverty, which it has pleased some declaimers to dignify with the appellation of virtuous simplicity.'

77. Gibbon, c. 2 fin. (Everyman edition, 1. 58). A variation of this reason to which he often refers is that long peace made the Romans degenerate and soft.

78. Gibbon, c. 5 init. (Everyman edition, 1. 101). See also c. 7 fin. and Bury's appendix 11, in his edition.

79. Gibbon, c. 35 fin. (Everyman edition, 3. 406): this is one of the favourite modern explanations, particularly since the financial administration of Roman Egypt has been revealed to us in great detail by recently discovered papyri.

80. Gibbon, c. 38 fin. (Everyman edition, 4. 103 f.). The 'four principal causes of the ruin of Rome' set out in Gibbon's last chapter (Everyman edition, 6. 550 f.) concern only the destruction of the city, not that of the empire and its civilization; but they take us back to the young man sitting in the ruins of the Temple of Jupiter (see p. 352). J. W. Swain, 'Edward Gibbon and the Decline of Rome' (*South Atlantic Quarterly*, 39 (1940), 1. 77–93), says the essay in c. 38 was written before 1772, and perhaps as early as 1767. Professor Swain points out interesting parallels between Gibbon's changing attitude (altering from one volume to another) to the real cause and significance of Rome's decline, and the changes in his own political situation, and the changing fortunes of the British empire, with particular reference to the loss of the American colonies.

81. Walter Moyle, *Works* (London, 1726), v. 1. On Spengler see pp. 267–8.

82. Gibbon, c. 10 init. (Everyman edition, 1. 238).

83. Gibbon, c. 10 fin. (Everyman edition, 1. 274).

84. There is a fine survey by Professor N. H. Baynes, 'The Decline of

Roman Power in Western Europe—Some Modern Explanations', in *JRS*, 33 (1943).

85. The date was 15 Oct. 1764: see Gibbon's autobiography, p. 167.
86. The arguments advanced by Gibbon's opponents are usefully summarized in S. T. McCloy's book *Gibbon's Antagonism to Christianity and the Discussions that it Provoked* (Chapel Hill, North Carolina, 1933).
87. Gibbon, c. 28: see especially the last pages (Everyman edition, 3. 145–7).
88. Gibbon, c. 50 fin. (Everyman edition, 5. 290–2).
89. Gibbon, c. 71 (Everyman edition, 6. 553). See an interesting reinterpretation by A. J. Toynbee, *A Study of History* (Oxford, 1939), 4. 56–63.
90. Gibbon, c. 2 (Everyman edition, 1. 28 f.).
91. Gibbon, c. 23 (Everyman edition, 2. 371).
92. See Gibbon, c. 37 (Everyman edition, 4. 16 f.).

Notes on 19. THE TIME OF REVOLUTION, § 1: INTRODUCTION

1. The word *romance* means a work written in one of the vernacular languages of Roman origin—and so a popular work in the ordinary speech of the Mediterranean peoples (as opposed to a serious book in Latin, the language of culture), and particularly a story of chivalrous adventure. Catalan, French, Italian, Portuguese, Rumanian, and Spanish are still known as 'Romance' languages. An even stranger relic of the Romans is the word for modern colloquial Greek, which is called 'Romaic', the speech of the (eastern) Roman empire.
2. See pp. 61, 514.
3. So also Wordsworth's note on his return to classical symbols in the *Ode to Lycoris* (1817):

'No doubt the hacknied and lifeless use into which mythology fell towards the close of the 17th century, and which continued through the 18th, disgusted the general reader with all allusion to it in modern verse; and though, in deference to this disgust, and also in a measure participating in it, I abstained in my earlier writings from all introduction of pagan fable, surely, even in its humble form, it may ally itself with real sentiment.'

4. Byron, *Don Juan*, 2. 194. Probably the actual group of which Byron was thinking was a Cupid and Psyche in the Uffizi Gallery. See J. A. Larrabee, *English Bards and Grecian Marbles* (New York, 1943), 167 and his note 16.
5. See C. Justi, *Winckelmann und seine Zeitgenossen* (Leipzig, 1898²) 1. 202 f., for Winckelmann's radical views and the authors he read to confirm them.
6. The whole of Hugo's *Les Orientales* is an expression of the excited hatred of Turkey and the passion for liberty which moved the more generous spirits of the revolutionary age. To Greece! he shouts in 4,

En Grèce, ô mes amis! vengeance! liberté!
Ce turban sur mon front! ce sabre à mon côté!
Allons! ce cheval, qu'on le selle!

G. Deschamps, in L. Petit de Julleville's *Histoire de la langue et de la littérature française*, 7. 275 f., describes the assertion of Greek independence by British, French, and Russian forces as a triumph of the enthusiasm of poets and intellectuals over cautious officialdom. In France Chateaubriand's propaganda was really more efficient than the rhodomontades of Hugo.

7. See p. 262 f.

8. On the conflict of the Olympians and the Nazarene, see Heine's *Reisebilder: Die Stadt Lucca* 6, quoted, translated, and discussed by J. G. Robertson in "The Gods of Greece in German Poetry' (*Essays and Addresses on Literature*, London, 1935), 136 f., and in E. M. Butler's brilliant and tendentious *The Tyranny of Greece over Germany* (Cambridge and New York, 1935), 256 f.

9. E. M. Butler (cited in n. 8), 118–19.

10. There is another striking expression of this hatred for Christianity in Shelley's *Ode to Liberty*, which in stanza 8 says the fall of Greco-Roman culture was caused by 'the Galilean serpent' creeping forth 'from its sea of death' (an allusion to the Dead Sea), and in stanza 16 says that the name of PRIEST was an emanation of hell and the fiends.

11. Lessing, *Wie die Alten den Tod gebildet.*

12. For the word *macabré* and its associations, see J. Huizinga, *The Waning of the Middle Ages* (London, 1937), 129–30.

13.   Happy is England! I could be content
               To see no other verdure than its own;
               To feel no other breezes than are blown
            Through its tall woods with high romances blent:
            Yet do I sometimes feel a languishment
               For skies Italian, and an inward groan
               To sit upon an Alp as on a throne,
            And half forget what world or worldling meant.
            Happy is England, sweet her artless daughters;
               Enough their simple loveliness for me,
               Enough their whitest arms in silence clinging:
            Yet do I often warmly burn to see
               Beauties of deeper glance, and hear their singing,
            And float with them about the summer waters.

                      Keats, Sonnet 17 (*Poems published in* 1817).

'World and worldling' mean the modern commercial and industrial life of Britain, as in Wordsworth's *The World is too much with Us* (on which see p. 436 f.).

14. This is emphasized for the Germans by W. Rehm in *Griechentum und Goethezeit* (Das Erbe der Alten, second series, 26, Leipzig, 1936), 1 f. Winckelmann got as far as the temple at Paestum (Rehm, 34). Rehm's book is very learned, but seems to me to be vitiated by the German nationalistic assumption that there was a special spiritual affinity (he calls it a *Wahl-Verwandtschaft* on p. 18) between the Greeks and the Germans —rather than between the Greeks and all the thinkers and aesthetes of the revolutionary age in every land. Considering the opposition between

Greece and Germany which some of the most important German writers
have felt (p. 366), it is difficult even to make sense out of an assertion like
this: 'Der Glaube an Griechisches ist also im letzten nur ein Gleichnis
für den Glauben an das Hoch- und Rein-Menschliche und darum auch für
den Glauben an das Deutsche' (17–18).

15. Goethe, Diary 1786, quoted and translated by H. Trevelyan,
Goethe and the Greeks, Cambridge, 1942, 121.

16. Goethe, *Venezianische Epigramme*, 76:

> Was mit mir das Schicksal gewollt? Es wäre verwegen,
> Das zu fragen: denn meist will es mit vielen nicht viel.
> Einen Dichter zu bilden, die Absicht wär' ihm gelungen,
> Hätte die Sprache sich nicht unüberwindlich gezeigt.

So, in the same book (29), after saying that he has tried painting and
drawing and so forth, he writes.

> Only one single skill could I bring near to success:
> writing in German. And so, I am wasting (unfortunate poet)
> on the vilest of stuff, wasting my life and my art.

> Nur ein einzig Talent bracht' ich der Meisterschaft nah·
> Deutsch zu schreiben. Und so verderb' ich unglücklicher Dichter
> In dem schlechtesten Stoff leider nun Leben und Kunst.

17. E. M. Butler (cited in n. 8), 203.

18. See Vernon Lee, *Studies of the Eighteenth Century in Italy* (London,
1927²), c. 2, 'The Musical Life', especially 139 f. and 153 f.

19. See L. Hautecœur, *Rome et la renaissance de l'antiquité à la fin du
XVIIIe siècle* (Bibliothèque des écoles françaises d'Athènes et de Rome,
105, Paris, 1912), 1. 1, on the increasing popularity of tours in Italy and
their stimulating effect.

Notes on 19. THE TIME OF REVOLUTION, § 2: GERMANY

1. 'Alle Völker haben eine Renaissance gehabt, diejenige, die wir für
gewöhnlich so bezeichnen, mit einer einzigen Ausnahme, nämlich
Deutschland. Deutschland hat zwei Renaissancen gehabt; die zweite
Renaissance liegt um die Mitte des 18. Jahrhunderts und knüpft sich an
Namen wie Herder, Goethe, Schiller, Lessing, Winckelmann. Da stehen
die Griechen ebenso im Vordergrund wie in der ersten die Lateiner,
die nationale Wesensverwandtschaft der Deutschen und Griechen ist
entdeckt worden. Daher kommt es, dass die Deutschen ebenso stark
Griechen, wie die Engländer, Franzosen und Italiener bis auf den heutigen
Tag Lateiner sein können. Für uns steht in erster Linie Homer, nicht
Virgil, Thukydides, nicht Titus Livius, Plato, nicht Seneca, das ist ein
grundlegender Unterschied. Wir denken zunächst ganz instinktiv an das
Griechische, dann an das Römische, die Leute zur Zeit der ersten Renaissance und die grossen Kulturnationen des Westens machen es gerade
umgekehrt, und darin ist vielleicht ein gutes Teil des Grundes zu sehen,
weshalb die Deutschen so unbekannt und missverstanden in der Welt

stehen.'—Paul Hensel, 'Montaigne und die Antike' (*Vorträge der Biblio-thek Warburg* 1925–6, Leipzig, 1928), 69.

2. *Don Giovanni* and *Le nozze di Figaro* are the results of the collaboration of Mozart and Lorenzo da Ponte. (Da Ponte, by the way, ended his singular career as professor of Italian at Columbia College, New York.)

3. 'Storm and Stress' is the usual translation of *Sturm und Drang*, the title of a drama by Klinger (1777), whose hero, 'glutted by impulse and power', was a Byron before Byron was born.

4. Winckelmann read Greek until midnight, wrapped in his coat by the fireside, slept in his chair until four, woke up and studied Greek again until six, and then started his school-teaching. In summer he used to sleep on a bench, with blocks of wood tied to his feet, so that when he moved they would make a noise and wake him. See E. M. Butler, *The Tyranny of Greece over Germany* (Cambridge and New York, 1935), 14.

5. *Gedanken über die Nachahmung der griechischen Werke in der Malerei und Bildhauerkunst.* A good summary of Winckelmann's thought, with an interesting account of the reactions (not all favourable) which it provoked in Germany, will be found in H. C. Hatfield's *Winckelmann and his German Critics 1755–81* (New York, 1943).

6. Shaftesbury was one of Winckelmann's two favourite authors, and many of his ideas reappear in Winckelmann's work: C. Justi, *Winckelmann und seine Zeitgenossen* (Leipzig, 1898[2]), 1. 208, 211, 215–16.

7. The fine Greek buildings and streets of late-eighteenth-century and early-nineteenth-century Britain are well known. Russia has many Greek-style buildings dating from the same period and created by the same impulse. In Berlin the style appeared in the Brandenburg Gate which Langhans built on the model of the Propylaea at Athens in 1789–94, in Schinkel's State Theatre (1819–21), and in Schinkel's portico for the Old Museum (1824–8). On Jefferson and classical architecture in revolutionary America see p. 400 f. The Greek current ran strong in the minor decorative arts too, as is shown by the work of Wedgwood the famous potter, and by such portrait-busts as those of Goethe made, in the Greco-Roman style, by A. Trippel (1787) and M. G. Klauer (1790).

8. See J. E. Sandys, *A History of Classical Scholarship* (Cambridge, 1908), 2. 431–2.

9. On this work see also p. 383; Sandys (cited in n. 8), 2. 432–3, and G. Finsler, *Homer in der Neuzeit von Dante bis Goethe* (Leipzig, 1912), 258 and 368–72.

10. Chandler's description of Ionia was eagerly read by Goethe and Hölderlin (W. Rehm, *Griechentum und Goethezeit* (Das Erbe der Alten, 2nd series, 26, Leipzig, 1936), 3). Wood's *Essay* and Blackwell's *Enquiry into the Life and Writings of Homer* (1735) were the books which opened Goethe's eyes to Homer (E. Maass, *Goethe und die Antike* (Berlin, 1912), 87). Wood was privately printed in 1769, then published posthumously in 1775, going into several editions and translations. On Blackwell, see Finsler (cited in n. 9), 332–5.

11. *Eine edle Einfalt und eine stille Grösse* (*Gedanken* 21).

12. *Geschichte der Kunst des Alterthums.* On the essays which Winckel-

mann published in the *Bibliothek der schönen Wissenschaften*, see H. C. Hatfield (cited in n. 5), 9 f.

13. The phrase is E. M. Butler's, in her book cited in n. 4, p. 26. E. Fueter, *Geschichte der neueren Historiographie* (ed. D. Gerhard and P. Sattler, Munich, 1936³), 390 n., points out that Winckelmann invented both the word *Kunstgeschichte*, 'history of art', and the idea.

14. *Monumenti antichi inediti*: see J. E. Sandys, *A History of Classical Scholarship* (Cambridge, 1908), 3. 23.

15. The legend is in Vergil, *Aen.* 2. 40 f.

16. For the date 25 B.C. see C. Blinkenberg, 'Zur Laokoongruppe', in *Mitteilungen des deutschen archäologischen Instituts, römische Abteilung*, 42 (1927), 177–92. The group was carved by two brothers, Athanodorus and Hagesandros, who were made priests of Athana Lindia as a reward from the state of Rhodes. Blinkenberg thinks the group was not known to Vergil, but was brought to Rome by Titus in A.D. 69. There is also a good article by M. Pohlenz in *Die Antike*, 9 (1933), 54 f., suggesting that the date is certainly within the decade 32–22 B.C. On the question whether Laocoon is shrieking, Pohlenz points out that the later Stoics (whose most prominent spokesman Panaetius came from Rhodes) held that a shriek was quite impermissible in pain, but that a groan was allowable, as an expression of the effort of will made to overcome pain. In view of the extreme anguish in Laocoon's face, I do not feel this is quite convincing. He is not shrieking; he is groaning, but it is scarcely a groan of Stoical resistance. The group was rediscovered in January 1506, and at once identified as that described in Pliny, *Hist. Nat.* 36. 37. On the history of its reputation there is an interesting treatise by M. Bieber, *Laocoon: the Influence of the Group since its Rediscovery* (New York, 1942).

17. Julius Caesar was exceedingly interested in the connexion between Troy and Rome; Varro (d. 27) wrote a work *De familiis Troianis*, on the Roman families which traced their descent back to Troy; Vergil began the *Aeneid* in 29 B.C.

18. On 'Dares the Phrygian' see p. 51 f.

19. 'De toutes les statues qui sont restées jusqu'à présent, il n'y en a point qui égale celle de Laocoon': quoted by S. Rocheblave in L. Petit de Julleville's *Histoire de la langue et de la littérature française*, v. 5, c. 12. The works of art which the Académie Royale admired most were, for compositions containing several figures, Poussin's paintings; and, for isolated figures, Greco-Roman sculpture, particularly *Laocoon*.

20. See c. 15, particularly p. 290 f.

21. The German titles are *Briefe, die neueste Litteratur betreffend* (1759–65) and *Hamburgische Dramaturgie*. There is a very full analysis of the latter, and of Lessing's other critical writings on theatrical subjects, by J. G. Robertson: *Lessing's Dramatic Theory* (ed. E. Purdie, Cambridge, 1939). The name *Dramaturgie* was taken from a catalogue of plays by the Italian critic Allacci published in 1666 and called *Drammaturgia*: Lessing intended it to mean something like 'dramatic activity in Hamburg'. (See Robertson, 120 f.) On Lessing's imaginative but erratic criticisms of Homer see Finsler (cited in n. 9), 420–6.

22. See p. 287.

23. This was in the early *Beyträge zur Historie und Aufnahme des Theaters*: Lessing wrote it as a reply to criticism of his essay on Plautus and his translation of the *Captiui*. See Robertson (cited in n. 21), 94 f.

24. 'Von den lateinischen Trauerspielen, welche unter dem Namen des Seneca bekannt sind', in the *Theatralische Bibliothek*: a polemic against Brumoy's depreciation of Latin drama as compared with Greek. See Robertson (n. 21), 110 f.

25. The attack was in *Briefe, die neueste Litteratur betreffend*, 17 (Feb. 1759): Robertson (n. 21), 205 f.

26. It is often said that Lessing's criticism in the *Hamburgische Dramaturgie* is based on his interpretation of Aristotle's *Poetics*. Robertson (cited in n. 21), 342 f., points out that this is not so. Lessing began to work hard at the *Poetics*, using Dacier's translation and commentary, as late as March 1768. See also Robertson's summary, on p. 489 f.

27. See H. Trevelyan, *Goethe and the Greeks* (Cambridge, 1942), 50. On Herder's eulogies of Homer see Finsler (cited in n. 9), 429–36.

28. There is a useful thesis by W. J. Keller, *Goethe's Estimate of the Greek and Latin Writers* (Madison, Wisconsin, 1916), which describes the stages of Goethe's developing interest in each of the classical authors, and contains a chronological table showing what he was reading each year from 1765 to 1832. See also E. Maass, *Goethe und die Antike* (Berlin, 1912), a standard work, supplemented by K. Bapp, *Aus Goethes griechischer Gedankenwelt* (Das Erbe der Alten, 2nd series, 6, Leipzig, 1921).

29. Schiller, *An die Freude*:

> Freude, schöner Götterfunken,
> Tochter aus Elysium . . . .

30. Schiller, *Die Götter Griechenlands*, stanza 9:

> Damals trat kein grässliches Gerippe
> vor das Bett des Sterbenden. Ein Kuss
> nahm das letzte Leben von der Lippe,
> seine Fackel senkt' ein Genius.

(Cf. p. 364 f.)

31. On this poem see p. 437 f.

32. For details of these attacks see F. Strich, *Die Mythologie in der deutschen Literatur von Klopstock bis Wagner* (Halle, 1910), i. 273 f.

33. After Hölderlin went mad he changed his name so as to become a different person. There is a sympathetic chapter on him by E. M. Butler (cited in n. 4).

34. On Hölderlin's hymns see also p. 251.

35. There are some superficial remarks on this in G. Wenzel's *Hölderlin und Keats als geistesverwandte Dichter* (Magdeburg, 1896).

36. Plato, *Symposium*, 201 d f.

37. Keats, *When I have Fears* (1817). Hölderlin, *An die Parzen*:

> Nur einen Sommer gönnt, ihr Gewaltigen!
> Und einen Herbst zu reifem Gesange mir,
> Dass williger mein Herz, vom süssen
> Spiele gesättiget, dann mir sterbe.

38. On this see Keller (cited in n. 28), 9–10, and pages 73 (Aeschylus), 96 (Aristophanes), 111 (Aristotle's *Poetics*), 125 (the Greek Anthology), 140 ('Longinus'), and 141 (Lucian).

39. See H. Trevelyan (cited in n. 27), c. 1, and E. Maass (cited in n. 28), c. 3. Goethe himself speaks of this in *Dichtung und Wahrheit* (Vienna edition), 161–2, and in *Winckelmann und sein Jahrhundert*.

40. See Keller (cited in n. 28), 17; see his c. 1 generally.

41. Goethe, *Römische Elegien*, 5.

42. Goethe, *Römische Elegien*, 1. 13–14:

Yes, Rome, you are a world indeed. And yet, without love, the
world would not be the world; neither could Rome still be Rome.

Eine Welt zwar bist du, o Rom, doch ohne die Liebe
Wäre die Welt nicht die Welt, wäre denn Rom auch nicht Rom.

He is using mythology quite like Propertius and Ovid when, in *Römische Elegien*, 3, he tells his mistress that she must not be ashamed of her quick surrender to him, because the gods and goddesses of the heroic age took their lovers swiftly and without hesitation. One of those sudden unions produced the wolf-twins, who made Rome queen of the world.

43. See E. Maass (cited in n. 10), c. 7, and Rehm (cited in n. 10), 128 f.

44. E. Maass (n. 10) compares her on p. 341 to Cordelia and Imogen.

45. There is a careful analysis of the sources of the *Römische Elegien* by F. Bronner, 'Goethes römische Elegien und ihre Quellen', in *Neue Jahrbücher für Philologie und Paedagogik*, 148 (1893). Bronner points out, among other things, that Goethe did not read Catullus and Propertius in Rome, but started them later, when Knebel (who had translated Propertius into prose) sent him a volume of the elegists. He cared little for Tibullus; he got some material from Martial and the *Priapea*; and he probably knew Ovid best of all—the motto for the *Römische Elegien* comes from *The Art of Love* (1. 33).

46. This is *Römische Elegien*, 6, with an exquisite ending in the manner of the Greek Anthology.

47. Take, for instance, the opening of Longfellow's *Evangeline*:

1 This is the forest primeval. The murmuring pines and the hemlocks
4 Stand like harpers hoar, with beards that rest on their bosoms.

Line 1 is all dactyls: stress light light, stress light light . . ., The next line is supposed to begin with four spondees: stress stress, stress stress, stress stress, stress stress:

Stand like / harpers / hoar with / beards that . . . .

But in fact 'harpers' and 'hoar with' cannot be made into pairs of equally stressed syllables, and it is difficult to force 'beards that' into the same balance. They are really stressed syllables followed by unstressed syllables: trochees. Therefore such hexameters always tend to become alternations of dactyls and trochees, even feet against uneven feet, and so they acquire a limp. As for the efforts made by some classicists who were more scholars than poets to create hexameters and pentameters based on quantity—the metre satirized by Tennyson in

/   /   /   /   /   /
Barbarous experiment, barbarous hexameters—

Goethe had too good taste to pay any attention to them.

48. J. H. Voss, the translator, had already produced some poetry of this type in hexameters, but without so much plot as Goethe put into *Hermann und Dorothea*. See V. Hehn, *Über Goethes Hermann und Dorothea* (Stuttgart, 1913³), 139 f., on Voss's *Luise*.

49. Goethe, *Hermann und Dorothea*, 1. 78 and *passim*:

der edle verständige Pfarrherr.

50. F. A. Wolf, *Prolegomena ad Homerum, sive de operum homericorum prisca et genuina forma variisque mutationibus et probabili ratione emendandi.* There is a good edition with notes by Bekker (Berlin, 1872); an old but still useful survey of its influence by R. Volkmann, *Geschichte und Kritik der Wolfschen Prolegomena zu Homer* (Leipzig, 1874); and a handy summary in Sandys (cited in n. 8), 3. 51 f. The treatment of Wolf in Finsler's book on Homeric criticism (see n. 9), 463 f., is definitely hostile. Finsler says he got nearly all his ideas from others, starting by rediscovering D'Aubignac's *Dissertation sur l'Iliade* (1664) and then pillaging Wood, Heyne, Macpherson's Ossian, and others; and on p. 210 accuses him of deliberately falsifying his debt to D'Aubignac.

51. See p. 270 f. Another instance of this is Voltaire's attack on Homer in his *Essai sur la poésie épique*, introductory to the second edition of his own epic *La Henriade* (1726). See Finsler (cited in n. 9), 237–8.

52. On Wood see p. 370, and Finsler (cited in n. 9), 368–72. Almost equally important in changing the direction of eighteenth-century thought was the picture of Homer as an untutored but widely travelled and experienced genius, building up his poems by improvisation, striking off piece after piece at white heat and slowly moulding the whole into its final form. This was found in Thomas Blackwell's *Enquiry into the Life and Writings of Homer* (1735): see Finsler, 332–5.

53. On Mabillon see Sandys (cited in n. 8), 2. 293 f.; on Bentley see p. 283 f. of this work. What actually started Wolf on his *Prolegomena* was the publication by the French scholar Villoison, in 1788, of the Marcianus A manuscript of Homer, with the attached scholia.

54. *Il.* 6. 168–70, 7. 175 f. See Wolf, *Prolegomena*, c. 19: 'accurata interpretatio facile vincet eos [locos] non magis de scriptura accipiendos esse quam celebrem illum Ciceronis [*N.D.* 2. 37] de typographia nostra.' See also pp. 3–4 of this book on the runes.

55. Wolf, *Prolegomena*, c. 12.

56. Wolf, *Prolegomena*, c. 26: 'Videtur itaque ex illis sequi necessario, tam magnorum et perpetua serie deductorum operum formam a nullo poeta nec designari animo nec elaborari potuisse sine artificioso adminiculo memoriae.' He goes on, in this important chapter, to declare that the

feat is impossible to mortal man. This is an odd relic of medieval thinking. Before making such an outright assertion it would have been safer to make sure, by inquiry and experiment: for now it is known that the feat is not only possible, but in certain stages of civilization customary.

57. Wolf quotes this, in his c. 26, n. 84, from Bentley's *Remarks upon a Late Discourse of Free-thinking* (1713), c. 7.

58. It was largely because they looked like 'folk-poetry' that Herder admired them so greatly. But in his essay *Homer ein Günstling der Zeit* (1795) he attacked Wolf for missing the fundamental point that the epics are great poetry, and were therefore designed not by an editor but by a great poet.

59. Wolf, *Prolegomena*, cc. 33-4.

60. Livy's early books were thus dissolved by Niebuhr (see p. 472 f.), and in the later nineteenth century the same solvent was applied to many poets and philosophers who little needed it. Ribbeck, for example, having grasped the obvious fact that Juvenal's satires grew gentler and more discursive as the poet grew older, wrote *Der echte und der unechte Juvenal* to prove that the early satires were written by Juvenal and the later satires by an imitator.

61. For discussions of the poems from the point of view of modern scholarship see C. M. Bowra, *Tradition and Design in the Iliad* (Oxford, 1930); Rhys Carpenter, *Folk Tale, Fiction, and Saga in the Homeric Epics* (Sather Classical Lectures, 20, Berkeley, Cal., 1946); G. Murray, *The Rise of the Greek Epic* (Oxford, 1924³), and W. J. Woodhouse, *The Composition of Homer's Odyssey* (Oxford, 1930).

62. So in the elegiac poem introducing *Hermann und Dorothea* he calls for a toast to Wolf the liberator:

Erst die Gesundheit des Mannes, der, endlich vom Namen Homeros
   Kühn uns befreiend, uns auch ruft in die vollere Bahn.
Denn wer wagte mit Göttern den Kampf? und wer mit dem Einen?
Doch Homeride zu sein, auch nur als letzter, ist schön.

63. Goethe expressed his reconversion in a little poem, *Homer wieder Homer*, as well as in various prose utterances. For an account of his varying opinions on the Homeric question, see Dapp (cited in n. 28), c. 4.

64. See p. 251. The famous *Wanderers Nachtlied* is an adaptation of a fragmentary lyric by Alcman.

65. See p. 72 f.

66. This suggestion was made, with good supporting evidence, by E. Maass (cited in n. 28), 255 f. Goethe had another reason for introducing a 'classical' witches' sabbath: he wished to compose a scene corresponding, on the 'classical' plane, to the 'Gothic' sabbath which in Part I followed the seduction and despair of Gretchen, and thus to link the two appearances of the woman physical and the woman aesthetically apprehended.

67. See p. 459.

68. See n. 14 on p. 662. Another fine example of this peculiar nationalist assumption appears in Mommsen's *Römische Geschichte* (Berlin,

1865⁴), 1. 15. 233: 'Nur die Griechen und die Deutschen besitzen den freiwillig hervorsprudelnden Liederquell; aus der goldenen Schale der Musen sind auf Italiens grünen Boden eben nur wenige Tropfen gefallen.'

Notes on 19. THE TIME OF REVOLUTION, § 3: FRANCE AND THE UNITED STATES

1. 'Ces républicains étaient la plupart des jeunes gens qui, nourris de la lecture de Cicéron dans les collèges, s'y étaient passionnés pour la liberté. On nous élevait dans les écoles de Rome et d'Athènes, et dans la fierté de la République, pour vivre dans l'abjection de la monarchie, et sous le règne des Claude et des Vitellius.'—Camille Desmoulins, *Histoire des Brissotins* (Archives parlementaires de 1787 à 1860, 1st series, 3 Oct. 1793), 622, n. 1: quoted by J. Worthington, *Wordsworth's Reading of Roman Prose* (Yale Studies in English, 102, New Haven, 1946), p. 5, n. 5.

2. See p. 399.

3. W. Rehm, *Griechentum und Goethezeit* (Das Erbe der Alten, 2nd series, 26, Leipzig, 1936), 61. On David's early triumphal success with 'Les Horaces', and on the rapid spread of his influence to painters like Tischbein, see L. Hautecœur, *Rome et la renaissance de l'antiquité à la fin du XVIIIᵉ siècle* (Bibliothèque des écoles françaises d'Athènes et de Rome, 105, Paris, 1912), 2. 2. 2 and 2. 2. 3. Hautecœur points out that one of the most powerful formative influences on David himself was Poussin.

4. See p. 141.

5. There is a good chapter on Gluck in D. J. Grout's *A Short History of Opera* (New York, 1947), v. 1, c. 15. Mr. Grout stresses the revolutionary nature of Gluck's work by quoting Metastasio's remark that he was a composer of 'surpassing fire, but . . . mad'. I believe, however, that Mr. Grout underestimates Gluck's power as a teacher and model. His pupils may have been few, but they were important. One was Cherubini, favourite composer of the French Revolution; another was Berlioz; perhaps Bellini was a third; and the greatest was Mozart.

6. Gluck, preface to *Alceste*, quoted and translated by D. Tovey, s.v. 'Gluck', *Encyclopaedia Britannica*.

7. He tried to learn Greek in 1749 (*Correspondance générale*, 1. 287, 27 Jan. 1749), but gave it up. In 1757, refusing the post of librarian at Geneva, he wrote, 'Je ne sais point de grec, très-peu de latin' (*Corr. gén.* 3. 14, 27 Feb. 1757); but this was a characteristic exaggeration. He read a lot of Plato in a Latin version; he read Seneca, and even translated his difficult satire, the *Apocolocyntosis*, into French (*Works*, Hachette edn., 12. 344–54). I owe these references to G. R. Havens's excellent critical edition of Rousseau's *Discours sur les sciences et les arts* (*PMLA*, New York and London, 1946).

8. Lists of the books Rousseau read will be found in M. Reichenburg's *Essai sur les lectures de Rousseau* (Philadelphia, 1932).

9. J.-E. Morel, 'Jean-Jacques Rousseau lit Plutarque' (*Revue d'histoire moderne*, 1 (1926), 81–102), has analysed this commonplace-book, which

Rousseau started immediately after publishing the first *Discourse*. It contains many anecdotes which fed the subterranean springs of Rousseau's mind.

10. See p. 188. Montaigne's other favourite author was Seneca, also a favourite of Jean-Jacques.

11. There is a lucid discussion of the Lycurgus legend and the real Sparta in W. Jaeger's *Paideia*, 1 (Oxford, 1939), 78–84. On the idealization of Sparta by the Greek philosophers, see F. Ollier, *Le Mirage spartiate*, part 2 (Annales de l'Université de Lyon, 3rd series (Lettres), fasc. 13, Paris, 1943).

12. For this idea see C. W. Hendel, *Jean-Jacques Rousseau Moralist* (Oxford, 1934), 2. 320 f.

13. Similarly, Montesquieu held that the ideal form of government was a democracy, and in describing democracy he drew his models from Greco-Roman history and philosophy. See L. M. Levin, *The Political Doctrine of Montesquieu's 'Esprit des lois': its Classical Background* (New York, 1936), for a general account of Montesquieu's wide classical learning; and p. 67 f. for this particular point.

14. Quoted from Lord Russell's discussion in *A History of Western Philosophy* (New York, 1945), 694 f.

15. There is a useful analysis of his dependence on Plutarch, in respect of these moral ideals, in his famous *Discourse*, by A. C. Keller, 'Plutarch and Rousseau's first *Discours*' (*PMLA*, 54 (1939), 212–22): see also G. R. Havens (cited in n. 7), introduction, 63 f.

16. Nevertheless, Plutarch was on the whole in favour of the arts and sciences. Rousseau altered his version of the Prometheus myth in order to make civilization out to be a nuisance and a corruption (see G. R. Havens, cited in n. 7, 209). A. Oltramare, 'Plutarque dans Rousseau', in *Mélanges d'histoire et de philologie offerts à M. Bernard Bouvier* (Geneva, 1920), 185–96, asks the question so often asked before—where did Rousseau get the paradox on which his first *Discourse* is based (that the progress of art and science has injured humanity)?—and replies, convincingly enough, that he got it from Plutarch. The proof is that the first words of the *Discourse* Rousseau wrote, the first jet of his inspiration set down 'in pencil, under an oak' on his way out to see Diderot at Vincennes, was the apostrophe to Fabricius, the primitive Roman warrior (consul 282 B.C.) who, according to Plutarch, rejected the bribes of the condottiere Pyrrhus, defended his country successfully, and died in virtuous poverty. This apostrophe contains the entire paradox, that Rome was good while it was simple, and, like all states, grew corrupt as it grew more highly civilized.

17. On the conception of *paideia*, see W. Jaeger, *Paideia* (New York and Oxford, 1939–44), and pp. 547–9, 552 of this book.

18. H. T. Parker, *The Cult of Antiquity and the French Revolutionaries* (Chicago, 1937), 28 f. and (quoting Mme Roland's letter) 96 f.

19. R. Hirzel, *Plutarch* (Das Erbe der Alten, 4, Leipzig, 1912), c. 19, covers some aspects of the subject, but it deserves much more detailed and thoughtful discussion.

20. Parker (cited in n. 18), 142 f.

21. Parker (n. 18), 178 f., shows that this fashion soon palled: the reaction to it appeared in 1795.

22. Quoted by F. Beck, reviewing the second edition of Hosius' edition of Lucan in *Gött. gel. Anz.* 1907, 780, n. 1. The line is Lucan, *Bell. ciu.* 4. 579:

> ignoratque datos, ne quisquam seruiat, enses.

The subject, as the text stands, is *libertas*. Housman therefore read *ignorantque*, to make the subject 'people' in general, i.e. the enslaved populace of Lucan's time.

23. Cic. *Pro Sex. Rosc. Am.* 56–7.

24. I owe these connexions to T. Zielinski, *Cicero im Wandel der Jahrhunderte* (Leipzig, 1912³), 264 f., where other instances will be found. Livy and Tacitus also exercised their influence on the French revolutionaries, although in a far less important degree than Cicero. Next to Cicero's speeches, the greatest source of material and rhetorical patterns for the revolutionary orators was a collection of the speeches in Livy's history, translated by Rousseau (Zielinski, 362). Tacitus was less often used because his style was so difficult, but his sentiments were admired. The third issue of the journal called *Le Vieux Cordelier* (dated *quintidi frimaire, troisième décade, an II*), edited and largely written by Desmoulins, is a tissue of anti-monarchic extracts from Tacitus. (See L. Delamarre, *Tacite et la littérature française*, Paris, 1907, 110–15, for details.)

25. Parker (cited in n. 18), 80 f.

26. Parker (n. 18), 132 f. and 158 f.

27. See p. 391.

28. The title was also applied to Romulus, Camillus, and Marius; thereafter (in the form *parens patriae*) to Julius Caesar and Octavian. (See Mayor on Juvenal, 8. 244.) Mommsen, *Römisches Staatsrecht*, 2. 2 (Leipzig, 1877²), 755 n. 1, attempted to make a fundamental distinction between Cicero's honorific title and Julius Caesar's honorific title, saying that Cicero's was *natürlich etwas ganz Anderes*. The distinction existed only in Mommsen's mind, and was due to his hatred for Cicero and his adoration of Caesar: see pp. 476–7. Those who applied the phrase to Washington were certainly thinking of the title as borne by Cicero.

29. *E pluribus unum* apparently comes from the pastoral idyll attributed to Vergil and called the *Moretum*, line 104. As the salad which the poor farmer has mixed is mashed in the bowl, the herbs lose their distinctive hues, and

> color est e pluribus unus.

The three words had been used as a tag on title-pages as early as 1692. St. Augustine, *Conf.* 4. 8, also has *ex pluribus unum facere*, but he was not much read by the Founding Fathers, and the hexameter rhythm suggests that the real source of the phrase is the *Moretum*.

30. Vergil, *Buc.* 4. 5:

> magnus ab integro saeclorum nascitur ordo.

(Shelley, *Hellas*, 1060 f., on which see p. 422.)

31. Vergil, *Georg.* 1. 40 (addressed to Octavian!):

> da facilem cursum atque audacibus adnue coeptis.

Also, *Aen.* 9. 625:

> Iuppiter omnipotens, audacibus adnue coeptis.

(See G. Hunt, *The History of the Seal of the United States*, published by the Department of State, Washington, 1909, 13 f., 33 f.)

32. I owe the facts in this paragraph to G. R. Stewart's fascinating work, *Names on the Land* (New York, 1945), c. 21, pp. 181–8.

33. There is an excellent book on this aspect of his work by Karl Lehmann, *Thomas Jefferson—American Humanist* (New York, 1947), to which I am indebted for many of these facts. Jefferson kept a commonplace-book in which he copied out quotations he thought worth preserving. It has been reprinted and analysed by G. Chinard, *The Literary Bible of Thomas Jefferson* (Baltimore, 1928). The Greek quotations in it come from Homer, Herodotus, Euripides, Anacreon, and Quintus Smyrnaeus. In Latin Cicero predominates—largely the *Tusculan Discussions*. There are twelve quotations from Horace, including that which characterized both Horace and Jefferson:

> O rus, quando ego te aspiciam? (*Serm.* 2. 6. 60.)

There are a few from Ovid, and fewer than we should expect from Vergil. A. Koch, *The Philosophy of Thomas Jefferson* (New York, 1943), c. 1, also explains how Jefferson's education was built on classical literature, and gives illuminating details.

34. There is a fine biography of Chénier by Paul Dimoff, *La Vie et l'œuvre d'André Chénier jusqu'à la révolution française 1762–1790* (2 vv., Paris, 1936). A survey of Chénier's knowledge of and adaptations from the classics will be found in v. 2, bk. 3, cc. 6 and 7. The much shorter *André Chénier* by Émile Faguet (Paris, 1902) is also good. On the late rise of Chénier's reputation see R. Canat, *La Renaissance de la Grèce antique (1820–1850)* (Paris, 1911), 6 f.

35. Des lois, et non du sang!

36. Details in A. J. Dingham, *Marie-Joseph Chénier, Early Life and Political Ideas 1789–94* (New York, 1939), 56 f. and 167.

37. On both these large projects see P. Dimoff (cited in n. 34), 1. 387 f.

38. As well as Theocritus, Chénier loved the melancholy epigrams of the Greek Anthology, and echoed their elegiac minor chords in several poems—notably his famous *La Jeune Tarentine*. (On this point see J. Hutton, *The Greek Anthology in France and in the Latin Writers of the Netherlands to the Year 1800* (Ithaca, N.Y., 1946), 73 f.).

39. Chénier did something to relax the strict rules which had manacled French metre. His idylls contain what the French used to think of as bold enjambements: for instance—

> Ce n'est pas (le sais-tu? déjà dans le bocage
> Quelque voile de nymphe est-il tombé pour toi?)
> Ce n'est pas cela seul qui diffère chez moi. (*Lydé.*)

40. Autour du demi-dieu les princes immobiles
   Aux accents de sa voix demeuraient suspendus,
   Et l'écoutaient encor quand il ne chantait plus. (*Hermès*, 2. 11.)

41. Fielding, in writing his 'comic epic', *Tom Jones*, did exactly the same, for the same reason: see p. 343.

42. We have already touched on this point in tracing the growth of the novel out of epic and romance: see p. 344.

43. Chateaubriand, *Le Génie du christianisme*, 12 init.

44. This point is well made by C. Lynes, Jr., in his *Chateaubriand as a Critic of French Literature* (The Johns Hopkins Studies in Romance Literatures and Languages, 46, Baltimore, 1946). However, Mr. Lynes points out that, in spite of his praise of Christian literature, Chateaubriand really preferred Vergil and Homer to Racine and Fénelon—so that his work might be called *Le Génie du classicisme*. René Canat (cited in n. 34) deals in c. 1 with Chateaubriand as a Philhellenist, and speaks of *Le Génie de l'hellénisme*. Chateaubriand's knowledge of Homer and Vergil was really very deep and sensitive. The reflections of it in his work have been classified and analysed by B. U. Briod, *L'Homérisme de Chateaubriand* (Paris, 1928); C. R. Hart, *Chateaubriand and Homer* (The Johns Hopkins Studies in Romance Literatures and Languages, 11, Baltimore and Paris, 1928); and L. H. Naylor, *Chateaubriand and Virgil* (same series, 18, Baltimore, 1930).

45. Hugo, *Les Orientales*: see p. 661.

46. These examples, including Chênedollé's

   Les mortels qu'ont noircis les soleils de Guinée,

are taken from an admirable chapter on the subject by F. Brunot, c. 13 of v. 8 of L. Petit de Julleville's *Histoire de la langue et de la littérature française*. See also p. 274.

47. Delille, quoted by A. Guiard, *Virgile et Victor Hugo* (Paris, 1910).

48. *Les Contemplations*, 1. 7: *Réponse à un acte d'accusation*:

   Les neuf Muses, seins nus, chantaient la Carmagnole.

49. A. Guiard, *Virgile et Victor Hugo* (Paris, 1910). Hugo's monsters— the blood-drinking Han of Iceland and the irresistible one-eyed solitary Quasimodo—are clearly children of Cacus and the Cyclops (Guiard, 51 f.). *Les Contemplations*, 5. 17, is a short poem called *Mugitusque boum*, which begins

   Mugissement des bœufs au temps du doux Virgile,

and recalls *Georgics*, 2. 470.

50. *Voix intérieures*, 7: *A Virgile*.

51. *Les Contemplations*, 1. 13. The first outbreak ends:

   Grimauds hideux qui n'ont, tant leur tête est vidée,
   Jamais eu de maîtresse et jamais eu d'idée!

52. See p. 413.

675

Notes on 19. THE TIME OF REVOLUTION, § 4: ENGLAND

1. Shelley, preface to *Hellas*: 'We are all Greeks. Our laws, our literature, our religion, our arts have their roots in Greece. But for Greece— Rome, the instructor, the conqueror, or the metropolis of our ancestors, would have spread no illumination with her arms, and we might still have been savages and idolaters.'

2. Wordsworth, *On a Celebrated Event in Ancient History*, and *Upon the Same Event*, in *Poems dedicated to National Independence and Liberty*.

3. Wordsworth, *The Excursion*, 9. 210.

4. Keats in a letter to Shelley, 1820.

5. D. Bush, in 'Wordsworth and the Classics' (*University of Toronto Quarterly*, 2 (1932–3), 359–79), discusses the poet's interest in classical literature, and points out that he was a keen reader, having nearly 3,000 books in his library, many of them classics, although he could not afford to buy books for show. In his note on the *Ode to Lycoris* he says Ovid and Homer were his favourites when he was young. He wrote to Landor (20 April 1822) 'My acquaintance with Virgil, Horace, Lucretius, and Catullus is intimate'; and he had some idea of translating the *Aeneid*— there is a fragment of book 1 among his published works. In 1795 he was planning with Wrangham to write a modern translation and adaptation of Juvenal's eighth satire on true and false nobility (as Johnson modernized the third and tenth satires); see U. V. Tuckerman, 'Wordsworth's Plan for his Imitation of Juvenal' in *Modern Language Notes*, 45 (1930), 4. 209–15. But Horace, as he himself said, was his favourite. It seems strange at first, but on reflection we can see the sympathy between the two—both lovers of nature, retirement, and tranquillity, both strong moralists and patriots. For details see M. R. Thayer, *The Influence of Horace on the Chief English Poets of the Nineteenth Century* (Cornell Studies in English, 2, New Haven, 1916), 53–64.

6. The phrase is G. L. Bickersteth's, in his lecture *Leopardi and Wordsworth* (Proceedings of the British Academy, 1927), 13.

7. See W. Jaeger, *Paideia*, v. 1 (Oxford, 1939), preface, p. xxvii f. and *passim*.

8. See W. Jaeger, *Paideia*, v. 3 (Oxford, 1944), o. 9.

9. Wordsworth, *London, 1802*.

10. Wordsworth, *September, 1802. Near Dover.*

11. Wordsworth, *Lines composed a few miles above Tintern Abbey*.

12. Wordsworth, lines from a MS. note-book, printed in De Selincourt's edition of *The Prelude*, p. 512.

13. Wordsworth, *The Excursion*, 4. 324 f.; the Seneca reference is *Nat. Quaest.* 1, praef. 5. See J. Worthington, *Wordsworth's Reading of Roman Prose* (Yale Studies in English, 102, New Haven, 1946), 44.

14. Wordsworth, *Ode to Duty*, 47–8.

15. For further remarks on this ode see pp. 251–2. The ideas in it are Platonic; but Wordsworth may have received them, either directly or indirectly through Coleridge, from the Neoplatonists. 'Our birth is but a sleep and a forgetting' is almost a translation of a sentence in Proclus.

Coleridge bought Ficino's Latin translation and edition of selections from Iamblichus, Proclus, Porphyry, and others, as early as 1796. It has been suggested that he discussed its contents with Wordsworth during the crisis of imagination from which they both felt themselves suffering in the spring of 1802; that, as a result, Coleridge started *Dejection: an Ode* and Wordsworth wrote the first four stanzas (the 'question') of his own immortality ode; and that both poems were in a Pindaric form because the two poets had been discussing Ben Jonson (on whose odes see p. 238). A few days after the discussion, on 23 March, Wordsworth read Jonson's lyrics; and his composition of *Intimations of Immortality* began on 27 March. It has also been possible for us to see Coleridge's little son Hartley in the 'six years' darling of a pigmy size' in whom Wordsworth here sees his own dead self; and even to trace the fine phrase 'trailing clouds of glory' back to a spring night when William and Dorothy Wordsworth watched the moon coming out through a multitude of fleecy clouds. For these reconstructions see J. D. Rea, 'Coleridge's Intimations of Immortality from Proclus' (*Modern Philology*, 26 (1928–9), 201–13), and H. Hartman, 'The "Intimations" of Wordsworth's *Ode*' (*Review of English Studies*, 6 (1930), 22. 129–48). Mr. Rea also suggests that in the sonnet, *The World is too much with Us*, which is closely allied to the ode in content and inspiration, Wordsworth intended Proclus by the 'Pagan suckled in a creed outworn', and identified the sea-god Glaucus, mentioned by Proclus, with 'Proteus, rising from the sea'. In spite of the authority of Mr. Douglas Bush—*Mythology and the Romantic Tradition in English Poetry* (Harvard Studies in English, 18, Cambridge, Mass., 1937), 59—this suggestion can scarcely be accepted. (1) Wordsworth is saying that, rather than be like the matter-of-fact materialistic men of the nineteenth century, he would be a pagan who would see nature-spirits everywhere. This is the same thought as Schiller's in *Die Götter Griechenlands* (p. 376 f.), and it is another version of the thought in *Intimations of Immortality*, where Wordsworth regrets that he is no longer a child, to see all external nature as miraculously alive. But Proclus was not a childlike pagan. He neither saw nor believed in sea-gods and Tritons. He merely followed Plato in using the appearance of the weed-grown and shell-encrusted merman as an image for the earthbound human soul (*Rep.* 611c f.). (2) Wordsworth knew too much mythology to confuse Proteus (who rises from the sea in *Odyssey*, 4, and was well known to him from that passage and allusions in English poetry) with Glaucus: this sonnet was not written on the strange level of consciousness where half-remembered images fuse into one another, as described in *The Road to Xanadu*.

Mr. F. E. Pierce, 'Wordsworth and Thomas Taylor' (*Philological Quarterly*, 7 (1928), 60–4), points to Vaughan's *Silex scintillans* as another source for the thought of the first four stanzas of the ode, and suggests that Wordsworth got his Neoplatonic ideas, not from Coleridge, but from the illustrative parallels in Taylor's translated *Works of Plato*—which, however, he does not show that Wordsworth ever possessed. But Vaughan's *Resurrection and Immortality* and *The Retreat* are among the main channels through which Plato's thought flowed into this magnificent poem.

16. Wordsworth, preface to *Lyrical Ballads*.

17. See p. 387 f.

18. An interesting and percipient book on this whole topic, S. A. Larrabee's *English Bards and Grecian Marbles* (New York, 1943), has a good section on 'Byron and the Elgin Marbles' (151–8). Byron attacked Elgin not only in *Childe Harold's Pilgrimage* (2. 11 f.) but in *English Bards and Scotch Reviewers, The Curse of Minerva*, and one of his violent letters (Larrabee, 157, n. 11).

19. A particularly striking example of this power to re-create the past is *Childe Harold's Pilgrimage*, 4. 44–5, where Byron tells how he repeated (in a Byronic pose, lying along the prow of his boat) the voyage which Servius Sulpicius made among the ruins of the Greek cities, and which 'the Roman friend of Rome's least mortal mind' made into the occasion of a noble consolation to the heart-broken Cicero (Cic. *Fam.* 4. 5).

20. 'Pope is a Greek Temple, with a Gothic Cathedral on one hand, and a Turkish Mosque and all sorts of fantastic pagodas and conventicles about him. You may call Shakespeare and Milton pyramids if you please, but I prefer the Temple of Theseus or the Parthenon to a mountain of burnt brickwork'—Byron's letter to Moore from Ravenna, 3 May 1821 (*Works of Lord Byron*, ed. R. E. Prothero, London, 1901, *Letters and Journals*, 5. 273, letter 886).

21. Hor. *Carm.* 1. 9.

22. Byron, *Childe Harold's Pilgrimage*, 4. 75–6. In spite of his abhorrence, what he learnt of Horace remained with him. For his many reminiscences of Horace, see M. R. Thayer (cited in n. 5), 69–84.

23. See p. 407.

24. Swinburne, *Letters*, ed. E. Gosse and T. J. Wise (New York and London, 1919), 2. 196.

25. For a further discussion of this subject see p. 490 f.

26. So D. Bush, *Mythology and the Romantic Tradition in English Poetry* (Harvard Studies in English, 18, Cambridge, Mass., 1937), 75.

27. Byron wrote his own fine *Prometheus* in 1816, after Shelley had translated Aeschylus' tragedy, reading aloud to him. It was one of the favourite myths of the revolutionary era, not only in literature, but in music too—witness Beethoven's overture (1810). The Medici Venus is described with passionate worship in *Childe Harold's Pilgrimage*, 4. 49–53. See Larrabee (cited in n. 18), 158 f.

28. Keats, *Sonnet to Homer*.

29. The collection, edited by Alexander Chalmers, was published in 1810: see O. P. Starick, *Die Belesenheit von John Keats* (Berlin, 1910), 5.

30. Keats, *On seeing the Elgin Marbles for the first time* and *To Haydon* (*with the above*). See S. A. Larrabee, *English Bards and Grecian Marbles* (cited in n. 18), 210 f.

31. W. Sharp, in *The Life and Letters of Joseph Severn*, quoted by Larrabee (n. 18), 212, n. 16.

32. There is a detailed discussion, suggesting that the Urn is largely a blend of the Sosibios volute krater and a Dionysiac vase both in the Louvre, by C. M. Bowra, *The Romantic Imagination* (Cambridge, Mass., 1949) 129–135.

33. The passages Shelley chose were *Buc.* 10. 1–30 and *Georg.* 4. 360 f.
34. Ov. *Met.* 9. 715. There is also a naughty Latin epigram on a lady's watch among Shelley's juvenilia, as well as a rather poor Horatian version of the epitaph in Gray's *Elegy.*
35. See A. S. Droop, *Die Belesenheit Percy Bysshe Shelley's nach den direkten Zeugnissen und den bisherigen Forschungen* (Weimar, 1906), to which I am indebted in this section.
36. In *The Wandering Jew*, which Shelley and Medwin wrote when they were boys, the epigraph to the fourth canto was Aeschylus, *Eumenides,* 48 f.
37. Shelley, letter to Gisborne, 22 Oct. 1821.
38. See N. I. White, *Portrait of Shelley* (New York, 1945), 465.
39. See, for instance, H. Agar, *Milton and Plato* (Princeton, 1925). On Shelley, there is L. Winstanley's 'Platonism in Shelley' (*Essays and Studies by Members of the English Association,* 4 (1913), 72–100).
40. See J. G. Frazer, *The Golden Bough,* for the interpretation of this legend as a symbol of the annual death of the fertility of nature. (This appears in cc. 29–33 of the one-volume abridged edition, New York, 1940.)
41. There is a list of the unexpectedly numerous parallels between *Adonais* and its chief models, Theocritus' lament for Daphnis, Bion's lament for Adonis, and the anonymous lament for Bion, by George Norlin, in *University of Colorado Studies,* 1 (1902–3), 305–21.
42. Shelley, *Adonais,* stanza 9.
43. Shelley, *Adonais*: the dragon, stanza 27 = Bion, 60–1; the poison, stanza 36 = *Lament for Bion,* 109–12.
44. This was in 1818 (N. I. White, cited in n. 38, 271). *Swellfoot the Tyrant* was begun in August 1819.
45. See R. Ackermann, *Lucans Pharsalia in den Dichtungen Shelley's* (Zweibrücken, 1896).
46. Shelley, letter to Hogg, Sept. 1815.
47. So Shelley, *Adonais,* stanza 38.
48. Lucan, *Bell. ciu.* 9. 700 f.
49. Milton, *Paradise Lost,* 10. 521 f.
50. Shelley, *The Revolt of Islam,* 8. 21; *Prometheus Unbound,* 3. 1. 40, 3. 4. 19, &c.
51. Demogorgon has a complex ancestry. His name is evidently a blend of the monstrous terrifying Gorgons and the great Craftsman, *Demiourgos,* who Plato says made the universe. He is mentioned in Lucan, 6. 498, and invoked by the witch in Lucan, 6. 744 f.; then in Statius, *Theb.* 4. 513 f.; he appears as Daemogorgon in Boccaccio's *Genealogia deorum,* and reaches English poetry in Spenser through Ariosto. Pointing to 'the terror of the earth' in *Prometheus Unbound,* 3. 1. 19, Miss J. F. C. Gutteling in *Neophilologus* 9 (1924), 283–5, suggests that Shelley may have combined the simple elements *demos* ('people') and *Gorgon* to indicate the element of religion which he himself hated most, its power to terrorize the people.
52. Shelley, *Adonais,* stanza 45.

53. See N. I. White (cited in n. 38), 22.

54. This is Vergil, *Bucolics*, 4: see also pp. 72 f. and 399.

55. These words are from Tennyson's fine ode *To Virgil*.

56. There is a description of Shelley's varied and active interest in Greco-Roman sculpture in S. A. Larrabee's *English Bards and Grecian Marbles* (New York, 1943), c. 8.

57. Shelley, *Epipsychidion*, 149 f.

Notes on 19. THE TIME OF REVOLUTION, § 5: ITALY

1. Leopardi, *Canti* 3, *Ad Angelo Mai*, 69–70:
   Ahi dal dolor comincia e nasce
   L'italo canto.

2. Plato, *Rep.* 491e.

3. 'All' udire certi gran tratti di quei sommi uomini, spessissimo io balzava in piedi agitatissimo e fuori di me, e lagrime di dolore e di rabbia mi scaturivano del vedermi nato in Piemonte ed in tempi e governi ove niuna alta cosa non si poteva nè fare nè dire ed inutilmente appena forse ella si poteva sentire e pensare.' (*Vita di Alfieri, scritta da esso*, ed. Linaker, Florence, 1903, 95.)

4. At first he was enthusiastic over the Revolution. He went to the ruins of the Bastille and gathered some of its stones as a memento: see G. Megaro, *Vittorio Alfieri, Forerunner of Italian Nationalism* (New York, 1930), 110 and notes. Wordsworth did the same thing (*The Prelude*, 9. 67 f.).

5. Not all are strictly definable as tragedies. *Abele* he called a *tramelogedia*; *Alceste seconda* is based on a straight translation of Euripides' *Alcestis*; *Merope* and *Timoleone* do not end tragically (though their last-minute deliverances ally them to some Euripidean plays).

6. The story is in Ovid, *Met.* 10. 298 f.

7. Alfieri's play makes Arnold's *Merope* (p. 451 f.) look even paler by contrast.

8. For instance, he read Aeschylus' *Seven against Thebes* (in translation) for his *Polinice*, and wrote *Agamemnone* and *Oreste* under the inspiration of Seneca; *Virginia* came from Livy, *Timoleone* from Plutarch, *Ottavia* from Tacitus and from the play attributed to Seneca; *Antigone* was inspired by Statius' *Thebaid*. Alfieri was particularly devoted to the Roman historians, Tacitus, Sallust, and Livy. In this, as in his passion for Plutarch, he was very close to the men who made the French Revolution. On his debt to the classics in general see G. Megaro (cited in n. 4), c. 4.

9. Alfieri lays this down in his treatise *Della tirannide*, 1. 1. He also wrote a comedy, *I troppi*, which is full of abuse of the common people.

10. On Chénier's career see p. 401 f. A reconstruction of his friendship with Alfieri is given in P. Dimoff, *La Vie et l'œuvre d'André Chénier* (Paris, 1936), 1. 220 f.

11. Alfieri's *Del principe e delle lettere* is analysed in Megaro (cited in n. 4), c. 2.

12. There is an analysis of the character of the tyrant as depicted by Alfieri, *Der Tyrann in Vittorio Alfieris Tragödien*, by M. Schwehm (Bonn, 1917).

13. This is what Montesquieu calls 'commencer par faire un mauvais citoyen pour faire un bon esclave' (*De l'esprit des lois*, 4. 3); according to Helvétius, it is the beginning of the collapse of a despotic state.

14. Wordsworth, *The Prelude*, 11. 108–9.

15. He produced a translation of Catullus, 66 (*The Hair of Berenice*), with a commentary. Homer and Plutarch were among his favourite authors: see A. Cippico, 'The Poetry of Ugo Foscolo' (*Proceedings of the British Academy*, 1924–5). On his eminently successful but unfortunately incomplete experiments in translating Homer (*Iliad*, 1 and 3) see G. Finsler, *Homer in der Neuzeit* (Leipzig, 1912), 116–17.

16. The first words in Foscolo's collected works, the opening of an admirable sonnet—

> Non son chi fui; perì di noi gran parte

are Horace's

> Non sum qualis eram (*Carm.* 4. 1. 3) + magna pars mei (*Carm.* 3. 30. 6)

with the mellow Horatian irony deepened by youthful gloom. There are also two charming odes, which he calls Aeolian, but which are really more Horatian in manner: *A Luigia Pallavicini* and *All' amica risanata*. Like a real revolutionary, although he admired Horace's artistic skill, he despised Horace personally as an apostate from the republic and a flatterer of the 'tyrant' (L. Pietrobono in *Orazio nella letteratura mondiale*, Rome, 1936, XIV, 127).

17. On this idea see p. 364 f., on Lessing's *Wie die Alten den Tod gebildet*.

18. See p. 315 f. on Parini's *Il giorno*.

19. Foscolo, *Dei sepolcri*, 293–5:

> Ove fia santo e lagrimato il sangue
> Per la patria versato, e finchè il sole
> Risplenderà su le sciagure umane.

20. Foscolo spent many years on a didactic poem to be called *Le Grazie*, of which the unfinished fragments are published as *Inni*: it was intended to glorify the Greek divinities as the true inspirers of civilization, as the creators of beauty, and as the patrons of philosophy and poetry, the two methods of appreciating the world. In this positive paganism he appears to me to be a direct ancestor of Carducci and Leconte de Lisle (on whom see pp. 455, 456).

21. Details, with analyses of his separate works, are given in F. Moroncini's *Studio sul Leopardi filologo* (Naples, 1891).

22. These were Dio Chrysostom, Aelius Aristides, Hermogenes, and Fronto.

23. In Rome he found no one who knew Greek and Latin—the Romans cared for nothing but antiquarianism; in Milan it was worse, he could not find a single edition of a Greek or Latin classic published later than the seventeenth century; in Bologna, philological studies were 'in uno stato che fa pietà, anzi non esistono affatto'; in Florence, supreme

disdain of classical literature; in Naples, despite its pretence of admiring antiquity, utter indifference. See Moroncini (cited in n. 21), 25 f., quoting Leopardi's own letters.

24. Towards the end of his life (1833–) when he had abandoned the ideals of patriotism and progress, he wrote a *Supplement to the Battle of Frogs and Mice* (*Paralipomeni della batracomiomachia*), which, under the inspiration of Casti's *Talking Animals*, satirizéd the attempts of the Italians to free themselves from the Austrians, and at the same time poured scorn on Germanic culture.

25. See Moroncini (cited in n. 21), 169 f. In the same year Leopardi translated book 2 of the *Aeneid*, the *Moretum*, and Hesiod's description of the battle of the gods and the Titans.

26. Leopardi's *Alla primavera* (*Canti* 7), like Schiller's *Die Götter Griechenlands* (on which see p. 376 f.), asks if it is really true that the spirits which once made all nature alive have for ever disappeared.

27. *All' Italia* and *Sopra il monumento di Dante* (*Canti* 1–2) were written in 1818 and published together in early 1819 as *Canzone sullo stato presente dell' Italia*. The Mai poem (*Canti* 3) was composed in 1820. On the career of the brilliant Jesuit scholar Mai (1782–1854), see J. E. Sandys, *A History of Classical Scholarship* (Cambridge, 1908), 3. 241. There were several unusual things about his discovery of Cicero's *De re publica*. (1) The book had been entirely lost, and was known only through excerpts. (2) Mai did not find it in an ordinary manuscript, but in a palimpsest—i.e. in a manuscript which had been cleaned off in the Dark Ages in order to receive the text of St. Augustine's commentary on the Psalms. He detected the faint traces of earlier writing beneath the later text, and was able to read them and copy them. (3) The political doctrine of the book, although not new to students of Greco-Roman political theory, confirmed the aspirations of the revolutionary generation in its recommendation of the division of powers within the state, and in its assertion that abstract justice was superior to the will of the monarch.

28. Leopardi, *Canti* 3, *Ad Angelo Mai*, 61 to the end.

29. Leopardi, *Canti* 1, *All' Italia*, 61 f.

30. De Quincey, *Levana*.

31. Leopardi, *Canti* 27, *Amore e morte*, 27 311

> Quando novellamente
> Nasce nel cor profondo
> Un amoroso affetto,
> Languido e stanco insiem con esso in petto
> Un desiderio di morir si sente. . . .

32. Leopardi, *Canti* 9, *Ultimo canto di Saffo*.

33. His belief that crushing boredom (*noia, tedio*) was the central condition of human life is clearly the same as Baudelaire's view of *ennui*: see, for instance, the four poems called *Spleen* in *Les Fleurs du mal*, 77–80.

34. Leopardi, *Operette morali* (1824–32). English is not well enough supplied with diminutives to permit a good translation of *operette*.

35. He himself said that his poems were not to be regarded as imitations of any one author (*Scritti letterari*, ed. Mastica (Florence, 1899),

2. 283–5). I owe this quotation to J. Van Horne's *Studies on Leopardi* (Iowa University Humanistic Studies, 1. 4, 1916)—a useful introduction to Leopardi's *Zibaldone*, slightly marred by the attempt to explain Leopardi through the antithesis 'romantic')('classical', and by the idea that Greek and Roman culture is an 'extinct phase of human life' (p. 22).

36. Leopardi had the greatest admiration for the style of Greek and Latin prose and poetry. 'The men of antiquity', he wrote, 'devoted to the art of style an infinitely greater amount of study than we give to it; they understood a thousand secrets whose existence we do not even suspect or which we comprehend with difficulty when explained by Cicero or Quintilian' (*Pensieri di varia filosofia e di bella letteratura*, 5. 407–8, quoted and translated by J. Van Horne (n. 35)).

37. Leopardi, *Canti* 30, *Sopra un basso rilievo antico sepolcrale dove una giovane morta è rappresentata in atto di partire accomiatandosi dai suoi*, 27–8:

> Mai non veder la luce
> Era, credo, il miglior.

Cf. Sophocles, *Oedipus Coloneus*, 1224 f., and Theognis, 425–8. It is interesting to compare this gloomy poem with another lyric on Greek sculpture, Keats's *Ode on a Grecian Urn* (which is full of life), and with Lessing's exposition of the calm and natural attitude to death expressed by Greek gravestones (p. 364 f.). Here Leopardi's thought is far less Greek than Christian, and he was probably influenced by his devout mother. See his next poem (*Canti* 31), which, like a medieval sermon, reflects that the beautiful woman whose portrait appears on her tomb is now only 'mud and bones' beneath it.

38. Ovid, *Heroides*, 15. Lines 65–8 are an adaptation of Vergil, *Georg.* 3. 66–8.

39. Leopardi, *Canti* 15, *Il sogno*; Propertius, 4. 7; Petrarch, *Trionfo della Morte*, 2.

40. It is strange to see Lucretius beginning a poem designed to prove, among other things, that the gods know nothing of our world, by an invocation to Venus.

41. See the fine comparison of a disturbed ant-hill to the eruption of Vesuvius, in *Canti* 34, *La ginestra*, 202 f.: an idea which reappears in the work of the contemporary American pessimist, Hemingway, in the last chapter of *A Farewell to Arms*. While the hero's mistress is dying in childbed, he remembers how once he had thrown a log full of ants on to a camp-fire, and how little their agony and death meant to him.

Notes on 19. THE TIME OF REVOLUTION, § 6: CONCLUSION

1. Oswald Spengler ends his preface to *Der Untergang des Abendlandes* by saying that he is 'proud to call it *a German philosophy*', and (in a sentence omitted in the English translation) hopes it will be worthy of the achievements of the German armies:

> 'Ich habe nur den Wunsch beizufügen, dass dies Buch neben den militärischen Leistungen Deutschlands nicht ganz unwürdig dastehen möge.'

2. Ovid, *Tristia* and *Ex Ponto*.

3. The minor poets of this period in England—Leigh Hunt, Peacock, and others—are well expounded in D. Bush's *Mythology and the Romantic Tradition in English Poetry* (Harvard Studies in English, 18, Cambridge, Mass., 1937), c. 5.

4. Sébastien Mercier, who hated both the classics and the moderns, denounced both Horace and Boileau for killing originality:

> Nés tous originaux, nous mourrons tous copies.
> Eh bien, qui rétrécit la sphère des génies?
> C'est ce code vanté, si froid et si mesquin,
> Que Boileau composa d'après l'auteur latin.
> Il défend tout essor; abondance, vigueur,
> Style mâle, hardi, fierté, tout lui fait peur.

(Quoted by J. Marouzeau, in *Orazio nella letteratura mondiale*, Rome, 1936, XIV, 77.)

5. Blake, *Prophetic Writings* (ed. Sloss and Wallis, Oxford, 1926), 1. 640, quoted by D. Bush (n. 3), 131–2. On 'Barbarism and Religion' see p. 352 f.

Notes on 20. PARNASSUS AND ANTICHRIST

1. Wordsworth, *The World is too much with Us*. On this poem see also pp. 377, 676.

2. Arnold, *Consolation*.

3. Wordsworth, *The World is too much with Us*.

4. Sainte-Beuve coined the phrase 'ivory tower' in his poem A. M. Villemain' (*Pensées d'août*, *Œuvres*, Paris, 1879, vol. 2, p. 287).

5. Milton, *Paradise Lost*, 1. 6–7:

6.   What was the great Parnassus' self to Thee,
       Mount Skiddaw?

—asked Wordsworth in a sonnet (*Pelion and Ossa flourish side by side*: *Miscellaneous Sonnets* 5) which he composed in 1801, but did not publish until 1815.

7. For instance, Leconte de Lisle and Landor were spiritually brothers. There is a good deal of useful literature on the French Parnassiano and their own interpretation of these ideals. See H. Peyre, *Bibliographie critique de l'Hellénisme en France de 1843 à 1870* (*Yale Romanic Studies* 6, New Haven, 1932); P. Martino, *Parnasse et Symbolisme* (Paris, 1925); and M. Souriau, *Histoire du Parnasse* (Paris, 1930).

8. Hugo, *Notre-Dame*; *L'Homme qui rit*; *Les Travailleurs de la mer*.

9. Keats, *Ode to a Nightingale*.

10. D. Nisard, *Poètes latins de la décadence* (1834); see also his manifesto *Contre la littérature facile*.

11. Carducci, *Classicismo e romanticismo* (*Rime nuove*, 69).

12. *Les Trophées*, published in 1893 after circulating in manuscript for years. Heredia was the favourite pupil of Leconte de Lisle, and edited Chénier's *Bucoliques*.

13. Heredia, *Antoine et Cléopâtre*:

> Et sur elle courbé, l'ardent Imperator
> Vit dans ses larges yeux étoilés de points d'or
> Toute une mer immense où fuyaient des galères.

There is an echo which I have often admired in the sonnet *Après Cannes* —all the more admirable because it has converted a satiric sneer into a frown of real grandeur. Juvenal derides the desire of great generals for military glory, and cries (10. 157–8):

> O qualis facies et quali digna tabella
> cum Gaetula ducem portaret belua luscum!

Heredia describes the panic in Rome after Cannae, and pictures the mob going out every evening to the aqueducts:

> Tous anxieux de voir surgir, au dos vermeil
> Des monts Sabins où luit l'œil sanglant du soleil,
> Le Chef borgne monté sur l'éléphant Gétule.

Petronius would have called that *curiosa felicitas*—the image of the one red Cyclops-eye of the sun glaring over the elephant-backed hills, like Hannibal's.

14. Carducci, *Odi barbare* (1877). These poems, he said, were partly inspired by Goethe's *Roman Elegies* (on which see p. 380 f.).

15. The system is an adaptation of that invented by Chiabrera (on whom see p. 235 f.), and is explained by G. L. Bickersteth in his introduction to his excellent volume of selections from Carducci (London, 1913).

16. Hor. *Carm.* 3. 1. 1: 'Odi profanum uolgus et arceo.'

17. Cf. also Carducci's *Intermezzo*, 9: he says that he hopes, in life, to sing the songs of Horace's master Archilochus of Paros, and, in death, to be buried in a tomb of Parian marble, as pure and lasting as the poems written in that tradition.

18. Gautier, *L'Art*:

> Point de contraintes fausses!
> Mais que pour marcher droit
>   Tu chausses,
> Muse, un cothurne étroit.

19. Gautier, *L'Art*:

> Tout passe. — L'art robuste
> Seul a l'éternité,
>   Le buste
> Survit à la cité.

20. Leconte de Lisle: 'Le Beau n'est pas le serviteur du Vrai.' After abandoning socialism, he wrote, 'Les grandes œuvres d'art pèsent dans la balance d'un autre poids que cinq cents millions d'almanachs démocratiques et sociaux. L'œuvre d'Homère comptera un peu plus dans la somme des efforts moraux de l'humanité que celle de Blanqui.' (Quoted by P. Martino, *Parnasse et Symbolisme*, Paris, 1925, 52.)

21. Hugo, *William Shakespeare*, 6. 1. On the whole question see L. Rosenblatt, *L'Idée de l'art pour l'art dans la littérature anglaise pendant la période victorienne* (Bibliothèque de la Revue de littérature comparée, 70, Paris, 1931), especially pp. 12–13 and 58–61. Miss Rosenblatt, following R. F. Egan, 'The Genesis of the Theory of "Art for Art's Sake" in Germany and in England' (*Smith College Studies in Modern Languages*, 2. 4, Northampton, Mass., 1921, and 5. 3, Northampton, Mass., 1924), suggests that the intermediaries were Crabb Robinson (who knew many German philosophers) and Benjamin Constant (to whom he passed the idea).

22. *Zweckmässigkeit ohne Zweck* (see Rosenblatt, cited in n. 21, 63).

23. Gautier's attacks on the type of criticism which insisted that all literature should be fit for the Young Person were made in his prefaces to *Mademoiselle de Maupin* and *Albertus*, and were echoed, almost word for word, by Swinburne in *Notes on Poems and Reviews*. (See Rosenblatt, cited in n. 21, 146 f. and 159. For Pater's dependence on Swinburne, see Rosenblatt, 195 f.)

24. For an exhaustive discussion of the moral purpose of Greek literature, see W. Jaeger, *Paideia* (Oxford, 1939–44).

25. This point is well made by Rosenblatt (cited in n. 21), 16–51, with quotations from the periodicals (often highly influential) of the early Victorian age.

26. Pater, *The Renaissance: The School of Giorgione* (London, 1888³), 140.

27. J.-K. Huysmans, *A rebours*: the symphonies of perfume, c. 10; the books, c. 12; the corruption of Langlois, c. 6.

28. The 'poisonous book' which influenced Dorian Gray more than any other, and which he had bound in nine different colours, to 'suit his various moods and the changing fancies of a nature over which he seemed, at times, to have almost entirely lost control', was Huysmans's *A rebours* (Wilde, *The Picture of Dorian Gray*, c. 10 fin., c. 11). Details will be found in A. J. Farmer's *Le Mouvement esthétique et 'décadent' en Angleterre* (*1873–1900*) (Bibliothèque de la Revue de littérature comparée, 75, Paris, 1931), bk. 2, c. 2.

29. In *Dover Beach* Arnold compares himself, musing by the sea, with Sophocles listening to the Ægean. Once, in a sonnet written during the hard eighteen-forties, he says that his consolations 'in these bad days' are Homer, the Stoic Epictetus, and most of all Sophocles—not for his remoteness from the present, but because, in times of similar disaster, he 'saw life steadily and saw it whole'. On Swinburne's knowledge of Greek see W. R. Rutland's *Swinburne, a Nineteenth Century Hellene* (Oxford, 1931).

30. Quoted by E. de Selincourt, 'Classicism and Romanticism in the Poetry of Walter Savage Landor', *Vorträge der Bibliothek Warburg 1930–1* (ed. F. Saxl, Leipzig, 1932), 230–50. In 1815 and 1820 Landor published collections of 'heroic idylls' in Latin, which he only much later translated into English verse. His *Latine scribendi defensio* (1795) is a slight thing: it is now a bibliographical rarity, but can be read in the

Modern Language Association rotograph 279. It is prefaced by a number of Landor's Latin poems, beginning with a set of hendecasyllables addressed to Catullus.

31. There is an exhaustive discussion of Browning's changing and developing interest in Greek and Latin literature by Robert Spindler, *Robert Browning und die Antike* (Englische Bibliothek, 6, Leipzig, 1930). Apparently Browning began Latin about 6 and Greek a year or two later; he got well on with them at school; but he was badly taught at London University, so that his interests turned away to medieval things. In later life his wife rekindled his delight in Greek, which never died thereafter. He himself has sketched the growth of his knowledge of Greek in a charming poem called *Development*, built round a fine tribute to his father's gay and clever teaching. Of his three large Hellenic works, *Balaustion's Adventure* has much charm (see p. 452 f.); but in *The Last Adventure of Balaustion*, and still more in his translation of *Agamemnon*, he was overcome by the innate vices of his own style: pedantic allusions, bewildering crowds of proper names, and grotesquely strained rhythms which make the poems difficult to study and impossible to act. It is strange to see him, when plunging deep into Greek poetry and history, committing just the same faults that spoiled his youthful exploration of the Italian Middle Ages, *Sordello*. Those who wish to study the precise extent of Browning's debt to the different Greek and Roman authors whom he read will find the facts in Spindler, and also, in tabular form, in T. L. Hood, 'Browning's Ancient Classical Sources' (*Harvard Studies in Classical Philology*, 33 (1922), 79–180).

32. On Leconte de Lisle's knowledge of Greek, see H. Peyre, *Louis Ménard* (Yale Romanic Studies, 5, New Haven, 1932), 478 f. The effect of Leconte de Lisle's translations on Louÿs was like that of Chapman's upon Keats.

33. Tennyson, *The Lotos-eaters*, expressing almost the same mood as his *Hesperides* and *Sea-fairies*.

34. Browning's description of Aristophanes, in *The Last Adventure of Balaustion*.

35. See J. Vianey, *Les Poèmes barbares de Leconte de Lisle* (Paris, 1933), for a short analysis of these interesting pieces, and A. Fairlie, *Leconte de Lisle's Poems on the Barbarian Races* (Cambridge, 1947), for a sensitively written analysis of the sources to which he went for his imaginative material. *Barbares* (as Miss Fairlie points out) is used from the Greco-Roman point of view, to mean 'non-Greek and non-Roman'.

36. So H. Peyre, *Bibliographie critique de l'Hellénisme en France* (cited in n. 7), 38.

37. Landor, *Homer, Laertes, Agatha*, 2. 218 f.

38. *Ulysses* was written after the death of Tennyson's much-loved friend Hallam, to express 'the sense of loss . . . but that still life must be fought out to the end'. See the admirable analysis by D. Bush, in *Mythology and the Romantic Tradition in English Poetry* (Harvard Studies in English, 18, Cambridge, Mass., 1937), 210 f. Mr. Bush points out very appositely that when Tennyson treats a serious problem both in an

antique setting and in a modern setting, the antique treatment is always far superior.

39. Tolstoy, *Anna Karenina*, tr. Garnett, pt. 7, c. 30.

40. There is a clever analysis of these plays in D. Bush's book cited in n. 38: *Merope*, 260–2; *Atalanta in Calydon*, 331–44; *Erechtheus*, 344–9. W. R. Rutland, *Swinburne, a Nineteenth Century Hellene* (Oxford, 1931), praises both Swinburne's dramas very highly and analyses them with much insight and knowledge: though few will agree with him in placing *Erechtheus* beside *Samson Agonistes*.

41. There is a full analysis of *Balaustion's Adventure*, and of the translation of *Alcestis* which it contains, in R. Spindler's *Browning und die Antike* (cited in n. 31), 1. 17–85, 2. 278–94. Spindler's bibliography is also useful.

42. Prologue to *Fifine at the Fair*.

43. On the Battle of the Books see c. 14.

44. There is a useful edition of the *Prière sur l'Acropole* by E. Vinaver and T. B. L. Webster (Manchester, 1934), which shows that—although Renan said he took the text of his prayer from 'an old manuscript' he had written during his visit to Athens—it was in fact composed in several stages and carefully revised. The editors also point out striking resemblances to ideas expressed in Chateaubriand's *Itinéraire de Paris à Jérusalem*.

45. France dedicated his *Poèmes dorés* to Leconte de Lisle.

46. *Le Procurateur de Judée* is stated to have been suggested to France by Renan. 'He and Renan were talking together, and Renan declared that the things described in the Gospels must have made a deep impression on those who took part in them. This France denied, and Renan, smiling, said something tantamount to 'Then, in your view, Pontius Pilate, in old age . . .'' (M. Belloc Lowndes, *Where Love and Friendship dwelt* (London, 1943), 178).

47. Carducci's bitterest personal attack on the Pope was *Per Giuseppe Monti e Gaetano Tognetti*, which describes him as rubbing his old hands with delight at the thought of the execution of two Italian agitators. On this subject see also S. W. Halperin, 'Italian Anticlericalism 1871–1914' (*Journal of Modern History*, 19 (1947), 1. 18 f.). For Argument 1 in Carducci see *In una chiesa gotica*: 'Addio, semitico nume!'

48. On Alfieri's opposition to the Roman Catholic church see G. Megaro, *Vittorio Alfieri* (New York, 1930), c. 3.

49. The victorious locomotive engine appears again at the end of *Alle fonti del Clitumno*: the last words are *fischia il vapore*.

50. Leconte de Lisle, *Poèmes antiques: Hypatie*: 'Le vil Galiléen t'a frappée et maudite.' He has an even stronger denunciation, called *Les Siècles maudits*, in *Poèmes barbares*. In tones which Gibbon would have admired, even if he disapproved their violence, he calls the Catholic Middle Ages 'siècles d'égorgeurs, de lâches et de brutes', and denounces the church as

la Goule
Romaine, ce vampire ivre de sang humain.

51. There is a brilliant monograph on Ménard by Henri Peyre (*Yale Romanic Studies*, 5, New Haven, 1932), to which I am much indebted. Mr. Peyre points out that Ménard was a direct heir of the revolutionary poets: among his early works were a *Prométhée délivré* (inspired by Shelley) and an *Euphorion* (inspired by Goethe). Like most of the men of that generation, he never saw Greece itself, although he had an opportunity to visit it. He was, of course, a fervent opponent of the naïve nineteenth-century ideal of progress ('every day in every way we get better and better'): for two reasons—first, because it is impossible for us to surpass the Greeks (a Battle of the Books argument); and second (a new one) because it is immoral to expect that the tide of progress will carry us forward, and we should reconcile ourselves to work and the difficulties of this world. The quotation in the text is on p. 203 of Mr. Peyre's book.

52. This is from the first chorus of Swinburne's *Atalanta in Calydon*. His *The Last Oracle* is a hymn to Apollo, representing the Greek spirit as ruined by Christianity with its gloom and ugliness:

> Fire for light and hell for heaven and psalms for paeans
> Filled the clearest eyes and lips most sweet of song,
> When for chant of Greeks the wail of Galilaeans
> Made the whole world moan with hymns of wrath and wrong.

And his poem *For the Feast of Giordano Bruno, Philosopher and Martyr* equals Carducci's hatred for the churches, calling Bruno a

> soul whose spirit on earth was as a rod
> To scourge off priests, a sword to pierce their God.

It ends by placing Bruno in an atheists' heaven between Lucretius and Shelley.

53. See K. Franke, *Pierre Louÿs* (Bonn 1937).

54. Louÿs himself wrote:

'La poésie est une fleur d'*Orient* qui ne vit pas dans nos serres chaudes. La Grèce elle-même l'a recue d'Ionie, et c'est de là aussi qu'André Chénier ou Keats l'ont transplantée parmi nous, dans le désert poétique de leur époque; mais elle meurt avec chaque poète qui nous la rapporte d'*Asie*. Il faut toujours aller la chercher à la source du soleil.' *Poésies* (Paris, 1930), introductory note.

This identification of Ionia with Asia, and the idea that Greece got her poetic genius from the Orient, is almost entirely bosh.

55. On 'Dares the Phrygian' see p. 51 f.

56. Wilamowitz's review is reprinted from the *Göttinger gelehrte Anzeigen*, 1896, 623 f., in his *Sappho und Simonides* (Berlin, 1913). He points out that even the name Bilitis is un-Greek, and conjectures that it comes from Beltis, one of the appellations of the Syrian sex-goddess. It must be said, however, that Louÿs had great talent for description, and in the early poems of the Bilitis book showed a real pastoral genius: they evoked three exquisite songs by Debussy.

57. Louÿs, *Aphrodite* (*Poésies*, p. 163).

58. Nietzsche, *Die Geburt der Tragödie aus dem Geist der Musik* (1872). Wilamowitz's reply was *Zukunftsphilologie*, a name which neatly alludes to the description of Wagner's music (then much admired by Nietzsche) as

Zukunftsmusik. Later, Nietzsche made a personal adaptation of the Theseus and Ariadne myth, in which he became Dionysus and Cosima Wagner Ariadne: see Crane Brinton, *Nietzsche* (Cambridge, Mass., 1941), 70.

59. Nietzsche, *Zur Genealogie der Moral*, 1. 5. Theognis says ἀγαθοί and κακοί, ἐσθλοί and δειλοί. 'Gentlemen' are men who have a family (a *gens*) with land and a coat of arms; 'villains' are serfs attached to a *villa*, a gentleman's estate. The primary meanings of 'noble' and 'vulgar' show a similar distinction. On Theognis see also W. Jaeger, *Paideia*, 1. 186 f.

60. Callicles in Plato's *Gorgias* and Thrasymachus in *The Republic* both say that justice is really the interest of the stronger.

61. Nietzsche, *Jenseits von Gut und Böse*, part 3, para. 62.

62. Nietzsche, *Jenseits von Gut und Böse*, part 5, para. 195. Cf. also *Zur Genealogie der Moral*, cc. 7–11; *Jenseits von Gut und Böse*, paras. 44, 46, 201; and *Antichrist*, cc. 24–5.

63. Nietzsche, *Die Geburt der Tragödie*, cc. 13 and 15.

64. Nietzsche, *Jenseits von Gut und Böse*, 7, para. 218: 'Flaubert... der brave Bürger von Rouen.'

65. This is the main implication of his story *Un Cœur simple*, at the end of which an old housemaid has a vision of the Holy Ghost in the form of her pet parrot. This is significantly juxtaposed to the noble legend of St. Julian the Hospitaller.

66. *Paganisme, Christianisme, muflisme.*

67. Flaubert, *Madame Bovary* and *Bouvard et Pécuchet.*

68. Pater, 'Style', in *Appreciations.*

69. On *Les Martyrs* see pp. 103–4.

70. On Hypatia see p. 456.

71. Lygia is the daughter of the chief of the Lygians, allied to the Suevi; her huge retainer, the bear-man Ursus, is also a Lygian. This is as near first-century Polish as makes no matter.

72. Unfortunately Sienkiewicz made the common mistake of searchers after local colour, and believed that the vulgar millionaire Trimalchio, whose banquet is described by Petronius in his *Satirica*, was a typical Roman gentleman. As a matter of fact, everything that Trimalchio does is either silly or vulgar or both, so that it is a sure guide to how the upper-class Romans did *not* behave. Petronius himself would be politely amused to see the vulgar superstitions and ostentations, which he observed in Levantine freedmen, transferred to his own life. The same mistake has been made, among others, by Mr. J. Carcopino, *Daily Life in Ancient Rome* (tr. Lorimer, New Haven, 1940). It was pointed out by M. Johnston, 'Sienkiewicz and Petronius' (*Classical Weekly*, 25 (1932), 79); and see G. Highet, 'Petronius the Moralist' (*Trans. Am. Phil. Assn.* 72, 1941, 178 f.).

73. On the advance in history during the nineteenth century see p. 472.

74. On Fénelon's *Télémaque* see p. 336 f. J. J. Barthélemy's *Voyage du jeune Anacharsis en Grèce*, published towards the end of the eighteenth century, was reissued surprisingly often, long after his death: in 1845, in 1860, and so on.

75. On Niebuhr's theory and Macaulay's *Lays* see also p. 472 f.

76. For Argument 1 see the Battle of the Books see p. 262 f.

Notes on 21. A CENTURY OF SCHOLARSHIP

1. Browning, *A Grammarian's Funeral shortly after the Revival of Learning in Europe.*

2. One of the strangest types of publication to be found in university libraries is the annual 'programme' issued by German schools during the nineteenth century. It was a paper-bound pamphlet of some thirty pages, prepared for the prize-giving day. Usually it contained a list of all the classes, with the names of all the boys and masters, and a schedule of the subjects taught; and then a dissertation in Latin or German by one of the masters, *On the Comet mentioned in Juvenal's Sixth Satire* or *The Sources of Gildas.* That kind of publication brought credit to the school, earned some kudos for the master, and—if there was anything in his article —helped him towards a university position.

3. Sid. Ap. *Ep.* 6. 4. 1. Some have thought that the warning in *Carm.* 17. 15 f., 'do not expect wines from Gaza, Chios, and Italy', implies that the trade-routes were broken; but it is more commonplace, being only the favourite theme of the poet's frugal meal (cf. Juvenal, *Sat.* 11). See C. E. Stevens, *Sidonius Apollinaris and His Age* (Oxford, 1933), c. 4.

4. Niebuhr befriended Leopardi (p. 430) when he was ambassador at Rome. *En route,* he discovered the *Institutes* of Gaius in Verona Cathedral, and helped to found the modern study of Roman law. There is an agreeable essay on him by W. Warde Fowler in *Roman Essays and Interpretations* (Oxford, 1920), 229–50—and an even more charming one on Mommsen (250–68).

5. On Niebuhr's 'romantic' background see G. P. Gooch, *History and Historians in the Nineteenth Century* (New York, 1913), 15 f., who points out that, as a boy, he was enraptured by Voss's translation of the *Odyssey* (see p. 375). He was also much interested in Wolf's *Prolegomena* (p. 383 f.): he dreamt that the Romans, too, had had a magnificent balladry, or rather a cycle of heroic poems: 'eine Epopoë, die an Tiefe und Glanz der Phantasie alles weit zurücklässt, was das spätere Rom hervorbrachte' (*Römische Geschichte,* 1. 259).

6. Fueter, *Geschichte der neueren Historiographie* (ed. D. Gerhard and P. Sattler, Munich, 1936³), 467, points out that L. de Beaufort, in his *Considérations sur l'incertitude des cinq premiers siècles de l'histoire romaine* (1738), had already shown that the truth about the early centuries of Rome's existence was virtually unobtainable. The Dutch scholar Perizonius, in his *Animadversiones historicae* (1685), anticipated Niebuhr in distinguishing history from myth in such early traditions.

7. The phrase comes from Ranke's preface to the first edition of his *Geschichten der romanischen und germanischen Völker von 1494 bis 1514* (1824):

'Man hat der Historie das Amt, die Vergangenheit zu richten, die Mitwelt zum Nutzen zukünftiger Jahre zu belehren, beigemessen: so hoher Aemter unterwindet sich gegenwärtiger Versuch nicht: er will blos zeigen, wie es eigentlich gewesen.'

In archaeology, the work of Schliemann was a practical method of following out Ranke's principle. By digging up the actual sites, Schliemann got nearer to finding out what really happened. In literature, the 'realistic' novelists, who professed only to record facts, without choosing or commenting, were his colleagues.

8. The criticism is the appendix to Ranke's *Geschichten* (cited in n. 7). It is called *Zur Kritik neueren Geschichtsschreiber*, and contains his famous dissection of Guicciardini. G. P. Gooch (cited in n. 5), 24 and 79, is the authority for Mommsen's remark, and for Ranke's honouring the bust of Niebuhr.

9. So G. P. Gooch (cited in n. 5), 460.

10. E. Fueter, *Geschichte der neueren Historiographie* (cited in n. 6), 553. Mommsen's son-in-law Wilamowitz saw the problem, but dodged it in a way unusual for him. In his *Geschichte der Philologie* (Einleitung in die Altertumswissenschaft, ed. Gercke and Norden (Leipzig, 1927³), 1. 70–1) he says that when Mommsen had, with Caesar's autocracy, reached the goal which he had deliberately set himself *on artistic grounds*, he broke off; and then started the preliminary work which was necessary to make a perfect history of Rome—chronology, numismatics, &c. All that was preparation for his history of the Caesars. 'Dass er von ihr nur den 5. Band geschrieben hat, werden die Laien beklagen; er urteilte richtiger.' How Mommsen's judgement was more correct Wilamowitz does not tell us, nor even if it was a historical or an artistic decision.

11. A. J. Toynbee, *A Study of History* (Oxford, 1939), 1. 3.

12. A somewhat similar explanation was given by R. G. Collingwood, in *The Idea of History* (Oxford, 1946), part 3, sect. 9, 131 f. However, he overstated the antithesis between Mommsen's earlier and later work, and his explanation that Mommsen was affected by the positivistic attitude to history (treating it only as a group of microscopic problems) is inadequate in view of such books as the *Römisches Staatsrecht*.

13. N. M. Butler, *Across the Busy Years* (New York, 1939–40), 1. 125. President Butler confirmed this to me in conversation.

14. T. Zielinski's *Cicero im Wandel der Jahrhunderte* (Leipzig, 1912³), to which all students of this subject owe so much, was written partly in order to correct Mommsen's falsification. Although it traced the 'Cicero-caricature' back to its beginnings in the late republic, it did not entirely face the problem raised by Mommsen. This has lately been taken up with great seriousness by W. Rüegg in *Cicero und der Humanismus* (Zürich, 1946). In a thoughtful preface, called 'Deutschland und der Humanismus', Rüegg suggests that both the nature of Mommsen's attack on Cicero and its success were major symptoms of the collapse of German culture, its abandonment of the liberal, humane, European tradition which Cicero largely created.

15. Fustel's fault as a historian, which is apparent as early as *La Cité antique*, was that although he insisted that every assertion must be supported by a document, he did not criticize the documents themselves so far as to recognize that even a contemporary narrative may be vitiated by mistakes, or lies, or interpolations. There is a good description of his work by C. Seignobos in Petit de Julleville's *Histoire de la langue et de la littérature française*, 8. 279–96.

16. Although Monod (*Portraits et souvenirs*, Paris, 1897, 148 f.) says Fustel gave utterance to these ideas before 1870, it is difficult to believe that he was not moved (perhaps unconsciously) by the spirit of resistance to German aggrandizement. His theory was of course seized upon with delight by French nationalists and attacked by their opponents. There is an amusing chapter in Charles Maurras's *Devant l'Allemagne éternelle* (Paris, 1937), describing the uproar which went up when the newly established *Ligue d'Action Française* organized a celebration of Fustel's seventy-fifth birthday in 1905.

17. Ranke also insisted that it was impossible to write the history of one nation by itself: in extreme old age he attempted to compose a 'universal history', but it was too much for him.

18. F. W. Newman, brother of the famous Catholic convert who became a cardinal, traversed during his long life (1805–97) almost all the crusades and eccentricities, laudable and ridiculous, of the nineteenth century: antivivisection, vegetarianism, utilitarian clothing designed by himself, &c. On him, and on the controversy with Arnold, more details will be found in L. Trilling's competent *Matthew Arnold* (New York, 1939), 168–78; and there is a fuller sketch of his character in I. G. Sieveking's *F. W. Newman* (London, 1909).

19. These quotations come from Newman's preface to his translation, pp. iv–v and x.

20. Newman's translation of *Iliad*, 20. 499–500. 'Ditty' is his own explanation of 'ballad'.

21. When I read Arnold's 'Since I have been reproached with undervaluing Lord Macaulay's *Lays of Ancient Rome*, let me frankly say that, to my mind, a man's power to detect the ring of false metal in those Lays is a good measure of his fitness to give an opinion about poetical matters at all', I wince: for, having enjoyed the *Lays* since boyhood, I can with an effort detect the ring of false metal, but it is usually drowned for me by the clang of true steel.

22. Housman, in his inaugural lecture on being appointed as a successor to Newman at London University, pointed out one of the worst errors, Arnold's mistranslation of *Il.* 24. 506 in *Last Words*; but agreed that the effect of the lectures as criticism outweighed all the writings of all the scholars. And Arnold was 'tortured' by bad taste in translation, because it ruined passages of poetry he had always loved: see his remarks on Maginn's rendering of *Od.* 19. 392 f. in the second lecture. Therefore, in spite of his studied urbanity, he was cruel to Newman. The motto of his lectures, *Numquamne reponam?*, comes from the savage cry of the satirist Juvenal (1. 1) forced to listen all day to bad poetry.

23. 1 Cor. xvi. 22: ἀνάθεμα = 'dedicated' to a pagan god, = 'accursed'. *Maran-atha* is Syriac for 'O Lord, come!'

24. Rev. xiii. 16–17. Matt. v. 3.

25. Job xix. 20, a passage which many commentators have tried to explain or emend.

26. See R. E. C. Houghton, *The Influence of the Classics on the Poetry of Matthew Arnold* (Oxford, 1923), 8 f., who mentions:

Balder Dead, 1. 174–7 = Vergil, *Aen.* 6. 309 f.
Balder Dead, 2. 157 f. = Hom. *Od.* 11. 35–40 and Verg. *Aen.* 6. 305 f.
Balder Dead, 2. 265 f. = Hom. *Od.* 11. 488 f.
Balder Dead, 3. 160 f. = Hom. *Il.* 23. 127 f.
Sohrab and Rustum, 111–16 = Hom. *Il.* 2. 459–68.
Sohrab and Rustum, 480–9 = Hom. *Il.* 17. 366 f.

To these might be added:

Balder Dead, 2. 101 f. = Verg. *Aen.* 6. 388–416.
Balder Dead, 3. 65 f. = Hom. *Il.* 24. 723 f.

and many other adaptations ranging from a single word and phrase to a repeated convention or the broad framework of a scene.

27. *Sohrab and Rustum*, 556 f.

28. e.g. in *Sohrab and Rustum*, the pedlars from Cabool crossing the Caucasus (160 f.), the moonlit cypress (314 f.), the Chinese painter (672 f.), and the pillars of Persepolis (860 f.); in *Balder Dead*, the spring thaw (3. 313 f.), the lonely woodcutters (3. 200 f.), and the storm-tossed sailors (3. 363 f.). One or two images which reflect Victorian England seem oddly out of place: the rich lady ('I read much of the night, and go south in the winter') in *Sohrab* 302 f., and the traveller in the English lane (*Balder*, 1. 230 f.).

29. The lost dog (*Balder*, 3. 8 f.), the captive stork (*Balder*, 3. 565 f.), the cut hyacinth (*Sohrab*, 634 f.), the dying violets (*Sohrab*, 844 f.), and a number of those mentioned in note 28.

30. 'Faint Homeric echoes' is from *The Epic*, Tennyson's introduction to *Morte d'Arthur*. On Tennyson's adaptations of Homer, see W. P. Mustard, *Classical Echoes in Tennyson* (New York, 1904), c. 1. There are more and subtler Homeric echoes in Tennyson than most of us imagine.

31. On Tennyson and Vergil see also p. 446. The quotation in the text is from the conclusion of *Morte d'Arthur*.

32. Butler, *The Authoress of the Odyssey*, c. 15, p. 256.

33. For all these judgements see Lawrence's preface.

34. Lawrence's translation of *Od.* 23. 350–1.

35. T. S. Eliot, *Euripides and Professor Murray* (1918), reprinted in *Selected Essays 1917–1932* (New York, 1932), 46–50.

36. Pierre Louÿs, who had good taste nevertheless, bitterly attacked the academic translators of his day. In the preface to his *Lectures antiques* he wrote of the best-known French translations from the Greek:

'Il suffit d'examiner les plus célèbres pour admirer avec quelle attention zélée certains universitaires s'appliquent à corriger l'original. Avec eux, plus d'épithètes hardies, plus de métaphores à double image; ils répandent sur l'auteur qu'ils daignent embellir une élégance qui leur est personnelle et surtout un 'goût' qui supprime ou ajoute, au hasard des phrases, ce qu'il convient de biffer ou d'introduire çà et là. C'est une collaboration dont le Grec a tout l'honneur et le savant toute la peine. Tel est leur désintéressement. Je l'admire. Je ne l'imiterai point.'

In his own translations he actually kept the Greek word-order, even if it was inharmonious in French. What he most admired was the translations of Leconte de Lisle—because, although they were harsh and to some eyes pedantic, they were challenging and original.

37. Quoted from Osler's article, 'Science in the Public Schools' (*The School World*, London, 1916), by Harvey Cushing, *The Life of Sir William Osler* (New York and Oxford, 1932), 1. 29 f.

38. See H. Cushing, *The Life of Sir William Osler*, 2. 124–5, for an illuminating extract from Osler's Linacre Lecture.

39. Nicholas Murray Butler, *Across the Busy Years* (cited in n. 13), 1. 65 f. President Butler later found his graduate work in classical philology equally uninspiring:

'In addition to my graduate study of philosophy I continued my work in Greek and Latin, getting some glorious experiences from the study of Plato but finding little benefit from the work given me by Professor Short. How unimportant his work was for my particular intellectual interest may be seen from a very technical philological paper which I contributed at Professor Gildersleeve's request to the *American Journal of Philology* in October, 1885, with the title 'The Post-positive *Et* in Propertius'. (Ibid. 94.)

And yet he records that another member of the Greek and Latin department who organized a *boulé*, a voluntary class to read Homer, collected a number of willing and delighted students who got through a great deal of both epics, and learned to enjoy them.

40. W. L. Phelps, *Autobiography with Letters* (New York and London, 1939), 136 f.

41. E. F. Benson, *As We Were* (London, 1930), 133–4.

42. Gibbon, *Memoirs of my Life and Writings* (Everyman ed.), 46.

43. Byron's note on *Childe Harold's Pilgrimage*, 4. 75–7.

44. Quoted from C. M. Bowra's presidential address to the Classical Association, *A Classical Education* (Oxford, 1945).

45. Here Housman's shyness and defensive arrogance led him into one of the errors which have helped to injure the study of the classics in our time. By refusing to say that the literature of Greece and Rome contained much of the best art and thought in the possession of the human race, and that it was directly relevant to us (as, for example, Hindu literature or Mayan art is not), he made it easy for those who were ignorant, mistaken, or short-sighted, to say that all the study of the past, of art, and of literature was entirely useless. Henry Ford, for instance, is reported to have declared 'History is bunk'—although it is not easy to reconcile that with his personal passion for collecting antiques. Descartes put it more gracefully but not less forcibly:

'Il n'est plus du devoir d'un honnête homme de savoir le grec et le latin, que le suisse ou le bas-breton, ni l'histoire de l'empire germano-romanique, que celle du plus petit estat qui se trouve en Europe. . . . Savoir le latin, est-ce donc en savoir plus que la fille de Cicéron au sortir de nourrice?' (Quoted by Gillot, *La Querelle des anciens et des modernes en France*, Paris, 1914, 289 n. 1.)

All Housman's readers must have felt that there was something lacking in his attitude to the subject on which he spent his life. Perhaps it was humanity. 'Humanismus', says a Swiss scholar, 'ist mehr als Wiederbelebung der Antike; Humanismus ist auch nicht die Beschäftigung mit der Antike an und für sich . . .: sonst wären die Altertumswissenschafter die grössten Humanisten, was durchaus nicht der Fall ist.' (W. Rüegg, *Cicero und der Humanismus*, Zürich, 1946, 6.)

46. A. S. F. Gow, *A. E. Housman: a Sketch* (New York, 1936), 43. The chart on Mr. Gow's p. 90 shows that Housman preferred to lecture on the fourth book.

47. From a letter written by Mrs. T. W. Pym, and quoted in Grant Richards, *Housman 1897–1936* (O.U.P., 1942), 289.

48. Quoted by C. Seignobos, in L. Petit de Julleville's *Histoire de la langue et de la littérature française*, 8. 259. Renan himself held that writing history was 'as much an art as a science. . . . There is no exaggeration in saying that a badly arranged sentence always corresponds to an inexact thought.' (Quoted from *Essais de morale et de critique*[2], 131, by E. Neff, in *The Poetry of History* (New York, 1947), 162. On the subject of this entire chapter, Mr. Neff's c. 8, 'History as Science', is of much interest.)

49. After writing this I was fortunate enough to find the same thought expressed by a distinguished scholar who is himself a sensitive critic and an admirable writer. Dr. Gilbert Norwood of Toronto, in his *Pindar* (Sather Classical Lectures 1945, Berkeley, Cal., 1945), says on p. 7:

'We should hope . . . for a seemly elegance in our editions and resent it as an outrage if we open a copy of Theocritus only to find a horrible *apparatus criticus* lurking at the bottom of the page like some open sewer at the end of a gracious promenade.'

50. Housman has a memorable sneer at this, in the preface (p. xxviii) to his edition of Juvenal:

'The truth is, and the reader has discovered it by this time if he did not know it before hand, that I have no inkling of *Ueberlieferungsgeschichte*. And to the sister science of *Quellenforschung* I am equally a stranger: I cannot assure you, as some other writer will assure you before long, that the satires of Juvenal are all copied from the satires of Turnus.* It is a sad fate to be devoid of faculties which cause so much elation to their owners; but I cheer myself by reflecting how large a number of human beings are more fortunate than I. It seems indeed as if a capacity for these two lines of fiction had been bestowed by heaven, as a sort of consolation-prize, upon those who have no capacity for anything else.'

*Turnus was a satirist who is known to have written not long before Juvenal, but whose work has almost entirely disappeared.

Notes on 22. THE SYMBOLIST POETS AND JAMES JOYCE

1. The term 'symbolists' was (like the term 'Parnassian') appropriated by one comparatively small school of French writers—of whom Mallarmé has been called 'the conclusion and crown' (C. M. Bowra, *The Heritage of Symbolism* (London, 1943), 1); but it is very difficult to assert that, in poems such as Eliot's *The Waste Land* and *Ash Wednesday*, symbols do not play a part quite as important as in Baudelaire's poetry. The modern poets who can—on this wider definition—be called symbolists are much

more numerous than the four dealt with in this chapter, but cannot all be considered. Some of them make little or no use of classical symbolism: Yeats, for instance, feels Celtic imagery much more deeply, and his references to Helen and Byzantium are decorative but superficial.

2. Valéry said that was why he never wrote a novel: he could not bring himself to write down 'The countess went out at five o'clock'.

3. Goethe repeated this idea at the end of *Faust* II:

> Alles Vergängliche
> Ist nur ein Gleichniss . . .

although his idea of the relation between symbol and truth was far from Plato's.

4. Mallarmé, *Las de l'amer repos*:

> Je veux délaisser l'Art vorace d'un pays
> Cruel, et . . .
> Imiter le Chinois au cœur limpide et fin.

5. H. Levin, *James Joyce* (Norfolk, Conn., 1941), 76.

6. Ulysses is a latinized, or italianized, form of the Greek hero's name Odysseus. Like Tennyson, Joyce used it because it was more thoroughly naturalized in English: as he preferred Dedalus to Daedalus or the original Daidalos.

7. In particular, Stuart Gilbert, to whose *James Joyce's 'Ulysses'* (New York, 1931) I am indebted for the identifications in the text. In the preface Mr. Gilbert explains that Joyce 'never gives lectures or interviews, never employs any of the devices by which certain modern writers are enabled to "explain themselves" to the public'. He then goes on to acknowledge his indebtedness to Joyce, 'to whose assistance and encouragement this work owes whatever of merit it may possess'—evidently including the merit of allowing Joyce to 'explain himself' to the public. His work contains a great deal of information which could scarcely have been derived from any source except detailed coaching by Joyce: names of obscure books, intricately concealed parallels, &c. (It was probably Joyce who surrendered himself to Bérard's theory of the *Odyssey*, on which much of Mr. Gilbert's exposition is based.) All this is valuable; but the defect of Mr. Gilbert's book is that it leaves much unexplained and almost everything uncriticized. Joyce is reported to have said that what he demanded of his reader was to give up a lifetime to reading Joyce's books. Apparently he imagined himself as a modern Aquinas, and Gilbert as the first commentator on his *Summa Dublinensis*. There are good criticisms of his technique, and discussions of his background, by S. F. Damon, 'The Odyssey in Dublin' (*Hound and Horn*, 3 (1929), 1. 7–44), and Edmund Wilson, *Axel's Castle* (New York and London, 1931), 211 f.

8. As a caricature of O. St. J. Gogarty, who evidently irritated and stimulated him in his youth, Mulligan was important for Joyce, but not for Joyce's readers.

9. Mallarmé, *Le Tombeau d'Edgar Poe*:

> Tel qu'en Lui-même enfin l'éternité le change.

10. Some of the pastoral elements are as old as Theocritus. The setting is Sicily, the faun plays the syrinx, Venus Erycina may appear. But this is not the pastoral of lovelorn shepherds and shepherdesses: it is something more primitive and more real, a satyr dreaming of 'the breasts of the nymph in the brake'. Martino, *Parnasse et Symbolisme*, says it was inspired partly by a Parnassian poem (Banville's *Diane au bois*) and partly by the rococo painter Boucher's *Pan et Syrinx*. This is another interesting example of the way in which classical influence passes on from one artist to another, taking new shapes and producing new transformations in the work of every different generation.

11. Debussy also wrote settings of great beauty for three pastorals from Pierre Louÿs's *Chansons de Bilitis*, on which see p. 458.

12. In

les sanglots suprêmes et meurtris
D'une enfance sentant parmi les rêveries
Se séparer enfin ses froides pierreries

the word *pierreries* seems to carry both images: 'jewels' and 'stonework'.

13. In fact, the young Fate is Mallarmé's princess, one night later than the night of *Hérodiade*.

14. For analysis and commentary, see C. M. Bowra, *The Heritage of Symbolism* (London, 1943), c. 2, especially pp. 20–7, and A. R. Chisholm, *An Approach to M. Valéry's 'Jeune Parque'* (Melbourne, 1938).

15. For instance, *diamants extrêmes* of distant stars, and *tonnantes toisons* of trees.

16. The fragments are an elaboration of Valéry's early poem *Narcisse parle*, and contain certain themes which are apparently developed from, and beyond, *La Jeune Parque*. He treated the same theme again, with more emphasis on the tempting nymphs, in the *Cantate du Narcisse* (1938).

17. For a fuller discussion of *La Pythie*, see C. M. Bowra, *The Heritage of Symbolism* (cited in n. 1), 39–44.

18. Stephen also means 'crown' and implies 'martyr'. The early version of the *Portrait* (written in 1901–2, published in 1944 with an introduction by T. Spencer) was actually called *Stephen Hero*. There the pseudonym was spelt Daedalus. No doubt Joyce altered it in *Ulysses* to Dedalus in order to make it look more like Irish names such as Devlin and Delaney. It is the Greek for 'cunning' ('silence, exile, and cunning') and has entered English as the adjective *daedal*.

19. Daedalus' son Icarus flew too high, too near the sun: his wings melted, and he fell. Gide interprets this myth in *Thésée* as a symbol of the metaphysician who soars so near the ultimate truths that they blind and destroy him; and Goethe in *Faust* adapted it to the career of Byron (see p. 387 f.). If Joyce himself was the skilful Daedalus in *Ulysses*, he became Icarus in *Finnegans Wake*.

20. Ov. *Met.* 8. 183–235; cf. *A. A.* 2. 21–96. Joyce quotes line 188:

dixit, et ignotas animum dimittit in artes

—'he spoke, and turned his mind to unknown arts'. The reference is misprinted 18 in Joyce's text.

21. This point is further discussed in chapter 23, p. 523.

22. *Odyssey*, 11. There is an even earlier Babylonian legend, in which a hero passes over the waters of death and speaks with the dead; but this was lost to literature until the discovery of the epic of Gilgamesh in the nineteenth century.

23. Aeneas' journey through the underworld is the subject of *Aeneid* 6. Perhaps the golden bough is a Celtic myth. Norden agrees that Vergil was the first to introduce it into literature (*Aeneis Buch VI erklärt von Eduard Norden*, Berlin, 1916², 173), and suggests that he took it from the Mysteries, where boughs were used by initiates. But the golden bough is not an ordinary branch. It is likened to the mistletoe which flourishes in winter when other plants are dead (thus symbolizing life in death) and which was sacred to the Druids. Celtic elements in the poetry of the north Italian Vergil have often been divined. By calling the great book in which he gave new life to the buried religion of our ancestors *The Golden Bough*, Sir James Frazer testified to the fertility of the legend.

24. Instead of going to Homer, Pound apparently took his text from the word-for-word Renaissance translation of Homer into Latin by Andreas Divus (Venice, 1537: see G. Finsler, *Homer in der Neuzeit* (Leipzig, 1912), 47 on it), so that the story is obscured by a double layer of mistakes. Yet his eloquence still makes it readable.

25. W. B. Yeats, *A Packet for Ezra Pound* (Dublin, 1929), 2.

26. S. Gilbert, *James Joyce's 'Ulysses'* (cited in n. 7), 2. 6. 143 f.

27. S. Gilbert (n. 7), 2. 15. 293 f.

28. Joyce, *A Portrait of the Artist as a Young Man*, section 3.

29. Mr. H. Levin, on p. 71 of his *James Joyce* (cited in n. 5), says 'Joyce shuns heroics. The relation of the *Odyssey* to *Ulysses* is that of parallels that never meet.' This is less than the truth. Joyce does not merely avoid heroics, he inverts them. The two books do not run along side by side, they move in opposite senses.

30. See c. 14, p. 272.

31. Joyce, *Ulysses*, the last words of section 2. The apparition is possibly adapted from the stuffed parrot which appears as the Holy Ghost in Flaubert's *Un Cœur simple*: see p. 689.

32. See p. 151 f.; and cf. Shakespeare's *Merchant of Venice*, 5. 1. 1 f., in which the lovers make their love more beautiful by recalling famous lovers of the past, who loved with the same magical intensity on such a night.

33. Eliot, *Sweeney erect*. In stanza 3 Eliot makes Sweeney still more repulsive by comparing him to the Cyclops Polyphemus, and the frail hysterical girl to the young princess Nausicaa: both Homeric characters.

34. See J. P. Marquand's novel, *The Late George Apley* (Boston, 1937).

35. The Roman satirist Juvenal sardonically warns a friend that, if his wife takes it into her head, she will poison him; and if that fails, 'your Clytemnestra will take the axe'. It is the same use of the myth, but Juvenal (6. 655 f.) is emphasizing the ruthlessness rather than the meanness of his times.

36. Ov. *Met.* 6. 424–674. Its medieval version, *Philomena*, is mentioned on p. 61.

37. Swinburne, *Itylus*, in which the nightingale Philomela sings to Procne.

38. Eliot, note on line 218 in *The Waste Land*.

39. Ov. *Met.* 3. 316–38. The figure of Tiresias may have been partly suggested to Eliot by Guillaume Apollinaire's surrealist play, *Les Mamelles de Tirésias* (largely written in 1903, produced as a play in 1917 and as an opera with Poulenc's music in 1947), where an emancipated woman makes the opposite change, into Tiresias from Thérèse. Eliot's idea that the poet must pay for his second sight, by suffering the pangs of those whom he sees, appears earlier in Matthew Arnold's fine classical poem, *The Strayed Reveller*:

> —such a price
> The Gods exact for song;
> To become what we sing.

Tiresias figures in it too: his age, weakness, and second sight are shared by the poet who sees him. It is a strange poem. Imagination, the poet's vision, says Arnold, is a rare gift;

> But oh, what labour!
> O Prince, what pain!

In his later *Philomela* he uses almost the same words in almost the same rhythm, of that other Greek symbol of poetry, the nightingale:

> What triumph! hark—what pain!

40. Eliot, *The Waste Land*, 228.

41. Eliot, *The Waste Land*, 243 f.

42. Eliot, *Ash Wednesday*, 1. 6.

43. Petronius, *Satirica*, 48. 8:

'Nam Sibyllam quidem Cumis ego ipse oculis meis uidi in ampulla pendere, et cum illi pueri dicerent: Σίβυλλα, τί θέλεις; respondebat illa: ἀποθανεῖν θέλω.'

Cf. Ov. *Met.* 14. 130–53.

44. Mallarmé, *Salut*.

45. Eliot, *A Cooking Egg* and *Coriolan* 1 (*Triumphal March*).

46. Eliot, *The Waste Land*, 426 f.

47. See Pater, *Marius the Epicurean*, c. 7; and p. 220 of this book.

48. In this, Eliot's poem touches Chénier's most famous work, *La Jeune Tarentine*, which is a blend of the mourning elegy and the briefer epitaph.

49. Pound, *Nunc dimittis*, in *Personae* 183.

50. *Papyrus* occurs in Pound's *Lustra*, a collection of short poems containing many adaptations of classical models.

51. The name occurs in E. Lobel's edition of Sappho (Oxford, 1925) at ᾱ 11. 10 and ἔ 4. 4.

52. Joyce, *A Portrait of the Artist as a Young Man*, section 5, init. He emphasizes his training in Aristotle and Aquinas, and the fact that he began Latin with Ovid's *Metamorphoses*—like Wordsworth and

Montaigne and many another. In *Stephen Hero* he outlines a firmly classicist theory of poetry.

53. Pound has proclaimed again and again that it is essential for poets and readers to know a wide range of literature, in which certain Greek and Roman poets are high peaks: see his *How to Read* and *Polite Essays*. His most interesting classical work is *Homage to Sextus Propertius* (1917). This is a very free translation of some of Propertius' elegies. It is individual, and bold, and charming; it vibrates with the southern warmth and Latin energy of Propertius himself. Only it is sometimes repulsive and often unintelligible, because Pound makes schoolboy mistakes in both English and Latin. In English he is capable of writing

> may I *inter* beneath the hummock (= be buried)

and

> Have you *contempted* Juno's . . . temples?

(See *Homage to Sextus Propertius*, 3 and 8.) His mistakes in understanding Propertius' own language are the delight of connoisseurs in dog-Latin. The best known is so bad that it might have been meant to be funny. Propertius says that he would rather write love-poetry than epics, and then mentions a number of heroic subjects, including

> Cimbrorum . . . minas et benefacta Mari

—'the challenge of the Cimbrians (who invaded Italy and threatened Rome) and the services of Marius'. Pound translates this

> Nor of Welsh mines and the profit Marus had out of them

(*Homage to Sextus Propertius*, 5. 2; Propertius, 2. 1. 24). The verbal mistakes, delicious as they are, do not matter too much; but the spirit is false. Pound should have known that no poet would dream of writing a heroic work about coalmining dividends.

Nevertheless, *Homage to Sextus Propertius* is often eloquent and effective. Its vocabulary is far more vivid than the boring elderly language into which even the most passionate classical poems are too often translated: thus—

> 'You are a very early inspector of mistresses.
> Do you think I have adopted your habits?'
> There were upon the bed no signs of a voluptuous encounter,
> No signs of a second incumbent.

(*Homage to Sextus Propertius*, 10; Prop. 2. 29. 31–2, 35–6.) The medium is not the strict stopped couplet of Propertius, but a free unrhymed variation on the five-foot and six-foot iambic line, with some dramatic half-lines. Because of the fine sense of rhythm that made Eliot call Pound 'the better artist' and praise his discoveries in the art of writing verse, his variations on Propertius, although eccentric and often incorrect, are still alive and memorable. Ignorant and brash though he is, Pound is a sincere and sensitive admirer of classical literature.

54. Eliot, *The Waste Land*, 265, 288–91.

Notes on 23. THE REINTERPRETATION OF THE MYTHS

1. See F. Jacoby, 'Euemeros', in Pauly–Wissowa's *Real-Encyclopädie der classischen Altertumswissenschaft*, 6. 952 f.

2. J. D. Cooke, in 'Euhemerism: a Mediaeval Interpretation of Classical Paganism' (*Speculum*, 2 (1927), 396–410), shows how eagerly the early Christian propagandists seized on the theory, and used it (*a*) to harmonize with the explanation of idolatry given in the Book of Wisdom (that idols were originally commemorative statues of loved and revered human beings); (*b*) to confirm the stories of Hercules and other deified mortals; (*c*) to account for the stories of the human frailties of the gods. They concluded that *all* the Greco-Roman deities were originally men. Lactantius (in the *Divinae institutiones*) was the chief elaborator of this theory. It was transmitted through Isidore of Seville to such late medieval writers as Vincent of Beauvais (see p. 101), Guido de Columnis (p. 55), and Chaucer's pupils Lydgate and Gower.

3. See p. 150, and note 23 on the passage.

4. Genesis vi. 2–4.

5. *Paradise Regained*, 2. 172 f. Similarly, in *Paradise Lost*, 1. 738 f., the devil who built Pandemonium is identified with Hephaestus/Mulciber/Vulcan.

6. Creuzer's *Symbolik und Mythologie der alten Völker* was keenly attacked in Germany on two main counts. One—represented in Lobeck's brilliant *Aglaophamus* (1829)—was that the elaborate interpretations and deep significances which Creuzer saw in ancient religious practices were invented by himself, and that there was little evidence to show that the Greeks themselves felt them at all. The other—represented in Voss's *Anti-Symbolik* (1824–6) and his articles in the *Jena Litteratur-Zeitung*—was that it was calculated to overthrow the Protestant faith, in favour of mysticism, priestcraft, and theocracy. In a handsomely written article ('Les Religions de l'antiquité', reprinted in *Études d'histoire religieuse*, Paris, 1857) Renan dismissed the second of these, and elaborated the first, comparing Creuzer with the Neoplatonist mystics Proclus and Porphyry. Creuzer's influence on Schelling's philosophy is pointed out by E. Cassirer, in his *Philosophie der symbolischen Formen* (Berlin, 1923–9), 2. 21. See the documents edited by E. Howald, *Der Kampf um Creuzers Symbolik* (Tübingen, 1926).

7. Ménard and Leconte de Lisle are discussed on pp. 456 f., 446 f. of this book. See H. Peyre, *Bibliographie critique de l'Hellénisme en France de 1843 à 1870* (Yale Romanic Studies, 6, New Haven, 1932), 60 f., and of course his admirable monograph on Ménard (number 5 in the same series), to which I am much indebted, both here and in chapter 20.

8. On *Ovide moralisé* see p. 62.

9. See, for instance, the tenth lecture ('Symbolism in dreams') in Freud's *A General Introduction to Psychoanalysis* (tr. J. Riviere, Garden City, New York, 1943). The connexions between myth, ritual, and psychical symbolism have been further investigated in the periodical

Imago, started by Freud's pupils Sachs and Rank, and in a number of penetrating books on ritual by Theodor Reik.

10. For a poetic version of this myth see p. 72. A contemporary version (inspired by the fourth of Vergil's *Bucolics*) is W. H. Auden's ode to John Warner: *The Orators*, 3. 4.

11. There is an interesting statement of his point of view in his *Réponse à une enquête de 'La Renaissance' sur le classicisme* (1923), in volume 10 of his collected works:

'Je ne pense pas que les questions que vous me posez au sujet puissent être comprises ailleurs qu'en France, la patrie et le dernier refuge du classicisme. Et pourtant, en France même, y eut-il jamais plus grands représentants du classicisme que Raphaël, Goethe ou Mozart?

'Le vrai classicisme n'est pas le résultat d'une contrainte extérieure; celle-ci demeure artificielle et ne produit que des œuvres académiques. Il me semble que les qualités que nous nous plaisons à appeler classiques sont surtout des qualités morales, et volontiers je considère le classicisme comme un harmonieux faisceau de vertus, dont la première est la modestie. Le romantisme est toujours accompagné d'orgueil, d'infatuation. La perfection classique implique, non point certes une suppression de l'individu (peu s'en faut que je ne dise: au contraire) mais la soumission de l'individu, sa subordination, et celle du mot dans la phrase, de la phrase dans la page, de la page dans l'œuvre. C'est la mise en évidence d'une hiérarchie.

'Il importe de considérer que la lutte entre classicisme et romantisme existe aussi bien à l'intérieur de chaque esprit. Et c'est de cette lutte même que doit naître l'œuvre; l'œuvre d'art classique raconte le triomphe de l'ordre et de la mesure sur le romantisme intérieur. L'œuvre est d'autant plus belle que la chose soumise était d'abord plus révoltée. Si la matière est soumise par avance, l'œuvre est froide et sans intérêt. Le véritable classicisme ne comporte rien de restrictif ni de suppressif; il n'est point tant conservateur que créateur; il se détourne de l'archaïsme et se refuse à croire que tout a déjà été dit.

'J'ajoute que ne devient pas classique qui veut; et que les grands classiques sont ceux qui le sont malgré eux, ceux qui le sont sans le savoir.'

12. For a recent discussion of Wilde's knowledge of Greek and Latin see A. J. A. Symons, 'Wilde at Oxford', in *Horizon*, 1941.

13. I am here indebted to an article by Winifred Smith, 'Greek Heroines in Modern Dress' (*Sewanee Review*, July–Sept. 1941, 385 f.). Hasenclever, exiled in France, killed himself in 1940 to escape the Gestapo ('Letter from France' in *Horizon*, March 1941).

14. See F. Brie, 'Eugene O'Neill als Nachfolger der Griechen', in *Germanisch-romanische Monatsschrift*, 21 (1933), 46–59; B. H. Clark, 'Aeschylus and O'Neill', in *The English Journal*, 21 (1932), 699–710; and D. Bush, *Mythology and the Romantic Tradition in English Poetry* (Harvard, 1937), c. 15, on the entire subject.

15. No one who saw Judith Anderson's performance of Medea in 1947–8 in New York will ever forget how she blended the two passions—how, as the weeping nurse told her of her rival's fearful death, she laughed as luxuriously as a happy lover. Jeffers's violent abbreviation of the *Oresteia* into a single piece, half-drama, half-poem, *The Tower beyond Tragedy* (New York, 1925), contains some fine poetry, some wonderful

imaginings—for instance, Agamemnon's voice speaking after his murder
through the body of Cassandra; but the physical violences of lust and
murder are so extreme as to be incredible or repulsive rather than truly
tragic.

16. *Icaro*, translated by Ruth Draper, with a preface by Gilbert Murray
(New York, 1933).

17. See in particular the first chorus (modelled on the first chorus in
Sophocles' *Antigone*) and Icarus' rhapsodical speeches in Act 1.

18. A. Camus, *Le Mythe de Sisyphe: essai sur l'absurde* (Paris, 1942).
He has also written a play on Caligula, the Roman emperor, whom he
admires for treating life as 'absurd'. There is a searching criticism of his
philosophical attitude by A. J. Ayer in *Horizon* (March 1946).

19. Byron, *Prometheus* (*Poems of July–September 1816*).

20. The best single book on Spitteler is R. Faesi, *Spittelers Weg und
Werk* (Frauenfeld, 1933), which has a large bibliography. See also
W. Adrian, *Die Mythologie in Carl Spittelers Olympischem Frühling*
(Berne, 1922); F. Buri, *Prometheus und Christus* (Berne, 1945); J. Fränkel,
Spitteler, Huldigungen und Begegnungen (St. Gallen, 1945); O. Hofer,
Die Lebensauffassung in Spittelers Dichten (Berne, 1929); C. G. Jung's
essay on *Prometheus und Epimetheus* in *Psychologische Typen* (Zürich,
1921); R. Messleny, *Karl Spitteler und das neudeutsche Epos* (Halle, 1918);
F. Schmidt, *Die Erneuerung des Epos* (Beiträge zur Ästhetik, 17, Leipzig,
1928); an excellent essay by A. H. J. Knight in *The Modern Language
Review*, 27 (1932), and a sound introductory article by J. G. Robertson in
his *Essays and Addresses on Literature* (London, 1935). I have not seen
J. G. Muirhead's translation of *Prometheus und Epimetheus* (London,
1931). E. Ewalt's *Spitteler oder George?* (Berlin, 1930) is not worth reading, except for its collection of Spitteler's verbal effects.

21. Prometheus was a favourite of Goethe (p. 637), Shelley (p. 419),
Byron, and others.

22. In spite of their strong resemblances, Spitteler's book and
Nietzsche's book were written quite independently. Neither author knew
or understood the other. See Spitteler's own statement 'Meine Beziehungen zu Nietzsche' (*Süddeutsche Monatshefte*, 1908), Nietzsche's sneer
in *Ecce Homo*, c. 1, and J. Nagaz, *Spittelers Prometheus und Epimetheus
und Nietzsches Zarathustra* (Chur, 1912).

23. See A. H. J. Knight's essay, *The Modern Language Review*, 27
(1932), 443–4, on Spitteler's knowledge of Greek. I am also indebted to
this essay for the remarks on Spitteler's pessimism.

24. Spitteler, *Olympischer Frühling*, 1. 3:

Und sieh, am Horizonte droben auf der Weid
Wuchs aus dem blauen Himmel eine schlanke Maid,
In Tracht und Ansehn einer schlichten Hirtin gleich,
Doch schimmernd wie ein Engel aus dem Himmelreich.
Die hohlen Händ als Muschel hielt sie vor dem Mund,
Draus stiess sie Jauchzerketten in den Alpengrund.
Jetzt hat ihr Blick die Lagernden erspäht. 'Juchhei!'
Und mit verwegnen Sprüngen kam sie flugs herbei.

It is impossible not to think of the first appearance of Venus to her son in *Aeneid*, I. 314 f., as a bare-kneed hunting girl with a jolly 'heus, iuuenes!'

25. On Spitteler and Böcklin see Faesi (cited in n. 20), 238 f. There is a two-volume work on the subject, *Spitteler und Böcklin*, by S. Streicher (Zürich, 1927).

26. André Obey's *Le Viol de Lucrèce* (1931) is an interesting experiment in bridging the gap between audience and actors by introducing a Récitant and Récitante (masked) who sit at each side of the stage throughout the action. Sometimes they report offstage action, sometimes they comment on the events shown on the stage, sometimes they speak for crowds, and now and then they quote the poem of Shakespeare on which the play is based: 'poor bird', they say, and 'poor frighted deer', *pauvre biche effrayée*—which is changed in the last words of the drama to *pauvre biche égorgée*.

27. See p. 51 f.

28. Gide has this thought in *Considérations sur la mythologie grecque* (*Works*, v. 9), init.

29. The real books are *Notre inquiétude* by Daniel-Rops, and an essay called *Un Nouveau Mal du siècle* by Marcel Arland of the *Nouvelle revue française*.

30. My colleague Justin O'Brien points out that Gide is interested in the idea that sin is infectious—as Molière was. Just as the hypocrisy of Tartuffe and the greed of Harpagon affected those who came into contact with them, so the unconscious incest of Oedipus (or was it quite unconscious?) spreads out from him to infect his whole family.

31. Gide, *Le Roi Candaule*, 2 fin.

32. Gide, *Thésée*, 11. The exchange of a sister for a brother is one of Gide's obsessions: see *Corydon* 1.

33. Gide, *Thésée*, 11.

34. Ovid, *Her.* 10. 41–2:

> candidaque imposui longae uelamina uirgae,
> scilicet oblitos admonitura mei.

35. Gide, *Thésée*, 4.

36. Giraudoux, *Électre*, 2. 6.

37. Giraudoux, *La Guerre de Troie n'aura pas lieu*, 2. 8.

38. This is an atrocious pun on Oedipus' incestuous marriage-bed: 'On peut dire qu'il s'est mis là dans de mauvais draps.' For a man of his lyrical imagination Giraudoux committed a surprising number of such vulgarities. In *Électre*, 1. 2, one of the little Eumenides says to the gardener: 'Le destin te montre son derrière. Regarde s'il grossit!' And in his *Elpénor* (1929) there is a poem about the seduction of Helen, ending

> C'est un péché, je le confesse,
> Mais Pâris vaut bien une messe!

39. Cocteau, *La Machine infernale*, 2 (pp. 116–17).

Notes on 24. CONCLUSION

1. For details, see P. C. Wilson, *Wagner's Dramas and Greek Tragedy* (New York, 1919). Wagner was very well trained in the classics at school, and took up Greek again with great enthusiasm at 35: even his theatre at Bayreuth was, he said himself, a Greek inspiration.

2. Thoreau, *Familiar Letters*, 19 Nov. 1856.

3. Quoted and translated by E. J. Simmons, *Leo Tolstoy* (Boston, 1946), 288–9, 311.

4. On Pitt's father, see p. 329; on Casaubon's, p. 639; on Browning's, his poem *Development*, and p. 686; on Montaigne's, p. 186. There is another such tribute in Edmund Gosse's *Father and Son*, which shows how strangely the child's imagination can be kindled and how necessary it is to kindle it. Gosse, who became an eminent literary critic, was brought up in a dreary religious household. He found it hard to learn Latin, which was made as repulsive for him as possible: 'strings of words, and of grim arrangements of conjugation and declension, presented in a manner appallingly unattractive' (cf. p. 490 f.). But his father, hearing him repeating these strings of words, took down the old Delphin Vergil which 'had been an inestimable solace to him' during his field-trips as a young naturalist, 'by the shores of Canadian rapids, on the edge of West Indian swamps . . . there was a great scratch on the sheepskin cover that a thorn had made in a forest of Alabama'. He thought of the happy months of his youth spent in the wilds, and of the beloved wife he had lost; and he began to repeat the first of Vergil's bucolic poems by memory. The little boy could not understand a word, but was struck by the beauty of the sounds. He listened 'as if to a nightingale' until his father reached

> tu, Tityre, lentus in umbra
> formosam resonare doces Amaryllida siluas.

Then he asked for a translation; but the lines meant nothing to him when they were translated: how could a boy of 11 brought up among Plymouth Brethren understand the pagan shepherd singing about his sweetheart? And yet he was haunted by the music of the words. 'I persuaded my Father, who was a little astonished at my insistence, to repeat the lines over and over again. At last my brain caught them.' And thenceforward he went about repeating them to himself in a kind of glory: 'as I hung over the tidal pools at the edge of the sea, all my inner being used to ring out with the sound of

> formosam resonare doces Amaryllida siluas.'

This is the same 'Amaryllis in the shade' who charmed Milton's imagination more than 200 years earlier: see *Lycidas*, 68.

5. Plato, *The Republic*, 372 *d* 4.

INDEX

Important references are shown by bold figures, thus: **123**. A page-number in parentheses (123) shows that a subject is mentioned on that page, but not explicitly named. Titles are given in the same forms as in the body of the book —that is, in English translation when cited from the main text, and in the original languages when cited from the notes alone. The index will be more helpful if used together with the table of contents on pages xiii–xxxvi.